ZURICH
TAX
HANDBOOK
2011–12

Lisa Macpherson

PKF

PEARSON EDUCATION LIMITED
Edinburgh Gate
Harlow CM20 2JE
Tel: +44 (0)1279 623623
Fax: +44 (0)1279 431059
Website: www.pearson.com/uk

This edition first published in Great Britain in 2011 by Pearson Education

© Zurich Financial Services 2011
www.zurichadvice.co.uk
The right of L. Macpherson to be identified as author of this
Work have been asserted by her in accordance with the
Copyright, Designs and Patents Act 1988.

Pearson Education is not responsible for the content of third-party internet sites.

ISBN: 978-0-273-75963-8

British Library Cataloguing in Publication Data
A CIP catalogue record for this book can be obtained
from the British Library

Crown copyright material is reproduced with the permission of the Controller
of Her Majesty's Stationery Office and the Queen's Printer for Scotland.

Typeset by 30
Printed and bound in Great Britain by Clays Ltd, Bungay, Suffolk

CONTENTS

Readers can access the accompanying website:

www.pearson-books.com/zurichtaxhandbook

for relevant and up-to-date changes that occur throughout the year between Budgets. The glossary can also be accessed on the website.

PREFACE

The prime purpose of this book is to enable you, the reader, to understand how the UK tax system applies to your own situation, especially in relation to what is expected of you in terms of reporting and payment of tax, and to identify situations where it may be possible for you (possibly with professional advice) to save tax. This involves setting out the basic principles and at the same time providing commentary on problem areas and opportunities for saving tax. I have reproduced, as in previous years, the relevant pages of HMRC forms, cross-referenced to the relevant sections of the text, and explained ways in which readers may obtain further details from Government publications. The advice given varies from the basics of filling in the forms to interpretations of the often overly-complicated British legal system. Throughout the text, you will see numerous places where our advice to you is to take professional advice or independent financial advice. This is not ducking the issue; many of these areas are truly complex and the correct answer can only be reached by considering your specific circumstances – a general 'one-size-fits-all' answer is genuinely not possible.

This text also provides detailed information aimed at professionals whose daily work brings them face to face with our complex tax system – accountants, solicitors and company secretaries – and I continue to refer them to other reference material, especially the material provided by the HMRC for professional advisers via its website and its *Tax Bulletin* newsletter.

This book is, as always, very much a team effort and I believe that this helps to make it more useful and relevant. Readers can e-mail any of us with queries and suggestions.

Finally, I would like to thank my contributors for all their help as well as Linda Dhondy and Tony Quinn, my long-suffering editors.

This book is dedicated – with all my love, always – to my lovely husband, David.

Lisa Macpherson

CONTRIBUTORS

Anne-Marie Boden is an employment taxes and reward senior manager with PKF (UK) LLP in London. She has 20 years' experience in tax investigation work, including PAYE audits of large businesses, Government departments and charities. She also specialises in employment-related securities, including the arrangements in respect of expatriates. She has a wealth of experience in the negotiation of settlements with HMRC and is well versed in its new risk based approach. Email: anne-marie.boden@uk.pkf.com

Dale Butcher is a personal tax manager with PKF (UK) LLP in Guildford. He deals with wealthy individuals, owner-managed businesses, professional partnerships and Lloyd's Underwriters. He is a member of the Chartered Institute of Taxation. Email: dale.butcher@uk.pkf.com

Sarah Campbell is a corporate tax senior manager with PKF (UK) LLP in London and specialises in direct tax issues for charities and the wider not-for-profit sector. Email: sarah.campbell@uk.pkf.com

John Cassidy is a tax investigations and dispute resolution partner with PKF (UK) LLP in London. His work covers offshore evasion, lengthy fraud investigations carried out by the HMRC's specialist units, disputes with HMRC (or between taxpayers), professional negligence claims relating to tax and detailed self assessment enquiries into companies and individuals. He is also an experienced expert witness in court cases. E-mail: john.cassidy@uk.pkf.com

Graham Chase is a partner at Olswang LLP. He is a fellow of the Chartered Institute of Taxation and a member of the Institute of Indirect Taxation. Graham has a particular interest in stamp taxes and is a member of the Stamp Taxes Practitioners Group; this interest is reflected in his contribution as a consulting editor of this book. E-mail: graham.chase@olswang.com

Viran De Silva is a corporate tax manager with PKF (UK) LLP in London. He has advised clients ranging from owner-managed businesses to multi-national groups. His expertise covers corporate as well as personal tax, in particular, advising on maximising capital allowances, group reconstructions and demergers, company sales, purchase of own shares and capital gains tax planning. Email: viran.desilva@uk.pkf.com

Philip Fisher is a partner with PKF (UK) LLP in London and heads the employment tax and rewards team. He has a particular interest in share schemes and expatriate issues. He is a regular contributor to the taxation press on employment tax issues. He is also the author of *Employee Share Schemes* and was, for a number of years, editor of *Income Tax & NIC for the Employed*. Philip is a consultant editor of this book. Email: philip.fisher@uk.pkf.com

Tony Foreman was a PKF partner between 1988 and 2010 and is now a consultant for the firm. He specialises in personal tax planning. He has served on the ICAEW's Tax Technical Committee and is the author of a number of books on taxation and personal financial planning. Email: tony.foreman@uk.pkf.com

Mark Francis is a trust manager with PKF (UK) LLP in Guildford and has dealt with trusts throughout his career. He has in-depth experience in all matters relating to trust and estate taxation, administration and accounting. Mark is a very active member of STEP (Society of Trust and Estate Practitioners). Email: mark.francis@uk.pkf.com

Jenny Grasham-Whalley is the Head of Risk Management within PKF Financial Planning Ltd. Jenny is Diploma qualified and has over 19 years of industry experience in a number of roles within Administration, Compliance and Risk Management. During this time she has gained a wealth of knowledge in all areas of Financial Planning and is involved in developing all areas of the client proposition within the Company. Email: jenny.grasham-whalley@uk.pkf.com

Marios Gregori is a corporate tax partner with PKF (UK) LLP in London. He has advised clients ranging from owner-managed businesses to multinational groups. Whilst he has expertise in a wide number of tax matters, he specialises in tax issues for the real estate, construction and hotel sectors. E-mail: marios.gregori@uk.pkf.com

Sarah Halsted is a VAT technical senior manager based in PKF (UK) LLP's National Tax Directorate in London. She is responsible for researching, analysing and reporting on VAT developments, both for PKF's VAT Practice and its client publications and events. E-mail: sarah.halsted@uk.pkf.com

Gordon Hopkins is a tax senior manager with PKF (UK) LLP in Ipswich. He qualified as a chartered tax adviser with the firm in 1999. He advises a wide range of family-owned businesses on compliance and tax planning issues. Email: gordon.hopkins@uk.pkf.com

Richard Jones is a tax technical senior manager based in PKF (UK) LLP's National Tax Directorate in London. He is responsible for providing internal technical support and training across all direct taxes. E-mail: richard.jones@uk.pkf.com

Brian Lovie is director of employment taxes & reward with PKF (UK) LLP based in Edinburgh. He specialises in all matters relating to PAYE / NIC, employee benefits, Construction Industry Scheme and PAYE investigations. E-mail: brian.lovie@uk.pkf.com

Lisa Macpherson is national director of tax with PKF (UK) LLP in London and heads up PKF's tax technical team, which supports the firm's tax teams on policy and technical issues across its national network of 23 offices. She specialises in dealing with inheritance tax planning, onshore and offshore trust taxation, residence and domicile issues, capital gains tax and pre-owned assets tax for a number of high net worth clients and is a member of the Society of Trust and Estate Practitioners. E-mail: lisa.macpherson@uk.pkf.com

Chris Martin is a tax IT senior manager in PKF (UK) LLP's National Tax Directorate, based in Leeds. He is responsible for providing internal technical support and training across all direct tax software. E-mail: christopher.martin@uk.pkf.com

Gerald A. Mowles was formerly a personal tax manager with PKF London. He is a US Enrolled Agent and specialises in US tax and its interaction with UK tax. Gerald is a partner with BBL (UK) Services LLP. E-mail: gerald@ukservicesllp.com

Sue Parr is the tax librarian and research officer with PKF (UK) LLP's National Tax Directorate in London. Her main role is the provision of information to the professional tax staff in the firm; she is also responsible for PKF's tax library. E-mail: sue.parr@uk.pkf.com

Hilary Sharpe is a tax partner with PKF (UK) LLP in Manchester. Hilary qualified as a chartered accountant in 1989 and has specialised in the taxation of owner-managed businesses ever since. Her experience includes capital tax planning and shareholder issues in respect of buying and selling businesses together with all aspects of company taxation. E-mail: hilary.sharpe@uk.pkf.com

Nick Warner is a VAT Partner with PKF (UK) LLP with responsibility for London and the South East, with over 25 years experience in HMRC, industry and the profession covering all aspects of VAT. A member of the VAT Practitioner's Group and The Institute of Indirect Taxation, he is a regular speaker on issues affecting the insurance industry, where he specialises in providing VAT and IPT advisory services to a wide range of insurers and outsourcers. His wider clients range from owner-managed business and charities to FTSE 100 companies. E-mail: nick.warner@uk.pkf.com

Mike Wilkes is a personal tax specialist and a partner with BBL (UK) Services LLP. He trained with the Revenue and a leading firm of chartered accountants. Mike has particular expertise in international tax planning for individuals. E-mail: mike@ukservicesllp.com

Graham Yeatman is a tax senior manager in PKF (UK) LLP's National Tax Directorate based in London and specialises in analysing tax developments to identify tax planning opportunities and how these should be communicated to the firm's clients and contacts. E-mail: graham.yeatman@uk.pkf.com

1

INTRODUCTION: PRINCIPLES OF TAX PLANNING AND HOW TO USE THIS BOOK

This chapter contains the following sections:

(1) Introduction

Managing your tax affairs

(2) General strategy
(3) Planning points if you are employed
(4) If you are thinking of becoming self-employed
(5) If you are already in business
(6) Investments and capital gains tax
(7) Business tax and finance
(8) Managing your investments and your family's financial affairs
(9) Tax issues if you are non-resident or have a foreign domicile

Good housekeeping

(10) Ensure that all important deadlines are kept.

1.1 INTRODUCTION

Why would you want to read a book on tax? Almost certainly because you want to have a better understanding of how taxes are assessed and administered in general, and how they can be made as painless as possible in your particular case. The hope is that this book will help empower you so that you can deal with the annual task of filing your self-assessment tax return (or better understand when you may need to instruct a professional), stay on top of your tax obligations and identify tax planning opportunities.

Any reference book can easily become just a miscellany of facts and figures. There is a particular danger of this here because the UK tax system has developed in a piecemeal way. A new set of specific rules and regulations come in every year and are superimposed on last year's version. The cumulative effect of this process is to make things incredibly complicated and, in so doing, obscure any coherent structure which reflected the reasons why that particular aspect of the tax 'system' was originally designed.

With all this in mind, this book is split into six parts so that you can more easily distinguish the chapters that are particularly relevant to you:

Part 1: The self-assessment process

The first part of this book deals mainly with the practical aspects of filing your annual tax return.

It also looks at how you deal with HM Revenue & Customs (HMRC) and its various offices.

As you read through the various aspects of self-assessment, it identifies some tax saving possibilities. HMRC will always give good advice on your obligations to file forms and pay taxes but it is not within its remit to tell you how you might save taxes and avoid unnecessary filing.

Part 2: Business tax and finance

This part covers aspects of the UK tax regime of which you need to be aware in your business life, especially if you are running your own business. For example, how business profits are computed, CGT as it affects business transactions, getting relief for financing costs and your duty to act as an unpaid tax collector by withholding tax and paying it over to HMRC. You need to know the specific filing obligations that apply to you as a sole trader, a member of a partnership or LLP, or as a shareholder in a company.

There is another aspect on which there has been increasing focus in recent editions. It is important when you are in business to plan ahead, not least in relation to your ultimate exit from the business on retirement. At regular intervals in this book, it is recommended that you take professional advice. Saying this is not ducking the issue; the best course of action for you to take can only be ascertained when the full facts have been established. But as in so many matters, the facts often speak for themselves when you ask the right questions.

Part 3: Tax and wealth planning

A few years ago, the Office of National Statistics told us that we were getting older and wealthier. It hasn't felt like that lately (well, older, maybe …). Hopefully things will eventually get back to normal and there are therefore several chapters that concentrate on how you can build up capital and increase your wealth. The chapters cover matters such as:

- tax privileged investments (eg ISAs, EIS and VCT investments);
- the tax treatment of life assurance policies;
- pension schemes;
- some ways of reducing capital gains tax;
- inheritance tax;
- the taxation of trusts;
- passing on your family business.

Part 4: Anti-avoidance legislation

We all want to keep tax down to the minimum but successive governments and HMRC have constructed a series of barriers and traps to ensure that the UK Exchequer is not diminished (a kind of fiscal Maginot Line). This part of the book deals with areas of taxation on which you will normally need to consult a tax accountant or lawyer for specialist advice. The intention is to make you aware of the pitfalls in certain wealth creation tax schemes and to give you a strong indication of when you might stray into areas where you need specialist advice.

Part 5: Residence, domicile and international matters

The chapters in this part cover international issues arising out of an individual's residence and domicile status.

Part 6: Other taxpayers and taxes

Finally, the book deals with some miscellaneous tax matters and some taxes that do not fit easily into any one section. An example of this is stamp duty, one of the UK's oldest taxes given new teeth by the introduction of SDLT in the Finance Act 2003.

MANAGING YOUR TAX AFFAIRS

Managing your tax affairs and planning ahead are inextricably connected: you cannot plan in an effective way unless you are on top of your responsibility to file returns and you are aware of the deadlines. In recent years, HMRC has acquired sweeping new powers to investigate and to impose penalties for late filing and/or late payment as well as the potential to withhold participation in certain beneficial tax regimes where your filing record has been poor. It is therefore more important than ever before to ensure you meet your obligations in good time.

1.2 GENERAL STRATEGY

There is no water-into-wine solution to the question of how to pay less tax – if only there were! And there are plenty of ways of getting it wrong and increasing your tax problems. However, you should not go too far wrong if you bear in mind the following advice:

1 Carry out some background research

Your tax affairs need to be taken seriously. It is important to fill out your tax return in a meticulous way. You should carefully read the notes issued with the tax return and, if there are areas on which you are not quite sure, you should seek advice, either from HMRC itself by calling the Self-Assessment Helpline number 0845 9000 444, or from a practising accountant.

2 Deal with your self-assessment return issued in April 2011

You need to submit your 2011 (2010–11) Self Assessment (SA) tax return by either 31 October 2011 (paper filers) or 31 January 2012 (online filers), and settle your outstanding tax by 31 January 2012. If you fail to do this, you automatically become liable for interest and penalties. You may not receive a tax return form or a notice to make a return, but you still have a duty to notify HMRC by 5 October following the end of the tax year, if you need to make a return of income or gains for that year.

3 Check on back years

Mistakes do happen, and in the past you may have failed to claim all the allowances to which you were entitled. You should therefore carry out a periodic check or 'audit' to ensure that you (and family members, eg your minor children or elderly dependent relatives) have claimed all the tax allowances and reliefs to which you – and they – are entitled. The time limits for claiming repayments from earlier years changed in 2009–10, from six to four years. The new and transitional time limits for old 'five years and 10 month' claims are as follows:

Year of assessment	Old time limit	Self-assessment New time limit	PAYE and non-SA New time limit
2005–06	31 January 2012	5 April 2010	31 January 2012
2006–07	31 January 2013	5 April 2011	31 March 2012
2007–08	31 January 2014	5 April 2012	5 April 2012
2008–09	31 January 2015	5 April 2013	5 April 2013
2009–10	n/a	5 April 2014	5 April 2014

For corporation tax, the new four-year limit took effect for accounting periods ending after 31 March 2006. For accounting periods ending between 31 March 2004 and 31 March 2006 (transitional periods) the time limit was effectively a fixed date of 31 March 2010.

If you find that mistakes have occurred in relation to your tax for 2007–08, you need to file a repayment claim by 5 April 2012. If you do not, the overpaid tax will be lost to you forever.

4 Steer clear of tax evasion

Arguably this should be point number 1.

Before you commit yourself to any course of action, make sure that you would be happy for all the facts and documentation to be laid out before the Inspector of Taxes. If a scheme or arrangement relies on non-disclosure, you may be getting involved in tax evasion. People who are found out become liable for interest and punitive penalties and are sometimes prosecuted.

Tax evasion is illegal; tax avoidance *is* legal but may still lead to problems with HMRC (see below).

5 Take professional advice

Unless your affairs are extremely straightforward, you could probably do with a financial 'health check' from time to time, ie a discussion with an accountant or tax adviser to go over your affairs to look at how you might improve your situation and pay less tax. A good accountant should be able to more than cover the fees charged by pointing out ways in which you can reduce personal taxes or avoid penalties.

If your affairs are more complex, you probably need to take professional advice regularly. It also makes sense for a tax accountant or adviser to take over the detailed work of preparing your tax return, agreeing payments and making sure that deadlines are not missed.

6 Plan ahead

Part of practical tax planning is to anticipate what could change in the future. For example, it may be that you are likely to sell your present home in two or three years' time when you reach retirement. If you have let the property in the past, you need to look into the position now to see whether there could be a CGT charge when you sell it and, if there is a potential problem, what steps you might take to mitigate it. If you are going to sell your business when you retire in a few years' time, you need to find out what tax may be payable and what you can do to reduce this.

7 Take all taxes into account

It is important to be aware that steps you might take to avoid one tax will have consequences for other taxes, and may even result in an increase in the amount you pay overall. For example, you may be able to obtain a tax deduction if you set aside part of your home for work. However, if a couple of rooms are set aside exclusively for business purposes, this may affect your main residence exemption and could result in a CGT charge when you sell the property. There may well be ways in which you could both have your cake and eat it, but you need to look into the fine detail of the rules concerning the main residence exemption.

Whilst looking at the income and capital taxes effects of any tax planning or business structuring you intend to implement, the transactional taxes can tend to be forgotten, and you should always ensure you find out the VAT and SDLT consequences before proceeding.

8 Be flexible

It makes no sense to invest in a savings plan because the return is free of tax if the plan is not suited to your personal requirements and the capital is tied up for, say, ten years but you require access to liquid funds within a shorter timescale. You should bear in mind that circumstances may change. It may therefore be unwise to put all your spare investments into a trust for the benefit of your children if your own situation might change for the worse. In recent years, many individuals have suffered unexpected demands on their capital and some people are now regretting that they gave away capital that they thought was surplus to their requirements.

9 Do not forget the rules might change

Tax legislation is subject to a review at least once a year in the Chancellor's Budget. One only has to look at recent changes to the rules relating to relief for interest, company cars, charitable giving, foreign domiciliaries, residence (and so the list goes on) to realise that tax law is in constant flux and changes often leave taxpayers, their advisers and sometimes even HMRC staff, trailing behind.

Before you carry out any tax planning that will affect your situation in future years, put down on paper how much the various tax reliefs are worth to you and the extent to which you could rearrange your affairs if the law were changed and the reliefs curtailed or abolished.

Court decisions constantly result in changed interpretations or sometimes HMRC simply decides to interpret the legislation in a different way. It could be unwise to rely too heavily on tax breaks afforded by the present rules. A recent example is HMRC's attack on situations where a husband and wife took out profits from a company in the form of dividends and the spouse who contributed most to the business took what HMRC regarded as an unrealistically low salary (see 33.5.3). HMRC suddenly picked up on this and demanded extra tax for past years, which the individuals concerned had thought to be long since settled. The taxpayers eventually won their case, after a lengthy battle, but at only at the cost of years of stress and uncertainty.

10 If it sounds too good to be true, it probably is ...

All professional advisers complain that clients invariably know someone who assures them that, quite legitimately, he or she is paying virtually no tax at all. Be wary of advice given over a 'gin and tonic': very often, your helpful friend does not really understand all the ramifications of his or her own affairs, let alone yours. Worse still, some of the schemes put forward often turn out to involve evasion (which is illegal) rather than avoidance. Even where there is some substance to what is being said, your friend's or colleague's situation may be quite different from yours. For example, someone who advises you that he or she pays no tax on his or her earnings from work carried out outside this country may have a foreign domicile (see Chapter 35) and so be entitled to reliefs that are not available to you as a UK domiciliary.

11 Bear in mind the anti-avoidance provisions

One definition of tax avoidance is that it involves 'really smart people doing things that would be absolutely dumb if it were not for the tax advantages'. Unfortunately, this (and previous) Governments do not see the funny side. The tax legislation now contains extensive anti-avoidance provisions intended to make sure that you cannot save tax by carrying out transactions in a roundabout way. In particular, much of this legislation is already aimed at preventing a person from converting income into capital gains and in view of the current differential in tax rates for income and capital, further action can be expected if there is wide-spread abuse in this area. There are also provisions aimed against the use (or, to be more specific, the abuse) of settlements. In the main, you will be assessed on income arising to trustees of a settlement if you created that settlement and there is any way in which you, your spouse or registered civil partner, or minor children may benefit under the settlement.

If you are considering taking steps for tax planning that you hope will help you to escape tax, but that are contrary to the spirit of the legislation, you need to take a particularly close look at the anti-avoidance provisions. This is a situation where it is normally imperative to take professional advice.

12 Artificial tax avoidance schemes are likely to be challenged

Lord Clyde commented, in 1929, that:

> No man in this country is under the smallest obligation, moral or other, so to arrange his legal relations to his business or to his property as to enable the Inland Revenue to put the largest possible shovel into his stores. The Inland Revenue is not slow – and quite rightly – to take every advantage which is open to it under the taxing statutes for the purpose of depleting the taxpayer's pocket. And the taxpayer is, in like manner, entitled to be astute to prevent, so far as he honestly can, the depletion of his means by the Inland Revenue.

Seven years later, Lord Tomlin's dictum in the *Duke of Westminster* case made it clear that in his view, taxpayers were under no obligation to arrange their tax affairs in such a way that they maximised their tax liability.

> Every man is entitled if he can so order his affairs so that the tax attaching to them ... is less than it otherwise would be. If he succeeds in ordering them so as to secure this result, then however unappreciative the Commissioners of the Inland Revenue or his fellow taxpayers may be of his ingenuity, he cannot be compelled to pay an increased tax.

However whilst many people recall these famous judicial sentiments, few people other than tax professionals appear to be aware of the many developments in this doctrine in the intervening 75 years. In recent years, the courts have drawn a clear distinction between acceptable tax planning and unacceptably artificial avoidance, applying a purposive rather than the previous more restrictive, literal, interpretation of anti-avoidance legislation and in doing so, have sought to give effect to the assumption that Parliament – when deciding on new anti-avoidance measures – fully intends to catch a wide variety of avoidance devices.

The Government has increasingly employed this distinction between acceptable planning and unacceptable (albeit legal) avoidance. Dawn Primarolo summarised the then Government's policy on 1 April 2004 as follows:

> the Government takes steps to close down tax avoidance schemes ... where they create economic distortions, provide commercial advantages over compliant taxpayers, redistribute tax revenues in an unfair or arbitrary manner, or represent an abuse that conflicts with or defeats the will of Parliament.

Using unacceptably artificial avoidance schemes is like playing with fire (your wallet may certainly require urgent medical attention as a result). The Government has naturally encouraged HMRC to challenge tax avoidance schemes with the utmost vigour. It has also reinforced HMRC's information powers by requiring tax advisers to register tax avoidance schemes. Someone who uses a tax scheme must therefore expect wide-ranging and searching questions from the taxman. If there is significant money at stake, you are likely to be dragged through the courts. If you lose in the High Court, or one of the superior courts, you will normally have to bear HMRC's legal costs on top of your own costs – and of course the underpaid tax, interest and, potentially, penalties.

Furthermore, FA 2004 introduced income tax and CGT charges that operate – according to the then Government – 'retroactively' rather than retrospectively (see pre-owned assets (33.7) and trusts and main residence exemption (33.13)), although that distinction may not be apparent to those caught by these measures. The Government also threatened to use specifically retrospective measures in respect of employment taxes avoidance in December 2004 and there must be a danger that similar tactics will be used if further examples of widespread or endemic avoidance are discovered in future. FA 2008 contained a measure to deal with perceived avoidance using double-taxation treaties, which also has retrospective application and the taxpayers' appeal against the legality of such measures was roundly quashed at judicial review proceedings in January 2010 (*Huitson, R (on the application of)* v *Revenue and Customs* [2010] EWHC 97 (Admin)). This is a trend that tips the balance of risk versus reward even further against tax avoiders.

See also the *Ramsay* doctrine (33.19) on the way that the courts will ignore purely artificial steps inserted for tax avoidance purposes.

If you have used a tax avoidance scheme in the past, you should seek professional advice to ensure that the year concerned is now closed (see 3.4.9 on HMRC's powers to issue a discovery assessment where relevant facts were not fully disclosed). If the scheme is still being challenged, you need an up-to-date prognosis as to the chances of HMRC succeeding.

1.3 PLANNING POINTS IF YOU ARE EMPLOYED

Whether you are a company director, a senior executive, a manager or an ordinary employee, there are still legal ways in which you may be able to reduce your tax liabilities.

1.3.1 Claim expenses

It is important to claim all genuinely allowable expenses (see 4.3). There are fixed deductions for workers in certain industries (eg nurses, dental nurses, midwives and radiographers can now claim £100 pa, uniformed police officers can claim £140 pa and pharmacists £60 pa without having to produce any receipts). Go to the HMRC website and type in EIM 32712 for a copy of the full list.

If you have to belong to a professional institute in connection with your job, the subscription is normally an allowable expense. If you are required to provide certain equipment yourself (eg a fax machine at home), make sure you put in a claim for the expenses associated with it, and claim capital allowances. If you have to use your own car for business trips, consider claiming mileage allowances (see 4.4.9).

1.3.2 Keep records

If you are required to travel extensively, especially overseas, keep a note of your itinerary and the expenses you incur. By doing this, you will be well placed to answer any queries from the Inspector and you should be able to demonstrate that there is no benefit-in-kind provided all the expenses are business related.

Again, if you need to use your own car in the course of your employment, find out whether your employer pays the authorised mileage rates (see 4.4.9). If it does not, or if the mileage payments exceed the authorised rates, you need to keep a detailed note of your business and private mileage so that any benefit-in-kind can be calculated. Under SA, keeping good records is no longer simply a matter of 'good housekeeping' but a necessity (see 3.3.2 and 3.6).

1.3.3 Reduce car scale benefits and consider cash options

The company car rules changed back in 2002–03 and since then the taxable benefit has been increased each year. If you have a company car, but your employer would be prepared to give you cash instead, you should check that having the car still makes sense. You need to work out the after-tax value of having a company car and compare this with your after-tax position if you were to run your own car and claim approved mileage allowances when you use it for business (see 4.4.9).

1.3.4 Go for benefits that do not attract NIC

The cost of traditional benefits packages became much more onerous for employers because of the imposition of the Class 1A NIC charge at 13.8% (see 23.1.8). Why not suggest a package of benefits that are not subject to Class 1A NIC, such as approved share schemes?

1.3.5 Other tax-efficient benefits

If you have any influence over the way your remuneration package is made up, take account of the fact that some benefits are more tax efficient than others. For example, it is well worth having an interest-free loan of up to £5,000 since no benefit-in-kind is assessed whatsoever. Indeed it may be worth considering the idea of a loan above this limit as the tax charge may be more favourable than the commercial options. The benefit of having the right to occupy a company flat can compare favourably with the cost of providing accommodation personally, especially where it originally cost your employer £75,000 or less (see 4.8).

1.3.6 Pension schemes

Pension benefits are particularly attractive as they are not normally taxable. If you do not need all your salary to cover your living costs, it may well be attractive if you can reach a 'deal' with your employer so that it makes contributions towards your pension instead of giving you a larger annual pay rise. However such 'salary sacrifice' arrangements were ineffective for reducing liability to the pensions 'special annual allowance charge' which had effect for the period from 22 April 2009 to 5 April 2011. If you are a high earner, you will probably need professional help to consider the new restrictions on pensions tax relief and the complex transitional rules which operated in 2009–10 and 2010–11, especially their interaction with the transitional rules concerning the reduction in the annual allowance to £50,000 for pension input periods commencing before 14 October 2010, but ending in 2011–12. If your employer has gone to the trouble of setting up a pension scheme for you, make sure that you get the maximum possible benefit from it. Recent changes in legislation mean that anyone who employs more than five employees can be *required* by the employees to offer a pension scheme.

Quite separately from this, do carefully consider the merits of making additional voluntary contributions, but again, remain aware of the new £50,000 annual allowance (and potential tax charges for exceeding this limit, from 6 April 2011). The coalition Government has abandoned Labour's planned tapering of tax relief for those on incomes between £150,000 and £180,000. Instead it has reduced the amount on which tax relief can be given from the previous £255,000 pa to £50,000 pa. If you are not in a company pension scheme, you are most strongly advised to start a personal pension scheme or at least review your retirement planning strategy. See generally Chapter 26.

1.3.7 Share incentives

Company directors and senior executives are often offered an opportunity to acquire shares in their company. However, there are various pitfalls that can apply if you acquire shares through a non-approved scheme (see 6.3), so you need to seek professional advice. You need to plan ahead; for example, there can be situations where you can elect to pay tax up front on the receipt of restricted shares and this can be a sensible course of action if it results in any future capital growth being subject to only 28% (or even 18% or 10%) CGT. Also, if you have been given approved share options in the past (see 6.4), consider how you will reap the benefit in a way that involves the least CGT cost.

Approved schemes offer significant advantages (see Chapter 6). The all-employee share scheme provides total exemption from tax after five years; Enterprise Management Incentive (EMI) options are designed to provide larger equity profits that may – in limited circumstances – be taxed at just 10%, or more usually, at 18% or 28% depending on your other income.

It is particularly important to take advice if you are offered the opportunity to subscribe for shares on a partly-paid basis as a particularly punitive tax charge can arise on a sale of such shares (see 6.6).

You should also take advice if you are offered a chance to participate in a management buy-out (MBO) as there are a number of tax considerations (see 11.5.2 and 37.12) of which you should be aware.

1.3.8 'Disguised' remuneration

This year's edition has a new chapter dealing with the new rules on disguised remuneration. Company directors and senior executives have in the past often been offered the opportunity to be rewarded with an interest in an employee benefit trust (EBT) or employer financed retirement benefit scheme (EFRBS). Successive governments have considered that such structures have been abused, so (subject to transitional rules which came into force on 9 December 2010) from 6 April 2011, new legislation makes it virtually impossible to reward employees in this way without incurring an up-front PAYE charge.

If you already have funds accruing in an EBT or EFRBS, you really should seek professional advice as a matter of urgency, as the new rules are highly complex and can operate in a draconian manner, catching situations which appear to be innocent of any avoidance motive.

1.4   IF YOU ARE THINKING OF BECOMING SELF-EMPLOYED

1.4.1 Will HMRC accept that you are self-employed?

The first question to address is whether HMRC is likely to accept that you are self-employed. If the main thing that you have to sell is your time, and you are subject to supervision in the way in which you carry out your work, you may well be regarded as an employee. It cuts no ice that your contract may state that you are self-employed.

One reason why HMRC will look into this so closely is that, if you are self-employed, you will be able to claim tax relief for certain expenditure that is not allowable as a deduction for employees. So you should take all possible steps to ensure that your claim for self-employed status can stand up to scrutiny by HMRC (see 7.2).

In theory, the risk of HMRC's reclassifying a self-employed person as an employee lies with the employer. If its view is eventually upheld, the employer is liable to pay Class 1 NIC and HMRC may well require it to pay over the tax that the employer ought to have withheld under PAYE as well. Where this happens, the consequences can be disastrous. In law, an employer is precluded from collecting arrears of Class 1 NIC by deducting them from subsequent payments to the individual concerned. In other words, if the employer does not get it right first time round, it cannot correct its mistake later on. Similarly, the primary responsibility for deducting tax under PAYE and paying it over to HMRC lies with the employer. HMRC is normally reluctant to get into time-consuming disputes with the employee and will simply demand the tax from the employer, leaving it to make any adjustment by agreement with the employee. Nevertheless, most self-employed individuals also have a vested interest in HMRC's accepting that they are genuinely self-employed. If a dispute arises with someone to whom you provide services, he or she is unlikely to want to deal with you again in the future, certainly not on a self-employed basis.

1.4.2 **Keep HMRC informed**

Once you start to be self-employed, your best interests are safeguarded by keeping HMRC advised about what you are doing. You are legally obliged to make your existence known to your local tax district by either completing a form available at www.hmrc.gov.uk/startingup or by calling on 08459 15 45 15. This will enable you to register both with HMRC for tax purposes, and to pay Class 2 NIC.

Where a new business commenced on or after 6 April 2009, a penalty is potentially payable where there is a failure to notify that event to HMRC by 31 January following the end of the tax year in which the liability to pay Class 2 NIC first occurred. The amount of the penalty is geared to the amount of the 'potential lost revenue', ie the amount of contributions which were due from commencement to 31 January following the first year of assessment (ie a maximum of 22 months' contributions, for an April start-up), even where these are later paid when notifying HMRC of the liability. The gearing of the penalty to the lost contributions closely follows the model used for income tax errors under Schedule 24, FA 2007 although the issue here is a failure to notify rather than a misdeclaration. Where the liability to pay a Class 2 contribution first arose before 6 April 2009, the penalty for failure to notify liability within three months of commencement was a flat £100. So, it is more important than ever before to ensure that you register with HMRC in good time.

An Inspector of Taxes, like anyone else, is likely to be more inclined to be reasonable if treated with civility and respect, rather than irritated by the fact that he or she constantly has to chase you for information.

There are various other practical matters. You have a statutory duty to register your business for VAT if you have exceeded (or are likely to exceed) the registration threshold.

HMRC's website gives plenty of helpful advice on what to do – visit www.hmrc.gov.uk/vat/start/register/when-to-register.htm for details (see also 22.4.1). You will also find other useful advice about starting your business, including employing people, via www.businesslink.gov.uk.

HMRC also issues a starter pack for new employers, which can be obtained by either visiting www.hmrc.gov.uk/employers or calling 08457 646 646.

1.4.3 Should you employ your spouse or civil partner?

Depending on the type of business you carry on, it may be appropriate for you to employ your spouse or civil partner, or even to have him or her as a business partner (see 1.5.4). This may be a particularly good idea if he or she would otherwise have little or no taxable income. However, if you employ your spouse or civil partner, do not pay an unrealistic salary. HMRC will challenge any situation where the salary is disproportionate. Its argument is that you will be due a deduction only for a reasonable rate of remuneration paid to him or her in return for actual services and expertise provided.

Do be careful on this; in principle you could suffer double taxation if you get it wrong since your spouse will still be taxed on his or her full salary, even if only part of that salary is allowed as a deduction in arriving at your business profits for tax purposes. Alternatively, where the work done by your spouse or civil partner is truly not commensurate with the payments made and he or she has no 'capital' interest in the business and does not share in the risks, this may be open to attack under the settlement provisions, and potentially, the amounts paid could be taxed on you, at your marginal tax rates, instead. This is an area in which it would be prudent to take professional advice. Problems will also arise if you are deemed to be paying your spouse or civil partner (or yourself) too little; you should also obtain advice on the implications of the minimum wage legislation.

1.4.4 Provide for tax

Finally, when you commence self-employment, do think ahead and make provision for the tax payments that you will need to make over the next 18 months to two years. Get into the habit of setting aside part of your income each month so that you will have something in hand to pay HMRC when the time comes. Under self-assessment, the first tax payment can often be crippling as it represents a payment of tax for your first year plus a 50% payment on account for the next tax year.

Example – 50% payment on account

S becomes self-employed during the tax year to 5 April 2012 and draws up his accounts on a fiscal year basis. He was formerly an employee who paid all his tax under PAYE and was therefore not required to make payments on account. On 31 January 2013, S will have to pay a balancing payment for all of the tax due for the year to 5 April 2012 plus a payment on account in respect of the year to 5 April 2013 equal to 50% of the 2011–12 tax.

1.4.5 Take advice on IR35 and managed services companies

If you are setting up a limited company to supply your services, bear in mind that the company may have to pay over PAYE tax on notional salary that you have not actually taken out. The legislation is aimed at individuals who provide their services via intermediary companies (or partnerships) and who would otherwise be regarded as employees of the end customer. The effect of the rules is that your company is required to account for tax on its income from 'relevant engagements' as if that income was your earnings subject to PAYE. See 21.3 on this. The coalition Government had tasked the Office of Tax Simplification (OTS) with looking at the IR35 provisions prior to the 2011 Budget to see if they could be simplified or replaced. However the Government has decided that it cannot put substantial tax revenue at risk at this time and has therefore decided to retain IR35 and to achieve simplification by making improvements to the way in which it is administered.

These improvements are to:

- provide greater pre-transaction certainty, including a dedicated Helpline staffed by specialists;
- provide greater clarity by publishing guidance on those types of cases HMRC views as outside the scope of IR35;
- restrict reviews to high risk cases carried out only by specialists teams; and
- promote more effective engagement with interested parties through an IR35 Forum to monitor HMRC's new approach.

FA 2007 made matters even more complicated by introducing rules to stamp out the use by individuals of managed services companies to avoid PAYE. A number of promoters are still selling schemes that purport to skirt around the managed service companies' legislation. You are advised to be very wary of these – they are, almost without exception, disclosable to HMRC and in the writer's experience often do not work as advertised in any case.

1.4.6 VAT

Research the VAT implications relating to your business. Check regularly to make sure you comply with registration requirements (see 22.4.1). The onus is on you to notify HMRC if you exceed the VAT registration threshold. Make sure that you charge VAT where appropriate and allow for VAT in costings. VAT is a transaction tax, not a tax on profit, so forgetting VAT can be costly and putting mistakes right can often wipe out any profit.

1.5 IF YOU ARE ALREADY IN BUSINESS

1.5.1 Keep good records

Much of the above applies to the same extent if you have already been in business for a number of years. In many businesses, some figures have to be estimated (eg the extent to which a trader's telephone bill relates to business, as opposed to private, calls). There is nothing wrong with estimates, but do try to keep as complete a record as possible, so that the estimate can be supported if HMRC challenges it. For example, where you regularly need to include estimates for business usage, it may be worth separately noting either personal or business usage (whichever will be easier, eg if you know your private use is only in the region of 10% it will be much quicker to note private calls, or mileage, etc rather than noting the business proportion) over a sample period of a month – or during four or five separate weeks spread throughout a year – to be able to show HMRC a representative sample of your private usage, to support the estimates you make. HMRC is instituting a programme of business records checks from 2011 (see 3.6) so now is the time to sort your records out, rather than waiting until you have been visited and a penalty has been charged!

You must indicate estimated entries on your SA return. HMRC may enquire into this and the Inspector may well want to go back to previous years if he or she later looks into the position and decides the estimate is unreasonable. The main defence against this would be where the Inspector was already on notice about the way in which estimates were arrived at.

Discovery is a whole topic in itself, but there are certain simple rules to follow regarding disclosures in the 'white space' of the tax return, which should help to protect you from the danger of HMRC making discovery assessments in future (see 3.4.12).

Keep your records: HMRC may call for them up to five years and ten months after the end of the tax year. Remember that this applies to all your tax affairs, not just the records relating to your business.

If you are a partner, keep tabs on the partnership's tax affairs. One of the partners (the 'representative partner') is responsible for filing a partnership return and you will not be able to complete your personal return without reference to this.

1.5.2 Do not cut corners on PAYE

Beware of situations where you should withhold tax, especially where you are paying casual or freelance workers whom HMRC may regard as employees. HMRC has teams of investigators who carry out regular reviews of PAYE compliance.

1.5.3 Take VAT seriously

VAT is a constant source of problems. It is a complex regime, and subject to frequent changes in European, as well as domestic, case law. Whenever you carry out a major transaction you should always ask a VAT specialist for advice. Also, bear in mind that HMRC makes regular control visits to examine accounting records. Penalties can be levied if mistakes are uncovered during visits, so it is well worth having a review carried out in good time for errors to be corrected before a visit.

If you are VAT-registered, you are effectively an unpaid tax collector. Make certain that VAT works for you by taking account of opportunities to improve cash flow. Ideally you should organise matters so that suppliers send you invoices before the end of the return period. Ensure that you take full advantage of recovering input VAT. Consider whether special accounting schemes or flat rate schemes may be best for you (see 22.6).

1.5.4 Remunerating your spouse or civil partner

Think carefully about the salary you pay to your spouse or civil partner. If it is less than you have to pay to an ordinary employee, increase the amount (it must be at least that required under the minimum wage legislation). Consider setting up a pension scheme for your spouse or civil partner, as your contributions will be tax deductible.

Think also about bringing your spouse or civil partner into partnership. This is a complex matter on which it is best to seek professional advice that will take account of the nature of your business, and the time, expertise or capital brought to the business by him or her.

1.5.5 Financing a partnership

There are some interesting possibilities for accelerating tax relief by you and your partners raising personal loans to put money into the firm to enable it to clear borrowings. Suppose your firm makes up accounts to 30 April 2012: interest on the firm's borrowings will be an expense in arriving at 2012–13 taxable profits, whereas interest paid in 2011–12 by the partners on personal loans invested in the partnership business will be a deduction from their taxable income for 2011–12, so you actually get your tax relief one year earlier (see 11.4).

1.5.6 Relief for losses

If your business has not been going well and you have suffered losses, look into the best way you can get relief. In some cases, you may be able to carry back the losses and set them against your other income (see 7.7). In other situations, the choice open to you is to set your losses against your income for the year of the loss, or against the following or preceding year's income, or carry forward the losses to be set against trading income received in later years. Obviously, it will make a great difference if you take relief in a year in which you will otherwise be subject to tax at 40% or 50% rather than in a year in which your other income is relatively low and tax relief will be obtained at only 20%. Also remember the extension to the loss carry back rules for individuals for losses arising in accounting periods ending in 2008–09 and 2009–10, and for companies for losses arising in accounting periods ending between 24 November 2008 and 23 November 2010. This allowed a further £50,000 for each loss making period to be carried back for up to three years instead of the normal one year, generating much needed tax repayments.

1.5.7 Pension schemes (see Chapter 26)

It is particularly important for self-employed individuals to provide for their retirement since they qualify only for the basic State pension and not for S2P.

Contributions to a personal scheme are tax deductible. Furthermore, the scheme is not generally subject to tax and so the fund is likely to grow at a far faster rate than investments that are subject to tax.

Up to 25% of the fund may be taken as a tax-free lump sum. The balance must be used to provide a pension.

1.5.8 If you are a partner in a large professional firm

Make sure that tax relief is due for interest on loans used to finance your investment in the partnership (see 11.4).

You must liaise with your firm's 'nominated partner' to obtain the information required for your SA return (see 7.4.6). If you incur any expenses, or buy plant and machinery used for the firm's business (eg a fax machine), you must arrange for the appropriate relief to be claimed in the partnership return (see 7.4.7).

Your firm may be considering conversion into a limited liability partnership (LLP) (see 7.5). The tax legislation makes allowance for this. However, there may be other considerations, for example a bank manager or landlord may be happy to take a guarantee from a normal partnership as he or she knows that each partner is jointly and severally liable, whereas he or she may not be inclined to accept a guarantee from an LLP, where each partner's liability is limited to their share of the capital. Also the rules regarding interest on qualifying loans can give rise to problems where an investment LLP is involved (see 11.4).

1.5.9 Should you transfer your business to a company?

If your business is going very well, you should consider incorporating your business, ie transfer your business to a company. Some general principles are set out in Chapter 20, but once again this is a matter where you would probably be best advised to consult an accountant or tax adviser. You will also have to consider the rules in respect of service companies, discussed at 21.4. Another option is to set up an LLP (see 7.5).

1.5.10 If you already have a private company

A key issue is whether it makes sense to take a smaller salary and take the rest of your income in the form of dividends (which are not subject to NIC). Another issue concerns the ownership of shares; if shares are held by your spouse or civil partner, he or she may pay a lower rate of tax on dividends. However, bear in mind that HMRC is looking at these situations much more closely of late (see 33.5.3).

You should fund your pension scheme to the maximum extent you can afford. A small self-administered scheme may have much to commend it if you wish to be able to take loan-backs or have the fund buy a property to rent to your company (see 26.3).

Do you see an opportunity to start a new business or extend your company's existing business to a new location? You might establish a subsidiary company but this may not necessarily be the best approach (amongst other considerations, having two companies is likely to affect your existing company's rate of corporation tax (see 18.4.3)). One way of organising matters, which is worth investigating, is to have a LLP with the members being yourself (and possibly your spouse) and your existing limited company. The terms of the LLP can mean that your company bears most of the risk but you and your spouse are entitled to a share of profits in return for the work that you put into the venture. Your share of the profits should only attract NIC at the additional 2%, assuming that your company remuneration takes you over the upper limit for Class 1 and Class 4 contributions. See 7.5 on LLPs in general.

Do you need to recruit or retain key managers? If so, consider share schemes because these can have great motivational value and (provided you take suitable professional advice) can be taxed more beneficially than cash bonuses and benefits-in-kind (see 4.13–4.16). Bear in mind that your company may get tax relief for such schemes (see 18.3.2) and you may also qualify for CGT relief on sales to approved employee trusts (see 13.7).

1.5.11 Plan for retirement and handing the business on

Finally, do plan ahead, both for retirement and for passing on your business in due course to your family. Try not to leave pension funding until the last few years as this will inevitably make it much more expensive.

Key questions need to be addressed in relation to CGT planning: make sure that you take full advantage of entrepreneur's relief, which commenced on 6 April 2008 at £1m, doubled in value to £2m on 6 April 2009, increased from 23 June 2010 to £5m and again doubled, from 6 April 2011, to a £10m lifetime allowance.

Will IHT be payable on your death? It may be possible to organise your affairs so that either 100% or 50% business or agricultural property relief will be due, see 30.8–30.9 on this.

Finally, see Chapter 32 on passing on a family business.

1.6 INVESTMENTS AND CAPITAL GAINS TAX

Chapters 8–10 explain how various types of investments are dealt with for tax purposes.

We cover CGT in Chapter 13.

Your home may well be your most valuable asset. See Chapter 14 on the detailed rules that determine whether the whole of any gain is exempt when you sell a property which has been your main residence.

1.7 BUSINESS TAX AND FINANCE

We have already touched on a number of issues in passing that affect people in business. However, this part of the book is aimed specifically at business people.

The following chapters cover matters that are particularly relevant for a proprietor of an unincorporated business or a shareholder/director in a limited company:

- Chapter 16 Computation of business profits and capital allowances
- Chapter 17 Capital gains tax and business transactions
- Chapter 18 Tax and companies
- Chapter 19 Financing your business
- Chapter 20 Should you operate through a company?
- Chapter 21 Deducting tax at source and paying it over to HMRC
- Chapter 22 Outline of VAT
- Chapter 23 National insurance contributions

1.8 MANAGING YOUR INVESTMENTS AND YOUR FAMILY'S FINANCIAL AFFAIRS

We focus on this subject in Chapter 24.
Relevant issues include the following:

- How can you make best use of investments that carry 'tax breaks'? See Chapter 25.
- How much can you pay into a pension scheme? See Chapter 26.
- How can you take the benefits from your pension scheme in the most advantageous way? See 26.2.
- The technical aspects and advantages of investing in life assurance policies – see Chapter 28.
- How can you keep CGT liabilities down to a minimum? See Chapter 29.
- When is IHT charged and what can you do to save this? See Chapter 30.
- How are trusts taxed? See Chapter 31.
- Passing on your family business – see Chapter 32.
- What are the obstacles to tax saving that arise from the anti-avoidance legislation? See Chapter 33.

1.9 TAX ISSUES IF YOU ARE NON-RESIDENT OR HAVE A FOREIGN DOMICILE

We address these issues in Part 5 of this book.
Chapter 34 deals with questions such as:

- What are the tests that determine whether you will be treated as resident and/or ordinarily resident in the UK?
- How will your income tax and CGT liabilities be affected by your being non-UK resident or not ordinarily resident?

Chapter 35 deals with issues such as:

- What does it mean to say that someone has foreign domicile?
- How does having foreign domicile affect your tax position?
- Tax planning.

The 2008 Budget introduced changes in the taxation of non-UK domiciliaries that will have a profound effect on individuals who have been resident in the UK for at least seven of the previous nine tax years. Further changes in Finance Act 2012 will introduce a higher charge on those who have been resident here for 12 years or more from 6 April 2012.

In Chapter 36, we look at considerations for people who are caught up (to varying degrees) in more than one tax regime – something that happens increasingly often now that many of the barriers to travel and individuals relocating abroad have fallen away.

GOOD HOUSEKEEPING

1.10 ENSURE THAT ALL IMPORTANT DEADLINES ARE KEPT

It is pointless trying to arrange your affairs tax efficiently unless you get the basics right and keep your affairs tidy. This means watching deadlines for action (eg paying tax) and for making elections.

The most important tax planning deadlines are listed below. Note that this section should be read subject to three cautions:

(1) Most of the deadlines are dates by which returns, payments, claims or elections must be received by HMRC. A document or payment must be posted a minimum of three working days before the deadline and, because of the danger of postal delays, ideally at least a week. Filing and paying online can provide certainty that your return or payment has been received by the due date and in many instances, is now compulsory.

(2) To keep this checklist to a manageable size, only those deadlines likely to apply to the majority of people have been included; the checklist is not fully comprehensive.

(3) Many deadlines cannot be included because they are fixed by reference to the facts of the individual case. For example, most corporation tax deadlines are fixed by reference to the end of the company's accounting period.

1.10.1 Outstanding deadlines for tax year 2010–11

5 October 2011	To avoid the danger of incurring penalties, individuals with new sources of income in 2010–11 should have notified HMRC by 4pm today if no tax return has been received.
19 October 2011	Amounts agreed under 2010–11 PSAs due for payment – interest starts to run.
31 October 2011	Paper filers: the self-assessment tax return for 2010–11 needs to be filed by this date if it was issued to you before 31 July 2011.
31 January 2012	Online filers: the self-assessment tax return for 2010–11 needs to be filed and 2010–11 tax paid by this date.

1.10.2 Main 31 January 2012 deadlines for tax year 2009–10

Personal tax

(1) Claiming a set-off for industrial buildings allowances on enterprise zone investments made in 2009–10 (see 25.7 and 8.7.6–8.7.7).

(2) Electing for the tests for furnished holiday accommodation to be computed by reference to an average (see 8.5.1).

(3) Claiming relief against income tax for 2009–10 for a loss on the disposal of shares in a qualifying trading company (see 17.2).

Capital gains tax

(1) Claiming that an asset became of negligible value during 2009–10 under s 24(2) TCGA 1992 (see 13.5.9).

(2) Electing under s 138A TCGA 1992 where an earn-out is to be satisfied by the issue of securities (see 17.9).

(3) Electing under s 261B TCGA 1992 for 2009–10 trade losses to be relieved against gains.

(4) Electing under s 261D TCGA 1992 for 2009–10 post-cessation expenses to be relieved against gains.

Business tax

(1) Claiming that a trading loss incurred in 2009–10 should be set against other 2009–10 income under s 64 ITA 2007 (see 7.7.2).

(2) Claiming that a trading loss incurred in 2009–10 should be set against a capital gain realised in 2009–10 under s 71 ITA 2007 (see 7.7.7).

(3) Claiming that a trading loss incurred in 2009–10 be carried back, where permitted under the 'new business' rules under s 72 ITA 2007 (see 7.7.6).

(4) Electing under s 162A TCGA 1992 to disapply CGT incorporation relief (see 17.6.5).

(5) Electing under s 83 CAA 2001 to treat plant or machinery purchased in 2009–10 as a short-life asset for capital allowance purposes (see 16.2.11).

(6) Electing under s 257 ITTOIA 2005 for post-cessation receipts received in 2009–10 to be taxed for the year the trade was discontinued (see 16.4).

1.10.3 Last chance deadline for 2006–07

Claims for 2006–07 should have been made by 5 April 2011. If you do not have to complete a SA return, or are taxed solely under PAYE, the applicable deadline is slightly longer – you have until 31 March 2012 to make any necessary changes for 2006–07. For companies, the new four-year limit took effect for accounting periods ending after 31 March 2006, so for claims for 31 March 2007 year ends, the time limit was 31 March 2011 and for 31 March 2008 year ends, it will be 31 March 2012.

1.10.4 Last chance deadlines for 2007–08

The following claims for 2007–08 must be made by 5 April 2012.

Personal tax

(1) Claiming personal allowances (see Chapter 12).
(2) Claiming relief for interest paid.
(3) Claiming relief for pension contributions paid.
(4) Claiming 'top-slicing' relief in respect of life assurance policy gains (see 28.3.4).
(5) Claiming relief to correct an error or mistake made by the taxpayer that resulted in an excessive assessment being made in the year.

Business tax

(1) Claiming to carry forward trade losses under ss 83 and 88 ITA 2007.
(2) Claiming to carry back terminal losses under s 89 ITA 2007.

Capital gains tax

(1) Claiming roll-over and hold-over relief in respect of disposals (see 17.3 and 17.5).
(2) Claiming a set-off against capital gains assessed in respect of a loss incurred on a qualifying loan to a trader under s 253 TCGA 1992 (see 17.1).

1.10.5 Deadlines for next year's diary

5 April 2012	The deadline for maximising the use of your ISA allowance for 2011–12.
6 April 2012	Most employers are now required to file online. Penalties may be charged if you use paper filing when required to file online.
19 April 2012	PAYE/NIC payments due at the Accounts Office by today. Interest chargeable after this date (see 21.1).
19 May 2012	Employers who do not file end-of-year returns (on Forms P14, P35 and P38/P38A, CIS36) by today may be fined (see 21.1.7).
31 May 2012	Last date for giving a 2011–12 form P60 to each relevant employee.

6 July 2012	Substantial fines may be imposed on any employer who does not submit Form P9D/P11D (returns of benefits, etc provided for employees) by today (see 4.4.1 and 21.1.8). Details of benefits shown on P9D or P11D forms must be supplied to each employee.
	Deadline for submission of form 42 covering reportable events under the legislation on employment-related securities (see 6.1).
19 July 2012	Due date for payment for 2011–12 Class 1A NIC (see 23.1.8).
	PAYE quarterly payment date for small employers (see 21.1.1).
31 July 2012	Second interim tax payment for 2011–12 due (see 2.1.4).

PART 1

SELF-ASSESSMENT

31 January is firmly established in the UK taxpayer's mind as the most important day in the tax year. However, since 2007–08 31 October has been the deadline for most people filing paper returns, with only online filers and a few exceptional cases retaining the 31 January filing deadline. 31 January is still the day that tax falls due for payment.

This part of the book looks at the practicalities surrounding the annual task of filing your form. The part is broken down into the following chapters:

2 Self-assessment (SA)

3 HMRC and you

4 Employment income

5 Employment income through third parties: disguised remuneration

6 Share incentives

7 Self-employment

8 Income from UK property

9 Savings income

10 Other income

11 Allowable deductions

12 Allowances and tax credits

13 Capital gains tax

14 Your main residence

15 The tax calculation

2

SELF-ASSESSMENT

This chapter contains the following sections:

(1) Self-assessment (SA)
(2) Filing SA tax returns online
(3) Short tax return 2012
(4) Ten golden rules for dealing with your 2012 tax return
(5) Common errors
(6) Providing additional information
(7) Finding your way around the SA form

2.1 SELF-ASSESSMENT (SA)

2.1.1 An overview of the SA system

Try not to be put off by the fact that the form and filing instructions seem complicated: HMRC has produced a number of helpsheets and will be only too pleased to clarify anything that is not covered by the notes. Indeed you may even be one of the individuals selected for the simplified forms (see 2.3), which will hopefully make the annual chore a little easier.

The SA system is a great improvement on what went before. It is a properly designed system rather than an arbitrary set of procedures that evolved gradually in a piecemeal fashion over 200 years. For example, you now only need to deal with one point of contact. Also, you or HMRC work out the tax that you owe (or are owed) as a global figure, whereas in the past many taxpayers had to contend with several different tax districts making assessments on particular types of income, sometimes from opposite ends of the country.

The HMRC form (SA100 for individuals) contains a 'core' section that applies to all taxpayers. Beyond that, there are special schedules that you need to complete only if you have specific types of income, etc.

The principle is that by completing the form you should work out your own tax liability and settle what you owe by 31 January each year. However, provided a paper SA return is filed not later than 31 October following the end of the tax year, HMRC will calculate the amount of tax payable for you. Filing online provides instant gratification in that the tax payable is calculated automatically, whenever the return is filed.

2.1.2 'Incentives' to make you comply

The legislation contains a number of 'incentives' to ensure that people comply with their obligations. If a person does not file his or her SA return by the 31 October or 31 January deadline, he or she currently becomes liable for a fixed penalty of £100. If the return has still not been sent in by 31 July (or 30 April for paper returns), there is another £100 fixed penalty. If a return is filed more than 12 months late, further penalties, up to 100% of the amount of tax outstanding (but usually reduced) may be imposed after the return is filed. For tax years up to 2009–10, where the tax due was paid by 31 January, so that the outstanding balance remaining due at that date was less than £100, the penalty was reduced to the amount of the tax outstanding, and to nil, if applicable – this no longer applies.

These penalties for late submission of the return forms are in addition to surcharges that may be imposed on outstanding tax (see 2.1.7).

Schedule 55 FA 2009 contains details of changes to this penalty system, and has applied since 6 April 2011. In addition to the £100 penalty for submitting a return late, a penalty of £10 may be applied for each day that the failure continues during the period of 90 days beginning with the date specified in a notice given by HMRC. The reduction of the minimum basic late filing penalty of £100, where the outstanding tax is less than this figure, has ceased to apply, with effect for 2010–11 returns.

If a return is more than six months late, the penalty will be the higher of 5% of any liability to tax which would have been shown in the return in question, and £300. If the failure continues for more than 12 months and the taxpayer has deliberately withheld information which would enable HMRC to assess the tax due, this becomes the greater of 100% of any liability to tax which would have been shown in the return in question, and £300.

If the withholding of the information is deliberate *and* concealed, the penalty is the greater of 100% of any liability to tax which would have been shown in the return in question, and £300. If the withholding of the information is deliberate but not concealed, the penalty is the greater of 70% of any liability to tax which would have been shown in the return, and £300. In any other case, the penalty will be the greater of 5% of any liability to tax which would have been shown in the return, and £300. Higher penalties (up to double the amount of tax due) can be charged where the withheld information concerns offshore matters.

2.1.3 Steps that HMRC will eventually take if you do not file your return

The current rules are that, if an individual continues to be dilatory, HMRC may apply to the Tribunal for more penalties to be imposed of up to £60 per day that the return remains outstanding. As a last resort, HMRC will issue a 'determination' (which it must do within three years of the filing date for the return) which shows the tax that HMRC estimates is due for the year. This tax is then due and payable and the determination may only be set aside by the taxpayer submitting the outstanding tax return. HMRC can take you to court to enforce collection of tax payable under a determination.

Once issued, a determination can only be replaced by the taxpayer filing a return (including a Self Assessment (SA)) within three years from the statutory filing date or 12 months from the issue of the determination if later. Some taxpayers fail to meet these deadlines and do not have a reasonable excuse for doing so. In the past, by concession, HMRC has only collected the sum that would have been due for the period had the taxpayer filed the return on time, rather than the determined amount. HMRC had intended to abolish this concession, which is known as 'equitable liability', but following sustained pressure from tax advisers and professional bodies, it was proposed (in the 2009 PBR) to legislate for this treatment in FA 2010. A consultation document (including draft legislation to enact the concession) was issued on 12 July 2010, for comment by 1 October 2010, and legislation (which is to have effect from 1 April 2011) has been included in the Finance Bill 2011. In the meantime, HMRC has confirmed that it will continue to apply the concession.

2.1.4 The process

The chances are that if you are going to receive a 2012 SA tax return or Notice to Complete a Tax Return (SA316), you will receive it just after the start of the new tax year in April. If you do not receive a form and you had a new source of income or capital gains in the year ended 5 April 2012, you should report this to HMRC by 5 October 2012. If you have received the paper form, this must be filed by 31 October 2012, but if you intend to file online you have until 31 January 2013.

If you want HMRC to work out your tax for you or have underpayments collected under PAYE in the following tax year, you need to file your paper return by 31 October 2012. The online filing date is 31 January 2013 and the online system will work out your tax liability, though you will still need to file by 30 December 2012 if you want any tax to be collected by a PAYE adjustment in 2013–14 (see Figure 2.1).

Figure 2.1 – Deadlines

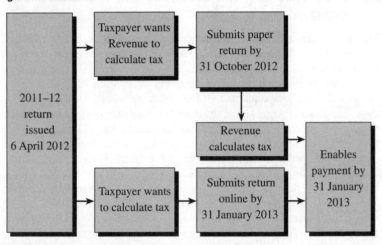

Tax notes

Your tax affairs need to be taken seriously. It is important to fill out the tax return in a meticulous way. You should read the notes issued with the tax return carefully and, if there are areas on which you are not quite sure, seek advice, either from HMRC itself from its website (www.hmrc.gov.uk), by calling the Self-Assessment Helpline number 0845 9000 444, or from a practising accountant or tax practitioner.

Table 2.1 – Diary under self-assessment

Date	Who is affected	What happens
6 April 2012	Everybody who gets a tax return	Paper self-assessment tax return for 2011–12 sent out or form SA316 sent out as a reminder to people who filed online last year.
31 May 2012	Employees	Employer should have given employee P60 for 2011–12 by this date
6 July 2012	Employees who receive expenses and benefits-in-kind (not covered by a dispensation)	Employer should have given employee details of expenses and benefits for 2011–12 by this date

31 July 2012	Some people: HMRC will notify in advance where it applies	Second interim payment on account of 2011–12 tax
5 October 2012	People with new sources of income or capital gains arising in 2011–12, who have not received a return	Report to HMRC by now or risk penalty
31 October 2012	Paper filers who want HMRC to calculate their 2011–12 tax. If you file a paper return after this date you may be charged a £100 fixed penalty	Report to HMRC by now or risk penalty
31 October 2012	Paper filers who pay tax under PAYE and want HMRC to collect any tax due (up to £2,000) through their PAYE code during 2013–14	Send in tax return by now
30 December 2012	Online filers who pay tax under PAYE and want HMRC to collect any tax due (up to £2,000) through their PAYE code during 2013–14	File tax return online now
31 January 2013	Online filers	This is the deadline for filing the online return and paying all the tax due (£100 penalty for those failing to comply)
31 January 2013	Everybody who had an income tax liability for 2011–12 of more than £1,000 and less than 80% of liability not accounted for by tax deducted at source	First interim payment on account in respect of 2013–14 tax
28 February 2013	Everybody who has not paid tax due on 31 January 2013	Automatic 5% surcharge will arise
6 April 2013	Start of new tax year	Paper return or SA316 for 2012–13 will be sent out.

If you read nothing else in this chapter read this!

The UK allows taxpayers more time to file tax returns than many other countries. Compare the US where the tax year ends on 31 December and the individual is required to file the return and pay the outstanding tax by the following 15 April! If the UK imposed the same timetable, the tax form you received in April would need to be filed in July of the same year, not October or even January of the following year. So what are you waiting for? Why wait until after Christmas to file your tax form; risk losing tax papers issued the previous summer; pay interest on missed payments on account; forgo the option to have unpaid tax collected under PAYE in the following tax year (in effect an interest-free loan)? If you organise your filing early you will have time to save for any payment due the following January and, better still, you may be owed a tax refund!

Tax notes

Organise your tax papers early and aim to file early to improve your tax position. You can turn this chore into something constructive as a tax return can serve a similar function to an annual set of accounts. Armed with this information you will be better placed to make informed financial decisions going forward.

2.1.5 Provisional figures, estimates and valuations

The maximum time permitted for completion and submission of a return is 10 months (ie for 2011–12, 6 April 2012 to 31 January 2013) if you file online. Final figures may not always be available by the submission deadline and therefore it may be necessary to estimate these amounts.

HMRC's current policy is that it will accept a return (assuming there are no other problems) where the taxpayer has used a provisional or estimated figure and it will not send back a return just because it does not contain an adequate explanation for why such figures are needed or which does not give a date for the supply of final figures. However, the omission of such explanations or information will be a factor to be taken into account in deciding whether to open an enquiry into the return. Furthermore, HMRC also believes that it is possible for the use of provisional or estimated figures to result in an incorrect return for which a penalty may be charged. This might apply where the taxpayer has not taken reasonable care when calculating the figures or because final figures could have been obtained before the return was sent to HMRC.

There will be situations where an estimated figure is submitted that will not be amended in the future (eg where there is inadequate information to reach a precise figure). If the estimate is considered to be sufficiently reliable to make a complete return (eg where it is based on detailed records for a sample representative period in the case of private proportion expenses such as motoring expenses), it is not necessary to refer specifically to the estimate. However, if the figure is not reliable (eg because the records may have been lost or destroyed), HMRC requires identification of the amount and an explanation of its calculation.

HMRC also draws a distinction between estimates and judgemental figures. A valuation at 31 March 1982 for CGT is a good example of a judgemental figure. That is, there is no right or wrong answer. The figure to be included is basically the taxpayer's best judgement (preferably based on professional valuations) as to the figures, which should be agreed with HMRC. Again, HMRC requires identification of, and details about, the valuation. This may be enquired into during the 12-month enquiry period. HMRC has stated (in SP1/06) that most taxpayers who state that a valuation has been used, by whom it has been carried out, and that it was carried out by a named independent and suitably qualified valuer if that was the case, on the appropriate basis, will be able, for all practical purposes, to rely on protection from a later discovery assessment, provided those statements are true.

2.1.6 Payment of tax

Having filed the SA return, the taxpayer must settle any tax liability for the year concerned. Of course, some income will have borne tax during the course of the year, either under PAYE or for example, a bank may have deducted tax from interest paid. A self-employed person may also have made payments on account of his or her tax liability (see 2.1.8).

2.1.7 Surcharges

If tax is still outstanding after the 31 January payment date, interest is charged and the following surcharges are imposed:
(a) a 5% surcharge on any tax that is unpaid by 28 February after the end of the tax year (a month after the tax fell due);
(b) a further 5% surcharge on any tax still outstanding by 31 July (six months after the date that the tax fell due for payment on 31 January).

Tax notes

Try not to get into this situation but, if you find it impossible to submit your tax return within 30 days of the filing date, make a payment on account of the tax that is owing to keep any surcharge to the minimum.

2.1.8 **Payments on account**

A person who files an SA return may be required to make payments on account of the tax liability for the current year. Basically, the person should take the total tax liability for the previous year (ie the year covered by the SA return) and deduct CGT and tax withheld at source. If less than 80% of the tax has been deducted at source (ignoring any CGT), and the balance is £1,000 or more, the taxpayer must make equal payments on account on 31 January and 31 July, which together add up to this amount.

Example

> A files a SA return for 2011–12 in January 2013. There is tax to pay of £10,000, but £4,500 of this is CGT. A must pay £2,750 on 31 January 2013 as a payment on account for 2012–13 and must make a similar payment on account on 31 July 2013.

Tax notes

You can apply for a reduction in your 2012–13 payments on account if you have reason to believe that your tax liability will be lower than that for 2011–12, but if you turn out to be mistaken you will be charged interest. Penalties may be charged where HMRC contends that the payments on account were improperly reduced, ie where the taxpayer was aware that the tax was due, but merely sought to defer payment until 31 January following the tax year.

2.1.9 **Return amendments by the taxpayer and HMRC**

The taxpayer may within 12 months of the filing date give a notice to HMRC amending an SA return.

HMRC may repair an SA return within nine months of receiving it to correct obvious errors of principle, transpositions of figures and arithmetical errors. HMRC is required to issue a notice of this correction and the taxpayer can then either accept the repair or file an objection.

2.1.10 **Tell HMRC to issue a return if you owe tax**

(s 7 TMA 1970)

A taxpayer who has not received a return form is still obliged to inform HMRC of any taxable income or gains (other than income taxed under PAYE, income taxed by deduction at source, and income and gains already assessed) within six months of the end of the year of assessment (ie by

5 October following the end of the tax year). The penalty used to be 100% of the tax found to be due: however, from 1 April 2010, any taxpayer who fails to do so instead becomes liable to a penalty under Schedule 41, FA 2008:

(a) for a deliberate *and* concealed act or failure, 100% of the potential lost revenue;
(b) for a deliberate but not concealed act or failure, 70% of the potential lost revenue;
(c) for any other case, 30% of the potential lost revenue, ie the tax unpaid at the filing date.

2.2 FILING SA TAX RETURNS ONLINE

Over the years HMRC has tried to encourage people to file their tax returns electronically. The benefits for HMRC are obvious and – as stated on Californian state tax returns – no tree wants to grow up to be a tax return! It is advisable for confidentiality that you use your own personal computer to file online and that you ensure that you have adequate anti-virus software installed on your machine.

You will also have to register at www.hmrc.gov.uk before you can file and will need the following details to hand:

- your UTR – unique taxpayer reference, which is ten digits long;
- your national insurance number;
- your postal code.

The site asks also for an email address and a password of your choice. Once you have successfully registered, an ID number will be generated on screen and an activation PIN (Personal Identification Number) sent in the post.

The online filing set up process is summarised by HMRC in the steps shown in Figure 2.2:

Figure 2.2 – Steps in the activation process

1	2	3	4	5	6
Terms and conditions	About you	Create password	Note user ID	Enter details	Receive activation PIN

The following forms can be filed online:

- Self-assessment tax returns SA100 (individuals) and supplementary pages for employment, self-employment; partnership (to report the income you receive as a partner), UK property, capital gains and for-eign income can be filed using HMRC's online filing software. Non-UK residents are also able to register to use HMRC online services.

- Amended tax returns for 2007–08 onwards (but only for 12 months after the usual filing date for that return).
- Compulsory online filing for companies has been introduced from 1 April 2011 for accounting periods ending after 31 March 2010 – see Chapter 18 for details. Smaller companies may be able to use HMRC's online filing software, but generally, commercial software will be needed to file online.
- It is necessary to use commercial software in order to file SA800 (partnerships) and SA900 (trusts) forms online, and to file supplementary pages for non-UK residence, trust income, Lloyds underwriting or income earned as a Minister of Religion or Member of Parliament.

The following are not available online:

- non-resident company tax returns (SA700) or self-administered pension schemes returns (SA 970).

The preferential 31 January deadline still applies for individuals', partnerships' and trusts' online filing, ie the tax return for the year ended 5 April 2012 must be filed no later than 31 January 2013, but there is an extension to the 31 October deadline for individuals who wish to have payments of up to £2,000 collected via the PAYE code operated against their earnings in the tax year commencing 6 April 2013. For the 2012 SA, this online deadline is 30 December 2012. If you do miss the 31 October deadline for paper filing it may therefore be worth considering filing online by the December deadline.

There are certain individuals who will be unable to file online eg Members of Parliament. There also continue to be exclusions and 'special cases' for certain returns due to technical issues with the online filing system. In these circumstances the paper form will be accepted within the deadlines that apply to returns filed online, ie the filing deadline is 31 January not 31 October. If your paper return is filed between 1 November and 31 January, due to technical issues, your return should be accompanied by an explanation of the circumstances.

Tax notes

HMRC states the advantages of filing online are that it is: 'secure, accurate and you will get an immediate acknowledgement of receipt, plus you should receive a repayment significantly faster if you are owed money. Our Self Assessment Service checks your Tax Return as you fill it in and automatically calculates your tax for you.'

2.3 SHORT TAX RETURN 2012

HMRC has tried to make things easier by issuing a short tax return to some taxpayers (see pages 55–58). Issue of the short form is at HMRC's discretion, ie the taxpayer cannot simply choose to complete the short form. On the other hand, taxpayers who have been sent the short form have the right to request the long form or to file online, if they choose, or their tax affairs for that year warrant it.

2.4 TEN GOLDEN RULES FOR DEALING WITH YOUR 2012 TAX RETURN

The SA system requires that you carry out certain tasks by fixed deadlines. If you fail to deal with your tax affairs in a business-like way, you will be charged interest and surcharges (and penalties, including the increased penalty rates in Schedule 55, FA 2009, which entered into force on 6 April 2011 for income tax self-assessment).

The SA tax return may still be unfamiliar but is not as difficult as it seems at first glance. A review carried out by HMRC showed that 30% of returns contained clerical errors that needed correction (eg arithmetical mistakes, figures entered in the wrong columns, etc), but 90% of the mistakes could be readily identified to enable the return to be 'processed' and the taxpayer's details entered on the HMRC computer. The standard return may need to be supplemented by additional schedules so this is probably your first task: to see if you have been sent all the extra schedules that you will need. The tax legislation can be very complicated but HMRC has gone to considerable expense to provide detailed notes and helpsheets that accompany the extra schedules and these should enable you to cope with most straightforward situations.

The next thing to take on board is that HMRC has powers enabling it to check up on taxpayers. Tax officials will be using these powers and will not find it amusing if you are audited and found wanting, even where the shortcomings amount only to carelessness. The HMRC Enquiry Manual makes it quite plain that SA will not be allowed to degenerate into 'pay what you like'. Furthermore, even though there is a set time limit for HMRC to announce that a return will be audited ('selected for enquiry'), it will be able to reopen back years if the taxpayer has omitted key information (this is called 'discovery': see 3.4.12).

Therefore, you are advised to do the following:

(1) Get organised; start to collect together the information you will need (see Table 2.2).
(2) Do not throw anything away for the time being. In fact, you should keep your 2011–12 records until 31 January 2014 (2018 if you run a business or receive rental income). Remember that HMRC's policy

is 'process now, check later'. HMRC will be able to open an enquiry into your 2011–12 return by serving a notice within 12 months of the date it receives the SA form – and it will not have to give any justification for doing so.

(3) Do not leave everything until the last minute. There will be an automatic £100 penalty if you are late in filing your return, with additional penalties if the failure continues and in any case, it will be easier to tackle the return while things are fresh in your mind. If there are any gaps in your records, you may be able to reconstruct them by getting down to the task before the trail goes cold.

(4) Do not send in an incomplete return because it will be rejected. If you had benefits-in-kind, such as a company car, you will need to put down a figure for your taxable benefit: just reporting 'per form P11D' or 'as PAYE' is not acceptable.

(5) Start to put cash aside now so that you can settle your 2011–12 tax and make a payment on account for 2012–13 the following 31 January. If you are short of funds after Christmas you may find yourself exposed to interest. Worse still, if you are unable to clear your 2011–12 tax by 28 February 2013, you will be liable for an automatic 5% surcharge, with a further 5% charge falling due if the tax remains unpaid by the next 31 July.

(6) Consider filing early. HMRC has given repeated assurances that filing early will not increase the likelihood of your return being selected for enquiry. On a positive note, HMRC will collect underpayments of up to £2,000 via the PAYE system if you submit your paper return by 31 October or online by 30 December. This may be much more convenient than having to make a lump sum payment.

(7) Work on the basis that your return will be selected for enquiry. HMRC selects about 10,000 returns each year randomly; this means there is a less than 1% chance of being selected, but you are considerably more likely to be selected for random enquiry than to win the National Lottery for instance. Tax offices are also expected to check another 30,000 returns with the selection being made on a more scientific assessment of risk factors.

(8) Remember to tick box 20 if your return contains any estimated or provisional figures. It will probably be in your own best interests to give an explanation of how you have arrived at the figures concerned as this may pre-empt queries from HMRC. It may also afford a degree of protection against HMRC reopening the 2011–12 tax year after the 12-month enquiry deadline by making a 'discovery assessment'.

(9) Think twice about not drawing attention to any assumptions you have made in completing your return where these could be challenged by HMRC. You do not have to follow HMRC's line on everything, especially if you receive professional advice that HMRC's interpretation of the legislation is open to doubt, but you should not

be coy about this. From time to time HMRC is shown to be wrong, but HMRC wins more often than it loses. You could be liable for penalties if the courts uphold HMRC's interpretation and it emerges that you had not put all your cards face up on the table. Bear in mind the case of *Langham* v *Veltema*, which is covered at 3.4.12. Consider investing in a certificate of tax deposit to cover exposure to interest if HMRC challenges your interpretation (see 3.4.11).

(10) Finally, get professional advice if your affairs are complicated. DIY tax returns may be a false economy if your situation is non-standard, however hard HMRC has tried to explain the rules in its helpsheets.

Table 2.2 – Information you will need

If you are employed:	
Form P60, ie the annual certificate of pay and tax deducted at source	Your employer should have provided this automatically by 31 May 2012
Taxable figures for any benefits-in-kind (company car, cheap loans in excess of £5,000)	Your employer should have provided this automatically by 6 July 2012
Details of amounts paid to you as approved mileage payments for using your own car for company business (see 4.4.9)	Your HR dept may be able to provide this but you would do better to keep a log of business travel and amounts claimed from your employer
If you changed jobs during the year ended 5 April 2012, details of benefits and pay provided by your previous employer	You may have to ask for this
Advice from your employer as to what to report if you received free shares or exercised (or were given) a share option in 2011–12	Speak to your HR department about this
If you were self-employed:	
You will need to prepare accounts or ask an accountant to do this for you. HMRC requires your details in a set format so that it can use its computer to assist it in identifying cases that should be taken up for enquiry	See 7.1.4

If you have rental income:	
You should keep an analysis of rents receivable and a note of any bad debts, details of expenditure such as fees paid to managing agents, repair bills and redecoration, replacement of electrical goods and furniture. If you have borrowed to fund your property business, the interest should be an allowable expense	Rent charged for 2011–12 will normally be taxable even if you did not receive it until after the end of the year
If you have income from savings:	
Keep a copy of your bank account statements, your building society passbook and dividend vouchers	Most banks include details of the interest earned on an account, and any tax deducted, on a statement within a couple of months following 5 April
If you had trust income:	
You need form R185, which sets out the amount of income paid to you and the tax deducted at source	
If you have made capital gains:	
You will need any stockbroker's contract notes for sales of shares and copies of the sale contract and completion statement if you made real estate sales. If you gave assets to your children or other family members you may be liable for CGT as if you had sold at market value so seek advice in such situations	The gains are exempt if they totalled less than £10,600. See 13.1.1. Remember that the date of disposal for CGT is the contract date, not the date payment is received.

2.5 COMMON ERRORS

HMRC's Press Office has, over the years, kindly provided us with a note of the more common errors on the SA form:

(1) Not explaining unusual variations – there is an area on the return that allows you to explain variations. By filling in this section you can avoid follow-up requests for extra information to explain any apparent discrepancies.
(2) Misclassifying expenses – any anomalies may trigger a request for further explanation.
(3) Not including relevant supplementary pages – any supplementary pages indicated as relevant must be sent with the return.

(4) Using rounded-up figures or estimates – these can be a sign that a person's affairs have not been properly maintained and could trigger further enquiry.

(5) Not including actual information on the main Tax Return – it is important to provide specific figures where appropriate on the return itself – reference to supplementary sheets or accounts can lead to delays.

(6) Capital expenditure v capital allowances – another common mistake is entering your capital expenditure in the Self-Employment section instead of your capital allowances, resulting in a claim to undue tax relief.

(7) Highlighting 'private use' items – it should be made clear where items have been used for private purposes, and the relevant adjustments made to reflect this.

(8) For paper returns, not signing and dating the return.

Tax notes

Deal with the self-assessment return issued in April 2012. Under self-assessment (SA), you need to submit your tax return either by 31 October 2012 if you file the paper form or 31 January 2013 if you file online and settle your outstanding tax by 31 January 2013. If you fail to do this, you automatically become liable for interest and penalties.

Enabling letters

In recent years HMRC has taken to issuing what are referred to as 'enabling letters' to (amongst other targeted groups) self-employed individuals with turnover of up to £150,000. The letters are not enquiries into the taxpayer's affairs and do not reflect upon the character of either the taxpayer or tax agent, but can be taken as a warning over common areas of inaccuracies and reporting. HMRC's objective in issuing these letters is to ensure that the taxpayer is aware of their obligations.

Typically the letter will highlight the fact that most formal inquiries result in additional tax due together with interest and penalty charges. The following general points will be made:

- read the SA form guidance notes;
- include all business income;
- claim only actual expenses;
- have records that support both income and expenditure;
- file and pay your taxes on time.

The letter then highlights specific areas where errors are likely to occur when reporting self-employed income.

- **Turnover** – taxpayers should ensure that the gross income received and not the net is shown, eg if you are a freelance self-employed consultant and receive a fee subject to deduction of tax, it is the gross figure that needs to be declared. (If you are VAT registered, the VAT element should not be included.) Payments in kind, tips and insurance proceeds for loss or damage to stock should also be included. Conversely, tax credits, business-start up allowance, funds introduced by the taxpayer and proceeds from the sale of a fixed asset need not be included.

- **Goods taken from stock for private use** – goods that a trader takes from trading stock, for the personal use and enjoyment of him or herself and/or members of his or her household, should be credited at market value. The relevant legislation is in ss172A–172F ITTOIA 2005 for income tax and Chapter 10, Part 3, CTA 2009 for corporation tax. In brief, any disposal of trading stock not made in the course of the trade should be dealt with for taxation purposes as if it were a sale at market value.

- **Plant and machinery** – the cost of repairing, but not of buying, equipment is an allowable business expense, although capital allowances may be claimed on the latter (see 16.2).

- **Dual purpose expenditure** – if an expense is for both private and business purposes, it is said to have a duality of purpose. If the two elements are inseparable, no tax relief is due (see 16.1.5). For instance, a claim for everyday clothing, albeit only worn whilst undertaking the duties of the employment or business (*Mallalieu* v *Drummond* and more recently, *S. Williams* TC00397). It was held that there was an intrinsic duality of purpose, because although the clothes were bought to maintain a professional and business-like appearance, the individuals concerned had to wear clothing for the purposes of warmth and decency.

- **Motoring costs** – remember that travel between your home and place of work is not deductible. The object of home to work travel is not to allow you to undertake your business, but to enable you to live away from it.

- **Business trips** – only reasonable costs are allowable. However, attempts by HMRC officers to define 'reasonable costs' by reference to their own, internal, civil service guidelines for incurring travelling and hotel expenditure should be strenuously resisted.

- **Cost of home office** – these should be accurately calculated to reflect only that part of the home which is used for business. Remember that home office expenditure is a double-edged sword in that it might give rise to a capital gains tax charge on disposal (see 14.2.1). In practice, where there is only minor use of the home for business, HMRC will accept a claim of up to £3 per week without detailed enquiry.

- **Salaries** – where sums are paid from the business to the self-employed individual these are effectively drawings and are not deductible. Any payments to spouses, civil partners or minor or young adult children may give rise to the question as to whether any services performed by the family member were commensurate with the salary paid, in allowing them as a deduction. Remember the national minimum wage rules must also be considered.
- **Cost of services** – where provided to friends and family these are non-deductible.

2.6 PROVIDING ADDITIONAL INFORMATION

At the end of the SA form, HMRC has left a number of blank spaces for additional information. You may be tempted to think that this is HMRC's way of giving you enough rope to hang yourself, but in reality it should be grasped as a lifeline. There may be aspects of the form where either you or your tax adviser has relied on a certain interpretation of the tax law. HMRC may not agree with your interpretation but will be unaware of the basis on which you have completed the form unless you draw its attention to this. If this emerges later on, HMRC may seek to re-open your self-assessment and possibly charge interest and penalties. One way of covering yourself is to make appropriate entries in the additional information box, 19 (sometimes referred to as the 'white space'). If you make your assumptions and interpretations explicit, you will protect yourself against HMRC using its discovery powers (see 3.4.12).

Tax notes

Protect yourself against penalties or discovery assessments by making entries on the tax return in the white space.

2.7 FINDING YOUR WAY AROUND THE SA FORM

When you examine your return, you will see that we have referenced the following questions to this book (see following pages).

What makes up your tax return

To make a **complete** return of your taxable income and gains for the year to 5 April 2011 you may need to complete some **separate supplementary pages**. Answer the following questions by putting 'X' in the 'Yes' or 'No' box.

Chapter 4

1 Employment

If you were an employee, director, office holder or agency worker in the year to 5 April 2011, do you need to complete *Employment* pages? Please read page TRG 3 of the tax return guide before answering.

Fill in a separate *Employment* page for each employment, directorship etc., for which you need to complete an *Employment* page and say how many sets of pages you are completing.

Yes ☐   No ☐   Number ☐

2 Self-employment

Did you work for yourself (on your 'own account' or in self-employment) in the year to 5 April 2011? (Answer 'Yes' if you were a 'Name' at Lloyd's.) Fill in a separate *Self-employment* page for each business and say how many sets of pages you are completing.

Yes ☐   No ☐   Number ☐

Chapter 7

3 Partnership

Were you in partnership? Fill in a separate *Partnership* page for each partnership you were a partner in and say how many sets of pages you are completing.

Yes ☐   No ☐   Number ☐

4 UK property

Did you receive any income from UK property (including rents and other income from land you own or lease out)?

Yes ☐   No ☐

5 Foreign

If you:
- were entitled to any foreign income, or income gains
- have, or could have, received (directly or indirectly) income, or a capital payment or benefit from a person abroad as a result of any transfer of assets
- want to claim relief for foreign tax paid

please read the notes on page TRG 4 to decide if you have to fill in the *Foreign* pages.

Do you need to fill in the *Foreign* pages?

Yes ☐   No ☐

6 Trusts etc.

10.10 and Chapter 31

Did you receive, or are you treated as having received, income from a trust, settlement or the residue of a deceased person's estate?

Yes ☐   No ☐

7 Capital gains summary

Chapters 1 and 17

If you disposed of any chargeable assets (including, for example, stocks, shares, units in a unit trust, land and property, goodwill in a business), or had any chargeable gains, or you wish to claim an allowable loss or make any other claim or election, read page TRG 5 of the guide to decide if you have to fill in the *Capital gains summary* page.

Do you need to fill in the *Capital gains summary* page?

Yes ☐   No ☐

8 Residence, remittance basis etc.

Chapters 3 and 35

Were you, for all or part of the year to 5 April 2011, one or more of the following – not resident, not ordinarily resident or not domiciled in the UK and claiming the remittance basis; or dual resident in the UK and another country?

7.4–7.6

Yes ☐   No ☐

9 Supplementary pages

If you answered 'Yes' to any of questions 1 to 8, please check to see if, **within this return**, there is a page dealing with that kind of income etc. If there is not, you will need separate supplementary pages. Do you need to get and fill in extra loose supplementary pages?

Chapter 8

Yes ☐   No ☐

If 'Yes', you can go to www.hmrc.gov.uk to download them, or phone 0845 9000 404 and ask us for the relevant page.

10.1, 10.2, 10.5 and 10.6

*Some less common kinds of income and tax reliefs (not covered by questions 1 to 8), and details of disclosed tax avoidance schemes, should be returned on the **Additional information** pages enclosed in the tax return pack. Do you need to fill in the **Additional information** pages?*

33.4

10.4

Yes ☐   No ☐

Student Loan repayments

Please read page TRG 6 of the tax return guide before filling in boxes 1 and 2.

21.1.9

1 If you have received notification from the Student Loans Company that repayment of an Income Contingent Student Loan began before 6 April 2011, put 'X' in the box

☐

2 If your employer has deducted Student Loan repayments enter the amount deducted

£ ☐☐☐☐☐☐☐ . 0 0

Income

Interest and dividends from UK banks, building societies etc. ———————— Chapter 9

1 Taxed UK interest etc. - *the net amount after tax has been taken off (see notes)*

£ [   ] • [0][0]

2 Untaxed UK interest etc. - *amounts which have not been taxed (see notes)*

£ [   ] • [0][0]

3 Dividends from UK companies - *do not include the tax credit (see notes)*

£ [   ] • [0][0]

4 Other dividends - *do not include the tax credit (see notes)*

£ [   ] • [0][0]

5 Foreign dividends (up to £300) - *the amount in sterling after foreign tax was taken off. Do not include this amount in the Foreign pages*

£ [   ] • [0][0]

6 Tax taken off foreign dividends - *the sterling equivalent*

£ [   ] • [0][0]

UK pensions, annuities and other state benefits received ———————— Chapter 40

7 State Pension - *the amount due for the year (see notes)*

£ [   ] • [0][0]

8 State Pension lump sum

£ [   ] • [0][0]

9 Tax taken off box 8

£ [   ] • [0][0]

10 Pensions (other than State Pension), retirement annuities and taxable triviality payments - *give details of the payers, amounts paid and tax deducted in the 'Any other information' box, box 19, on page TR 6*

£ [   ] • [0][0]

11 Tax taken off box 10

£ [   ] • [0][0]

12 Taxable Incapacity Benefit and contribution-based Employment and Support Allowance - *see notes*

£ [   ] • [0][0]

13 Tax taken off Incapacity Benefit in box 12

£ [   ] • [0][0]

14 Jobseeker's Allowance

£ [   ] • [0][0]

15 Total of any other taxable State Pensions and benefits

£ [   ] • [0][0]

Other UK income not included on supplementary pages

Chapters 6, 9.4, 9.9

Do not use this section for income that should be returned on supplementary pages. Share schemes, gilts, stock dividends, life insurance gains and certain other kinds of income go on the *Additional information* pages in the tax return pack.

16 Other taxable income - *before expenses and tax taken off*

£ [   ] • [0][0]

17 Total amount of allowable expenses - *read page TRG 14 of the tax return guide*

£ [   ] • [0][0]

18 Any tax taken off box 16

£ [   ] • [0][0]

19 Benefit from pre-owned assets - *read page TRG 15 of the guide*

£ [   ] • [0][0] ———— 33.7

20 Description of income in boxes 16 and 19 - *if there is not enough space here please give details in the 'Any other information' box, box 19, on page TR 6*

[   ]

[   ]

[   ]

8–10.9   Chapter 27

Tax reliefs

Paying into registered pension schemes and overseas pension schemes —————— Chapter 26

Do not include payments you make to your employer's pension scheme which are deducted from your pay before tax or payments made by your employer.

1 Payments to registered pension schemes where basic rate tax relief will be claimed by your pension provider (called 'relief at source'). Enter the payments and basic rate tax

£ _____ · 0 0

2 Payments to a retirement annuity contract where basic rate tax relief will not be claimed by your provider

£ _____ · 0 0

3 Payments to your employer's scheme which were not deducted from your pay before tax

£ _____ · 0 0

4 Payments to an overseas pension scheme which is not UK-registered which are eligible for tax relief and were not deducted from your pay before tax

£ _____ · 0 0

Charitable giving ———————————————————————————————— 11.9–11.11

5 Gift Aid payments made in the year to 5 April 2011

£ _____ · 0 0

6 Total of any 'one-off' payments in box 5

£ _____ · 0 0

7 Gift Aid payments made in the year to 5 April 2011 but treated as if made in the year to 5 April 2010

£ _____ · 0 0

8 Gift Aid payments made after 5 April 2011 but to be treated as if made in the year to 5 April 2011

£ _____ · 0 0

9 Value of qualifying shares or securities gifted to charity

£ _____ · 0 0

10 Value of qualifying land and buildings gifted to charity

£ _____ · 0 0

11 Value of qualifying investments gifted to non-UK charities in boxes 9 and 10

£ _____ · 0 0

12 Gift Aid payments to non-UK charities in box 5

£ _____ · 0 0

Blind Person's Allowance ——————————————————————————————— 12.6

13 If you are registered blind on a local authority or other register, put 'X' in the box

14 Enter the name of the local authority or other register

15 If you want your spouse's, or civil partner's, surplus allowance, put 'X' in the box

16 If you want your spouse, or civil partner, to have your surplus allowance, put 'X' in the box

Other less common reliefs are on the *Additional information* pages enclosed in the tax return pack.

Service companies ———————————————————————————————————— 21.3

1 If you provided your services through a service company (a company which provides your personal services to third parties), enter the total of the dividends (including the tax credit) and salary (before tax was taken off) you withdrew from the company in the tax year - *read page TRG 21 of the guide*

£ _____ · 0 0

Tax return: Page TR 4   HMRC 12/10

Finishing your tax return

ⓘ **Calculating your tax** – if we receive your tax return by 31 October 2011, or if you file online, we will do the calculation for you **and** tell you how much you have to pay (or what your repayment will be) before 31 January 2012.

But if you want to calculate your tax ask us for the *Tax calculation summary* pages and *notes*. The *notes* will help you work out any tax due or repayable, and if payments on account are necessary.

Tax refunded or set off

1 If you have had any 2010-11 Income Tax refunded or set off by us or Jobcentre Plus, enter the amount

£ _____ . 0 0

If you have not paid enough tax ———————————————————— 2.1

Use the payslip at the foot of your next statement (or reminder) from us to pay any tax due.

2 If you owe tax for 2010-11 and have a PAYE tax code, we will try to collect the tax due (if less than £2,000) through your tax code for 2012-13, unless you put 'X' in the box - *read page TRG 22 of the guide*

3 If you are likely to owe tax for **2011-12** on income other than employed earnings or pensions, and you do **not** want us to use your 2011-12 PAYE tax code to collect that tax during the year, put 'X' in the box - *read page TRG 22 of the guide*

If you have paid too much tax

We will repay direct to your bank or building society account - this is the safest and quickest method. Tell us where you would like us to make any repayment by filling in boxes 4 to 14.

If you would like us to send some, or all, of your repayment to charity please use the *Giving your tax repayment to charity* form in your tax return pack. ———————————————————————— 11.9.3

4 Name of bank or building society

5 Name of account holder (or nominee)

6 Branch sort code

7 Account number

8 Building society reference number

9 If you do not have a bank or building society account, or if you want us to send a cheque to you or to your nominee, put 'X' in the box

10 If you have entered a nominee's name in box 5, put 'X' in the box

11 If your nominee is your tax adviser, put 'X' in the box

12 Nominee's address

13 and postcode

14 To authorise your nominee to receive any repayment, you must sign in the box. A photocopy of your signature will not do

Your tax adviser, if you have one

This section is optional. Please see the note on page TRG 24 about authorising your tax adviser.

15	Your tax adviser's name	17	The first line of their address and the postcode

| 16 | Their phone number |

| 18 | The reference your adviser uses for you |

Any other information ——————————————— 2.7

19 Please give any other information in this space

Signing your form and sending it back

20 If this tax return contains provisional or estimated figures, put 'X' in the box

21 If you are enclosing separate supplementary pages, put 'X' in the box

22 If you give false information, you may have to pay financial penalties and face prosecution. Please sign and date this form.

The information I have given on this tax return and any supplementary pages is correct and complete to the best of my knowledge and belief

Date *DD MM YYYY*

Signature

23 If you have signed on behalf of someone else, enter the capacity. For example, executor, receiver

25 If you filled in boxes 23 and 24 enter your name

24 Enter the name of the person you have signed for

26 and your address

Finally, please send us your completed form in the envelope provided.

HM Revenue & Customs

Additional information
Tax year 6 April 2010 to 5 April 2011

These pages:
- are for less common types of income, deductions and tax reliefs, and for other information
- if completed, are to be sent back with your tax return (but we do not want these pages back if you have made no entries on them, please).

If you think you need to complete them, go to **www.hmrc.gov.uk** or phone **0845 9000 404** and ask us for the *Additional information notes*.

Other UK income ———————————————————— 9.4–9.7

Interest from gilt-edged and other UK securities, deeply discounted securities and accrued income profits

1 Gilt etc. interest after tax taken off	3 Gross amount before tax
£ · 0 0	£ · 0 0

2 Tax taken off	
£ · 0 0	

Life insurance gains ——————————————————————— 28.3

4 UK life insurance policy etc. gains on which tax was treated as paid – *the amount of the gain*	8 UK life insurance policy etc. gains from voided ISAs
£ · 0 0	£ · 0 0

5 Number of years the policy has been held or since the last gain – *whichever is less*	9 Number of years the policy was held

6 UK life insurance policy etc. gains where no tax was treated as paid – *the amount of the gain*	10 Tax taken off box 8
£ · 0 0	£ · 0 0

7 Number of years the policy has been held or since the last gain – *whichever is less*	11 Deficiency relief – *see notes*
	£ · 0 0

Stock dividends, non-qualifying distributions and loans written off ——— 9.8–9.10

12 Stock dividends – the appropriate amount in cash/cash equivalent of the share capital – *without any tax*	13 Non-qualifying distributions and close company loans written off or released
£ · 0 0	£ · 0 0

Business receipts taxed as income of an earlier year ————————— 16.4

14 The amount of post-cessation or other business receipts	15 Tax year income to be taxed, for example 2009-10 *YYYY YY*
£ · 0 0	—

Share schemes and employment lump sums, compensation and deductions

				Chapter
1 Share schemes - the taxable amount - *excluding amounts included on your P60 or P45* £ · 0 0	**8** Exemptions for amounts entered in box 4 £ · 0 0	
2 Tax taken off box 1 £ · 0 0	**9** Compensation and lump sum £30,000 exemption - *see page AiN 15 of the notes* £ · 0 0	
3 Taxable lump sums - excluding redundancy and compensation for loss of your job - *see notes starting on page AiN 15 and Working Sheet 8* £ · 0 0	**10** Disability and foreign service deduction £ · 0 0	4.15–4.
4 Lump sums or benefits received from an Employer Financed Retirement Benefits Scheme excluding pensions £ · 0 0	**11** Seafarers' Earnings Deduction - *the total amount (and give the names of the ships in the 'Additional information' box on page Ai 4)* £ · 0 0	37.13
5 Redundancy and other lump sums and compensation payments £ · 0 0	**12** Foreign earnings not taxable in the UK £ · 0 0	35.4
6 Tax taken off boxes 3 to 5 £ · 0 0	**13** Foreign tax for which tax credit relief not claimed £ · 0 0	4.15–4.
7 If you have left box 6 blank because the tax is included in box 2 on the *Employment* page, put 'X' in the box	**14** Exempt employers' contributions to an overseas pension scheme £ · 0 0	

Other tax reliefs

				Chapter
1 Subscriptions for Venture Capital Trust shares - *the amount on which relief is claimed* £ · 0 0	**6** Post-cessation expenses and certain other losses £ · 0 0	25.6
2 Subscriptions for shares under the Enterprise Investment Scheme - *the amount on which relief is claimed (and provide more information on page Ai 4)* £ · 0 0	**7** Maintenance payments (max £2,670) - *only if you or your former spouse or civil partner were born before 6 April 1935* £ · 0 0	16.5 / 11.1 / 25.5
3 Community Investment Tax Relief - *the amount on which relief is claimed* £ · 0 0	**8** Payments to a trade union etc. for death benefits - *half the amount paid (max £100)* £ · 0 0	11.13 / 11.15
4 UK royalties and annual payments made £ · 0 0	**9** Relief claimed for employer's compulsory widow's, widower's or orphan's benefit scheme - *(max £20)* £ · 0 0	11.12 / 11.5–11.
5 Qualifying loan interest payable in the year £ · 0 0	**10** Relief claimed on a qualifying distribution on the redemption of bonus shares or securities £ · 0 0	9.9

Age-related Married Couple's Allowance
Chapter 12

you are the **husband** (marriages up to 5 December 2005), or the **spouse or civil partner, with the higher income** (marriages and civil partnerships on or after 5 December 2005) you should complete box 1 and, where appropriate, boxes 2 to 5 and box 9. you want to claim or transfer surplus allowances, complete box 10 or box 11 as well.

you are the **wife** (marriages up to 5 December 2005), or the **spouse or civil partner, with the lower income** (marriages and civil artnerships on or after 5 December 2005) please read the notes on page AiN 23. These notes will help you fill in boxes 6 to 11.

If you, or your spouse or civil partner, were born **before** 6 April 1935, complete the relevant boxes

1 Your spouse's or civil partner's full name

2 Their date of birth if older than you (and at least one of you was born before 6 April 1935) *DD MM YYYY*

3 If you have already agreed that **half** the minimum allowance is to go to your spouse or civil partner, put 'X' in the box

4 If you have already agreed that **all** of the minimum allowance is to go to your spouse or civil partner, put 'X' in the box

5 If, in the year to 5 April 2011, you lived with any previous spouse or civil partner, enter their date of birth

6 If you have already agreed that **half** of the minimum allowance is to be given to you, put 'X' in the box

7 If you have already agreed that **all** of the minimum allowance is to be given to you, put 'X' in the box

8 Your spouse's or civil partner's full name

9 If you were married or formed a civil partnership after 5 April 2010, enter the date of marriage or civil partnership *DD MM YYYY*

10 If you want to have your spouse's or civil partner's surplus allowance, put 'X' in the box

11 If you want your spouse or civil partner to have your surplus allowance, put 'X' in the box

Other information
7.7

Income Tax losses
17.2

Other income losses

1 Earlier years' losses – *which can be set against certain other income in 2010-11*
£   · 0 0

2 Total unused losses carried forward
£   · 0 0

Trading losses
7.7

3 Relief now for 2011-12 trading, or certain capital, losses
£   · 0 0

4 Tax year for which you are claiming relief in box 3, for example 2009-10 *YYYY YY*
–

Pension savings tax charges and taxable lump sums from overseas pension schemes —— Chapter

5 Value of pension benefits in excess of your Available Lifetime Allowance, taken by you as a lump sum

£ [   ] · [0][0]

6 Value of pension benefits in excess of your Available Lifetime Allowance, not taken as a lump sum

£ [   ] · [0][0]

7 Lifetime Allowance tax paid by your pension scheme

£ [   ] · [0][0]

8 Amount saved towards your pension, in the period covered by this tax return, in excess of the Annual Allowance

£ [   ] · [0][0]

9 Amount saved towards your pension in excess of the Special Annual Allowance taxed at 20%

£ [   ] · [0][0]

10 Amount saved towards your pension in excess of the Special Annual Allowance taxed at 30%

£ [   ] · [0][0]

11 Amount of unauthorised payment from a pension scheme, not subject to surcharge

£ [   ] · [0][0]

12 Amount of unauthorised payment from a pension scheme, subject to Surcharge

£ [   ] · [0][0]

13 Foreign tax paid on an unauthorised payment (in £ sterling)

£ [   ] · [0][0]

14 Taxable short service refund of contributions (overseas pension schemes only)

£ [   ] · [0][0]

15 Taxable lump sum death benefit payment (overseas pension schemes only)

£ [   ] · [0][0]

16 Taxable refunds of contributions (overseas pension schemes only)

£ [   ] · [0][0]

17 Foreign tax paid (in £ sterling) on boxes 14, 15 and 16

£ [   ] · [0][0]

Tax avoidance schemes ————————————————————————— 33.20

18 The scheme reference number

[   ]
[   ]

19 The tax year in which the expected advantage arises, for example 2009-10 YYYY YY

[   ]—[ ]
[   ]—[ ]

Additional information

20 Please give any additional information in this space

Personal details

21 Your name

22 Your Unique Taxpayer Reference (UTR)

[   ] [   ]

Tax return: Additional information: Page Ai 4

HM Revenue & Customs

Short Tax Return 2011
Tax year 6 April 2010 to 5 April 2011

70115   8010102YC01135
846

UTR
Tax Reference
Employer Reference

Date   6 April 2011

HM Revenue & Customs
CUSTOMER OPERATIONS 284601
GEORGE STEPHENSON HOUSE
ST MARKS COURT
THORNABY
STOCKTON ON TEES
TS17 6QP

Telephone 0845 302 1409

Your tax return

This notice requires you, by law, to make a return of your taxable income and capital gains, and any documents requested, for the year from 6 April 2010 to 5 April 2011.

Before you start to fill in this tax return, please read pages 1 and 2 of the enclosed guide to check that it is the right tax return for you.

Deadlines
We must receive your tax return by these dates:
- if you are using a **paper return** – by **31 October 2011**, or
- if you are filing a return **online** – by **31 January 2012**.

If your return is late you will be charged a **£100 penalty**. If your return is more than 3 months late, you will be charged daily penalties of £10 a day.

If you pay late you will be charged interest and a late payment penalty.

How to file your return
To file online, go to **www.hmrc.gov.uk/online**

To file on paper, please fill in this form using the rules below.

Use black ink and capital letters

Cross out any mistakes and write the correct information below

1.1 Name of bank or building society

A N Y B A N K

Please round up tax paid: £4,700.21 would be £4701

Pay from all employments before tax was taken

2.4 2 4 5 0

2.8 Tax taken off box 2.4 4 8
4 7 0 1

+

- Enter your figures in whole pounds – ignore the pence. Round down income and round up expenses and tax paid – it is to your benefit.
- If a box does not apply, please leave it blank – do not strike through empty boxes or write anything else.

Your personal details and Student Loan repayments

Before you start to fill in this form, please read pages 1 and 2 of the guide to check whether you can use the Short Tax Return.

1.1 Your date of birth *DD MM YYYY*

1.2 Your name and address – *if it is different from what is on the top of this page, please write the correct details underneath the wrong ones, and put 'X' in the box*

1.3 Your phone number

1.4 Your National Insurance number – *leave blank if it is shown above as your 'Tax Reference'*

1.5 If you have received notification from the Student Loans Company that repayment of an Income Contingent Student Loan began before 6 April 2011, put 'X' in the box

1.6 If your employer has deducted Student Loan repayments enter the amount deducted

£   . 0 0

SA200 2011

PG 1

200228:00060443:001

55

+

Employment income

This section is for PAYE earnings - any self-employment income goes in boxes 3.1 to 3.13. ———————— Chapter

| 2.1 | The number of employments you had in the year | 2.4 | Benefits and taxable expenses received - *read the notes* |
| | | | £   · 0 0 |

| 2.2 | Pay from all employments before tax was taken off | 2.5 | Allowable expenses |
| | £   · 0 0 | | £   · 0 0 |

| 2.3 | Tax taken off box 2.2 | 2.6 | PAYE tax reference of your main or last employer |
| | £   · 0 0 | | / |

Self-employment income ———————————————————— Chapter

3.1 What work do you do? *For example, plumber, bookkeeper*

3.7 Turnover (include balancing charges) - *you cannot use this form if your annual turnover was £70,000 or more*

£   · 0 0

3.2 If you began working for yourself after 5 April 2008, enter the date you began *DD MM YYYY*

3.8 Expenses allowable for tax (excluding any capital allowances - *they go in box 3.9*)

£   · 0 0

3.3 If you stopped working for yourself before 6 April 2011, enter the date you stopped

3.9 Capital allowances

£   · 0 0

+

3.4 Date you made your books up to - *please read the notes in the guide*

3.10 Profit (box 3.7 minus (boxes 3.8 + 3.9))

£   · 0 0

3.11 Loss (boxes 3.8 + 3.9 minus box 3.7)

£   · 0 0

3.5 Class 4 National Insurance contributions. Put 'X' in the box if they are excepted - *read the notes in the guide*

3.12 Business losses brought forward from earlier years

£   · 0 0

3.6 Business Start Up Allowance - *do not include in box 3.7*

£   · 0 0

3.13 Deductions on payment and deduction statements from contractors - *construction industry subcontractors only*

£   · 0 0

UK pensions and State benefits received

This section is for the pensions and benefits you get - pensions you are paying into go in boxes 9.1 and 9.2. ———— Chapter

4.1 State Pension - *enter the amount for the year (not the weekly, or 4-weekly amount)*

£   · 0 0

4.4 Tax taken off boxes 4.2 and 4.3

£   · 0 0

4.2 Total of other pensions etc. - *before tax was taken off*

£   · 0 0

4.5 Jobseeker's Allowance

£   · 0 0

4.6 Total of other taxable State benefits

£   · 0 0

4.3 Taxable Incapacity Benefit and contribution-based Employment and Support Allowance - *read the notes*

£   · 0 0

+

interest, dividends and other investment income

e read the notes in the guide before filling in boxes 5.1 to 5.3.

Chapters 9 and 10

Taxed UK interest etc. - *the net amount after tax has been taken off*

£ [ ] . [0][0]

5.2 Untaxed UK interest etc. - *total amounts which have not been taxed*

£ [ ] . [0][0]

5.3 Company dividends (but do not include the tax credits)

£ [ ] . [0][0]

property

annot use this form if your UK property income was £70,000 or more - if it was, please contact us.

Chapter 8

Income

£ [ ] . [0][0]

6.4 Loss

£ [ ] . [0][0]

Expenses allowable for tax

£ [ ] . [0][0]

6.5 UK property losses brought forward from earlier years

£ [ ] . [0][0]

Profit

£ [ ] . [0][0]

er UK income and capital gains

section is **not** to be used for the types of income listed in the guide.

Other income

£ [ ] . [0][0]

7.3 Where does box 7.1 income come from? *For example, commission, tips, locum fees*

[ ]

+

Any tax taken off income in box 7.1

£ [ ] . [0][0]

7.4 Capital gains - *read the notes to see if you need to fill in the Capital gains summary pages. If so, put 'X' in the box*

[ ]

Aid

11.9

Gift Aid payments made in the year to 5 April 2011 - *read the notes in the guide*

£ [ ] . [0][0]

8.2 Total of any 'one-off' payments included in box 8.1

£ [ ] . [0][0]

ing into registered pension schemes or overseas pension schemes

ments to your pension scheme are deducted from your pay before it is taxed, do not include them here - *read the notes.*

Chapter 26

Payments to registered pension schemes where basic rate tax relief will be claimed by your pension provider (called 'relief at source'). Enter the payments and basic rate tax

£ [ ] . [0][0]

9.2 Gross payments - *payments made without basic rate tax relief*

£ [ ] . [0][0]

d Person's Allowance

12.6

If you are registered blind on a local authority or other register, put 'X' in the box

[ ]

10.2 Enter the name of the local authority or other register

[ ]

200 2011   PG 3

+

Married Couple's Allowance ——————————————————— 12.

Married Couple's Allowance is only due if you, or your spouse or civil partner were born before 6 April 1935. It is made up of two amounts - a minimum amount (worth up to £267), plus an age-related amount. *Read the notes in the guide.*

11.1 To claim the full allowance, enter your spouse or civil partner's first name

11.3 Your spouse or civil partner's date of birth *DD MM YYYY* - *if older than you and you filled in boxes 11.1 or 11.2*

11.2 If, as a couple, you have already asked us to give all of the minimum amount to you, or your spouse or civil partner, put 'X' in the box

11.4 Date of marriage or formation of civil partnership - *if between 6 April 2010 and 5 April 2011*

If you have paid too much tax or not enough tax

Please carefully fill in boxes 12.1 to 12.6 to tell us how you would like any repayment to be made. If you also want some of your repayment to go to charity, fill in boxes 12.8 to 12.10 as well. But if you would like all of your repayment to go to charity, just fill in boxes 12.7, 12.9 and 12.10.

12.1 Name of bank or building society

12.8 But if you want only some of your repayment to go to charity, enter the maximum amount we can send

12.9 Enter the charity code - go to www.hmrc.gov.uk and under *Charities & Donors* select *Charities search* ——— 11

12.2 Branch sort code

12.3 Account number

12.10 If you want Gift Aid to apply to the payment to charity, put 'X' in the box

12.4 Building society reference number

12.11 2010-11 tax already refunded

12.5 Name of account holder

12.12 If you owe tax for 2010-11 and have a PAYE tax code, we will try to collect the tax due (up to £2,000) through your tax code for 2012-13, unless you put 'X' in the box

12.6 If you have entered a nominee's name in box 12.5, put 'X' in the box

12.13 If you are likely to owe tax for **2011-12** on income other than employed earnings or pensions, and you do **not** want us to use your 2011-12 PAYE tax code to collect that tax during the year, put 'X' in the box

12.7 If you would like all of your repayment to go to a charity, put 'X' in the box

Signing your form and sending it back

13.1 Please sign and date this form. If you give false information, you may face financial penalties and prosecution. (If you have asked us to send any repayment to a nominee's account, your signature will be our authority to pay that person.)

The information I have given in this tax return is correct and complete to the best of my knowledge

Signature   Date

Finally, please send us your completed form in the envelope provided.

3

HMRC AND YOU

JOHN CASSIDY

'We want you to pay the right amount of tax: no more, no less.'

HMRC

This chapter looks at the way in which the taxpayer and HMRC will interact during the lifetime of your SA tax return and following its submission. We also look at the extent and limits of HMRC's powers, your rights as a taxpayer and other practical aspects such as making complaints or seeking HMRC rulings.

This chapter contains the following sections:

(1) Understanding your responsibilities and rights
(2) Information available from HMRC
(3) The tax return process
(4) HMRC enquiries into tax returns
(5) What penalties can HMRC impose?
(6) Other initiatives
(7) Disclosure facilities relating to offshore bank accounts and other assets
(8) Remission of tax by HMRC
(9) Error or mistake relief/recovery of overpaid tax
(10) Equitable liability
(11) Complaints and compensation
(12) Revenue Adjudicator
(13) HMRC rulings

3.1 UNDERSTANDING YOUR RESPONSIBILITIES AND RIGHTS

3.1.1 Background

HMRC is increasingly run more like a business. It has limited resources which are becoming more thinly spread, hence must be allocated efficiently to ensure that tax is not lost. At the same time, the Government requires it to operate quality management and to assess its efficiency in terms of 'satisfied customers'.

It is HMRC's stated policy to help taxpayers understand their rights and obligations, get their tax affairs right and pay their tax on time, whilst at the same time tackling those who seek to pay less tax than HMRC believes is due.

3.1.2 The Taxpayers' Charter

The Government decided that HMRC must publish a charter and various consultations took place throughout 2009. Originally titled 'HMRC's Charter', the final document published in late 2009 is called 'Your Charter', thereby recognising that the focus of the Charter is the service provided by HMRC to its 'customers'. It sets out standards and values to which HMRC will aspire in dealing with taxpayers and others and what HMRC expects in return. HMRC will have to report annually on progress in meeting those standards.

One practical problem is that the activities undertaken by HMRC are so wide and diverse. They range from the SA system, running the tax credit system, assessing death duties (all these activities relate to private individuals) to administering corporation tax and VAT (often dealing with large companies). HMRC also exists to prevent criminal activities such as smuggling. Can a single charter properly do justice to the standards applicable to dealing with such a diverse range of customers?

A summary of the Charter's contents is shown in Figure 3.1.

Figure 3.1 – Summary of the Charter

Your rights

What you can expect from HMRC:

- Respect you
- Help and support you to get things right
- Treat you as honest
- Treat you even-handedly
- Be professional and act with integrity
- Tackle people who deliberately break the rules and challenge those who bend the rules
- Protect your information and respect your privacy
- Accept that someone else can represent you
- Do all we can to keep the cost of dealing with us as low as possible

Your obligations

What HMRC expects from you:

- Be honest
- Respect our staff
- Take care to get things right

3.1.3 **What this means in practice**

HMRC expects taxpayers to deal with their tax obligations (filing returns, paying tax, replying to HMRC queries) in an honest and business-like way, ie conscientiously and in a timely fashion.

In practice, this means that a taxpayer should attend promptly to correspondence from HMRC and complete tax returns accurately and within a reasonable period. If you find there are some aspects of your tax return that are complex and prevent you from completing the entire form, you should contact the Inspector and explain the reason for the difficulty. In return, HMRC promises to deal with you in a professional, fair and reasonable way, to assume that you are honest unless it has good reason not to and to avoid making unnecessary demands on your time.

3.2 INFORMATION AVAILABLE FROM HMRC

3.2.1 **Codes of practice and fact sheets**

HMRC has published codes of practice (COPs), some of which are examined in this chapter, explaining its approach and procedures in certain areas of work, which set out the legal rights of taxpayers (and HMRC) and explain what the taxpayer can expect to happen. The COPs (which can be found at www.hmrc.gov.uk/leaflets) include the following:

- COP8   Specialist Investigations (fraud and avoidance). Cases other than suspected serious fraud;
- COP9   Civil investigation into cases of suspected serious fraud;
- COP10   Information and advice;
- COP24   Stamp duty land tax enquiries for individuals;
- COP25   Stamp duty land tax enquiries for companies and partnerships
- COP26   Overpayments of tax credits.

The information provided by COPs is also supplemented by Fact Sheets. These are typically shorter than COPs at around 1–5 pages and are designed to help understand how the changes to HMRC investigation powers brought in by FA 2008 have altered the way HMRC officers check a person's tax position. Links to the fact sheets can be found at www.hmrc. gov.uk/compliance/factsheets.htm. Examples of the Fact Sheets are:

- FS1   General information about compliance checks;
- FS2   Requests for information and documents;
- FS3–5   Visits to business premises;
- FS6–7   What happens when inaccuracies are found and penalties;
- FS13   Publishing details of deliberate defaulters;
- FS14   Managing deliberate defaulters;
- FS15   Self assessment and old penalty rules.

A further fact sheet, *HMRC1 – HM Revenue & Customs decisions – what to do if you disagree* may also be useful.

3.2.2 Statements of practice and extra-statutory concessions

It is extremely important that HMRC operates a uniform interpretation of the tax legislation.

In cases where the legislation is obscure or its precise implication is uncertain, HMRC publishes statements of practice (SPs). These operate as a shield for the taxpayer rather than a sword for HMRC. You can rely on HMRC applying these SPs but they do not affect your statutory rights and, if you believe that HMRC's interpretation is wrong, it is still open to you to appeal to the Tax Tribunal.

HMRC also publishes extra-statutory concessions (ESCs). These apply in cases where the legislation is quite clear but the letter of the law produces an unreasonable result. In effect, HMRC recognises that Parliament could never have intended to impose certain tax liabilities, and ESCs are common sense rules that HMRC applies so as to avoid an unreasonable result. Once again, HMRC publishes these ESCs because it recognises the need to treat all taxpayers alike. In general, unless your circumstances are special, or you are seeking to apply an ESC so as to avoid tax, you can rely on HMRC applying a published ESC if it covers your particular circumstances.

Following the House of Lords decision in *Wilkinson* in 2007, HMRC became concerned that it had been acting outside its powers in making such concessions. It has therefore legislated for a number of these, others are now considered obsolete, and a considerably reduced number remain in operation.

3.2.3 General information available from HMRC

The following information is available from HMRC:

- explanatory leaflets, booklets and help sheets, designed to explain different aspects of the tax system and provide assistance with tax return completion;
- press releases, which announce a proposed change in the law, in HMRC practice or other change;
- the *Tax Bulletin*, which provides insight into the thinking of HMRC specialists on technical issues and interpretation of tax law: from 1 January 2007 this was replaced by *HM Revenue & Customs Brief* (see below);
- the *Revenue & Customs Brief* is a short bulletin giving information on developments and changes of interest, and is generally used to announce changes in policy or to set out the legal background to an issue: they have a six-month life span;
- the internal guidance *Manuals*, which cover HMRC's interpretation of tax law and the operation of the tax system.

Most of the above information is on HMRC's website, www.hmrc.gov.uk which also includes a 'top stories and what's new' section where the latest announcements can be found. The website is valuable for not only the large amount of information it makes available, but also for the speed with which it is updated. As well as providing information, SA return forms and employer's forms can be downloaded. In addition to covering tax generally there are also more specialist areas covering matters such as:

- Construction industry scheme;
- Coming to the UK;
- Starting a business;
- Trusts and estates;
- Tax credits.

HMRC's internal Manuals are largely in the public domain. They are available for reference at www.hmrc.gov.uk/manuals.

The HMRC manuals do not have the force of law, nor can they be used as aids to statutory construction. The manuals merely provide HMRC's interpretation of legally binding statutes, case law and practice. They are, therefore, open to challenge through the courts.

3.3 THE TAX RETURN PROCESS

3.3.1 Processing of tax returns

HMRC has designed the SA return with its own data processing needs in mind. Returns are normally read electronically or figures are input by people who have little or no tax knowledge.

The basic principle adopted by HMRC is 'process now, check later'. The fact that the return is processed does not imply that it has been accepted.

Past experience has shown that many returns need correcting because of arithmetical errors, figures being transposed, amounts being entered in the wrong column, etc. When an HMRC officer identifies such obvious mistakes he or she issues a notice to the taxpayer advising him or her of the correction (or 'repair') needed. The taxpayer can object, but if HMRC does not hear further within 30 days, the correction is deemed to form part of the return. In recent years HMRC has taken a more pragmatic approach to this process by phoning the taxpayer or his or her agent to discuss any simple amendments that show up on the processing of the forms.

Tax notes

If you receive a phone call from HMRC it is important that you keep a note of the HMRC officer's name, date of call, topic discussed and any agreement made.

Routine checking and making corrections must not be confused with HMRC officers carrying out an enquiry or other compliance check (see 3.4).

3.3.2 **Keeping proper records**

Because HMRC operates on a 'process now, check later' basis, you need to keep records to be able to back up the entries on your SA return. The length of time that you need to retain your records depends on whether you have a business or are letting property. If you do, the required period is five years and ten months after the end of the tax year (six years for a company). If you do not have either of these sources of income, the minimum period for retaining your records is normally one year and ten months after the end of the tax year concerned.

The duty to preserve records may be discharged by preserving them in any form, eg on an electronic filing system, or by preserving the information contained in those records.

3.4   HMRC ENQUIRIES INTO TAX RETURNS

3.4.1 **HMRC enquiries and other compliance checks**

Once HMRC has received a tax return, it has 12 months to issue a notice that it is carrying out an enquiry into a tax return.

When an enquiry is completed, or if no enquiry is opened before the deadline, the position becomes final and HMRC cannot reopen enquiries into that year unless it can show 'discovery', ie that the taxpayer acted negligently or fraudulently or that key information was not made available to HMRC.

Enquiries can be made into partnership returns under the same rules as apply to individual returns, but any amendments to partnership profits then need to be taken through to each partner's tax returns.

Powers introduced in FA 2008 enable HMRC to undertake compliance checks outside of the enquiry regime. These include powers to visit business premises and to demand documents and information. There is no necessity for the tax year in question to have ended, or for an enquiry to be open, although other criteria may need to be met in such circumstances, such as HMRC having reasonable grounds to suspect a discovery exists.

3.4.2 **Selection of returns for HMRC enquiries**

HMRC has the statutory power to enquire into any tax return without giving a reason. However, because of its limited resources, it has to be selective. It is more likely to look into cases where tax is perceived to be at risk perhaps, for example, because of known intelligence concerning the taxpayer's reliability or, at the other extreme, a new entry appearing on the return when compared to prior years. A number of returns not suspected of being incorrect will also be selected at random each year, although these will be very few as the vast majority of cases will be based on risk assessment.

Even without evidence of inaccuracies, HMRC's employees (and its computer systems) are more likely to choose certain returns for enquiry based on other factors such as:

- returns filed late;
- payments made late;
- returns that include provisional figures;
- cases that involve large capital gains or loss claims;
- changes in accounting date.

3.4.3 HMRC procedure for enquiries

HMRC must give written notice that an enquiry is to be made into an SA return. This notice must be served within 12 months from the date HMRC receives the form.

Historically, HMRC has not given reasons for having opened an enquiry, although it is becoming more open about this issue in the interests of moving matters smoothly forward. In any case it should soon become apparent whether it is initially an enquiry into one particular aspect of the return or a full enquiry under which HMRC is reviewing the entire return and usually requires access to all the taxpayer's records. An aspect enquiry can extend into a full enquiry as HMRC receives information, so the distinction is not completely clear cut.

The opening of an enquiry is not meant to imply that HMRC believes that anything is untoward; merely that it is carrying out checks to test the return's accuracy and reliability.

The Enquiry Manual states repeatedly that HMRC officers should adopt a non-confrontational approach and keep an open mind. HMRC intends that the opening of enquiries should be less contentious, and its aim is to develop a more neutral and less confrontational approach in this area. It is acknowledged that the information initially available in the return and elsewhere is unlikely to be sufficient to establish whether the return is incorrect, and even where it appears incorrect it could be that the information is incomplete, misleading or capable of explanation. The Manual advises officers that unless they are reasonably certain that there have been omissions (and often it will not be possible for them to be certain), they should ask the taxpayer in a neutral way whether there is anything more that he or she has to say, taking account of what has already been said. They should make it clear that no allegations are being made at this point. When HMRC opens an enquiry or compliance check, it will issue details of its code of practice and/or fact sheets as appropriate.

3.4.4 Information required

The HMRC officer is instructed to request informally any information needed, in most cases, rather than using HMRC's formal powers to require the production of the data. A formal notice will, however, be issued for documents and information in the taxpayer's power or possession if he or she has refused to co-operate with the informal request or has failed to comply within the specified timescale. Such a notice must allow the taxpayer a reasonable amount of time to comply; how long is 'reasonable' depends on the particular circumstances, but there is no longer the 30-day minimum period that existed under pre-FA 2008 legislation. The taxpayer may appeal to the Tax Tribunal in some, but not all, circumstances: for example if he or she thinks that the notice is invalid because the data requested is not reasonably required to check his or her tax position. There is no right of appeal against demands for 'statutory records' (broadly, being those records required in order to be able to prepare a complete a correct return) nor is there an appeal mechanism to determine if something is a 'statutory record' in the first place. However, that point may well be covered in any appeal as to the validity of a penalty issued for non-compliance with the statutory notice.

HMRC should only request information and documents that are relevant and reasonably required to determine whether the tax position (which in practice will usually mean the self-assessment return) is correct. Its approach varies according to whether the taxpayer is a business taxpayer (ie a taxpayer who is in self-employment or in receipt of income from property). In the case of a full enquiry into the business taxpayer's affairs, HMRC considers that the following items can be reasonably requested without providing an explanation:

- business records generally;
- cash book, petty cash book, sales and purchase invoices and bank account statements;
- details of how any adjustments made by the accountant have been calculated;
- an analysis of drawings;
- details of any balancing figures or estimates used in the accounts.

Private bank and credit card statements should not normally required at the initial stage of an enquiry but may be required as matters progress. The advice to officers is that they should not ask to see private bank statements at this early stage unless it can be demonstrated that the statements are relevant to the return and can be reasonably required for checking the return's accuracy.

Where there is a full enquiry into a non-business taxpayer that is a complex case, officers should seek to verify in the first place the income and gains declared by reference to any third-party information held (eg a form P11D). The information requested directly might then comprise:

- dividend vouchers;
- certificates of loan interest paid;
- form PPCC (a certificate confirming payment under a personal pension scheme);

- a detailed CGT computation;
- a copy of a property valuation;
- an account of the precise use made of a company asset, such as a private plane.

In aspect cases (where HMRC focuses on just one aspect of the return), the request should, unsurprisingly, concentrate on information relevant to the particular point under review.

3.4.5 Meetings with HMRC

Taxpayers are not obliged to attend any meeting requested by HMRC, but are expected to provide promptly any information considered essential to the enquiry. HMRC believes that meetings allow taxpayers to clarify and explain any points that might have been misunderstood, and to ask questions. The taxpayer will be told if HMRC considers correspondence is an inadequate substitute for a meeting. HMRC has confirmed that the taxpayer should be sent an agenda in advance of such a meeting. The Enquiry Manual states:

> An agenda covering the main areas for discussion at a meeting with the taxpayer should always be provided [...] It should be case specific but not a detailed list of questions and should not be seen by either party to be exhaustive or restrictive [...] It would, however, be unusual for a completely new major agenda item to be introduced at the meeting unless something unexpected is revealed during the course of the meeting.

However, an HMRC officer cannot insist that a taxpayer attends any meeting, and his or her only option in terms of asking questions of the taxpayer face-to-face is to take an appeal to the Tax Tribunal and put his or her questions to the taxpayer during cross-examination (assuming the taxpayer is put forward as a witness).

There is no reason in principle why enquiries should not be conducted entirely through correspondence. The relevant Codes of Practice instruct the HMRC officer to be mindful of the taxpayer's compliance costs and it may be possible to agree with the officer that matters should proceed by way of correspondence without this being viewed as lack of co-operation on the taxpayer's part. It should be borne in mind, however, that a refusal to attend a meeting might, in certain circumstances, be seen as a lack of co-operation when it comes to assessing penalties in the event that the enquiry reveals an under-declaration of tax.

A request for a meeting can often be taken as an indication that the officer, having considered the information initially supplied, has concluded that there are grounds for doubting the return's accuracy or that there are matters that require further detailed enquiry. Officers are instructed that where irregularities are suspected they would need to consider how to give the taxpayer the opportunity to disclose them and to co-operate actively in quantifying them. Whether the taxpayer takes this opportunity could have a bearing on the level of penalty that might be levied on him or her. HMRC officers are instructed to seek early meetings.

3.4.6 Visits to business premises

FA 2008 introduced new legislation allowing HMRC to inspect business premises, assets and documents. Although a formal enquiry does not need to be open, it is likely that most visits that are not part of a traditional VAT or PAYE review will take place as part of an enquiry. HMRC's review may well cover several taxes at once, perhaps requiring several officers to visit. Hence, in practice, it will not be straightforward and careful follow-up will be needed if off-the-cuff responses are given.

The legislation provides for only seven days' notice of a visit which does not have to be in writing. It may be that less, perhaps no, notice will be given if the visit is approved internally or by the Tax Tribunal.

Once on the premises, HMRC officers can only inspect those documents which could be required under a formal information notice. They are also only allowed to 'inspect', not to 'search'. HMRC's guidance confirms that this means to inspect by eye rather than by hand, although in practice the distinction is unlikely to be straightforward. HMRC's manuals give examples of a room with various files on the table as requested by the Inspector. In the corner is a filing cabinet. The Inspector cannot go over and open the filing cabinet to see what is in it; that is considered to be searching. However, if, for example, he or she has been told that the invoices backing up the books he or she is reviewing are stored in the filing cabinet then he or she can open it at will to inspect the invoices.

It should also be noted that the new legislation only creates a power to inspect, it does not give HMRC officers any power to interview or to demand answers to questions at all.

When the new legislation was drafted it did not preclude HMRC turning up at an individual's home. An amendment was later made so that the power could not be used to visit premises used 'solely' as a dwelling. The key word is, of course, 'solely'. In practice, very few visits will be made to private homes as the legislation also includes the express caveat that visits can be made only 'if the inspection is reasonably required for the purposes of checking that person's tax position'.

In the vast majority of cases how can it be 'reasonably required' that the records are reviewed at home rather than anywhere else, such as at an agent's or the business's main premises? HMRC officers are in fact instructed that, wherever practicable, they should avoid inspecting at a person's home as there will normally be an appropriate alternative location.

In addition to buildings, 'premises' also includes any means of transport. Hence there may be requests for access to those premises, for example for a car boot to be opened, subject to whether those actions constitute a search as opposed to an inspection. In reality HMRC recognises that the definition primarily covers things such as mobile chip vans and market stalls run from vans and its manual instructs that officers should not routinely enter all the transport used in a business. The instructions also state, however, that in certain circumstances, officers may open the door of a delivery van in the business's yard and be allowed to look at the boxes inside; climb inside the van to look at the boxes not visible from outside; and to ask the trader to open any box in order to check the tax position of what is inside.

Finally it is worth noting that, if the taxpayer refuses access or asks that the Inspector leaves, HMRC's instructions are simply to withdraw. The right of refusal of entry is not overridden by the inspection notice. There is normally no penalty for doing this; only if the Tax Tribunal has authorised the visit can a penalty can be levied, for deliberately obstructing an HMRC officer during a visit. Even if a tribunal has authorised the visit but no advance notice has been given there should be no penalty, at least initially. The Government is on record as stating that the new powers must be used reasonably so HMRC will surely have to concede that it is unreasonable to levy a penalty for obstruction if all the taxpayer has asked is that the visit is delayed until such time as he or she can arrange representation to deal with issues that he or she is far from expert in.

3.4.7 Closure of the enquiry

The legislation does not specify any time limit within which HMRC must complete its enquiries. However, any taxpayer who feels that the HMRC officer has had sufficient information may appeal to the Tax Tribunal for it to direct HMRC to bring the enquiry to an end.

When the HMRC officer who has conducted the enquiry has completed his or her investigation, he or she must issue a notice stating this and setting out the conclusions of the correct amount of tax that should be payable for the year in question. Once the notice has been issued, HMRC is debarred from starting new enquiries in relation to that return.

3.4.8 If you cannot reach agreement with HMRC

There will be cases where a HMRC officer and a taxpayer (or professional adviser) will form different conclusions about whether, or how, tax should apply to a particular transaction. In such cases where there is an honest difference of opinion, or even in cases where there is an argument about the actual facts, HMRC does not have the last word. The procedure for resolving such disputes is ultimately to require an appeal to be heard by the Tax Tribunal.

Prior to that, an 'independent' internal review may be offered by the HMRC officer or requested by the taxpayer or his or her adviser. This means that an HMRC officer totally unconnected with the case will review it and then report back with his or her views. Whilst this is clearly not truly independent, such reviews can be useful and the contents of the reviewer's report can be enlightening. Whichever way the review goes, the taxpayer can still appeal to the Tax Tribunal.

3.4.9 Tax Tribunals

A new tribunal system came into force on 1 April 2009. The previous bodies, the General Commissioners and Special Commissioners, have been abolished. Most appeals will initially be heard by the First-tier Tribunal. However, some complex cases may be heard by the Upper Tribunal.

Appeals to the Upper Tribunal may be taken on a decision by a First-tier Tribunal on matters of law, but not on matters of fact. Appeals on decisions of the Upper Tribunal will be heard by the Court of Appeal.

Costs

Both the First-tier and the Upper Tribunal have discretion to award costs in certain limited circumstances. In the main, the First-tier Tribunal will award costs only where the unsuccessful party has acted unreasonably. Where the case heard by the First-tier Tribunal is a complex one, the Tribunal has the power to award costs but an appellant can opt out of this in advance.

The Financial Secretary to the Treasury stated on 27 March 2009:

> The general rule in the appeal courts is that the losing party risks having to pay the other side's costs, and I do not think it would be right to treat tax cases differently as a matter of course.

> However, HM Revenue and Customs (HMRC) exercise their discretion and are willing in appropriate circumstances, and in particular where it is they who are appealing against an adverse decision, to consider waiving any claim to costs in cases before the Upper Tribunal or the appeal courts, or to consider making other arrangements – this may also extend to cases before the First-tier Tribunal.

> In the minority of cases categorised as complex, where costs can be awarded in the Tax Chamber of the First-tier Tribunal other than for unreasonable behaviour, the appellant can ensure that there is no risk of them bearing HMRC's costs by opting for the costs rules not to apply.

> In considering the exercise of HMRC's discretion, influential factors include the risk of financial hardship to the other party, the involvement of a point of law the clarification of which would be of significant benefit to taxpayers as a whole and the efficient collection and management of revenue for which HMRC have responsibility.

> If HMRC are to come to an arrangement of this nature, they would expect to do so in advance of the hearing and following an approach by the taxpayer involved.

3.4.10 What happens if the SA return is found to be incorrect?

If the outcome of the enquiry is that a taxpayer has paid too much tax, the difference is refunded, together with interest (normally from the due date of payment).

If the enquiry reveals material errors in the taxpayer's favour, he or she is likely to be charged interest from the 31 January filing date. He or she may also be charged a penalty (see below).

3.4.11 Certificates of tax deposit

There is a way of protecting yourself against interest charges that might otherwise arise if HMRC successfully challenges your tax return.

A taxpayer can make deposits with the Collector of Taxes. A certificate is issued and the deposit is held for the general benefit of the individual until such time as he or she surrenders all or part of the certificate to cover tax liabilities.

Where a deposit is used to cover a tax liability, interest on overdue tax no longer runs from the date that the deposit was made. Deposits are therefore commonly used to cover a tax liability that cannot easily be quantified, for example a capital gain on a sale of unquoted shares where a value at 31 March 1982 needs to be negotiated with the Shares Valuation Division.

Interest is credited from the date the deposit is made to the date it is used (or cashed) for a maximum of six years. The interest is taxable. Interest is paid at a lower rate where deposits are encashed rather than used to settle tax liabilities.

3.4.12 Discovery assessments

If errors revealed in an enquiry were also made in previous tax years, HMRC is likely to raise discovery assessments for those years. Such assessments may be made even though the normal time limit for starting an enquiry may have expired. The time limit for raising such an assessment is normally four years after the end of the year in question, rising to six years in cases of failure to take reasonable care (in effect, negligence) and 20 years where the inaccuracy was deliberate (ie fraud).

HMRC may revisit the past in this way only if fresh information comes to light or if it turns out that the taxpayer had negligently or fraudulently withheld that information.

No discovery assessment may be made where HMRC could reasonably have been expected to identify the point at issue from information provided in a SA return. Moreover, information provided in SA returns for the two previous years is also to be taken into account in this connection. It follows that taxpayers should provide HMRC with too much information rather than too little to avoid discovery assessments. The provision of business accounts is particularly useful in this context, although HMRC's guidance notes for taxpayers state that it is not necessary to send them.

The case of *Langham* v *Veltema* (2004) STC 544 sheds interesting light on all this. The taxpayer had bought a property from his company and it did not occur to the Inspector that the valuation needed to be agreed. The Court of Appeal held that a discovery assessment could be made as the return should have contained an explicit reference to the fact that the valuation had not been agreed with HMRC and hence the insufficiency in the amount of tax emanating from the figures returned. Subsequent discovery cases have followed the same line. HMRC's position and guidance on the implications of this case for taxpayers who wish to ensure finality by filing tax returns which draw its attention to potentially contentious aspects is contained in SP1/06.

An additional form of protection may be secured by obtaining post-transaction rulings (see 3.12).

3.5 WHAT PENALTIES CAN HMRC IMPOSE?

There have been numerous changes to various penalty regimes in all four Finance Acts between FA 2007 and FA 2010. The main ones are:

- 2007 – penalties for incorrect returns;
- 2008 – penalties for failure to notify;
- 2009 – penalties for late filing and late payment of tax;
- 2010 – penalties of up to 200% related to offshore bank accounts.

All follow similar principles, with later Finance Acts building on the format introduced by FA 2007. This section will therefore concentrate on the penalties for incorrect returns which are in practice likely to be the most commonly argued.

In view of these changes, we are presently in a situation where two different penalty regimes might apply as the new rules only apply to documents which were due to be filed on or after 1 April 2009.

3.5.1 Penalties for 2007–08 and earlier years

If a taxpayer has submitted an incorrect return for 2007–08 or an earlier year, he or she could be liable to a maximum penalty equal to the difference between the tax charged on the income or gain returned and the true income or gain. Strictly, such a penalty is chargeable only if the taxpayer has been fraudulent or negligent, but HMRC officers routinely assume that the mere fact that the return is wrong proves that the taxpayer must have been guilty at least of negligence (this is actually a non-sequitur).

A taxpayer will normally encounter resistance from HMRC if he or she tries to get out of a penalty by blaming a third party (eg an accountant) for an error, although he or she may be able to insist that the accountant reimburses any penalty suffered.

Similar provisions apply for partnership returns; penalties for incorrect partnership returns may be levied on each partner.

3.5.2 Mitigation of penalties under the old regime

The penalty for an error in a return (including a set of business accounts submitted with a return) was a potential doubling of the tax chargeable on the income or gains under-declared. This could be levied in addition to any interest charge. However, HMRC's practice was to reduce or mitigate the potential penalty by reference to three factors. Taking the maximum penalty as a surcharge of 100%, the possible reductions were as follows:

(1) For disclosure, a maximum of 30% if the taxpayer had gone to HMRC admitting that a mistake had been made and a maximum of 20% if the taxpayer made a complete disclosure as soon as he or she was challenged by the Inspector.

(2) For co-operation, a maximum of 40%. 'Co-operation' means, for example, answering HMRC's questions and providing any back-up documentation within a reasonable time span.

(3) For reduced seriousness, a maximum of 40%. For example, 0–15% might have been allowed under this heading if it was clear, even though the HMRC officer could not prove it, that the taxpayer had set out deliberately to cheat HMRC. A reduction of perhaps 15–30% would have been allowed if the taxpayer had been guilty of negligence and between 30% and 40% where he or she had simply misunderstood information supplied by a third party (eg where he or she had entered the net instead of the gross interest received on a building society account). HMRC also took into account the size of the adjustment in both relative and absolute terms.

The usual procedure was for the HMRC officer to suggest an overall settlement figure to include underpaid tax, interest and any penalty. However, he or she would also provide a computation showing how the overall figure was calculated and it was open to the taxpayer to argue for a bigger reduction of the penalty element. If the HMRC officer did not agree, a penalty assessment was raised, following which an internal review could be requested and/or an appeal made to the Tax Tribunal.

Payment by instalments was possible where the taxpayer did not have readily realisable capital, but this increased the interest (though not the penalty) payable.

3.5.3 The new penalty regime

A new penalty regime came into effect for return periods starting on or after 1 April 2008 where the due date for filing is on or after 1 April 2009. The first tax returns affected are therefore those for the year ended 5 April 2009 (year ended 31 March 2009 for companies). The new provisions require that three conditions must be satisfied before HMRC can charge a penalty:

- a person delivers a return or other document (such as accounts or a document which is likely to be relied upon by HMRC to determine without further inquiry a question about the taxpayer's liability to tax) to HMRC;
- the return or document contains an inaccuracy which amounts to or leads to
  - an understatement of a person's tax liability; or
  - a false or inflated statement of loss by that person; or
  - a false or inflated claim to repayment of tax;
- the inaccuracy was careless or deliberate.

3.5.4 Different types of inaccuracy

These are defined as follows:

- 'careless' if the inaccuracy is due to the taxpayer failing to take proper care;
- 'deliberate but not concealed' if the inaccuracy is deliberate but the taxpayer did not take steps to conceal it;
- 'deliberate but concealed' if the taxpayer made arrangements to conceal a deliberate misrepresentation.

3.5.5 Taking reasonable care

The HMRC manual (the Compliance Handbook) states:

> Where an inaccuracy in a document has been made despite the person having taken reasonable care to get things right, no penalty will be due.

The manual gives examples of situations where a penalty would not be applicable. These include:

- taking a reasonably arguable view of situations that is subsequently not upheld;
- an arithmetical or transposition inaccuracy that is not so large either in absolute terms or relative to overall liability as to produce an obviously odd result or be picked up by a quality check;
- the taxpayer has followed advice from HMRC that subsequently proves to be wrong;
- the taxpayer has acted on advice from a competent tax adviser (having provided that adviser with a full set of accurate facts) which turns out to be wrong.

The manual also instructs HMRC staff that they should treat a person as taking reasonable care where arrangements or systems have been put in place which could reasonably be expected to produce an accurate basis for the calculation of tax.

The guidance in the Compliance Handbook stresses that HMRC officers should accept that it is possible for taxpayers to make simply careless – rather than intentional – errors and that not every error is automatic evidence of a deliberate attempt to pay the wrong amount of tax.

There have, however, been worrying reports of cases where – rather than following the clear guidance in the Compliance Handbook – HMRC has taken a hard line and sought to charge the full, unmitigated, penalty for a deliberate but unconcealed error in inappropriate circumstances. This is one of the situations in which expert advice from a tax investigations specialist can be invaluable as he or she will be able to ensure that not only does HMRC act within the law, but also according to its own guidance.

3.5.6 Penalties – amounts

In cases not covered by the 'reasonable care let-out' the maximum penalties (or 'starting point') are as follows:

Action	Penalty
Careless action	30% potential lost revenue
Deliberate but not concealed	70% potential lost revenue
Deliberate and concealed	100% potential lost revenue

3.5.7 Discounts for disclosure

A taxpayer may identify an error and volunteer it to HMRC. Alternatively he or she may be challenged ('prompted') and decide to come clean. The following discounts may be allowed:

Maximum penalty	Disclosure	Minimum penalty (irreducible minimum)
30%	unprompted	0%
30%	prompted	15%
70%	unprompted	20%
70%	prompted	35%
100%	unprompted	30%
100%	prompted	50%

3.5.8 Discounts depend on the quality of disclosure

The above discounts are not automatic, they depend upon the quality of the taxpayer's disclosure which is, essentially, how co-operative the taxpayer has been.

The HMRC manual tells its staff to take into account three elements:

- **telling** HMRC what is wrong;
- giving HMRC reasonable **help**;
- allowing HMRC **access** to records.

The discount between the maximum and minimum penalty is then allocated as follows:

Element of disclosure	Percentage
Telling HMRC	30%
Helping	40%
Giving access	30%

3.5.9 Penalties for careless mistakes can be suspended

A penalty may be suspended as part of a process of encouraging a person to improve his or her reporting systems. Suspended penalties then become payable if further careless mistakes arise during the suspension period.

3.5.10 Accepting an under-assessment

Knowingly accepting an under-assessment of tax by HMRC is an offence within the 'careless' category and up to a 30% penalty may be charged.

3.5.11 Appeals against penalties

A taxpayer may appeal against a penalty (and/or request an internal review). The appeal will be heard by the Tax Tribunal.

3.5.12 Naming and shaming

For tax periods commencing on or after 1 April 2010, a non-financial penalty, included in FA 2009, allows HMRC to publish the names of persons who incur penalties for serious irregularities. This will apply to companies and individuals who have deliberately understated more than £25,000 of tax. The details published will include not only the relevant names and amounts, but also addresses, the business sector, periods affected and any other information considered appropriate by HMRC to make clear the person's identity.

Those who make a full unprompted disclosure or a full prompted disclosure within the required time will not be affected. This is on the basis that the penalty is reduced for the quality of the disclosure to the full extent permitted.

Those who have deliberately evaded a much smaller figure, just £5,000 of tax, will be monitored by HMRC (see 3.6 below) and required to submit returns for up to the following five years showing more detailed tax information, for example, detail of the nature and value of any balancing adjustments within business accounts.

> **Tax notes**
>
> Minimise penalties by co-operating fully in an investigation. Don't make matters worse by digging your heels in if you are in the wrong.

3.6 OTHER INITIATIVES

HMRC has, in recent years, stepped up its efforts to monitor areas it regards as posing risks to the Exchequer, whether in the form of common errors, inadequate records, or more serious and deliberate evasion.

The first initiative is the provision of 'toolkits' covering a number of areas of tax. These toolkits were originally intended for advisers, however, since they only cover certain aspects of each specific area, and given HMRC's views rather than the strict legal position, they will mainly be of use to unrepresented taxpayers to provide general guidance on areas of error that HMRC frequently sees in returns and set out the steps that can be taken to reduce those errors. The toolkits will be updated at least annually, but remember, if your affairs are complex, you are likely to save money in the long run by paying a tax adviser to look after your tax affairs.

HMRC has also announced that four new 'products' are suitable for the self-employed, sole traders and small businesses:

- **Keeping records for business** – this is a basic guide, which includes details of where to obtain further information (www.hmrc.gov.uk/ factsheet/record-keeping.pdf).
- **A general guide to keeping records for your tax return** – this provides more detailed guidance on record-keeping covering what type of records you may have to keep, common problems and examples for different types of business (www.hmrc.gov.uk/sa/rk-bk1.pdf).
- **How to set up a basic record-keeping system** – this guidance gives examples of spreadsheets and information about setting up a record-keeping system (www.businesslink.gov.uk/recordkeeping).
- **Finding out what records you should be keeping** – the guidance details the records you need to keep and will help you assess how well you are keeping them. If you are thinking of starting a business the guidance provides you with a checklist. If you are established it will give feedback and advice on any improvements you may need to make (www.businesslink.gov.uk/recordkeepingcheck).

This guidance has been produced by HMRC to help businesses improve their record-keeping, in advance of the launch of HMRC's new Business Record Checks programme later in 2011, which will impose penalties for significant record-keeping failures. HMRC has – at the time of writing – commenced pilot business record checks. If HMRC contacts you to arrange a record check, it is likely that it regards your business as being at high risk of having inadequate records, although it will carry out a small number of random checks. It is expected that HMRC officers will visit your business premises to carry out the record checks and they will seek to make an appointment within the following seven days to carry this out. However, some record checks may be carried out over the telephone.

HMRC has legal powers enabling its inspectors to visit your business premises and in some circumstances it does not even require your permission do to so. Therefore, it is vital that you take this process seriously and notify your adviser as soon as you are contacted by HMRC. It should be noted that, although a factsheet issued with the letters in the pilot project refers to the possibility of penalties for poor records, HMRC has confirmed that no such penalties will be levied at all during the pilot period.

It remains to be seen over the next year what HMRC's attitude to record-keeping standards will be. It may be that some inspectors – who are of course not accountants or generally experienced in running a business – stick to a rigid checklist of what sort of records ought (in HMRC's opinion) to be kept for a business of a particular size. However, it is hoped that inspectors will be more practical than this and take account of what records are strictly needed for each business in question.

In the consultation document HMRC recognised that a simple 'money in' and 'money out' record may be all that is needed for many small businesses. Examples were given of traders who simply put all receipts into a box, not necessarily knowing which of the expenses were capital, disallowable or deductible as revenue, to be sorted out later, perhaps by the business's accountant. That was described as sufficient, on the basis that those records were capable of being turned into a correct and complete return of taxable business profits. Your adviser will be able to help you tidy up your records and get things in order before a records check visit takes place and, if you wish, can be on hand during the visit to protect your interests. Even if HMRC just wants to do a record check over the phone, it is important to contact a suitably qualified professional for guidance before the check takes place: a telephone interview with HMRC could still lead to a tax penalty.

HMRC is also monitoring what it refers to as 'deliberate defaulters'. Deliberate defaulters are taxpayers who have deliberately evaded tax in the past, whether by failing to make returns or by deliberately making incorrect entries on returns. HMRC will notify taxpayers who it intends to monitor in this way and tell them what obligations they will have to meet. Those individuals who trigger the rules will be required to supply additional information with their self-assessment returns. This additional burden can last for up to five years and is unlikely to last for less than two years.

Whilst in the programme (which HMRC refers to by the acronym of MDD) defaulters will be closely monitored to ensure that all tax obligations are being fully met. Where there is any failure to meet and maintain those obligations or HMRC considers the taxpayer presents a high risk to the Exchequer, further compliance activity will be undertaken in accordance with HMRC's new inspection and information powers. Any further failures to meet tax obligations or continuing deliberate defaults are likely to result in the imposition of penalties and may ultimately lead to criminal proceedings being taken against the defaulter.

3.7 DISCLOSURE FACILITIES RELATING TO OFFSHORE BANK ACCOUNTS AND OTHER ASSETS

In 2007 HMRC made an attempt to encourage individuals to come forward if they had offshore bank accounts and had not disclosed taxable income and gains (the Offshore Disclosure Facility).

Errant taxpayers were expected to self-assess the tax lost to HMRC. This involved tax on the source of the monies deposited offshore as well as the interest which had arisen on the overseas bank accounts. Interest and a standard penalty (usually at 10%) were then added in.

This was followed up with an almost identical facility (the New Disclosure Opportunity) which ran until March 2010. A similar facility relating to the medical profession (but not necessarily linked to offshore assets) also closed in 2010; then in March 2011, HMRC announced the Plumbers' Tax Safe Plan (PTSP).

Tax notes

Despite its name, and HMRC's reluctance to publicise the fact, the Plumbers' Tax Safe Plan (PTSP) is actually open to anyone who has not fully disclosed their income in the past and offers very similar terms to any UK resident who wants to make a full tax disclosure.

Only individuals who had the opportunity to use a previous amnesty – those who held offshore accounts before 4 January 2010 and doctors and dentists practising before 31 March 2010 – are barred from using the PTSP. However, in many circumstances, offshore account holders may still be able to take advantage of the current Liechtenstein Disclosure Facility (see 3.7.1), even if they do not currently have a financial presence in Liechtenstein.

While many are calling the PTSP an amnesty it is worth remembering that it is not a total amnesty: it will cost business owners money to use it and bring their tax affairs up to date. Once individuals have registered for the scheme (by the deadline of 31 May 2011) they will need to work out how much tax has been underpaid in past years – possibly as far back as 1991–92 where HMRC has been deliberately misled. The settlement payment covering the tax plus interest and the reduced penalties must be made by 31 August 2011.

It is the reduced tax penalties that are the best part of the deal for individuals. Where individuals have underpaid tax because of making careless mistakes with their tax returns or have forgotten to tell HMRC that they have started up in business, tax penalties will be limited to between zero and 10% of the tax due – cheaper than the 30% penalty that could otherwise be charged in such situations. Where individuals have deliberately understated their income or not told HMRC that they have started trading, tax penalties will be limited to 20% – a bit more expensive than previous amnesties, but still much cheaper than the penalties of up to 100% that can otherwise be charged if HMRC catches you out.

3.7.1 Liechtenstein Disclosure Facility

All of the above facilities have now closed, but another remains open (until 2015 in theory) for those with accounts or other assets held in Liechtenstein. This operates in a fundamentally different way to the other facilities and provides an opportunity for significant tax savings in certain circumstances. The reason for this is that it was negotiated directly between Liechtenstein and HMRC so its terms are unusual and bespoke rather than general in nature.

A key principle of the Liechtenstein Disclosure Facility (LDF) is that Liechtenstein financial intermediaries (such as banks) must identify any clients who may have a tax liability in the UK, for example if a UK address is somehow linked to the account in question. Those persons must then register for and use the LDF (assuming there is a UK tax problem) otherwise the bank must cease acting. Anyone with an account in Liechtenstein who is already fully UK tax compliant must provide an accountant's certificate to that effect; otherwise the Liechtenstein bank or other financial intermediary must again cease to act entirely.

If anyone has tax to declare that is linked to an offshore account but did not use the previous (now closed) facilities, it may still be possible to use the LDF even if there is currently no link with Liechtenstein. There are various complexities to consider before ascertaining if the beneficial terms of the LDF will be available but, in principle, a Liechtenstein presence can be validly created in order to make a disclosure under the LDF.

If you have not disclosed taxable income, you should take advantage of this facility because much more severe penalties will be imposed if your transgressions emerge later, particularly if they come to light as a consequence of an HMRC investigation, potentially up to 200% under the provisions in FA (No. 1) 2010.

3.7.2 Agreement with Switzerland?

There have been reports in the press regarding a potential deal between the UK and the Swiss regarding some sort of facility for settling undeclared tax on assets held in Swiss bank accounts.

Negotiations have been going on with Switzerland for about four months now, but much of what has been written is guesswork so it simply is not known how any deal will be structured. At the time of writing, it is true that HMRC has stated that an agreement may be made public in May/June 2011 but it has also stated that it will be incorporated into a double tax treaty, which will need ratification, so is unlikely to happen before the end of this year. Hence, it seems that a facility is not just around the corner.

Speculation is rife as to what it might include, and whether it will be better than the LDF. HMRC again has stated that any agreement will have some 'novel features' and that there is no plan for it to undermine the LDF.

Overall, the best intelligence now is that any Swiss deal will retain client privacy, so HMRC will not know about the accounts, and will use a withholding tax system. However, we do not know how the mechanism for disclosing past irregularities will work whilst retaining secrecy. Will HMRC be content to waste potentially huge amounts of valuable resources gathering data on apparent tax evaders only to find there is no tax due as everything was previously settled without it knowing the details of the settling taxpayer and his or her Swiss accounts? Other areas of doubt are whether it will have the same advantages as the LDF:

- Will there be immunity from prosecution?
- Will users have the ability to disclose worldwide irregularities?
- Will the penalty be 10%, nil or, based on the new FA 2010 rules, up to 150%?
- Will settlement of past taxes under any Swiss deal cover an even shorter period than 5 April 1999 onwards (as under the LDF) or will it cover 20 years (as is normal)?

With so many unknowns, the LDF still looks like the best deal – an excellent deal in fact. The Swiss deal may eventually prove to be better for some people, but in the author's view, it does not make sense to sit back and hope it will be great for you. We know of cases where HMRC has already acted on stolen bank data to open Code of Practice 9 investigations into individuals with Swiss bank accounts who could have used the LDF but chose to delay. They are now subject to a much more stressful and intrusive investigation, 20-year settlements, much higher penalties, and far higher professional fees.

It would be great if a favourable Swiss deal does come along, but for now, it is not good advice to let clients or prospective clients ignore the certainty of the LDF based on speculation.

3.8 REMISSION OF TAX BY HMRC

(ESC A19)

HMRC's policy is to give up arrears of tax that have arisen because of its failure to make proper and timely use of information supplied. Remission of tax in this way is normally available where the taxpayer could have reasonably believed that his or her tax affairs were in order and was notified of the arrears more than 12 months after the end of the tax year in which HMRC was informed. Alternatively, in the case of an over-repayment, it is available if the taxpayer was notified after the end of the tax year following the year in which the repayment was made.

3.9 ERROR OR MISTAKE RELIEF/RECOVERY OF OVERPAID TAX

(s 33 and Schedule 1AB TMA 1970 inserted by Schedule 52, FA 2009)

Sometimes errors are made against the taxpayer and relief can be claimed against any over-assessment to income tax or CGT owing to an error or mistake in a return. However, relief does not extend to an error or mistake in a claim included in the return. Relief will not be available on the grounds of an alleged error in the basis of computation of liability if the return was made on the basis of, or in accordance with, the practice generally prevailing at the time when the return was made.

The term 'error or mistake' includes errors of omission such as the non-deduction of an admissible expense, errors of commission (eg computational or arithmetical errors), errors arising from a misunderstanding of the law and erroneous statements of fact.

The relief is also available for an error or mistake in a partnership statement where the partners claim that their self-assessments were excessive. If the claim results in an amendment to the partnership statement, any necessary amendments to the partners' individual self-assessments are made by notice by the Board of HMRC.

The rules at s 33 TMA were replaced by Schedule 52 FA 2009 in relation to claims made on or after 1 April 2010. New Schedule 1AB goes into much more prescriptive detail than its predecessor. The gist of the rules has, however, not changed, although eight prescribed circumstances are now listed where such claims will not be entertained. These include cases where the taxpayer knew (or ought to have known) that relief could have been claimed before a certain period expired (such as the tax return amendment window or the time limit to appeal against an assessment) but did not do so.

Relief may be claimed within four years of the tax year to which the return relates.

3.10 EQUITABLE LIABILITY

When HMRC has sought to collect unpaid tax on income and gains for back years, it has sometimes allowed reliefs even though claims have not been made by the appropriate deadlines (see *Tax Bulletin* August 1995). This practice was set to cease from 1 April 2010 but it was announced in December 2009 that the concession was to be put into formal legislation 'at the first opportunity'. It has now been announced that this concession will be given statutory force in FA 2011, and applies from 1 April 2011.

3.11 COMPLAINTS AND COMPENSATION

A taxpayer who is not happy with the way he or she has been treated by HMRC is entitled to complain. In this first instance, it is recommended that the complaint be raised with the person or officer who has been dealing with the case to see if matters can be resolved before entering into the formal complaints procedure. If matters cannot be resolved (or if the complainant does not want to approach the officer who has been working the case) the complaint will be referred to a complaints handler. If this proves unsatisfactory, the complaint should be raised with the Adjudicator (see leaflet AO1 at www.hmrc.gov.uk/leaflets/ao1.pdf); failing that, the case could be referred through the taxpayer's local MP to the independent Parliamentary Ombudsman. Further details of how to complain and who to contact are provided in leaflet C/FS Complaints (www.hmrc.gov.uk/factsheets/complaints-factsheet.pdf), the complaints fact sheet.

If HMRC makes a mistake or causes unreasonable delay, the taxpayer is entitled to an apology, an explanation of what went wrong and, if appropriate, details of the steps taken to ensure the mistake does not happen again. If reasonable and possible, HMRC will also have the mistake corrected.

In addition, the taxpayer may receive some form of financial redress such as the payment of costs incurred by the taxpayer; a (small) payment to reflect the worry and distress caused; and waiving of interest. The redress payments are ex-gratia and HMRC is under no legal obligation to pay them.

3.12 REVENUE ADJUDICATOR

If you are dissatisfied with the treatment you receive from HMRC and have exhausted HMRC's own complaints procedure you can ask an independent body to investigate your complaint. The matter should be referred to:

The Adjudicator's Office, 8th Floor, Euston Tower, 286 Euston Road, London, NW1 3US; Tel: 030 0057 1111 or 020 7667 1832; Fax: 030 0057 1212 or 020 7667 1830; www.adjudicatorsoffice.gov.uk.

If this fails you can ask your Member of Parliament to refer the case to the Parliamentary Ombudsman (www.ombudsman.org.uk).

3.13 HMRC RULINGS

There are two types of HMRC rulings: post-transaction and advance rulings.

3.13.1 Post-transaction rulings

Post-transaction rulings are rulings on the application of tax law to a specific transaction after it has taken place. Although ultimately a matter for the courts, HMRC will consider itself bound by its rulings unless material information is withheld.

The following information has to be submitted before a ruling can be obtained:

- the taxpayer's name and tax reference number;
- full particulars of the transaction or event in question;
- copies of all relevant documents with the relevant parts or passages identified;

- the taxpayer's opinion of the tax consequences of the particular transaction along with reasons for that opinion;
- an explanation of the particular point(s) of difficulty that led to the request;
- details of what sections of the Taxes Acts, case law, extra-statutory concessions or statements of practice are considered to be relevant;
- when submitting an application for a transaction for which there is also the disclosure of an avoidance scheme which covers all or part of the transaction, it is important that explicit mention is made of any related disclosures, preferable by including a copy of the disclosure or, where available, by reporting the allocated DOTAS scheme reference number;
- a statement that, to the best of the taxpayer's knowledge and belief, the facts given are correct and all relevant facts have been disclosed;
- full details, including tax reference numbers, of any other parties involved;
- if advice on HMRC's interpretation of tax law is sought, the taxpayer must make it clear that he or she is seeking considered guidance and say how he or she intends to use it, for example by publishing it.

Tax notes

After a tax return is filed, a ruling will only be given up to the deadline for HMRC opening an enquiry. Make use of the post-transaction rulings procedure before you need to file your return so that when you file that particular aspect has been agreed in advance. For example, you may want to agree the value of unquoted shares at the time that you acquired them if that value determines your tax liability under the employment income provisions. Or if you have sold shares in a private company, you may need confirmation that the gain qualifies for entrepreneurs' relief.

3.13.2 Advance clearances

HMRC also has a system for giving clearances and advance transactions rulings to 'business customers'. HMRC aims to provide some certainty for businesses and will, normally within 28 days, provide clearances on areas of material uncertainty arising within four Finance Acts of the introduction of any new legislation (although for years – like 2010–11 – where there is more than one Finance Act, by concession HMRC will provide clearances on areas of material uncertainty arising in Finance Acts for the last four years). Older legislation will also be considered where there is material uncertainty around the tax outcome of a real issue of commercial significance to the business itself, determined by reference to the scale of the business and the impact of the issue upon it.

Similar details to those noted above for non-business clearances must be provided.

4

EMPLOYMENT INCOME

PHILIP FISHER AND ANNE-MARIE BODEN

This chapter deals with the following matters:

(1) Basis of assessment
(2) How tax is collected
(3) Allowable expenses
(4) Benefits-in-kind in general
(5) Company cars
(6) Free use of assets
(7) Beneficial loans
(8) Living accommodation
(9) Miscellaneous benefits
(10) Share incentives
(11) Options to acquire gilts
(12) Options to acquire company assets
(13) Golden hellos
(14) Restrictive covenants
(15) Redundancy payments
(16) Golden handshakes, other termination payments and continuing benefits
(17) Designing a 'tax efficient' remuneration package

4.1 BASIS OF ASSESSMENT

4.1.1 Introduction

An individual who holds an office or employment is taxed under the Income Tax (Earnings and Pensions) Act (ITEPA) 2003, which came into force on 6 April 2003.

Employment income is taxed according to the residence status of the individual concerned. The rules are set out in Table 4.1.

Table 4.1 – Different treatment according to residence/domicile of employee

---

Individual resident and ordinarily resident in the UK: tax is due on total remuneration (s 15 ITEPA 2003).

Individual resident but not ordinarily resident in the UK: tax is due on total remuneration (subject to special treatment of foreign earnings (see 35.4)).

Individual not resident in the UK: tax is due on total remuneration for duties performed in the UK (s 27 ITEPA 2003).

Individual resident but not ordinarily resident in the UK where the duties are performed outside the UK. Tax is due on earnings brought into or enjoyed in the UK.

Individual resident and ordinarily resident but not domiciled in the UK where all the duties are performed abroad ('foreign earnings', see 35.4). Tax is due on earnings brought into or enjoyed in the UK (s 26 and s 22 ITEPA 2003).

The remainder of this chapter concentrates on UK resident and ordinarily resident employees who are taxed under s 15 ITEPA 2003. See Chapters 34 and 35 for the taxation of non-ordinarily resident and non-UK domiciled individuals.

4.1.2 Receipts basis

(s 10 ITEPA 2003)

The amount that is assessable for a tax year is the amount of earnings chargeable in any year.

4.1.3 Date remuneration is deemed to be received

(s 18 ITEPA 2003)

Special provisions define the date that an individual is deemed to receive remuneration as the earlier of:

(1) the date when payment is actually made; and
(2) the time when the employee becomes entitled to payment.

In the case of directors, the date can be earlier than above, in that payment is deemed to take place on the earliest of (1) and (2); and

(3) the date that sums are credited to the director in the company's accounts or records (whether or not there is any restriction on the right to draw those sums); or
(4) the end of a period if the director's earnings for a period are determined before the period has expired; or
(5) if earnings are not determined until after the end of a period the date when the amount is determined.

The employer is required to operate Pay As You Earn (PAYE) when payment is deemed to have taken place (see 21.1).

4.1.4 Amounts deducted in arriving at pay

(s 713 ITEPA 2003)

Contributions to a payroll giving scheme ('give as you earn') are deducted from an individual's salary in arriving at taxable pay for both PAYE and for assessment purposes. Note that NIC is based on pay before such amounts are deducted (see 23.1).

4.2 HOW TAX IS COLLECTED

4.2.1 Tax deductions under PAYE

Earnings paid to directors and employees are subject to PAYE. Earnings for this purpose are all cash payments (salary, wages, bonus, etc) and a limited number of benefits and expense payments.

PAYE code numbers

HMRC issues code numbers that determine the amount of PAYE deductions. Such code numbers are based on the latest information available to HMRC and are intended to ensure that the amounts withheld under PAYE approximate closely to an individual's actual liability. Nevertheless, deduction of tax under PAYE is provisional in that if the actual liability exceeds the amount withheld under PAYE, HMRC may collect the balance either by increased PAYE deductions in subsequent years or by raising an assessment and similarly, overpayments can be recovered by the individual. HMRC may issue 'K codes' under which increased deductions may be taken, of up to 50% of an individual's pay. The principle behind K codes is that notional pay is added to an employee's actual pay, and PAYE is operated accordingly. This is intended to cover the situation where taxable benefits-in-kind exceed a person's allowances.

What the letters in your code mean

L   Basic personal allowance.
P   Full personal allowance for those aged 65–74.
Y   Full personal allowance for those aged 75+.
T   Any other items HMRC needs to collect through a tax code or if someone asks HMRC not to use any of the other tax code letters listed. This has also been in use from 2010–11 for those expected to lose some or all of their personal allowances because income is expected to exceed £100,000.

K   Total allowances in a code are less than the total deductions. Sections PAYE11095 and PAYE11096 in HMRC's PAYE Manual explain how a K coding works.

BR   Tax deducted at the basic rate, currently 20%.

D0   Tax deducted at a flat rate of 40%.

D1   Tax is deducted at the additional rate of tax – currently 50% (most commonly used for a second job or pension)

NT   No Tax, usually used for non-UK residents being paid from the UK.

How HMRC tax code is worked out

Step one

Your tax allowances are added up (in most cases this will just be your personal allowance and any blind person's allowance; in some cases it may include certain job expenses).

Step two

Income you have not paid tax on (for example, untaxed interest or part-time earnings) and any taxable employment benefits are added.

Step three

The total amount of income you have not paid any tax on ('deductions') is taken away from the total amount of tax allowances. The amount you are left with is the total tax-free income you are allowed in a year.

Step four

To arrive at your tax code, the amount of tax-free income you are left with is divided by ten and added to the letter that fits your circumstances.

As an example, the tax code 177L means:

- you are entitled to the basic personal allowance;
- £1,770 must be taken away from your total taxable income after accounting for untaxed income etc.

How tax is worked out using this code 177L for 2011–12

Pay from employment or pension	£21,840
Minus tax free amount for the year	£1,770
Pay on which tax will be paid	£20,070
On £20,070 the tax payable is	
Basic rate 20% =	£4,014.00
So tax to be paid in the year =	£4,014.00

Tax notes

It is important that you pay attention to the tax code being operated against your monthly income to ensure that when you come to filing your tax form there are no surprises. Two areas to highlight are as follows:

(1) You start a new job part way through a tax year and you do not have a form P45 from your previous employer and a form P46 is not filed. In previous years, your payroll department would have operated a basic rate (BR) tax code which would have resulted in an underpayment for a higher rate taxpayer and an overpayment for a basic rate taxpayer but rarely the right amount of tax being deducted. From 6 April 2011 your employer will be required to deduct tax using the 0T (zero T) code on a non-cumulative basis. Tax code 0T will ensure that tax is deducted at the basic, higher and additional rates where necessary. This is likely to result in you overpaying tax until your code is corrected.

(2) You file an annual SA form but HMRC includes some of your investment income in the code to be operated against your earnings. Consider whether you want to be taxed on this basis, ie paying tax via your coding, or if you would prefer to continue to pay tax via the self-assessment system.

4.2.2 Foreign employers unable to operate PAYE

Where a person is employed by a foreign employer that has no place of business in the UK, PAYE is not normally operated. Tax is payable by the employee as if he or she were self-employed, ie two payments on account based on the previous year's tax bill plus a balancing payment on 31 January following the end of the tax year.

4.2.3 Self-assessment

An employee has until 31 January following the year of assessment to file a return and pay any additional tax due (ie for 2011–12, by 31 January 2013). If the employee wants the tax underpaid (of up to £2,000) to be collected by way of an adjustment in the code operated against his or her salary, he or she is requested to file a paper return by 31 October following the year of assessment (ie for 2011–12, by 31 October 2012). The 31 October filing date is extended to 30 December (ie for 2011–12, by 30 December 2012) for individuals who file their returns online.

Where the taxpayer fails to notify HMRC, and pays any tax due by 31 January, interest, penalties and surcharges may arise (see Chapter 2).

4.3 ALLOWABLE EXPENSES

4.3.1 Strict conditions must be satisfied for expenses to be allowed

(s 327 ITEPA 2003)

The rules governing the amounts that may be deducted for tax purposes from remuneration subject to tax as employment income are extremely strict. The legislation provides for a deduction to be made only in respect of expenses that are wholly, exclusively and necessarily incurred in the performance of the duties of the employment or office.

Wholly, exclusively ...

The courts have held that the following expenses are **not** deductible for employment income purposes because they are not deemed to have been incurred wholly and exclusively in the performance of the employment duties:

(1) meal expenses paid out of meal allowances;
(2) the rent of a telephone installed for business reasons but not used wholly and exclusively in the performance of duties;
(3) the cost of domestic assistance where the taxpayer's wife is employed;
(4) the cost of looking after a widower's children; and
(5) the cost of ordinary clothing.

... and necessarily ...

The situation often arises that the employer has reimbursed the expense because it is regarded as essential. This is helpful, but not conclusive. HMRC will assess the amount paid to a director or P11D employee (see 4.4.1) but may then seek to disallow the individual's expenditure claim on the grounds that it is not *necessary*. Two of the leading cases won by HMRC involved reimbursed expenditure by journalists on newspapers and other periodicals. The point at issue was whether reading such newspapers was part, or inherent in the performance, of the journalists' duties. The key point here is that it is not the employer's decision that determines the case. The employer may be fully prepared to reimburse the expenditure but HMRC may still argue that it fails to meet the very strict guidelines on what constitutes 'necessary'.

... in the performance of the duties

Other expenses were rejected on the grounds that they were not incurred in the performance of the duties of the relevant employment:

(1) employment agency fees (although entertainers specifically are now entitled to claim a deduction for such expenses of up to 17.5% of their earnings);
(2) a headmaster's course to improve background knowledge;
(3) an NHS registrar's costs of attending training courses that had to be completed so that he could apply for a position as a consultant (*HMRC* v *Decadt* [2007] ER (D) 139)
(4) an articled clerk's examination fees;
(5) travelling costs from home to the place where the employment duties were performed;
(6) expenses paid out of living allowances given to an employee when working away from home;
(7) expenditure by a rugby league player on diet supplements to improve and maintain his fitness (*Ansell* v *Brown* 2001 STC 1166);
(8) expenses incurred by a supply teacher in keeping a room at her home for preparation of lessons, marking, etc (*Warner* v *Prior* 2003 SpC 353);
(9) expenses incurred by a Civil Servant who was allowed to work from home in Norfolk but was required to travel to the department's offices in Leeds each week (*Kirkwood* v *Evans* 2002 STC 231).

Cases where the taxpayer has succeeded

There have been cases where travelling expenses have been allowed because the courts were satisfied that a person's duties started as soon as he or she left home. For example, in *Gilbert* v *Hemsley* [1981] STC 703, a plant-hire company director's duties involved him using his home as a base and travelling to various sites. The court held that once he left home he was travelling in the course of his duties. Similarly, in *Pook* v *Owen* (1969) 45 TC 571 a doctor was 'on call' and his duties started once he was telephoned by the hospital to ask him to attend.

In *HMRC v Banerjee* [2010] EWCA Civ 843, a trainee doctor's course costs were allowed because the expenditure on training was held to be incurred solely for the purpose of meeting the requirements of her employment contract.

4.3.2 Expenses that *are* allowable

(ss 333–360 ITEPA 2003)

Certain expenses are specifically allowable, such as the cost of professional subscriptions to an approved body that is relevant to the individual's employment (eg the annual subscription to the Institute of Chartered Accountants or The Law Society – see www.hmrc.gov.uk/list3/list3.pdf). Also, flat rate expenses are given to employees in certain industries to cover expenditure on tools, overalls, special clothing, etc.

Tax notes

HMRC publishes a list of approved bodies whose subscriptions qualify as allowable expenses.

Despite the very restrictive rules outlined in 4.3.1, you may be able to secure a deduction if you pay interest on a loan applied to purchase equipment used in the course of your employment (eg a computer or a fax machine at your home that you use for business purposes).

In addition to claiming a deduction for loan interest, relief may be due for expenses such as running costs and (in the case of a fax machine) the line rental. Capital allowances may also be due, subject to restrictions if the equipment is used for private purposes as well as for your employment.

At one time, directors or employees could not obtain tax relief for expenditure on items such as directors' and officers' liability insurance, or professional indemnity insurance. Relief from tax and NIC is now specifically due for such premiums. Moreover, tax relief is also available where an employee has to meet his or her own uninsured liability.

The relief for insurance or payment of uninsured liabilities is also available to former employees who incur such expenses within a six-year period after the year in which the employment ceased.

4.4 BENEFITS-IN-KIND IN GENERAL

Part 7A, ITEPA 2003 entered into force on 6 April 2011, subject to additional anti-forestalling provisions which applied between 9 December 2010 and 5 April 2011. In considering whether a benefit-in-kind charge arises, particular care should be taken where benefits are paid, or assets or loans are made available, via a third party such as a trust, as the provisions in Part 7A may in certain circumstances apply rather than the applicable benefit-in-kind charge. If this is the case, in some cases not only will the tax charge be accelerated, but it may be substantially increased as the charge will be on the full capital value of what has been made available, rather than an annual 'usage' value. The disguised remuneration provisions are considered in detail in Chapter 5.

These provisions are extremely complex and if you think you might be affected, it would be advisable to take specialist professional advice, as any errors could prove very costly.

4.4.1 Directors and 'higher paid' employees

(s 201 ITEPA 2003)

An employer is required to submit form P11D in respect of most employees who may then be assessed on the cost to the employer of benefits-in-kind received by them. In rare cases, employees may only be taxed on benefits if they are convertible into cash.

Some employers tax benefits-in-kind via the payroll (in a horrible mutilation of the English language, this is commonly known as 'payrolling' benefits). However, unless prior agreement has been obtained from HMRC, they are currently still required to complete and submit forms P11D, otherwise penalties will be charged. Where employers have taxed some expenses and benefits for some or all of their employees via the payroll and file P11D information online, they are advised to telephone the Employer Helpline at least a week in advance of any online submission of forms P11D, advising HMRC that payrolling has taken place in that year, in order to avoid incorrect processing of the data (ie double charging!). The employer should then complete the *amount made good or from which tax deducted* box (where this box is available for the relevant benefit) and, separately on paper, submit P11D information for other payrolled benefits (where the *amount made good or from which tax deducted* box is not available). These separate P11Ds and lists must be clearly marked 'payrolled'. Form P11D(b) should then be completed as normal. Where paper returns are still being made, all relevant forms must be clearly marked 'payrolled' and form P11D(b) completed as normal.

An employee will fall within the P11D category where remuneration, together with benefits and reimbursed expenses, is paid at the rate of £8,500+ pa. Such employees formerly were called 'higher paid' employees! Possibly because this rate is below the level of the National Minimum Wage, the Office of Tax Simplification (OTS) has recently suggested that it should either be increased to a reasonable level reflecting current norms for 'higher pay', or scrapped entirely. As yet the Government has not acted on this suggestion.

For example, a person whose employment began on 1 January 2012 and who had received a salary of £2,000 and reimbursed expenses of £200 by 5 April 2012 would be within the P11D category as the total amount of £2,200 would give an annual rate greater than £8,500.

All reimbursed expenses and other benefits have to be reported on form P11D and count towards the £8,500 pa limit (even though they may be validly incurred for business purposes and ultimately no taxable benefit-in-kind arises) unless a dispensation has been agreed by HMRC (see 4.4.2).

Directors are normally within the P11D regime, regardless of whether their remuneration reaches or exceeds the £8,500 pa limit (subject to one exception: see below). Furthermore, individuals who control a company's affairs and take management decisions may be treated as directors, even if they do not hold a formal position with the company and may have another title or job description within the company.

A person remunerated at a rate below £8,500 pa by a particular company is still within the P11D category if a directorship is held with another company in the same group, or if the total remuneration from group companies amounts to £8,500+ pa whether or not any directorships are held. Certain directors are exempt from these rules by virtue of s 223(8) and therefore are excluded from the definition. To qualify for this favourable treatment, certain conditions need to be satisfied. The director:

(1) must not hold more than 5% of the company's ordinary share capital (holdings by his or her associates may need to be included as if he or she held the shares); and

(2) must be employed on a full-time basis (or the company must be a non-profit making organisation); and

(3) must be receiving remuneration and benefits that in aggregate are less than £8,500 pa.

An employer must provide the employee with details of the taxable amounts for benefits shown on his or her form P11D. This must be done before 6 July following the tax year unless the employee had left employment before the end of the tax year (in which case the employer must provide the information within 30 days of the former employee requesting him or her to do so). The P11D must include the cost of benefits provided by third parties where these were arranged by the employer.

Anyone earning at a rate below £8,500 and in receipt of chargeable benefits should receive a form P9D showing those benefits.

4.4.2 Dispensations

HMRC may grant a dispensation so that certain reimbursed expenses that would not, in any event, give rise to a tax charge need not be reported on form P11D. This is useful in reducing administration and accounting work and, wherever possible, employers should apply for a dispensation. HMRC will set out expenses covered by it; any expenses not covered must still be reported. Any changes in the method of reimbursing expenses or scales of allowances must be notified to HMRC.

4.4.3 Benefits-in-kind provided by third parties

(s 265 ITEPA 2003)

It is not uncommon for wholesalers and distributors to offer benefits-in-kind to employees of retailers with whom they do business. Subject to certain *de minimis* rules, such benefits are taxable just as if they had been provided by the retailer him or herself. This can also apply in other situations.

However, non-monetary gifts costing no more than £250 received by an employee or his or her family from someone other than his or her employer are generally exempt from income tax. Likewise, no income tax liability usually arises on entertainment that an employee receives from a third party. These exemptions apply only where the gift or entertainment is not provided directly or indirectly by their own employer and, furthermore, where it is not provided as a reward for, or in recognition of, specific services done or to be done by the employee.

Where the third party benefits have not been arranged by the employer, the provider must give the employee details of any taxable benefits by 5 July following the tax year.

4.4.4 Benefits for a director's family

(s 201(2) ITEPA 2003)

A fundamental point is that an assessment may arise even though the director or employee has not personally received a benefit-in-kind. A tax liability may arise if a benefit is made available to a member of the director's or employee's household by reason of his or her employment. HMRC may argue that substantial benefits-in-kind enjoyed by a director's family are provided by reason of the director's employment even though the recipient may also be a company employee. HMRC is especially likely to argue this where a director's spouse or civil partner is employed by the company and receives abnormally large benefits-in-kind for an employee of that particular category.

The legislation defines an individual's family or household as his or her spouse or civil partner; children and their spouses or civil partners; parents, domestic staff, dependants and guests. Note that this definition does not include grandparents, brothers, sisters and grandchildren, although there can be situations where such relatives count as dependants.

4.4.5 Scholarships

(s 213 ITEPA 2003)

There is a general exemption for scholarships, but a scholarship provided to a child by reason of his or her parent's employment is normally treated as a benefit-in-kind of the parent. The benefit is taxable unless it can be shown that the scholarship was not awarded by reason of the employment and 75% of the scholarships awarded by the fund are awarded to children whose parents are not employed by the company.

4.4.6 Benefits that may result in a tax charge for non-P11D employees

The general rule is that employees not within the P11D category are assessable only on benefits capable of being converted into cash or on any benefits provided by an employer meeting an employee's personal liability. This principle has been modified to some extent so that, for example, credit vouchers are an assessable benefit even if the employee is not within the P11D category. However, the principle continues to hold good with regard to benefits such as the provision of a company car, free use of assets, beneficial loans, etc. Table 4.2 sets out the position.

Table 4.2 – Treatment of benefits received by non-P11D employees

	Taxable	Non-taxable
Benefits capable of being turned to pecuniary account, ie convertible to cash	✓	
Luncheon vouchers* in excess of 15p per working day	✓	
Credit tokens and vouchers	✓	
Transport vouchers (ie any ticket, pass or other document or token intended to enable a person to obtain passenger transport services)	✓	
Living accommodation	✓	
Payment of employees' personal liabilities	✓	
Company cars		✓
Free use of assets		✓
Beneficial loans		✓
Medical insurance		✓

* The tax exemption for luncheon vouchers up to 15p per day is to be abolished following a period of consultation.

4.4.7 Tax treatment of specific benefits when received by a non-P11D employee

Benefits capable of being converted into cash

Where the benefit is convertible into cash, the measure of assessable benefit is the amount of cash that could be realised. For example, an employee provided with a new suit by the employer would be taxable on its second-hand value.

Credit tokens and vouchers

(s 90 ITEPA 2003)

The taxable amount in respect of credit tokens and vouchers is the cost to the employer of providing them. Vouchers other than cheque vouchers are deemed to be taxable earnings as and when they are allocated to a particular employee, not when they are used by that employee.

Transport vouchers

(s 82 ITEPA 2003)

Specific legislation was introduced some years ago to ensure that season tickets provided by employers should be taxable. Once again, the measure of the assessable benefit is the cost to the employer of providing the ticket or voucher.

Living accommodation

(s 97 ITEPA 2003)

The assessable amount is the greater of the property's gross rateable value or the rent payable by the employer, less any amount made good by the employee. Following the abolition of domestic rates, estimated values are used for new or substantially altered properties. No assessable benefit arises where the employee occupies representative accommodation (see 4.4.8).

Payment of employee's personal liabilities

A liability arises where the employer pays a personal liability of the employee. This would include such items as home heating, lighting bills and water rates, but special rules apply where the employee is in representative accommodation (see 4.4.8).

4.4.8 Benefits not taxable for any category of employees

There are certain benefits that are not usually taxable even when the employee is within the P11D category. The most widely used tax-free benefits are as set out below.

Retirement benefits

As a general rule, payments by an employer to an approved occupational pension scheme to secure retirement benefits for an employee do not give rise to an income tax liability for that employee, unless the payment causes the lifetime allowance to be exceeded. From 22 April 2009, new rules were introduced which meant that a tax charge may be levied where large contributions are made by the employee or employer into a registered pension scheme for someone earning £150,000 or more. These rules were extended to apply to those earning £130,000 or more (not taking into account employer contributions) from 9 December 2009. These lapsed on 5 April 2011, with the introduction of the new, lower annual allowance of £50,000 (albeit this had actually been in effect since 14 October 2010 in certain transitional cases – see 2.5).

Payments by the employer into an 'unregistered' scheme are treated as payments to an employer funded retirement benefits scheme (EFRBS). Previously, no tax or NIC was payable on contributions into the scheme (but neither the employee nor the employer received tax relief on contributions). Instead, when relevant retirement benefits were paid out, the employee (or ex-employee) was subject to tax at his or her marginal rate at that time. Payments out could be free of NIC provided certain strict conditions were met. With the introduction of Part 7A ITEPA, such payments are likely to give rise to an immediate tax charge under the 'disguised remuneration' rules – see Chapter 5.

To secure approval, a **registered** pension scheme must be established for the sole purpose of providing 'relevant benefits' (ie pensions, death-in-service payments and widows' and dependants' pensions). The pension benefits payable by a registered scheme must not exceed certain limits. Pension schemes are covered in more detail in Chapter 26.

Luncheon vouchers

Non-transferable luncheon vouchers that are not capable of being exchanged for cash are currently exempt from income tax up to a generous limit of 15p per working day! Vouchers for larger amounts are partly exempt, with the excess over 15p being taxable in full, whether or not the employee is within the P11D category. However, this is amongst the reliefs reviewed by the OTS, and is to be abolished following a period of consultation.

Staff canteen and dining facilities

No taxable benefit-in-kind arises where the canteen, etc is available to all staff. Furthermore, the use of a separate room by directors and more senior staff does not prejudice this exemption, unless the meals provided are superior. HMRC also accepts that facilities provided by a hotel or restaurant for staff to 'eat in' may come within the definition of a 'canteen', provided that the meals are taken at a time or place when they are not being served to the public or where part of the restaurant or dining room is designated specifically as being for staff use only. From 6 April 2011, this relief will only be available where it is not linked to relevant salary sacrifice or flexible remuneration arrangements.

Where an employer provides meals in a canteen by giving employees a smart card which is topped up periodically by the employer, but to which the employee can also add funds, this is regarded as the provision of money rather than the provision of free or subsidised meals. See HMRC manual EIM 21675. Employers should operate PAYE and NIC in these circumstances.

Sports facilities

(s 261 ITEPA 2003)

No taxable benefit arises in respect of the use or availability of sports facilities owned by the employer. HMRC's view is that the exemption is not available for use of facilities that are available to the general public, eg under a corporate subscription to a sports club.

Medical check-ups

The provision of routine health checks or medical screening does not constitute a taxable benefit provided the check-ups are available to all employees or all those employees who have been identified in a health screening as requiring a medical check-up.

The exemption does not apply to payment for any medical treatment which follows such a check-up.

Eye tests and corrective glasses

Employers are required by law to pay for eye tests and corrective glasses where employees use computer screens. HMRC does not charge tax in these circumstances, whether the benefit is provided directly or through the provision of a voucher. However, where spectacles are for general use, but include a special prescription for VDU use, only a proportion of the cost relating to the special prescription will be exempt from tax.

Workplace nurseries and crèches

Employees are exempt from income tax on the benefit derived from the use of a workplace nursery provided by the employer. The exemption applies only to nurseries run by employers alone or jointly with other employers or bodies, either at the workplace or elsewhere.

The provision by an employer of cash allowances to employees for childcare, or the direct meeting of an employee's childcare bills by an employer, are at present taxable benefits. An employer can provide a tax free benefit of up to £55 pw (restricted to £28 pw and £22 pw for higher rate and additional rate taxpayers first joining the scheme from 6 April 2011, respectively) by either contracting with an approved childcarer or providing vouchers that the employee can use to pay an approved childcarer. This relief is no longer available at all where the benefit is provided through a salary sacrifice arrangement.

Pool cars

(s 167 ITEPA 2003)

No tax charge arises by reason of the use of a pooled car. A car qualifies as a pooled car only if all of the following conditions are satisfied:

(1) It is available for, and used by, more than one employee and is not used ordinarily by any one of them to the exclusion of the others.
(2) Any private use of the car by an employee is merely incidental to its business use.
(3) It is not normally kept overnight at or near the residence of any of the employees unless it is kept on the employer's premises.

These requirements are interpreted strictly. Employers need to be able to demonstrate that the conditions for the car to be a pool car have been met, for instance by keeping detailed mileage records to show when the car was used, by whom and for what journeys.

Note that a car only qualifies as a pooled car by reference to a tax year. There is a danger, therefore, in a car being taken out of pooled use and allotted to a specific employee towards the end of a tax year. As the car now no longer qualifies as a pooled car, any employee who has had the car available for private use during the same tax year may be assessed. So, if the car is ordinarily parked overnight near the home of one of the users, it will not qualify as a pooled car and creates a tax problem for any other employees who use it.

Emergency service vehicles

Emergency service workers in the fire, police and ambulance services are entitled to a specific exemption from the benefit charge which might otherwise arise from having to take their emergency vehicles home when on call.

Disabled employees' travel costs

Assistance with travelling costs between home and work is not taxable where it is given to disabled persons. This includes contributions towards the cost of travel by public transport. A car provided for travel between home and work is not taxed where:

- the employee is severely and permanently disabled; and
- the car has been specially adapted; and
- no private use is made other than travel between home and work.

'Green commuting' facilities

There is no taxable benefit in respect of:

- works buses with a seating capacity of nine or more;
- subsidies to public bus services, provided the employee pays the same fare as other members of the public;
- bicycles and cycle safety equipment made available for employees to get to and from work; and
- workplace parking for bicycles and motorcycles.

For employees who may need to shower and change clothes after arriving at the office because, for example, they cycle or run to work, tax is not chargeable on the free use by employees of changing and shower room facilities at an employer's premises, provided they are generally available to all employees. The employer can also currently provide breakfast on designated 'cycle to work days' without this constituting a taxable benefit, but this latter relief is to be abolished, following a period of consultation.

Late travel

There is also currently an exemption for the cost to an employer of providing transport to get an employee home (after 9 pm) where public transport is not available or it is not reasonable for the employer to expect the employee to use it. The exemption does not apply if the employee has to work late on a regular or frequent basis. There is an overall limit of 60 occasions on which transport can be provided.

The exemption has been extended to cover extra travel costs where car-sharing arrangements temporarily break down. This can include situations where the employee travels home at his or her normal time (eg where the employee whose car he or she shares is unexpectedly kept late).

The OTS has also recommended the abolition of this relief (following a period of consultation).

Employees' rail strike costs

(s 245 ITEPA 2003)

There is a statutory exemption covering the extra costs incurred by employees in getting to work because of a rail strike. The exemption (which may also cover the cost of hotel accommodation near the place of work) means that no tax is payable where the employer meets these expenses.

Homeworking allowance

An exemption is available for payments of up to £3 per week to cover extra expenses where the employee is required to work from home. This mirrors the amount that HMRC will accept for minor use of home by self-employed individuals. Alternatively, employees can reclaim the actual additional costs incurred in working at home but must be prepared to justify any claim.

Relocation expenses

(s 271 ITEPA 2003)

There is an exemption from tax on certain removal expenses borne by an employer when an employee has to change his or her residence to take up a new job within the same organisation, or to take up completely new employment. It is not necessary for the employee to sell his or her former home, but the exemption is available only where it would be unreasonable to expect him or her to work at the new location without moving closer to it. Abortive costs where a particular purchase falls through can be covered by the exemption provided the employee does eventually move house. The exemption is subject to a ceiling of £8,000 for any one move.

Qualifying expenses and benefits must fall into one of the six categories below:

- the employee's sale of their old residence;
- their purchase of a new residence;
- transporting the employee's belongings to the new residence;
- associated travel and subsistence costs;
- domestic goods for the new premises;
- bridging loans.

Payments made to compensate employees for losses on the sale of their former houses are regarded as taxable.

Sometimes employers provide guaranteed selling prices for the employee's former home, either directly or through a relocation agency. HMRC published its views on the tax consequences of such arrangements in *Tax Bulletin 11,* May 1994, available from HMRC Press Office (or www.hmrc.gov.uk/bulletins/tb11.htm#anchor252234). These will not come within the exemption.

Gifts by third parties

The exemption for non-monetary gifts by third parties covered at 4.4.3 applies to all categories of employees.

Long service awards

(s 323 ITEPA 2003)

Awards to directors and employees to mark long service are exempt provided the period of service is at least 20 years and no similar award has been given to the employee within the previous ten years. The gift must not consist of cash and the cost should not exceed £50 per year of service. The exemption also applies to gifts of shares in the company that employs the individual or in another group company.

Awards under suggestion schemes

(ss 321–322 ITEPA 2003)

Provided the employee is not engaged in research work, he or she may receive a tax-free payment under a firm's suggestion scheme. Making suggestions should not, however, be regarded as part of the employee's job. The size of the award should be within certain limits, ie £25 or less where the suggestion, although not implemented, has intrinsic value. Where the suggestion is implemented, the amount should be related to the expected net financial benefit to the employer. In any event, any excess over £5,000 is taxable.

Representative accommodation

(s 99 ITEPA 2003)

Living accommodation qualifies as representative accommodation and as such is not treated as a taxable benefit if any one of the following conditions is satisfied:

- it is necessary for the proper performance of the employee's duties that he or she should reside in the accommodation;
- the accommodation is provided for the better performance of the employee's duties and it is customary to provide accommodation for such employees; or
- the employee has to live in the accommodation because of a special threat to his or her security.

Under the first two conditions, if the employee is a director, the exemption is usually only available if he or she (together with his or her associates) holds 5% or less of the company's ordinary share capital and is a full-time working director.

HMRC strongly resists the application of the third exemption to any but the most clear-cut cases. However, in 2004, the Special Commissioners upheld a claim by the late Lord Hanson that he was entitled to the security exemption.

Where the employer pays for heating, lighting, repairs, maintenance, etc, the representative occupiers cannot be assessed, in respect of such benefits, on more than 10% of their earnings from the employment.

The main occupations that satisfy the conditions for exemption are:

- agricultural workers living on farms or agricultural estates;
- lock-gate and level-crossing gatekeepers;
- caretakers who live on the premises for which they are responsible: this only covers those with a genuine full time caretaking job who are on call outside normal working hours;
- stewards and greenkeepers who live on the premises they look after;
- managers of public houses who live on the premises;
- wardens of sheltered housing who live on the premises and are on call outside normal working hours;
- police officers and Ministry of Defence police;
- prison governors, officers and chaplains;
- clergymen and ministers of religion, unless engaged on administrative duties only;
- members of the armed forces;
- members of the Diplomatic Service;
- managers of newspaper shops that have paper rounds;
- managers of traditional off-licences (ie those with opening hours that are the same as for public houses);
- head teachers and teachers at boarding schools who have pastoral responsibility, if the accommodation is at or near the school;
- stable staff of racehorse trainers who live on the premises and certain key workers who live close to the stables.

In addition, provided that the accommodation is necessary for the better performance of their duties, the following two categories can also qualify

(1) veterinary surgeons who live near their practice; and
(2) managers of camping and caravan sites living on or near the premises.

Retraining

(ss 311–312 ITEPA 2003)

Where an employer pays the cost of a course undertaken by a full-time or part-time employee (or former employee) to provide him or her with skills for future employment elsewhere, that cost can be a deductible expense of the employer, and may not be a taxable benefit of the employee. The employee must have completed at least two years' service.

The exemption is normally dependent on the employee leaving his or her job no later than two years after completing the course.

Sandwich courses

(SP4/86, as revised in April 2005)

Where an employer releases an employee to take a full-time educational course at a university, technical college or similar educational institution that is open to the public at large, payments for periods of attendance may be treated as exempt from income tax. There are various conditions that attach to this exemption:

- the course must last for at least one academic year with an average of at least 20 weeks of full-time attendance; and
- the annual rate of payment including lodging, subsistence and travelling allowances, but excluding any tuition fees payable by the employee to the university must not exceed £15,480.

Where the rate of payment exceeds £15,480, the full amount is taxable; where the amount of payment is increased during a course, only subsequent payments are taxable.

Education and training

(ss 255–260 ITEPA 2003)

No tax charge arises on payments made to a provider in respect of the costs of providing 'qualifying education or training' for a fundable employee. Similar relief is available for payment or reimbursement of any incidental costs incurred wholly and exclusively as a result of the employee undertaking the course. The exemption is available only where participation is available on similar terms to all employees.

'Qualifying education or training' is education or training which qualifies for grants under the Learning and Skills Act 2000 and its Scottish equivalent. A fundable employee is one who holds an account qualifying under s 104 Learning and Skills Act 2000 or who is a party to arrangements under s 105 or s 106 of that Act.

4.4.9 Expenses relating to directors and P11D employees

This section deals with problem areas that arise regularly in practice where expenses are paid on behalf of directors and senior employees or where the employer reimburses them.

Travelling expenses

(ss 336–340 ITEPA 2003)

Travel between home and the ordinary place of work does not rank as business travel and therefore will be treated as a taxable benefit-in-kind if it is funded by the employer. Where an individual is 'on call' and assumes the responsibilities of the employment upon leaving home, it may be possible to argue that home to work travel is business, not private travel, but this applies only in exceptional cases. Other travelling expenses are not normally treated as a benefit-in-kind so long as the individual has a 'normal place of work' that he or she attends the majority of the time. The Special Commissioners decided in 2003 that site-based employees of an agency did not meet these requirements (*Phillips* v *Hamilton* 2003 SpC 366).

Where an employee performs incidental duties of the employment at another location and travels there directly to or from his or her home, the expense is usually allowable. However, if the temporary workplace is close to the normal place of work, this will not apply.

If an employee is obliged to attend a place of work for a period that it is reasonable to assume will exceed two years then that is regarded as a permanent workplace from the time that assumption is made.

To secure tax relief on reimbursed travelling expenses, the employee must keep adequate records so as to distinguish business from non-business travel. Ideally, expenses claims to the employer should show the actual cost of such travel and, if the employer is to obtain a dispensation, HMRC will need to be satisfied that such internal controls exist.

Approved Mileage Allowance Payments (AMAP)

There is a statutory scheme of flat-rate allowances for business mileage. The following rates apply for 2011–12 and future years unless changed by HMRC.

Cars and vans:	*Per mile*
First 10,000 miles in tax year	45p
Each additional mile	25p
Motorcycles	24p
Bicycles	20p
Passengers (including volunteers)	5p

The employee cannot claim tax relief for interest on a loan used to buy his or her car.

Tax notes

Where an individual is required to use his or her own car for business, and he or she is reimbursed at less than the authorised rates, he or she can claim a deduction equal to the shortfall. Form P87 is designed to be used by employees who make such claims. You should keep a log of your business travel to back up your claim.

In addition to the mileage allowance payment, an employer can also pay up to 5p per passenger per mile free of tax and NICs for fellow employees (from 2011–12, including volunteers) carried in the employer's or employee's car or van where the journey constitutes business travel for both driver and passengers. The employee cannot claim any relief if the employer does not pay the passenger rate.

Mileage allowances for business travel in a company car

Where an employer reimburses fuel costs relating to business mileage, the following rates may be paid tax free (rates published 1 March 2011).

	Petrol	*Diesel*	*LPG*
1,400cc or less	14p	13p	10p
1,401–2,000cc	16p	13p	12p
Over 2,000 cc	23p	16p	17p

These rates are normally reviewed twice a year with any changes taking effect on 1 June and 1 December and will be published on the HMRC website shortly before the date of change. HMRC will also accept the figures in the table for VAT purposes though employers will need to obtain the relevant fuel receipts from employees in line with current legislation.

Employee car ownership schemes

HMRC has been reviewing employee car ownership schemes that take maximum benefit of the approved mileage allowances and this could lead to a more restrictive approach in future.

Using a bicycle for business

Employees can claim capital allowances on bicycles used for business travel. A tax-free cycling allowance of 20p per business mile can be paid. Where the employer pays less than this rate, the employee can claim a tax deduction for the difference.

Subsistence

HMRC's view is that it is strictly only the extra costs of living away from home that are allowable. If there are continuing financial commitments at home, the whole cost of living away from home is normally allowed. This concession is not available if the employee has no permanent residence, for example an unmarried person who normally lives in a hotel or club and who gives up that accommodation when away on a business trip. There is a specific exemption where an employee performs his or her duties wholly overseas and needs board and lodging abroad to do so.

Personal incidental expenses

There is a statutory exemption for employees' miscellaneous personal incidental expenses when they are required to stay away from home overnight on business. This exemption allows employers to meet expenses of up to £5 a night (£10 if overseas).

Benchmark scale rates for subsistence

In April 2009, HMRC published benchmark scale rates for employees who incur subsistence expenses while travelling on business but are not away from home overnight. These rates apply only where the following conditions are satisfied:

- the travel must be in the performance of the employee's duties or to a temporary workplace;
- the employee should be absent from his or her normal workplace or home for a continuous period which either exceeds five or ten hours;
- the employee has incurred a cost on a meal after starting the journey.

The scale rates vary between £5 and £15.

Higher rates may be negotiated for a particular set of circumstances or actual sums validly incurred can be claimed instead of scale rates. However, if a higher rate is paid without such an agreement, HMRC says that the excess should be subject to PAYE tax and NIC.

For further details see www.hmrc.gov.uk/briefs/income-tax/brief2409.htm

Travel costs

Site-based employees

A deduction is allowed for the costs of travel to or from any place where attendance at that place is in the performance of the duties of a person's employment. The subsistence costs of site-based employees are also an allowable expense.

This is subject to certain conditions and in particular, if it is reasonable to assume that the worker will be based at the site for two years or longer, no relief is available.

Temporary absence from normal place of work

Where an employee is required to work temporarily at a place other than his or her normal workplace, the deductions for travel expenses described above are available.

Temporary relocation to another office, etc

HMRC has clarified the circumstances in which employees who are temporarily absent from their normal place of work can claim a deduction for travelling and subsistence expenses. Normally an employee is regarded as temporarily absent from his or her normal place of work if:

- the absence is not for more than 24 months; and
- the employee returns to the normal place of work at the end of the period.

If these conditions are satisfied, the employer can pay a subsistence allowance free of tax.

HMRC takes the view that an individual may also qualify if these conditions are expected to be satisfied at the outset but circumstances subsequently change. Relief is available for the period up to the time when it becomes clear that either condition will be breached.

There are special rules for subsistence allowances given to employees of overseas companies who are seconded to work in the UK for periods of up to two years. These rules are dealt with in 35.4.

Overseas travelling expenses

(s 370 ITEPA 2003)

Where some or all of the employment duties are performed abroad, travelling expenses to and from the UK in connection with the carrying out of such duties are specifically regarded as having been necessarily incurred in the performance of the overseas employment. It follows that if those expenses are reimbursed by the employer, no benefit-in-kind arises.

Where an employee travels between places where different jobs are performed, and one or more of these jobs is performed wholly or partly overseas, the expenses incurred in travelling overseas are also deemed to be necessarily incurred in performing the duties carried out overseas, so that once again no benefit-in-kind arises. In many cases, there is dual purpose in travelling and a taxable benefit-in-kind arises on the private element. Consequently, where travel expenses relate partly to a foreign holiday taken at the end of the business trip, there would be a taxable benefit-in-kind.

Similarly, a benefit-in-kind may be assessed on the expense relating to a spouse or civil partner who accompanies a director or employee on a trip unless this is necessary for business purposes.

When he or she is abroad, the maximum allowance to cover an employee's personal incidental expenses is £10 per night.

A director or employee who travels overseas must be able to substantiate a claim that expenses were necessarily incurred for business purposes by producing details of the expenses and the time spent away from home. A brief itinerary should be available where travel is undertaken within the overseas country or countries. HMRC expects that an employer will properly control expenditure and in certain cases may wish to inspect receipted bills or other vouchers.

HMRC has published benchmark scale rates that employers can use to reimburse accommodation and subsistence expenses incurred by employees while visiting various countries. See the HMRC Employment Manual at EIM 05255.

Tax notes

Keep records of your travel costs to avoid arguments with HMRC. These records should include details of the purpose of each trip and the business undertaken.

Spouse's travelling and subsistence expenses

HMRC are rarely persuaded that there is a business need for a spouse or civil partner to accompany a director or employee. Where a spouse, civil partner or other member of the family accompanies a director abroad on a business trip, a Board minute stating that it is necessary for the person to accompany the director may assist in attempts to persuade HMRC that no benefit-in-kind arises. However, this is not generally sufficient in itself and it must be shown that the spouse, etc performed tasks that could not be carried out by the director.

It may be possible to show this if the spouse or civil partner has some practical qualification, for example an ability to speak the appropriate foreign language. A relative's expenses may also be allowable where the director or employee is in poor health and to travel alone would be impracticable or unreasonable. Where the individual's presence is for the purpose of accompanying his or her spouse or civil partner at business entertainment functions, the expenses of his or her trip may be disallowed in calculating the employer's tax liability under the entertainment legislation, even if the expenses are not included in the employee's tax liability.

Tax notes

Be prepared for HMRC to contend that the cost of your spouse or civil partner's travel is a benefit-in-kind and collect evidence to show that his or her accompanying you was necessary for business purposes.

Employees working overseas: family visits

(s 371 ITEPA 2003)

Where an employee is abroad for a continuous period of 60 days or more, there is an exemption for amounts borne by the employer in respect of the travelling expenses for visits by the employee's spouse and minor children. The exemption is available for up to two journeys by the same person in each direction in a tax year. There is no relief if the employee bears the expense personally.

Entertaining expenses and allowances

It is not uncommon for directors or employees to have a round-sum allowance to cover such things as travelling, subsistence and entertaining. In the case of travelling and subsistence, the allowance counts as the director's or employee's taxable income charged to PAYE and NIC, but a tax deduction may be claimed in respect of any part of the allowance that can be shown to have been spent for business purposes. It is very important to keep records that enable such claims to be substantiated. It may be better to dispense with entertainment allowances and reimburse the director or employee for properly substantiated expenditure, since no benefit-in-kind should then arise.

The situation is more complex for entertaining expenditure. If an employer reimburses entertaining expenditure or pays an amount that is specifically intended for client entertaining, the expense to the employer is disallowed for tax purposes. The reimbursement or allowance is entered on the director's or employee's P11D, but a deduction may be claimed for expenditure which is for genuine business purposes. If the payment relates to staff entertaining, then it will be a taxable benefit-in-kind and no deduction can be claimed.

Once again, if the employer pays a round-sum allowance for entertaining this must be charged to PAYE and NIC.

Where an employer does make payments for business-related expenses that will ultimately lead to a claim for a tax deduction for the employee, it is advisable to apply for a dispensation so that the expense does not need to be included on forms P11D. This will generally not be available in connection with round sum allowances.

4.5 COMPANY CARS

(s 114 ITEPA 2003)

4.5.1 Car benefits

In 2002, a more environmentally friendly regime for calculating the cash equivalent of the benefit where an employer provides a car to an employee or member of his or her family or household was introduced. This is based on the published carbon dioxide (CO_2) emissions figure (in grams per kilometre) for a given car. Since 1 March 2001 that figure has appeared in the car log book. For cars registered between 1 January 1998 and 1 March 2001, the emissions figure can be obtained from a booklet published by:

The Vehicle Certification Agency
1 The Eastgate Office Centre
Eastgate Road
Bristol BS5 6XX
Website: www.vca.gov.uk

The emissions figure is rounded down to the nearest whole 5g below and is then converted to a percentage using the HMRC table (see Table 4.3). The maximum percentage to be applied to the list price of the car is 35%.

The list price used to be subject to an overall limit of £80,000. However, with effect from 6 April 2011, the £80,000 cap has been abolished so drivers of very expensive cars will see a large hike in their tax bills.

Diesel cars have a low CO_2 figure but produce other emissions. To maintain an environmental balance with petrol vehicles, the percentage is increased by 3% (up to the maximum 35%), for example if diesel emissions in 2011–12 are 220 grams per kilometre, the percentage is 35% (33% + 2%).

Electric cars were taxed on 9% of their list price for periods up to 5 April 2010. For the following five years, this rate has been reduced to zero.

Cars registered before 1 January 1998 do not have a listed CO_2 emissions figure and the percentage for these vehicles continues to be based on engine size, but with no discounts for age or business use, as follows:

Engine size (cc)	Percentage of car's price taxed
0–1,400	15%
1,401–2,000	22%
2,001 and over	32%

A limited number of cars produced on or after that date will also not have a CO_2 figure and the percentage to be used then is:

Engine size (cc)	Percentage of car's price taxed
0–1,400	15% *
1,401–2,000	25% *
2,001 and over	35%

*Plus 3% supplement for diesel cars

Diesel cars

Add a 3% supplement to the relevant percentage scale charge to arrive at the amount of the car's price to be taxed. This is subject to a maximum charge based upon 35% of the car's list price.

Automatic cars

These have higher CO_2 emissions.

Disabled employees who need to drive automatic cars

For some years, where an employee is disabled (ie holds an 'orange badge') and can only drive an automatic car, the emission figure has been taken as that of the 'equivalent manual car', ie the closest non-automatic variant of the car concerned. This concession has applied only in relation to the emissions figure, the taxable benefit has still been computed by reference to the actual cost of the car. However, FA 2009 provided that the concessionary treatment should apply in relation to the cost of the car as well, with effect from 2009–10.

Second cars

Second and subsequent cars are charged at the same rate as first cars.

Table 4.3 – CO_2 emissions: cars registered from 1 January 1998

CO_2 emissions in grams per kilometre					Percentage of car's price taxed
2010–11	2011–12	2012–13	2013–14	2014–15	
0	0	0	0	0	0
1–75	1–75	1–75	1–75	1–75	5
76–120	76–120	76–99	76–94	76–94	10
n/a	n/a	100	95	95	11
n/a	n/a	110	105	105	13
121–130	121–125	120	115	115	15
135	130	125	120	120	16
140	135	130	125	125	17
145	140	135	130	130	18
150	145	140	135	135	19
155	150	145	140	140	20
160	155	150	145	145	21
165	160	155	150	150	22
170	165	160	155	155	23
175	170	165	160	160	24
180	175	170	165	165	25
185	180	175	170	170	26
190	185	180	175	175	27
195	190	185	180	180	28
200	195	190	185	185	29
205	200	195	190	190	30
210	205	200	195	195	31
215	210	205	200	200	32
220	215	210	205	205	33
225	220	215	210	210	34
230	225	220	215	215	35

A number of changes to the chargeable benefit-in-kind on company cars and vans, effective for five years from 6 April 2010 to 5 April 2015, were introduced in FA (No.1) 2010 and Finance Bill 2011:

- The first change gives full relief from the chargeable benefit-in-kind on company cars and vans which cannot produce more than 0 g/km CO_2 engine emissions under any circumstances when driven (ie electric cars). The taxable benefit is due to revert to 9% of the list price in 2015–16.
- The percentage reductions that had applied for alternative fuels will no longer be available from 6 April 2011.

4.5.2 Reductions in the scale benefit

The scale figures are reduced proportionally where an employee was provided with a company car part way through the tax year, or where he or she ceases to have a company car. However, there is no reduction where the car was not available for use because it was being repaired, unless it was incapable of being used for at least 30 consecutive days. Contributions made by an employee for private use of the car can be deducted from the chargeable benefit.

Tax notes

If you are not using your company car while you are away on holiday, your scale benefit would be reduced if your employer required you to hand back your car for this period so that it was not available for your use.

4.5.3 Private petrol

(s 149 ITEPA 2003)

For 2011–12, the fuel scale charge is based on multiplying the relevant CO_2 rate by £18,800 (increased from £18,000). The scale figures apply regardless of the amount of private fuel provided. If any is provided at all, the fuel scale charge is always applied unless the employee reimburses the employer for the full cost. It may well be cost effective for the employee to do this so the position should be reviewed before the start of each tax year.

The charge is reduced if the car is not available for part of the tax year (see 4.5.2), the employee makes good the cost during part of the tax year or where fuel is withdrawn during a tax year and not subsequently reinstated. Care has to be taken as there is no apportionment for days before provision of free fuel commenced.

4.5.4 Car parking spaces

(s 266(1) ITEPA 2003)

The provision of a car parking space at or near the employee's place of work is not treated as a taxable benefit. Where an employee pays for car parking him or herself, he or she cannot claim a deduction for those charges.

4.5.5 Private use of company vans

(s 154 ITEPA 2003)

There is a scale charge for employees who have private use of company vans. An employee may be assessed on a standard amount of £3,000 pa in respect of private use of a van irrespective of its age and since 2010–11 an additional charge of £550 applies if the employer provides fuel for private use (previously £500). Any vehicles in excess of 3.5 tons are exempt from tax altogether (unless the vehicle is used wholly or mainly for the employee's private purposes). From 6 April 2010 to 5 April 2015, the £3,000 charge is reduced to nil for electric vans.

The scale charge is reduced if the van was not available for private use throughout the year. Where an employee has two or more vans made available for private use at the same time, tax is charged on the scale figure for each van. The standard amount is reduced pro rata where the van is only available part of the year. As for company cars, a £1-for-£1 reduction is made for any contributions made by the employee towards the private use. Where a van is shared among several employees, the standard amount is apportioned among the employees.

4.5.6 Congestion charge

No tax charge arises where an employer pays the congestion charge on a company car or van. It does apply where the congestion charge relates to a vehicle that is not owned by the employer unless the travel into London was an expense incurred wholly and necessarily in the performance of the employee's duties.

4.5.7 Hands-free phone kit

HMRC accepts that no additional benefit arises where an employer pays for a hands-free phone kit to be fitted in a company car.

4.6 FREE USE OF ASSETS

(s 203 ITEPA 2003)

A taxable benefit arises where an employer makes an asset available for use by a director or P11D employee. The annual benefit is 20% of the asset's market value when it was first made available for use by the employee. Virtually any asset apart from living accommodation and company cars may be involved including yachts, furniture, television sets and stereo equipment. If the employer rents or hires the asset for a sum in excess of 20% of its original market value, the higher rental charge is substituted as the assessable benefit. A deduction is allowed for any contribution or rental paid by the employee.

A further charge may arise if the ownership of an asset is eventually transferred to the employee. The amount will be determined by either the asset's market value at the time of transfer of ownership or, where a higher figure results, its original cost at the time it was first made available as a benefit for any person, less any amounts already charged as benefits in connection with its availability. Care must be taken that the disguised remuneration provisions are not triggered – Chapter 5 deals with this charge.

Example – Transfer of assets

> A company provides an employee with the use of a yacht that costs £40,000, with the employee paying a rental of £2,000 pa. After two years the yacht is sold to the employee for its second-hand market value of £20,000. The assessable benefit would be:
>
> | | | Benefit £ |
> |---|---|---:|
> | Year 1: | £40,000 × 20% | 8,000 |
> | | *Less*: rental paid | (2,000) |
> | | | 6,000 |
> | Year 2: | £40,000 × 20% | 8,000 |
> | | *Less*: rental paid | (2,000) |
> | | | 6,000 |
> | Year 3: | Cost of yacht | 40,000 |
> | | *Less*: benefits assessed in Years 1 and 2 | (12,000) |
> | | Amounts paid by employee | (24,000) |
> | | | 4,000 |

Where an asset previously made available to an individual is transferred to him or her (or to another employee) at a time when its market value is still high, it is possible that the total amount charged as a benefit for tax purposes exceeds the original cost. In other cases, the rules may operate to impose a high benefit charge on the transfer of an asset despite its value having depreciated rapidly during the period of use.

Such rules must therefore be considered carefully when planning the provision of an asset for use by an employee or arranging for its transfer to him or her. It may be that where a tax-efficient remuneration package is desired, transfer of ownership should be avoided where assets have a relatively short useful life.

Example – Ownership of assets

A company provides employees with the use of suits that remain the property of the company. The suits cost £200 and have a useful life of two years, after which they are scrapped. An employee could therefore have an effective benefit of £200, but would be charged tax on only £40 for each of the two tax years.

4.6.1 Assets where this charge does not arise

In the case of a car, the charge is calculated only by reference to the market value at the time that the car is transferred to the employee. Thus if a car had been purchased for £40,000 and after two years the employee buys it for £20,000, a tax charge will arise only if the £20,000 is less than market value.

Similarly, since 6 April 2005, the tax charge on a transfer to an employee of a computer or bicycle previously made available to him or her, or another employee, is based only on the market value at that time.

4.7 BENEFICIAL LOANS

(s 184 ITEPA 2003)

4.7.1 Type of loans caught

A charge generally arises for directors and P11D employees on the annual value of beneficial loan arrangements. A loan's 'annual value' is taken as interest at the 'official rate' less the amount of interest (if any) paid by the employee. The official rate is now generally set annually in advance and was 5% from 2002–03 to 2006–07; 6.25% for 2007–08; 6.10% for 2008–09; and 4.75% for 2009–10. It then reduced to 4% with effect from 6 April 2010 and has remained at that level for 2011–12. An additional taxable benefit arises if the loan is subsequently written off or forgiven. The beneficial loan provisions can also apply if a loan is made to a member of an employee's family. In some circumstances, the disguised remuneration provisions can create an upfront tax charge on the full capital amount of the loan; see Chapter 5 for details.

Moreover, HMRC can assess benefits where credit has been involved, even though there may be no formal loan. In particular, a director who overdraws his or her current account with the company is regarded as having obtained a loan.

Almost all loans by employers (and persons connected with them) are caught as the legislation deems such loans to have been given by reason of the employment. There is an exception where the employee is related to the employer and it could be shown that the loan was given for family reasons. Loans made by an employer whose business includes lending money to the general public do not give rise to a charge on the employees provided the loans are made on similar terms to those available to the public.

4.7.2 Beneficial loans used for qualifying purpose

No benefit-in-kind charge arises in respect of a cheap loan where the money borrowed has been applied for a qualifying purpose, for example to purchase shares in a close company in which the individual has a material interest or where he or she is employed full time in the conduct and management of the company's business. However, it is possible that a disguised remuneration charge might still apply in these circumstances.

4.7.3 *De minimis* exemption

Provided that the total of all cheap or interest-free loans made to an individual employee do not exceed £5,000 at any point in a tax year, no benefit-in-kind charge arises. This figure excludes loans used to buy shares in employee-controlled companies (see 11.6).

4.7.4 Employee loans written off

If the loan is written off, the amount forgiven is treated as assessable income for that year even if the company no longer employs the person concerned. The main exception here is if the loan is forgiven on the employee's death – however, despite the relief in s 190 ITEPA, in most cases, the loan write off will be taxable under s 62 ITEPA as general earnings in any case. Where the employee is also a shareholder in a close company, there will be no charge as employment income and instead, the individual is deemed to receive a distribution on their shares.

Some care must be taken if it is decided to clear a loan by making an *ex gratia* or compensation payment to an employee on termination of employment. An income tax liability will arise if the loan is formally written off. However, no liability normally arises if the employee receives a cheque as an *ex gratia* or compensation payment and uses that sum to clear his or her outstanding loan. It is recommended that professional advice be taken in such circumstances.

4.7.5 Further information

HMRC guidance on how loans provided by employers to employees are taxed can be found at www.hmrc.gov.uk/manuals/eimanual/eim26100.htm.

4.8 LIVING ACCOMMODATION

(ss 105–106 ITEPA 2003)

4.8.1 Introduction

The income tax charge that generally applies where an employee is provided with accommodation (unless it is representative accommodation: see 4.4.8) depends on whether the property is rented or owned by the employer.

Where the property is rented by the employer, the assessable amount is the greater of the rent paid and the annual value. In addition, a charge may arise on the annual value of any furniture and fixtures and on any occupier's expenses borne by the company such as water rates, decorations, gardener's wages, etc.

Where an employer purchases a leasehold interest in a property on or after 22 April 2009, and that lease has less than ten years to run, the lease premium may be treated as if it were rent for the period of the lease.

Where the employer owns the property, the assessable amount was originally confined to the gross annual value for rating purposes. Despite the abolition of domestic rates, this treatment continues to apply for properties on existing rating lists (see 4.4.7). For new properties and those where there have been major improvements, HMRC makes an estimate of what the gross annual value (GAV) would have been had rates continued. Over the years, this has meant that the GAV is far less than a market rent. Accordingly, the Government has introduced an additional charge for more expensive properties.

This additional charge arises where the employer paid more than £75,000 to acquire the property. The additional amount assessable is a percentage of the excess of the property's cost over £75,000. The percentage to be applied is the official rate of interest used for beneficial loans (see 4.7) at the beginning of the tax year.

Example – Charge on living accommodation in excess of £75,000

For several years a company director has occupied a property owned by the company that has a gross annual value of £2,000. The cost of the property in 2005 was £95,000. The director will be assessed on the following amount for 2011–12:

	£	£
Gross annual value		2,000
Additional charge:		
Cost in 2005	95,000	
Less:	(75,000)	
	20,000	
Assessment on £20,000 at official rate of 4%		800
		2,800

Where a property is unavailable for any part of the year, this will reduce the amount chargeable. It is emphasised that this will not apply merely because an employee chooses not to stay in a property that is available for his or her use.

In addition, the benefit charge is reduced by any rent or expenses reimbursed by the employee.

4.8.2 Properties owned for more than six years

Where the company has owned the property for at least six years before it was occupied by the employee and the employee first occupied it after 30 March 1983 then, rather than the cost, the figure taken into account in computing the additional charge is the market value at the time it was first made available to the employee, plus any amounts that had been spent on improving it after the employee took up occupancy and before the start of the tax year.

The actual cost (including improvements) to the employer is still used to determine whether the provisions apply. Consequently, properties where the actual cost was less than £75,000 (including the cost of any improvements) are not within the scope of this additional charge even if their market value exceeds £75,000. Where the actual cost exceeded £75,000, the additional charge is based on the market value.

Example – Charge on living accommodation purchased more than six years ago

In the example in 4.8.1, assume the company has owned the property for more than six years before the director moves in. Also assume that in May 2004, when the director first occupies it, the market value is £225,000. As the original cost of the property exceeded £75,000, the director will be assessed on the following amount for 2011–12:

	£	£
Gross annual value		2,000
Additional charge:		
Market value in 2004	225,000	
Less:	(75,000)	
	150,000	
Assessment on £150,000 at official rate of 4%		6,000
		8,000

4.8.3 Possible reductions in taxable amount

It may be possible to reduce the taxable amount where the employee is required to occupy a property that is larger than would normally be needed for his or her own purposes. In *Westcott* v *Bryan* (1969) 45 TC 476 a director was required to live in a large house so that he or she could entertain customers. He was allowed a reduction in the taxable amount to cover the relevant proportion of the annual value and the running expenses.

Some care is needed if it is intended to claim relief in this way. This claim succeeded because the house was larger than needed for the director and his family. It would not have succeeded had the property merely been more expensive than he would have chosen. It was also helpful that the company directors had approved board minutes setting out their requirement and the business reason for it.

Where part of the property is used exclusively for work, the taxable amount may be reduced on a pro rata basis. Revenue Helpsheet IR202 contains working sheets that enable you to compute your taxable benefits in this situation.

4.8.4 Possible increase in taxable benefit

It is sometimes the case that an employer offers a choice: salary of £x or salary of £y plus a house. In this situation, if the difference between £x and £y calculated along the lines set out in 4.8.1–4.8.2 exceeds the normal benefit-in-kind it may be taxed as additional remuneration.

4.8.5 Holiday accommodation and foreign properties

Some employers buy holiday flats, cottages, etc for use by staff. In practice, generally HMRC apportions the assessable amount for the year among those employees who have occupied the property. However, where only a single employee or director has access to the property, they will usually be liable to pay a benefit charge for the whole year, not just the time that they occupy it.

The assessment can be reduced by letting the accommodation to third parties when directors and employees do not require it.

A practical problem arises with overseas properties. Because there is no rateable value, the benefit is the annual rent that the property would normally command on the open market. Where this applies, there is normally no additional charge based on the excess of the property's cost over £75,000 (see 4.8.1).

4.8.6 Overseas holiday homes held in a single purpose company

It is common for a UK individual who is acquiring a home overseas to set up a company to buy the property. Where the individual is a director, he or she is potentially subject to the tax charge under s 105 ITEPA 2003. FA 2008 provides an exemption from this (with full retrospective effect) as long as the following conditions are satisfied:

- the company must be owned by individuals;
- the company's main activity must be to own the property, any other activity being incidental;
- the property must be the only or main asset of the company;
- the company must not be funded directly or indirectly by a connected company.

4.9 MISCELLANEOUS BENEFITS

Council tax

Where an employer pays council tax on behalf of an employee, this is normally chargeable as part of the employee's remuneration package, resulting in a charge to both income tax and NIC. The one exception to this is where the employee is a representative occupier (see 4.4.8).

Mobile phones

(s 319 ITEPA 2003)

No tax charge arises on the provision of one telephone for each employee. However where an employee has more than one phone, for example a mobile phone plus a BlackBerry, a charge will arise on the second phone. A charge will also arise if the employer pays for the use of a mobile phone owned by the employee, unless the payment is for business calls only and can be fully substantiated.

No benefit-in-kind arises where an employer pays for a hands-free mobile kit to be fitted in an employee's car provided the employer retains ownership of the kit.

Telephone line rental

HMRC treats the full amount of the rental paid by the employer as a taxable benefit-in-kind even though the phone may be partly (or mainly) used for business calls. The decision in *Lucas* v *Cattell* (1972) 48 TC 353 was that the expenditure on rental had a dual purpose (ie that a phone was intended to be used for both business and personal use) and therefore no part of it was allowable.

Liability insurance and payment of uninsured liabilities

Section 349 provides that employees are not subject to tax on a benefit-in-kind where their employer pays premiums on items such as directors' and officers' liability insurance or a professional indemnity insurance policy. Furthermore, the Act also provides that payment of an employee's uninsured liabilities does not give rise to a benefit-in-kind provided they arise from the employee's work. This is subject to the overriding requirement that the liabilities could have been insured against and this means that those arising from, for example criminal convictions, cannot attract relief.

Medical insurance

The cost of medical insurance is normally assessable on P11D employees. Where the employer has a group scheme, a proportion of the total premiums is related to individual employees. There is an exception in that the premiums are exempt to the extent that they provide cover for an employee working outside the UK.

Club subscriptions

A benefit-in-kind is deemed to arise where an employer pays or reimburses an employee's subscription to a club, even though the employee may only belong to the club to entertain the employer's customers.

In-house tax and financial advice

This is a type of expenditure that HMRC has ignored in the past as the marginal cost of providing such advice is inconsequential, but certain Inspectors of Taxes are now treating this as a benefit-in-kind where there is a cost that can clearly be allocated to particular employees. HMRC will also seek to assess directors on a benefit-in-kind where work on their personal taxation affairs has been carried out by the company's auditors or other external advisers.

Christmas parties and other functions

HMRC does not assess a benefit in respect of 'modest' expenditure on a Christmas or other annual party for staff, provided the party is open to all staff. The limit regarded as modest in this context is £150 per head. If the cost (including VAT) amounts to over £150, the whole amount is taxable, not just the excess. Although this rule is generally attributed to Christmas parties, it may apply to a function at another time of year. The £150 can be used to cover the cost of more than one function.

Legal fees

There may be expenditure incurred for the benefit of the company's business but which nevertheless is deemed to give rise to a benefit-in-kind. A leading case in this connection concerned a company director who was accused of dangerous driving. It was necessary for the company's business that he should not be imprisoned and the company paid his legal expenses. Although the lawyers engaged by the company were more expensive than the director would have used himself, the expenditure by the company was treated as a benefit-in-kind.

Outplacement counselling

(s 310 ITEPA 2003)

The value of outplacement services provided to employees made redundant is exempt from income tax. Such services may include assistance with CVs, job searches, office equipment provisions and advice on interview skills.

Goods and services provided at a discount to the normal price ('in-house benefits')

Where employees are allowed to purchase goods or services from their employer, no tax charge arises provided they pay an amount equal to the employer's cost. The House of Lords eventually decided that 'cost' meant marginal, and not average, cost (*Pepper* v *Hart* [1992] STC 898). This will normally produce a significantly lower benefit.

Following this case, HMRC published a statement of their practice with regard to teachers, employees within the transport industry and other employees who receive goods or services from their employer. It stated that the *Pepper* v *Hart* decision means that:

- rail or bus travel by employees on terms that do not displace fare-paying passengers involves no or negligible additional costs;
- goods sold at a discount that leave employees paying at least the wholesale price involve no or negligible net benefit;
- where teachers pay 15% or more of a school's normal fees, there is no taxable benefit;
- professional services that do not require additional employees or partners (eg legal and financial services) have no or negligible cost to the employer (provided the employee meets the cost of any disbursements).

Employer Financed Retirement Benefit Schemes (EFRBS)

(ss 393–400 ITEPA 2003)

Some employers make contributions to an EFRBS for the benefit of their employees. The creation of an EFRBS must be reported to HMRC under normal rules for reporting the creation of trusts. No taxable benefit charge arises for 2006–07 and later years, however from 6 April 2011, an upfront tax charge will arise under new Part 7A ITEPA. See Chapter 5 and 26.7 for details.

Making good benefits-in-kind for previous years

The cash equivalent of any benefit chargeable to tax under s 203 ITEPA 2003 is the cost of the benefit 'less so much (if any) of it as is made good by the employee to those providing the benefit'. HMRC accepts that there is no time limit for making good and, provided the relevant year's assessment has not been determined, there could be some merit in the person concerned taking further remuneration now and using the net cash left to him or her, after PAYE, to make good benefits provided for earlier years. This could be a particularly good idea where a director of a family company is faced with an income tax assessment plus penalties and interest in respect of prior year incorrect returns because benefits have not been reported properly.

For beneficial loans, however, the cash equivalent can be reduced by a payment in a later year only if the interest is paid under an obligation that existed at the time of the loan.

4.10 SHARE INCENTIVES

We cover the subject of share incentives in Chapter 6, both from the employee's point of view and from the employer's perspective.

There are many situations where a gift of shares or the exercise of an option gives rise to a liability for the employer to account for PAYE or alternatively, the employee must pay tax through self-assessment. Where this happens, the taxable income should be included in the figure for taxable pay on form P60.

There are also situations where shares are made available through an HMRC approved scheme and no income tax charge will arise on the acquisition of such shares provided the necessary conditions are satisfied.

In the case of other share incentives ('unapproved schemes'), the employee will need to complete a special schedule to his or her tax return (HS305, Employee Share Schemes).

4.11 OPTIONS TO ACQUIRE GILTS

FA 2003 introduced rules that apply to options over other securities such as British Government securities ('gilts') granted after 15 April 2003. These rules can now be found in ss 471–487 ITEPA 2003.

A profit on the exercise of such an option granted after 15 April 2003 will generally be subject to income tax as employment income. Furthermore, the profit will normally be subject to PAYE.

4.12 OPTIONS TO ACQUIRE COMPANY ASSETS

The rules regarding options to acquire shares or other employment-related securities are set out in Chapter 6. The treatment of options involving other assets is quite different. An income tax charge may arise at the time that an option over assets other than securities is granted if the option has a market value. However, if the price at which the option may be exercised is higher than the asset's present market value, it is arguable that the option has little or no value at the time it is granted.

No employment income tax charge would normally arise on the exercise of the option. Furthermore, on a subsequent disposal of the asset there would normally be liability only for CGT on the profit over the amount paid. Special care needs to be taken where the director or employee is connected (perhaps as a shareholder) with the company that grants the option.

Example – Option to acquire assets

> A company director, who is not a shareholder, is granted the option to purchase a house owned by the company for £150,000. She has not occupied it at any time. The house has a market value of only £125,000 at the time the option is granted and the option, therefore, has no real value at that time. When the option is exercised the house has a market value of £250,000 and the director has in effect acquired a capital asset at a discount of £100,000 on its current market value. This discount would not normally be subject to income tax.

4.13 GOLDEN HELLOS

These are payments made to induce a prospective employee to take up employment with the company and are (very) occasionally not taxable. In *Pritchard* v *Arundale* (1971) 47 TC 680, which involved a firm of chartered accountants, a senior partner was approached by a client to leave his practice and become a director of the client's company. In order to induce him to do this, he was given shares in the company that were held to be not a reward for services to be rendered in the future but an inducement to leave his practice and take up the employment. They were therefore not taxable.

In *Vaughan-Neil* v *IRC* [1979] STC 644 a barrister received £40,000 to induce him to give up his practice and join a company as its 'in-house adviser'. Once again it was held that the payment was not taxable. By contrast, in *Glantre Engineering Ltd* v *Goodhand* [1983] STC 1 a payment by an engineering company to induce an employee of a firm of accountants to join them was held to be taxable.

The principles that emerge from these three cases are as follows:

- it must be clear from the facts that the payment is an inducement and not a reward for future services;
- the payment must not be returnable if the person does not take up the employment; and
- it is probably more likely that the payment will be accepted as non-taxable if the recipient has previously been in practice or self-employed rather than an employee of another company.

Shilton v *Wilmshurst* [1991] STC 88 extended these principles by deciding that a payment made by a football club to a footballer about to transfer as an inducement to him to join his new club was taxable. The House of Lords held that an emolument from an employment meant an emolument for being or becoming an employee and therefore would include a sum paid by a third party as an inducement to enter into a contract of employment to perform services in the future. It was not necessary for the payer to have any interest in the performance of those services.

In *Silva* v *Charnock* (2002) SpC 332, the taxpayer had taken a career break to study for an MBA. Her tuition fees cost her £18,000. After getting her MBA, she took a new job and received a signing-on bonus of £18,000. It was held that this was not taxable as it fell within the exemption contained in s 200B ICTA 1988 (now s 250 ITEPA 2003).

4.14 RESTRICTIVE COVENANTS

(s 155 ITEPA 2003)

Where the present, past or future holder of an office or employment gives an undertaking that restricts his or her conduct or activities, any sum paid in respect of that restrictive covenant is treated as remuneration from the office or employment for the year in which the payment is received. This rule applies even where the covenant is not legally valid. In some cases, valuable consideration other than money is given for the restrictive covenant and in such a situation a sum equal to the value of that consideration is treated as having been paid. The payment may not necessarily come from the employer and so a payment to an employee that was made by a major shareholder in a family company may well be caught under these provisions.

4.15 REDUNDANCY PAYMENTS

(s 309 ITEPA 2003)

A statutory redundancy payment made under the Employment Rights Act 1996 is exempt from tax, although it may need to be taken into account in computing the tax payable on a termination payment (see 4.16). HMRC generally treats payments to an employee under a non-statutory redundancy scheme as exempt under SP1/94 where payments are made only on account of redundancy as defined in s 139 of the Employment Rights Act 1996. Further, it is usually expected that payments will be made to all relevant employees and not merely to a selected group of employees and the payments should not be excessively large in relation to earnings and length of service.

In such situations, HMRC is willing to give advance clearance confirming that payments will fall within the exemption. Employers are strongly advised to take advantage of this facility.

In *Mairs* v *Haughey* [1993] STC 569 HMRC sought to tax a payment made to an employee for giving up contingent redundancy rights. HMRC argued that the payment constituted an emolument of the employment, but it was held that a redundancy payment is not an emolument and a lump sum paid in lieu of a right to receive such payment is equally not an emolument.

4.16 GOLDEN HANDSHAKES, OTHER TERMINATION PAYMENTS AND CONTINUING BENEFITS

(s 401 ITEPA 2003)

4.16.1 Introduction

Where a director's or employee's contract of service is terminated, it may be possible for a compensation or *ex gratia* payment to be made that is either wholly or partly tax-free provided the employee is not entitled to the compensation under a contract of service, the anti-avoidance provisions relating to disguised remuneration are not triggered and the payment is not deemed to be a benefit under a retirement benefit scheme. Where the individual receives compensation under a term of his or her employment contract, HMRC's view is that it is taxable in the usual way. A payment made to a director as compensation for accepting a reduced salary or any other variation of his or her service contract is not regarded as a termination payment, and the amount received is normally taxable in full. However, HMRC lost in the case of *Wilson* v *Clayton* where an employer was required by an employment tribunal to reinstate an employee and make a payment of £5,060.

HMRC succeeded in a 2004 case (*Allum & Allum* v *Marsh* SpC 446) in arguing that voluntary payments to outgoing directors were, in fact, no more than a payment for past services and therefore taxable in full as earnings.

4.16.2 Exemptions from the charge under s 401

There are various types of termination payment that are exempt:

(1) Payments made because of termination of employment through death, injury or disability. Disability covers not only a condition arising from a sudden affliction, but also a continuing incapacity to perform the duties of an office or employment because of the culmination of a process of deterioration of physical or mental health caused by chronic illness (see SP10/81).
(2) Terminal grants and gratuities to members of HM forces.
(3) Lump sum payments from Commonwealth government superannuation schemes or compensation for loss of career owing to constitutional changes in Commonwealth countries.
(4) A special contribution by an employer into an approved retirement benefit scheme (ie a registered pension scheme).
(5) A lump sum payment where the employment has constituted foreign service that exceeds any of the following limits:
    (a) three-quarters of the whole period of service;
    (b) the last ten years;
    (c) one-half of the period of service provided this amounted to at least 20 years and subject to at least ten of the last 20 years of service being foreign service.

(6) 'Foreign' service is defined as meaning a period of service during which the earnings were not taxable because either the individual was not resident in the UK or the 100% deduction was available because the period spent working overseas exceeded 365 days.

4.16.3 Basic £30,000 exemption

(s 403 ITEPA 2003)

Where a termination payment is not wholly exempt, the first £30,000 can often be paid tax free and only the balance is chargeable. Where an individual receives both statutory redundancy payments and a termination payment, the statutory redundancy payments use up part of the £30,000 exemption and only the balance is available to cover the remainder of the termination payment. Whilst the tax exemption is limited to £30,000, the full amount paid may be exempt from NIC provided it is essentially compensatory in nature.

4.16.4 Employment includes a period of foreign service

The £30,000 exemption may be increased where the employment has included 'foreign service'.

Example – Increased exemption owing to foreign service

B was non-resident in the UK, working overseas from 1991 to 2001. B retired in December 2012 and received compensation of £80,000. The exemption is found by using the fraction:

$$\frac{\text{Foreign services}}{\text{Total period of employment}}, \text{i.e. in this case } \frac{10 \text{ years}}{21 \text{ years}}$$

This fraction is applied to the amount of the golden handshake after deduction of the £30,000 exemption. The taxable amount would be arrived at as follows:

	£
Compensation	80,000
Less: 'normal exemption'	(30,000)
	50,000
$^{10}/_{21}$ thereof	(23,809)
Taxable amount	26,191

4.16.5 Year for which a termination payment may be taxed

It used to be the case that the timing of a termination payment did not affect the tax liability because it was always treated as taxable income for the year in which the employment was terminated. However, termination payments are now taxed as income of the year in which they are received.

4.16.6 Taxation of continuing payments and benefits

Redundancy and other termination settlements often include provisions for payments to be made or benefits to continue after termination. Such benefits are taxable only as they arise. So, both benefits and payments are taxable in the year when received or enjoyed (not in the year of termination).

Example – Benefits-in-kind following redundancy

M was made redundant on 6 October 2010 and received a lump sum of £20,000 plus a further £20,000 on 6 April 2011. She also continued in the company medical insurance scheme for 18 months at a continuing cost to the employer of £350 in 2010–11 and £650 in 2011–12.

In 2010–11 *M* received a combined redundancy package of £20,350 that is covered by the £30,000 exemption. The £9,650 exemption balance is carried forward to the following year. In 2011–12 she received the balance of the package of £20,650, of which £9,650 is exempt. The medical benefit of £650 is covered by the balance of the exemption as is £9,000 of the cash payment, leaving £11,000 to be taxed at her marginal rate under PAYE.

4.16.7 Certain benefits are not taxed on former employees

(The Employer-Financed Retirement Benefits Schemes (Excluded Benefits for Tax Purposes) Regulations 2007 (SI 2007 No 3537))

No charge arises where an employer continues to provide certain benefits after an employment has ceased. These benefits are:

- living accommodation and related benefits;
- health screening and annual medical check-ups (from 2006–07);
- welfare counselling;
- recreational benefits;
- annual parties and similar functions;
- writing of Wills, etc;
- equipment for disabled employees.

The exemption for health screening is contained in s 320B ITEPA 2003 which was inserted by FA 2009.

4.16.8 *Ex gratia* payments

There has been concern that *ex gratia* payments may be subject to tax as relevant retirement benefits under s 393 ITEPA 2003. If this charge arises, the £30,000 exemption is not available. An *ex gratia* payment is normally regarded as a retirement benefit taxable under ss 393–400 only where it is paid in connection with an individual's retirement. Please note that from 9 December 2010 the rules on disguised remuneration may have created an upfront tax charge on payments made into an EFRBS, EBT or other structure. In that case, amounts received by the employee will only be taxable under ss 393–400 to the extent that a tax charge has not already arisen.

HMRC has also given guidelines on hypothetical situations. In particular, it regards it as possible for a person to retire from one employment and draw benefits from that employer's EFRBS while taking up employment with a new employer – see Table 4.4, which defines the position for EFRBS purposes. It does not follow that the same treatment will necessarily apply when considering whether a termination payment is taxable as a contribution to an unapproved retirement benefits scheme.

Table 4.4 – Guidelines on hypothetical situations

Situation	*Retirement position*
A long-service employee leaves to take a senior executive position in another company at the age of 60	The employee has retired
A division of the company is sold and the 55-year-old manager responsible for running it leaves to take a job with the purchaser	The manager has retired
A person in his 50s has a heart attack and is advised by his doctor to leave and seek a less stressful position	If the person were re-employed in an entirely different capacity with the same employer or finds employment with another employer, HMRC would generally accept the member had retired early from the original employment (possibly on ill-health grounds or possibly on normal early retirement grounds – depending on scheme rules and exact medical advice). But if the *ex gratia* payment made is purely consolation for loss of health that results in the premature termination of employment, it would not be regarded as made in connection with retirement)

Situation	Retirement position
An employee aged 35 is involved in an accident and suffers disabilities that make it impossible to continue with the job	A lump sum paid on retirement solely by reason of disability from an accident is not taxable as a benefit from an employer-financed retirement benefits scheme
An employee aged 50 leaves to take a job nearer home to be able to nurse her aged parents	Employee has retired

4.16.9 Payments in lieu of notice (PILONs)

PILONs have featured increasingly in employment contracts in recent years as employees have tried to formalise their rights and employers have wanted to be able to enforce restrictive covenants and prevent ex-employees using confidential information that they have acquired in the course of their employment. HMRC set out its opinion in a lengthy article in *Tax Bulletin 24* (August 1996). In large measure, HMRC's interpretations have been upheld by the courts (see *EMI Electronics Group Ltd* v *Coldicott*). Also see *SCA Packaging Limited* v *HMRC* [2007] EWHC 270.

The term 'PILON' is sometimes used loosely to include payments to employees on 'garden leave'. This is not correct. An employee on garden leave is still an employee: he or she cannot take another job until the end of the notice period. All that has changed is that he or she is not required to carry out any duties. Payments to such an employee are taxable in the normal way and the employer should deduct tax under PAYE.

There are also situations where the employee's service contract actually provides for a PILON, usually at the employer's option. HMRC's view is that where an employer decides to make a PILON, the payment is made under the contract rather than as compensation for the contract having been broken. As such, it remains taxable in full and PAYE deductions should be made.

Rather more controversially, HMRC argues that there may be an implied term to an employment contract where an employer customarily makes PILONs. This is common in certain industries (IT, stockbroking, asset management, etc) where the last thing an employer wants is for an employee who is serving out a notice period to have continued access to confidential information or to clients. You should take professional advice if you are an employer who has a history of regularly making PILONs.

Virtually the only circumstances in which you can be completely confident that a PILON will be treated as a golden handshake (see 4.16) is where the payment is a 'one-off' exception to your normal rule, and there is no reference to the possibility of such a payment in the service contract or related documents such as the staff handbook. In this situation, the first £30,000 (including other elements of the termination package) is normally exempt from tax.

4.17 DESIGNING A 'TAX EFFICIENT' REMUNERATION PACKAGE

Where an individual has a real degree of influence over the way his or her total remuneration package of salary and benefits is made up, the following should be borne in mind.

(1) Pension schemes are very tax efficient.
(2) Approved share options are treated more favourably than non-approved options.
(3) The legislation on benefits-in-kind still leaves some scope for manoeuvre.
(4) Golden handshakes are not always taxable.

4.17.1 Advantages of pension funds in general

From a tax perspective, there can be no better medium to long-term investment than a pension scheme. The fact that pension schemes are not subject to tax internally because of the funds' exemption from UK income tax and CGT, combined with the facility to take one quarter of the fund as a tax-free lump sum at retirement, means that the overall return will almost certainly beat any comparable investment. Furthermore, an employer's contribution does not attract NIC.

4.17.2 Employer can contribute up to £50,000 pa

From 6 April 2011, an employer can make contributions of up to £50,000 pa (plus any of the employee's unused allowances – limited to £50,000 pa – for the last three tax years) provided that the contributions do not take the employee's pension fund over the lifetime allowance (see 26.1.2). This allowance is currently £1.8 million and is due to reduce to £1.5 million from 6 April 2012, subject to the availability of an election to protect the fund (which is expected to work in a similar way to 'enhanced protection' following the 'A' Day changes).

4.17.3 Employee shares

With CGT at 28%, or 18% for basic rate taxpayers, an employee share scheme can form part of a very attractive benefits package. However, close attention needs to be given to the rules on special shares (see 6.6). Bear in mind the election at 6.6.7 where restricted shares have only a small initial value as it could be well worth accepting a modest income tax charge upfront in order to ensure that the capital appreciation will be subject only to CGT.

4.17.4 Approved share option schemes

The tax treatment of an individual who exercises an approved share option is significantly better than that for someone who benefits via an unapproved arrangement. Basically, no tax charge arises on the exercise of an approved share option provided that certain conditions have been observed (see 6.4.4).

The conclusion must be that wherever an individual has a choice, he or she should participate via an approved rather than a non-approved scheme to the maximum extent permitted.

4.17.5 Tax efficient benefits-in-kind

Despite the Government's long-term intention to remove any discrimination between the tax treatment of benefits-in-kind and cash remuneration, there are still certain benefits that are treated favourably for tax purposes. If a person is a company director, or someone else who has a degree of say in the way his or her remuneration package is made up, significant tax benefits can be secured by a judicious choice of benefits-in-kind.

Company cars or cash allowance?

You need to check that you will be better off with a company car as opposed to receiving a cash allowance with which you can buy your own car and then charge for business mileage at the flat-rate mileage allowances (see 4.4.9). Similar considerations apply to car fuel.

It may pay to buy your company car

Because of the high rate of depreciation in the first year, it may be advantageous for a director to arrange for his or her company to purchase a car with a view to its being sold to him or her after it has been used for a period. Provided he or she pays the full market value for the car in its second-hand condition, there will be no tax charge on the difference between the cost of the car to the company and the amount at which the director purchases it. Admittedly, there is a scale benefit for the period the company owns the car, but this is often significantly less than the vehicle's depreciation during the period concerned.

Car fuel

Where an employee or director has a company car, it is clearly beneficial that he or she should have as much free petrol as possible as the scale benefit does not vary according to how much private petrol is provided. However, as the taxable benefit is so high, it is often better for the employee to pay for fuel then claim for reimbursement of business mileage.

Interest-free loans

There is a *de minimis* limit so that, if an individual has a beneficial loan from his or her company, no income tax charge arises unless the loan exceeds £5,000.

Company accommodation

It may be possible to secure a favourable result when a director or employee occupies a company property. This is a complex area where you should take professional advice.

4.17.6 Golden handshakes are not always taxable

A termination payment can still be treated favourably, either because of the £30,000 exemption or because it qualifies for total exemption (see 4.16).

5

EMPLOYMENT INCOME THROUGH THIRD PARTIES: DISGUISED REMUNERATION

This chapter deals with the following matters:

(1) Introduction to the rules
(2) Anti-forestalling
(3) The transition to the new rules
(4) The old rules
(5) The new rules
(6) Relevant steps
(7) Exclusions
(8) The charge to tax
(9) Deductibility
(10) Summary

5.1 INTRODUCTION TO THE RULES

(ss 554A–554Z20, Part 7A ITEPA 2003; Schedule 2 Finance Act 2011)

These wide-ranging anti-avoidance provisions were introduced as part of Finance Act 2011. The main provisions took effect from 6 April 2011, with anti-forestalling rules in effect from 9 December 2010 to 5 April 2011. The rules will apply in circumstances where employees and their employers enter into arrangements which result in a payment of money or the provision of an asset by a third party rather than the employer. It is understood that the main motivation of Government in introducing this legislation was to prevent tax avoidance through the use of employee benefit trusts (EBTs) and employer funded retirement benefit schemes (EFRBSs). These are often complex offshore structures with value passed to employees in diverse ways (eg cash or asset loans or asset transfers) either during their employment or after they have retired or left the company.

Initially, this legislation only applies for income tax purposes but HMRC has stated that equivalent legislation to extend the rules for NIC will follow.

Tax notes

The provisions are extremely complex and if you think you might be affected, it is essential that you take specialist professional advice, as any errors could prove very costly.

The layout of new Part 7A ITEPA 2003 is as follows.
Chapter 1:

- s 554A states when chapter 2 (the charge to tax) applies;
- ss 554B to 554D specify what constitutes a 'relevant step';
- ss 554E to 554X contain exclusions from the rules;
- ss 554X and 554Z contain definitions.

Chapter 2:

- ss 554Z1 to 554Z7 contain detailed rules on the income tax treatment of relevant steps;
- ss 554Z8 to 554Z10 deal with the remittance basis; and
- ss 554Z11 to 554Z14 deal with other miscellaneous points.

Chapter 3:

- ss 554Z15 to 554Z20 deal with situations where security is given for an undertaking to make contributions to an EFRBS in future.

The new rules create a tax charge which will apply to certain loans of money or assets by third parties to the employee; the earmarking of money or assets for the employee by a third party; and to the outright payment of money or transfers of assets to the employee by a third party where these are not otherwise charged to tax as earnings from the employment. Throughout the rules, references to employees also include prospective or former employees.

HMRC has recently released a set of frequently asked questions (FAQs) (see www.hmrc.gov.uk/budget-updates/disguised-remuneration-faqs.pdf and www.hmrc.gov.uk/budget-updates/march2011/drl-faq.pdf), dealing with the main queries it has received so far on the application of the draft rules. Full guidance is unlikely to be issued until Finance Bill 2011 has received Royal Assent, ie at least three months into the operation of the new rules (and after the date of publication of this book).

There will always be those who claim to have schemes that 'get round' the rules. It should be borne in mind that this is anti-avoidance legislation and, as such, the courts can be expected to give these provisions their widest possible meaning in order to circumvent the mischief at which the legislation is aimed.

Realistically, any scheme which seeks to side-step new Part 7A ITEPA 2003 will be disclosable under the Disclosure of Tax Avoidance Schemes (DOTAS) Regulations and it is therefore expected that HMRC will make changes reactively if genuine loopholes have been discovered as is demonstrated by the late addition of Chapter 3 in May 2011. HMRC also released Spotlight 11 (www.hmrc.gov.uk/avoidance/spotlights.htm) on 3 March 2011 making it clear that it does not consider that schemes which involved withdrawing the funds as a loan prior to 5 April 2011, retaining value in a different (and accessible) structure and arranging repayment of the original loans prior to 5 April 2012 succeeded in skirting the new legislation. Whilst no further changes tightening up the legislation have been announced at the time of writing, this should be taken as a warning that HMRC is monitoring disclosures in this area particularly carefully.

There are a number of areas which are unintentionally included and in places the draft legislation has been amended to put this beyond doubt. There is no doubt however that some situations that both taxpayers and advisers would have regarded as completely innocent will now be caught.

For employees that could benefit from such arrangements and have a need for short-term liquidity, it may be possible to ensure that any new loans are made directly by the employer rather than, say, an EBT. Some companies will be able to do this easily, whilst others may require shareholder approval. Employers will need to ensure that they have robust processes in place to identify when a tax charge under the new provisions arises so that they can be sure that they can comply with the tight deadlines for compliance.

5.2 ANTI-FORESTALLING

(Paras 53–58, Schedule 2 Finance Act 2011, applying from 9 December 2010 to 5 April 2011)

Any relevant step (except where a charge arises in whole or in part in connection with qualifying recognised overseas pensions schemes (QROPs)) taken between 9 December 2010 and 5 April 2011 will be treated as a relevant step occurring on 6 April 2012 (to the extent the value of the relevant step has not been repaid by that date), with the resulting income being treated as income of 2012–13. The amount which would otherwise count as employment income of the individual will be reduced by so much of the sum as has been repaid (or where a readily convertible asset had been made available, the asset is returned) to the employer or third party making the payment, before 6 April 2012 by the person to whom the payment was made.

The anti-forestalling rules only bit when a person:

> paid a sum of money to a relevant person, or made available an asset for use as security for a loan made or to be made to a relevant person, or otherwise as security for the meeting of any liability, or the performance of any undertaking, which a relevant person has or will have, or the asset is a readily convertible asset which is made available to secure the payment of a sum of money.

Therefore the following actions, which are caught from 6 April 2011, were not caught by the anti-forestalling rules:

- earmarking;
- transferring the property in a non-readily convertible asset to a relevant person;
- taking a step by virtue of which a relevant person acquired securities, interests in securities, and securities options, as defined in s 420 ITEPA (assuming these were not readily convertible to cash);
- granting a lease of any premises, the effective duration of which was likely to exceed 21 years, to a relevant person.

HMRC was fully aware of these lacunae but it was faced with either implementing the legislation in its entirety on 9 December 2010, which would have caused a widespread outcry and political fall-out, or giving a transitional period (which it did) when only cash or near cash transactions would be caught. Accordingly, the 2011 Budget did not contain any 'retroactive' amendments to the anti-forestalling rules. There were however changes to the rules which operate from 6 April 2011, both to implement the policy responses to the FAQs and potentially to block any schemes which have been disclosed in the interim.

This meant that it was still possible to get value out of structures prior to 5 April 2011, but that any later relevant step taken in connection with such assets after 5 April 2011 will trigger the Part 7A charge. Therefore there were opportunities for employers to make further additions to EBTs and for trustees to allocate cash or assets to sub-funds before 6 April 2011 whilst deferring any income tax liability until such time as the employee receives a benefit from the EBT.

Possibilities also existed where funds were allocated (but had not been transferred) to the employee prior to 9 December 2010, either by appointing out an asset which was not readily convertible to the spouse, civil partner or other family member, or alternatively, appointing out the right to repayment of an outstanding loan, provided this was for a stated (lengthy) term rather than repayable on demand.

5.3 THE TRANSITION TO THE NEW RULES

Sums 'earmarked' (however informally) for an employee from 6 April 2011 will be subject to income tax (and, it is expected, NIC). From 6 April 2011, it is therefore important that no further allocations, however notional or informal – potentially including discussions between the trustee and the employer – are made, so that unallocated funds cannot be said to have been earmarked. The legislation requires that a 'step' be taken to earmark, pay, transfer or make available a sum or asset to trigger a tax charge. Sums already allocated to sub-trusts before 9 December 2010 should therefore be unaffected, until such time as a further step is taken post-6 April 2011.

Loans that were already in existence on 9 December 2010 will not trigger the new rules, until such time as a further relevant step is taken (this could be waiving the loan, or simply renegotiating the terms, or receiving an extra advance). HMRC has however confirmed that simply changing trustees will not trigger a charge under Part 7A.

A loan made prior to 9 December 2010 – so long as no later relevant step is taken with respect to it (which might be as simple as changing the terms sufficiently that it actually constitutes a new loan) – does not fall within the charge. Because the subject matter (the loan) is never within Part 7A in those circumstances, the nastier provisions (see s 554D) which effectively impose a charge after the cessation of the employment, by creating a new tax charge on the capital value, will not bite as they can only operate on something which is within the Part 7A charge to begin with.

The landscape changes for individuals where (say) an earmarking step is taken on or after 6 April 2011, or who receive cash or assets or benefit from an asset, and those who have received money (including loans) or 'readily convertible assets' from 9 December 2010.

In those cases, a Part 7A charge will arise on the occasion of an earmarking (s 554B) or the receipt of value within s 554C (cash/near cash/other assets), or s 554D (use of assets). Subject to conditions, Chapter 2 does not apply where the relevant step involves a sum of money or an asset which was derived from or acquired using the proceeds from a sum of money or asset which was the subject of an earlier relevant step within s 554B (ie earmarked), and Chapter 2 applied by reason of that earlier relevant step in respect of the employee's employment with the employer.

So, say the first relevant step was the earmarking of a sum of money for X; a Part 7A charge would arise on X for that year. Then, in a later tax year, the earmarked funds are loaned to X. No new Part 7A charge *should* arise, provided that the earmarked fund – or an asset purchased with the earmarked funds – is loaned rather than some other asset (ie if £500,000 was earmarked and a charge arose, then instead of giving X £500,000, the trustees appointed a £500,000 house to him which was not purchased with the earmarked funds, this would be a new relevant step which would be separately chargeable in the later year).

Some commentators have expressed concerns that the benefit-in-kind charge on loans is extended where the employment does not continue; however, this is not the case. The reason for this is that where a loan is made, this is specifically defined as being cash, so there is an upfront Part 7A charge on the capital value of the loan, rather than an on going benefit-in-kind charge on interest not paid each year. For the avoidance of doubt, new s 554Z1(3) specifies that, in a case in which the relevant step is the making of an employment-related loan (within the meaning of Chapter 7 of Part 3), the loan is not to be treated for any tax year as a taxable cheap loan.

However where an ex-employee is given the use of an asset (probably something more than 'use of' is implied – see FAQ 7), s 554D basically extends the charge so that it applies whenever the asset is made available. (This is in contrast to the previous position where an asset made available in a different tax year to that in which the employment ceased would escape a benefit-in-kind charge.) The s 554D charge is not a benefit-in-kind charge; it is a charge on the capital value of what is transferred, ie it may be out of all proportion to any actual benefit derived. Factors which determine whether s 554D applies include any limitations on the way in which the relevant person may benefit from the asset, such as the period over which the asset is being made available and (if relevant) the extent to which that period covers the expected remaining useful life of the asset; the extent to which the relevant person has, or is to have, a say over the disposal of the asset; and the extent to which the relevant person may benefit from any proceeds arising from the disposal of the asset or otherwise have a say in the way the proceeds are used.

Only loans made between 9 December 2010 and 5 April 2011 (inclusive) will be within the scope of the anti-forestalling provisions. However, the anti-forestalling provisions do apply to loan arrangements entered into before 9 December 2010 if the loan is actually paid on or after that date. For example, where there is a loan arrangement which was entered into on 1 December 2010 but the loan was not paid until 15 December 2010, the loan is not excluded from the anti-forestalling provisions simply because the agreement to make the loan was entered into before 9 December 2010.

Where a loan was advanced between 9 December 2010 and 5 April 2011, a Part 7A charge will only arise if the loan is not repaid in full before 6 April 2012. However, where the making of a loan on or after 6 April 2011 gives rise to a relevant step, a tax charge will arise at the time of payment whether or not the loan is subsequently repaid by 6 April 2012.

Loans which were paid and assets made available before the legislation applied are outside the scope of Part 7A. But, for example, if an asset provided before 6 April 2011 is subsequently reallocated to somebody else, this will trigger a new charge under s 554C or s 554D.

Part 7A applies to money or assets in a sub-fund or sub-trust of an employee benefit trust established before 9 December 2010 despite remaining undistributed (including by way of a loan) on 6 April 2011 only to the extent that a relevant step under ss 554C or 554D occurs on or after 6 April 2011 (or on or after 9 December 2010 if the anti-forestalling provisions apply). It will also apply to new acts of earmarking in relation to the sub-trust or fund on or after 6 April 2011.

5.4 THE OLD RULES

5.4.1 Benefits conferred on an employee during the relevant employment

Such benefits were chargeable under s 62 ITEPA. Benefits-in-kind may also have been chargeable under the benefits code, with the overall charge being on the higher amount, as any amount taxable as earnings under s 62 was deducted from the amount of the benefit-in-kind charge.

5.4.2 Benefits conferred on an employee after termination of the relevant employment

A benefit conferred on a beneficiary after the termination of his or her employment constituted 'earnings under s 62'. The benefits-in-kind code however does not apply in a tax year in which the employment is not held. Depending on the form which the benefit took, it might also have been chargeable as a pension, payment of relevant benefits, or under the transfer of assets abroad provisions.

5.4.3 Benefits conferred on a person other than the employee during the relevant employment

A benefit conferred on a person other than an employee during the continuance of the relevant employment could give rise to a charge to income tax under the benefits-in-kind code. The person chargeable was the employee and the income charged was deemed to be his or hers, even if he or she personally did not benefit. A charge might also arise on annual payments or under the transfer of assets abroad provisions if it could be matched with unmatched 'relevant income' in relation to the beneficiary, which had arisen within the trust structure.

Subject to the above, a payment or transfer of capital by the trustees of an employee benefit trust to, or the conferral of benefit on, a person other than the employee in a year during which the relevant employment was held would not give rise to a charge to income tax.

5.4.4 Benefits conferred on persons other than the employee in a year in which relevant employment was not held

The benefit-in-kind provisions did not apply in such a situation, however, charges might arise on the payment of relevant benefits or pensions, or under the transfer of assets abroad provisions.

145

5.5 THE NEW RULES

The new rules apply from 6 April 2011.

5.5.1 Chapter 1: arrangements falling within Chapter 2, Part 7A, ITEPA

(ss 554A–554D Chapter 1, Part 7A ITEPA 2003)

New s 554A introduces the concept of 'relevant steps' (taken in pursuance of, or connected to, 'relevant arrangements') which will count as employment income of the employee, or prospective or former employee. The rules are not restricted to arrangements involving EBTs and EFRBS. Some new concepts, such as *earmarking* and persons *linked with* an individual are introduced.

This encompasses virtually anything that a [legal] person might choose to do. Anyone (whether the employee, or employer, or any third person – including corporate trustees, etc) who creates a trust, or holds funds, of which the discretionary beneficiaries are past, current or future employees (or persons linked with them) might arguably be said to have 'earmarked' funds with a view to these being used in a later relevant step.

The rules apply to arrangements to make money or assets available to current, former and prospective employees of a person where:

- It is reasonable to suppose that, in essence:
    (i) the relevant arrangement, or
    (ii) the relevant arrangement so far as it covers or relates to the employees, is (wholly or partly) a means of providing, or is otherwise concerned (wholly or partly) with the provision of, rewards or recognition or loans in connection with the employees' employment, or former or prospective employment, with the employer.

- Or a relevant step is taken by a relevant third person (ie either the employee or the employer acting as a trustee of an arrangement, **or any other person**), and it is reasonable to suppose that, in essence:
    (i) the relevant step is taken (wholly or partly) in pursuance of the relevant arrangement, or
    (ii) there is some other connection (direct or indirect) between the relevant step and the relevant arrangement.

Section 554A was amended at the 2011 Budget to make clear that arrangements between groups of companies or LLPs and their subsidiary companies were not intended to be caught where there was no tax avoidance motive, ie in such circumstances, another group company would not fall within the definition of 'any other person acting as a trustee'.

At its broadest, a relevant arrangement is one relating to an employee and concerned with providing him or her with rewards, while a relevant step is any step connected with the arrangement. 'Connected' in this sense simply means 'having to do with', which is an extremely wide definition.

Prior to the publication of HMRC's FAQs, there had been concern that, as the legislation was drafted, placing funds on discretionary trust, of which the class of beneficiaries included past, present or future employees or persons linked with them, could constitute earmarking. It has been confirmed by implication that 'something more' would be needed, but you should note that this 'something more' may often be undertaken inadvertently by the employer, ie by telling staff what level of bonus or share ownership they can look forward to (and indeed, the staff may insist on knowing what level of bonus they can expect). At that stage, it is earmarked and therefore caught by the rules, and the employer would be forced to account for PAYE and NIC on the sums so earmarked.

Insofar as an arrangement relates to the employee, it must be reasonable to suppose that, in essence, the arrangement is (wholly or partly) a means of providing rewards or recognition, or loans, in connection with his or her employment with the employer. It does not matter if at the time it is made the arrangement does not include certain details, such as the sum of money to be provided. References to 'the payment of sum of money' in this context include loans.

For a tax charge to apply, a relevant step must be taken by a relevant third person.

The definition of an 'arrangement' includes any agreement, scheme, settlement, transaction, trust or understanding (whether or not it is legally enforceable). This is very widely defined and seems to bring in rather more than the IT and CGT anti-avoidance on trusts where an element of bounty is required. The wording covers virtually anything one might do to pay high-performing employees at some future date. Quite how HMRC would prove that such a decision has been taken, where it is not otherwise documented, is not clear, but the breadth of the definition clearly encompasses the full range from discretionary or fixed interest trusts to bare trust arrangements through to simple verbal agreements.

The definition of trustee has been narrowed to exclude group companies and subsidiary companies of LLPs, as noted above.

These changes will be subject to an anti-avoidance rule. Other than in very limited circumstances, a group company will now only be a relevant third person if it is acting as the trustee of an arrangement or where there is some underlying tax avoidance motive.

A new concept of persons 'linked with' the employee is introduced and references to the employee include references to any person linked with him or her.

A person linked with the employee is a person within the 'connected persons' definition at s 993 ITA 2007 plus:

- a close company in which the employee or a linked person is or has been a participator; or
- a company in which the employee or a linked person is or has been a participator and which would be a close company if it were a UK resident company; or
- a company which is a 51% subsidiary of a company within either of the above bullet points.

For the purposes of this section people living together as if they were spouses or civil partners are treated as if they were spouses or civil partners of each other.

5.6 RELEVANT STEPS

5.6.1 Earmarking

(s 554B(1) ITEPA)

A person takes a relevant step if he or she (or it) formally or informally 'earmarks' a sum of money or asset held by or on behalf of an individual, with a view to a later relevant step being taken in relation to a relevant sum or asset (by that or any other person, on the meeting of any condition or otherwise). Earmarking is a somewhat woolly concept – it is not defined but it is expected that the courts will give the term its normal English meaning, which is to designate something for a particular purpose, or select and reserve something to be used for a particular purpose.

It does not matter whether the details of the later relevant step have been worked out, or whether the employee or a linked person has a legal right to have a relevant step taken in connection with the sum or asset (or a sum or asset arising or deriving from it).

As previously noted, anyone (whether the employee, or the employer, or any other person) who creates a trust, or holds funds, of which the discretionary beneficiaries are past, current, or future employees, or persons linked with those employees – and an indication has been made of how funds are to be allocated to the beneficiaries – can be said to have 'earmarked' funds with a view to these being used in a later relevant step.

A letter of wishes could constitute earmarking if it sets out details of how much the employer wishes to have allocated to certain employees, whether now or in future.

HMRC has stated that where shares or funds to acquire shares are put into an EBT to meet future requirements of an employee share plan or a long-term incentive plan (LTIP), but are not earmarked in relation to named employees, this transaction on its own will not give rise to a charge.

HMRC has stated that the policy objective is to tackle arrangements established for the purposes of tax avoidance and to achieve this in a proportionate and well-targeted way. To address this concern, the legislation has been amended so that arrangements which have the following characteristics do not give rise to a charge on earmarking at the time that the shares are earmarked.

- The payment of the shares must be subject to conditions which, if not met, will mean that there will be no possibility of the employee (or a person linked with the employee or chosen by the employee) receiving them or retaining any form of current or future entitlement to the amount they do not receive.
- The arrangement must specify a date for the vesting of the shares. This must be at most five years from the date of grant. Where this condition is fulfilled, if vesting does not take place within five years of the date of grant, a Part 7A charge will arise unless an event has happened which means there is no possibility of the employee (or a person linked with the employee or chosen by the employee) receiving their benefit from the plan.
- The nature of the arrangements must be such that, if vesting does occur on or before the vesting date, there will be a charge to tax on employment income.
- The deferral or avoidance of tax must not be the main purpose, or one of the main purposes, of entering into the arrangement.

If an earmarked sum, on which a charge has already arisen, will in fact never be made available to the individual, relief can be claimed. An application for relief may be made by the individual (or, if he or she has died, his or her personal representatives) to HMRC if an event occurs (which is not a relevant step) by reason of which no further relevant step is or will be taken and there is no connection (direct or indirect) between the relevant event and a tax-avoidance arrangement. This means that if an earmarked sum, on which a charge has already arisen, will in fact never be made available to the individual, relief can be claimed.

5.6.2 Paying a sum of money or transferring an asset

(s 554C(1) ITEPA 2003)

A person takes a relevant step if he or she:

- pays a sum of money;
- transfers the property in an asset;
- takes a step by which a relevant person acquires securities, interests in securities or securities options to make available a sum of money or asset for use as security for a loan to a relevant person, or as security for the meeting of any other liability or undertaking; or
- grants a lease of premises which is likely to exceed 21 years.

The scope of Part 7A is very wide in relation to loans. Any loan made by any third party to an employee on or after 9 December 2010 will be caught. HMRC has confirmed that this is intentional.

If a loan is made by a relevant third person on or after 9 December 2010 under an arrangement to which s 554A applies, it is within the scope of Part 7A. Unless the loan meets the tests for the 'commercial transactions' or employee benefits packages exclusions, the making of the loan will be a relevant step.

Part 7A is not specifically targeted at particular types of intermediary structure (eg EBTs and EFRBS). This also is intentional; targeting particular types of intermediary would, in HMRC's view, encourage the use of alternative vehicles for tax-avoidance purposes. Similarly, excluding loans made by particular types of intermediary would inevitably result in the structuring of loan arrangements through excluded third parties.

5.6.3 Arrangements not intended to be caught

The policy intention is that the new rules should apply to arrangements involving a third party to reward employees and directors which seek to avoid, defer or reduce income tax and NICs and also to arrangements that are used as a tax-advantaged way to save for retirement, such as using an EFRBS as an alternative to, or to top up, savings in a registered pension scheme.

However, HMRC has accepted that as originally drafted, the legislation would have brought forward an income tax charge in genuine deferred remuneration arrangements, including those put in place to meet the requirements of the FSA's recently published Remuneration Code, and the legislation has been amended to address this issue, subject to certain conditions.

5.6.4 Making an asset available

(s 554D(1) ITEPA 2003)

A person takes a relevant step if, without transferring the property in an asset to a relevant person, he or she (or it):

- at any time, makes the asset available for the relevant person to benefit from (irrespective of whether the relevant person actually benefits) as if the property in the asset had been transferred to the relevant person at that time, or
- at or after the end of the relevant period, makes the asset available for the relevant person to benefit from.

If before the end of the relevant period any person makes available an asset for the employee (or ex-employee) to benefit from and, at the end of the relevant period, continues to make it available in this way, that person is treated as taking a relevant step at the end of the relevant period.

5.6.5 Arrangements not intended to be caught

HMRC has been asked to clarify this. For example, would the normal provision of a company car under a lease agreement or the occasional use of a holiday home be capable of meeting the test? HMRC has confirmed that this is not caught.

HMRC has commented that the test is intended to cover circumstances that are, in essence, the same as the way in which the employee could have benefited from the asset had the employee been the outright owner. This requires something more than the asset simply being at the employee's disposal or available for his or her private use. HMRC has given examples of the 'something more' that would point to the employee being able to benefit from an asset in much the same way as the outright owner. These include:

- where the employee can directly influence decisions about whether to sell or replace an asset;
- where it is clear that the employee is likely to benefit from any eventual disposal proceeds of an asset (eg because they will be ploughed back into the employee's sub-trust).

5.6.6 Relevant sum of money or asset

(s 554B(4) ITEPA)

The 'relevant sum' of money or asset is the earmarked sum of money or asset, or a sum of money or asset deriving from the earmarked sum of money or asset.

5.6.7 Relevant period

(s 554D(4) ITEPA 2003)

The relevant period means the period of two years starting with the day on which the employee's employment with the employer ceases.

5.6.8 Relevant person

(ss 554C and 554D ITEPA 2003)

A relevant person for these purposes is the employee, or any person chosen by the employee, or any person within a class of persons chosen by the employee; including, if any person takes a step on the employee's behalf, or otherwise at the employee's request, any other person. References to the employee include any person linked with the employee.

References to 'the payment of a sum of money' include a loan and once such a charge has been made, it is irrevocable.

The anti-forestalling rules allow credit for repayment of any part of a loan made in the period from 9 December 2010 to 5 April 2011 inclusive. Where such a loan is made the Part 7A charge will be based on the amount of the loan less any repayments made before 6 April 2012. However, there is no provision for credit to be given for the repayment of any loan made by a third party on or after 6 April 2011, and no intention to rectify this punitive provision. Therefore, once a Part 7A charge has arisen, the recipient would be advised not to repay the loan, as no credit will be obtained for doing so.

5.7 EXCLUSIONS

(ss 554E–554X ITEPA 2003)

5.7.1 Steps under 'certain schemes and arrangements'

The legislation in Part 7A does not apply to:

- an approved SIP (as defined by Chapter 6, Part 7 ITEPA 2003);
- an approved SAYE option scheme(as defined by Chapter 7, Part 7 ITEPA 2003);
- an approved CSOP scheme (as defined by Chapter 8, Part 7 ITEPA 2003);
- an arrangement the sole purpose of which is the issue of qualifying EMI options (as defined by Chapter 9, Part 7 ITEPA 2003);
- an arrangement the sole purpose of which is the provision of excluded benefits within s 393B(3) ITEPA 2003 (broadly on ill health, accidental death or disablement during service, or payment of benefits under a relevant life policy);
- a registered pension scheme; or
- an arrangement the sole purpose of which is making payments (as defined by s 161 FA 2004) which are authorised by s 160(1) FA 2004 (broadly permitted pensions, permitted lump sums, recognised transfers, scheme administration member payments and payments pursuant to a pension sharing order).

HMRC may, by regulation (and with retrospective effect), also exclude payments under a 'relevant non-UK scheme' where migrant member relief has been given; relief has been given (after 5 April 2006) under a double-tax arrangement; there has been a relevant transfer at any time (after 5 April 2006) when the scheme was a QROPS, or s 307 ITEPA 2003 (exemption for provision made by employer for retirement or death benefit) has applied in respect of provision made under the scheme (at any time after 5 April 2006) when the scheme was an 'overseas pension scheme'. Overseas pension schemes are only exempt from the new rules so far as employer payments to these schemes would be subject to the reduced £50,000 annual allowance.

Protection is limited, ie qualifying registered overseas pension schemes (QROPS), which accept transfers from pensions which have been subject to the rules and limits for registered pensions, are protected, but not currently qualifying non-UK pension schemes (QNUPS) although these may later be removed from the charge by regulation.

Section 554E does not provide any exemption for 'genuine' EFRBS. The exclusion applies only where the sole purpose of an arrangement is to make payments to or in respect of a member and the payments are deemed by statute to be paid by a registered pension scheme (although not actually paid by such a scheme). The most common example is where a registered pension scheme provides a pension by purchasing an annuity from a life insurer for payment to the member. The exclusion does not apply where the payments under the arrangement would have been authorised payments if they had been paid by a registered pension scheme but are not so paid nor treated as so paid for the purpose of Finance Act 2004.

5.7.2 Commercial transactions

(s 554F ITEPA 2003)

Chapter 2 does not apply to a relevant step which is the payment of a sum of money by way of a loan that is a commercial loan made in the ordinary course of the lender's business, where similar loans were available to members of the public, or any variations in terms were made in the ordinary course of the lender's business, provided it is not (and is not connected, whether directly or indirectly, with) an arrangement which has a tax-avoidance purpose.

The new charge also does not apply to a relevant step taken by a person (which is not a payment of a sum of money by way of a loan) for the purposes of a transaction that person has with the employee in the ordinary course of that person's business and a substantial proportion of that person's business involves similar transactions with members of the public, and the terms are substantially the same as those applying to transactions with members of the public, provided it is not (and is not connected, whether directly or indirectly, with) an arrangement which has a tax-avoidance purpose. Substantial in this context is taken to mean at least 50%.

No protection is given for loans to invest in a close company, which might have been expected to be included, on purely commercial grounds.

An arrangement has a tax-avoidance purpose if the main purpose, or one of the main purposes, of the person entering into the arrangement is the avoidance of tax or NIC. As is the case throughout Part 7A, references to the employee include any person linked with the employee.

5.7.3 Transactions under employee benefit packages

(s 554G ITEPA 2003)

Chapter 2 does not apply to a relevant step which is taken by a person for the purposes of a transaction that person has with the employee in the ordinary course of his or her (or its) business if:

- the step is not taken under a pension scheme;
- where the step is the payment of a sum of money by way of a loan, a substantial (>50%) proportion of the person's business involves making loans to members of the public for similar purposes; or
- the transaction is part of a package of benefits that is available to a substantial (>50%) proportion of the employer's employees or of employees whose status as employees is comparable with the individual's status as an employee (taking into account, for example, levels of seniority, types of duties and levels of remuneration); and
- the terms on which similar transactions are offered are generous enough to enable substantially all the employees to whom the package is offered to take advantage of it, if they want to; and
- the terms for the employee are substantially the same as those for other employees; and
- a majority of the employer's employees (assume >50%) to whom the package is available do not have a material interest in the employer (ie holding alone or together with associates, >5% of the shares or alone or together with associates, entitlement to acquire on a winding-up of the company >5% of the assets available for distribution); and
- provided it is not (and is not connected, whether directly or indirectly, with) an arrangement which has a tax-avoidance purpose; and
- unless any feature of the package of benefits is likely to mean that it is directors, senior employees or employees of the employer who receive (or would as a result of the package of benefits receive) the highest levels of remuneration on whom the benefit will be wholly or mainly conferred.

This is intended to – and will – hit plans where in reality, it is understood that only the very senior people and owners of the business will benefit.

There has been concern that salary or bonus sacrifice arrangements involving a third party where the third party allocates tax-exempt or favoured benefits in return for the sacrifice might not fall within the exclusion.

HMRC has accepted that – on its own – sacrificing salary in favour of provision of tax-exempt or tax-advantaged benefits does not constitute tax avoidance. However, it has not ruled out the possibility that particular salary sacrifice arrangements could involve tax avoidance.

There is now some provision for the tax and NIC charged under Part 7A to be refunded if the employee ultimately receives less or no benefit. Credit will still not be given for any repayment of a loan or the return of an asset made after 5 April 2011.

Relief is available where an earmarking charge has arisen and subsequently there is an event which makes it clear that there will be no future relevant step with regard to the earmarked funds, ie the employee will never benefit.

5.7.4 Deferred remuneration and share schemes

Where remuneration is deferred (whether under the FSA code, or for other business reasons) or there is an employee share scheme, and certain conditions are met, a charge will not apply unless at the end of the deferred term (ie the vesting date) the funds remain earmarked for specific employees, or, if earlier payment is made, a charge will arise at that time.

The conditions are – broadly – that:

- The deferred reward is subject to specific conditions which, if not met, will mean there is no possibility of the employee (or a person linked with him or her) receiving the reward or retaining any form of entitlement to the reward.
- A vesting date must be specified which is a maximum of five years from the date of grant.
- The deferred reward must be such that if it is received on or before the vesting date, it is chargeable to tax as employment income.
- The deferral or avoidance of tax must not be the main purpose, or one of the main purposes of the arrangement.

5.7.5 Employment-related securities

(s 554M ITEPA 2003)

Chapter 2 does not apply by reason of:

- an acquisition of employment-related securities if s 425(2) ITEPA 2003 (restricted securities acquired by conversion, at less than market value, or by an option) applies (or would apply apart from s 421E(1)): or
- an acquisition of an employment-related securities option if s 475(1) applies (or would apply apart from s 474(1)); or
- a chargeable event within s 426 (restricted securities: charge on post-acquisition chargeable events), s 438 (convertible securities: charge on post-acquisition chargeable events), or s 476 (securities options: charge on post-acquisition chargeable events); or
- an event which gives rise to the discharge of a notional loan for the purposes of s 446U, or a disposal to which Chapter 3D (securities disposed of for more than market value) of Part 7 applies.

In addition, Chapter 2 does not apply where a loan is made and used solely for the purpose of enabling the employee to exercise a share option, and the exercise of the option by the employee gives rise to employment income chargeable to income tax, or which is exempt income, and there is no connection (direct or indirect) between the relevant step and a tax-avoidance arrangement. 'Share option' in this context means a right to acquire shares (including stock) in a company.

This is to be expected, as a defined tax regime already exists to deal with such matters.

5.7.6 Employee car ownership schemes

Where an employee car ownership scheme is run by the employer (or a group company or subsidiary company of an LLP) the arrangements fall outside the new rules. Where a third party is involved, an exclusion applies where the employee purchases a new car from another person using a loan made to him or her by a licensed lender.

● The agreement must specify the date by which the car loan must be fully repaid which must be no later than four years after the date on which the car loan is made; and
● must permit the employee, in order to obtain funds to repay the car loan, to sell the car back on a specified date at a specified price based on an estimate (made at the time the car ownership arrangement is made) of the likely outstanding amount of the car loan on the specified date; and
● the employee actually purchases the car using the car loan.

Chapter 2 does not apply by reason of a relevant step taken for the sole purpose of the purchase of the car or its sale-back as provided for by the car ownership arrangement, or the making of the car loan, so long as the car ownership arrangement is not a tax-avoidance arrangement and there is no other connection (direct or indirect) between the relevant step and a tax-avoidance arrangement. Where by the repayment date, the loan has not been fully repaid, a relevant step will be treated as taking place, valued at the amount of the outstanding loan.

5.7.7 Employment income exemptions

Where benefits are exempt from tax, this legislation will not be in point. If the exemption relating to benefits that are not taxable applies to only part of a relevant step, the relevant step is treated as being two separate relevant steps (on a just and reasonable basis), one of which is exempt, and one of which is chargeable.

5.7.8 Income arising and acquisitions from earmarked funds

If income arises from an earmarked sum or asset, and when the income arises, it is received by or on behalf of the third party who holds the earmarked sum or asset, and that sum or asset had been the subject of a relevant step within s 554B taken by that person, Chapter 2 will not apply provided:

- before the income arises, the sum or asset was the subject of a relevant step within s 554B taken by that person;
- Chapter 2 applied by reason of the earlier relevant step in respect of the employee's employment with the employer (or would have so applied apart from ss 554P, 554Q, any of ss 554H to 554L or s 554S);
- immediately before the income arises, the sum or asset is still earmarked; and
- it is not reasonable to suppose that, taking into account the type of investments from which the income derives (directly or indirectly), in essence, the income represents a more than commercial return from the sum or asset.

5.7.9 Pension provision

As originally drafted, Part 7A would have applied to all transfers from one unregistered pension scheme to another. Now, transfers between corresponding overseas schemes will be exempted from a charge but only to the extent that the transfer value is referable to contributions made before 6 April 2011. Transfers of sums or assets deriving from personal contributions will also be excluded from the Part 7A charge.

If an employer earmarks a sum or asset with a view to a relevant third person paying a pension or other relevant benefits, the intention is that this earmarking will be a relevant step. HMRC has stated that there will be only two exceptions to this rule.

First, if the relevant third person is:

- a registered pension scheme;
- an overseas pension scheme; or
- a scheme in respect of contributions to which the employer may claim either transitional corresponding relief under Article 15 of SI 2006 No. 572 (the Taxation of Pension Schemes (Transitional Provisions) Order 2006) or relief under double-taxation arrangements.

Second, if the earmarking is carried out with the sole purpose of actually paying an immediate contribution.

QNUPS settled by the employer will get a corporation tax deduction and the protection of s 12(2) IHTA 1984, but will be vulnerable to a charge under Part 7A.

QNUPS settled by individuals will not have the protection of s 12(2) IHTA 1984, ie there may be a transfer of value, but will not be vulnerable to Part 7A.

Broadly speaking, relevant benefits under EFRBS will be subject to tax under s 394 only to the extent that the value of the benefits exceeds amounts charged to tax in respect of the relevant arrangement either as earnings or under Part 7A.

As originally drafted, Part 7A taxed lump sums and retirement benefit arrangements (including annuity purchase and s 615 ICTA 1988 trusts) that would previously have been exempt, for example under ESC A10. Part 7A has since been amended to keep the exemptions, but only to the extent that the benefits provided are referable to contributions or rights accrued before 6 April 2011 (FAQ 19).

Pension payments will be subject to tax under Part 9 ITEPA as pension income in priority over Part 7A, including pensions paid by corresponding overseas schemes. As a result, the remittance basis and the 10% abatement for foreign pensions given under Part 9 will continue to apply where appropriate.

All pension schemes not excluded under s 554E will, however, be liable to the Part 7A charge on any new earmarking on or after 6 April 2011, with credit given against the Part 9 charge for earlier Part 7A charges.

5.7.10 Unfunded schemes (UFRBS)

HMRC has confirmed that Part 7A will not create tax charges for wholly unfunded unapproved retirement benefit schemes. However, a number of arrangements exist whereby the employer promises to provide retirement benefits through a relevant third person and instead of the employer paying contributions at the time of giving the promise, he or she (or it) gives employees various levels of security, backed by assets that they hold. These arrangements are neither funded upfront nor wholly unfunded. Accordingly, Part 7A has been amended to make it clear that the employer itself will be treated as a relevant third person where it earmarks a sum of money or asset and takes a step with a view to meeting an undertaking to pay or secure contributions.

To the extent that funds were taxable on the way into a structure pre-6 April 2006, the removal of funds will not constitute part of the value of a relevant step taken. There will be apportionment where the fund comprises pre- and post- 'A' Day contributions.

The purchase of an annuity out of pension rights accrued in a scheme prior to 6 April 2011 and relevant benefits provided under a relevant scheme by way of a payment of a lump sum wholly out of pre-6 April 2011 rights which the employee has under the scheme are both exempt. So are transfers between overseas pensions and s 390 pensions to the extent that the transfer is made out of rights accrued before 6 April 2006. Transfers arising from post-5 April 2006 contributions, which were neither tax-relieved or exempt, remain chargeable.

To the extent that other payments under retirement benefit plans might come within the ambit of new Part 7A, the draft legislation does not alter the character of pension/retirement income under double-taxation treaties. It will not therefore change the way the UK's treaties allocate taxing rights.

5.8 THE CHARGE TO TAX

5.8.1 Treatment of relevant step for income tax purposes

(s 554Z1 ITEPA 2003)

Employment income

The value of the relevant step counts as employment income of the employee, arising from his or her employment with the employer, either for the tax year the relevant step is taken, or – if before the employment commences – the tax year the employment starts.

There is a priority rule where a relevant step otherwise gives rise to an amount which is treated as earnings under the benefits code, or any income from UK dividends to which Chapter 3, Part 4 ITTOIA 2005 (dividends from UK resident companies) applies. In both, Part 7A takes priority.

Value of relevant step

(s 554Z2 ITEPA 2003)

If the relevant step involves a sum of money its value is the amount of the sum. In any other case, the value of the relevant step is the higher of the market value of the asset, or the cost of the step, unless the relevant step is that a relevant person acquires securities, interests in securities or securities options and any of the provisions of Chapters 2–4A, Part 7 ITEPA 2003 (ie restricted securities; convertible securities; securities with artificially depressed or enhanced market values; securities acquired for less, or disposed of for more, than market value; post-acquisition benefits from securities and shares in research institution spin-out companies), in which case the value of the relevant step is the market value of the asset

Non-UK residence

(s 554Z3 ITEPA 2003)

Sections 16 and 17 ITEPA 2003 will apply as if the value of the relevant step were general earnings. If all or part of the value of the relevant step is for a tax year in which the employee is non-UK resident, the value is reduced so far as it is in respect of duties not performed in the UK, on a 'just and reasonable' basis.

Where an arrangement gives rise to a relevant step, the value of which relates to non-UK duties of an individual who is not domiciled in any part of the UK and claiming the remittance basis in any of the years related to the relevant step, the value is apportioned to the appropriate tax years.

The individual must then check if he or she paid tax under the remittance basis for any of those years. If so, any amount for that year which is not in respect of duties performed in the UK is not taxable until or unless it is remitted to the UK. It is then taxable in the year it is remitted unless the amount is remitted before the relevant employment starts when it is taxable in the year the employment begins.

The new rules have the effect that any part of a relevant step, which is 'for' duties performed within the UK, will remain subject to income tax and NIC. Where a relevant step is taken in a year before the employment has started or after it has ceased and the value can't be attributed to a particular period, the full value of the relevant step is treated as being 'for' the first or last tax year in which the employment was held. If the individual was UK resident in the tax year which the value of the relevant step is 'for' it is chargeable to tax under Part 7A in the tax year in which the relevant step is taken, whether or not the individual is non-UK resident at that time. This is no different from the existing position.

Overlaps with earlier relevant steps

(s 554Z4 ITEPA 2003)

If there is an overlap between the sum of money or asset which is the subject of a relevant step, and a sum or asset which was the subject of an earlier relevant step, the value of the later relevant step is reduced (to a minimum of nil, ie cannot create a 'loss') on a 'just and reasonable basis', depending on the proportion of overlap.

The value of the earlier relevant step is determined after applying s 554Z3 (reduction for non-UK duties) and s 554Z4 (overlaps) but before applying ss 554Z5 to 554Z7.

Overlaps with certain earnings

(s 554Z5 ITEPA 2003)

If the relevant step gives rise to relevant earnings for a tax year, the value of the relevant step (after applying ss 554Z3 and 554Z4) is reduced (to a minimum of nil, ie cannot create a 'loss') by the amount of the relevant earnings.

Relevant earnings are:

- any salary, wages or fee, any gratuity or other profit or incidental benefit of any kind obtained by the employee if it is money or money's worth, or anything else that constitutes an emolument of the employment;
- payments which are treated as earnings;
- deemed employment payments (or any part thereof) arising under the provisions relating to workers provided under arrangements by intermediaries.

However, anything which is exempt income is not relevant.

Where a charge to tax on earnings arises when shares are transferred to an employee, there will not be a double charge under Part 7A.

Sums paid to exercise share options

(s 554Z6 ITEPA 2003)

Section 554Z6 allows a deduction from the value of a relevant step in some circumstances where under the terms of the share option, a sum has to be paid to acquire the shares.

Transfer of assets: consideration given at the time the relevant step is taken

(s 554Z7 ITEPA 2003)

Where the relevant step is within s 554C (ie payment of a sum, transfer of an asset, etc), and before – or at or around the time – the property is transferred, the employee gives the transferor consideration in the form of a sum of money or asset (but not a loan), the value of the relevant step is reduced (to a minimum of nil, ie cannot create a 'loss') by the amount of the consideration given. References to the employee include references to a person linked with the employee. HMRC has advised that 'at or about' means a few days either side of the relevant step – perhaps up to a week, and possibly longer depending on the individual circumstances. This relief is subject to an anti-avoidance purpose test.

This also applies where, for instance, an EBT buys back shares at or below market value from employees who are leaving the company, allowing credit for the market value of the asset sold by the employee.

5.8.2 Remittance basis

(s 554Z8 ITEPA 2003)

Ordinarily resident individuals

If the value of the relevant step is for a tax year in which the remittance basis automatically applies or is claimed, and

- the employee is ordinarily resident;
- the employee's employment in the relevant tax year is with a foreign employer; and
- the duties of the employment, in the relevant year, are performed wholly outside the UK

The individual's employment income by virtue of s 554Z1(1) is taxable so far as it is remitted to the UK in a tax year. Any income which is remitted before his or her employment starts is treated as being remitted in the tax year that the employment starts.

Where there are 'associated employments' which are not performed wholly outside the UK, then the amount of the employee's income which is available to be taxed on the remittance basis is limited subject to a just and reasonable apportionment, having regard to:

- income from all associated employments, together with the income from the employment with the employer;
- the proportion of that income that is general earnings under s 22 (chargeable overseas earnings) or to which s 41A (taxable specific income from employment related securities) applies;
- the nature of, and time devoted to, performing duties inside and outside the UK; and
- any other relevant circumstances.

However, where the amount of the employment income to which the remittance basis would otherwise apply exceeds that limit, the amount of employment income to which the remittance basis can be applied is instead to be taken as an amount which is 'just and reasonable'.

Not ordinarily resident individuals

(s 554Z9 ITEPA 2003)

If the value of a relevant step is for a tax year in which the remittance basis automatically applies or is claimed, and

- the individual is not ordinarily resident; and
- the value of the relevant step is in respect of duties which are performed outside the UK;

then the individual's employment income by virtue of s 554Z1(1) is taxable specific income for the tax year, so far as it is remitted to the UK in that year. Any income which is remitted before his or her employment starts is treated as being remitted in the tax year that the employment starts. The question of whether or to what extent the value of the relevant step (or part thereof) relates to duties performed outside the UK is to be determined on a just and reasonable basis.

5.8.3 Supplementary – calculation

(s 554R ITEPA 2003)

Where the value of the relevant step is in respect of duties which are performed outside the UK, and has been determined to be taxable specific income for a tax year, the reductions in the value of the relevant step under ss 554Z4–554Z7 are to be made so that only a percentage of the reduction is made to the relevant part.

For example, if you have a relevant step valued at £500,000 and £350,000 of it is taxable specific income to which the remittance basis is available, and you are due reductions of:

- £50,000 for overlaps with earlier relevant events;
- £20,000 for overlaps with relevant earnings; and
- £40,000 for consideration given for assets before they were transferred;

then the reductions to be applied to the £350,000 which is subject to the remittance basis are 70% (ie £350,000/£500,000), rather than the whole amounts, as follows:

- £35,000 for overlaps with earlier relevant events (£50,000 × 70%);
- £14,000 for overlaps with relevant earnings, and (£20,000 × 70%);
- £28,000 for consideration given for assets before they were transferred (£40,000 × 70%).

New s 554Z12 gives relief for double charges 'to the extent it is just and reasonable to do so' where there has been a relevant event chargeable under Chapter 7A and a later event occurs, which (apart from Part 7A or Chapters 2–5, Part 7 – ie restricted securities; convertible securities; securities with artificially depressed or enhanced market values; securities acquired for less, or disposed of for more, than market value; post-acquisition benefits from securities, shares in research institution spin-out companies and securities options, or Part 9 – foreign pension income) would give rise to a charge to income tax for *the employee or any other person*.

In that case, the income tax charge on the later event is reduced in respect of the asset or the sum of money which was the subject of the earlier relevant step.

5.9 DEDUCTIBILITY

A relevant arrangement (or an arrangement connected to a relevant arrangement) under new Part 7A ITEPA is an employee benefit scheme for the purposes of determining whether something is an employee benefit contribution and qualifying benefits are provided by an employee benefit scheme (and a deduction becomes available) if a relevant step giving rise to a tax charge under Chapter 2, Part 7A ITEPA is taken.

5.10 SUMMARY

This legislation is incredibly widely targeted. It will, even with the reliefs and exclusions outlined in the text above, catch far too many innocent transactions. It is also likely to create considerable uncertainty which is contrary to one of the Government's stated targets for the tax system.

As drafted, tax liabilities can arise in circumstances where the employee receives no value at all from the arrangement, either when the taxable 'step' is taken or at any later time. All that is required for the charge to apply is that there is a 'step' that may or may not lead to some form of advantage for the employee later.

If you think you may be affected by this legislation, you need to take professional advice, as errors can be very expensive.

6

SHARE INCENTIVES

PHILIP FISHER

Shares are seen as an especially attractive form of employee compensation. Share incentive schemes are often a way in which an employee can acquire a capital asset and an opportunity to make gains that are based on the increase in value of shares and which can vastly exceed his or her salary.

The lengthy and complex legislation in this area contains many wide-ranging anti-avoidance provisions, which may apply if the share incentive arrangements do not form part of an approved scheme where the tax advantages are still very attractive. Even so, many employers prefer to establish unapproved arrangements because of the extra flexibility in the way schemes can be operated or because either they do not qualify for the selective schemes currently available or the limits are inadequate for the organisation's needs.

This chapter contains the following sections:

(1) Shares acquired at a discount
(2) Non-approved share options
(3) Approved share option schemes
(4) Special shares, etc
(5) Extra-statutory concession A11
(6) The employer's perspective
(7) Some tax planning ideas

6.1 SHARES ACQUIRED AT A DISCOUNT

Shares offered to an employee at below their market value are normally taxable as employment income. The charge is based on the difference between that market value and the amount, if any, that the employee pays to acquire the shares. This applies regardless of who provided the shares, so that they could come by subscription or from an existing shareholder.

If the shares are given to the employee by a shareholder, he or she is normally treated as if he or she had made a disposal of the shares at their market value, and therefore may be liable for CGT. This would not apply where the employee subscribed for new shares.

A company must report the acquisition of shares by an employee as a 'reportable event' on form 42. This return must be submitted to HMRC by 6 July following the end of the tax year.

Tax notes

You should take advice on your CGT position if you are considering making a gift of some of your shares to an employee.

PAYE must be accounted for if either the shares are readily convertible assets (see 20.1) or trading arrangements are in place. There is then a further liability for PAYE if the individual does not reimburse the company within 90 days of the date on which the shares were acquired.

6.2 NON-APPROVED SHARE OPTIONS

6.2.1 Introduction

An income tax charge may arise on the exercise of a share option that was granted by reason of the individual's office or employment.

6.2.2 Non-approved share options

(s 471 ITEPA 2003)

A tax charge may arise on the exercise of the option. The grant of the option is not an event that gives rise to an income tax charge.

Exercise of the option

A person who is subject to tax under s 15 ITEPA 2003 (see 4.1.1) may be subject to an income tax charge when he or she exercises a non-approved share option that has been granted by reason of an office or employment. The charge is not dependent on his or her selling the shares, but arises on any profit or gain that he or she is deemed to have made by exercising the option and thereby acquiring shares at less than their current market value. Normally the profit is simply the difference between the shares' market value at the time the employee exercises his or her option and the price payable under the option, although if he or she paid anything for the option grant, that can be deducted as well.

Example – exercise of share options

A was granted an option to acquire 1,000 shares in XYZ Ltd at a price of £2 per share. After five years have elapsed, he exercises the option and pays £2,000 to acquire the 1,000 shares. By this time the shares have grown in value to £5 per share. *A* will be assessed for the year in which he exercises the option. His profit will be assessed as £3,000, ie:

	£
Market value of 1,000 shares	5,000
Less: amount paid	(2,000)
	3,000

If the employee agrees to pay the employer's NIC on the profit from exercising the option, the employer's NIC is deducted in arriving at the taxable amount.

6.2.3 Employee's residence status

Before 6 April 2008, no charge arose under s 471 unless the employee was resident and ordinarily resident in the UK at the date the option was granted. However, a charge can now arise on the exercise of an option granted on or after 6 April 2008 to an individual who was resident but not ordinarily resident in the UK. It can also arise if an option was granted whilst he or she was not resident in the UK, if the option was granted in contemplation of his or her performing duties after taking up residence in the UK.

The tax treatment of options exercised by an individual who is resident but not ordinarily resident may depend upon whether the option relates to duties performed outside the UK. See further at 34.3.1 on this.

An income tax charge still applies where an individual who was resident and ordinarily resident when the option was granted exercises his or her option after he or she has ceased to be resident in the UK. In some cases, the income tax charge may be reduced because of relief due under a double taxation agreement or on general principles. There is a helpful article on the way HMRC applies these rules to internationally mobile employees in *Tax Bulletin 76,* April 2005.

6.2.4 Other employee share options

(ss 193–197 ITEPA 2003)

In limited circumstances, where no other charging provision applies, if an individual exercises an option that was granted to him or her as an employee at a time when he or she was either not resident in the UK or not ordinarily resident, and retains the shares, an income tax charge may arise on their eventual disposal. The legislation contains deeming provisions that treat the difference between the shares' market value at the time the option is exercised and the amount paid to exercise the option as if it were a loan. On a subsequent sale or disposal of the shares, the loan is deemed to be written off and an income tax charge arises if the individual is UK-resident at that time. If you think you may be in this situation, you should seek professional advice.

6.2.5 Reporting requirements

The grant or exercise of options must be notified on form 42 by 6 July following the end of the tax year.

PAYE must be accounted for on profits from options where the shares are readily convertible assets at the time of exercise. A further charge can arise unless the employee reimburses his or her employer within 90 days (see 21.1.4).

6.2.6 Capital gains tax

See 13.10.3 on the CGT consequences of disposing of shares acquired under an unapproved share option.

6.2.7 Retrospective legislation on options that form part of tax schemes

Section 443(1A) contains legislation that imposes a charge on certain options granted on or after 2 December 2004.

The legislation contains a 'purpose test' – basically, special rules apply where the right or opportunity to acquire a securities option was granted mainly to avoid tax or NIC. Options caught by this rule are taken out of the tax regime described in 6.3.1–6.3.12 and are taxed under legislation that applies to convertible securities (see the last part of 6.4.10), which would not otherwise be applicable to options.

HMRC has published the following example of the tax consequences where an option after 1 December 2004 fails the purpose test.

Example of the charge under s 443

An option to purchase securities is used as part of an avoidance scheme. This brings into play anti-avoidance legislation first enacted in FA (No.2) 2005 that applies where convertible securities are acquired under an avoidance scheme. The application of this legislation means that the individual is taxed on the acquisition of the convertible security and the measure of the tax charge is based on a notional market value which assumes that the entitlement to convert is immediate and unconditional. The effect is to bring into charge the maximum possible gain.

6.3 APPROVED SHARE OPTION SCHEMES

(ss 517–526 ITEPA 2003)

6.3.1 Introduction

The types of approved share option schemes for employees are:

- save as you earn share option scheme (SAYE) – 6.3.2;
- share incentive plan (SIP) – 6.3.4;
- company share option plan (CSOP) – 6.3.10; and
- enterprise management incentives (EMI) – 6.3.13.

6.3.2 Approved SAYE-linked share option scheme

These schemes utilise an option for employees to purchase company shares at a price that must not be 'manifestly less' than 80% of their market value at the time the options are granted. The employee is required to take out an SAYE-linked savings scheme (maximum £250 pm) with a bank or building society and may use the proceeds to exercise the share option three, five or seven years later, depending on the rules of the particular scheme. No income tax liability arises on the grant or exercise of the options. CGT is charged on an eventual disposal of the shares.

6.3.3 Reporting requirements

The grant or exercise of options must be notified on Form 34 by 6 July following the end of the tax year.

> **Tax notes**
>
> SAYE schemes are a 'one way bet'. If the share price goes up, exercise the option. If the share price goes down, take your cash from the SAYE scheme instead.

For more details, see www.hmrc.gov.uk/manuals/ersmmanual/ERSM 302100.htm.

6.3.4 Share incentive plan (SIP)

(ss 488–515 ITEPA 2003)

These plans may involve one or more of the following elements:

- free shares;
- partnership shares;
- matching shares;
- dividend shares.

The principle is that all employees should participate on similar terms. However, if an employer awards free shares, the award may made be partly or wholly by reference to performance targets. Under the plan, trustees acquire shares in the employing or holding company of a group. No income tax or NIC is payable on the award of shares to individual employees. All income and capital growth that arises while the trustees hold shares will normally be tax-free. The shares must be fully paid-up ordinary shares in a company that is not controlled by another company or shares in a quoted subsidiary of a company that is not a close company (see 18.14).

6.3.5 Free shares

An employee may be awarded free shares with a value of up to £3,000 pa. The shares may be awarded partly by reference to objective criteria including salary and length of service. In such a case, the highest performance-linked award must not exceed four times the highest award by reference to non-performance linked criteria. In other cases (eg where all awards are by reference to performance), the employer must demonstrate to HMRC's satisfaction that the performance targets are broadly comparable.

Wherever awards are to be made by reference to performance, the targets and other criteria must be communicated to employees in advance. Performance criteria may be linked to individual, team, divisional or corporate performance.

Free shares must be held by the trustees for a period of between three and five years. Shares can, at the employer's discretion, be awarded so that they will be forfeited if the employee leaves within three years.

Where an employee withdraws from the scheme within three years, income tax and NIC is payable on the shares' market value at the date of withdrawal. Where he or she withdraws between three and five years from an award, the employee is charged on the lower of the shares' initial value or their market value at the time that he or she withdraws.

Where an employment comes to an end because of death, disability or redundancy, the shares may be withdrawn tax free even if this occurs within the three-year period.

6.3.6 Partnership shares

Employees may relinquish up to £1,500 pa of their pay in return for 'partnership' shares. No income tax or NIC arises on salary forgone in this way, but the employing company receives a deduction in arriving at its taxable profits equal to the amount relinquished. The partnership shares cannot be subject to forfeiture, but the scheme rules can require the trustees to repay the sums invested if the employee leaves before acquiring shares.

Where an employee withdraws from the scheme within three years, income tax and NIC is payable on the shares' market value at the date of withdrawal. Where he or she withdraws between three and five years from an award, the employee is charged on the lower of the shares' initial value or their market value at the time that he or she withdraws.

Where an employment comes to an end because of disability or redundancy, the shares may be withdrawn tax free even if this occurs within the three-year period.

6.3.7 Matching shares

If an employer so wishes, matching shares can be awarded to employees on a basis of up to 2:1 (ie matching shares worth up to £3,000 pa can be offered to an employee who relinquished salary of £1,500 in order to 'buy' partnership shares). An award of matching shares may be made on the basis that they are forfeited if the employee leaves within three years or withdraws his or her partnership shares during that period. The tax treatment is similar to that for free shares.

6.3.8 Dividends

The legislation gives employers a choice of whether to offer dividend reinvestment. If dividends are paid out they are taxable income for the employees. However, dividends may be reinvested tax-free up to £1,500 pa.

6.3.9 Reporting requirements

Each year, a form 39 return is required for each approved scheme. The trustees will also receive a Trust SA Return for completion. For more details see www.hmrc.gov.uk/manuals/ersmmanual/ERSM303100.htm.

6.3.10 Company share option plan (CSOP)

The general principle is that if an employer agrees to abide by relatively strict constraints, he or she can offer employees tax-efficient share options worth up to £30,000 per individual.

6.3.11 Conditions for approval

To receive HMRC approval, the following conditions must be satisfied:

(1) Participation in the scheme must be open only to full-time directors or to full or part-time employees. Part-time directors may not participate in this scheme: HMRC has indicated that it regards a director who works 25 hours pw as full-time. The employer may choose which employees are to be permitted to participate in the scheme.
(2) Where the employer is a close company, no participant must (together with associates) own (or be entitled to acquire as a result of the grant of the option) more than 25% of the company's shares. Furthermore, no individual who has owned more than 25% of the company's shares within the previous 12 months can participate.

(3) The price at which the option is to be exercised must not be 'manifestly less' than the shares' value at the time the option is granted.
(4) There is a limit on the value of shares over which a particular employee may be granted options. The scheme must limit the employee's options to shares with a market value at the time the options are granted that does not exceed £30,000.
(5) The shares issued under the scheme must be fully paid ordinary shares of the company or its parent company. They must be shares either quoted on a recognised stock exchange or in a company not under the control of another company.
(6) Options must not be transferable.
(7) The exemption from income tax applies only to options exercised between three and ten years after they are granted or where the option is exercised within three years because of the individual's employment coming to an end by reason of death, retirement, redundancy, injury or disability.

6.3.12 Reporting requirements

The grant or exercise of options must be notified on form 35 by 6 July following the end of the tax year. For more details see www.hmrc.gov.uk/manuals/ersmmanual/ERSM301100.htm.

Tax notes

These approved options mean that you are not subject to an income tax charge unless you exercise the option within the first three years. You will be subject to CGT but only when you sell the shares. If you transfer some of the shares to your spouse or civil partner (and you have no other capital gains in the year), you can each realise tax-free capital gains of £10,600 (in 2011–12).

6.3.13 ENTERPRISE MANAGEMENT INCENTIVES (EMI)
(ss 527–541 ITEPA 2003)

The main aspects of the EMI option scheme are as follows:

(1) Share options, with a value of up to £120,000 per employee, can be issued to employees. This refers to the value of underlying shares at the time the options are granted.
(2) The total value of shares over which options can be granted by a company or group of companies is £3m.

(3) The price at which options may be exercised may be more or less than market value at the time the options are granted.

(4) The only income tax charge is on exercise of the options and is equal to the difference between the shares' market value at the time of grant (or if lower at exercise) less the exercise price. If the options are granted at market value, no tax is payable.

(5) If the shares are readily convertible assets at the time the option is exercised any tax is collected through PAYE and NIC is charged on the same basis as the income tax charge.

(6) Where the conditions for entrepreneurs' relief are satisfied, see 16.8, the effective rate of CGT may be 10%. However, among other conditions, a minimum 5% holding (and 5% of voting power) must have been held for 12 months from the date that the EMI option is exercised.

Only certain companies can operate the arrangement, and certain employees may be ineligible. A summary of the rules is as follows:

(a) the company must be independent and not under the control of another company;

(b) the company or, where relevant, a group member must be carrying on a qualifying trade defined as for EIS purposes (see 19.3.4) – this trade must be carried on through a permanent establishment in the UK;

(c) its gross assets cannot exceed £30m at the time the options are granted. The £30m test is applied on a consolidated basis where the company is the parent of a group of companies. There is a relieving provision that prevents a company from failing the £30m test simply by reason of its transferring an intangible asset within the group;

(d) the company or group must have fewer than 250 employees;

(e) the employee must be employed for at least 25 hours pw or, if less, 75% of his or her working time;

(f) the option ceases to qualify once the employee no longer meets the 25 hours pw 75% requirement;

(g) the employee must not own or control more than 30% of the shares in the company.

The grant of an EMI option must be notified to HMRC within 92 days.

Where an individual exercises an EMI option, the shares may be restricted shares (see 6.4.2 below). He or she is regarded as automatically making the election described at 6.4.7 if there is no income tax charge under (4) above (as this will always be to his or her advantage).

Where a company is taken over by another company which itself is able to establish an EMI scheme, an individual can surrender his or her options for replacement options in an EMI scheme operated by the new parent company. The value of the shares over which the new options are granted must not exceed the value at the time of the takeover of the shares to which the original options related.

6.3.14 Reporting requirements

The grant of EMI share options must be notified to HMRC no more than 92 days from the date of grant. Adjustments or exercises of options should be notified on form EMI 40 by 6 July following the end of the tax year. For more details see www.hmrc.gov.uk/manuals/ersmmanual/ERSM304100.htm.

Tax notes

EMI options are the most favourable type of options because they are flexible in that there is no minimum holding period and the share valuation can be agreed with HMRC before the options are granted. Where the conditions for entrepreneurs' relief are satisfied, the rate of CGT may be 10%.

6.4 SPECIAL SHARES, ETC

(ss 417–440 ITEPA 2003)

6.4.1 Background

The legislation on employee shares (also called 'employment-related securities') was substantially amended by Schedule 22, FA 2003, which focused on special shares such as restricted shares and convertible shares. It also dealt with situations where employee shareholders are treated in an especially favourable way.

In the main, the amended rules apply only to securities acquired on or after 16 April 2003 (but note the exception to this for conversion of employment-related securities – see 6.4.10 below).

Sections 6.4.2–6.4.7 below will not apply to events that occur more than seven years after the individual has ceased to be an employee of the company awarding the shares.

Further information is available on HMRC's website (www.hmrc.gov.uk/shareschemes).

6.4.2 **Restricted securities**

Until 5 April 2008, the charge on restricted securities applied only if the securities were acquired at a time when the employee was resident and ordinarily resident in the UK. It now also applies to restricted securities acquired by employees who are resident but not ordinarily resident in the UK where the securities are awarded on or after 6 April 2008. We cover the treatment of internationally mobile employees at 34.3 and 34.6.1. See also 6.5 on ESC A11 which may apply to income arising in the year in which an individual becomes resident in the UK or in which he or she ceases to be resident.

Sometimes shares or other securities subject to special restrictions, eg in relation to voting rights or freedom to sell are given (ie 'awarded') to employees. The shares may become much more valuable once the restrictions cease to apply. Similarly, shares may be awarded on the basis that they will be forfeited if a target is not met or if the employee leaves within a certain period. In such a situation, the employee only acquires full ownership of the shares when the forfeiture provisions fall away. Forfeiture provisions are really just a special type of restriction on the individual's ownership of his or her shares.

6.4.3 **Meaning of 'restrictions'**

Restrictions include the following:

- restrictions on dividend rights;
- restrictions on voting rights;
- restrictions on transferability.

The legislation provides that shares are not to be treated as restricted if the only restrictions are that:

- partly-paid shares will be forfeited if outstanding calls are not paid;
- the shares have to be sold if the employee is dismissed for misconduct;
- the shares are redeemable for payment.

For further details, see Figure 6.1.

Figure 6.1 – Does removal of restrictions mean there is an income tax charge?

6.4.4 Charge depends on whether the restrictions can apply for more than five years

Schedule 22 made a significant distinction on restrictions that might last for more than five years.

6.4.5 Restrictions capable of lasting more than five years

If the shares or securities are subject to longer-term restrictions, an income tax charge will arise on the award of the shares and a further charge on the restrictions ceasing to apply. This is not a double charge; the amount taxed on the award of the shares is the market value of those shares, taking into account the effect of the restrictions, less anything paid by the employee for the shares. When these restrictions are lifted, the amount taxed is based on the increase in value as a result of lifting the restriction.

Example

> *T* was given shares on 1 June 2007 that had an open market value of £1,000. However, *T* will forfeit them if he leaves his employer before 1 July 2013. The effect of this restriction is to depress the value on acquisition to £650 (ie a 35% discount). When the forfeiture provisions cease to apply on 1 July 2013, the shares are worth £5,000.
>
> A tax charge arose for 2007–08 on £650 and will arise for 2013–14 on £1,750, ie 35% of £5,000.

6.4.6 Restrictions not capable of lasting more than five years

Where the restrictions involve forfeiture provisions that can apply only for a period of five years or less, there will normally be no income tax charge on the shares or securities being awarded. The charge will normally be triggered by the release of the restrictions or the forfeiture provisions coming to an end and will be based on the market value at that time. Thus, if in the previous example the restrictions had been due to expire within five years, *T* would not have been taxed on £650 for 2007–08 but he would have been taxed on £5,000 for the year in which the restrictions ceased to be operative.

6.4.7 Election to accept the tax charge upfront

(ss 430–431 ITEPA 2003)

There is an election that is available. The employee can choose to accept a tax charge at acquisition on the full value, ignoring the effect of the restrictions. If he or she adopts this course of action, there will be no further income tax charge on the restrictions being lifted, the employee will have 'taken his or her medicine' upfront.

This election is available regardless of whether the restrictions are capable of remaining in force for more than five years. It must be made within 14 days of the shares being acquired.

Tax notes

Take advice on the value of shares at the time you receive them because it may be better to accept a modest upfront tax charge or even no charge to avoid having to pay tax when the forfeiture provisions expire.

6.4.8 Charge where value is extracted

(s 446A ITEPA 2003)

If value is extracted by artificial means, this will generally give rise to a chargeable event, with income tax and NIC becoming due on the value derived.

6.4.9 Special rules where restrictions are part of a tax-avoidance scheme

FA 2004 varied Schedule 22. There is an exception to the general rule that no employment income tax charge arises on the acquisition of shares which are subject to forfeiture for up to five years (see 6.4.6 above). The legislation imposes a charge where the market value of the shares at the date that the restrictions are lifted has been artificially decreased by things done other than for genuine commercial purposes.

The legislation is drafted in wide terms and can apply where transactions are part of a scheme or arrangement designed to avoid tax or NIC. A charge can also arise where the market value of shares is artificially increased as part of such a scheme or arrangement.

6.4.10 Convertible securities

(s 439 ITEPA 2003)

An income tax charge can arise on the value of any new shares received when a share conversion takes place and the original shares were employment-related securities. It can also arise on an employee selling convertible securities to a third-party or on his or her receiving a payment for relinquishing the conversion rights. The amount charged takes account of any amount already charged on the acquisition of the original shares.

This charge is intended to catch arrangements where an employee receives shares with a low value that are later converted to shares with a much higher value. The charge does not normally arise where the event is triggered by the employee being disabled.

Section 439 can apply where employment-related securities were held before the 2003 Budget and are converted after 1 September 2003. There is some concern that s 439 could also apply to a gain realised by a former owner of a company on the completion of an earn-out satisfied by the issue of loan notes or other securities. This is likely to be a problem where the individual is required to remain with the company after selling out and he or she is receiving more than other vendors or where the earn-out is closely linked with his or her personal performance.

FA (No.2) 2005 introduced special rules where convertible securities are acquired as part of a tax avoidance scheme. Income tax may be charged on a notional market value of the option at acquisition, with this value being arrived at on the assumption that the right to convert is immediate and unconditional. The effect is to bring into charge the maximum possible gain.

6.4.11 Additional rights

(s 446K ITEPA 2003)

An income tax charge can arise where the value of employment-related securities is enhanced by means of non-commercial transactions. Once again, this charge can apply even where the individual was not resident and ordinarily resident at the time that he or she acquired the securities in question.

For the charge to apply, the market value of the employment-related securities must be increased by at least 10% by transactions carried out other than for genuine commercial purposes. The taxable amount is the increase in value and this is charged as employment-related income for the year in which the transactions take place.

6.4.12 Sale of shares by an employee at an overvalue

(s 446Y ITEPA 2003)

An income tax charge arises where an employer or connected person purchases employment-related securities from an employee for more than market value. The amount taxed as income is the over-value. Again this is not limited to situations where the employee was resident and ordinarily resident at the time that he or she acquired the securities in question.

6.4.13 Employee can elect to pay employer's NIC

Sections 428A and 442A provide tax relief if an employee bears his or her employer's NIC on a charge relating to restricted or convertible shares. This works in a similar way to the relief where an employer pays the NIC on exercising a non-approved option over readily convertible assets (see 6.2.2).

6.4.14 Partly-paid shares or shares acquired by borrowing from the employer

(s 446Q–U ITEPA 2003)

Where an employee acquires partly-paid shares, he or she is treated as if he or she had received a notional loan. An annual charge may arise on the interest that would have been payable if the 'loan' had carried interest at the official rate (see 4.7).

Where the employer lifts the obligation to pay up the outstanding amount, the employee is deemed to have received employment income for that year (s 446U). Furthermore, a sale of the shares will also normally be treated as a discharge of the obligation so that once again a tax charge arises on the amount of the notional loan.

These provisions could also apply where there is an actual loan, eg a loan from a major shareholder.

Section 446U can apply even though the individual was neither resident nor ordinarily resident at the time that he or she acquired the partly-paid shares if he or she subsequently carried on his or her employment whilst resident in the UK.

Tax notes

In many cases, it may be better for you to make shares fully paid before you sell them to avoid a tax charge under s 446U. This is a situation where you should take professional advice.

6.5 EXTRA-STATUTORY CONCESSION A11

The residence status of an individual is decided for a complete tax year. There is no provision in the statutory rules for splitting a tax year into different residence categories. However, by concession, when an individual's tax liability is affected by residence the tax year may be split. Liability to UK tax which is affected by residence is computed by reference only to that part of the year when the employee is resident.

HMRC, EIM42850

HMRC has clarified the application of ESC A11 (split year treatment) to charges under the employment-related securities legislation. This issue has become more significant since radical reforms to the remittance basis were introduced by FA 2008 (see 34.3).

- **Year of arrival in the UK**: HMRC's view has always been that the ESC did not apply to taxable income arising during the year of arrival but before the individual came to the UK under the legislation on employment-related securities. However, it has emerged that many employers, taxpayers and advisers were not aware of this. HMRC has therefore stated that it will allow the ESC to cover income from employment-related securities other than where there is a notional loan charge in respect of shares acquired at an undervalue (see 6.1). This will apply both in relation to past years where a taxpayer's liability has not been finalised, and going forwards (until further notice).

- **Year of departure from the UK**: Previous HMRC guidance had made it clear that ESC A11 did not apply during the year of departure but after the individual left the UK where a charge arose on the notional loan treatment of shares acquired at an undervalue (see 6.1). However, HMRC has reluctantly accepted that it had not made clear that the concession did not cover other tax charges under the employment-related securities legislation. It has therefore confirmed that ESC A11 may apply in the year of departure to prevent a tax liability arising under these other provisions of the employment-related securities legislation.

In both cases, HMRC reserves the right to withhold the ESC where tax avoidance is involved. Also, it will not be possible to re-open past years that have already been agreed.

All extra-statutory concessions are currently under review. It is intended that in the fullness of time ESC A11 will be put on a statutory basis.

Tax notes

Extra-statutory concession A11 may mean that you do not have to pay tax on certain income from employment-related securities which arises either in the year of arrival or in the year of departure.

6.6 THE EMPLOYER'S PERSPECTIVE

An employer will often not wish to be tied into the 'democratic' aspects of some of the approved schemes, ie the principle that all employees must be allowed to participate on a similar basis (see 6.3.1–6.3.9). The managing director will often want to reserve the incentive for 'key employees' whose input to the business is likely to make a significant difference to its profitability. Enterprise Management Incentives (6.3.13) are one type of approved scheme that is aimed primarily at such people but there are limits, both to the equity available and the types of companies that can operate an EMI (eg a company that is a subsidiary of another company cannot do so). Other approved schemes contain a much lower ceiling for the value of shares that can be provided without a tax charge (see 6.3.11 on the £30,000 limit for CSOPs).

Employers will also be concerned that additional costs such as employer's NIC are kept to a minimum. If the company is going to receive a corporation tax deduction for the costs of establishing and operating a share scheme, this will reduce the net cost for the employer. See 18.3.2 on the circumstances in which the company may qualify for such relief.

6.7 SOME TAX PLANNING IDEAS

6.7.1 Subscription for shares

In some cases, it may be possible to keep things simple. Instead of having
an option, the company pays a cash bonus and the amount that is left after
PAYE and NIC is used by the individual to subscribe for new shares. This
would make a lot of sense where a company has been set up relatively
recently and the shares do not have a great deal of value (even though they
are seen as capable of becoming very valuable if the business takes off).

Example

> A company pays a bonus of £20,833 to a key employee. After 50% income tax
> and 2% NIC, he or she is left with £10,000 and uses this to subscribe for shares.
>
> There will generally be some timing differences but overall the company's
> position could work out as follows:
>
> | | £ |
> |---|---|
> | Bonus | 20,833 |
> | Employer's NIC | 2,875 |
> | | 23,708 |
> | Cash returned to company as subscription for shares | 10,000 |
> | Net cost to company | 13,708 |
> | Corporation tax relief | 4,742* |
> | Effective net cost | 8,966 |
>
> * received nine months after company's year end
>
> This example assumes corporation tax relief at 20%, ie the small companies'
> rate.
>
> However, if we were to assume that the company enjoys relief at the
> mainstream corporation tax rate (26% for 2011–12), and the employee is a
> basic rate taxpayer, paying 12% NIC, the figures could be:
>
> | | |
> |---|---|
> | Bonus | 20,833 |
> | Employer's NI | 2,875 |
> | | 23,708 |
> | Cash returned to company as subscription for shares | 10,000 |
> | Net cost to company | 13,708 |
> | Corporation tax relief | 6,164 |
> | Effective net cost | 7,544 |

6.7.2 Make the election within 14 days

When this method is adopted, it will often be the case that the employee's shares are subject to restrictions and it will therefore be important that the individual and company make an election under s 431 ITEPA 2003 (see 6.4.7) so as to ensure that any future growth in value is subject only to CGT. This election has to be made within 14 days of the shares being issued to the employee.

6.7.3 Use approved schemes where possible

In cases where the shares have significant value, it is advisable to use approved schemes provided these fit in with the commercial objectives. For example, it may be that the controlling shareholders of a long-established company believe that a key manager will be tied into staying with the company in the medium term by being given 5% of the equity. Simply giving him or her the shares would give rise to an immediate income tax charge. Giving him or her an option may therefore be a better idea, especially if the option can be granted under an EMI scheme (see 6.3.13). Such options can be granted over shares worth up to £120,000. Subject to the various conditions being satisfied, the individual need then have no income tax liability on acquiring his or her shares. In due course it may be appropriate for the employee to be given a cash bonus to give him or her sufficient cash to exercise his or her option. Where this happens, the overall effect is exactly the same as if the manager had been given the shares except that he or she will suffer no tax beyond the PAYE on his or her cash bonus.

CSOP and EMI options can be granted selectively, ie the legislation does not require similar options to be offered to other employees.

The company will qualify for a corporation tax deduction for the difference between the amount payable on exercising the option and the market value of the shares at the date of exercise (see 18.3.2).

6.7.4 Consider making loans or issuing partly-paid shares

Suppose that the employing company's shares are not eligible for approved share options or EMI schemes (eg the company may be a subsidiary of another company).

One possible way of designing a tax-efficient share scheme would be for a loan to be made to the employee (possibly from a parent company or another group company as this will be excluded from the 'disguised remuneration' charge under Part 7A ITEPA – see Chapter 5 – unless there is a tax avoidance motive) and for the employee to use this to buy shares, whether by subscribing for new shares or in purchasing existing shares. In such cases, employees must always be given the opportunity to understand that they will be liable to repay the loan at some future time, even if the shares are by then worthless.

No income tax charge will normally arise at the outset provided the shares are not acquired at an undervalue. Once again, an election under s 431 may well be appropriate so that any profit on an eventual sale should be subject only to CGT (see 6.4.7).

No income tax charge will normally be payable on the loan provided interest is charged at a rate no lower than the official rate (see 4.7) or the company is a close company and the employee meets either of the tests set out in 11.5 (ie the employee has a material interest or is engaged full-time in the management of the company's business).

The employee may be better off subscribing for new shares if this will mean that he or she can secure income tax relief under s 131 ITA 2007 in the event of suffering a capital loss (see 17.2).

On a disposal of the shares, an income tax charge may arise on the amount of the loan unless the loan is repaid beforehand (see 6.4.14 on this)

6.7.5 Other possibilities

Recently, unquoted companies have explored the advantages of creating a separate class of growth shares. The idea is that these will have no intrinsic value unless the company is successful after their acquisition. Therefore they cannot give rise to an income tax charge on acquisition. If the company grows in value, any gain on these shares will be subject to income tax.

Listed companies have begun to use Joint Share Ownership Plans. These are complex structures that require shares to be jointly acquired by an employee benefit trust and an employee, with the employee's interest having little or no value at acquisition. If set up effectively, they have a similar tax treatment to growth shares.

In both cases, it is advisable to seek professional guidance before entering into such arrangements as they can easily go wrong.

7

SELF-EMPLOYMENT

GORDON HOPKINS

If you are self-employed in business on your own, or in a partnership, you will be taxed under s 5 ITTOIA 2005.

In practice, the rules for determining taxable profits of trades and professions are almost the same and therefore all references in this chapter to a person carrying on a trade apply equally to a person who is engaged in a profession.

This chapter contains the following sections:

(1) How self-employed individuals pay tax
(2) Are you really self-employed?
(3) Basis of assessment
(4) Partnerships
(5) Limited liability partnerships (LLPs)
(6) Partnerships controlled outside the UK
(7) Relief for trading losses

We cover the detailed rules governing the computation of profits for tax purposes in Chapter 16. This chapter focuses on the way in which a self-employed individual should deal with his or her tax affairs once the amount of the taxable profit or loss has been ascertained, usually by an accountant.

7.1 HOW SELF-EMPLOYED INDIVIDUALS PAY TAX

7.1.1 Payment of tax

Unlike employees who suffer deduction of tax from their earnings under PAYE, self-employed individuals pay tax directly to HMRC. Tax payable by them for 2011–12 needs to be paid in two instalments, on 31 January 2012 and 31 July 2012. The amount payable for each instalment is normally half the income tax liability for 2010–11. Any balance of tax for 2011–12 is then payable on 31 January 2013.

If you are in the construction industry scheme (CIS) and are not registered to receive gross payments, the contractor will deduct an amount (currently 20%) before he or she pays you and he or she is then responsible for paying this over to HMRC. You will still need to pay tax and NIC on your income through your tax return (as explained above), but HMRC will set any deductions that have already been made from your income against this bill.

If you started self-employment fairly recently, and previously over 80% of your tax was collected under PAYE, you may find that you do not have to make instalment payments for 2011–12. However, the system will catch up with you on 31 January 2013 as you will then have to settle the whole of your 2011–12 tax and make the first payment on account for 2012–13.

Tax notes

Bear in mind that self-employed individuals have to pay instalments on account of their tax liability for the year, the first instalment falling due on 31 January within the tax year.

7.1.2 Completing your tax return

You will need to complete a special schedule as part of your SA tax return; this asks for details of the type of business you are carrying on. If your sales for the year ending in 2011–12 do not exceed £73,000, you can complete an abbreviated self-employment schedule (SA103S). You have the option of completing the tax return on the basis of four entries: sales, expenses, capital allowances and profit. Alternatively, a more detailed breakdown of expenses can be provided on the full length form, SA103F.

7.1.3 Ascertaining taxable profits based on accounts

There is no obligation to prepare accounts, although it may well be advisable to do so for other reasons. If accounts have been prepared it is advisable to send them with the SA return (or attach them as a .PDF file for online filing), whether or not HMRC wants them, as this limits the scope for HMRC to reopen back years by making 'discovery assessments'.

Very often, accounts are drawn up for other reasons as well (eg for production to banks and other lenders) and it is important to bear in mind that there may need to be adjustments for tax purposes. There are also specific rules that govern the amount of capital allowances that a trader may claim – in broad terms, capital allowances are an adjustment for depreciation or wear and tear on equipment, etc used in the business.

7.1.4 Self-assessment tax return

The full tax return for a self-employed individual with a turnover of more than £73,000 contains a schedule, which consists of boxes designed to adjust accounts figures for tax purposes.

Example – Profit and loss account

Z's profit and loss account for the year ended 31 December 2010 shows the following:

	£	£
Income		97,500
Expenses		
Wages	27,500	
Rent	6,000	
Insurance	1,650	
Utilities	1,060	
Repairs	2,100	
Telephone	980	
Accountancy	500	
VAT surcharge	400	
Depreciation	1,400	
Entertaining	1,200	
Miscellaneous	250	
		(43,040)
Net profit		54,460

Notes:

(1) Goods taken out for personal use: £600 without payment (at selling price).
(2) Telephone costs not relating to business: £200.
(3) Non-staff entertaining: £565.
(4) Capital allowances of £1,900.

The way the information has to be entered on the HMRC form is shown on pages 188–191. The computation of profits is dealt with in greater detail in Chapter 16 along with capital allowances because the principles that apply to a self-employed individual also apply to partnerships and companies.

The return also directs you to submit a balance sheet if your business accounts include one.

Self-employment (full)

Tax year 6 April 2010 to 5 April 2011

Read page SEFN 1 of the *notes* to check if you should use this page or the *Self-employment (short)* page.

Your name	Your Unique Taxpayer Reference (UTR)

Business details

1 Business name - *unless it is in your own name*

2 Description of business

3 First line of your business address - *unless you work from home*

4 Postcode of your business address

5 If the details in boxes 1, 2, 3 or 4 have changed in the last 12 months, put 'X' in the box and give details in the 'Any other information' box

6 If your business started after 5 April 2010, enter the start date *DD MM YYYY*

7 If your business ceased after 5 April 2010 but before 6 April 2011, enter the final date of trading

8 Date your books or accounts start - *the beginning of your accounting period*

9 Date your books or accounts are made up to or the end of your accounting period - *read page SEFN 3 of the notes if you have filled in box 6 or 7*

Other information

10 If your accounting date has changed permanently, put 'X' in the box

11 If your accounting date has changed more than once since 2005, put 'X' in the box

12 If special arrangements apply, put 'X' in the box - *read page SEFN 4 of the notes*

13 If you provided the information about your 2010-11 profit on last year's tax return, put 'X' in the box - *read page SEFN 4 of the notes*

Business income

14 Your turnover - *the takings, fees, sales or money earned by your business*

£ 97500 · 00

15 Any other business income not included in box 14 - *excluding Business Start-up Allowance*

£ · 0 0

Business expenses

Read pages SEFN 7 to SEFN 9 of the *notes* before completing this section.

Total expenses If your annual turnover was below £70,000 you may just put your total expenses in box 30		**Disallowable expenses** Use this column if the figures in boxes 16 to 29 include disallowable amounts	
16 Cost of goods bought for resale or goods used	£ · 0 0	**31**	£ · 0 0
17 Construction industry – *payments to subcontractors*	£ · 0 0	**32**	£ · 0 0
18 Wages, salaries and other staff costs	£ 2 7 5 0 0 · 0 0	**33**	£ · 0 0
19 Car, van and travel expenses	£ · 0 0	**34**	£ · 0 0
20 Rent, rates, power and insurance costs	£ 8 7 1 0 · 0 0	**35**	£ · 0 0
21 Repairs and renewals of property and equipment	£ · 0 0	**36**	£ · 0 0
22 Phone, fax, stationery and other office costs	£ 9 8 0 · 0 0	**37**	£ 2 0 0 · 0 0
23 Advertising and business entertainment costs	£ · 0 0	**38**	£ 5 6 5 · 0 0
24 Interest on bank and other loans	£ · 0 0	**39**	£ · 0 0
25 Bank, credit card and other financial charges	£ · 0 0	**40**	£ · 0 0
26 Irrecoverable debts written off	£ · 0 0	**41**	£ · 0 0
27 Accountancy, legal and other professional fees	£ 5 0 0 · 0 0	**42**	£ · 0 0
28 Depreciation and loss/profit on sale of assets	£ 1 4 0 0 · 0 0	**43**	£ 1 4 0 0 · 0 0
29 Other business expenses	£ 6 5 0 · 0 0	**44**	£ 4 0 0 · 0 0
30 Total expenses in boxes 16 to 29	£ 4 3 0 4 0 · 0 0	**45** Total disallowable expenses in boxes 31 to 44	£ 2 9 6 5 · 0 0

Net profit or loss

46 Net profit - *if your business income is more than your expenses (if box 14 + box 15 minus box 30 is positive)* £ 5 4 4 6 0 · 0 0	**47** Or, net loss - *if your expenses are more than your business income (if box 30 minus (box 14 + box 15) is positive)* £ · 0 0

Tax allowances for vehicles and equipment (capital allowances)

There are 'capital' tax allowances for vehicles, equipment and certain buildings used in your business (you should not have included the cost of these in your business expenses). Read pages SEFN 10 to SEFN 15 of the *notes* and use the examples to work out your capital allowances.

48 Annual Investment Allowance £ · 0 0	**54** 100% and other enhanced capital allowances - *read page SEFN 13 of the notes* £ · 0 0
49 Capital allowances at 20% on equipment, including cars with lower CO_2 emissions £ 1 9 0 0 · 0 0	**55** Allowances on sale or cessation of business use (where you have disposed of assets for less than their tax value) £ · 0 0
50 Capital allowances at 10% on equipment, including cars with higher CO_2 emissions £ · 0 0	**56** Total allowances (total of boxes 48 to 55) £ 1 9 0 0 · 0 0
51 Restricted capital allowances for cars costing more than £12,000 - *if bought before 6 April 2009* £ · 0 0	**57** Balancing charge on sale or cessation of business use (only where Business Premises Renovation Allowance has been claimed) £ · 0 0
52 Agricultural or Industrial Buildings Allowance £ · 0 0	**58** Balancing charge on sales of other assets or on the cessation of business use (where you have disposed of assets for more than their tax value) £ · 0 0
53 Business Premises Renovation Allowance (Assisted Areas only) - *read page SEFN 13 of the notes* £ · 0 0	

Calculating your taxable profit or loss

You may have to adjust your net profit or loss for disallowable expenses or capital allowances to arrive at your taxable profit or your loss for tax purposes. Read pages SEFN 15 and SEFN 16 of the *notes* and fill in the boxes below that apply.

59 Goods and services for your own use - *read page SEFN 15 of the notes* £ 6 0 0 · 0 0	**62** Total deductions from net profit or additions to net loss (box 56 + box 61) £ 1 9 0 0 · 0 0
60 Total additions to net profit or deductions from net loss (box 45 + box 57 + box 58 + box 59) £ 3 1 6 5 · 0 0	**63** Net business profit for tax purposes (if box 46 + box 60 minus (box 47 + box 62) is positive) £ 5 5 7 2 5 · 0 0
61 Income, receipts and other profits included in business income or expenses but not taxable as business profits £ · 0 0	**64** Net business loss for tax purposes (if box 47 + box 62 minus (box 46 + box 60) is positive) £ · 0 0

Calculating your taxable profit or loss (continued)

If you start or finish self-employment and your accounting period is not the same as your basis period (or there are overlaps or gaps in your basis periods), or in certain situations or trades or professions, you may need to make further tax adjustments – *read pages SEFN 16 to SEFN 19 of the notes*. In all cases, please complete boxes 72 and 75, or box 76, as applicable.

65 Date your basis period began *DD MM YYYY*

`0 1` `0 1` `2 0 1 0`

66 Date your basis period ended

`3 1` `1 2` `2 0 1 1`

67 If your basis period is not the same as your accounting period, enter the adjustment needed to arrive at the profit or loss for the basis period – *if the adjustment needs to be taken off the profit figure, put a minus sign (-) in the box*

£ `▬` · `0 0`

68 Overlap relief used this year – *read page SEFN 17 of the notes*

£ · `0 0`

69 Overlap profit carried forward

£ · `0 0`

70 Adjustment for change of accounting practice – *read page SEFN 17 of the notes*

£ · `0 0`

71 Averaging adjustment (only for farmers, market gardeners and creators of literary or artistic works) – *if the adjustment needs to be taken off the profit figure, put a minus sign (-) in the box*

£ `▬` · `0 0`

72 Adjusted profit for 2010-11 (see Working Sheet on page SEFN 18) – *if a loss, enter it in box 76*

£ `5 5 7 2 5` · `0 0`

73 Loss brought forward from earlier years set off against this year's profits – *up to the amount in box 63 or box 72, whichever is greater*

£ · `0 0`

74 Any other business income not included in boxes 14, 15 or 59 – *for example, Business Start-up Allowance*

£ · `0 0`

75 Total taxable profits from this business (box 72 minus box 73 + box 74 – *or use the Working Sheet on page SEFN 18*)

£ `5 5 7 2 5` · `0 0`

Losses

If you have made a net loss for tax purposes (in box 64), or if you have losses from previous years, read page SEFN 19 of the *notes* and fill in boxes 76 to 79, as appropriate.

76 Adjusted loss for 2010-11 (see Working Sheet on page SEFN 18)

£ · `0 0`

77 Loss from this tax year set off against other income for 2010-11

£ · `0 0`

78 Loss to be carried back to previous year(s) and set off against income (or capital gains)

£ · `0 0`

79 Total loss to carry forward after all other set-offs – *including unused losses brought forward*

£ · `0 0`

CIS deductions and tax taken off

80 Deductions on payment and deduction statements from contractors – *construction industry subcontractors only*

£ · `0 0`

81 Other tax taken off trading income

£ · `0 0`

7.2 ARE YOU REALLY SELF-EMPLOYED?

7.2.1 Introduction

It is not possible to elect to be self-employed; whether you are self-employed is a matter of fact. However, since the Taxes Acts do not define 'self-employment', the rules have evolved through decisions handed down by the courts.

The real distinction between being self-employed and an employee is that there is no 'master-servant' relationship. Yet in practice it is often difficult to discern the dividing line and HMRC may take a different view from the parties concerned. For example, freelance workers may not necessarily be recognised as being self-employed and salaried partners may be classified as employees. At one time, the position could be complicated further in that the Contributions Agency was responsible for assessing liability for NIC and occasionally reached a different conclusion from HMRC. Such grey areas have sometimes resulted in companies treating freelance workers as if they are employees and deducting tax and NIC under PAYE accordingly. This is essentially to protect the employer, as it is HMRC's practice to seek unpaid tax from them in cases where the company has not operated PAYE correctly. As a result, it is very difficult, for example, for workers in the computer industry to secure payment as being self-employed. Similar problems are often experienced by workers in the TV industry, journalists, actors and artistes, and many other industries where freelance workers are required to work 'on-site'.

HMRC has addressed this issue by the introduction of legislation (in April 2000) known colloquially as IR35. These rules are covered in more detail at 21.3 as they deal primarily with individuals who offer their services through a service company. During the consultation period leading up to the introduction of this legislation, HMRC consolidated its statements on the dividing line between being employed and self-employed: see *Tax Bulletin* 48, available at www.hmrc.gov.uk/bulletins/tb48.htm#f, and www.hmrc.gov.uk/ir35/index.htm.

The Government recently asked the OTS to review IR35 to see if it could be replaced or improved upon. However, it looks as though we are going to be stuck with it for some time to come, as the Government's conclusion following the review was that it could ill afford to give up on this source of revenue. It is however considering whether the administration of the charge can be simplified.

7.2.2 HMRC's criteria

Guidelines issued by HMRC to clarify employment status (leaflet ES/FS1, www.hmrc.gov.uk/leaflets/es-fs1.pdf) include the following points:

(1) An employee generally does the work in person (and does not hire someone else to do it), working at times and places and in the way specified by the firm for whom the work is done and normally paid at hourly, weekly or monthly rates, possibly including overtime.

(2) A self-employed person may hire and pay others to do the work, or do it personally, in either case specifying the time and the way it is done, providing major items of equipment, being responsible for losses as well as profits and correcting unsatisfactory work in his or her own time and at his or her own expense.

These criteria are only for guidance and in some cases the courts have held that a person who did not fulfil the requirements in (2) above was nevertheless self-employed. Thus, a journalist who worked as a freelance sub-editor at various national newspapers was held by the Special Commissioners to be self-employed even though she carried out all her work at the newspapers' offices. Similarly, a test case sponsored by Equity resulted in the Special Commissioners finding that actors engaged in London West End theatre work were not employees.

First-tier Tribunal (previously Commissioners') decisions, unlike court decisions, do not set binding legal precedents. It was therefore even more important that the Court of Appeal held in *Hall* v *Lorimer* [1994] STC 23 that a TV vision mixer was self-employed even though he failed to satisfy virtually all of the above tests. The taxpayer used extremely expensive equipment provided by the TV companies concerned and his work was controlled rigorously.

However, the First-tier Tribunal, in *ITV Services Ltd* v *HMRC* [2010] UKFTT 586 (TC), has recently re-evaluated the position of entertainers and decided that there is a liability for Class 1 NIC for all actors on existing Equity contracts (even where the production is dependent on them for box-office success). HMRC was obliged to apply the law immediately to all Equity contracts that were either newly entered into, revised, renewed or extended from 2 March 2011 and from 6 April 2011 in respect of all current Equity contracts that continued beyond the end of the 2010–11 tax year, which were of a type that had been previously accepted by HMRC as falling outside of the regulations. It is unclear whether this represents the start of a general trend towards finding that employed – rather than self-employed –status applies.

The decision in *Castle Construction (Chesterfield)* v *HMRC*, SpC 723 shows how difficult it is for HMRC to show that freelance workers are employees rather than self-employed. See also *HMRC* v *Larkstar Data Ltd*.

The Government is pushing ahead with its plans to tax 'false self-employment in the construction industry' by deeming that sub-contractors who do not meet set criteria are to be treated as 'deemed employees' and taxed accordingly. Legislation is expected in FA2012.

> **Tax notes**
>
> Take professional advice if you are a borderline case rather than simply accepting a 'ruling' from HMRC. The rules can work in an unexpected way; for example FA 2000 contains provisions that can treat certain partnership income as if it were employment income subject to PAYE.

7.3 BASIS OF ASSESSMENT

7.3.1 The way in which residence status affects liability

(s 5 ITTOIA 2005)

A person is taxed on the profits of a trade carried on by him or her if he or she is resident in the UK regardless of where that trade is carried on. If he or she is not resident in the UK, he or she is taxed on the profits of the trade if it is carried on in the UK. If part of a trade is carried on in the UK, a non-resident person is taxed on the profits of that part of the trade.

7.3.2 Basis of assessment

The same rules apply for both trades and professions. A self-employed person may draw up accounts to any date he or she chooses; there is no requirement that accounts be made up to 5 April to fit in with the fiscal year (albeit HMRC may encourage him or her to do so). All self-employed individuals are now taxed on the 'current year' (CY) basis.

7.3.3 Current year basis

A business's assessable profits are dealt with on the CY basis. The basic principles of the current year basis are to tax 12 months' profits in each tax year of the business other than the first and last years; and over the life of a business, for profits taxed to equal profits actually earned. The CY basis of assessment is determined by the profits for the accounting year that ends in the year of assessment. Thus a business with a 31 May year end will be assessed for 2011–12 on its profits for the year ended 31 May 2011. Taxable profits for these purposes are those after deducting capital allowances (see 16.2).

Special rules govern the first tax year since there are normally no accounts that end in that tax year (see below).

Opening years

Special rules apply for the opening years:

Tax year	Taxable profits
Year one	the profits from the date of commencement to 5 April following
Year two	the profits in the 12-month accounting period ending in year two (if the period is more than 12 months long, only 12 months worth of profit is included), *or*
	if the period to the accounting date in year two is less than 12 months from commencement, the profits of the first 12 months (apportioned from two sets of accounts), *or*
	if there is no accounting date in year two, the profits of the 12 months to 5 April.
Year three onwards	the profits of the 12 month accounting period ending in the tax year, *or*
	12 months to 5 April if accounts not drawn up to a date in year three and there has been no change of accounting date.

Example – Opening years rules under the CY basis

A started in business on 6 October 2011. Accounts for the year to 5 October 2012 showed profits of £48,000. Profits for the year ending 5 October 2013 are £72,000. A will be assessed as follows:

	£
2011–12 'actual' basis	
$(^6/_{12} \times £48,000)$	24,000
2012–13 first 12 months' profits	48,000
2013–14 CY basis	72,000

Example – Position where first accounts not drawn up for 12-month period

---

The precise way in which the opening year rules work is slightly more complicated when there are no accounts for a period of 12 months ending in the second tax year. This is covered by the following examples:

(1) *B* started in business on 1 January 2011. The first set of accounts was made up to 30 April 2011, then to 30 April 2012. *B* will be assessed on profits computed as follows:

2010–11 Profits of period 1 January to 5 April 2011.

2011–12 Profits of first 12 months, ie

$\frac{4}{4}$ profits of period 1 January to 30 April 2011

Plus $\frac{8}{12}$ of profits for year ended 30 April 2012.

(2) *C* started up on 1 March 2011 and the first set of accounts was made up to 30 April 2012, ie there are no accounts ending in the second tax year. *C*'s assessable profits are:

2010–11 $\frac{1}{14} \times$ profits for 14 months ended 30 April 2012.

2011–12 Profits of first tax year, ie

$\frac{12}{14}$ profits for 14 months ended 30 April 2012.

2012–13 $\frac{12}{14} \times$ profits for 14 months ended 30 April 2012.

7.3.4 Final year of trading

An individual who ceases to carry on a business is taxed under the CY basis on the profits for a notional period that starts immediately after the basis period for the previous tax year and ends on the date that he or she ceases to trade. This can be illustrated by a case where a person makes up accounts to 30 April. Assume the profits for the year ended 30 April 2011 are £80,000. He or she ceases business on 30 November 2011 and profits for the final seven months amount to £50,000. The assessable income for 2011–12 is his or her profit for the period 1 May 2010 to 30 November 2011, ie £80,000 plus £50,000 (but subject to either overlap or transitional relief: see below).

7.3.5 Overlap relief

Because of the way a new business is assessed under the CY basis for the first two tax years, some profits may be taxed more than once. To compensate for this, and to ensure that over the life of the business tax is paid only on the actual amount of profits, overlap relief is given when the business is discontinued or, in the case of partners, when they leave the firm, and partially, on a change of accounting date closer to 5 April.

If the overlap relief exceeds the taxable profits for the final year, the balance may be treated as an allowable loss and either set against the individual's other income for that year or the preceding year, or carried back against profits of the last three years as terminal loss relief (see 7.7.7).

Example – Overlap relief

In the first example at 7.3.3, in which A's first accounts end on 5 October 2011, $183/365$ of the first 12 months' profits are assessed twice. Accordingly, a figure of £24,000 is carried forward and is deducted from A's profits for the final year of trading. Thus, if A retires on 5 October 2020 and the final year's profits are £60,000, the assessment for 2020–21 will be as follows:

	£
CY basis	60,000
Less: overlap relief	(24,000)
Taxable profits	36,000

Change of accounting dates

Unless a business – from the date of commencement – draws up annual accounts ending in the period 31 March to 5 April, there will be overlap relief.

Example – Change of accounting dates (1)

G started trading on 1 October 2008. The profit for the first year of trading was £45,000. The basis of assessment for the opening years would be:

2008–09	1 Oct 2008 to 5 Apr 2009
2009–10	12 months to 30 Sept 2009
2010–11	12 months to 30 Sept 2010

The overlap period is the 187 days to 5 April 2009 that will be assessed both in 2008–09 and 2009–10. The overlap profit is £23,055.

If during the business's lifetime the accounting date were extended to bring it nearer to 5 April, the overlap relief would be utilised in part. The intention of the legislation is to give relief in full when accounts are drawn up on a fiscal year basis, ie for the year to 5 April, so if the accounting reference date is changed to 31 March or 5 April, the relief will be given in full. If the accounting period is shortened, additional overlap relief is created.

Example – Change of accounting dates (2)

G changes his accounting date to 30 April 2012. The profit in the year to 30 September 2011 is £90,000.

| 2011–12 | 12 months to 30 September 2011 |
| 2012–13 | 12 months to 30 April 2012 |

The period of overlap is 1 May 2011 to 30 September 2011. The overlap profit is therefore £37,726 over 153 days, which is combined with the earlier overlap profit to give an overlap profit of £60,781 over 340 days.

If G extends his basis period towards 5 April, the overlap relief is used: logically, if G were to extend the accounting date to 5 April, all of the relief would be used.

Tax notes

Give consideration to the fact that the value of the relief will diminish in real terms with time. Professional advice should be taken in respect of using this relief during the course of the business by advancing the accounting date towards the following 5 April.

7.3.6 Transitional relief

The basis of assessment for a pre-6 April 1994 business changed to the CY basis in 1996–97. This meant that a self-employed individual with, for example a year end of 5 May was assessed for 1996–97 on the whole of his or her profits for the period from 6 May 1994 to 5 May 1996 even though he or she had already been assessed for 1995–96 on a full year's profits, albeit profits that were computed in a different way. Thus, if a business made up accounts to 5 May, the 1996–96 assessment was based on profits for the two years ended 5 May 1996 and the transitional overlap relief is 336/731 of those profits. The assessment for 1997–98 was based on the 12 months to 5 May 1997.

Tax notes

Overlap relief is properly computed on a daily basis, however, HMRC is content to split years in these situations by either months or days providing there is consistency. Transitional relief will be allowed against current profits when the accounting date is moved to a point later in the tax year, or the individual ceases to carry on business.

7.4 PARTNERSHIPS

A partnership's profits are computed in the same way as a sole trader's (see 7.3). However, there are complications.

7.4.1 Salaried partners

A salaried partner is engaged under a contract of employment. His or her profits are normally taxed as employment income. His or her remuneration is treated as a normal employee cost in arriving at the firm's profits. Sometimes partners have a fixed share of profits and it is not always easy to determine whether they are self-employed or salaried partners. The main indicators that a partner is self-employed are that the individual has capital at risk and that he or she is not subject to the control and direction of the other partners.

7.4.2 Treatment of partners under CY basis

Partners assessed individually

Assessments under the CY basis have always been made on individual partners rather than on the firm itself. Each partner is responsible for settling his or her own tax liabilities and is not jointly and severally liable for the total amount of tax (apart from VAT) payable by the partners. There may be a minor exception to this where there are non-resident partners in the firm.

Application of CY basis to partners

Basically, each partner is treated separately and the rules described at 7.3.1–7.3.3 are applied.

Example – How partners' taxable income is computed

> *K* and *L* start a firm on 6 October 2010. They share profits equally. On 6 January 2012, M joins them and takes a one-third entitlement to profits. Accounts to 5 October 2011 show a profit of £132,000. The accounts for the years to 5 October 2012 and 5 October 2013 show a profit of £240,000 and £300,000 respectively. The position is as follows:
>
> 2010–11 *K* and *L* are each assessed on the actual basis, ie the firm's profits of £66,000 for 2010–11 ($\%_{12}$ × £132,000 profits for the year ended 5 October 2011) are divided equally between them, so *K* and *L* are each assessed on £33,000.
>
> 2011–12 *K* and *L* are assessed on their share of the firm's profits for the first 12 months, ie profits of £132,000 are divided equally and each is assessed on

£66,000. *M* is assessed on the actual basis, because 2011–12 is her first tax year as a partner in this firm, so she is assessed on £20,000 (3/12 × her one-third share of the profits for the year ended 5 October 2012).

2012–13 *K* and *L* are assessed on the CY basis on their share of the firm's profits for the year ended 5 October 2012, ie £80,000 each. *M* is assessed on the profits for her first 12 months (ie 9/12 × £80,000 plus 3/12 × £100,000).

From 2013–14 all three partners are assessed on the CY basis, ie their one-third share of the firm's profits for the year ended 5 October 2013 of £300,000.

Similarly, the provisions on overlap relief are applied separately in relation to each partner. Thus, in the above example, if *K* retired on 5 October 2013, he would be entitled to overlap relief in arriving at his taxable profits for 2013–14. The other on going partners will get their overlap relief only when they retire or the firm changes its accounting date (see below). Their overlap relief is as follows:

	£
K	33,000
L	33,000
M	45,000 (3/12 × £80,000 + 3/12 × £100,000).

7.4.3 Partnership interest and other investment income

A partner may be entitled to a share of interest earned by the firm on surplus cash – or indeed any other investment income.

Each partner is assessed on his or her share of such income, but it is assessed on the CY basis. Thus, if a firm makes up accounts to 31 May, the partners will be assessed for 2011–12 on their share of investment income in the firm's accounts for the year ended 31 May 2011 – even though the relevant income may actually have been received during the tax year 2010–11. Overlap relief and transitional overlap relief therefore applies to partnership untaxed investment income such as gross interest or rental income. The exception to this is investment income taxed at source, which is assessable on a tax-year basis, ie bank interest received net.

7.4.4 Catching-up charge: partnerships formerly on cash basis

The catching-up charge for businesses taxed on the cash basis up to 1998–99 is described at 16.1.11.

7.4.5 Partnership tax returns

As well as requiring returns from individual partners, HMRC issues a partnership tax return to the 'nominated partner'. The return requires full details of the firm's profits and capital gains and the way profits (and losses) are divided between the partners.

7.4.6 Expenditure incurred personally by a partner

The legislation requires that all business expenses must be claimed on the partnership return, even where the expenditure is borne by an individual partner (eg his or her car expenses or the purchase of a fax machine for business use at home). HMRC states in Helpsheet HS231 that:

> The only legal basis for giving relief for expenditure that qualifies for capital allowances is as a deduction in the calculation of the profits of the partnership business (unless there is a formal leasing agreement between the partner and the partnership, when the allowances will be due against the leasing income).

However, this does not mean that any legitimate expenditure incurred by a partner – that is any expense that would be allowable if met from partnership funds – can only be relieved if it is formally included in the partnership accounts. Nor does it mean that capital allowances can only be claimed on vehicles, or other assets, that feature in the partnership accounts. Provided that:

- any expenditure, or claim to capital allowances, is correctly calculated for tax purposes; and
- records relevant to those calculations are made and kept as if the expenditure, or assets, were part of the partnership accounts.

HMRC will accept entries in the relevant sections of the Partnership Tax Return that, although based on the partnership accounts, include adjustments for such expenditure, or allowances. But once the adjustments have been made the expenditure will be treated, for all practical purposes, as if it had been included in the partnership's accounts.

7.4.7 Interest paid by partners on personal loans

Where a partner has taken a personal loan to finance buying into the firm or to provide part of its working capital, he or she can claim relief for the interest paid on such borrowings. However, this relief is given by way of a deduction from his or her total taxable income rather than as an expense in computing his or her trading profits (see 11.4).

7.5   LIMITED LIABILITY PARTNERSHIPS (LLPs)

7.5.1 Background

The legislation on limited liability partnerships (LLPs) came into effect on 6 April 2001. In essence, an LLP is a hybrid. Legally, it takes the form of a body corporate (a company) with its own legal personality, but for tax purposes it may be treated as transparent. Provided the LLP is carrying on a lawful business with a view to profit, its members are taxed as if they were partners in a partnership.

Members are assessed on their share of the LLP's profits and capital gains. Unlike a conventional partnership, there is no joint and several liability between the members. Members' liability, in most cases, is limited to the capital contributed to the LLP, together with any further capital they may have agreed to contribute in the event of winding up the LLP. Undrawn profits do not automatically become part of a member's capital contributed (unless otherwise agreed). The member ranks equally with other unsecured creditors for repayment of his or her current account balance. This contrasts with conventional partnerships where the partner is jointly and severally liable for partnership debts other than tax to the full extent of his or her personal assets. An LLP may therefore have attractions as compared with conventional partnerships, but there can also be drawbacks. For example, the LLP is technically a company and has to file accounts and disclose certain financial information, broadly in line with companies of a similar size.

7.5.2 Restriction of loss relief

If a loss arises, there may be a restriction on the member's ability to set the loss against his or her other income. The limit is the amount of capital contributed by the member.

This restriction does not apply where the LLP carries on a profession. Guidance notes on LLPs can be obtained from Companies House (www.companieshouse.gov.uk).

7.6   PARTNERSHIPS CONTROLLED OUTSIDE THE UK

(ss 857–858 ITTOIA 2005)

A UK resident may be a partner in a partnership controlled outside the UK. His or her earnings from such a partnership are taxable in the same way as if they arose from a partnership controlled in the UK unless he or she is not domiciled in the UK. A foreign domiciled partner's share of profits from a trade (or part of a trade) carried on outside the UK are taxed on the remittance basis, subject to making the relevant election (see 35.2).

7.6.1 Current year basis

A partner in a foreign partnership is assessable on the CY basis (see 8.3.3).

7.6.2 Classification of overseas entities

In practice, it is often not clear whether an overseas legal entity will be treated as a partnership or a company for UK tax purposes. This is so especially where an entity combines some of the characteristics of UK partnerships and companies. HMRC sets out its opinion of the correct tax treatment of various US and European entities in its International Manual (www.hmrc.gov.uk/manuals/intmanual/INTM180000.htm).

7.7 RELIEF FOR TRADING LOSSES

Relief may be available for a loss incurred by an individual in a trade or profession. Relief may also be due for pre-trading expenditure treated as a loss incurred when the trade was commenced (see 16.3). The provisions that govern the relief for trading losses are complex and there are several ways in which it is possible to claim for losses to be utilised.

Tax notes

FA 2009 enables losses arising in 2008–09 and 2009–10 to be carried back three years as opposed to the usual one year (see 7.7.3). However, there is a £50,000 pa cap on using losses in this way.

7.7.1 Carry forward relief against subsequent assessments

(s 83 ITA 2007)

A loss incurred by a sole trader or a partner's share of his or her firm's trading loss may be carried forward and deducted in assessments for later years in respect of the same trade or profession. With the introduction of the CY basis of assessment (see 7.3.3), capital allowances are treated as trading expenses and can therefore increase or create a loss. Where losses are carried forward in this way, they must be used against the assessable profits for the first subsequent year in which profits arise. The loss carried forward in this way may also be relieved against certain income connected with the trade even though it is assessed under different provisions (eg interest earned on temporary investment of trade receipts and dividends from trade investments). There is no limit on the number of years for which a loss may be carried forward provided the same trade is carried on.

The loss must be claimed within four years of the tax year end (ie for a loss arising in 2007–08, by 5 April 2012).

Table 7.2 – Losses under self-assessment for 2011–12

Reference	Description	Deadline
ss 261B and 261C TCGA 1992	Deduction from gains for 2011–12	31 Jan 2014
s 64 ITA 2007	Deduction from income or gains for 2011–12	31 Jan 2014
s 72 ITA 2007	Loss in first four years of trade carried back	31 Jan 2014
s 83 ITA 2007	Carry forward against future profits	5 April 2016
s 89 ITA 2007	Terminal loss relief	5 April 2016

7.7.2 Relief against general income

(s 64 ITA 2007)

Where a sole trader or partner incurs a loss and the trade was carried on with a view to profit, the loss may be relieved against his or her general income for the year of assessment in which it was incurred (ie his or her total income for the year). Relief may also be claimed against general income for the preceding tax year. The claim for a loss to be set against his or her general income for the preceding tax year is an alternative to the claim for the loss to be relieved against income of the year of loss. In other words, either the loss may be set against income of the current year (with any balance being set against income of the previous year) or the individual may forgo the chance to set the loss against his or her income for the current year and set the full amount against income of the preceding year.

Where an individual takes relief for trading losses against his or her general income, he or she must use up the losses to the extent to which he or she has taxable income. It is not possible for a claim to be made to restrict the amount of losses so as to enable sufficient income to be left to make use of personal allowances. On the other hand, the legislation permits the deduction of certain items before arriving at the general income against which trading losses can be offset. These items include relief for allowable expenses for employment income purposes, retirement annuity and personal pension contributions, interest relief and relief for donations to charities by deed of covenant or Gift Aid.

Relief for losses against other income must be claimed within 22 months of the end of the tax year in which the loss arises (ie one year after the filing date for the return relating to that year of assessment) so that a 2009–10 loss must be claimed by 31 January 2012.

7.7.3 Carrying losses back to previous years

The right to carry a loss back against the individual's income of the preceding year was temporarily extended in FA 2009 to cover three tax years. However, in the second and third year back, the loss may only be offset against income from that trade. Moreover, this is subject to a ceiling or 'cap.' A carry-back to the previous tax year is unlimited but only a further £50,000 can be carried back to the previous two tax years.

This relief only applies for losses realised in 2008–09 and in 2009–10.

Example – Carry-back of losses against income of the previous three years

A sole trader or member of a partnership realises a loss of £100,000 in 2009–10. His or her income for the previous three years was as follows:

Year ended	Profits
5 April 2009	35,000
5 April 2008	45,000
5 April 2007	58,000

£85,000 of the current year loss could be utilised by carry-back with £15,000 being carried forward. The revised amounts assessed would be as follows:

Year ended	Profits
5 April 2009	Nil
5 April 2008	Nil
5 April 2007	53,000

7.7.4 Relief by aggregation

Where the profits of different accounting periods are time apportioned (eg on commencement of a business), a loss may be relieved by aggregation with a profit. This situation could arise if a first period of trading were less than 12 months.

Example – Loss relief by aggregation

W started business on 1 January 2011. She made a loss of £6,000 for the period ended 30 September 2011 and a profit of £24,000 for the year ended 30 September 2012. Relief by aggregation would produce the following result:

Profits assessable 2010–11	Nil
Profits assessable 2011–12	Nil
Profits assessable 2012–13	£24,000

This is because the first 12 months' trading would be deemed to produce a net loss computed as follows:

	£
Loss for period 1 Jan to 30 Sept 2011	(6,000)
3/12 of profit for year ended 30 Sept 2012	6,000
	Nil

If a loss is set against other income, it cannot also be relieved by aggregation. Thus, if W had claimed relief for the £2,000 loss that she had incurred in 2010–11, only the balance of the loss for the period ended 30 September 2011 which relates to the period 6 April to 30 September 2011 could be taken into account in arriving at the profits of the first 12 months' trading. The 2011–12 assessment would then be £2,000.

Example – Loss set against other income

Y commenced trading on 1 August 2010. He has a loss during the nine months ended 30 April 2011 of £36,000. He has profits for the year ended 30 April 2012 of £60,000.

If the 2010–11 and 2011–12 losses were used by being set against Y's other income, the taxable income would be:

		£
2010–11		Nil
2011–12	Profits of first 12 months:	
	9 months ended 30 April 2011	Nil
	3/12 × profits for year ended 30 April 2012	15,000
		15,000
2012–13	CY basis profits for year ended 30 April 2012	60,000

Contrast this with the situation where relief for the loss is obtained by aggregation:

2010–11		Nil
2011–12	Loss for 9 months to 30 April 2011	(36,000)
	3/12 × Profits for year ended 30 April 2012	15,000
	Loss carried forward	(21,000)
2012–13	Profits assessed on CY basis	60,000
	Less: loss brought forward	(21,000)
		39,000

7.7.5 Losses arising from a business taxed under CY basis

Under the CY basis (see 7.3.3), losses are attributed to a tax year in the same way as profits are assessed. This means that once the business has got past the opening years, a loss will be treated as arising in the tax year in which the trader's accounting period ends. Losses for the opening years are computed on exactly the same basis as profits.

7.7.6 Losses in early years of a trade

(s 72 ITA 2007)

In certain circumstances, relief may be claimed against an individual's general income for the three years of assessment preceding the year in which the loss is incurred. Relief is given against income for the earliest year first. The carry-back is not restricted to £50,000 as with the temporary relief introduced by FA 2009 (see 7.7.3).

There are certain preconditions for a loss to be claimed in this way:

(1) The loss must arise during the first four tax years in which the business is carried on.
(2) Where a trade is acquired from a spouse or civil partner, the four years run from the date the spouse first commenced trading (unless the trade is taken over on the spouse's death).
(3) The trade must be carried out on a commercial basis and with a reasonable expectation of profits.

The claim for a 2009–10 loss must be made by 31 January 2012, to be relieved in this way.

Tax notes

Many new businesses take time before generating substantial profits. In the past you might have been in a job that paid well and a large part of your earnings was taxed at 40% or 50%. Carrying back losses in this way could enable you to recover tax paid at higher rates whereas setting the losses against your income for the current year or carrying them forward may give you only limited benefit.

7.7.7 Relief for trading losses against capital gains

(ss 261B and 261C TCGA 1992)

An individual who has incurred a trading loss may claim to have it set against any capital gains that arise in the same or preceding year. It is not possible to claim relief for losses in this way without first having made a claim for relief for the loss to be set against the individual's general income for the year (see 7.7.1 for the time limit for making such a claim).

Tax notes

If you have a substantial loss, you should look into the possibilities for relieving it against capital gains. However, this is generally a 'last resort', especially as trading losses which are used in this way attract a maximum rate of relief of 28% as opposed to the 40% or 50% relief which may be achieved by setting losses against income that would otherwise be taxed at the top rate.

7.7.8 Terminal loss relief

(s 89 ITA 2007)

Where a trade, profession or vocation is permanently discontinued, a loss incurred during the last 12 months can be deducted from the profits charged to tax in the three tax years before the final year. The relief can include a claim for the loss arising in the tax year in which the cessation takes place as well as a proportion of the loss for the previous tax year.

Capital allowances for the final tax year may also be claimed, as can an appropriate proportion of the preceding year's capital allowances, representing the allowances due for the period beginning 12 months before the cessation.

The terminal loss may be carried back against profits from the same trade for the three tax years immediately preceding the year of cessation. The relief is given against the latest year's profits first.

If interest and dividends would have been included as trading profits (except for the fact that they were subject to deduction of tax at source), the terminal loss may be set against such income.

7.7.9 Anti-avoidance provisions

Losses from limited partnerships

(ss 104 to 106 ITA 2007)

Limited partnerships have, in the past, been widely used in tax avoidance arrangements. The House of Lords decided in *Reed* v *Young* [1986] STC 285 that a limited partner could be entitled to loss relief for an amount that exceeded his or her actual liability under the Limited Partnership Act. This led to specific legislation to limit the amount of loss relief to the capital that is 'at risk'. Any losses incurred beyond this amount must be carried forward to be set against any future share of profits received by the limited partner from the firm. The s 104 provisions apply to individuals who are limited partners or members of a joint venture arrangement under which their liability is limited to a contract, agreement, guarantee, etc.

'Non-active partners'

A partner who devotes less than ten hours a week to the partnership business cannot secure relief against other income for losses that exceed the capital he or she has contributed to the firm. Losses that exceed this capital must be carried forward and used only to offset profits from the firm for a later year. This rule came into effect on 10 February 2004.

Further legislation that came into effect on 2 March 2007 prevents any sideways relief where participation in the partnership forms part of tax avoidance arrangements. Furthermore, even where no such avoidance arrangements are present, FA 2007 restricts the tax relief available to non-active partners to £25,000 a year. The perceived abuse occurred where a non-active partner contributed capital to a partnership to take advantage of tax losses.

'Non-active sole traders'

As a result of the numbers of individuals switching from taking part in loss-making partnership arrangements to sole trader structures, following the FA 2007 anti-avoidance legislation, similar provisions were introduced from 12 March 2008 for sole traders who devoted less than ten hours a week to a loss-making business. Once again, loss relief against other income is restricted to £25,000 (and sideways relief is excluded altogether where the business forms part of tax avoidance arrangements). These provisions do not apply to Lloyd's Names or qualifying film expenditure.

Loss relief for film partnerships, etc

FA 2004 contained anti-avoidance provisions aimed at individuals who participate in partnerships only for tax planning purposes. We deal with these provisions at 25.8.

7.7.10 Loss relief where business transferred to a company

(s 86 ITA 2007)

Where a business has been carried on by an individual (either as a sole trader or in partnership) and is transferred to a company, it is possible for any unused trading losses to be relieved against his or her income from the company in subsequent years. This relief is available only if the business is transferred to a company wholly or mainly in return for an allotment of shares and then only if the individual has retained ownership of those shares throughout the tax year concerned. In practice, HMRC is unlikely to withhold relief provided the individual has retained at least 80% of the shares.

7.7.11 Losses from an overseas partnership

(s 95 ITA 2007)

A UK resident partner's share of profits from a trading partnership that is managed or controlled abroad are taxed under s 852 ITTOIA 2005 (formerly Schedule D Case V). If a loss should arise, relief is calculated in the same way as for a loss incurred in a UK trade, profession or vocation. Relief for such losses is then given in the same way as relief is given for UK trading losses, except that where a loss is to be set against other income, the loss can be deducted only from:

- profits from other foreign trades;
- foreign pensions and annuities where a 10% deduction is available;
- foreign emoluments taxed as employment income.

INCOME FROM UK PROPERTY

VIRAN DE SILVA

This chapter deals with rental income from land or property in the UK. Rents received from letting an overseas property are dealt with separately in the tax legislation and are covered in 10.1.

This chapter contains the following sections:

(1) Basis of assessment and administration
(2) How to calculate your taxable profit
(3) Lump sums deemed to be rent (premiums)
(4) 'Rent-a-room' relief
(5) Furnished holiday accommodation
(6) 'Buy to let' investments
(7) Capital allowances on investment properties
(8) Mineral royalties
(9) Woodlands
(10) Property investment companies
(11) VAT considerations
(12) Interest earned on trust funds for service charges and sinking funds

8.1 BASIS OF ASSESSMENT AND ADMINISTRATION

8.1.1 All rental activities treated as single business

All rental income received by an individual from UK properties is assessed under s 264 ITTOIA 2005, whether the property is let unfurnished or furnished. All income and expenses are brought together in a single business of letting UK property. Income and expenses on overseas properties are totally excluded when computing the profits of an individual's UK property business and deficits on overseas properties cannot be offset against profits that fall into the other category.

The income from a UK property business is determined using normal commercial accountancy principles, on an accruals, rather than a cash, basis. Expenses are allowed if they satisfy the test that the expense is incurred wholly and exclusively for business purposes and this rule applies to interest (including overdraft interest) just as for any other expense.

8.1.2 Exceptional types of rental income

Rental income includes ground rents. It also includes 'other receipts from an estate' in land such as charges levied by a landlord in return for maintaining a block of flats and payments made to a landowner for sporting rights. It does not include admission charges made by hotels, boarding houses, theatres, etc, since the profits of such businesses are chargeable to tax as trading income.

Income from taking in lodgers is generally treated as trading income rather than UK property business income. However, see 8.4 on 'rent-a-room' relief.

8.1.3 Property income assessed on fiscal year basis

An individual must report income on a tax-year basis, ie accounts must be drawn up to 5 April.

8.1.4 Partnership income dealt with separately

Rental income received by a partnership is treated as a separate source. If the partnership does not have any trading income, the rental income is assessed on a fiscal-year basis, irrespective of the date to which the partnership draws up accounts. In contrast, if the partnership also has some trading income, its UK property income is assessed on the same basis. Thus, if a trading partnership has a 30 April year end, the partners will be assessed for 2011–12 on their share of the partnership's UK property income for the year ended 30 April 2011.

8.1.5 UK property income is investment income

(ss 118, 120 ITA 2007)

Although all UK rental income is treated as arising from a single business of letting property, the income is still treated as investment income. Any losses can only be carried forward for offset against UK property income and cannot be set against the individual's other income for the year. There are exceptions; where capital allowances are available, the lower of the net capital allowances and the loss itself may be set against other income, and for deficits arising from letting agricultural properties, the deficit may be set against other income (see below).

8.1.6 Deficiency on agricultural property

(s 120 ITA 2007)

Where an estate consists of or includes agricultural land, a deficiency may be set against any UK property income. Any balance that cannot be relieved in this way may be set against the individual's other income for the year, or the following tax year.

'Agricultural land' is defined as land, houses or other buildings in the UK occupied wholly or mainly for husbandry purposes. 'Estate' means any land and buildings managed as one estate. Where only part of the estate is used for husbandry, only a proportion of any deficiency can be relieved in this way.

8.2 HOW TO CALCULATE YOUR TAXABLE PROFIT

The legislation requires that landlords should calculate their income and expenses in accordance with normal accountancy principles but subject to the same specific rules that apply for computing trading profits (see Chapter 16).

You should study the notes and help sheets issued by HMRC to enable landlords to complete their SA tax returns. HMRC's guide to the SA return sets out the normal treatment of certain common expenses.

8.2.1 Rent receivable

HMRC confirms in its manuals that you do not bring rent into a year's tax computation merely because you receive it, or it is due to be paid to you, in the year. Equally, you do not exclude rent merely because you receive it outside, or it is due outside, the tax year. You bring in the proportion of rent earned in the year from the tenants' use of the property in the year. You exclude the proportion earned from the tenant's right to use the property outside the year. So, you may need to make an adjustment where rent is receivable, say, quarterly, either in advance or in arrears. Incidentally, HMRC's notes to the SA return point out that rental income includes receipts-in-kind as well as in cash.

8.2.2 Bad debts

A landlord can claim a deduction for rent that is due to him or her but has not been paid where the debt is clearly irrecoverable. A deduction can also be claimed for doubtful debts. Such a deduction is available only where the landlord has taken all reasonable steps to recover the debt. Furthermore, if the outstanding rent is collected in a later tax year, he or she should bring the recovery into his or her accounts as a receipt for his or her rental income for that year.

No deduction is available for a general bad debt reserve (ie a landlord cannot deduct 5% of the outstanding rents due to him or her at the year end just to be on the safe side). Tax relief is available for provisions for doubtful debts only if the provisions relate to specific debts and the facts relating to each debtor have been taken into account. Furthermore, as

HMRC literature makes clear, you cannot deduct a bad or doubtful debt merely because the tenant is always a slow payer. There has to be good reason for thinking the debt is likely to be bad.

8.2.3 Rent-free periods

HMRC's approach follows the accounting principles set out in SSAP21. If the landlord, for example, grants a lease for a five-year period with no rent being payable in year one and rent of £10,000 being payable in years two to five, the landlord should spread the total amount of rent receivable over the five years (ie £40,000) and bring into his or her accounts one-fifth of that total income for each year of the lease. In other words, the treatment reflects the substance of the transaction; in essence there is not really a rent-free year at all since the £40,000 payable over the first five years is rent for the whole of that period.

8.2.4 Expenses

Expenses should also be brought into account on normal accountancy principles. This means that a landlord should deduct any allowable expenses that relate to work done, or goods or services supplied to him or her, for a particular year. There is no requirement that the supplier should have been paid during the tax year. Thus if you have raised a loan for the purchase or improvement of repairs of properties that are let out, you can claim relief for interest that has accrued up to 5 April even though the bank or building society may debit interest on a different basis (eg at 30 June and 31 December).

Expenses are deductible only if they meet the 'wholly and exclusively' rule (ie expenditure that is part business/part private is not allowable). For example, the cost of travelling to Wales to supervise repairs to a holiday cottage is not an allowable deduction for tax purposes if the landlord also takes a holiday while there (ie the visit had a dual purpose). But where a definite part or proportion of an expense is wholly incurred for business purposes, that part may be deducted. This may well arise where a landlord lives in part of the property that is rented out: here, a proportion of the insurance premium relating to the property as a whole may be deducted in arriving at the landlord's UK property income. Remember that where expenditure is partly for business and partly for personal use, you have to complete a specific box on the SA return.

8.2.5 Repairs, maintenance and renewals

Examples of common repairs normally deductible in computing income for tax purposes are:

- exterior and interior painting and decorating;
- stone cleaning;
- damp and rot treatment;
- mending broken windows, doors, furniture and machines such as cookers or lifts;
- re-pointing;
- replacing roof slates, flashing and gutters.

Improvements are generally treated as capital expenditure. However, if the replacement of a part of the 'entirety' is like-for-like, or the nearest modern equivalent, HMRC generally accepts the expenditure is allowable revenue expenditure. For example, HMRC has confirmed that the cost of replacing worn out single-glazed windows with double glazing may be an allowable expense in computing UK property income (see *Tax Bulletin* 59). Substantial repairs carried out shortly after a landlord has occupied a property to put it into a fit state are generally disallowed as constituting capital expenditure.

The *Jenners* case (see 16.1.9) means that a specific and scientifically calculated provision for the cost of repair work to be carried out in the future might be allowable. You need to take specialist advice on whether making such a provision accords with the generally accepted accountancy principles set out in FRS12.

8.2.6 Energy saving allowance

Until 5 April 2015, landlords of residential property are allowed a deduction for expenditure of up to £1,500 per dwelling on the installation of the following energy saving items:

- loft insulation;
- cavity wall insulation;
- solid wall insulation;
- draught proofing;
- hot water system insulation;
- floor insulation.

The maximum deduction for a tax year is £1,500, but the way in which this limit applies depends on when the expenditure was incurred.

Up to 5 April 2007, the limit applied to all the expenditure incurred in relation to a building, irrespective of how many separate dwellings there were in the building and how many possibly eligible claimants there might be for the building, ie only one £1,500 allowance was available, even if the property contained ten eligible flats.

From 6 April 2007 the limit applies to all expenditure incurred in relation to each separate dwelling. So if there are three flats in a building, relief of up to £4,500 per tax year may be available. The relief is also available to corporate landlords who let residential property.

8.2.7 Refurbishing business premises in disadvantaged areas

Business Premises Renovation Allowances (BPRA) became available on 11 April 2007, for an initial period of five years. The Government confirmed in the 2011 Budget that the allowance is now to be retained until at least 2017 but that flat renovation allowances and land remediation relief will be abolished after April 2012.

The BPRA provides relief against the cost of renovating business property which has been empty for at least one year in designated 'disadvantaged areas'. The whole of Northern Ireland qualifies. Go to www.dtistats.net/regional-aa/aa2007.asp to see whether an area in England, Wales or Scotland qualifies. The capital costs of such renovations would normally not be relieved immediately, but the relief means that a 100% allowance should be available.

Relief is claimed on page 2 of the 'UK Property' supplementary SA form in Box 31 with any balancing charge shown in Box 29. For details on the computation of capital allowances and balancing charges generally see 16.2.

8.2.8 Renewals

The landlord can claim the cost of replacing furniture, furnishings and machinery. However, expenditure on renewals is not available where the landlord claims the standard 10% wear and tear allowance (see 8.2.11).

Where expenditure on renewals is claimed, the landlord should bring into account of his or her income any amounts received for items that have been scrapped or sold. Also, expenditure on renewals should not normally include the cost of items that represent a significant improvement or addition to the furniture and furnishings, etc previously made available to the tenant.

8.2.9 Legal and professional costs

HMRC's view is as follows:

Non-allowable expenses

(1) Expenses in connection with the first letting or subletting of a property for more than one year (including eg legal expenses, such as the cost of drawing up a lease, agents' and surveyors' fees and commission).
(2) Any proportion of the legal, etc costs that relate to the payment of a premium on the renewal of a lease.
(3) Fees incurred in obtaining planning permission or on the registration of title when buying a property.

Allowable expenses

(1) Expenses for granting a lease of a year or less.
(2) The normal legal and professional fees incurred on the renewal of a lease, provided it is for less than 50 years (HMRC confirmed in its property income manual (at PIM2205) that the costs of granting a lease to a new tenant are normally allowable provided the replacement lease follows closely on the previous one and is broadly similar in terms).
(3) Professional fees incurred:
   (a) in evicting an unsatisfactory tenant, with a view to re-letting;
   (b) on an appeal against a compulsory purchase order; and
   (c) in drawing up accounts.

8.2.10 Costs of services provided, including wages

A landlord who provides any service to a tenant (eg gardening, the provision of a porter, cleaning, etc) can claim the cost of these services, provided they are incurred wholly and exclusively for the purposes of the letting.

8.2.11 10% wear and tear allowance

(ESC B47)

A landlord who lets a dwelling-house as furnished accommodation can claim (instead of claims on a renewals basis) an allowance amounting to 10% of the rent received after deducting charges or services that would normally be borne by the tenant but are, in fact, borne by the landlord (eg council tax). This allowance, known as 'wear and tear allowance', is accepted by HMRC as broadly covering the cost of normal renewals of furniture.

A landlord who lets non-residential property (eg offices) can normally claim capital allowances for any items provided (eg furniture).

Table 8.1 – Computing your 2011–12 property income (straightforward situation)

For each property, bring in the rental income that relates to the tax year (ie if rent is receivable on 25 March 2012 for the quarter ending 24 June 2012, include a proportion for the period 25 March to 5 April 2012).

Deduct

- charges made by an agent for rent collection and management;

- any rent you have to pay on the property (eg ground rent);

- any service charges you have to pay (particularly likely to apply if you are letting out a flat);

- insurance premiums paid for the period covered by the tax year: if you pay insurance for a calendar year, include $3/12$ of the premium for 2012 + $9/12$ of the premium for 2011;

- repairs and similar expenses (eg gardening) incurred in the tax year. Note that the expense need not actually have been paid in the tax year so long as it is clear that it relates to the tax year;

- interest on borrowings used to finance the original purchase of a property, improvements or repairs or against the value of the property at the time that it was brought into the UK property business.

Aggregate all the income and expenses for your different properties – except for properties not let on a commercial basis (any deficit on such properties will almost certainly not be allowable). Add in any lump sums taxable as premiums (see 8.3).

8.2.12 Interest

For many years, it was understood by most tax advisers, and virtually all HMRC staff, that relief for mortgage interest could only be set against rental income to the extent that it related to interest paid on loans used to *purchase* the property that was being let. We all thought relief was not available on any subsequent borrowings except to the extent that the money was borrowed to finance capital improvements. However, HMRC's updated *Business Income Manual,* (at BIM45700) contradicts this. The relevant section states:

Mr A owns a flat in central London, which he bought ten years ago for £125,000. He has a mortgage of £80,000 on the property. He has been offered a job in Holland and is moving there to live and work. He intends to come back to the UK at some time. He decides to keep his flat and rent it out while he is away. His London flat now has a market value of £375,000.

The opening balance sheet of his rental business shows

Mortgage	£80,000	Property at MV	£375,000
Capital account	£295,000		

He renegotiates his mortgage on the flat to convert it to a buy-to-let mortgage and borrows a further £125,000. He withdraws the £125,000, which he then uses to buy a flat in Rotterdam.

The balance sheet at the end of Year 1 shows

Mortgage		£205,000	Property at MV £375,000
Capital account			
brought forward	£295,000		
Less Drawings	£125,000		
carried forward		£170,000	

Although he has withdrawn capital from the business, the interest on the mortgage loan is allowable in full because it is funding the transfer of the property to the business at its open market value at the time the business started. The capital account is not overdrawn.

(*Source*: HMRC BIM 45700)

8.3 LUMP SUMS DEEMED TO BE RENT (PREMIUMS)

(s 277 ITTOIA 2005)

8.3.1 Introduction

A landlord faced with the choice of letting a property for five years at £10,000 pa, or taking a lump sum in return for granting a lease for five years at an annual rent of £100, would regard the two transactions as very similar in their overall consequences. The purpose behind the tax legislation that deals with lump sums (or 'premiums') is to ensure that the tax treatment of both transaction types is similar in nature. The principle is that a proportion of a premium received by a landlord for granting a lease of less than 50 years should be taxed as if it were rent.

The following sections apply only where the person who receives the premium is the landlord, ie a person who continues to hold a superior interest in the property. An outgoing tenant who assigns the whole of his or her interest in the property for a lump sum is not regarded as receiving a premium for income tax purposes.

8.3.2 How premiums are apportioned between income and capital

(s 277 ITTOIA 2005)

The rule is that the full amount of the premium is treated as rent except for 2% for every complete year of the lease after the first year. For example, if a ten-year lease is granted for a premium of £25,000, the amount subject to tax as income is 82% of £25,000, ie £20,500. See Table 8.2.

Table 7.2 – Extract from Revenue helpsheet

Working sheet for chargeable premiums – leases up to 50 years		
Premium	**A**	£
Number of complete periods of 12 months in the lease, ignore the first 12 months	**B**	£
50 minus box B	**C**	£
Box C divided by 50	**D**	£
Box A multiplied by Box D	**E**	£
Copy box E to box 20.		

Source: HMRC

8.3.3 Payments in kind

(s 278 ITTOIA 2005)

It is provided that if a tenant is required to carry out work as a term of his or her lease, the whole of the benefit accruing to the landlord is deemed to be a premium receivable at the commencement of the lease.

8.3.4 Deemed premiums

(s 281 ITTOIA 2005)

Any lump sum paid by a tenant to vary the lease can be treated as a premium receivable at the time the contract for the variation is entered into.

Example – Deemed premium

A is the landlord of a property used as offices and let on a 15-year lease. It is a term of the lease that the tenant should not use the premises for any other purpose.

The tenant secures planning consent to use the property for light industrial use. He makes a payment to A of £12,000 in Year 4 to induce him to vary the lease so that the property can be used for industrial purposes. A is deemed to receive a premium in Year 4. The taxable amount is:

	£
	12,000
Less: (10 × 2%)	(2,400)
	9,600

Similarly, if A had received a lump sum to induce him to waive the relevant term in the lease, the lump sum would be treated as a premium.

8.3.5 Sale with right to repurchase the property

(s 284 ITTOIA 2005)

Where the freehold or leasehold of a property is sold subject to a condition that at a future date the purchaser may be required to sell it back to the vendor at a lower price, the vendor must treat the excess of the sale price over the repurchase price as a premium. The excess, or notional premium, is reduced by 2% for each complete year between the date of sale and the date of resale less one year, the balance is taxed as income from property.

A similar rule applies where a vendor sells a property but retains an option to repurchase it.

8.4 'RENT-A-ROOM' RELIEF

(ss 309, 784–802 ITTOIA 2005)

Special relief is available to an individual who receives payment for letting furnished accommodation in a qualifying residence. The relief provides total exemption from income of £4,250 pa unless sums accrue to another person in respect of lettings of furnished accommodation in the same property, in which case the exemption is reduced to £2,125, regardless of the number of other people (ie if three people qualified in respect of the same property, the limit for all three would be £2,125 each).

A qualifying residence is a residence that is the individual's only or main residence at some time in the basis period for the year of assessment in relation to the lettings. If the receipts would otherwise be brought into account in calculating the profits of a trade, the 'income period' in s 786(1)(b) is the basis period for the tax year. Otherwise the income period is the tax year. 'Residence' means a building (or part of a building) occupied or intended to be occupied as a separate residence.

Rent-a-room relief is available automatically unless the taxpayer elects otherwise or the gross sums received exceed the £4,250 limit. Londoners in particular are likely to make a number of claims for this relief to apply, covering the period of the 2012 Olympic Games, as is already the case for annual events such as Wimbledon.

Where the gross sums received exceed the £4,250 limit for the year of assessment (or the £2,125 limit where some other person receives income from furnished lettings within the same property), the taxpayer may elect for his or her profits or gains for the basis period to be treated as equal to the excess. For example, if a taxpayer has gross rent of £5,000, he or she may compute his or her taxable income as £750 or he or she can compute it in the normal way by reference to the expenses actually incurred.

Need for caution

HMRC has commented on the suggestion that rent-a-room relief might be available where part of an individual's residence is let to a company for use as an office (or for some other trade or business purpose). HMRC's view is that the relief is available only where the person paying rent uses the premises for residential purposes.

8.4.1 Revenue leaflets

For further information on rent-a-room relief, obtain leaflet HS223, *Rent-a-Room for Traders.*

8.5 FURNISHED HOLIDAY ACCOMMODATION

(s 322–328 ITTOIA 2005)

8.5.1 Definition

While furnished holiday lettings (FHL) in the UK and other EEA countries will continue to qualify for the special tax reliefs available for FHL, the qualifying conditions have altered from April 2011 onwards.

In particular, it is now more difficult for a property to qualify as a holiday letting – it will have to be available for commercial letting as holiday accommodation for 210 days a year (previously 140 days) and actually let for 105 days (previously 70 days). However, to cater for fluctuations in lettings from year to year, it will be possible for owners to elect for continuation of a qualifying holiday letting to cover a break of one or two years where the letting thresholds are not reached.

FHL owners who may struggle to meet the new letting thresholds will have to decide whether or not to retain the property for personal use and/or hold it as an investment or take steps to ensure that the property is available and actually let for the appropriate periods (by advertising more widely etc). Owners who retain properties purely as an investment rather than letting them should remember that they will no longer get tax relief on any interest paid on the mortgage (if there is one). Therefore, it may be cost-efficient to repay such borrowing where possible, rather than pay the interest from post-tax income.

A qualifying FHL is regarded as a trade for CGT purposes and, therefore, qualifies for various CGT reliefs. For example, on selling a FHL, the owner can claim rollover relief on reinvesting the gain or, in some circumstances, entrepreneurs' relief (ER). These tax advantages will continue but only if the new letting thresholds are met.

For properties that do not meet the letting threshold and which were not sold before 6 April 2011, the holiday lettings trade will be deemed to have ceased on 5 April 2011 (if it had not actually ceased before then). It should still be possible to sell the property within three years of this deemed cessation and claim ER to obtain an effective 10% rate of CGT on the first £10m of gains.

8.5.2 Reliefs available

The following reliefs will be available if a property is treated as being let as furnished holiday accommodation.

Profits classified as earned income

Profits are treated as earned income. This is not dependent on the owner taking any active involvement in the lettings: the whole activity can be dealt with by an agent where desired.

Relief for interest

Interest on loans used to purchase the property and to finance the lettings should qualify as an expense incurred in the trade. In some cases, the inclusion of such interest may give rise to a loss for tax purposes.

Capital allowances for plant and machinery

Equipment, furniture and furnishings may attract capital allowances: see 16.2.

Relief for pre-trading expenditure

Expenditure incurred before the business of letting such properties actually commences may be allowed as a loss incurred at the point in time when the lettings commence, as pre-trading expenditure (see 16.3).

Relief for losses

FHL losses arising after April 2011 may only be set off against future profits from FHL businesses and losses from qualifying UK and overseas FHL must be segregated. Previously, losses arising from FHL businesses were treated as trading losses and set against other profits, income and gains of the owner.

Capital gains tax

Roll-over relief may be available (see 17.4).

The property is regarded as a business asset for entrepreneurs' relief (see 17.8).

Inheritance tax

In some circumstances, a furnished holiday letting business can qualify for 100% IHT business property relief, making it easy to pass such an asset to members of the family. In the past, HMRC generally allowed relief where the lettings were short term, and the owner, either him or herself or through an agent such as a relative, was substantially involved with the holidaymakers in terms of their activities on and from the premises.

HMRC has, in recent years, reconsidered its approach. In particular it will be looking more closely at the level and type of services, rather than who provided them.

8.6 'BUY TO LET' INVESTMENTS

8.6.1 General principles

The tax legislation does not recognise the term 'buy to let' investments but in practice the tax treatment of such investments falls within certain clearly defined rules:

(1) Interest paid on a buy to let mortgage can be offset against other UK property income if it exceeds the rent from the property.
(2) A buy to let investment will not attract roll-over relief unless it is to be let as furnished holiday accommodation (see 8.5 above).

8.6.2 Cashbacks

A feature in recent years has been the receipt by buy to let investors of cashbacks from developers. Sometimes the cashbacks have been conditional on the purchase going through by a given date. There are instances where the lender was not advised of the cashbacks and SDLT has been paid on the full price. In such cases, the cashback might have covered the purchaser's deposit so that the lender had effectively made a 100% loan against the discounted price.

No tax charge should arise on the receipt of the cashback (see SP4/97) as this is an ordinary discount to a retail customer.

8.6.3 Deficit situations

In the current market, with initial fixed-rate mortgage periods coming to an end, many over-stretched buy to let investors may face a situation where their borrowing costs exceed their rental income. Income tax legislation gives no sideways relief for such losses against the investor's other income (unless, for years up to 2010–11, the properties were let as furnished holiday accommodation: this relief is no longer available, even for FHL, from April 2011).

A possible solution would be for the investor to sell some or all of the properties to a company and raise new loans, which he or she lends on to the company to enable it to pay for the properties. The money received from the company could then be used to clear all or some of the investor's original borrowings. Interest paid on the individual's new loans could be relieved against his or her other income (see 11.5). The company would generally pay tax at the small companies' rate (currently 20%). However, the main problem with this strategy will be if the properties have fallen in value and their current value is substantially less than the investor's outstanding borrowings. Also, SDLT will be payable and the long-term CGT implications may not be attractive (the company's acquisition cost will be the market value of the properties at the time that it bought them).

There is no easy solution or 'quick fix' for this situation. If you find yourself in this boat, seek advice from an accountant.

8.7 CAPITAL ALLOWANCES ON INVESTMENT PROPERTIES

8.7.1 Introduction

Capital allowances are usually given when HMRC assesses the profits of a trade. It is also possible to qualify for capital allowances in respect of expenditure on investment properties, for example where a landlord installs a lift, air-conditioning, electrical equipment etc, or incurs capital expenditure on a flat over a shop (see 16.2.13). Plant or machinery provided for use in residential property is otherwise excluded. The allowances must first be set against the income of a defined class (see below), but any surplus of allowances may be set against the individual's other income for that year or the following tax year.

8.7.2 Expenditure that may attract allowances

The following are often installed by landlords and generally qualify as plant:

- electrical, cold water, gas and sewerage systems designed to meet the particular requirements of a trader to whom the building is let;
- water-heating systems;
- powered systems of ventilation, air cooling or air purification;
- lifts, hoists and moving walkways;
- sprinkler systems and fire alarms;
- burglar alarm systems;
- thermal insulation (deduction of £1,500 per dwelling house or capital allowances on all other buildings used for any qualifying business purpose).

8.7.3 Purchase of second-hand buildings

A landlord who acquires a building can often claim capital allowances for the plant contained in it (see 16.2.17).

8.7.4 Capital allowance changes from April 2008 onwards

- Integral fixtures. The writing down allowances for plant that is contained in a building (ie a fixture) have been reduced to 10%.
- Annual investment allowance. The first £100,000 of expenditure each year by businesses on most plant and machinery currently attracts tax relief in full. This limit will reduce to £25,000 from April 2012.
- General plant and machinery. From April 2008, the main rate of writing down allowances reduced from 25% to 20%.
- First-year allowance. For 2009–10 only, a 40% allowance applied for expenditure (excluding cars) in excess of £50,000 that would otherwise have qualified for 20% writing down allowances.
- From 2012–13 the rates of writing down allowances for general plant and machinery and integral features are to be reduced to 18% and 8% respectively.

8.7.5 Agricultural buildings allowances

(s 361 *et seq* CAA 2001)

Agricultural buildings allowances (see 16.2.20) used to be available for relief by 'discharge or repayment of tax' if the landlord did not carry on a farming trade. The allowances had to be first set against agricultural or forestry rental income.

It was necessary to make a claim for relief in a tax return, subject to the normal time limits. Agricultural buildings allowances have now been phased out, with the rate of the allowance being reduced over the last few years as follows:

2008–09	3%
2009–10	2%
2010–11	1%
2011–12 onwards	nil

8.7.6 Industrial buildings allowances

(s 271 *et seq* CAA 2001)

An individual who owned the relevant interest in an industrial building may in the past have qualified for industrial buildings allowances (see 16.2.21) because the property was occupied and used for a qualifying trade. Similarly, an individual who owned a property in an enterprise zone generally qualified for allowances where the building was occupied for commercial purposes.

Again, it was necessary to make a claim for relief in a tax return, subject to the normal time limits. Industrial buildings allowances have now also been phased out, with the rate of the allowance being reduced as follows:

2008–09	3%
2009–10	2%
2010–11	1%
2011–12 onwards	nil

8.7.7 Enterprise zone trust

It used to be possible to invest in properties in enterprise zones through a syndicate or 'enterprise zone property trust'. An individual who invested in the trust was treated as if he or she had incurred a proportion of the trust's expenditure on enterprise zone properties and the allowances could then be set against his or her other income. Enterprise zone allowances have been completely withdrawn from April 2011, but without the phasing-out rules applying to industrial and agricultural buildings allowances. If there is a chargeable period that crosses the cut-off date, the WDA for that chargeable period is given by:

$$\frac{DCPB \times WDA}{DCP}$$

Where DCPB = number of days in the chargeable period before the cut-off date

DCP = number of days in the chargeable period

WDA = the WDA that would have been made for the chargeable period before the introduction of the FA 2008 legislation. Where a person had bought a used building in an enterprise zone the WDA was based on the residue of qualifying expenditure after sale in the normal way.

8.8 MINERAL ROYALTIES

(ss157, 319, 340–343 ITTOIA 2005; ss201–203 TCGA1992)

Mineral royalties are normally received net of tax at the basic rate. However, only part of the royalties is taxable as income. Where the recipient is resident or ordinarily resident in the UK, one-half of the mineral royalties is treated as capital gains rather than income. Only 50% of any management expenses or other sums normally deductible in computing property income may be set against the part of the mineral royalties treated as income, and no deduction of any kind is allowed from the 50% of the receipt charged to CGT.

When the mineral lease comes to an end, the person may claim a capital loss as if he or she had disposed of the land at its market value at that time. The loss may be set against capital gains for the year in which the mineral lease expires or against capital gains taxed on mineral royalties during the preceding 15 years.

Mineral royalties is defined as including rents, tolls, royalties and other periodic payments relating to the winning and working of minerals (other than water, peat and topsoil) under a lease, licence or other agreement.

8.9 WOODLANDS

At one time, profits arising from the occupation of woodlands in the UK were taxed under Schedule B. This charge was abolished many years ago. Profits or gains arising from the occupation of woodlands are now exempt and woodlands are not chargeable as UK property income.

8.10 PROPERTY INVESTMENT COMPANIES

This is covered in Chapter 27.

8.11 VAT CONSIDERATIONS

Do not overlook VAT: it is possible to register many rental businesses for VAT purposes and this can mean you will recover input tax. However, doing this will mean you will have to charge VAT on the rent (see 22.3.6). Also, VAT will have to be charged when you sell the property. The treatment of VAT on property interests is a complex area, and one in which it is essential to take professional advice.

8.12   INTEREST EARNED ON TRUST FUNDS FOR SERVICE CHARGES AND SINKING FUNDS

Many landlords, or their agents, are required to hold service charges and sinking fund payments made by tenants and leaseholders. In general, these monies are held on trust, ie if the building were destroyed or for some other reason the money never had to be used, it would have to be returned to the tenants.

Interest earned on these funds used will normally be taxed at the rate of 20%. Prior to 2007–08, the rate of tax on such interest used to be 40%.

9

SAVINGS INCOME

This chapter deals with the types of income from savings that need to be reported on page 3 of the SA tax return (reproduced on p. 47). Apart from dividends, income from savings is always taxed at 20% for 2010–11 and 2011–12 unless the taxpayer is an individual liable for higher rate or additional rate tax (or whose non-savings income is insufficient to exhaust the starting rate band, ie it is less than the personal allowance plus £2,560). Dividends are subject to their own rates of tax of 10% for basic rate taxpayers, 32.5% for higher rate taxpayers and 42.5% for additional rate taxpayers (from 2010–11). This rate (together with the 50% rate on non-dividend income) applies where an individual's taxable income is over £150,000 a year.

After gains, savings income is taxed as the highest part of income, with dividends forming the highest part, so for an individual with 2011–12 employment income of £149,000 and savings income of £20,000 (including dividends of £5,000) he or she will be taxed on £5,000 at 42.5% (less a notional tax credit at 10%); £14,000 at 50% (if applicable, with a credit for basic rate tax deducted at source); £115,000 at 40% and £35,000 at 20%.

The types of savings income are:

Interest income received gross

(1) Bank and building society interest
(2) Other interest income
(3) Loans to individuals and other private loans
(4) Gilts and loan stocks

Interest received net of tax

(5) Rate of tax deducted at source

Interest-type income

(6) Accrued income scheme
(7) Deeply discounted securities

Dividends from UK companies

(8) Dividends

(9) Sundry receipts treated as dividends

Overseas interest and dividend income

(10) Foreign interest and dividends

Exchange-traded funds

(11) Tax treatment of exchange-traded funds

INTEREST INCOME RECEIVED GROSS

9.1 BANK AND BUILDING SOCIETY INTEREST

9.1.1 Interest receivable without tax deducted at source

The National Savings Bank (NSB) always pays interest without deduction of tax. The widely-known exemption for the first £70 interest paid on an ordinary NSB account is to be abolished later in 2011–12 as the NSB no longer offers this type of account (and has not done so since 2003–04!). Interest on an NSB investment account or from deposit bonds, income bonds or capital bonds is taxable in full.

Interest payments by UK banks or building societies on deposit accounts are normally subject to deduction of tax at source unless the depositor completes form R85. This form requires the depositor's full name, address, date of birth and national insurance number and contains a declaration that the depositor is unlikely to be liable for income tax.

Interest payments may be made without deduction of tax on certificates of deposit (qualifying time deposits) provided the deposit is for at least £50,000 and the bank or building society takes the deposit for a fixed period (which must not exceed five years). Interest may also be paid without deduction of tax on deposits where no certificate of deposit has been issued, but the depositor would be entitled to a certificate if he or she called for one to be issued. From 6 April 2012 tax will be deducted at source from taxable interest paid on new 'qualifying time deposit' accounts. This will be achieved by including newly opened accounts within the tax deduction scheme for interest operated by banks, building societies and other deposit takers. The Government will informally consult stakeholders on the implementation of the change during May 2011 and will legislate in Finance Bill 2012.

Interest may also be received without tax being deducted at source from loans to individuals; deposits held by a solicitor and on certificates of tax deposit (see 9.2).

9.1.2 How the taxable amount is arrived at

The assessable income is the actual income that arises during the tax year, ie the CY basis. This means that for the current tax year 2011–12 the assessable income is the income received for the year ending 5 April 2012. Similarly for the 2010–11 SA form, the income declared is that received in the year ended 5 April 2011.

9.1.3 Date of receipt

Interest is regarded as received when it is credited to the account. Occasionally, cases arise where an individual is required to make a deposit with a bank as a condition of the bank advancing money to a company. In some situations, he or she is precluded from making withdrawals from the deposit account as long as the company's borrowings are outstanding. The courts have held that an individual who has a deposit account subject to such a block may nevertheless be taxed on interest credited to that account. Furthermore, there is no relief if he or she never receives the interest because the company goes into liquidation and the bank appropriates the money outstanding to his or her credit on the deposit account.

9.1.4 Minor children's accounts

A parent who gifts capital to his or her unmarried, minor, child's account is generally charged tax on interest credited to it, unless the total income from that gift does not exceed £100 (see 33.5.4 on aggregation of minor children's income in general).

9.1.5 Rate of tax on income from savings

All interest income counts as income from savings. Tax is charged at 20% unless the recipient is liable for the 40% or 50% higher rates or is only liable for tax at the lower rate.

Example

	£

B received untaxed interest of £15,000 in the year ended 5 April 2011. She is single and has other income of £12,000, so she is not subject to higher rate tax. She will pay tax on the interest as follows:

	£
Non-savings income	12,000
Savings income	15,000
	27,000
Less: allowance	(7,475)
	19,525
Basic rate tax on £19,525 @ 20%	3,905.00
Less:	
Basic rate tax deducted at source	3,000.00
£15,000 @ 20%	
Tax due	905.00

9.1.6 Holocaust victims' bank accounts: compensation

Compensation paid by banks on dormant accounts opened by Holocaust victims and frozen during World War II is exempt from tax. Up to 1995–96, ESC A100 applied; following that s 756A ITTOIA 2005 was introduced in FA 2006, and is treated as having had effect from 1996–97.

9.2 OTHER INTEREST INCOME

9.2.1 Interest payable by a solicitor

Interest may be received without deduction of tax from client's accounts held by a firm of solicitors or accountants. Such income is taxed under s 369 ITTOIA 2005.

9.2.2 Interest receivable on compulsory purchase monies

Where a property is the subject of a compulsory purchase order (CPO) that goes to appeal, and the amount payable is increased, interest is generally payable on the increase. This is regarded as income for the year in which the entitlement arises, ie when the CPO appeal is settled by agreement or on appeal and the interest is received. This principle is not affected by the fact that the interest may have accrued over several years and may be calculated using six-monthly rests.

9.2.3 Certificates of tax deposit

Interest is credited to an individual who has invested in certificates of tax deposit that are either applied to cover tax payable by assessments or are encashed. The interest is taxable and is income for the year of receipt.

9.2.4 Exempt interest

Interest paid by HMRC on over-payments of tax (called 'repayment supplement') is not subject to tax for individuals. However, interest paid by Customs in respect of official error is taxable.

9.2.5 Interest awarded by the courts

This may be exempt. The treatment turns on whether the court order or arbitration award provides for payment of interest as such (taxable) or is merely an element taken into account in arriving at the amount to be awarded (which is capital and not taxable income).

Where an investor receives compensation for being mis-sold an investment, part of what he or she receives may be interest (see *Tax Bulletin 72* August 2004).

9.3 LOANS TO INDIVIDUALS AND OTHER PRIVATE LOANS

Interest on a private loan to an individual or trust is generally received without deduction of tax. Interest paid by cheque is received when the sum is credited to the recipient's account, not when the cheque is received.

Interest is not assessable where an individual waives the interest before it falls due for payment, provided he or she receives no consideration for the waiver.

9.4 GILTS AND LOAN STOCKS

Interest payments on British Government Securities ('gilts') will usually be received gross, although this must be requested where interest has previously been received net. There are two exceptions:

(1) Interest on 3½% War Loan is always paid without deduction.
(2) Where interest is paid on all other gilts interest is also automatically paid without deduction unless the holder sends a request to Computershare Investor Services plc for the interest to be taxed at source.

Interest payments on loan stocks issued by companies are normally subject to deduction of tax at source. Again, interest from gilts and loan stocks is regarded as income from savings and so qualifies for the 20% rate (see 9.1.5).

INTEREST RECEIVED NET OF TAX

9.5 RATE OF TAX DEDUCTED AT SOURCE
(Chapters 2 and 15, Part 15 ITA 2007)

Interest payments made by UK banks and building societies are normally subject to deduction of tax at source (for exceptions see 9.1.1).

Interest paid on local authority loan stocks and company loan stocks and debentures is subject to deduction of tax, as indeed is all interest paid by UK companies to persons other than group companies. Because such income is income from savings, tax is deducted at 20%.

Certain unit trusts that invest only in bank deposits or gilts are treated as 'transparent' so that distributions of income are treated as interest rather than dividends. Once again, 20% tax is withheld at source.

INTEREST-TYPE INCOME

9.6 ACCRUED INCOME SCHEME
(Part 12 ITA 2007)

References are given below to specific sections, but in order to fully understand the taxation of accrued income, the whole of Part 12 ITA 2007 will need to be considered, as in many cases a concept is now dealt with across five or six different – and non-consecutive – sections of the legislation.

9.6.1 Introduction

An individual who sells a gilt or fixed-interest loan stock may sell either cum- or ex-interest. In the former case, the buyer receives the next interest payment; in the latter, the seller receives the next interest payment even though it is paid after he or she has sold the gilt or loan stock. In practice, gilts, etc, are quoted on an ex-interest basis from six weeks or so before interest is due for payment.

The price at which a gilt or loan stock is sold generally reflects an adjustment for accrued interest. For example, if a gilt pays interest every six months, a person who sells at the end of month 4 will receive a price that reflects four months' accrued interest. Conversely, a person who sells at the end of month 5 would normally sell on an ex-interest basis and the purchaser would take a deduction for one month's interest (as the seller would receive this).

9.6.2 Accrued income taxable

The accrued income scheme may apply where the nominal value of gilts or loan stocks held at any point in the year exceeds £5,000. It brings into charge the interest credited to sellers of gilts and loan stocks. The interest deemed to accrue on a daily basis is treated for tax purposes as if it had been received by the seller. The amount of any adjustments in the other direction (interest received but not earned over the period of ownership) is deducted and the net amount charged to tax on the CY basis.

Example

C subscribes £30,000 for a new Government Stock, 4.5% Treasury Stock 2042 issued on 1 August 2011. He holds the stock for 86 days and then sells it to D, who holds the stock at 1 February 2012 when the first six months' interest is payable. C will be assessable for income tax purposes on £317, ie $^{86}/_{183}$ × £675 (the half-yearly interest payable on the stock). D will be entitled to a deduction of the same amount in computing his taxable income. His position will therefore be as follows:

	£
D receives six months' interest of	675
He or she deducts 'rebate interest'	317
Taxable income	358

9.6.3 Types of securities within accrued income scheme

(s 619 ITA 2007)

The scheme applies to acquisitions and disposals of virtually all types of fixed interest securities by UK-resident individuals. The securities must be loan stock and not shares, but the scheme may apply to foreign securities as well as to UK loan stocks.

Savings certificates, certificates of deposit and zero coupon bonds are excluded. Bills of exchange and Treasury bills are not regarded as securities because they are within the definition of certificates of deposit (see 9.2.3), which are also excluded.

9.6.4 Types of disposal that may be caught

(s 620 ITA 2007)

The scheme applies to transfers. This term is widely defined in ITA 2007 and includes:

(1) a sale (s 620(1)(a));
(2) an exchange (s 620(1)(a)) or a conversion of securities (s 620(1)(b));
(3) a gift (s 620(1)(a));
(4) any transfer other than under (1)–(3) above (s 620(1)(b));
(5) a change in the true ownership where a person entitled to securities becomes a trustee in relation to them (s 651).

9.6.5 Year of assessment

(s 617 ITA 2007)

The assessment is made for the tax year in which the interest period ends, ie if a loan stock pays interest on 30 April, a disposal of the stock on a cum-interest basis on 5 April 2011 produces taxable income for 2011–12.

9.6.6 Income from savings

Amounts of accrued income taxed under ITTOIA 2005 count as income from savings (see 9.1.5).

9.6.7 Calculation of accrued amount and rebate amount

(s 628 ITA 2007)

Where transactions go through the London Stock Exchange, the accrued and rebate amounts are calculated by the broker and appear on the contract note. Where the transaction does not go through the market, the calculation is made in the same way.

If there is more than one transaction in 'securities of the same kind', the accrued and rebate amounts can be netted off. This term is interpreted strictly: £5,000 4.75% Treasury Stock 2020 is 'of the same kind' as £10,000 4.75% Treasury Stock 2020, but is not 'of the same kind' as some other issue of Treasury stock.

Separate calculation is necessary of all accrued and rebate amounts. Relief is given for a rebate amount against the next interest received on that security or, if a transfer intervenes, against the accrued amount. Thus it is possible for a rebate amount in one tax year to be set against interest received in the next.

9.7 DEEPLY DISCOUNTED SECURITIES

(s 427 ITTOIA 2005)

9.7.1 Introduction

The legislation may also bring sums deemed to be interest income into charge.

A loan stock may be issued at a discount, or be redeemable at a premium. In either case, the borrower undertakes that when the loan is repaid the borrower will receive more than the amount originally paid on the issue of the stock. A typical situation is where a loan stock is issued at £80 for every £100 nominal and when the loan stock is redeemed the investor is entitled to receive £100. There are no provisions for the payer to deduct tax from the discount.

The discount or premium is charged to tax where the loan stock is within the definition of a deeply discounted security and the company that issues the bond is a UK company. If the issuer is an overseas company, the discount is treated as foreign interest income.

9.7.2 Definition of 'deeply discounted security'

(s 430 ITTOIA 2005)

A loan stock is not a deeply discounted security (DDS) just because it is issued at a discount; it must be issued at a deep discount. A discount is regarded as a deep discount only where it exceeds 0.5% for every year of the loan stock's intended life (up to a maximum of 30), or where the discount exceeds 15% in total.

The following cannot be deeply discounted securities (s 432):

- shares in a company;
- gilt-edged securities that are not strips;
- life assurance policies;
- capital redemption policies.
- securities (which might otherwise be DDS) issued under the same prospectus where the preponderance of the securities so issued are not DDS; and
- 'excluded indexed securities'.

Examples – Deeply discounted security

> (1) A five-year loan stock is issued at £95 for every £100 nominal. This is a deeply discounted security because the discount exceeds 0.5% pa.
> (2) A 35-year loan stock is issued at £80 for every £100 nominal. This is a deeply discounted security, even though the discount is less than 0.5% pa, because it exceeds 15% in total.

9.7.3 Events that give rise to a tax charge

(ss 437–439 ITTOIA 2005)

A disposal of a deeply discounted security can give rise to a tax charge. The whole of the profit is taxable as if it were interest.

Example – Disposal of deep discount security

> A bond is issued at £82, redeemable at £100 after two years. This reflects a compound interest rate of approximately 10.5% since $82 \times \left(\frac{110.5}{100}\right)^2 = 100$. If the holder sells for £93 after 12 months, he or she will be assessed on the difference between £82 and £93, ie £11. If the purchaser holds the bond until it is redeemed in Year 2 he or she will be chargeable on the redemption profit of £18 as income for that year.

9.7.4 Stripped gilts

(ss 443–452, 452A–452G and 453–456 ITTOIA 2005)

There is one exception to the general rule that individuals and trustees are taxed on discounted securities only when a disposal takes place. Where a stripped gilt is held, it is necessary to revalue it at the end of each tax year and the owner must pay tax on any increase in value as if it were income. These rules were extended with effect from 27 March 2003 so that they now also apply to strips of non-UK government securities.

9.7.5 Income from savings

Discounts taxed as interest-type income count as income from savings (see 9.1.5).

9.7.6 Losses

Loss relief was withdrawn by FA 2003 in relation to most losses realised on disposals of DDS made on or after 27 March 2003. Loss relief may still be available for quoted securities acquired before that date.

DIVIDENDS FROM UK COMPANIES

9.8 DIVIDENDS

9.8.1 Taxable for year in which they fall due for payment

(ss 383–385 ITTOIA 2005)

The dividends that need to be reported on a tax return, and that are income for a tax year, are the dividends that were due for payment in the year. If you have shares in a company that declares a dividend that is payable on 5 April 2012, you must report the dividend as 2011–12 income. This is not affected by the fact that you may not receive the dividend payment until early in the next tax year.

The period for which the dividend is paid is also not relevant. A final dividend for a company's year that ended on 31 December 2010 would be income for 2011–12 if it was paid in, say, June 2011.

Dividends from UK companies carry a tax credit (see 9.8.2).

9.8.2 Rate of tax on dividends received from UK companies

A shareholder is entitled to a tax credit of one-ninth of the dividend. This credit is non-refundable.

An individual whose income is within the basic rate band does not have to pay any additional tax on UK dividends; the tax credit is treated as covering his or her liability. Higher rate taxpayers pay a special 32.5% rate on dividends and are able to set the tax credit against this. In practice, this means that the effective rate of higher rate tax is 25% of the actual dividend receipt. Additional rate taxpayers pay tax on dividends falling within the additional rate band at a rate of 42.5%. The effect of this is that the effective dividend rate increases from 25% to 36.11%.

9.8.3 Dividends paid by unit trusts

Dividends from unit trusts are normally treated in the same way as dividends from companies except in regard to 'equalisation'. This is an amount paid to holders of units who have acquired them since the last dividend was paid. The equalisation payment is not taxable as income but is instead treated as a return of capital.

Unit trusts that invest in gilts and corporate bonds are treated differently (see 9.5).

9.8.4 Dividends paid by Real Estate Investment Trusts

REIT distributions should not be included in the figure entered in a tax return for UK dividends because they are instead treated as rental income.

Basic rate tax is withheld at source and this tax can be reclaimed by recipients who are not liable for tax, or who are 10% taxpayers (ie their non-savings income is less than £10,035).

9.8.5 Stock dividends

(s 409 ITTOIA 2005)

A company may make a 'scrip' or bonus issue so that shareholders receive new shares in proportion to their existing shareholdings. This is not taxable income because in reality all that has happened is that the company has subdivided its share capital by issuing new shares.

In contrast to this, a company may offer shareholders the choice between a cash dividend and additional shares to a similar value. This is called a 'stock dividend' and is taxable income.

'Enhanced scrip dividends' are a special type of stock dividend where the company offers a premium to shareholders who take stock rather than cash and makes prior arrangements to enable the shareholders to dispose of the shares that they have acquired by taking the stock alternative.

9.8.6 How stock dividends are assessed

(SP A8 and s 412 ITTOIA 2005)

A shareholder who accepts extra shares in lieu of a cash dividend is normally treated as if he or she had received a dividend equal to the cash that he or she could have taken. Tax is deemed to have been paid at 10%.

A slightly different treatment applies where the value of the shares taken as the stock dividend differs from the cash dividend by 15% or more. In such a case, the shareholder is deemed to have received a dividend equal to the shares' value at the date of issue. The shareholder may therefore be required to pay higher rate tax on the 'grossed up' value of the dividend or the shares. However, HMRC has said it is normally prepared to use the amount of the cash dividend when the difference between the market value of the share capital and the cash dividend is no more than one or two percentage points greater than 15%.

Example – Taxation of dividends

E is a 40% taxpayer. He was entitled to a dividend of £2,100 or extra shares in X plc. He took the shares. If the shares were worth £1,900, he will nevertheless be charged higher rate tax on £2,100 (the dividend he could have taken) plus an amount equal to the tax credit; the amount charged to higher rate tax for 2011–12 is £2,333 (£2,100 grossed up for the 10% tax credit).

If the shares were worth £2,600 when they were issued, he would be charged higher rate tax on £2,600 'grossed up', ie £2,889.

9.8.7 Consequences for CGT of taking a stock dividend

In the example in 9.8.6, *E*'s acquisition value for CGT purposes of the shares that he acquires through the stock dividend is the market value of the shares before grossing up. Where the market value rule does not apply, the base cost for CGT is the cash that would have been received had the dividend been taken (£2,100 above) before the inclusion of the 10% notional tax credit.

9.8.8 Demerger dividends

(ss 1075–1080 CTA 2010)

A dividend may take the form of an issue of shares formerly held by the company in a subsidiary. Where the necessary HMRC clearances have been obtained, such a dividend is treated as capital and not as taxable income. The documentation issued by the company normally states that clearance has been obtained from HMRC and that the demerger is an exempt distribution.

9.8.9 Other dividend income

See 9.9 on sundry receipts from UK companies that are treated as distributions. See also 9.10.1 on dividends paid by foreign companies that are treated as income from savings.

9.9 SUNDRY RECEIPTS TREATED AS DIVIDENDS

9.9.1 Deemed dividends

(s 1000 CTA 2010)

There are various transactions that can count as a distribution, particularly where a person holds shares in a close company (see 18.14). From the recipient's point of view, a distribution is for all practical purposes the same as a dividend.

9.9.2 Interest at more than commercial rate

(s 1000E CTA 2010)

Interest paid to a shareholder may constitute a distribution in so far as it exceeds a normal commercial rate.

9.9.3 Issue of redeemable shares

(s 1000C CTA 2010)

An issue to shareholders of redeemable preference shares (or other redeemable shares) counts as a distribution. The redeemable shares' value at the date they are issued is treated as if it were a dividend paid in cash at that time. This rule does not apply where the redeemable shares are issued for new consideration.

9.9.4 Bonus issue following repayment of share capital

(s 1000H CTA 2010)

Where a company has repaid share capital in the past, a subsequent bonus issue is treated as a dividend paid to the shareholders who receive the bonus shares. These shareholders may not be the same people whose shares were previously bought back by the company, but this does not make any difference to the way in which the current shareholders are taxed on receipt of a bonus issue of shares in these circumstances.

9.9.5 Benefits-in-kind provided to shareholders

(ss 1000(2), 1064 CTA 2010)

Where shareholders in a close company (see 18.14) are provided with benefits-in-kind, they may be assessed as employment income. If the shareholders are not employed by the company, it is not possible for HMRC to assess benefits-in-kind in this way. In these circumstances, the company may be deemed to have made a distribution equal to the value of the benefits-in-kind concerned.

9.9.6 Assets transferred by or to close company

(s 1020 CTA 2010)

A deemed distribution may arise where assets are transferred from the members of a company to the company at a price that exceeds their market value, or company assets are transferred to shareholders at a price that is less than market value.

9.9.7 Purchase by company of its own shares

(ss 1033–1043 CTA 2010)

The general rule is that where a company buys back its shares, the amount paid by the company is treated as a distribution in so far as it exceeds the shares' original issue price, except as noted below (see 9.9.8).

The amount treated as a distribution is not affected by the shares' value at the time they were acquired by an individual. Consequently, where a person has acquired shares by inheritance or bought them from an existing shareholder, his or her acquisition value may exceed the original issue price (ie the amount paid to the company in return for the shares being issued). In the event of a purchase of own shares by a company, it is the issue price that is important.

Example – Purchase by company of own shares

> F acquires 1,000 shares in Y Ltd for £10,000. The shares were originally issued at their par value of £1 per share. It subsequently transpires that F cannot get on with the company's directors. If her shares are bought back by the company at £9 per share, F is deemed to have received a distribution of £8,000, even though she has actually made a capital loss.

9.9.8 Relief under ss 1033–1043 CTA 2010

In certain circumstances it may be possible for a company to purchase its own shares without the transaction being treated as giving rise to a distribution. Clearance must be obtained from HMRC that the purchase of own shares is for the benefit of the company's trade. The conditions that must be satisfied are:

- the company is an unquoted trading company or the unquoted holding company of a trading group, and
- the redemption, repayment or purchase is made wholly or mainly for the purpose of benefiting a trade carried on by the company or any of its 75% subsidiaries,
- it does not form part of a scheme or arrangement, one of the main purposes of which is to enable the owner of the shares to participate in the profits of the company without receiving a dividend, or the avoidance of tax, and the other requirements set out in ss 1034–1043 (so far as applicable) are met.

Alternatively, s 1033 may apply where shares are being bought back within two years of the shareholder's death and the reason for this is that the personal representatives would not otherwise be able to pay the IHT due on the estate.

OVERSEAS INTEREST AND DIVIDEND INCOME

9.10 FOREIGN INTEREST AND DIVIDENDS

Interest on bonds issued by overseas governments or companies is received without deduction of UK tax.

9.10.1 Foreign interest and dividends

Prior to the enactment of ITTOIA 2005, non-UK income was generally assessable under Schedule D, Cases IV and V. ITTOIA 2005 takes a different approach to charging such income to tax, so that for 2005–06 onwards each type of non-UK income previously within Case IV or V is charged to tax under the provisions charging the equivalent type of UK income.

9.10.2 How the taxable amount is computed

Income is taxed on the CY basis.

A point to watch with all foreign investments is that income tax is charged on the interest credited or dividends received, without reference to any exchange gain or loss on the money deposited or invested.

Tax notes

With foreign investments, income tax is charged on the interest credited or dividends received, without taking into account any exchange gain or loss.

Example – Foreign currency deposit account

In June 2011, F deposited £10,000 with a foreign bank. At the then exchange rate of £1 = 20 units of foreign currency, that sum was credited as 200,000 units. In June 2012, when the exchange rate was £1 = 25 units, interest of 30,000 units was credited to the account. In June 2013, F closes the account, receiving back her original capital, the interest credited in June 2012 and a further 20,000 foreign currency units as interest to close. By then the exchange rate was £1 = 30 units, so the sterling equivalent of the 250,000 units was only £8,333.

In commercial terms, F has suffered a loss of £1,667, but for tax purposes she received interest of £1,200 in June 2012 (30,000 units at £1 = 25) and £667 in June 2013 (20,000 units at £1 = 30) and income tax must be paid on that interest. She has also made a capital loss of £3,534, calculated as follows:

			£	£
Proceeds of	250,000	Units		8,333
	200,000	units cost (June 2011)	10,000	
	30,000	units cost (June 2012)	1,200	
	20,000	units cost (June 2013)	667	
Capital loss				11,867
				(3,534)

> Unfortunately, that capital loss may only be used by set-off against capital
> gains on the disposal of other assets. If *F* has no such gains, she cannot
> utilise the loss and so has paid tax on a profit of £1,867 when she has in fact
> made an overall loss of £1,667.

9.10.3 Double tax relief

Relief may be claimed for foreign tax withheld from the interest or
dividends. This credit will be restricted to the amount of UK tax due on the
income source, and if the foreign tax does not meet the full amount of tax
due this shortfall will be payable.

Example – Relief by credit

> *G* has UK earnings of £17,500 in 2011–12 and foreign income from property
> of £3,000 on which foreign tax of £500 has been paid. She is entitled to a
> personal allowance of £7,475.
>
> | | | £ | |
> |---|---|---|---|
> | (a) | Tax on total income | | |
> | | Earnings | 17,500 | |
> | | Income from property | 3,000 | (foreign tax £500) |
> | | | 20,500 | |
> | | Personal allowance | 7,475 | |
> | | Taxable income | 13,025 | |
> | | Tax on £13,025 @ 20% | 2,605.00 | |
> | (b) | Tax on total income less foreign income | | £ |
> | | Earnings | | 17,500 |
> | | Personal allowance | | 7,475 |
> | | Taxable income | | 10,025 |
> | | Tax on £10,025 @ 20% | | 2,005.00 |
>
> The difference in tax between (a) and (b) is £600. The foreign tax is less
> than this and the full credit of £500 is available against the UK tax payable.
> If the foreign tax had been £750, the credit would be limited to £600 and the
> balance of £150 would be unrelieved.

9.10.4 Retention tax

Countries in the EU, and most offshore territories, introduced a system
during 2005 whereby a person who is not resident there and who is in
receipt of interest must either agree to his or her identity being revealed to
the revenue authorities of the country where he or she resides or have 20%

(15% to 30 June 2008) retention tax withheld at source. The retention tax is then paid over to the revenue authority of the country in which the person is resident but without the person's identity being disclosed.

The fact that interest has suffered retention tax does not alter the person's obligation to include the income on his or her tax return. Conversely, a person is allowed a credit for tax withheld in this way. If, exceptionally, he or she is not liable for the 20% tax, HMRC will repay this.

9.10.5 Foreign dividends not treated as savings income for 2008–09 onwards

Remittance basis users who bring foreign dividends into the UK will be taxed at 40% or 50% and not at the 32.5% or 42.5% rates. See the 2008–09 *Tax Handbook* at 9.10.6–9.10.7 for the situation regarding 2007–08 and earlier years.

9.10.6 Stock dividends and other peculiarities

(s 410 ITTOIA 2005)

As explained in 9.8.5, an investor who opts to take a stock dividend (ie additional shares in lieu of a cash dividend) from a UK company is taxed as if he or she had received an equivalent amount in cash. This rule does not apply where a non-UK resident company declares a stock dividend.

A higher or additional rate taxpayer offered the choice between a stock and a cash dividend is therefore usually better off taking the stock dividend. However, this assumes that the additional shares offered are worth at least as much as the cash option and that they are readily saleable. As always, the 'tax-saving' tail must not be allowed to wag the 'sensible investment policy' dog. Moreover, in one court case it was suggested that, if stock dividends are taken year after year, and the shares so obtained are sold to provide the shareholder with an income, then income tax may be charged on that income. HMRC is unlikely to take this view unless a substantial amount of money is at stake.

In some situations, payments by an overseas company may escape income tax where an equivalent payment by a UK company would be taxable as a dividend. The most common situation where this occurs is where a payment by an overseas company is treated under the relevant foreign law as a partial return of the shareholders' original investment. Such distributions are treated as capital even though a similar payment by a UK company would be treated as taxable income. This is an area where you will need to take professional advice.

9.10.7 Reporting untaxed income from abroad

If you have foreign dividends or interest, you will need to tick the box at Q5 on the second page of your tax return and complete a special schedule for foreign income.

9.10.8 Taxation of foreign dividends from 6 April 2008

Since 6 April 2008, owners of foreign shares have been entitled to a non-repayable tax credit of one-ninth of the dividend to align the treatment with that of dividends paid by UK companies. The notional tax credit covers any basic rate liability. Higher, or additional, rate taxpayers are charged at a rate of 32.5% or 42.5% respectively on the dividend and tax credit in the same way as if they had received a UK dividend.

This treatment did not apply where an individual owned 10% or more of the shares in the foreign company but from 22 April 2009, the availability of tax credits was extended to include offshore funds (provided that distributions from the fund are not treated as interest) and to some investors with shareholdings of 10% or more (see 9.10.9 below).

9.10.9 Taxation of foreign dividends from 22 April 2009

From 22 April 2009, however, a non-repayable tax credit is available to individuals on *all* dividends from non-UK companies. Where the recipient has a shareholding of 10% or more, the company must be resident in a 'qualifying territory' (ie a territory which has agreed a double taxation agreement with the UK with a non-discrimination article).

Also from 22 April 2009, all dividends from offshore funds will attract the non-repayable tax credit provided the fund concerned is largely invested in equities. However, where the fund is substantially invested in interest bearing assets, individuals in receipt of distributions from such funds will be treated as having received interest instead.

EXCHANGE-TRADED FUNDS

9.11 TAX TREATMENT OF EXCHANGE-TRADED FUNDS

These are a type of collective investment scheme that have become increasingly popular. An investor in such a fund gets an income and capital return that exactly matches the index chosen, whether that be the FTSE 100 share index, an index based on an overseas stock exchange or an index that reflects all the Investment Grade $ Corporate Bonds etc. Furthermore, the charges are usually rather less than those charged by managers of tracker unit trusts.

The tax treatment will generally follow the legal structure. Many exchange-traded funds are Luxembourg or Irish open-ended companies. As such, distributions of income are normally treated as dividends. No tax will normally be withheld from such dividends.

However, from 22 April 2009, distributions from exchange-traded funds invested in loan stocks may be treated as interest in the hands of an investor.

The realisation of an investment in an exchange-traded fund will give rise to a capital gain or loss. Bear in mind that an investor in an exchange-traded fund which is invested in qualifying corporate bonds may have a capital gain on realising his or her investment whereas no capital gain would have arisen if he or she had realised direct investments in such bonds.

10

OTHER INCOME

This chapter deals with other income received that will need to be reported on your tax return but does not fall easily into the 'fill the box category' of more standard investments and may require the filing of supporting SA schedules. Most of the various types of income from sources covered in this chapter are received without deduction of tax at source. The exceptions where basic tax rate will generally be deducted are covered at 10.10.

This chapter contains the following sections:

Untaxed income from abroad

(1) Foreign real estate income
(2) Alimony and maintenance payments
(3) Investment in overseas partnerships
(4) Double tax relief
(5) Foreign pensions

Miscellaneous investment income

(6) Sale of certificates of deposit
(7) Gains from roll-up, and other offshore, funds

Miscellaneous income

(8) Miscellaneous income
(9) Taxation of commission, cashbacks and discounts

Income received net of tax

(10) Annuities, trust income, etc

UNTAXED INCOME FROM ABROAD

10.1 FOREIGN REAL ESTATE INCOME

(s 265 ITTOIA 2005)

It is not unusual for a UK resident to have bought – or inherited – a villa or flat abroad. It is less usual to own commercial premises, but the tax rules are the same. In addition, the same rules apply to properties bought under 'timeshare' arrangements.

> **Tax notes**
>
> If you have untaxed income from abroad, a special schedule of your SA tax return must be completed. Advice on which form needs to be completed can be obtained by calling the number on the front of your tax form or by consulting a practising tax accountant.

10.1.1 How income is computed

In calculating the assessable rent, the landlord may deduct expenses paid: for example, repairs, redecoration, insurance, maid service, gardening, management fees and advertising. If the landlord sometimes uses the property him or herself, then an apportionment of these expenses must be made in the same way as for a UK property (see 8.2).

There are three important differences between the tax treatment of rent from real property in the UK and rent from property abroad:

(1) The 'rent-a-room' scheme (see 8.4) applies only to residential properties in the UK; this exemption cannot be claimed against rents from an overseas property.
(2) The special rules allowing the provision of furnished holiday accommodation to be treated as a trade (see 8.5) apply only where the relevant property is situated in the EEA.
(3) If the rental income statement for an overseas property shows a deficit for a year (ie if expenses excluding interest paid exceed rent received), that deficit may be carried forward and deducted from the rent received in respect of the same property in the next year (and the deduction may be rolled forward indefinitely until there is rental income against which it can be set). However, no other form of loss relief is available. In particular, the deficit may not be set against rents received from other properties, whether in the UK or abroad. Interest payments can be deducted even if the interest is paid overseas.

10.1.2 Accounts

In the past, rental income statements should have been drawn up to 5 April, but in practice HMRC often accepted statements drawn up to any convenient date. For example, the rental statement for the calendar year will often have been taken as the measure of the income for the tax year. This is no longer acceptable and it is necessary to report the income that has actually arisen in the tax year ie on a receipts rather than a cash basis.

One possible complication is that income may be received, and expenses incurred, in either UK or local currency. In practice, HMRC accepts any reasonable basis of currency conversion. For example, if a local agent collects the rents, disburses local expenses and remits a net sum to the landlord, that net amount may be converted at the spot rate for the day it was remitted. However, HMRC expects the same basis of conversion to be retained from one year to the next.

Tax notes

For 2009–10 onwards, properties in the European Economic Area which are let as furnished holiday accommodation may qualify for the same reliefs as apply to UK properties. During 2010–11, it may also have been possible to claim (by the applicable deadlines) these reliefs for years back to 2006–07. For 2007–08 claims, the cut-off will be 5 April 2012.

10.2 ALIMONY AND MAINTENANCE PAYMENTS

(s 727 ITTOIA 2005)

A UK resident may receive maintenance or alimony payments from a spouse, former spouse or civil partner, or a parent resident abroad. This income is almost always exempt from tax.

10.3 INVESTMENT IN OVERSEAS PARTNERSHIPS

(s 95 ITA 2007)

A UK resident may be a sleeping partner in a business carried on abroad. For example, an individual might provide the finance for his or her son to set up in business abroad in return for a share of the profits. It may be difficult to tell whether the parent has become a sleeping partner in the son's business or has made a loan at interest to the son. If the parent is entitled to a stated proportion of profits (say, one-quarter), then he or she is certainly a sleeping partner; if he or she is entitled to a fixed annual sum, he or she may be a sleeping partner or may simply have made a loan. In practice, since both interest and a sleeping partner's profit share are taxed in the same way, it will not normally be necessary to decide this.

The important question is whether the UK resident is a sleeping or an active partner. If he or she is an active partner, the partnership business is likely to be carried on at least partly within the UK, in which case complex questions arise that are outside the scope of this book and specialist advice should be sought.

If the sleeping partner is entitled to a fixed sum, at annual or other intervals, and that sum is stated in a foreign currency, then each instalment must, for tax purposes, be converted into sterling at the spot rate for the date it falls due. If he or she is entitled to a stated proportion of profits, and the business accounts are prepared in a foreign currency, the appropriate profit figure must be converted into sterling at the spot rate for the last day of the accounting period. If the sleeping partner is obliged to bear a share of a trading loss, that loss may be relieved against overseas trading and pension income, but not against overseas investment income or any UK income. In most cases, therefore, it is relieved by deducting the loss amount from the partnership profit share assessable for a later year.

10.4 DOUBLE TAX RELIEF

(s 18 TIOPA 2010)

Foreign tax paid can be deducted from the UK tax charged on the same income.

Example – Double tax relief

D, a basic rate taxpayer, receives an interest payment of £1,000 from abroad, on which the foreign tax is £150. The UK tax position is:

	£
Gross interest	1,000
Foreign tax deducted or paid	(150)
Net receipt	850
UK tax at 20% of £1,000	200
Less: foreign tax paid	(150)
UK tax to be paid	50
After-tax income	800

If *D* were liable for tax at only 10%, the foreign tax would bring his UK tax liability down to nil, but he would not be entitled to reclaim the difference of £50.

10.4.1 An important practical point

Relief for overseas tax is not given unless the individual can prove that he or she has indeed paid the tax. It is not sufficient simply to demonstrate that tax is payable under foreign law: the claimant must be able to show that he or she has indeed paid that tax by producing an official receipt or tax deduction certificate. In some jurisdictions it can be a lengthy and difficult process to obtain such certificates.

10.4.2 **Foreign tax adjustments**

HMRC must be notified if an amount of foreign tax paid is later adjusted and this means that too much credit has been allowed as double taxation relief. Failure to notify HMRC within one year of an adjustment results in a taxpayer becoming liable to a penalty (not exceeding the tax underpaid) because of the claim that has proved to be excessive.

If a foreign tax adjustment means that you have not claimed enough you are under no statutory duty to report this, but it is clearly in your own interests to do so.

10.5 **FOREIGN PENSIONS**

(s 573 ITEPA 2003)

Certain foreign pensions are taxable as foreign income:

- pensions paid by a person outside the UK;
- pensions paid on behalf of a person outside the UK;
- voluntary pensions paid by a person outside the UK.

Foreign pensions are taxed as follows:

(a) pensioner is resident, ordinarily resident and domiciled in the UK – 90% of the pension is charged to tax;
(b) pensioner is resident but not ordinarily resident in the UK – the pension is assessed on the remittance basis by reference to sums brought into the UK;
(c) pensioner is resident and ordinarily resident, but not domiciled, in the UK – the pension will automatically have been taxed on the remittance basis up to 2007–08 and may be assessed on the remittance basis in 2008–09 and subsequent years if the individual makes a claim to be taxed on that basis (and pays the £30,000 remittance basis charge if applicable).

Foreign pensions are taxed on the CY basis.

Nazi compensation pensions

(s 642 ITEPA 2003)

Annuities and premiums paid under German or Austrian law to victims of Nazi persecution are exempt from income tax. These are pensions paid because of serious damage to the individual's health; they are also exempt from tax in Germany and Austria.

In addition, some payments to victims or their heirs from dormant bank accounts are also exempted from tax.

MISCELLANEOUS INVESTMENT INCOME

10.6 SALE OF CERTIFICATES OF DEPOSIT

(s 551 ITTOIA 2005)

A certificate of deposit is a document that entitles the holder to receive the amount held on deposit. An owner of such a deposit can assign it to someone else. Where this is done for valuable consideration, the profit is taxable as income.

At one time it was possible to avoid having taxable income by assigning ownership of a deposit without there being a certificate of deposit. Profits on such transactions are now also caught as income taxable under s 551. They are not treated as income from savings. This income should be reported on the SA form as part of the answer to Q15 on page 3.

10.7 GAINS FROM ROLL-UP, AND OTHER OFFSHORE, FUNDS

(Offshore Funds (Tax) Regulations 2009)

The rules relating to the treatment of UK investors in offshore funds have been amended on several occasions over the years since they were first introduced in 1984, and the regime has been modernised by legislation contained within FA 2008 (by provisions inserted in FA 2009), supplemented by regulations contained within the Offshore Funds (Tax) Regulations 2009. The legislation in ss 757–763 ICTA 1988 was repealed at the time the new legislation took effect, although there are certain transitional arrangements.

The new regime has effect for the purposes of income tax for the tax year 2009–10 and subsequent tax years, and for distributions made on or after 1 December 2009; and for the purposes of corporation tax on income, for accounting periods ending on or after 1 December 2009.

The purpose of both the original and the replacement offshore funds tax regimes remains the same, and they work by charging realisations of an interest in an offshore fund investment to tax as income rather than as chargeable gains, unless certain conditions are met.

The previous tax regime for UK investors in offshore funds, worked on the basis that if an offshore fund did not distribute at least 85% of its income then, on disposal of interests in the fund, UK investors would be charged to tax on income rather than on chargeable gains. This was to prevent any roll-up of income in an offshore fund being subject only to tax on chargeable gains rather than being charged to tax as income, as would be the case for income arising on investments in UK funds.

The 2009 regime moves away from the requirement that income is distributed, to a basis where the CGT treatment will instead apply if an offshore fund's income is reported to UK investors in such a way that UK investors are charged to tax on their share of the 'reported income' of the fund, regardless of whether that income is distributed to them or accumulated in the fund. Funds will either be 'reporting funds' or 'non-reporting funds'.

The definition contained within s 40A FA 2008, inserted by FA 2009, detaches the tax definition of an offshore fund from the regulatory definition and instead bases the tax definition on certain characteristics of the fund.

The key features of the new regime for offshore funds rules include:

- a new tax definition of an offshore fund;
- a facility for an advance election to be a 'reporting fund';
- a requirement (for reporting funds) to report fund income to UK investors rather than the requirement to actually distribute the income;
- the consideration of only one 'layer' of funds for reporting funds;
- revised rules to deal with breaches of conditions, in particular to deal with occasions of minor or inadvertent breaches; and
- treating investments in non-reporting funds in the same way as under the old regime for investments in non-distributing funds.

Reporting funds

UK investors must make a return of their income to include both the actual distributions received, as well as the 'reported income' (ie their proportionate share of the fund's reportable income in excess of the sums distributed). They will be liable to income or corporation tax as appropriate on the total of those sums.

In most cases, providing the fund in question has been a reporting fund for the entire period that an investor has held their interest, then on any subsequent disposal of that interest the investor will be subject to tax on any chargeable gain (or loss) arising, subject to some transitional arrangements.

Non-reporting funds

UK investors in non-reporting funds remain chargeable to income or corporation tax on any distributions the fund actually makes to them. Alternatively, if the fund is transparent for income purposes then the investor will be chargeable to tax on income arising on the underlying investments. On disposal of an interest in a non-reporting fund, UK investors will be subject to tax on any gains arising as if those gains were income – that is, on an 'offshore income gain' (OIG). There are detailed rules relating to the calculation of OIGs and their effect on chargeable gains computations.

10.7.1 Transitional rules and further proposed changes

UK investors who held a material interest in a qualifying fund (ie one that held distributing fund status for all previous periods of account) and who continued to hold an interest in the fund when it became a reporting fund immediately following its last period as a qualifying fund will not be subject to a charge to tax on an OIG on disposal of their interest.

There are also transitional provisions where:

- an investor held a material interest in a qualifying (ie distributing) fund that is also within the new definition of an offshore fund but that does not become a reporting fund;
- an investor held a non-material interest in a non-qualifying (ie non-distributing) fund that is also subsequently within the new definition of an offshore fund applying for interests acquired on or after 1 December 2009; or
- an investor held an interest in a fund that did not come within the previous definition of an offshore fund but does subsequently come within the new definition of an offshore applying for interests obtained on or after 1 December 2009.

Further proposed changes to the regime were announced on 20 December 2010 and 28 February 2011.

Reporting funds

Adjustments are to be made to the calculation of reported income per unit where funds do not operate equalisation. The regulations will also include transitional provisions which will apply the new rules to reports made after they come into force, together with an election not to apply the new rules in respect of any reporting period already ended where the report remains to be made.

Amendments are to be made for offshore funds similar to UK qualified investor schemes considered to be 'equivalent to UK authorised investment funds' (so that those funds can, if they otherwise qualify, access the trading and investment 'white list', with the effect that the rules relating to transactions considered not to be trading can be applied in relation to the computation of reportable income).

Alterations are to be made to the Genuine Diversity of Ownership rule to allow it to apply at sub-fund level (and not just share class) and to permit the investors in a feeder fund to be considered when assessing a Master fund.

There are new rules for calculating the reportable income of a transparent reporting fund. The rules now include a provision to give more certainty to the computation of reportable income in an index tracking fund.

The time limits for application and withdrawal have been extended and the scope of the reporting requirements (to 'relevant' investors) has been clarified.

All offshore funds

There is an exception to the OIG tax charge where non-reporting funds are invested almost entirely in unlisted trading companies and gains arise on the disposal of such non-reporting funds.

Fiscally transparent funds will be outside the scope of legislation which treats holdings in certain funds as loan relationships (for corporate investors). This will have the effect that corporate holders will 'look through' all transparent offshore funds for tax purposes including those that are mainly invested in interest bearing assets. The loan relationships rules will therefore apply directly to the underlying assets where relevant. These changes account for the effect of equalisation arrangements in the calculation of reportable income where an offshore reporting fund operates equalisation arrangements.

The Government introduced these amendments to provide certainty for industry, in line with its commitment to improve tax policy making and the UK tax system's reputation for predictability, stability and simplicity.

It is intended that the transitional provisions will allow reporting funds to have the option of operating the new rules for previous reporting periods where a report has not already been issued.

The new rules also incorporate the following minor amendments to the regulations as follows:

- an amendment to provide for continuity of reported income in a case where s 106A TCGA 1992 applies to a disposal and acquisition covering the end of a reporting period;
- changes to the transitional rules in Schedule 1 to the regulations which widen slightly the ability to apply for distributing fund status in the transitional periods and ensure that the regulations cater for earlier periods. (There is also a correction to the end date for the transitional period as previously announced.)

10.7.2 Gains realised by foreign domiciliaries

A gain from a disposal of an offshore fund by a person of foreign domicile may be taxed on the remittance basis if this is claimed (see 35.12).

> **Tax notes**
>
> From 1 December 2009, investments in qualifying offshore funds will be treated in the same way for capital gains tax purposes as shares or units in unit trusts.

MISCELLANEOUS INCOME

10.8 MISCELLANEOUS INCOME

(ss 261, 575, 579, 609, 614, 687 ITTOIA 2005)

Tax is charged under ITTOIA 2005.

Post-cessation receipts (see 16.4) are charged as miscellaneous income, as are gains from roll-up funds, profits under the accrued income scheme and gains on foreign life policies. Furthermore, where tax is charged under various anti-avoidance provisions (see Chapter 33) the amounts charged to tax are normally miscellaneous income.

In addition, profits from certain 'one-off' or isolated business activities in the nature of a trade have been charged as miscellaneous income. Thus, the following were held by the courts to be this type of income:

- commission for guaranteeing overdrafts;
- underwriting commission on share issues;
- insurance commission;
- receipts for the use of copyright material;
- payments made to the wife of a train robber for their life story;
- profits realised by an 'angel', ie a person who sponsored a play and was entitled to a share of the profits.

Miscellaneous income can be earned income or investment income.

10.8.1 Miscellaneous income losses

(s 872 ITTOIA 2005)

Losses from activities that would be taxed as miscellaneous income can be set against any profits assessable as miscellaneous income, whether or not the profits arise from the same activity. However, they cannot be set against other types of income such as employment income or savings income.

10.9 TAXATION OF COMMISSION, CASHBACKS AND DISCOUNTS

10.9.1 Commission on insurance products, etc

HMRC published SP4/97 on the taxation of commission, cashbacks and discounts, further commenting on this subject in its business income manual; BIM40655 onwards and BIM64600 onwards. HMRC has offered its assurances to the 'ordinary retail customer' that there normally will be no tax liabilities on rebated commissions or discounts. However, the position is more complex with regard to insurance products. SP4/97 states:

Life insurance and personal pensions

Qualifying life insurance policies

36 Where commission in respect of a policy holder's own qualifying life insurance policy is received, netted off or invested, that policy will not be disqualified as a result of entitlement to that commission if the contract under which commission arises is separate from the contract of insurance. In practice, HMRC will not seek to read two contracts as one in a way that would lead to the loss of qualifying policy status.

37 Where a policy holder pays a discounted premium in respect of his or her own policy, the premium payable under the policy will be the discounted premium. It is this amount that must be used for the purposes of establishing whether the relevant qualifying rules are met.

Calculation of chargeable event gains in respect of life policies, capital redemption policies and life annuity contracts

38 Chargeable event gains are computed by reference to the premiums or lump sum consideration paid. The amount paid will be interpreted as follows –
    - where a policy holder pays a gross premium and receives commission in respect of that policy, the chargeable event gain is calculated using the gross amount paid without taking the commission received into account;
    - where an amount of commission is received or due under an enforceable legal right and subsequently invested in the policy, that amount is included as a premium paid when calculating the chargeable event gain (but see 10.9.2 below);
    - where a policy holder nets off commission from an insurer in respect of his or her own policy from the gross amount of premium payable and the commission is not taxable as income on the policy holder, the chargeable event gain is calculated using the net amount paid to the insurer;
    - where a policy holder pays a discounted premium, the chargeable event gain is calculated using the discounted amount of premium paid;
    - where extra value is added to the policy by the insurer (for example by allocation of bonus units), the premium for the purpose of calculating the chargeable event is the amount paid by the policy holder without taking the extra value into account.

Tax relief in respect of personal pension contributions

39 Tax relief for contributions to personal pension schemes is due in respect of 'a contribution paid by an individual'. The amount of the contribution will be interpreted as follows where the contract under which the commission arises is separate from the personal pension scheme contract
    - where a contributor pays a gross contribution and receives commission in respect of that contribution, tax relief is given on the gross amount paid without taking the commission received into account;

- where an amount of commission is received by, or is due under an enforceable legal right to, the contributor and subsequently invested in the personal pension that gave rise to the commission, tax relief is given on that amount;
- where a contributor deducts commission in respect of his or her own pension contribution from the gross amount payable, relief is due on the net amount paid;
- where a contributor pays discounted contributions, tax relief is due on the discounted amount paid;
- where extra value is added to the policy by the insurer (for example by allocation of bonus units), relief is due on the amount paid by the contributor without taking the extra value into account.

40 If commission were to be rebated to the contributor under the same contract as the personal pension contract, this would be an unapprovable benefit (since it would involve leakage of the pension fund to the member) which would jeopardise the tax-approved status of the arrangement.

41 The consequences of paying commission on transfers between tax-approved pension schemes may be different from those outlined if such payment is effectively a benefit not authorised by the rules of the pension scheme.

The statement also encompasses HMRC's two previous press releases by stating that:

(1) other commission rebates to ordinary customers will not be taxed; and
(2) cashbacks offered by banks and building societies as an inducement to take out a mortgage will not be regarded as chargeable to CGT.

Source: HMRC

10.9.2 Limit imposed by FA 2007

Since 21 March 2007, certain commission rebates on insurance bonds (single premium insurance policies) have had to be taken into account in computing chargeable gains on the encashment of the bond. This treatment is required where:

(1) premiums paid to the insurance company exceed £100,000 in a given year; and
(2) the bond is surrendered, matures or is assigned before three tax years have elapsed.

10.9.3 Payments arising from trade or employment

If a cashback is received in the course of either the recipient's business or employment, the cashback may be chargeable as income.

The income tax consequences of the statement of practice are that employees who receive commission arising from, and discounts in connection with, goods, investments or services sold to third parties are assessable regardless of whether the commission is passed on by them to the customer and whether the commission is paid by the employer or anyone else.

HMRC takes the view that PAYE will apply in any situation where the commission, etc falls to be taxed as employment income.

INCOME RECEIVED NET OF TAX

10.10 ANNUITIES, TRUST INCOME, ETC

10.10.1 Annuities

(s 422 ITTOIA 2005)

Annuities paid by an insurance company are dealt with at 28.5. Where an annuity is payable by an individual or a private company, the payer must deduct tax at the 20% basic rate.

Example – Annuity income received net of basic rate tax: 2011–12

M sells his business to *N* for a cash sum plus an annuity of £10,000 a year payable by *N* out of the business profits. In 2011–12, *N* paid *M* £8,000 (£10,000 less tax at 20%).

(1) *M* may set any available personal allowances against the annuity, so that if he is aged 67, is single and has no other income, the position will be:

	£	£
Annuity (gross amount)		10,000
Personal allowance (over-65 rate)		(9,940)
		60
Tax payable		
£60 charged at 20%	12.00	
Less: tax paid by deduction	(2,000.00)	
HMRC will repay	1,988.00	

---

(2) If M's other income is sufficient to utilise both his personal allowances and the lower rate band, there will be no repayment. If he is a higher rate taxpayer, he will have to pay additional tax on the annuity, as follows:

	£
Higher rate tax on annuity (40% of £10,000)	4,000
Less: Already paid by deduction	(2,000)
Additional tax payable	2,000

(3) The buyer, N, can obtain relief for the annuity paid to M not as a trading expense, but as a deduction in computing total taxable income.
    (a) If he is only a basic rate taxpayer, he obtains the relief to which he is entitled by keeping for himself the £2,000 difference between the gross amount of the annuity and the £8,000 actually paid to M.
    (b) If he is a higher rate taxpayer, additional relief is given by not charging higher rate tax on an amount equal to the gross annuity paid – a process usually referred to as 'extending the basic rate band'.

(4) Suppose N's profits are £50,000, he has no other income and is entitled only to the basic personal allowance of £7,475. If he did not have to pay the annuity, his tax position would be:

		£
Income		50,000
Personal allowance		(7,475)
Tax payable on		42,525
£35,000	charged at 20%	7,000.00
£7,525	charged at 40%	3,010.00
£42,525		10,010.00

(5) As he does have to pay the annuity, the basic rate band is extended by the gross amount of that annuity (£10,000), so the position becomes:

		£
£42,525	charged at 20%	8,505.00

This is a reduction of £1,505 and so overall the position is:

	£
Gross annuity	10,000
Net payment to M	(8,000)
Basic rate tax relief	2,000
Reduction in tax payable by assessment	1,505
Total tax relief	3,505

If N has more income within the 40% band, the total tax relief might be £4,000 (ie 40% of £10,000). Where N is an additional rate taxpayer, relief is not given at 50%. Section 10(6) ITA 2007 mentions only two circumstances in which the higher rate band, as well as the basic rate band, will be extended – Gift Aid and pension contributions.

10.10.2 Income from trusts

Income paid to a beneficiary of a fixed interest trust is normally taxed at source at 20%. However, tax will sometimes have been charged on the trustees at other rates, eg dividends will carry a 10% tax credit. In such a situation, the beneficiary will have a credit for basic rate tax on that element of his or her income from the trust that represents income that has borne 20% tax and a 10% tax credit on dividend income which he or she has received from the trust.

Income payments to discretionary beneficiary carry a credit of 50% (40% for 2009–10 and earlier years). In practice, a beneficiary will normally receive a form R185, which sets out his or her income from the trust and the tax withheld.

10.10.3 Estates of deceased persons

(ss 649–656 ITTOIA 2005)

When someone dies, it takes time for his or her executors or personal representatives to identify all his or her assets, pay all his or her debts, settle any IHT liability and work out the best way of dividing the estate between those entitled (eg one beneficiary may want to take specific investments, another may prefer cash). During this time, known as the administration period, it is quite likely that income will be received by the executors or personal representatives, both on the deceased's existing investments and, for example, as interest on a bank account into which the executors have paid money collected on behalf of the estate.

The executors or personal representatives must pay tax on all income received. Items such as share dividends and bond interest are received net of tax and this tax will cover the executors' liability. Income from savings is taxed at 20%. Other income is also subject to tax at the basic rate and, where no tax has been withheld at source (eg rental income), the executors will need to go through the self-assessment procedures.

The executors or personal representatives must therefore pool income on which tax has been paid. That pool must be divided between the beneficiaries in accordance with the terms of the deceased's Will, or of the laws of intestacy if he or she left no Will.

Example – Tax treatment of estate income

The gross income from an estate for 2011–12 is £200, on which the executors have paid tax of £40. The deceased's son is, under the Will, entitled to half that income. He will receive a cheque for £80 plus a certificate, signed by the executors, confirming that tax of £20 has been paid to HMRC. The son's income for tax purposes is £100, but he is treated as having already paid basic rate tax on that £100. If he has personal allowances or other reliefs available, he can obtain (from HMRC) a repayment of some or all of the £20 tax paid; if he is a higher or additional rate taxpayer, he will have to pay over to HMRC the difference between basic and higher or additional rate tax.

10.10.4 Allocation of estate income to particular tax years

Payments made to beneficiaries out of the income of the residue of an estate are taxable as income for the year of payment. If, following death, income which accrued before death is taken into account both in determining the value of the estate for the purposes of IHT, and in calculating the residuary income of the estate for a tax year, a reduction is made in the residuary income of the estate for that tax year in ascertaining the extra liability, if any, of a person with an absolute interest in the whole or part of the residue.

11

ALLOWABLE DEDUCTIONS

In this chapter, we look at the deductions you may claim either on the main SA form or on the Additional Information Schedule to the SA tax return.

This chapter contains the following sections:

(1) Alimony and maintenance
(2) Loans used to purchase an annuity from an insurance company
(3) Loans to purchase investment property
(4) Loans to invest in partnerships
(5) Loans to invest in close companies
(6) Loans to invest in employee-controlled companies
(7) Loans to purchase plant and machinery
(8) Alternative finance 'products'
(9) Gift Aid
(10) Gift of listed shares and securities
(11) Gift of land and buildings
(12) Annuities, etc
(13) Trade union and friendly society subscriptions
(14) Life assurance premiums
(15) Community Investment Tax Credit (CITC)

11.1 ALIMONY AND MAINTENANCE

No relief is normally given for any payments whatsoever made after 5 April 2000. The remaining relief is of limited relevance as it is only available where one of the parties to the agreement under which the payments are made was born before 6 April 1935. For those who qualify, an allowance of up to £2,800 can be claimed for 2011–12. Relief is given at 10%.

11.2 LOANS USED TO PURCHASE AN ANNUITY FROM AN INSURANCE COMPANY

(ss 353(1A), (1AA) and (1AB) ICTA 1988)

MIRAS relief, abolished from 6 April 2000, was given for interest on loans taken out before 9 March 1999, by individuals already aged 65 or over, and secured on the borrower's main residence, where at least 90% of the loan on which the interest was payable was used to buy an annuity for the remainder of his or her life. Interest payable on this type of loan continues to attract relief at 23% despite the general abolition of MIRAS and the reduction in the basic rate to 20%.

11.3 LOANS TO PURCHASE INVESTMENT PROPERTY

Interest on loans used to acquire a property that is let out may be allowed in computing the rental income assessable for tax purposes (see Chapter 8).

11.4 LOANS TO INVEST IN PARTNERSHIPS

(s 398 ITA 2007)

Tax relief may be obtained on loan interest which is paid in a tax year provided that the loan has been used to invest in a partnership that is not an investment LLP. Interest on qualifying loans may be set against the individual's general income, ie relief is not confined to an offset against income from the partnership.

11.4.1 Conditions for relief

It does not matter that such loans may be secured by way of a mortgage against the partner's main residence; the availability of relief depends on the purpose for which the loan is raised, not the way in which the lender secures its position. Relief is basically available where the loan is applied:

- in purchasing a share in a partnership; or
- in contributing capital to a partnership or advancing money to a partnership where the money advanced is used wholly for the purposes of the partnership's trade, profession or vocation; or
- in paying off another loan the interest on which would have been eligible for tax relief.

However, there are further conditions that must be satisfied. The borrower must be a member of the partnership throughout the period in which the interest accrues (and not just as a limited partner). Also, he or she must not have recovered any capital from the partnership since raising the qualifying loan.

11.4.2 Recovery of capital

(s 399(3) ITA 2007))

If, at any time after the application of the proceeds of the loan, a partner recovers capital from the partnership, he or she is deemed to have used the money withdrawn to repay the qualifying loan on which he or she is claiming interest relief. This applies whether or not the proceeds are actually used in this manner. It is therefore advisable to segregate the partners' capital and current accounts in the partnership's books so that any withdrawal can be clearly identified.

Tax notes

Relief is due for interest which is paid in a year. Interest that is 'rolled-up' will not normally be eligible for relief until it is actually paid.

11.4.3 Property occupied rent-free by partnership

Where a partner takes out a loan to purchase property occupied by the partnership for business purposes and the interest is paid by the partnership, technically no deduction is due to the partnership because the interest is not its liability but the partner's. However, in practice, the interest paid can be treated as rent so that it then becomes allowable as a deduction. In the partner's hands, the rent is taxable but the interest paid is allowed as a deduction in arriving at the amount taxable as income from property.

11.4.4 Incorporation of partnership

(ss 409(1), 409(2) and 410 ITA 2007)

Where a partnership business is transferred to a limited company in return for shares, any qualifying loan in existence at the time continues to attract tax relief provided the conditions for relief in 11.5 below would be met if a new loan was taken out.

11.4.5 Tax planning: withdrawing partnership monies and replacing working capital by raising qualifying loans

Where a partner has a surplus balance on either his or her current or capital account with a partnership and he or she does not already have a qualifying loan, he or she may withdraw the balance due to him or her (with his or her partners' consent), use the money to pay off non-qualifying borrowings and then borrow further funds to introduce capital into the partnership and obtain tax relief.

Example – Replacement capital

B is a partner in the XYZ partnership. She has a credit balance of £100,000 in her capital account. Outside the partnership, she has bought a yacht for her private use with the help of a £40,000 loan from her bank and she has a house mortgage of £20,000. B could withdraw £60,000 from her capital account in the partnership and use the money to make the following repayments:

	£
Yacht bank loan	40,000
Building society	20,000
	60,000

Once these transactions have been completed, B could borrow £60,000 as a loan (not overdraft) and use the funds to reintroduce capital into the partnership with full tax relief on the interest payable. Professional advice should be sought well in advance before setting up this sort of loan.

11.4.6 Raising qualifying loans to replace partnership borrowings

Another situation where it may be appropriate to restructure existing borrowings is where the partnership has taken a loan, typically to purchase another business or the property from which the business is carried on. In this situation, each partner is normally required to borrow privately his or her share of the partnership loan and introduce the monies raised into the partnership. The partner can then personally claim tax relief on the interest paid as a charge on his or her income.

The partnership collects the monies raised by each partner's loan and uses the funds to redeem the partnership loan. As a result, each partner's share of profits becomes correspondingly higher because no interest is now payable by the partnership. However, the situation redresses itself because the higher profits must be used to finance the private borrowing.

Rearranging matters in this way can provide significant cash-flow benefits because relief is available for interest up to one year earlier than where the borrowings remain within the partnership. For example, if the partnership makes up its accounts to 30 April, interest paid on partnership borrowings in the year to 5 April 2012 will normally attract tax relief in 2012–13 (ie as an expense in arriving at the partnership profits for its year falling in 2012–13), whereas replacing these borrowings with qualifying loans raised by the partners will mean that the interest attracts tax relief against their income for the tax year 2011–12.

11.5 LOANS TO INVEST IN CLOSE COMPANIES

(ss 392–395 ITA 2007)

Where interest is paid on a loan used to purchase ordinary shares in a close company, or in lending money to such a company that is used for the purposes of the close company's business, the interest may be eligible for tax relief. For the definition of a close company, see 18.14.1. Once again, relief is dependent on the way the loan is used, not on the way it is secured; the borrower may therefore have a qualifying loan that is secured by way of a mortgage on his or her home.

Interest on such a loan may be set against the individual's general income, ie relief is not restricted to an offset against income from the close company.

Tax notes

Interest on a qualifying loan may be set against any of your taxable income; it does not have to be set against the income from the close company first.

Relief is due for the year in which the interest is paid, not for the year in which it accrued.

11.5.1 Conditions for relief where the loan is used to buy shares

Relief is dependent upon conditions being satisfied by the borrower, the company and in relation to the shares that are acquired.

Conditions applicable to the borrower

(1) The borrower, either alone or together with certain associates, owns a material interest in the close company (defined broadly as more than 5% of the ordinary share capital).

(2) The borrower holds less than 5% of the ordinary share capital, but works for the greater part of his or her time in the actual management or conduct of the company or an associated company (a works manager, a production manager or a company secretary would normally satisfy this condition).

Conditions applicable to the company

The company must exist wholly or mainly for one of the following purposes:

(a) To carry on a trade or trades on a commercial basis.
(b) To make investments in land or property let commercially to unconnected parties.
(c) To hold shares or securities or make loans to 'qualifying companies' or an intermediate company, all of which are under its control. A qualifying company is one that is under the close company's control and satisfies the conditions at (a) and (b) above.
(d) To co-ordinate the administration of two or more qualifying companies.

If the company holds property, the individual must not reside in it unless he or she has worked for the greater part of his or her time in the actual management or conduct of the company.

Conditions applicable to the shares being acquired

A loan used to buy shares is a qualifying loan only if the shares are ordinary share capital. 'Ordinary share capital' includes any shares in the company other than fixed rate preference shares.

11.5.2 Close EIS companies

(s 161(2) ITA 2007)

Loan interest relief is not available in respect of shares issued under the Enterprise Investment Scheme.

Tax notes

FA 2009 contains tax avoidance legislation to counter arrangements designed to generate a certain (or almost certain) financial profit for individuals through the availability of income tax deductions for loan interest. The provisions apply to interest payable on or after 19 March 2009.

The new measure applies to interest payable on loans taken out to finance various forms of investment (such as an interest in a close company or a partnership) where the availability of interest relief means that, taking this into account, the investor cannot fail to make a post-tax profit from the overall arrangements.

11.5.3 Company ceases to be close after loan taken out

Relief can continue to be due for interest paid on a loan even though the company has ceased to be a close company provided the other conditions remain satisfied. For example, the individual must either have a material interest or be employed full-time in the management of the company or an associated company. This is often relevant where management form a company in a management buy-out (MBO) and it ceases to be close after outside institutions inject further share capital.

11.5.4 Close company taken over on share-for-share basis

Where an individual has borrowed to invest in a close company and that company is taken over by another close company on a share-for-share basis, his or her loan can continue to be a qualifying loan provided all the other conditions are satisfied.

11.5.5 Close company shares sold

If you sell the shares in a close company, and you have a loan that was used to finance the purchase of the shares, the loan interest ceases to qualify for relief from the date of disposal. Interest charged by a bank on the subsequent redemption of the loan does not attract income tax relief.

Furthermore, if you give away shares, you may also be regarded as having 'recovered capital'. This means you may cease to be eligible for relief on interest paid on your borrowings.

11.5.6 Borrowing to lend money to a close company

Relief is also available under s 392 if you borrow to lend money to a close company in which you have a material interest, or are a full-time director or manager, and the company uses the money in its business.

Once again, the loan ceases to be a qualifying loan to the extent that you recover capital from the company. There is a trap here in that a gift or other disposal of shares may constitute a 'recovery of capital' even though the money you have lent to the company has not been withdrawn.

Tax notes

You should make sure that your bank debits you for accrued interest just before you sell or give away the shares because interest charged after that date will not attract tax relief.

11.6 LOANS TO INVEST IN EMPLOYEE-CONTROLLED COMPANIES

(ss 396, 397 ITA 2007)

It is also possible for an individual to establish a qualifying loan where he or she uses it to buy shares in an employee-controlled company, even if it is not a close company. The conditions that need to be satisfied for a loan to qualify under this provision are:

- during the year of assessment in which the interest is paid, the company must either become employee-controlled for the first time or be employee-controlled for at least nine months;
- the individual or his or her spouse or civil partner must be a full-time employee throughout the period commencing with the application of the loan and ending with the date on which the interest is paid: he or she can also continue to obtain relief for interest paid within 12 months of his or her having ceased to be an employee;
- the shares must be acquired before, or not later than 12 months after, the date on which the company first becomes an employee-controlled company; and
- the individual must not have recovered any capital from the company during the period from applying the loan proceeds to paying the interest.

The legislation requires that the company be unquoted and resident only in the UK and either a trading company or the holding company of a trading group. A company is 'employee-controlled' if more than 50% of its ordinary share capital and voting power is owned by full-time employees or their spouses or civil partners. If a full-time employee owns more than 10%, the excess is disregarded. For this purpose, a spouse or civil partner's holding is attributed to the employee unless the spouse or civil partner is also a full-time employee.

11.7 LOANS TO PURCHASE PLANT AND MACHINERY

(ss 388–391 ITA 2007)

Where a partner incurs capital expenditure on the purchase of plant and machinery used for the partnership's business purposes and eligible for capital allowances, he or she can claim tax relief on interest paid if the plant is financed by a loan. The relief is available only in the tax year in which the loan is taken out and the following three tax years.

Example – Use of loans to purchase plant and machinery

> A partner borrowed £10,000 at 10% pa on 6 October 2011 to buy a van that is used for the partnership's business. His private use is agreed at 25%.
>
> Interest relief is available on £375 in 2011–12 and on £750 for the following three tax years.

Similar relief is available for employees who are required to purchase plant for use in carrying out their duties but the relief is not available for loans used to buy a car, van or motor cycle.

Tax notes

If you have realised some capital and are in a position to clear some of your borrowings, it will generally be best to repay non-qualifying loans where you get no tax relief for the interest.

11.8 ALTERNATIVE FINANCE 'PRODUCTS'

Where an individual enters into a shariah compliant contract with an Islamic bank or financial institution, he or she will not pay interest. However, the transactions may have similar economic consequences. For example, a diminishing musharaka contract is in essence a partnership arrangement which involves a buyer and a bank jointly purchasing a property. The buyer pays rent to the bank on its share of the property. The buyer also gradually acquires the bank's share and, as he or she does so, the rent payable to the bank reduces because the bank owns a smaller proportion of the property. In economic terms, the musharaka contract has the same consequences as a repayment mortgage.

The object of the tax legislation on alternative finance contracts is to provide a level playing field, ie the same tax relief should be obtained in respect of the bank's charges as would be available if those charges were interest. For example, in the case of a diminishing musharaka contract, the rent paid to the bank would attract relief if the property were let or used for business purposes.

11.9 GIFT AID

11.9.1 Introduction

(s 414 ITA 2007)

Gift Aid is a way in which the Government seeks to encourage taxpayers to support charities. The scheme originally gave income tax relief only for substantial donations to charity. Prior to 6 April 2000 there was a minimum limit for gifts to qualify under this scheme of £250.

Example – Gift Aid donation

In 2011–12, *A* gives £800 to a recognised charity. Under the Gift Aid scheme, it will be treated as a donation of £1,000, from which basic rate tax of £200 has been deducted. The charity can claim that tax from HMRC, so it will receive a total of £1,000.

If *A* is a basic rate taxpayer that is the end of the story: he has paid over £800 that HMRC has 'topped up' to £1,000. If *A* is a higher rate taxpayer, he may claim higher rate relief on the gift, calculated as follows:

	£
Gross donation made	1,000
Tax relief at 40%	400
Less: deducted when gift made	(200)
Reduction in *A*'s own tax liability	200

If *A* is not a taxpayer at all, HMRC will require him to make good the £200 it has paid to the charity.

If *A* is a 50% taxpayer in 2011–12, he will be able to claim tax relief at his highest marginal rate of tax. Relief can also be obtained against tax on an individual's capital gains.

11.9.2 Carrying back relief

Since 5 April 2003 it has been possible to carry back Gift Aid donations made. The amount that may be carried back is the amount of donations made by the time the individual submits his or her tax return, ie payments made up to 31 January 2012 can be set against the 2011 tax liability.

An individual will need to make a formal carry-back election either on the tax return when filing or as a stand alone claim. The deadline for making this election is the date that he or she files his or her tax return or (if earlier) 31 January following the year to which the donations are being carried back.

> **Tax notes**
>
> Carrying back Gift Aid donations will mean that you get the benefit of the higher rate relief 12 months earlier than if you simply take the relief for the year of payment. It could also be beneficial if you were a higher rate taxpayer for the previous year but only a basic rate taxpayer for the year of payment. The recent case of *John Cameron* v *HMRC* TC00415 highlights a potential pitfall with claims to carry-back donations. Mr Cameron had made a claim to carry back Gift Aid contributions made in 2006–07 to 2005–06 on an amended 2006 tax return, having submitted his tax return for the year in question in good time. The Tribunal judge reluctantly concluded that the relief was not due (although in the judge's view this ran contrary to the principles of common sense and fairness) because the claim had not been made by the date that Mr Cameron delivered his original return, and the legislation is worded in such a way that a claim made on an amendment to the return for a year cannot be valid.

11.9.3 Giving a tax refund to charity

Individuals can currently nominate any tax repayment, in full or part, to charity. Such donations can be made under Gift Aid and, if made by 31 January 2012, can be set against an individual's tax liability in computing his or her 2010–11 tax. This relief is claimed by completing the *Giving your tax repayment to charity* form in the Tax Return pack. A list of charities that are registered with HMRC for 'SA donate' (not all charities have chosen to register) can be found at the HMRC website, www.hmrc.gov.uk/charities/charities-search.htm, or by calling HMRC on 0845 302 0203.

It is not possible for the taxpayer to elect for a donation made in this way to be carried back under the procedure described in 11.9.2 above. SA Donate (the method described above by which taxpayers are able to nominate charities to receive their tax repayments) is to be withdrawn for repayments of tax due on tax returns for 2011–12 and all subsequent years as well as for any repayments made in respect of earlier tax years on or after 6 April 2012. Since its introduction in 2005, SA Donate has not been widely used and it is estimated that only £400,000 was donated to charities in most years.

Where it transpires that an error has arisen, and a repayment sent to a charity was not in fact due, HMRC's procedure will depend upon who has made the error. If the taxpayer has made a mistake and a repayment is not due, HMRC will seek reimbursement from him or her. If the error arose at HMRC's end, it will seek reimbursement from the charity.

11.9.4 Qualifying donations

Several conditions must be satisfied under the Gift Aid scheme:

(1) The recipient must be a recognised charity or a community amateur sports club (see 38.2). Many appeal funds and societies established for the public benefit are not technically charities. In case of doubt, intending donors should ask for evidence of charitable status or should consult:

Charity Commission Direct
PO Box 1227
Liverpool L69 3UG
Web: www.charity-commission.gov.uk

By way of exception, four bodies that technically are not charities are deemed to be charities for Gift Aid purposes: the British Museum, the National History Museum, the National Heritage Memorial Fund and the Historic Buildings and Monuments Commission for England.

(2) The gift must be of money: it is not possible to claim Gift Aid relief for donated works of art, or even for goods (eg clothing or blankets) to be used to assist distressed people. Also, it is not possible to give money on condition that it is used to buy something from the donor, a member of his or her family, or a company in which he or she has an interest.

(3) The gift may be made in cash, by cheque or bank transfer, or by credit card. However, HMRC does not accept that writing-off an existing loan to the charity is equivalent to a gift of money.

(4) There is no minimum or maximum donation.

(5) Any reciprocal benefit received from the charity (by the donor or a member of his or her family) must fall within prescribed limits (see 38.1.21).

11.9.5 Permissible benefits for Gift Aid donors

A charity may wish to give a token of its appreciation to donors for their donations. Modest benefits received in consequence of making a donation will not stop the donation from qualifying as a Gift Aid donation, provided their value does not exceed certain limits. If the benefits exceed the permitted limits, the donations cannot qualify as Gift Aid donations.

If a charity wishes to provide benefits to donors it should consider whether the proposed benefits fall within the limits in the donor benefit rules. We deal with this at 38.1.15.

At the 2011 Budget, the Chancellor announced changes to the donor benefit limits for Gift Aid. As part of a wider package of measures to encourage charitable giving, the benefit limit for donations over £10,000 has been increased. The current rule that any benefits to the donor must not exceed 5% of the donation will remain but the upper limit has been increased from £500 to £2,500. This new measure will enable charities to thank their larger donors in a more generous way, without disqualifying the donation from Gift Aid.

The new rules will take effect for benefits received as a consequence of donations made on or after 6 April 2011 by individual donors and from 1 April 2011 by corporate donors.

11.9.6 'Tainted' charity donations

See 38.1.21 for the rules on tainted charity donations which have replaced the rules for 'substantial donors' who give more than £25,000 pa to a charity.

11.10 GIFT OF LISTED SHARES AND SECURITIES

Individuals who make gifts to charity of listed shares and securities are able to claim relief in calculating their taxable income. The relief applies where listed shares or securities are given or sold at undervalue to a charity. The shares must be listed on a recognised stock exchange in the UK or overseas. A gift of AIM shares can qualify.

The deduction is equal to the market value of the shares or securities on the date of the gift (inclusive of the incidental cost of disposal) less any consideration received for or in consequence of the gift.

Example – Giving shares to charity

> C, a basic rate taxpayer, gives listed shares with a market value of £10,000 to a charity. The shares show an unrealised gain of £9,000. C obtains income tax relief at 20% on £10,000 and gains of £9,000 escape tax at 18%: giving total tax relief of £3,620). If C was a higher rate taxpayer, this would increase to £6,520.

Note that the deduction is given only against income, not against capital gains.

Anti-avoidance

FA 2004 introduced anti-avoidance legislation to prevent the abuse of this relief by the donor having a right to repurchase the shares at less than market value.

In recent years, a number of avoidance schemes exploiting the Gift Aid provisions have been disclosed to, or discovered by, HMRC. These schemes sought to exploit the rules which enable a charity to claim a repayment of tax at the basic rate on a qualifying donation by an individual, with the individual claiming relief for the donation on the difference between the higher and basic rates of tax.

One scheme depended upon a circular series of payments. It starts with the charity purchasing, say, gilts of £100,000 which pass through a third party to an individual taxpayer for perhaps £10. The taxpayer is expected to make a sale for £100,000 and pass the money to the charity. There is an option that ensures the gilts will be returned to the charity if it does not receive a cash gift of £100,000 within one or two days.

In these circumstances, HMRC does not accept that the charity is entitled to a repayment of tax or that Gift Aid relief is due to the individual.

In addition, there have been a number of schemes that seek to generate Gift Aid (and gift of shares) tax relief claims. A cash donation to a nominated charity is made and in return shares are received from an unnamed non-UK 'philanthropist'. These shares are claimed to be worth many times the amount of the cash donation but are in companies listed on a stock exchange that is not recognised by HMRC. The shares are then donated to the nominated charity.

No Gift Aid is due on the cash donation because the donor receives a benefit (the shares) that is in excess of the donation. No relief is due on the gift of shares because the requirement that the shares are listed on a stock exchange recognised by HMRC is not met.

Section 31 and Schedule 7 FA (No.1) 2010 introduced rules to block tax avoidance schemes that exploit the rules for tax relief on gifts of qualifying investments to charities under Chapter 3, Part 8 ITA 2007.

The anti-avoidance deals with gifts of certain shares, securities and land. The avoidance depends on the donor receiving tax relief at their highest marginal rate of tax on the full market value of the qualifying investments at the date of the gift where:

- the donor acquired the investments at below market value as part of a scheme or arrangement, or
- the market value of the investment is artificially inflated at the date of the gift to charity.

The new rules adjust the amount of relief to the donor to the economic cost of acquisition of the gift, to the donor, where:

- the qualifying investment gifted to the charity (or anything from which the investment derives) was acquired within four years of the date of disposal; and
- where the main purpose, or one of the main purposes, of acquiring the qualifying investment was to dispose of it to a charity and claim the tax relief.

Income tax relief in addition to CGT exemption

No CGT arises on a gift of shares to charity, so the donor's 40% income tax relief may be in addition to a significant saving of CGT that would apply if he or she were to sell the shares.

> **Tax notes**
>
> Bear in mind that in the same way that no capital gain is recognised on a gift to charity, no loss is allowed. Therefore, if you are making a gift of shares ensure first that there would be a chargeable gain if you actually disposed of the shares. If not, then a better option would be to actually sell the shares and realise the capital loss. You can then make a cash donation to the charity. This would be especially beneficial if you had other chargeable gains arising during the tax year.

11.11 GIFT OF LAND AND BUILDINGS

Provisions enacted in 2002 (now in Chapter 3, Part 8 ITA 2007) also give tax relief to a person who makes a charitable donation in kind by transferring land or buildings to the charity as gift or sale at an undervalue. The donor is allowed to deduct the value of land or buildings in arriving at his or her taxable income. The relief is basically the same as that for gifts of listed shares; therefore, the same considerations apply, including the anti-avoidance provisions introduced in FA (No.1) 2010. Note that again the deduction is given only against income, not against capital gains.

A reduced rate of inheritance tax (IHT) is to apply for deaths occurring on or after 6 April 2012 where 10% or more of a deceased's net estate (after the deduction of all IHT exemptions, reliefs and the nil rate band) is left to charity. In such cases, the current rate of 40% will be reduced to 36%. A tax reduction is also being considered for taxpayers who give works of art or historical objects of national importance to the State. A consultation will be held in summer 2011 to consider these proposals.

11.12 ANNUITIES, ETC

(ss 447–452 and 900 ITA 2007, s 727 ITTOIA 2005)

11.12.1 Introduction

Most annuities are payments under deed of covenant, ie a written promise to pay another person a certain sum of money each year (or each week, month, quarter, etc), either for a fixed number of years or for a period determined by events (eg until the payer's or the payee's death).

At one time, all deeds of covenant operated so as to transfer taxable income from the payer to the payee, so that the payer's taxable income was reduced by the amount of the covenanted payment and the payee's similarly increased. This could save a great deal of money where (as would usually be the case) the payee was subject to a lower rate of tax than the payer. As a result, deeds of covenant were often used to redistribute income around a family. Inevitably this led to anti-avoidance legislation that gradually became all-embracing and the position now is that, generally, the payer does not obtain a deduction from income, and the recipient's income does not include the covenanted amount.

11.12.2 Business purchase and partnership annuities

There are still two categories of payments where the gross payment is deducted in arriving at net income. For a basic rate taxpayer the tax deducted is effectively the income tax relief but a higher rate taxpayer is entitled to the benefit of the difference between the basic rate and the higher rate. This only applies where the payment is one that requires the deduction of income tax at the basic rate:

- patent royalties where the payment arises in the UK, and
- payments made for commercial reasons in connection with the individual's trade, profession or vocation – this would include annuities paid by a partnership to former partners. Again, the payment must arise in the UK and the recipient must be subject to UK tax on the amount.

For details of such annuities, see 10.10.1.

11.13 TRADE UNION AND FRIENDLY SOCIETY SUBSCRIPTIONS

(ss 457–460 ITA 2007)

Some trade unions provide pensions and/or death benefits (often called 'funeral benefits') for their members. Each member is entitled to tax relief on half of that part of his or her subscription that relates to the provision of such benefits (up to a maximum of £100). However, this relief is sometimes given by HMRC making a block payment to the union and the union then charging reduced subscriptions to its members.

The members of some friendly societies also pay a subscription that covers both a death benefit and a sickness benefit (ie a 'mixed policy'). Half of the amount referable to the death benefit qualifies for tax relief.

There is a distinction between relief under the special arrangements for trade union subscriptions and mixed friendly society policies and the general relief for life assurance premiums (see 11.14). Relief under the special arrangements is available only in the exact circumstances described – and not, for example, for a premium paid under a simple life assurance policy issued by a friendly society. Relief under the special arrangements is, however, available irrespective of the date the insurance came into force, whereas the general relief for life assurance premiums is available only for policies entered into force before 14 March 1984.

11.14 LIFE ASSURANCE PREMIUMS

(ss 266, 274 ICTA 1988)

Most life assurance polices that came into force before 14 March 1984 currently qualify for a form of tax relief. (The operative date is the day the policyholder's proposal was accepted by the insurance company, not the day the policy was issued.) HMRC makes a block payment to the insurance company, equal to 12.5% of the tax on the premiums payable on qualifying policies, and the insurance company correspondingly reduces the amount actually paid by the policyholder. For example, if the standard premium was £100, HMRC would pay £12.50 and the policyholder only £87.50. That £12.50 is the sum total of the relief available: no additional relief may be claimed if the policyholder is a higher rate taxpayer. Relief is lost completely if any material change is made to the policy – for example, if a term policy is converted into an endowment or if the insurance company makes a loan to the policyholder without charging a commercial interest rate. The 12.5% rate represents half the historic basic rate of tax. The percentage has not been amended with changes in tax rates since that time. The amount subject to the relief is limited to the greater of 1/6 of total income or £1,500. No tax relief is available for the premiums on life assurance policies that came into force on or after 14 March 1984.

Following the OTS review, the Government intends to completely abolish life assurance premium relief. However, it recognises the need to provide a period of notice before the abolition and therefore intends that it will be abolished after 2012, with a final date set out after a consultation period.

11.15 COMMUNITY INVESTMENT TAX CREDIT (CITC)

The Community Investment Tax Credit (CITC) scheme came into effect on 23 January 2003 and applies to investments in accredited Community Development Finance Institutions (CDFIs) made on or after 17 April 2002. The relief is intended to stimulate private investment in disadvantaged communities by providing a tax incentive to individuals and companies investing in not-for-profit and profit-seeking enterprises in or for those communities.

The tax relief is worth up to 25% of the value of the investment in the CDFI and is spread over five years, starting with the year in which the investment is made.

The relief for a year should normally be claimed on the tax return for that year, page 2 of the Additional Information schedule to the SA form. However individual investors who have received a tax relief certificate may also request a change to their PAYE code number, or claim a reduction in their self-assessment payments on account.

12

ALLOWANCES AND TAX CREDITS

DALE BUTCHER

This chapter looks at allowances and tax credits that may be claimed by taxpayers under the following sections:

(1) Personal allowances
(2) The basic personal allowance
(3) Married couple's allowance
(4) Pensioner couples
(5) Blind persons
(6) Time limits
(7) Tax credits from 6 April 2003

12.1 PERSONAL ALLOWANCES

(ss 35–37 ITA 2007)

Income tax is not charged on the whole of a person's taxable income. In calculating the amount on which tax must be paid, he or she may claim a personal allowance that depends on his or her individual circumstances (eg age).

Personal allowances may, in most circumstances, be claimed by anyone resident in the UK. There is no minimum age requirement so that, for example, a new born baby is entitled to a personal allowance. Sometimes it is possible, through the use of trusts or settlements, to redirect part of a family's income to a child, so that it may (being covered by his or her personal allowance) be enjoyed tax free (although the scope for transferring taxable income in this way has been whittled down by a succession of complex anti-avoidance provisions: see 33.5.4).

British subjects and certain other categories of people not resident in the UK may also claim personal allowances. However, from 6 April 2010, Commonwealth citizens are no longer entitled to claim UK personal allowances in these circumstances.

12.2 THE BASIC PERSONAL ALLOWANCE

(s 35 ITA 2007)

Subject to income limits (see 12.2.3), every individual resident in the UK is entitled to the basic personal allowance – often called the 'single person's allowance', a throwback to the days when there was also a 'married man's allowance' and 'wife's earned income relief'. See 12.2.3 below concerning changes to income tax rates and personal allowances from 6 April 2010 and 35.13 concerning the restriction of allowances for non-UK domiciliaries claiming the remittance basis. The allowance for 2009–10 and 2010–11 was £6,475. This increased to £7,475 from 6 April 2011 and is due to increase further to £8,105 from 6 April 2012. In order to pay for this proposal, the higher rate threshold has been decreased to £35,000 for 2011–12 and £34,370 for 2012–13. If the individual is born or dies halfway through a year of assessment, the allowance is not scaled down.

Example – Death during tax year

Suppose *D* died at the end of September 2011, by which time he had earned only half his annual salary. His tax bill for 2011–12 would be:

	£
Salary	10,000
Professional subscription paid	(135)
	9,865
Personal allowance	(7,475)
Tax payable on	2,390
£2,390 charged at 20%	478.00

Because the PAYE scheme assumes that personal allowances will be used in equal monthly (or weekly) instalments over the year, only about £3,738 will have been deducted from *D*'s salary while he was alive, so he will have paid tax of around £1,225 up to the date of death. On request, HMRC will therefore repay his executors the excess tax deducted.

12.2.1 Higher allowances for the over-65s

(ss 36 and 37 ITA 2007)

Higher allowances are given to those who have attained age 65 and are of limited means. The 2010–11 allowance was £9,490 for those between ages 65 and 74 and £9,640 for those aged 75+. These increased to £9,940 and £10,090 for 2011–12 and will increase in line with the retail prices index for 2012–13. If an individual attains age 65 or 75 during a year of assessment, he or she is entitled to the appropriate allowance for the whole of that year. For example, a man born on 1 June 1947 will attain age 65 on 1 June 2012 and will be entitled to the whole of the higher allowance for the 2012–13 tax year.

The higher allowance is also given where the individual was alive on the first day of the tax year and would have achieved age 65 or 75 within the tax year had he or she not died.

The allowance is designed to assist only those of limited means. The allowance is reduced by £1 for every £2 by which the individual's 'total income' exceeds £24,000 (for 2011–12), until it falls back to the level of the standard allowance for the under-65s.

Within this band, every £2 of income can cost 30p in tax (20p on the £2 itself, plus 10p on the £1 of allowances withdrawn). This is an effective percentage rate of 30%. For 2011–12, the £1-for-£2 reduction operates between 'total incomes' of £24,000 and £28,930 for those between the ages of 65 and 74 and between £24,000 and £29,230 for those aged 75+. Individuals with total income in excess of the higher figures noted above, receive personal allowances of £7,475 only.

Example – Reduced higher allowances

In 2011–12, E was aged 70. He received a state pension of £5,500 pa, an occupational pension of £19,500 and rental income of £1,000. His 'total income' was £26,000; his overall income tax liability for 2011–12 is therefore:

	£	£	£
Total income			26,000
Higher personal allowance		9,940	
Total income	26,000		
Income limit	24,000		
Excess	2,000		
Half of excess		1,000	
Reduced higher personal allowance[1]			8,940
Tax payable on			17,060
Tax at 20% on £17,060 = £3,412			

[1]This cannot be reduced below the standard personal allowance of £7,475, except where income is in excess of £100,000 pa where a similar £1-for-£2 clawback will operate which may reduce the available allowances to nil.

The definition of 'total income' is, accordingly, very important, especially as in certain circumstances it is possible for an individual to rearrange his or her investments so that his or her 'total income', as defined by ITA 2007, is less than his or her real income. This is explained in 12.2.2.

12.2.2 Calculating 'total income'

(ss 22–32 ITA 2007)

A person's 'total income', as defined by ITA 2007, differs from his or her real income, first because not all receipts count towards total income and secondly because certain deductions can be made from real income in calculating total income.

The first step in calculating total income is to add together all the income that is assessable to tax. Income not assessable to tax is excluded. Examples include letting income exempt under the 'rent-a-room' scheme (see 8.4), the interest credited to an ISA, the dividends earned by a PEP (see 25.2) or a Venture Capital Trust (see 25.6), the growth in value of National Savings certificates (see 25.3.1) and amounts withdrawn from insurance bonds up to the annual 5% limit (see 28.3.3). A person whose income falls within the marginal age relief band therefore, might consider placing his or her money in tax-exempt investments, although every individual should take independent investment advice before withdrawing funds from existing investments or making new investments.

The second step is to deduct, from the sum of assessable income, the following outgoings:

- interest paid, insofar as it qualifies for tax relief under the usual rules (ss 383–412 ITA 2007);
- Gift Aid donations, subject to the normal rules (ss 413–454 ITA 2007);
- contributions paid to an occupational or personal pension scheme;
- any surplus capital allowances arising from investment in enterprise zone property (up to 5 April 2011, see 25.7).

Tax notes

If your income for the past year means that you don't get the full benefit from the increased personal allowance, and you are effectively subject to the 30% marginal rate (see above), it may pay for you to relate back Gift Aid donations (see 11.9.2). Another idea is to consult an independent financial adviser about investing surplus cash in a way that does not produce taxable income as you go along (eg a roll-up fund, an insurance bond or National Savings certificates).

12.2.3 Changes to income tax rates and personal allowances from 6 April 2010

From 2010–11, for individuals with income over £100,000 per annum, the personal allowance is reduced by £1 for every £2 of total income over £100,000 per annum. 'Total income' has the same meaning as described above in 12.2.2. The effect of this is that the basic personal allowance will be reduced to nil where an individual's net income is over £114,950. This limit applies irrespective of age.

For individuals with income over £150,000 per annum, a 50% tax rate applies to taxable non-dividend income above £150,000 per year.

A 42.5% dividend tax rate applies where taxable income is over £150,000 per annum and dividend income falls into the 'additional' (over £150,000) rate band (after gains, savings and dividend income are treated as the 'top slice' of income). Taking into account dividend tax credits, this means that the effective dividend tax rate increases from 25% to 36.11%.

12.3 MARRIED COUPLE'S ALLOWANCE

This relief was abolished with effect from 6 April 2000 for those born on or after 6 April 1935, though it is still available to married couples and civil partners where either spouse or civil partner was born before 6 April 1935 – see 12.4 below.

12.4 PENSIONER COUPLES

(ss 42–46 ITA 2007)

The married couple's allowance is still available if either spouse or civil partner was born before 6 April 1935. The allowance for 2011–12 is £7,295 (£6,965 for 2010–11). Relief is restricted to 10%. The allowance is subject to claw-back if the individual's income exceeds £24,000 (see 12.2.1). However, a minimum allowance of £2,800 for 2011–12 (£2,670 for 2010–11) is due even where the income exceeds the limit (including where income exceeds the £100,000 limit).

The legislation (ss 45 and 46) still refers to the lower allowance available to pensioner couples in earlier years where neither party was aged over 75, however, since all people born before 6 April 1935 became 75 years old during the 2009–10 tax year (or would have barring death earlier in the tax year) this is no longer relevant. However s 45 does give a choice for those married prior to 5 December 2005. The s 45 rules allow the husband (where he or his wife was born before 6 April 1935) to claim the allowance however, he can elect for the s 46 rules to apply instead. Section 46 applies to couples married on or after 5 December 2005 and civil partners (and those who elect for it to apply) and the allowance is given to the higher earning spouse or civil partner.

12.4.1 Pensioner couples: transfer of excess allowances

(s 47–53 ITA 2007)

The whole of a higher, age-related married couple's allowance may be transferred to the wife if the husband has insufficient income to use it himself (where a s 45 claim has been made) or alternatively, the higher earning partner may elect under s 47 to transfer the allowance (for s 46 claims). Where either claim has been made, the couple can jointly elect (under s 48) to share the allowance between them in the desired proportions. An election to do this must be lodged with HMRC before the start of the first tax year for which it is to have effect, or during that year if the marriage takes place during the year, or within the first 30 days of the tax year in which it is to take effect if HMRC is given prior notice. Civil partners can also make such elections.

12.5 BLIND PERSONS

(ss 38–40 ITA 2007)

A person who is blind may claim a special, additional personal allowance of £1,980 for 2011–12 (£1,890 for 2010–11). A person counts as 'blind' if:

- he or she lives in England or Wales and his or her name appears on the local authority's register of blind persons; or
- he or she lives in Scotland or Northern Ireland and is so blind that he or she cannot perform any work for which eyesight is essential.

This definition means that a person resident abroad can never, for tax purposes, count as blind – an odd rule which is strictly enforced by HMRC.

A person who becomes blind during a year of assessment may claim the full blind person's allowance for that year.

12.5.1 Married couples

If both spouses or civil partners are blind, each may claim a separate blind person's allowance.

A blind person with insufficient income to use all his or her personal allowances may be able to transfer the whole or part of his or her blind person's allowance to his or her spouse or civil partner (whether or not he or she also is blind). This election must be made within four years of the end of the tax year to which it relates. However, the transfer of the pensioners' married couple's allowance will take priority, so a transfer of blind person's allowance is only possible for pensioners where the husband or higher earning spouse or civil partner's income was insufficient to use his or her basic personal allowance and the blind person's allowance itself.

Example – Blind married couple

G, who is sighted, earns £10,000 a year. His wife, H, who is blind, has a pension of £7,000. The position for 2011–12 is:

H	£	£
Pension		7,000
Basic personal allowance	7,475	
Blind person's allowance	1,980	
		(9,455)
Excess, transferable to husband*		2,455
G		
Salary		10,000
Basic personal allowance	7,475	
Transferred excess from wife*	1,980	
		(9,455)
Tax payable on		545
£545 charged at 20%		109

* capped at £1,980 as the personal allowance is non-transferable.

12.6 TIME LIMITS

As noted at 12.2, subject to the income limit, every individual resident in the UK is automatically entitled to the basic personal allowance.

These allowances must be claimed within four years of the end of the year to which they relate, for example a claim in respect of blind person's allowance relating to the year ended 5 April 2008 must be made by 5 April 2012.

In general, most claims for allowances are made annually in the tax return. However, where a claim is overlooked or a formal return is not issued, a claim can be made to the taxpayer's tax office, normally in writing, though in certain circumstances phone claims will be accepted.

12.7 TAX CREDITS FROM 6 APRIL 2003

From 6 April 2003, various tax credits were consolidated in to the child tax credit and the working tax credit. The coalition Government announced a number of changes to the tax credit system, which will have effect from 2011–12, during the 'emergency' Budget on 22 June 2010. These included reductions in the applicable income limits and the income disregard, as well as an increase in the withdrawal rate.

12.7.1 Child tax credit

As its name suggests, the child tax credit is meant to support families with children and can be claimed if you have responsibility for a child.

The credit, which can be claimed in addition to any child benefit or working tax credit, is available for the support of:

- a child until 1 September following their 16th birthday;
- a person aged 16–18 who
  - is in full time education, up to and inclusive of A levels or their equivalent (NVQ3/Scottish Highers); or
  - if not in education has no job/training place and has registered with the Careers or Connexions Service.

The 'child' must not be claiming income support or tax credits and must not be serving a custodial sentence of more than four months.

Table 12.1 is a guide to the maximum amount of child credit that can be claimed in the tax year 2011–12. The amount a claimant, or joint claimants, actually receive depends on their income.

Table 12.1 – Child tax credit for the year 2011–12

The Child Tax Credit elements	Details	Maximum amount for 2011–12
Family element – the basic element	The basic payment to responsible for one or more children.	£545
Child element	Paid for each child. It is paid on top of the basic family element and any baby addition.	£2,555
Disability element	An extra payment for each disabled child.	£2,800
Severe disability element	An extra payment for each severely disabled child. It is paid on top of any disability element.	£1,130

12.7.2 **Working tax credit**

The working tax credit is available as a top up for individuals in low paid jobs, with additional payments being available for working households in which an individual has a severe disability.

In general, a qualifying individual is:

- aged 16 or over, works 16 hours a week and is responsible for a child; or
- aged 25 or over and works at least 30 hours a week; or
- aged 16 and over, has a disability that puts him or her at a disadvantage in getting a job and works at least 16 hours a week; or
- the individual or his or her partner is aged over 50 and is returning to work for at least 16 hours a week after time spent on qualifying benefits.

Table 12.2 offers a guide as to the amounts that could be receivable in 2011–12. The working tax credit contains several elements, including additional amounts for working people with a disability, for people with a severe disability and the cost of registered or approved childcare. The maximum value of each element is listed below, but the amount a claimant or joint claimants actually receive depends on their income.

Table 12.2 – Working tax credit for the year 2011–12

Maximum value for each element	
Element	*Maximum annual rate: 2011–12*
Basic element	£1,920
Disability element	£2,650
30-hour element	£790
Second adult element	£1,950
Lone parent element	£1,950
Severe disability element	£1,130
50 plus element (16–29 hours a week)*	£1,365
50 plus element (30+ hours a week)*	£2,030

* The 50 plus elements are mutually exclusive: where an individual works enough hours to qualify for the 50 plus element (30+ hours a week), he or she cannot also receive the 50 plus element (16–29 hours a week).

Child care element

The maximum rate of childcare element is 70% of the maximum eligible cost.

Element	Maximum eligible cost
Families with one child	£175
Families with two or more children	£300

So, the maximum child care element a person can get is either:

£140 a week (£175 × 70%) for one child, or
£240 a week (£300 × 70%) for two or more children.

The general rule is that to qualify for tax credits you must be aged 16 or over and usually live in the UK (see Figure 12.1). You may also qualify if you do not live in the UK but you are:

- a citizen of another country in the European Economic Area (EEA) and you work in the UK, or
- a Crown Servant posted overseas, or
- a citizen of a country in the EEA (including the UK) living abroad and you receive a UK state pension or contributions-based Jobseeker's Allowance.

If you feel that you meet the requirements for tax credits then you should phone HMRC helpline 0845 300 3900. Details on tax credits and an assessment of whether you qualify can be found at www.hmrc.gov.uk/taxcredits.

12.7.3 Renewal of tax credits claim

It is necessary to renew tax credits annually and HMRC will send out review packs between April and July each year. This is an annual process of reviewing credits given for the previous year and ensuring that you have the correct entitlement for the current year. It is essential that you tell HMRC about any changes in your circumstances promptly, as adjustments will only be back-dated by up to three months; if you delay making a claim, when for instance if your self-employed income has decreased substantially during the year, you may lose out on your entitlement.

If you require help renewing your tax credits claim, the contact details for the Tax Credits Helpline are as follows. You will need to have your National Insurance number to hand:

By phone:
from the UK: 0845 300 3900
for customers who are deaf, or hearing, or speech impaired:
0845 300 3909 (textphone)
from abroad: +44 2890 538 192

The Tax Credits Helpline is available from 8am to 8pm, every weekday and 8am to 4pm on Saturday (closed on Sundays, Christmas Day, Boxing Day and New Year's Day).

12.7.4 Overpayments may be clawed back

The rules for clawing back credits when a claimant's income increases changed in 2006–07 and have changed again in 2011–12 and 2012–13. For 2006–07 to 2010–11 income increases of up to £25,000 were ignored (in previous years the limit was £2,500) until the next year's assessment is made. This 'disregard' has been reduced to £10,000 for 2011–12 and will reduce to £5,000 for 2012–13. In addition, a disregard of £2,500 for reductions in income is to be introduced from 2011–12. It is important to tell HMRC straight away if income increases by more than £25,000, as the applicable tax credits are likely to decrease and an overpayment will arise, which will have to be paid back. Any decrease in tax credits will be backdated to the date the income changed.

Figure 12.1 Are you entitled to working tax credit?

Source: HMRC

13

CAPITAL GAINS TAX

GRAHAM YEATMAN

This chapter contains the following sections:

Basic principles

(1) Outline of CGT
(2) CGT and the self-assessment form
(3) Who is subject to CGT?
(4) What assets are chargeable assets?
(5) Which types of transaction may produce a chargeable gain?
(6) Hold-over relief where a gift is a chargeable transfer for IHT purposes

Computing capital gains

(7) Amount to be brought in as disposal value
(8) What costs are allowable?
(9) Assets held at 31 March 1982
(10) Other acquisition values
(11) Working out your capital gain

Special rules for certain assets

(12) Assets that have attracted capital allowances
(13) How gains are computed on quoted securities
(14) Unquoted shares
(15) When may a chargeable gain arise on foreign currency?
(16) Special rules for disposals of chattels
(17) Specific rules that apply to disposals of land and investment properties
(18) Disposal of foreign property
(19) Gains and losses on second-hand insurance policies

Unless otherwise stated, the statutory references are to the Taxation of Chargeable Gains Act (TCGA) 1992.

BASIC PRINCIPLES

13.1 OUTLINE OF CGT

Capital gains are assessed for a tax year. Under self-assessment the due date for payment of the tax is 31 January following the tax year (ie for gains arising in the year ended 5 April 2012, tax is payable by 31 January 2013). There is no requirement to make payments on account: indeed capital gains do not form part of the payment on account calculation (see 2.1.3).

The way that chargeable gains are computed is quite different from the rules that determine assessable income for tax purposes. At the time of writing different rates of CGT apply for basic and higher rate taxpayers (see 13.1.4) although both pay at a rate of 10% where entrepreneurs' relief is available (see 17.8). From 6 April 2008 to 22 June 2010, a uniform 18% rate applied no matter how large the chargeable gain (subject to the availability of entrepreneurs' relief).

The rate of CGT for years up to 2007–08 depended on the individual's income for the year and any gain was effectively taxed at the rate or rates applying to his or her top slice of income. A range of exemptions and reliefs used to apply before 6 April 2008 with a major distinction between CGT and income tax being that capital gains could be reduced by taper relief (and by indexation allowance, an adjustment for inflation up to April 1998). For information on 2007–08 and earlier years, see the 2008–09 *Tax Handbook* at 12.9–12.12.

13.1.1 Annual exemption

(s 3 TCGA 1992)

You are not liable for CGT unless you make gains of more than the annual exemption, which for 2011–12 is £10,600. The exemptions for the previous four years are:

Tax year	£	Tax year	£
2010–11	10,100	2008–09	9,600
2009–10	10,100	2007–08	9,200

13.1.2 No gain/loss on spouse or civil partner transactions

(s 58 TCGA 1992)

Provided a couple has not separated permanently, there can be no chargeable gains on any assets transferred from one spouse or civil partner to the other, whether by gift or sale. The asset is treated as passing across on a no-gain/no-loss basis, with the recipient acquiring it at his or her spouse or civil partner's cost. There is an exception to this rule in respect of the transfer of an asset that becomes part of the trading stock used in the spouse or civil partner's business.

13.1.3 Losses

(ss 16, 16ZA–ZC, 16A TCGA 1992)

Capital losses may arise as well as capital gains. The normal rule is that capital losses cannot be offset against an individual's income but must be offset against gains arising in the same year with any excess loss carried forward against capital gains of future years. Losses arising from transactions involving connected persons may only be set against gains arising from transactions with the same person.

Where gains and losses are made in the same year, the individual can decide against which gains they are set so that they can be used in the most tax-efficient way (eg where gains are liable at different rates within the same tax year – see 13.1.4 – the taxpayer can ensure that his or her loss is set against the gain suffering the highest rate of tax).

Brought-forward losses do not need to be set against gains that are covered by the annual exemption. However, current year losses must be set against capital gains before using the annual exemption.

Tax notes

If you have already realised gains in the current tax year, and these will be covered by the annual exemption, it may pay to defer sales that will produce CGT losses until next tax year. You will then be able to carry the losses forward in full to offset against future gains.

13.1.4 Rate of tax for 2010–11 and later years

(s 4 TCGA 1992)

Once the gains for the year have been computed (net of any losses), the annual exemption is deducted. For basic, higher and additional rate taxpayers, gains realised between 6 April 2010 and 22 June 2010 are liable to CGT at 18% (subject to special rules for non-UK domiciliaries – see Chapter 35) – ie the flat rate of CGT that was introduced from 6 April 2008. However, in the Emergency Budget, the coalition Government increased the CGT rate to 28% for higher and additional rate taxpayers with effect from 23 June 2010.

This unprecedented change of CGT rates during a tax year means that gains realised between and 23 June 2010 and 5 April 2011 (and in the 2011–12 tax year) are liable to CGT at 18% for basic rate taxpayers but 28% for higher rate taxpayers and trustees, assuming no other reliefs are available. However, where a basic rate taxpayer realises chargeable gains that, when added to his or her income for the year, exceed the basic rate tax band for that year, the excess gains are taxed at 28%.

Note that for disposals of business assets, entrepreneurs' relief may apply and reduce the rate of tax to 10% – see 17.8.

The introduction of the 50% 'additional rate' of tax on income over £150,000 per year from 2010–11 onwards caused considerable debate over high income individuals rearranging their investments and assets to generate capital gains rather than income. Despite the increase in the CGT rate to 28% for higher and additional rate taxpayers, there is still a tax differential of up to 22% for those willing to rearrange their finances to save tax. However, it cannot be assumed that the current relatively low rate of CGT will continue for all future tax years.

13.1.5 Trading losses

If relief for trading losses has been claimed against income from other sources for the year, any balance of unrelieved loss may be set against capital gains for that year, or against income and capital gains of the preceding tax year.

A formal claim must be lodged with HMRC by one year and ten months after the tax year of loss, ie a claim to utilise a 2009–10 trading loss must be made by 31 January 2012. Similar claims can be made for losses arising from letting furnished holiday accommodation, from post-cessation expenditure or from post-employment deductions (see 8.5 and 16.5).

13.2 CGT AND THE SELF-ASSESSMENT FORM

An individual is required to complete the CGT pages of the SA form if:

- there is CGT to pay;
- total proceeds for the tax year are more than four times the annual CGT exemption, ie for 2011–12 £42,400 and for 2010–11 £40,400;
- chargeable gains exceed the annual exemption and are reduced by losses;
- a CGT relief is to be claimed;
- a CGT election is being made;
- CGT losses are being claimed (a loss cannot be used in later years unless it has been claimed).

13.3   WHO IS SUBJECT TO CGT?

An individual's residence and domicile status may have a crucial bearing on CGT liability.

13.3.1 Significance of residence status

(s 2 TCGA 1992)

An individual is subject to the CGT legislation only if he or she is resident or ordinarily resident in the UK for the year in which relevant disposals take place. Residence and ordinary residence are determined in the same way as for income tax (see 34.2). There are two exceptions:

(1) Where a non-resident and non-ordinarily resident person carries on a trade or profession through a branch or agency in the UK, CGT may be charged on a disposal of assets used in that branch despite the fact that normally that individual would be outside the charge on capital gains.
(2) An individual who has been non-UK resident for a period of less than five complete tax years may be taxed on his or her return to the UK. This applies only where the individual had been resident or ordinarily resident in the UK during at least four of the seven tax years prior to ceasing to be resident (see further at 13.3.2 and 34.5.4).

13.3.2 Individual non-resident for part of tax year

Technically, an individual is resident or non-resident for the whole of a tax year.

Strictly, an individual who moves abroad is taxed on all capital gains for the year of departure, even if the gains are realised after the date the individual leaves the UK. By concession (ESC D2) an individual who leaves the UK and is treated on departure as not resident and not ordinarily resident here is not charged to CGT on gains from disposals made after the date of departure, provided that the individual was not resident and not ordinarily resident in the UK in at least four out of the seven years of assessment immediately preceding the year of assessment in which he or she left the UK.

Strictly, where an individual has become resident in the UK part-way through a tax year, gains prior to the date of arrival will be chargeable to CGT in the same way as gains arising after residence here has commenced. By concession (ESC D2) HMRC will treat an individual who comes to live in the UK and is treated as resident here for any year of assessment from the date of arrival as chargeable to CGT only in respect of chargeable gains from disposals made after arrival, provided that the individual has not been resident or ordinarily resident in the UK during the five years of assessment immediately preceding the year of assessment in which he or she arrives in the UK.

HMRC will assess capital gains where an individual has returned to the UK during the year in question and was non-resident for less than five complete tax years. In such a case, capital gains and losses realised in the period of non-UK residence on disposals of assets held at the time of departure, will be treated as accruing in the tax year in which he or she resumes UK residence.

Example – Non-residence for part of tax year

C was classified as non-resident in the UK from 1 January 2008 when she took up a job in the Middle East. She returned to the UK on 24 July 2012. For income tax purposes she is regarded as not resident and not ordinarily resident from 1 January 2008 to 23 July 2012, but she would be subject to CGT for the whole of 2007–08 including disposals made during the period 1 January to 5 April 2008. ESC D2 cannot apply, as C was resident in the UK for more than four out of the seven tax years preceding the year of departure.

Gains realised in the period 6 April 2008 to 5 April 2012 are not subject to CGT for the tax year concerned as C is neither resident nor ordinarily resident in those years. However, these gains will be taxed as if they were realised in 2012–13, the year in which C resumes residence in the UK. C will be taxed on all her gains for 2012–13, not merely those realised after her return on 24 July 2012. (Again, ESC D2 cannot apply, as C was resident in the UK for more than four out of the seven tax years preceding the year of return and was non-resident for less than five tax years in total.)

13.3.3 Foreign domicile may make an important difference

(s 12 TCGA 1992 – see 35.1 on domicile)

An individual who is resident (or ordinarily resident) and domiciled in the UK is subject to CGT on a worldwide basis (ie on gains realised both in the UK and abroad). By contrast, a non-UK domiciled individual can elect for a special tax treatment called the 'remittance basis' (although he or she may have to pay £30,000 (or even £50,000) for this privilege, see 35.2). Under the remittance basis, the individual will be charged tax on gains from disposals of foreign assets only if the proceeds are brought into (or, as the legislation puts it, the gains are 'remitted' to) the UK. There are more details on the CGT treatment of foreign domiciled individuals in 35.15 – these are particularly relevant for 2010–11 as there are a number of special rules required to handle the mid-year change in the rate of CGT. The rest of this chapter deals only with UK-domiciliaries.

13.4 WHAT ASSETS ARE CHARGEABLE ASSETS?

13.4.1 Assets within the scope of CGT

(s 21 TCGA 1992)

Gains on virtually all types of assets are potentially subject to CGT, subject to certain stated exceptions. Section 21(1) TCGA 1992 states:

All forms of property shall be assets for the purposes of this Act, whether situated in the UK or not, including:

(a) options, debts and incorporeal property generally, and
(b) any currency other than sterling, and
(c) any form of property created by the person disposing of it, or otherwise coming to be owned without being acquired.

The asset need not be transferable or capable of being assigned. The term 'any form of property' is all-embracing. For example, the courts have held that CGT was due on an employer's right to compensation from an employee who wished to be released from his service agreement. In another case, the right to compensation for property expropriated by the USSR in 1940 was held to be a form of property and therefore an asset for CGT purposes. Similarly, the High Court held in *Zim Properties Ltd* v *Proctor* [1985] STC 90 (see ESC D33) that the right to bring an action before the courts constitutes an asset that can be turned to account by the potential litigant negotiating a compromise and receiving a lump sum.

The conclusion therefore is that virtually all forms of property that can yield a capital sum are subject to CGT unless they are specifically exempt.

13.4.2 What assets are specifically exempt?

The following are the main categories of exempt assets:

- main private residence (see 14.1) [s 222];
- chattels that are wasting assets, unless used in a business (see 13.16) [s 44];
- chattels where the sale consideration is less than £6,000: there is some alleviation of the charge when more than £6,000 is received (see 13.16) [s 262];
- decoration for valour as long as sold by the original recipient [s 268];
- foreign currency acquired for personal expenditure outside the UK, including money spent on the purchase or maintenance of any property situated outside the UK [s 269];
- winnings from betting (eg the pools, horses, bingo and lotteries) [s 51];
- compensation or damages for a wrong or injury suffered in a profession or vocation [s 51]; certain compensation from foreign governments for property lost or confiscated [by concession];

- debts, where disposed of by the original debtor [s 251];
- National Savings certificates and non-marketable securities, ie those that cannot be transferred or are only transferable with a Minister of the Crown or National Debt Commissioner's consent [s 121];
- gilt-edged securities and qualifying corporate bonds (QCBs) and any options to acquire or dispose of such investments [s 115]: a QCB is a loan stock that is not convertible and is not a deeply discounted security (see 9.7);
- shares held in ISAs (see 25.1) and PEPs (now obsolete, see 25.2) [s 151];
- shares issued by way of business expansion schemes after 18 March 1986 (provided the BES relief has not been withdrawn) where the shares are sold, etc by the original subscriber or their spouse or civil partner;
- shares that qualified for income tax relief issued under an Enterprise Investment Scheme (see 25.5) provided the EIS relief has not been withdrawn;
- shares in a Venture Capital Trust (see 25.6);
- motor cars, unless not suitable for use as a private vehicle or commonly used for the carriage of passengers [s 263]; and veteran and vintage cars;
- woodlands [s 250];
- gifts to charities and for national purposes to any one mentioned in Schedule 3 IHTA 1984 [s 257];
- works of art where they are taken by HMRC in lieu of death duties such as IHT [s 258];
- gifts to housing associations; a claim is made by both transferor and the association [s 259];
- mortgage cash-backs: HMRC accepts that mortgagees who receive cash inducements from banks and building societies are not liable to CGT on such receipts;
- compensation for mis-sold personal pensions taken out as a result of disadvantageous advice given between 29 April 1988 and 30 June 1994;
- life assurance policies, but only where the policy is disposed of by the original owner or beneficiaries or by a person who acquired it by way of a gift from a person who had not him or herself acquired it by purchase [s 210] (see 13.19 and 28.3.10).

Where an asset is exempt, no gain is assessable. Unfortunately, it follows that no relief is normally given for losses (losses on a disposal of shares in an EIS are an exception to this general rule).

13.5 WHICH TYPES OF TRANSACTION MAY PRODUCE A CHARGEABLE GAIN?

13.5.1 Introduction

The most obvious type of disposal is an outright sale with immediate settlement of the proceeds due, but there are many other transactions that count as a disposal for CGT purposes, for example:

- outright sale (possibly with payment by instalments);
- conditional sale;
- exercise of an option;
- exchange of property;
- compulsory acquisition of asset by local authority, etc;
- sums payable as compensation or proceeds under an insurance policy;
- gifts or sales at undervalue;
- asset destroyed or becoming of negligible value.

The liability to CGT is determined by the tax year in which the date of disposal falls.

13.5.2 Outright sale

(s 28 TCGA 1992)

The date of disposal is the day on which the unconditional contract is entered into, which may be different from the date the vendor receives payment.

Sale with payment by instalments

The date of disposal is fixed by the time the parties enter into an unconditional contract. It may be possible to pay CGT arising from such transactions as the instalments come in, over a period of up to eight years (provided the instalments are spaced over a period of more than 18 months: s 280 TCGA 1992). HMRC operates a concession where a vendor grants a mortgage to a purchaser who defaults and the vendor takes back the asset in satisfaction of the sums due to him. The disposal is effectively treated as if it had never happened (see ESC D18).

13.5.3 Conditional sale

(s 28 TCGA 1992)

A conditional sale is a contract that does not take effect until a stated condition is satisfied.

Example – Conditional sale

> D agrees to purchase E's shares in XYZ Ltd provided the local authority grants planning permission over land owned by XYZ by April 2012. Under this type of agreement, E remains the legal owner of her shares until the condition is satisfied. If the local authority does not in fact grant planning permission, D is under no obligation to buy E's shares.
>
> The date of disposal under such contracts is the day the condition is satisfied and the contract becomes unconditional; in the above example, the date planning permission is granted.

13.5.4 Exercise of an option

(ss 144, 144ZA–144ZD, 144A TCGA 1992)

A 'call' option is a legally binding agreement between the owner of an asset and a third party under which the owner agrees to sell the asset if the other party decides to exercise his or her option. The purchase price payable upon the exercise of the option is normally fixed at the outset; this constitutes one of the terms of the option.

A 'put' option is one where the other party agrees to buy the asset if the owner decides to exercise an option requiring him or her to do so.

The grant of either type of option does not constitute a disposal of the asset concerned. This happens only when the option is exercised and the day on which this happens is the date of disposal.

In some cases, payment is made for the option to be granted. This is treated as a disposal of a separate asset unless the option is subsequently exercised.

13.5.5 Exchange of property

An agreement to exchange an asset for another is a disposal of the old asset and an acquisition of the new asset. If there is any cash adjustment, this must also be brought into account. For example, if F exchanges his holding in ICI for G's shareholding in Glaxo, F is treated as if he has disposed of the ICI shares for the market value of the Glaxo shares at the time of the exchange. This type of transaction commonly occurs where an individual transfers portfolio investments to a unit trust in return for units.

There is an important exception to the rule that an exchange constitutes a disposal, which may apply where a shareholder takes securities offered on a company takeover. Provided certain conditions are satisfied, the exchange does not count as a disposal and the securities issued by the acquiring company are deemed to have been derived from the original shares, with the shareholder carrying forward his or her original acquisition value.

Example – Exchange of shares on company takeover

> *H* holds 1,000 shares in XYZ plc that he acquired in 1998 for £9,000. Another company, ABC plc, makes a takeover bid and offers all XYZ shareholders a share exchange whereby they receive one ABC share (worth £30 each) for every two XYZ shares that they own. The offer document confirms that agreement has been obtained from HMRC that s 136 TCGA 1992 applies.
>
> If *H* accepts, he will receive 500 ABC shares worth £15,000, but he will be deemed to have acquired them in 1998 for £9,000. No disposal is deemed to have occurred on the share exchange.

13.5.6 Compulsory acquisition of asset

(s22 TCGA 1992)

The transfer of land to, for example, a local authority exercising its compulsory purchase powers is a disposal for CGT purposes. In some cases, once the compulsory purchase order (CPO) has been served, contracts are drawn up and the land is transferred under the contract. The rules in relation to outright sales and conditional sales apply.

Where the CPO is disputed, the date of disposal is normally the earlier of:

- the date on which compensation for the acquisition is agreed or otherwise determined; and
- the date on which the local authority enters the land in pursuance of its powers.

13.5.7 Sums payable as compensation or proceeds under an insurance policy

(s 22 TCGA 1992)

In some cases, an asset (eg a building) may be destroyed or damaged and a capital sum received as compensation. In such cases, the asset is deemed to have been disposed of at the date the capital sum is received. Similarly, where a capital sum is received from an insurance policy following such damage, receipt of insurance monies is treated as constituting a disposal.

Section 268A exempts the disposal of the right to receive the whole or any part of a qualifying payment in respect of National-Socialist persecution, or the disposal of an interest in any such right for periods from 6 April 1996.

Section 268B replaced ESC D50 from 1 April 2010 for companies and 6 April 2010 for individuals. It covers the receipt of compensation from the following territories:

- the Baltic States under the UK-USSR 1969 agreement;
- the former Soviet Union under the UK–USSR 1986 agreement;
- Czechoslovakia under the UK–Czech 1982 agreement;
- the Czech Republic and Slovakia under their domestic legislation;
- China under the UK–China 1987 agreement;
- the former East Germany under the domestic legislation of Germany;
- Uganda under that country's domestic legislation;
- Iraq and the Persian Gulf under United Nations resolutions;
- Grenada under that country's domestic legislation;
- Portugal under that country's domestic legislation.

A relevant compensation award is an award or distribution made under an Order in Council made under the Foreign Compensation Act 1950, or arrangements established by the government of a territory outside the UK that are equivalent in effect to such an Order.

13.5.8 Gifts and sales at undervalue

(s 17 TCGA 1992)

A gift is treated as a disposal at market value (except where it is from one spouse or civil partner to the other: see 13.1.2). At one time it was possible for assets to be transferred at cost, but this general form of hold-over relief was abolished in 1989. In some specific situations the capital gains may still be held over (see 13.6). For example, hold-over relief may be available where the gift involves business property (see 17.4) or is a lifetime chargeable transfer for IHT purposes, such as a gift to a discretionary trust (see 30.12) – but not a PET (see 30.6.1).

Such a gift often constitutes a transaction between connected persons: see also 33.10.

13.5.9 Asset destroyed or becoming of negligible value

(s 24 TCGA 1992)

The total destruction or entire loss of an asset constitutes a disposal. This could be physical destruction (eg by fire) or legal/financial destruction (eg bankruptcy or winding-up).

The legislation also permits a person to elect that he or she should be treated as having disposed of an asset that has become of negligible value. Normally, a capital loss will arise on such an occasion.

'Negligible value' is interpreted by HMRC as meaning 'considerably less than small'. For example, HMRC will only agree that shares, loan stock and other securities are of negligible value on being satisfied that the owner is unlikely to recover anything other than a nominal amount on the liquidation of the company. The mere fact that shares have been suspended or de-listed by a stock exchange is not regarded as sufficient.

The legislation provides that a disposal is deemed to take place in the year during which HMRC agrees that the asset has become of negligible value (HMRC publishes a list of shares that it agrees are of negligible value at www.hmrc.gov.uk/cgt/negvalist.htm). However, HMRC permits a claim to take effect up to two tax years prior to the claim provided the asset was of negligible value in the prior year (see s 24(2)).

In practice it is not always beneficial for an individual to claim the benefit of s 24(2), or indeed for a claim to be made, until such time as there are gains against which the loss can be set (see 13.1.3).

> **Tax notes**
>
> Because the date of disposal is linked to the date that you submit a negligible value claim, you can choose to defer the loss to a later year if this will be beneficial.

HMRC does not accept that a claim may be made by someone who acquired his or her shares from a spouse or civil partner at a time when the shares were already of negligible value.

13.6 HOLD-OVER RELIEF WHERE A GIFT IS A CHARGEABLE TRANSFER FOR IHT PURPOSES

(s 260 TCGA 1992)

Where a gift or a sale at undervalue is a chargeable transfer for IHT purposes, and the donee is UK resident, the donor and donee can elect for any gain to be held over. This generally means that the asset is deemed to pass across to the donee on a no gain/no loss basis, with the donee inheriting the donor's acquisition cost. This relief is not available for transfers of assets to settlor interested trusts after 9 December 2003. In 2006–07, the definition of a settlor-interested trust was extended to include trusts under which the settlor's minor, unmarried children can benefit.

Section 260 relief is not available where the gift is a potentially exempt transfer for IHT purposes (see 30.6) but another type of hold-over relief may be available if the property being transferred is business property (see 17.4). You should obtain a copy of Helpsheet IR295 if you make such a chargeable transfer. Section 260 was extended to cover the various situations encountered on making transfers to and from trusts for bereaved minors (s 71A) and '18-25 trusts' (s 71D) with effect from 22 March 2006.

The held-over gain becomes chargeable if the donee ceases to be resident within six years.

> **Tax notes**
>
> The right to transfer shares to a (non-settlor interested) family trust without having to pay CGT is crucially important. Transfers to such trusts can save IHT but without hold-over relief the CGT consequences would often be unattractive.

COMPUTING CAPITAL GAINS

13.7 AMOUNT TO BE BROUGHT IN AS DISPOSAL VALUE

13.7.1 Market value

(s 17 TCGA 1992)

The general rule is that market value must be used unless the transaction is at arm's length. In the straightforward situation where a contract is entered into with a third party on a commercial basis, the disposal proceeds are the actual sale proceeds. An individual is not penalised because he or she has made a bad bargain and sold an asset for less than it is really worth. However, if the bargain is not at arm's length and the individual deliberately sells the asset for an amount less than its true value, the legislation requires market value to be substituted. If the disposal is to a connected person, for example a relative or the trustee of a family settlement or a family company, there is an automatic assumption that the bargain is not at arm's length and market value is always substituted for the actual sale proceeds if the two amounts are different. There are three exceptions:

- transactions between spouses and civil partners (see 13.1.2);
- gifts to charities and similar bodies (see 13.4.2);
- situations where a hold-over election can be made (see 13.6 and 17.4).

> **Tax notes**
>
> Take advice if you are intending to give (or sell) assets to a connected person otherwise you may end up paying a lot of tax on notional sale proceeds.

13.7.2 Contingent liabilities

(s 49 TCGA 1992)

There may be occasions where the sale contract may require part of the proceeds to be returned at some time in the future. This is known as a sale with 'contingent liabilities'.

Suppose a vendor receives £150,000 for the disposal of a plot of land, but is under an obligation to return £60,000 in certain circumstances. Will the capital gain be charged on sale proceeds of £150,000 or £90,000? In fact, s 49 provides that in these circumstances the capital gain must be computed in the first instance without any deduction for the contingent liability, ie £150,000. However, if and when the vendor is required to refund part of the sale proceeds because the contingent liability has become an actual liability, the CGT assessment is adjusted accordingly.

13.7.3 Contingent consideration: quantifiable

(s 48 TCGA 1992)

In a similar way, it is possible that the contract may provide that additional sums may be payable if certain conditions are satisfied in the future. If it is possible to put a value on the further amount of consideration that is 'contingent' (ie payable only if certain conditions are satisfied), the full amount that might be received is brought into account at the date of disposal without any discount. If the conditions are not satisfied, so that the further amounts are never received, an adjustment is made later to the CGT assessment.

13.7.4 Contingent consideration: unquantifiable

The position is different where the contingent consideration cannot be ascertained at the date of disposal (this is normally the situation where the contingent consideration may vary and is not a fixed amount). Basically, the legislation requires that the market value of the right to receive the future consideration should be regarded as the disposal proceeds. The difference between this amount and the amount eventually received forms a separate CGT computation for the year in which the final amount of the actual contingent consideration is determined. The treatment of contingent consideration, especially variable contingent consideration, is fairly complex. It normally arises in relation to either land or shares in private companies.

See also 17.9 on earn-outs.

Tax notes

A sale for contingent consideration can be a tax minefield and it is essential to take professional advice.

13.7.5 Deduction for amounts charged as income

(s 37 TCGA 1992)

In some cases the disposal of an asset may give rise to an income tax charge. Where this happens, the amount taken into account in arriving at taxable income is deducted from the sale proceeds and only the balance is brought into account for CGT purposes. This commonly arises where a private company buys back its own shares and the transaction is treated as a distribution (see 9.9.7).

13.8 WHAT COSTS ARE ALLOWABLE?

13.8.1 Certain specific types of expenditure

The legislation permits only a limited range of expenses to be deducted in computing capital gains and losses. Section 38(1) TCGA 1992 states:

The sums allowable as a deduction from the consideration in the computation of the gain accruing to a person on the disposal of an asset shall be restricted to:

(a) the amount of value of the consideration, in money or money's worth, given by the individual or on his or her behalf wholly and exclusively for the acquisition of the asset, together with the incidental costs to the individual of the acquisition or, if the asset was not acquired by the individual, any expenditure wholly and exclusively incurred by him or her in providing the asset,

(b) the amount of any expenditure wholly and exclusively incurred on the asset by the individual or on his or her behalf for the purpose of enhancing the value of the asset, being expenditure reflected in the state or nature of the asset at the time of the disposal, and any expenditure wholly and exclusively incurred by the individual in establishing, preserving or defending title to, or to a right over, the asset,

(c) the incidental costs of making the disposal.

13.8.2 The cost of the asset

The asset's market value at 31 March 1982 must be substituted for actual cost if the asset was held at that date (see 13.9.1).

13.8.3 Incidental costs of acquisition

These are limited to:

● fees, commission or remuneration paid to a surveyor, valuer, auctioneer, accountant, agent or legal adviser;
● transfer/conveyancing charges (including stamp duty); and
● advertising to find a seller.

13.8.4 Enhancement expenditure

The legislation permits a deduction to be claimed in respect of expenditure incurred in order to enhance the asset's value provided such expenditure is reflected in the state or nature of the asset at the time of disposal. The latter condition excludes relief for improvements that have worn out by the time the asset is disposed of. Certain grey areas are worth mentioning:

- Initial expenditure by way of repairs to newly acquired property that is let may be allowable if no relief has been given in computing UK property income.
- Expenditure means money or money's worth; it does not include the value of personal labour or skill.

Tax notes

HMRC will charge tax on notional sale proceeds if you give an asset away but it will not give relief for notional expenditure where you carry out the improvement work yourself.

13.8.5 Expenditure incurred in establishing, preserving or defending legal title

The case law concerned with the allowable nature of this expenditure hinges on the interrelationship between the words 'incurred', 'establishing', etc. The High Court held in *IRC* v *Richards' Executors* (1971) 46 TC 626 that the cost of making an inventory and providing a valuation for a grant of probate was allowable under this head (see SP2/04).

13.8.6 Incidental costs of disposals

The following expenses may be deductible under this head:

- fees, commission or remuneration for the professional services of a surveyor, valuer, auctioneer, accountant, agent or legal adviser;
- transfer/conveyancing charges (including stamp duty);
- advertising to find a buyer;
- any other costs reasonably incurred in making any valuation or apportionment for CGT purposes, including in particular expenses reasonably incurred in ascertaining market value where this is required. Professional costs incurred in getting a valuation agreed with HMRC are not allowable.

Tax notes

The costs of getting a valuation at 31 March 1982 are allowable in arriving at your capital gain but the valuer's charges for negotiating with HMRC and arriving at an agreed valuation are not allowable. You need to establish in advance what fees are likely to be incurred in such negotiations.

13.8.7 Part disposals

(s 42 TCGA 1992)

Where a person disposes of part of an asset, the cost is apportioned between the part disposed of and the part retained by the formula $[A \div (A + B)]$ where A is the consideration received or deemed to have been received and B is the market value of the part retained.

Example – Part disposals

> B holds 1,000 shares in XYZ Ltd that cost him £10,000. The company is taken over and he receives cash of £5,000 and convertible loan stock issued by the acquiring company worth £15,000 (assume that in this particular case no capital gain arises in respect of the loan stock because it is issued on the occasion of a takeover and the necessary clearances have been obtained from HMRC (see 13.15.3 and 13.15.4)). B's acquisition value will be apportioned as
>
> $$£10,000 \times \frac{5,000}{(5,000 + 15,000)} = £2,500$$
>
> ie the proportion of acquisition value that relates to the part sold. £7,500 is treated as the acquisition value of the part retained, ie it will be taken into account in computing any gain or loss as and when the loan stock is sold.

13.8.8 Small capital receipts

(s 122 TCGA 1992)

There are occasions where the formula $[A \div (A + B)]$ does not have to be used, and the amount received is simply deducted from the owner's acquisition value. The most common situation where this arises is where a shareholder sells his or her entitlement under a rights issue, normally on a nil-paid basis. Provided the amount received is small as compared with the asset's value, the receipt can be deducted from the owner's acquisition value. 'Small' in this context, (as interpreted by HMRC in IR Int. 157) can mean 5% or less of the value of the asset, or a receipt of £3,000 or less whether or not falling within the 5% test; exceptionally, taxpayers may suggest different limits in the context of their particular circumstances (see *O'Rourke* v *Binks* [1992] BTC 460).

> **Tax notes**
>
> Small capital proceeds received are deducted from the allowable cost on the eventual disposal of the asset.

13.8.9 Capital sums applied in restoring assets

(s 23 TCGA 1992)

Under normal circumstances, an asset is regarded as having been disposed of for CGT purposes if it is lost or destroyed. However, where a capital sum is received from such an asset (eg insurance policy proceeds), the owner may claim that the asset is not treated as disposed of if at least 95% of the capital sum is spent in restoring the asset.

13.9 ASSETS HELD AT 31 MARCH 1982

(s 35 and Schedules 2 and 3, TCGA 1992)

13.9.1 General rebasing

(s 35 TCGA 1992)

The general rule is that where assets were held at 31 March 1982, it is to be assumed that they were sold on that date and immediately reacquired at their market value at that time. This is known as 'rebasing'.

> **Tax notes**
>
> For disposals made on or after 6 April 2008, there are no exceptions to this rule.

Different rules applied in 2007–08 and earlier years (see the 2008–09 *Tax Handbook* at 12.9.1–12.9.5).

13.9.2 Assets acquired via a gift made between 1 April 1982 and 5 April 1988

(Schedule 4 TCGA 1992)

A special relief used to apply but was abolished for disposals on or after 6 April 2008. For further details, see the 2008–09 *Tax Handbook* at 12.9.3.

13.10 OTHER ACQUISITION VALUES

13.10.1 Assets acquired via inheritance or family trust

(ss 62, 71 and 274 TCGA 1992)

Where a person inherits an asset, he or she is generally deemed to have acquired it for its market value at the date of the testator's death (ie probate value). There is one exception to this: it is possible to claim a form of relief from IHT where quoted securities have gone down in value after the person has died (see 30.11.3). Where such relief has been claimed for IHT, a corresponding adjustment is made so that the person taking the assets concerned is deemed to have acquired them not at probate value, but at the value actually brought into account for IHT purposes after taking account of the fall in value.

Where assets have been acquired from a trust, the beneficiary's acquisition value is normally the market value at the time the asset is transferred to him or her. However, the acquisition value may be lower than this where the trustees have claimed hold-over relief under either the general hold-over relief provisions that prevailed up to 5 April 1989 or the more restrictive provisions that have applied subsequently (see 17.4).

13.10.2 Deemed acquisition value where income tax charged

(ss 120 and 141 TCGA 1992)

Where a person is subject to an income tax charge on earnings under ITEPA 2003 when he or she acquires an asset (eg where an individual exercises a non-approved share option), he or she is deemed to have acquired it for an amount equal to the value taken into account in computing the income tax charge on him or her. Similarly, where a person acquires shares by way of a stock dividend (ie where there is a choice between a cash dividend or further shares issued by a UK company), the shares are deemed to be acquired for a consideration equal to the amount brought into account for income tax purposes by reason of the stock dividend (see further 9.8.6).

13.10.3 **Share options exercised up to 9 April 2003**

A 2002 decision by the Court of Appeal in the case of *Mansworth* v *Jelley* [2002] STC 1013 revealed an anomaly. The Court held that where an employee acquired shares by exercising an option, his or her acquisition cost was market value at that date *plus* an amount equal to the sum on which he or she was assessed for income tax purposes. This amounted to a form of 'double-counting' and generally meant that a CGT loss would arise on the sale of those shares.

This anomaly was corrected in relation to share options exercised after 8 April 2003 but the amending legislation was not retrospective. You should take professional advice if you exercised such options.

In 2009, HMRC changed its view on pre-9 April 2003 transactions, see HMRC Tax Briefs 30/09 and 60/09. This may affect claims for unused capital losses against gains realised in 2008–09 or other years where a self-assessment remains open.

13.11 WORKING OUT YOUR CAPITAL GAIN

Table 13.1 can be used as a 'pro forma' when calculating capital gains or losses.

Table 13.1 – Computing your 2011–12 capital gains

Sale proceeds (consider whether the market value provisions may apply) – see 13.7).	A	
Deduct incidental costs of disposal (see 13.8.6).	B	
Net sale proceeds (A – B).		C
If the asset was acquired after 31 March 1982, enter cost.	D	
Amount of any enhancement expenditure.	E	
If the asset was owned at 31 March 1982, enter value at 31 March 1982 (see 13.9.1).	F	
Enter the amount of enhancement expenditure – if 31 March 1982 value is entered at F or G, include only post-31 March 1982 enhancement expenditure.	G	
Enter the total of figures entered in any of D and E, or F and G		H
Capital gain (C – H).		I

SPECIAL RULES FOR CERTAIN ASSETS

13.12 ASSETS THAT HAVE ATTRACTED CAPITAL ALLOWANCES

No CGT loss arises on a disposal of an asset whose cost has attracted capital allowances (see 16.2). On the other hand, the cost is fully deductible if the disposal gives rise to a gain.

The Special Commissioners have held that a loss on a disposal of units in an enterprise zone property trust is an allowable loss even though the individual had received 100% capital allowances (see 25.7). This decision was on the basis that the units were a distinct asset that was separate from the underlying properties on which the capital allowances arose. See *Smallwood* v *HMRC* 2005 SpC 509 and [2007] EWCA Civ 462.

13.13 HOW GAINS ARE COMPUTED ON QUOTED SECURITIES

'Quoted securities' means shares, loan stock, warrants, etc that are dealt in on the London Stock Exchange and other similar stock exchanges recognised by HMRC as having similar rules and procedures to the London exchange. This section deals with the tax treatment of transactions such as:

- sale of part of a shareholding;
- bonus issues and rights issues;
- takeovers and mergers.

13.13.1 Identification rules

Specific rules apply where a person sells part of his or her holding in securities of the same class. Securities are treated as being of the same class if they are treated as such under stock exchange practice. For example, all ICI ordinary shares are securities of the same class, whereas BP ordinary shares are not and form a different class.

Identification rules on disposals in 2011–12

Shares sold are identified as follows:

- with acquisitions on the same day;
- with acquisitions made within 30 days before or after;
- with acquisitions being treated as having come out of a pool. All acquisitions of shares of the same class are treated as forming a single pool, with shares coming out at average cost.

Different identification rules applied in 2007–08 and in earlier years, see the 2008–09 *Tax Handbook* at 12.15.

Special election for shares acquired under an employee share scheme

There is one exception to the 'same day' rule. Where an employee acquires shares from more than one employee share scheme and sells some of those shares all on the same day, the employee can elect as to which shares have been sold.

13.13.2 Takeovers and mergers

There is a special relief that may apply where a company issues shares or securities in order to take over another company or takes a 25% stake in the target company. The shareholders who accept this offer will not be treated as making a disposal provided they meet one of the following requirements:

- together with persons connected with them, they do not hold more than 5% of the company's share capital; or
- HMRC is satisfied that the share exchange is a bona fide commercial transaction that is not entered into with a view to tax avoidance.

In *Snell* v *HMRC* 2006 SpC 532, it was held that an exchange of shares for loan notes had a tax avoidance motive because the taxpayer intended to take up residence in Jersey before cashing in the loan notes and it was clear from the contemporaneous records that he had deliberately chosen to take loan notes rather than cash to enable him to defer the gain until after his UK residence had ceased.

So far as quoted securities are concerned, the position is generally straightforward. The offer document forwarded to shareholders normally states whether clearance has been obtained from HMRC under s 138 TCGA 1992 confirming that s 135 TCGA 1992 applies. Provided this is the case, no capital gain will arise on the exchange of shares for securities issued by the company making the takeovers.

What happens if there is a mixture of shares and cash?

Suppose a shareholder in X plc is offered a share in Y plc plus cash of £1 in exchange for every share that he or she holds in X plc. If he or she accepts this offer there will be a part disposal. The value of the new Y plc shares on the first day of trading is taken and the following computation is required:

Amount received via cash element Take proportion of cost of holding in X plc	A
$$\frac{\text{Cash received}}{(\text{Cash + Value of Y plc shares})} \times \text{Cost}$$	B
Capital gain/(loss) on cash element	C

What happens if there is a mixture of shares and loan stock?

Suppose the shareholder in X plc had instead accepted an offer of one share in Y plc plus £1.25 loan stock. Assume that when the new Y plc shares were first traded they had a price of £2 and the loan stock was traded at £80 for every £100 nominal. The cost of the two types of new securities would be determined as follows.

Example – Takeover by mixture of shares and loan stock

Apportioned to Y plc shares:

$$\frac{\text{Value of Y shares}}{\text{Value of Y shares + Y loan stock}}$$

ie $\dfrac{£2}{£2 + £0.80} \times \text{Cost of X shares} = \text{Deemed cost of Y shares}$

Apportioned to Y plc loan stock:

$$\frac{\text{Value of loan stock}}{\text{Value of loan stock + Shares}}$$

ie $\dfrac{£0.80}{(£0.80 + £2)} \times \text{Cost of X shares} = \text{Deemed cost of Y loan stock}$

This division of the cost of the original holding in X plc will be relevant as and when there is a disposal of either the Y plc shares or loan stock.

Tax notes

The part disposal rules can produce some unexpected results if one part of the 'package' subsequently increases in value quite substantially. This happened when BT demerged O_2: the way that a BT shareholder's cost was divided between BT and O_2 shares reflected the respective values of the BT and O_2 shares at the time of the split. The O_2 shares then increased in value far more than the BT shares.

13.13.3 Special rules where share exchange involves qualifying corporate bonds

(s 116 TCGA 1992)

Loan stock is often a type of qualifying corporate bond (QCB), ie an exempt asset for CGT purposes (see 13.4.2). The offer document sent to shareholders on a company takeover normally draws attention to whether the loan stock falls into this category. If it does, the investor is only entitled to entrepreneurs' relief on a subsequent disposal if he or she fulfilled the conditions at the time of the takeover. This contrasts with the treatment of non-QCBs. However, this may be a good way to lock in the relief where the qualifying conditions were met at the time of the original disposal and may not be met at the time of a later disposal of the new stock. Disposal of the loan stock creates a capital gain calculated according to values at the time of the takeover and not the loan stock's value when it is sold or redeemed.

As a matter of fact, the deferred gain is triggered by any kind of disposal of the QCBs. For example, a gift of the loan stock causes the deferred gain to become chargeable. Indeed, a chargeable gain could even arise on a deemed disposal such as would apply if the company that had issued the loan stock went into liquidation.

For QCBs acquired between 6 April 2008 and 22 June 2010 but which are disposed of after 22 June 2010, the special transitional rules for entrepreneurs' relief may need to be considered – see 17.8.

13.14 UNQUOTED SHARES

There are some special features to the way in which gains on unquoted shares are computed. Other aspects follow the principles already covered in this chapter. For example, the identification rules where a person disposes of part of a shareholding of unquoted shares are exactly the same as for quoted securities (see 13.13.3).

There are also practical considerations that do not arise in relation to quoted securities such as the need to negotiate a valuation of the shares at 31 March 1982.

In the case of gifts, the value used for CGT purposes is normally the value of the asset taken by the acquirer, not the reduction in value for the person making the disposal. From this point of view, CGT works differently from IHT (see 29.3.3).

13.14.1 Shares held at 31 March 1982

Inevitably, the market value of shares held at 31 March 1982 will be the subject of negotiation with HMRC's Shares Valuation Division and professional advice should be taken. The shares' value will reflect factors such as the nature of the company, its assets and the size of the shareholding. See www.hmrc.gov.uk/shareschemes/shares-valuation.htm.

The general approach adopted by the SVD is to determine the value of the unquoted shares and securities by reference to a completely hypothetical market. It is assumed that any prospective purchaser will have available all of the information that a prudent purchaser of the asset might reasonably require when proposing to purchase it from a willing vendor by private treaty and at arm's length. Open market value must be assumed and the yardstick is always the requirement of the willing and prudent purchaser and not the wishes, etc of the directors of the private company.

The company's underlying assets are largely irrelevant if a person has only a relatively small minority shareholding; they may be a more important consideration if an individual has control. Therefore, a quite different valuation might be placed on shares that form, say, a 7% shareholding from a 51% shareholding that gives the owner control. In the former case the valuers will be looking at factors such as the level of dividends paid in the past and the likelihood of such dividends being paid in the future. At the other extreme, a 51% shareholder would place great value on a 7/51 part of his or her shareholding as a disposal of such shares would lead that shareholder to lose voting control over the company.

On a practical note, it is possible to enter into negotiations with HMRC in advance of filing your SA tax return. If you wish to reduce any uncertainty to the minimum by trying to agree 31 March 1982 values before filing your return, ask HMRC for form CG34.

13.15 WHEN MAY A CHARGEABLE GAIN ARISE ON FOREIGN CURRENCY?

There is an exemption for foreign currency provided it was acquired for an individual's personal expenditure abroad. In all other situations, foreign currency is a chargeable asset and a gain (or loss) will arise when the currency is disposed of. A disposal may take place on the foreign currency being spent, converted into another foreign currency, or converted into sterling. In each of these situations, the sterling equivalent of the foreign currency at the date of acquisition is compared with the sterling equivalent at the date of disposal.

In theory, each separate bank account denominated in foreign currency counts as a separate asset. In practice, HMRC permits taxpayers to treat all bank accounts containing the particular foreign currency as one account (see SP10/84 and M03/2010). Anti-avoidance was introduced from 16 December 2009 to prevent losses from accruing to remittance basis taxpayers where amounts on foreign currency bank accounts have been taken into account for income tax purposes and, due to the operation of s 37, there has been no genuine economic loss.

13.16 SPECIAL RULES FOR DISPOSALS OF CHATTELS

(s 262 TCGA 1992)

A chattel is defined by the legislation as a tangible, movable asset. Examples are a picture, a silver teapot and a first edition of a famous novel.

13.16.1 Chattels that are wasting assets

(s 45 TCGA 1992)

Special rules apply to chattels that fall within the definition of 'wasting assets'. These are assets with a useful life expectancy of less than 50 years. They are exempt regardless of the amount of the sale proceeds. Equally, there is no relief for any losses realised on their disposal.

This exemption is not available for an asset on which the owner was entitled to capital allowances because it had been used in a trade.

13.16.2 Other types of chattel

(s 262 TCGA 1992)

A gain arising on the disposal of a chattel not covered by the exemption in 13.16.1 is exempt only if the sale proceeds do not exceed £6,000. However, there is a form of marginal relief under which, if the sale proceeds are more than £6,000, the maximum chargeable gain cannot exceed five-thirds of the excess. For example, if a picture costing £900 is sold for £6,900, the chargeable gain cannot exceed 5/3 × £900, ie £1,500.

In some cases the marginal relief will not help, for example if the sale proceeds were £6,900, but the picture had cost £5,800, the chargeable gain would be computed on normal principles.

Losses

A capital loss may arise on the disposal of a chattel. Where the sale proceeds are less than £6,000, the loss must be calculated on the basis that notional sale proceeds of £6,000 were received. For example, if an uninsured antique table costing £10,000 is destroyed by fire, the proceeds are taken to be £6,000, not nil.

Assets forming a set

Several chattels may be deemed to form a single asset, for example a set of antique chairs and a table. Where these are sold to the same person, or to persons acting in concert, they may be regarded as the disposal of a single asset. This rule may apply even though the sales take place at different times. As a consequence, gains that would otherwise be exempt because of the £6,000 limit may be brought into charge.

For example, someone may own four antique chairs each worth £6,000. If they were to be sold one at a time to the same person, the total sale would be regarded as the sale of a single asset for £24,000 and the £6,000 exemption would not apply.

13.17 SPECIFIC RULES THAT APPLY TO DISPOSALS OF LAND AND INVESTMENT PROPERTIES

13.17.1 Will the gain be subject to income tax?

Speculative or short-term transactions in land may well give rise to a claim by HMRC that the individual is dealing in land and therefore the transaction is subject to tax as trading income. Whether a trade is being carried on is a matter of fact. HMRC may cite the following 'badges of trade' in support of an assessment as trading income:

- evidence that an asset was acquired with a view to its being resold in the short term;
- a large part of the purchase price being financed by borrowings, especially short-term borrowings such as an overdraft;
- the taxpayer has a background of similar transactions or has special expertise that assists in achieving a profit on disposal of the asset.

In *Kirkby* v *Hughes* [1993] STC 76, the court held that the taxpayer was carrying out a trade and the following were regarded as badges of trade:

- the properties were larger than would be expected for sole occupancy;
- the periods of occupancy were short;
- another property was purchased while the taxpayer was still resident in the first without any clear intention of selling the first;
- there was no proof that the taxpayer had intended to acquire the first house as a personal asset.

Quite separately from the above, Chapter 3, Part 13 ITA 2007 may enable HMRC to assess a gain to income tax as miscellaneous income. Chapter 3, Part 13 may apply where a capital gain is realised and UK land:

- was acquired with the sole or main object of realising a gain on its disposal; or
- is developed with the sole or main object of realising a gain on the disposal of it when developed.

There are also circumstances where disposal of shares in a company that owns land may give rise to an income tax charge (see 33.2.3).

Chapter 3, Part 13 can apply whether or not the person is UK-resident. Furthermore, the capital gain may be received by a third party such as a company and yet still give rise to an assessment under these provisions if an individual has transferred the opportunity of making a gain to the third party. Moreover, the rules can also apply to one or more transactions that form a scheme and any number of transactions may be regarded as constituting a single arrangement or scheme if a common purpose can be discerned in them, or if there is other sufficient evidence of a common purpose. For a fuller account of Chapter 3, Part 13 ITA 2007, see 33.2.

The main disadvantage for a UK resident who is assessed to income tax on gains from land is the differential in the tax rates applying to income and gains and that he or she cannot deduct the annual exemption. Also, the fact that gains are assessed as income may mean that the individual cannot make use of capital losses that have been brought forward from earlier years or have arisen during the same year on other transactions. On the other hand, where an individual has borrowed to acquire the land, he or she may be able to deduct the interest in calculating the gain for income tax purposes, whereas no deduction is normally available for CGT purposes.

The main circumstances where HMRC is likely to argue that these rules apply is where the individual concerned is a builder, developer or estate agent or has entered into a large number of land transactions or the amounts involved in a particular transaction are substantial.

13.17.2 Specific points on computation of gains on transactions involving land

(Schedule 8 TCGA 1992)

Wasting assets

Where a person disposes of a wasting asset the individual's cost or acquisition value may need to be restricted. This applies where a person disposes of a leasehold interest in land and the lease has less than 50 years to run at the date of disposal. Table 13.2 shows how the cost of a lease must be adjusted.

Table 13.2 – Depreciation of leases

Years	Percentage	Years	Percentage	Years	Percentage
50 (or more)	100	33	90.280	16	64.116
49	99.657	32	89.354	15	61.617
48	99.289	31	88.371	14	58.971
47	98.902	30	87.330	13	56.167
46	98.490	29	86.226	12	53.191
45	98.059	28	85.053	11	50.038
44	97.595	27	83.816	10	46.695
43	97.107	26	82.496	9	43.154
42	96.593	25	81.100	8	39.399
41	96.041	24	79.622	7	35.414
40	95.457	23	78.055	6	31.195
39	94.842	22	76.399	5	26.722
38	94.189	21	74.635	4	21.983
37	93.497	20	72.770	3	16.959
36	92.761	19	70.791	2	11.629
35	91.981	18	68.697	1	5.983
34	91.156	17	66.470	0	0

The fraction of the cost of the lease which is not allowed is given by the fraction

$$\frac{P(1) - P(2)}{P(1)}$$

where

P(1) = the percentage derived from the table for the duration of the lease at acquisition

P(2) = the percentage derived from the table for the duration of the lease at the time of disposal

Example – Wasting assets

E purchases a 48-year lease in 1997 for £10,000. In 2005 she spends £2,000 on improvements that affect the value of the lease. She disposes of it with 33 years left in 2012. Her allowable expenditure is therefore as follows:

$$\text{Original cost } £10,000 \times \frac{(99.289 - 92.280)}{99.286} \qquad = £907$$

$$\text{Additional } £2,000 \times \frac{(95.457 - 90.280)}{95.457} \qquad = \underline{£108}$$

$$= \underline{£1,015}$$

$$\text{Total allowable expenditure} = £12,000 - 1,015 = £10,985$$

Enhancement expenditure

It commonly happens that a person has spent money over the years on improvements. This expenditure can be taken into account provided the improvements are reflected in the state of the property when it is sold.

Where such enhancement expenditure occurred after 31 March 1982, the expenditure is added to the acquisition value.

Enhancement expenditure prior to 31 March 1982 may be taken into account only if the total of original cost and pre-31 March 1982 enhancement expenditure exceeds the market value at 31 March 1982.

13.18 DISPOSAL OF FOREIGN PROPERTY

13.18.1 Gains must be computed in sterling

Just as a chargeable gain may arise on the disposal of foreign currency, there may similarly be a currency gain on the disposal of certain foreign assets, such as a house or flat in a foreign country. Where overseas assets are disposed of, it is not correct to calculate the gain or loss in terms of the foreign currency and then convert that gain or loss into sterling at the time of the disposal. Instead, the following formula should be used:

Market value of foreign currency received at sale (converted at exchange rate applying at that time)	X
Deduct sterling equivalent of cost of asset on acquisition (converted at exchange rate applying at the time of acquisition)	Y
Chargeable gain	Z

Example – Disposal of foreign property

G acquired a property in the USA in 1987 for $600,000 (exchange rate $2:£1) and sold it in 2012 for $720,000 (exchange rate $1.6:£1). The gain would be computed as follows:

	£
Sale proceeds	
(proceeds converted at $1.6:£1)	450,000
Less: cost at the conversion rate applicable at date of purchase	(300,000)
Chargeable gain	150,000

This can produce some unexpected consequences. Suppose that *G* had borrowed the purchase price in $. When she repaid the mortgage on selling the property, she might well be left with no cash in hand. In fact, the profit on the sale of the property in sterling terms was matched by the increase in the sterling value of her mortgage debt. However, there is no CGT relief for this increase and the gain of £150,000 would still be chargeable.

13.18.2 Relief for foreign tax

(ss 277–278 TCGA 1992)

Many overseas countries reserve the right to charge CGT on the disposal of real estate situated in that country, whether or not the owner is resident there. Where a UK resident has had to pay foreign tax in these circumstances, he or she may claim double tax relief. In effect, the overseas country's tax is available as a credit against the UK tax.

Example – Relief for foreign tax

H has a property in Italy that cost 160m lire (at the time of purchase this was the equivalent of £90,000). The property is sold for 120,000 euros and there is a chargeable gain for UK tax purposes of £50,000 (assume that Italian CGT of £7,000 is payable). If *H*'s £50,000 gain is chargeable to tax at 28%, the position would be:

	£
UK CGT	14,000
Less: double tax relief	(7,000)
UK CGT actually payable	7,000

However, there is no relief for any excess. Thus, if *H* had unrelieved losses brought forward such that his UK tax had been only £6,500, there would be no relief for the balance.

Sometimes there will be a liability for foreign tax, but no capital gains for UK tax purposes.

Example – Foreign CGT only

> *J* disposes of a property in Sierra Leone at a £40,000 loss in sterling terms. However, there was a gain in terms of local currency and the tax bill in Sierra Leone is £10,000. *J* can claim a deduction for this amount as if it were a deduction from his sale proceeds, and this would mean that his loss for UK CGT purposes would be increased from £40,000 to £50,000.

13.18.3 Foreign gains that cannot be remitted

(s 279 TCGA 1992)

Where a person realises a gain on the disposal of assets situated abroad, but is genuinely unable to transfer that gain to the UK because of restrictions imposed abroad or because the foreign currency is not convertible, the amount of the gain may be omitted from assessment for the year in which it arose. Instead, the gain will be assessed to CGT only when it becomes remittable. Claims for this relief to apply must be made within four years of the end of the tax year in which the gain was realised.

13.19 GAINS AND LOSSES ON SECOND-HAND INSURANCE POLICIES

An insurance policy will normally be an exempt asset for CGT purposes. However, there is an exception for some second-hand policies.

13.19.1 Is a second-hand insurance policy a chargeable asset for CGT purposes?

Until 2002–03, a second-hand insurance policy was a chargeable asset for CGT purposes only if the person making the disposal acquired it by purchase (as opposed to receiving it as a gift). This allowed a CGT charge to be avoided in many circumstances. For example, where the person who purchased a policy gave it to his or her spouse, he or she would not be regarded as disposing of a chargeable asset because he or she had acquired it by gift rather than purchase. This loophole was plugged from 9 April 2003, and now, a second-hand policy is also a chargeable asset where it is received as a gift from a person who acquired it by purchase.

The 2003 rules also cater for more complex situations where policies have at any stage been bought second-hand. However, these rules still allow exemption in three circumstances. The policy will not constitute a chargeable asset where consideration is given only on transfers between:

- spouses or civil partners;
- former spouses under the terms of a divorce settlement;
- two companies within a group of companies.

13.19.2 Computation of CGT losses

Where a second-hand insurance policy is sold, the amount brought into account in computing taxable income is excluded from the consideration used in computing a CGT gain (or loss). In practice, this used to produce substantial CGT losses. From 9 April 2003, the CGT loss is restricted to the economic loss, which will generally be negligible.

14

YOUR MAIN RESIDENCE

GRAHAM YEATMAN

Until the recent falls in the property market, owning a residential property had been regarded more as holding an investment rather than providing the owner with a place to live. The existence of a capital gains tax exemption for an individual's main residence added to the attractiveness of this 'investment' but many do not fully understand the complexities of the exemption: this is illustrated by the public uproar over MPs 'flipping' their main residence even though this is clearly permitted by the rules of the exemption.

This chapter contains the following sections:

(1) Main residence exemption
(2) Possible restrictions on exemption
(3) Living in job-related accommodation
(4) Treatment where property not occupied throughout ownership period
(5) Passing on the family home – CGT considerations
(6) Anti-avoidance provisions
(7) Stamp duty land tax

It is important to note that the main residence exemption is a complex topic, to which entire books have been devoted. The following chapter is a quick overview of some of the quirks and pitfalls in the legislation, but is not intended to be comprehensive nor is it a substitute for professional advice where substantial sums are at stake.

14.1 MAIN RESIDENCE EXEMPTION

14.1.1 Basic conditions that must be satisfied

(s 222 TCGA 1992)

There is a total exemption from CGT where a gain is realised by an individual on the disposal of a property that has been his or her sole or main residence throughout the period of ownership. The legislation also provides exemption for land that forms part of the property (the garden or grounds) up to the 'permitted area'. The permitted area is always at least 0.5 of a hectare (approximately one acre), but may be more where the land is required for the reasonable enjoyment of the property (see 14.1.3).

Tax notes

The same rules that exempt the gain also deny the loss, so if you are unfortunate enough to make a loss on your qualifying residence then it will not be an allowable loss for CGT purposes.

Married couples or civil partners living together can have the exemption in respect of only one property between them for a particular period. Note that the exemption can also apply to a property outside of the UK.

14.1.2 Occupation test

(s 223(2) TCGA 1992; ESC D49)

A delay of up to 12 months between a property being acquired and the owner taking up residence does not prejudice the exemption; the property is still treated as if it were his or her main residence. The 12-month period can be extended by up to a further 12 months if it can be shown that there were good reasons for the owner not taking up residence, for example, the need to carry out alterations or building work, or where there was an unavoidable delay in the owner being able to dispose of his or her previous residence.

The last three years of ownership are treated as qualifying for the exemption, whether the owner lives in the property or not, provided the property has previously at some time been his or her main residence (see also 14.2.3).

14.1.3 The permitted area

The legislation also provides exemption for an area of gardens or grounds larger than 0.5 hectare if it can be shown that it was 'required for the reasonable enjoyment' of the property as a residence. If the taxpayer and HMRC cannot agree on this, the First-tier Tribunal can determine the matter.

Relevant factors here include considerations such as the extent to which other similar properties have gardens or grounds larger than 0.5 hectare, the need for an area of land to provide either privacy or a buffer between the property and, for example, a motorway, and the need to have room for other facilities and amenities appropriate to the property.

The last-mentioned factor is often the most difficult to argue with HMRC, which relies on a judgment by Du Parcq J in a 1937 compulsory purchase case, the so-called *Newhill* case [1938] 2 All ER 163:

'Required' ... does not mean merely that the occupiers of the house would like to have it, or that they would miss it if they lost it, or that anyone proposing to buy the house would think less of the house without it ... 'Required' means ... that without it there will be such a substantial deprivation of amenities or convenience that a real injury will be done to the property owner ...

HMRC's interpretation is not free from doubt, as the CGT legislation is worded differently from the compulsory purchase legislation, but *Longson* v *Baker* [2001] STC 6 lent support to HMRC. Mr Longson had used land for equestrian pursuits, but the High Court upheld the Commissioners' decision that, while it might have been convenient for him to be able to stable his horses and exercise them on land attached to his home, the facility was not required for the reasonable enjoyment of the property.

This is an area where it is essential to take professional advice.

14.1.4 What is 'the residence'?

There have been several cases concerning property where servants occupy a part of the premises.

In *Batey* v *Wakefield* [1981] STC 521 the property consisted of the main house and a caretaker's lodge. The caretaker/gardener and his wife (who was the owner's housekeeper) occupied the lodge rent free. The main house and the lodge were separated by the width of a tennis court. The Court of Appeal upheld the taxpayer's claim that his residence consisted of the main house and all related buildings that were part and parcel of the property and were occupied for the purposes of the owner's residence.

Yet in *Lewis* v *Rook* [1992] STC 171 the Court of Appeal decided against a taxpayer who claimed the exemption should cover a gardener's cottage located some 170 metres away, as it was not within the same curtilage as the taxpayer's house. Following that decision, HMRC, has set out its views in its CGT manual at CG64245 *et seq.* This area is complex and specialist advice should be taken if substantial sums are involved.

14.2 POSSIBLE RESTRICTIONS ON EXEMPTION

14.2.1 Part of property used for business purposes

(s 224(1) TCGA 1992)

If part of the property has been used exclusively for the purposes of a trade, business, profession or vocation, the exemption does not cover the part of the gain attributable to that part. This restriction does not apply where the relevant rooms are used for part business/part personal reasons. So, if a journalist's living room doubles up as a workroom from which he or she carries on his or her business, there is no restriction under this provision.

14.2.2 Part of property let out

(s 223(4) TCGA 1992)

A similar restriction may apply where the owner has let out part of his or her home. Thus, if the owner had let approximately one-third of the house, the exemption would normally be confined to two-thirds of the gain on disposal. This rule may be overridden if the lettings are of residential accommodation: the gain on the part of the property let out in this way may still be exempt up to the lesser of:

- the exemption on the part of the property occupied by the owner; and
- £40,000.

Tax notes

Civil partners or spouses who own a property jointly can each claim a letting exemption of up to the lesser of their exempt gain or £40,000 against their share of the gain on the let property.

The period during which the property was let which may qualify for the additional exemption can be before or after the period during which the property was the owner's main residence.

14.2.3 Expenditure incurred with view to gain

(s 224(3) TCGA 1992)

The exemption is not available if a gain arises from the purchase of property made wholly or partly for the purpose of realising a gain.

Example – Expenditure with a view to gain

K, a partner, lived in a flat owned by his firm. He was offered the opportunity to buy it for £75,000. He accepted because he knew he could fairly quickly find a buyer at £120,000. He sold it, and realised a gain of £45,000. HMRC is likely to argue that the gain is a chargeable gain because of s 224(3). Similarly, a person who holds a leasehold interest and acquires the freehold because it will enable a better price to be obtained may suffer a restriction under s 224(3) if HMRC can show that this was the only purpose of buying the freehold.

Some guidance on the circumstances in which HMRC may seek to deny exemption on these grounds can be found in its manuals at CG65200 onwards. In particular, where it is clear that an individual who is a builder or property developer has purchased a property to renovate and resell, occupying a property while it is renovated prior to sale will not change the fact that any profit on the sale is likely to be regarded by HMRC as trading income so the main residence rules will not apply. See HMRC's manuals at CG65214.

A number of cases have been heard by the First-tier Tribunal in the last year; in *Springthorpe* [2010] UKFTT 582 (TC), the taxpayer's occupation was held to be for the purpose of renovating the property with a view to letting it. The Tribunal decided that the appellant's occupation was not occupation of the property as his residence. Instead, the evidence produced indicated that he had not definitely made up his mind, when doing the renovation work, whether to sell, let or live in the house when it was completed. Accordingly, the Tribunal concluded that, to the extent that the Mr Springthorpe did occupy the property, he did so for the purpose of renovating the property rather than occupying it as his home which he expected to occupy with some degree of continuity. Thus the quality of his occupation and his intentions in respect of his occupation of the property did not satisfy the test in s 222 TCGA.

Favell [2010] UKFTT 360 (TC) was also decided against the taxpayer. The First-tier Tribunal, dismissing the appeal, said that the question of whether the taxpayer's occupation was sufficient to make him resident was one of fact and degree for the tribunal to decide in the light of the nature, quality, length and circumstances of the taxpayer's occupation.

In this case, the taxpayer had not discharged the burden of proof required to demonstrate that he occupied the property as his only or main residence at any time. There was a complete absence of objective documentary evidence to show that the taxpayer resided at the property. In the circumstances the tribunal was not satisfied that the taxpayer had occupied the property at the relevant time.

In *Moore* [2010] UKFTT 445 (TC), the First-tier Tribunal (dismissing the appeal) said that, in order to be a person's 'residence' for the purpose of s 222, a property had to be that person's home and a place where he lived. Although an occasional and short residence might suffice, there had to be an assumption of permanence and a degree and expectation of continuity in order to turn mere occupation into residence (following *Sansom* v *Peay (HMIT)* (1976) 52 TC 1, *Frost (HMIT)* v *Feltham* (1980) 55 TC 10 and *Goodwin* v *Curtis (HMIT)* [1998] BTC 176).

In each case, the taxpayer had not demonstrated the necessary *quality* of occupation. In *Springthorpe*, during the period of supposed residence, the kitchen had no units, and although electricity and water supplies were connected throughout the period of the renovations, bills were minimal and the gas supply had been turned off and was only reconnected once a central heating system had been installed. An exemption from Council Tax had been obtained on the grounds that the works required were such that the property was uninhabitable, and there were no proper lavatory or washing facilities.

In *Favell*, the appellant had no documentary evidence (bills, bank statements, correspondence, etc) to show that he had occupied the property. Mr Favell did not notify any official body (eg his bank, utilities, etc) that he had moved to the property. All his official correspondence continued to be sent to his previous address. Accordingly, the Tribunal decided that he had not discharged the burden of proof required to demonstrate that he had occupied the property but noted that, had Mr Favell been able to establish such proof, it would have been minded to hold that his seven months' occupation did in fact amount to residence.

In the third case, *Moore*, again no documentary evidence had been retained and the appellant admitted that he had no furniture apart from a bed and a cooker at the property between the relevant dates. The Tribunal held that Mr Moore had not proved that he registered as a resident of the property for council tax purposes, water rates purposes or DVLA purposes, and noted that he could not produce any insurance or telephone bills demonstrating that he had in fact taken up occupation. The fact that his girlfriend – later his wife – had refused to live in the property, instead remaining at the second property throughout added weight to the Tribunal's finding that he had occupied the property for the purposes of renovating it for subsequent letting, but not for the purposes of residing there.

Tax notes

Interestingly, in the case of *Jones* v *Wilcock (SP C 92), [1996] SSCD 389*, HMRC successfully argued that a property had not been purchased for trading purposes and was, therefore, able to prevent the owners claiming a loss made on the same property because it was, in reality, their main residence.

14.2.4 Sale of part of gardens

Special care is needed if it is decided to sell surplus land for development. In *Varty* v *Lynes* [1976] STC 508 the taxpayer had owned and occupied a house and the garden was less than one acre (the permitted area at that time). He sold the house and part of the garden in June 1971. Slightly less than 12 months later, he sold the rest of the garden to a builder and realised a substantial gain because he had secured planning permission in the meantime. He was assessed on the gain on the land sold to the builder. The High Court decided that the main residence exemption did not apply. Brightman J held that the exemption for the garden or grounds could apply only in relation to garden or grounds occupied as such by the owner at the date of sale.

HMRC subsequently stated that it would invoke this only where land was sold with development value. Therefore, the following principles should be borne in mind:

(1) A sale of land out of a parcel of land greater than 0.5 hectare may be vulnerable even where the owner remains in occupation. The fact that the owner continues to live in the property suggests that the surplus land was not required for the reasonable enjoyment of the property.

(2) A sale of land with development value at the same time as the owner ceases to live in the property is not open to attack in the same way as in *Varty* v *Lynes*.

(3) A sale of land with development value after the owner has moved out is likely to result in a tax charge.

The case of *Henke & Another* v *HMRC* SpC 550 is also helpful on practical issues where land adjoining an individual's home is sold off for development.

14.2.5 What happens where there are two homes?

An individual may live in two (or more) properties without necessarily owning both (or all) of them. HMRC's view is that a person has two residences if, for example, he or she owns a large house in Yorkshire and rents a modest flat in London where he or she lives during the week.

If necessary, the First-tier Tribunal will decide which of an individual's two or more residences is his or her main residence. The test is not necessarily where the individual lives most of the time, and it is often not clear in a particular case what view the Tribunal might take.

14.2.6 Taxpayer's right of election

(s 222(5) TCGA 1992)

Fortunately, the owner can settle the matter by formally electing one property to be treated as his or her main residence. As we have seen from revelations concerning MPs, it is possible for you to elect for a property which is not actually your main residence. However, you must have lived in the property.

The election may be varied from time to time (known in the Press as 'flipping'), but only in relation to the last two years prior to the variation.

There is a time limit for a notice under s 222(5) of two years. HMRC's view has been that the time limit refers to the point in time the individual starts to have a second residence. This interpretation was upheld by the High Court in *Griffin* v *Craig Harvey* [1994] STC 54.

There is one circumstance in which HMRC will accept an election outside the two-year time limit. ESC D21 provides:

> Where for any period an individual has more than one residence, but his [or her] interest in each of them, or in each of them except one, is such as to have no more than a negligible capital value on the open market (eg a weekly rented flat or accommodation provided by an employer) the two-year time limit will be extended where the individual was unaware that such a nomination could be made. In such cases the nomination may be made within a reasonable time of the individual becoming aware of the possibility of so doing, and it will be regarded as effective from the date on which the individual first had more than one residence.

14.2.7 Two adjacent flats

A situation in which you should take professional advice is if you occupy two flats as a combined home. HMRC's manuals confirm that the two flats can sometimes be regarded as constituting a single residence where certain conditions are satisfied. One condition is that the flats are contiguous. Another condition is that the two flats are in the same block. However, even if you satisfy both these conditions you may still not qualify. Furthermore, you should be prepared for HMRC to resist such a claim, at any rate in the first instance.

14.3 LIVING IN JOB-RELATED ACCOMMODATION

14.3.1 Meaning of job-related accommodation

Job-related accommodation is defined as accommodation provided for an individual or spouse or civil partner by reason of the individual's employment where:

- it is necessary for the proper performance of the individual's duties that he or she should live there; or
- it is provided for the better performance of his or her duties and the employment is one where employers customarily provide accommodation; or
- the accommodation is provided as part of the special security arrangements for the employee's safety.

14.3.2 Right to nominate a property

(s 222(8) TCGA 1992)

Where an individual is required to live in job-related accommodation, a house owned by that individual and intended to be occupied as his or her residence in due course is treated as if it were his or her residence. Such a house may, therefore, qualify for exemption even if the owner had let it and never actually occupied it personally before disposing of it, provided it is nominated by the individual as his or her only or main residence.

14.3.3 Similar provisions for self-employed individuals

A self-employed individual who is required to live at or near his or her place of work (eg a publican) can nominate a property under s 222(8) for eventual use as his or her main residence. This also applies if his or her spouse or civil partner is required to occupy such premises. Only his or her residence in job-related accommodation after 6 April 1983 can qualify under this heading.

14.4 TREATMENT WHERE PROPERTY NOT OCCUPIED THROUGHOUT WHOLE OWNERSHIP PERIOD

14.4.1 Proportion of gain may be exempt

The s 222 main residence exemption is not necessarily an 'all or nothing' test. The legislation makes provision for a proportion of the capital gain to be exempt where the necessary conditions are satisfied for part of the period of ownership. The exempt proportion of the gain is normally:

$$\frac{\text{Period of qualifying use}}{\text{Total period of ownership}} \times \text{Gain}$$

14.4.2 Periods prior to 31 March 1982 ignored

A period of non-qualifying use is ignored if it is prior to 31 March 1982.

Example – Incomplete period of occupation

> A property was acquired in March 1975 but was not the owner's main residence until March 1988. Thereafter it was the owner's sole residence. It was sold in March 2009 for a gain of £340,000. The exempt proportion of the gain would be:
>
> $\frac{21}{27} \times £340,000 = £264,444.$

14.4.3 Last 36 months of ownership

(s 223(2) TCGA 1992)

Provided the property has at some time qualified as the owner's main residence, the last three years of ownership also qualify for exemption. This still applies if the property is let or another property is nominated as the individual's main residence for all or part of that three-year period. It also applies even where the period when the property was occupied as the individual's main residence was before 31 March 1982. This relief is intended to ensure taxable gains do not arise on the sale of a main residence at times when – as at present – it may take some time sell a property.

14.4.4 Periods spent working abroad

(s 223(3)(b) TCGA 1992)

If, during a period when a property is (or is nominated as) an individual's main residence, the owner has to work abroad, the property continues to be regarded as his or her main residence (and therefore exempt from CGT) if he or she was employed abroad under a contract of employment and all the employment duties were performed overseas. The property must be the individual's main residence both **before** and **after** the overseas employment. The condition requiring the property to be the owner's only or main residence after working abroad is treated as satisfied if the owner is unable to resume residence because the terms of his or her new employment require him or her to work elsewhere (s 223(3B)(b) TCGA 1992). The final 36 months of ownership is treated as actual occupation for these purposes, irrespective of physical presence at the property.

14.4.5 Periods spent working elsewhere in UK

A period of up to four years during which the owner's employment necessitated him or her living elsewhere in the UK is also a qualifying period. A period (or periods in total) that exceeds four years is covered to the extent of four years. Again, it is normally necessary that the period be followed by a period of occupation, but s 223(3B)(b) applies if the individual cannot resume occupation because his or her current employment prevents this. Again, the final 36 months of ownership is treated as actual occupation for these purposes.

14.4.6 Other qualifying periods

A further period of absence (for any reason) of up to three years can be treated as qualifying for exemption, provided the period is both preceded and succeeded by a period of actual occupation. The final 36 months of ownership is treated as actual occupation for these purposes.

14.4.7 Summary

Table 14.1 may help in computing the position. The exempt gain is (X) + (Y).

Table 14.1 – Computation of exempt gain on main residence

Number of complete months since 31 March 1982 when the property was actually occupied as the owner's main residence. See 14.1.2	(A)
The lesser of 36 months or such part of the last 36 months which does not already fall within A. See 14.4.3	(B)
Months spent working abroad when the property was not occupied as the individual's main residence provided that the individual resumed residence after his or her overseas employment ceased or would have done so if he or she had not been required to take up employment elsewhere in the UK, excluding any period which already falls to be included in B above. See 14.4.4	(C)
Number of months spent living elsewhere because the individual's employment required him or her to live in another part of the UK (subject to a maximum of 48 months). Again, exclude any period already included in B.	
Note, an entry is appropriate here only if the individual resumed occupation of the property at the end of the period, or did not do so and that period fell within the final 36 months. See 14.4.5	(D)
Any further period of absence which was both preceded and succeeded by the individual occupying the property as his or her main residence (subject to a maximum of 36 months). Again exclude any period already included in B. See 14.4.6	(E)
Apply the following fraction to the overall gain which arose on the disposal of the property: $$\text{Overall gain} \times \frac{A+B+C+D+E}{\text{Months of ownership since 31 March 1982}}$$	(X)
A further exemption may also be due where the property has been let during any of the periods of absence. The additional exemption is the lesser of X or £40,000. See 14.2.2	(Y)

14.4.8 Dependent relatives

(s 226 TCGA 1992)

In addition to the main residence exemption, an individual may qualify for exemption in respect of a property occupied by a dependent relative as his or her main residence provided the property was so occupied before 6 April 1988. To qualify for this exemption, the property must have been occupied by the dependent relative rent free, and without any other consideration.

A widowed mother (or mother-in-law) is automatically regarded as a dependent relative. In other situations, the relative is regarded as dependent only if prevented by old age or infirmity from maintaining him or herself. The exemption is not available for a property acquired after 5 April 1988, even if the property is a replacement for another property previously occupied by a dependent relative.

In some cases, it may be appropriate to form a settlement with the trustees owning the property occupied by the dependent relative as the trustees may still qualify for exemption in respect of a property occupied by a beneficiary as his or her main residence (see 31.4.11).

14.5 PASSING ON THE FAMILY HOME – CGT CONSIDERATIONS

One of the main concerns that people have nowadays (as far as taxation is concerned, anyway) is the way in which their property will pass to their heirs. The IHT issues are dealt with in Chapter 30. A gift of property in an estate planning exercise would give rise to a CGT liability were it not covered by the main residence exemption. However, there is another aspect. Many IHT mitigation schemes have, as one of their consequences, the outcome that the donor's children end up owning an interest in the family home that is not covered by the main residence exemption. To that extent, the family might have saved IHT only at the cost of taking on a long-term CGT liability that will crystallise when the property is sold.

14.6 ANTI-AVOIDANCE PROVISIONS

Bear in mind the restriction on the main residence exemption where hold-over relief has been obtained on a previous disposal (see 33.13).

14.7 STAMP DUTY LAND TAX

CGT is, unfortunately, not the only tax to be considered when purchasing a new main residence – stamp duty land tax (SDLT) is a major consideration. The rates of SDLT for 2011–12 are shown in Table 14.2.

Table 14.2 – Rates of SDLT

Rate	Land in disadvantaged areas: residential	Land in disadvantaged areas: non-residential	All other land in the UK: residential	All other land in the UK: non-residential
Zero	£0–£150,000	£0–£150,000	£0–£125,000 *	£0–£150,000
1%	£150,001–£250,000	£150,001–£250,000	£125,001–£250,000 *	£150,001–£250,000
3%	£250,001–£500,000	£250,001–£500,000	£250,001–£500,000	£250,001–£500,000
4%	£500,000–£1m	Over £500,000	£500,000–£1m	Over £500,000
5%	Over £1m	–	Over £1m	–

* First time buyers (only) will not pay SDLT on residential property transactions up to £250,000 between 25 March 2010 and 24 March 2012 albeit this relief is currently subject to review to assess its effectiveness and may be discontinued before March 2012.

We look at stamp duty in greater depth in Chapter 39.

15

THE TAX CALCULATION

DALE BUTCHER

'Tax doesn't have to be taxing' is the glib way in which HMRC advertises the self-assessment process to its 'customers'.

Remember you will normally only have to file a self-assessment tax form if you receive a return form, or if you owe or are owed tax. However, regardless of whether you have to file a self-assessment (SA) form or not, you should carry out an annual review of how much tax you should have paid and how much you have actually paid.

This chapter covers the main steps involved in calculating your tax liability.

Table 15.1 – Rates of tax on various types of income for 2011–12

Rates of tax on	Non-savings income	Savings income	UK dividends and tax credits
Starting rate for savings £0–£2,560	N/A	10%*	10%
Basic rate £0–£35,000	20%	20%	10%
Higher rate £35,001– £150,000	40%	40%#	32.5%#
Additional rate – all remaining taxable income	50%	50%#	42.5%#

* If your non-savings income is above this limit (after deducting personal allowances) then this starting rate is not applicable

\# Savings and dividend income is treated as the top slice of income

---

Tax notes

Since 6 April 2010, individuals have been subject to a 50% tax rate on taxable non-dividend income above £150,000 per year. A 42.5% dividend tax rate applies where total taxable income is over £150,000 a year. Savings and dividend income forms the top slice of income after gains, with dividends forming the highest part.

WORKING OUT YOUR TAX FOR 2011–12

If you file your 2011–12 SA return online, HMRC will work out your tax for you. It will also do this if you submit a paper return by 31 October 2012. This chapter should help you to follow such HMRC calculations.

Example – Tax calculation

Z has the following income and gains for the tax year ended 5 April 2012

	Income	Tax	
Salary	£45,000	£8,322.00	(figures taken from P60)
Private medical	£780		(figure taken from P11D)
Bank interest	£750 (net)	£187.50	
Dividends	£1200 (net)	£133.33	
Property income	£500		
Capital gain	£12,000		

In addition Z had paid £50 a month (grossed up) into his personal pension plan and had donated £20 (net) on his Visa card to Comic Relief during the tax year.

The tax calculation would look as follows:

	Income £	Tax £
Earned income		
Earnings per P60 and P11D	45,780.00	8,322.00
Total earned income	45,780.00	8,322.00
	£	£
Investment income		
UK land and property	500.00	
UK savings	937.50	187.50
UK dividends	1,333.33	133.33
Total investment income	2,770.83	320.83
Total income		
Total earned income	45,780.00	8,322.00
Total investment income	2,770.83	320.83
Total income	48,550.83	8,642.83
Taxable income		
Total income	48,550	8,642.83
Basic allowance	£7,475	
Taxable income	41,075	8,642.83

Basic rate band adjustments*

Basic rate band	35,000
Pension payments	600
Gift Aid and charitable payments	25
Extended basic rate	35,625

* The basic rate band is extended by grossed up payments which are made net of basic rate tax (eg pension and Gift Aid payments). This method ensures that where appropriate income tax relief is given only for higher rate tax purposes.

Tax payable	£		£
Income other than dividends			
Basic rate	35,625	@20%	7,125.00
Higher rate	4,117	@40%	1,646.80
Dividends			
Higher rate on dividends	1,333	@32.5%	433.23
			9,205.03

	£
Income tax after allowances and reliefs	9,205.03
Less: Tax credits	(133.33)
Income tax due	9,071.70
Tax deducted at source	(8,642.83)
Total income tax	428.87
Capital gains tax	
(£12,000 – £10,600) = £1,400 @28%	392.00
Total tax due for 2011–12	820.87

Once you have arrived at the net tax due figure, consider:

(1) Do you have payments on account to make? See 2.1.3.
(2) Has any of the tax liability for this year already been included in a notice of coding? See 4.2.3.
(3) Do you owe tax for an earlier year which should have been collected via the PAYE code for this tax year? See 4.2.3.

For more examples in respect of individuals with different circumstances and personal allowances, refer to Chapter 12.

HMRC might have sent you a tax calculation guide and notes on the guide. The HMRC form often seems akin to a 16-page Sudoko puzzle. The form gets the right results but only by using arcane methods which seem counter-intuitive. Using the above calculation for your own figures should give you a ready reckoner to see if you have under- or overpaid tax.

Common sense

Once you have completed your tax calculation you need to find out how the liability or tax refund arose. If you have only income from earnings, the tax paid under PAYE should more or less equal the tax liability. If it doesn't, your tax code is wrong and probably needs adjusting. One common area is incorrect benefits-in-kind. A quick cross reference of your P11D with your end of year tax code should highlight any discrepancies.

Tax notes

Initial reaction to a tax refund is positive and to a tax liability the opposite. However, another view of a tax refund is that HMRC has been holding your money and paying you no interest for over a year; likewise, a tax liability may indicate good deferral planning by yourself or your tax adviser.

15.1 SOME POINTS TO LOOK OUT FOR

Bank and building society interest

(1)   If you are not sure from your statements how much interest you received, ask your bank for an end of year certificate. They will in any case supply these details to HMRC.

(2)   Remember to gross up net payments received to get to the taxable amount.

Tax notes

If you have bank interest taxable at the higher rate, the additional tax liability will be equal (subject to small rounding differences) to the tax already deducted by the bank or society, ie 20%.

Dividends

(3) Tax credits on your dividends and unit trust income are not refundable, ie the credit is a notional credit. The effect of adding the tax credit to the dividend, computing tax at 32.5% or 42.5% thereon, and then deducting the tax credit, is that the higher rate tax comes to 25% or 36.11% of the actual dividend received.

(4) Do not include equalisation as part of your dividends from unit trusts.

(5) From 6 April 2008, if you received dividends from overseas companies and you did not have a 10% shareholding in the overseas company, you could include these dividends with your UK dividends. You could then get a 10% tax credit. This system was amended with effect from 22 April 2009. The availability of tax credits was extended to include offshore funds (provided that distributions from the fund are not treated as interest) and, to some investors with shareholdings of 10% or more. The conditions for obtaining relief for >10% shareholdings are that the payer is a company with issued share capital and the recipient is at the time of receipt a minority shareholder; or the payer company is an offshore fund; or the payer company is resident only in a qualifying territory (broadly those with which the UK has signed tax information exchange agreements) at the time the distribution is made; or, if the relevant distribution is one of a series as part of a scheme, each of the companies in the chain is similarly resident only in a qualifying territory - if the last condition is not satisfied, then the scheme must not be a scheme to obtain a tax advantage. Bear in mind that some countries levy a 15% withholding tax on dividends and you could get a credit for this higher amount by completing the *Foreign* pages.

Tax notes

From 6 April 2011, if you have other income in excess of £35,000, then any additional dividend income will be taxed at an effective rate of 25% of the dividend received. However, if you have other income in excess of £150,000, then any additional dividend income will be taxed at an effective rate of 36.11% of the dividend received.

Insurance bonds

(6) Gains on UK policies are paid subject to a 20% (basic rate) notional tax credit. The notional tax credit only applies to policies taken out with UK resident insurers or with foreign insurers who have been subject to a comparable EEA tax charge. Otherwise, the policy gain will have been paid gross.

Offshore roll-up funds

(7) The gains on offshore roll-up funds are offshore income gains, and are chargeable to income tax rather than CGT. Do not deduct your CGT annual exemption.

Pension contributions

(8) Personal pension payments will have been made net of basic rate tax and relief is given by extending the basic rate tax band by the gross amount of these payments. The HMRC tax calculation guide requires you to enter the 'grossed-up' amount.

(9) Contributions to Free Standing AVC payments will also have been paid net of basic rate tax.

(10) Retirement annuity contributions may have been paid gross. It will depend on the arrangement set up by the insurance company concerned.

Deductions from your income

(11) The self-assessment tax return form requires you to enter the net amount of Gift Aid payments. You are entitled to gross up the amounts that you pay and claim higher rate relief.

(12) Remember some reliefs, such as EIS and donations to charities can be carried back from the current year (see 11.9.2).

Generally

(13) Interest and penalties are not taxed and you cannot treat them as a tax credit in your calculation.

(14) Gains, dividends, and then savings, form the top slice of your income in deciding the tax rates to apply.

(15) See 28.3.4 re top-slicing on gains from insurance bonds.

(16) Talk to HMRC about what underpayments have been included in your tax code from the tax year for which you are preparing the calculation and also for previous years.

(17) Compare this year's tax calculation with last year. HMRC will!

(18) Use the above calculation as a financial health check. If you are paying higher rate tax on investment income are you using tax-free investments to the maximum? Is it worth transferring assets to a spouse or civil partner if they pay tax at a lower rate?

Tax notes

Don't believe the hype – tax is taxing!

PART 2

BUSINESS TAX AND FINANCE

This part contains the following chapters:

COMPUTATION OF BUSINESS PROFITS AND CAPITAL ALLOWANCES

VIRAN DE SILVA

The calculation of business profits and accounting principles applies not only to self-employed individuals, but carries over to other areas where accounts are required, for example companies, partnerships and landlords. The changes in law over recent years have, for better or worse, brought taxable profits more into line with accounting profits calculated by reference to generally accepted accountancy principles.

This chapter looks at the computation of profits and the closely related area of capital allowances. It contains the following sections:

(1) Computation of trading profits
(2) Capital allowances
(3) Pre-trading expenditure
(4) Post-cessation receipts
(5) Post-cessation expenses

16.1 COMPUTATION OF TRADING PROFITS

16.1.1 The accounts profit is generally the starting point

Most tax computations start with the words 'Profits per accounts' and then consist of a number of special adjustments to those accounts, which are required by tax legislation and case law.

16.1.2 What types of accounts are required?

The nature and complexity of accounts should be governed by the business. An individual in business as a window-cleaner can keep his or her accounts as simple as possible. Moreover, HMRC allows certain 'short-cuts'. For example, if you use your car for business and have not registered for VAT, you can generally use the approved mileage allowance rates designed for employees (see 4.4.9) and merely claim, say, 4,000 miles at the appropriate rate rather than keep all the motoring bills and claim capital allowances. Larger businesses require more complex accounting.

The following text covers the rules that govern the tax treatment of income and expenses and deals with adjustments to accounts that are required for tax purposes. For example, a set of accounts prepared for commercial reasons may include a provision for wear and tear to a building. Such a provision needs to be 'added back' (as no tax relief is available for depreciation as such, relief is due only via the capital allowances system).

See 2.6 on the types of adjustments that have been identified by HMRC in 'enabling letters' sent to self-employed individuals. These letters reflect common shortcomings in accounts received by HMRC.

16.1.3 Accounts should be on the 'accruals basis'

HMRC's view is that accounts should normally be prepared to reflect a trader's earnings for a year rather than just the cash received. For example, the accounts should include debtors, ie bills that have been issued but not paid by the year end. Similarly, the accounts should include work in progress.

16.1.4 Sound commercial accountancy principles

The Master of the Rolls stated in *Gallagher* v *Jones* [1993] STC 537, CA:

> Subject to any express or implied statutory rule ... the ordinary way to ascertain the profits or losses of a business is to apply accepted principles of commercial accountancy. That is the very purpose for which such principles are formulated. As has often been pointed out, such principles are not static: they may be modified, refined and elaborated over time as circumstances change and accounting insights sharpen. But as long as such principles remain current and generally accepted they provide the surest answer.

Accountancy principles are constantly being refined and are published by the Accounting Standards Board (ASB) as Financial Reporting Standards (FRS). In particular, FRS18 brought together and updated a number of statements on accounting policies. Some FRSs are mandatory only for businesses of a certain size; others apply more generally. Smaller businesses that do not require an audit are governed by the regularly updated Financial Reporting Standard for Smaller Entities (FRSSE).

Key concepts for accountants include the 'going concern' concept, the need for consistency and the accruals principle whereby income and the expenses related to earning it are matched. Until recently, the concept of prudence was also regarded as a fundamental principle, ie that income and profits should not be anticipated. However, accountants now place increasing weight on accounts showing a 'realistic' position, rather than an approach that might be regarded as excessively prudent.

16.1.5 Expenditure that is specifically disallowed

(ss 33–35 and 45 ITTOIA 2005)

As mentioned above, certain types of expenditure are disallowed for tax purposes, by statute, although it may be sound accounting practice to deduct such costs in a trader's accounts. See Table 16.1 for a summary based on HMRC's tax return guide. The rest of this section looks more closely at specific types of business expenses.

Capital expenditure

(s 33 ITTOIA 2005)

The acquisition of a capital asset is not a cost that may be deducted in arriving at profits for tax purposes. This may seem obvious where an asset such as a building is acquired, but the definition of capital expenditure goes a long way beyond the acquisition of tangible assets. The generally accepted definition was given by Lord Cave in *British Insulated and Helsby Cables Ltd* v *Atherton* (1925) 10 TC 155 in which he stated:

> when an expenditure is made … with a view to bringing into existence an asset or an advantage for the enduring benefit of a trade there is very good reason (in the absence of special circumstances leading to the opposite conclusion) for treating such expenditure as properly attributable not to revenue but to capital.

The acquisition of, for example goodwill, is capital expenditure. Less obviously, a lump sum payment to secure release from an onerous liability (eg a lease at a high rent or a fixed rate loan) is also regarded as capital expenditure.

Entertaining

(ss 45–46 ITTOIA 2005)

Any expenses relating to entertaining customers or suppliers that are included in a set of accounts normally need to be added back. There is a modest exemption that may apply where the entertaining is provided by an hotelier, restaurateur or someone else who provides entertainment in the ordinary course of his or her trade. Staff entertainment is also an allowable expense, but the individual employee may be assessed on a benefit-in-kind.

Gifts to customers, etc

(ss45, 47 ITTOIA 2005)

The cost of gifts to customers and to potential customers and introducers is also disallowed unless the gift carries a conspicuous advertisement and is neither food, drink, tobacco nor a voucher exchangeable for such goods, nor an item that costs more than £50 per recipient per year.

Table 16.1 – HMRC Summary of allowable and non-allowable business expenses (based on HMRC tax return guide)

	Allowable	*Not allowable*
Basic costs	Light, heat and power; telephone; insurance; stationery and postage; business rates and rent; advertising; protective clothing; repairs; replacement loose tools (unless capital allowances claimed instead); transport of goods to customers or materials from suppliers; subcontractors	Private and personal expenses; non-business part of running costs of premises used only partly for business; own insurance; ordinary, everyday clothing even if bought specially for business use; parking and other fines; buying, altering or improving fixed assets; depreciation or losses on sale of fixed assets
Employee costs	Employees' wages and salaries; employers' NIC; redundancy payments; pension contributions on employees' behalf; employees' expenses and benefits	Own wages or salary and drawings from the business; own pension payments and other benefits; own NIC
Finance costs	Interest on loans and overdraft used solely for business purposes; costs of arranging such finance	Repayment of loan or overdrafts (as opposed to the interest)
Professional	Accountancy fees; preparation of ordinary business costs agreement; debt recovery (if debt is for a taxable receipt); renewing leases of less than 50 years (where no premium is paid); defending business appeals against business rates	Costs of settling tax disputes; legal costs of buying fixed assets (treated as part of the cost of fixed asset); costs and fines or penalties for breaking the law

Travel	Travel on business to meet customers, suppliers, etc; travel between business premises; accommodation and reasonable cost of meals on overnight business trips; vehicle running expenses (less proportion of private use)	Travel between home and place of business (unless agreed with HMRC that your home is your base); costs of buying vehicles (but capital allowances can be claimed); meals (except on overnight business trips)
Bad debts	Irrecoverable debts written off, if taxed when they arose; recovery costs; provisions against specific doubtful debts; debts recovered later should be shown in box 15 on page SEF1of the self-assessment return	General bad debts reserve; debts not taxed when they arose, eg because they relate to sale of a fixed asset
Subscriptions	Payments to certain professional bodies (See www.hmrc.gov.uk/list3/list3.pdf for a list of approved bodies)	Payments to political parties; most payments to clubs, charities or churches
Entertaining	Costs of entertaining staff; gifts (not food or drink) up to £50 per person per year that advertise your business	All other entertaining and hospitality
VAT	Any VAT that is not recoverable is an allowable expense. This does not include any input VAT paid on capital items, or other amounts not allowable for tax purposes. However, input VAT can be included in the cost of items on which a claim can be made for capital allowances.	
	Where allowable expenses net of recoverable input VAT are shown, the turnover should be shown on the same basis, ie net of output VAT charged. Alternatively, you may prefer to show receipts and allowable expenses including VAT and the net payment to HMRC as an expense or the net repayment as a taxable receipt.	

Illegal payments

(s 55 ITTOIA 2005)

A specific provision disallowing illegal payments such as bribes came into force on 11 June 1993. The disallowance was subsequently extended to cover payments made on or after 30 November 1993 in response to threats, menaces, blackmail and other forms of extortion. The disallowance in respect of bribes was further extended for expenditure incurred after 31 March 2002 to cover any payment that would constitute a criminal offence if made in the UK, effectively amending the law to cover bribes made outside the UK. The Bribery Act 2010 has greatly extended the definition of what constitutes bribery for these (and other) purposes. The Act is due to come into force on 1 July 2011, following the issue of detailed guidance by the Government.

Lease rentals on expensive cars

(s 48 ITTOIA 2005)

Before April 2009, where a trader used a leased car, or provided a car to an employee, and the original cost when new, or the retail price, was over £12,000, part of the lease rentals had to be added back as a disallowable expense. The amount disallowed was the following proportion of the lease rentals paid before April 2009:

$$\frac{1}{2} \times \frac{(\text{Cost of car} - £12,000)}{\text{Cost of car}}$$

This treatment did not apply to maintenance costs included in the lease rentals provided they were identified separately under the terms of the leasing agreement. Amounts paid under an HP agreement were dealt with differently (see 16.1.6).

From April 2009, the special rules that restrict the amount that can be deducted for tax purposes were reformed. The restriction has been changed to a flat rate disallowance of 15% of relevant payments for cars with CO_2 emissions exceeding 160g/km; this applied with effect from 2009–10 onwards. There is no restriction for cars with emissions of less than 160g/km. Expenditure under leases that commenced before 6 April 2009 (that is where the car was made available before 6 April 2009) continues to be subject to the 'old' rules until the end of the lease.

Provisions for bad debts

(s 35 ITTOIA 2005)

A general provision against bad debts is not allowable, but provisions against specific debts are an allowable deduction for tax purposes provided it can be shown the amount is a reasonable provision (see 16.1.8).

Remuneration not paid within nine months of year end

(s 36 ITTOIA 2005)

Bonus payments to employees may be made after the end of a year. If they clearly relate to a period of account, it would be normal for the trader's accounts to include a provision. However, this provision is allowable only if the remuneration is actually paid within nine months of the year end.

Pension contributions for employees

(s 196 FA 2004)

A deduction is due only if the contribution is paid during the course of the trader's year, whether to an approved or unapproved scheme. In some circumstances, large contributions may be subject to the spreading provisions in s 197. Large contributions may be spread over a period of up to four years. This spreading applies where the contribution is more than 210% of the contribution paid in the previous chargeable period and exceeds 110% of the contribution paid in that previous period by at least £500,000.

Pension contributions for the trader him or herself are not an allowable deduction in computing profits, although relief is available as a deduction from the profits taxable on him or her (see 26.1 for details of the method of dealing with personal pension contributions).

Expenditure not wholly for trade purposes

(s 34 ITTOIA 2005)

In practice, s 34 imposes a double test:

The expenditure must be incurred for the purposes of the trade

Powell v *Jackman* 2004 STC 645 concerned the expenses of a self-employed milkman who had his office at home but collected milk from a depot 26 miles away. He claimed that his travel to the depot was business travel from the base of his business operations but the High Court held this could not be justified on the facts and that his base of operation (place of work) was the area that constituted his round. The travel costs were incurred in getting to his place of work rather than in carrying on his business operations and were not allowable. As Lord Denning put it in a previous case, the cost of getting to one's place of work 'is a living expense as distinct from a business expense'. This case can be distinguished from *Horton* v *Young* 49 TC 60 where the Court of Appeal held that the base of operations for a self-employed bricklayer was his home.

> **Tax notes**
>
> It is, essentially, a matter of fact as to whether the base of the business is a trader's home.

The expenditure must be incurred wholly and exclusively for trade

The 'wholly and exclusively' test means that expenses incurred partly for trade purposes and partly for personal reasons are not allowable. For example, the cost of black dresses worn in court by a female barrister was disallowed on the grounds that the expenditure had a dual purpose (warmth and decency as well as the need to dress for court), as was the cost of meals incurred by a self-employed carpenter when he was working away from home.

Where an expense is incurred for mixed purposes the whole amount is disallowed; this rules out relief where an individual travels abroad mainly to have a holiday but carries out some work while there. However, where it can be shown that an additional cost was incurred wholly for business reasons, a deduction may be due for this. Consequently, if a person uses part of his or her home for business, the extra heat and light bills are an allowable expense for tax purposes. It should be noted that HMRC's Employment Income Manual, at EIM01476, suggests a guideline rate of £3 pw from 6 April 2008 (previously £2 pw) for employers reimbursing employees working from home and, in practice, HMRC has said that it will accept claims at this guideline rate from self-employed individuals also, without further enquiry. This is not a maximum; higher amounts can of course be claimed where there is evidence to justify them.

In practice, quite a number of expenses are apportioned between private (not allowable) and business (allowable) use. Phone bills and car expenses are two particular examples that arise often.

Arguments often arise where expenses relate to the preservation of a trader's reputation as HMRC will generally assume that the expenditure was at least partly incurred for personal reasons. In *McKnight* v *Sheppard HL* 1999 STC 669, a stockbroker incurred legal expenses in defending charges brought by the London Stock Exchange. He was found guilty of gross misconduct and suspended from trading. Because a suspension would have resulted in the destruction of his business, he appealed and his suspension was reduced to a fine. He was allowed tax relief for his legal expenses because these had been incurred wholly and exclusively for the purposes of the trade, but the fines imposed were disallowed.

Arguments will also arise where the expense relates to an activity that is regarded by HMRC as a hobby. However, this is a question of fact, as illustrated by a case involving expenditure by a coach company on motor rallying. It was held that this was an allowable expense even though the owner of the business was a motor sports enthusiast and he drove the company cars. See *McQueen* v *HMRC* SpC 601.

Payments of reverse premiums

(s 99 ITTOIA 2005)

Relief is due to a builder or developer who pays a reverse premium to induce a tenant to take a lease. However, no relief is due to a tenant who pays a reverse premium in order to be released from an onerous lease.

Sums recoverable from insurance policy, etc

(s 106 ITTOIA 2005)

Where a trader can get back from an insurance company the money that he or she has paid out, there is no deduction due for the expenditure. The same treatment applies where a trader has been indemnified against a particular cost.

Patent royalties and other annual payments

Certain annual payments (eg patent royalties) generally need to be paid net of basic rate tax. The payments are not deductible in arriving at profits of the trade or profession, although higher rate tax relief is available when computing the payer's liability.

16.1.6 Other expenditure where adjustments may be required

Interest

Relief for interest payments on qualifying loans taken by partners are given against the partner's general income (see 11.4). Interest paid by a sole trader or partnership may be deducted in arriving at the business's taxable profits provided it passes the 'wholly and exclusively' test (see above). See *Dixon* v *HMRC*, 2006 SpC 531 concerning the apportionment of interest where the loan was partly used to buy the flat over the trader's shop.

Problems may arise where overdraft interest is shown as a deduction in a set of accounts and the proprietor's capital account is overdrawn. HMRC is likely to argue that the interest (or, at any rate, part of it) was not incurred for business purposes, but to finance drawings. If you find yourself in this situation you should take advice from an accountant.

Cost of raising business finance

(s 58 ITTOIA 2005)

There are often certain costs in raising long-term finance, and a statutory deduction is available provided the costs:

- were incurred wholly and exclusively for the purposes of obtaining loan finance, providing security or repaying a loan; and
- represented expenditure on professional fees, commissions, advertising, printing or other incidental expenses in relation to raising finance.

In some cases a deduction will be available even though the expenditure fails and the loan finance is not in fact obtained.

Plant and machinery lease rentals

The way that lease rentals are treated depends on the type of lease. If it is an 'operating lease', ie a lease for a period that is less than the asset's anticipated useful life, it is normal for rentals to be deducted in arriving at the profits for the period to which the rentals refer. In practice, most leasing agreements provide for rentals to be payable in advance. So, if on 1 December a trader pays lease rentals of £12,000, which cover a period of six months, and he or she makes up accounts to the following 31 March, the amount deducted in arriving at the profits for the year ended 31 March will be:

$$\frac{4 \text{ months}}{6 \text{ months}} \times £12,000 = £8,000$$

A different accounting treatment is required where a trader pays rentals under a 'finance lease', ie a lease agreement under which the trader acquires almost all the benefits of outright ownership. HMRC's view is that the amount that should be deducted is that charged in the trader's accounts in accordance with SSAP 21 (ie the relevant Statement of Standard Accounting Practice that governs the accounting treatment of such leases).

Since 1 April 2006, the above provisions have not applied to 'long funding' leases; essentially, leases for periods of at least seven years (these provisions may also apply to certain leases for periods of between five and seven years where the lease is not a finance lease). FA2006 introduced rules that changed the taxation treatment of long funding leases of plant and machinery, which had previously been treated under the rules for finance leases or operating leases. The broad effect of these changes is that a lessee will be able to claim capital allowances as if he or she had bought the asset he or she is leasing. These capital allowances will be computed on the 'straight line' basis. In addition, he or she will be able to claim relief for the financing charges contained in the lease as if they were interest. The legislation also provides that a lessor and lessee may jointly elect for other post-31 March 2006 leases to be dealt with in this way.

Hire purchase

Where equipment is acquired under an HP contract, its cost counts as capital expenditure (and in most cases capital allowances will be available). The 'interest' element is apportioned over the contract term and relief is given for the amount of interest that relates to the accounting period concerned.

Example – Adjustments for HP contracts

A trader acquires a computer under a three-year HP agreement. The cost of the computer was £12,000, but the trader pays 36 monthly HP payments of £420.

The interest payable over the three years totals £3,120. This would normally be allocated roughly as follows:

Year 1:	£1,715
Year 2:	£1,040
Year 3:	£365

This type of allocation reflects the amount of the HP 'loan' outstanding during each year.

Legal and professional expenses

When HMRC examines a trader's business accounts, it normally asks for an analysis of any substantial amounts relating to legal and professional expenses. Legal costs in connection with the acquisition of capital assets are disallowable as capital expenditure, as are legal costs in connection with renewing a lease of more than 50 years. In contrast, legal costs incurred to protect a capital asset are generally allowable as a revenue expense.

Tax notes

Professional costs incurred in connection with tax appeals are not allowable on the grounds that such costs relate to tax on profits rather than an expense incurred in earning profits. However, in practice the costs of preparing and agreeing tax computations are usually allowed.

363

16.1.7 **Relief for premiums**

(ss 60, 287 ITTOIA 2005)

A trader may be required to make a lump sum payment to a landlord to obtain a lease. Where the lease is for a period of less than 50 years, part of the lump sum may be treated as income in the landlord's hands (see 8.3) and the trader may claim a deduction for this amount as if it were rent payable over the period of his or her lease. The part taxed in the landlord's hands is 100% of the premium less 2% for each complete year of the lease other than the first year.

There is no relief if the lease is for more than 50 years or if the premium is paid to someone other than the landlord because such a third party (eg an outgoing tenant) is not subject to income tax on income from the property.

Sometimes the lease will require a tenant to have certain building work carried out that will increase the value of the landlord's interest in the property. The landlord's UK property income should indicate the notional premium in this regard (see 8.3.4). Where this applies, the tenant can claim a deduction just as if he or she had been required to pay a premium in cash. However, the notional premium is generally far less than the actual cost of carrying out the work concerned.

Example – Treatment of premiums

> *B* pays a premium of £40,000 for a lease of ten years. Of this sum, 82% (ie £32,800) is taxed in the landlord's hands as rental income for the year in which the premium is payable (see 8.3).
>
> *B* can claim a deduction in his accounts for the ten years as if he had paid rent of £3,280 pa. If it were not for s 60, the expenditure would be treated as capital expenditure and would attract no relief.

16.1.8 **Provision for bad or doubtful debts**

HMRC has explained its approach with regard to provisions for bad or doubtful debts. Its interpretation is that a trader may be entitled to a deduction provided the following circumstances are satisfied:

- the debt existed at the balance sheet date; and
- before the accounts were finalised, the company's trader/directors discovered that the debtor's financial position at that date was such that the debt was unlikely to be paid.

HMRC has stated that a common example of this is where a debtor at the balance sheet date goes into administration or liquidation shortly after that date and before the date on which the trader approves the financial statements. Where the administration or liquidation commences after the balance sheet date, its occurrence before the accounts were finalised normally sheds light on the debtor's financial position at the balance sheet date. If the period between the balance sheet date and approval of the accounts is short, it is unlikely that a debtor would have gone from financial good health to insolvency in that period. In these circumstances it would normally be reasonable for the trader to regard the debt as doubtful. The acceptable amount of provision would depend on the information available.

HMRC contrasts this with a situation where a debtor is a habitually slow payer and there are no grounds to believe his or her financial position has changed. In such a case, HMRC argues that the length of time a debt has been outstanding is not in itself a sufficient reason to regard it as doubtful.

16.1.9 Provisions against liability to pay sums after year end

This is an aspect of a trader's accounts to which HMRC pays particular attention. It needs to be satisfied that relief is not sought for expenditure that will be incurred only in the future. Consequently, HMRC will almost certainly withhold relief unless the liability arose before the year end. For example, in the past it was not generally possible to secure a deduction for redundancy costs unless the necessary redundancy notices were served by the end of the trader's accounting period. Similarly, HMRC will often argue that a provision for an amount that may be due to a client for professional negligence is not allowable unless the client's claim has been admitted by the year end.

HMRC's approach may be challenged where the accounts comply with generally accepted accountancy principles, but you should seek professional advice if sizeable amounts of tax are at issue.

HMRC's rather restrictive approach was challenged successfully in *Johnston* v *Britannia Airways Ltd* [1994] STC 763. Civil Aviation Authority rules required each aeroplane to have a certificate of airworthiness. This would not be issued unless each engine was overhauled every 17,000 flying hours, which, in Britannia's case, meant every three to five years. Accordingly, a provision for the overhaul costs was made in each year's accounts based on the average cost of the overhaul per hour flown and the number of hours flown in the period.

HMRC took the view that the correct treatment was to make no provision before the cost of the overhaul was incurred, to capitalise the overhaul cost when incurred and then to write it off gradually over the period up to the next overhaul. The Special Commissioners found that the accruals method used by Britannia gave the most accurate picture of the airline's profits and was more effective in matching costs with revenue than the 'capitalise and amortise' method favoured by HMRC. Furthermore, the company's method was in accordance with ordinary principles of commercial accountancy. Accordingly, since there was nothing in statute or case law to contradict it, the company's appeal succeeded. This decision was upheld by the High Court.

Bear in mind that accountancy principles are being refined and updated constantly and FRS12 now sets out 'best practice' on provisions for sums payable after the year end. HMRC will resist an accounting treatment that does not comply with FRS12. The *Britannia Airways* decision has since been overtaken by changes in generally accepted accountancy principles.

There are sometimes circumstances where a payment will almost certainly be required in the future, although the precise amount has yet to be ascertained. For example, an insurance broker who may be required to refund commission to an insurance company if clients allow policies to lapse. HMRC has accepted that a provision may be allowable in these circumstances provided it is arrived at scientifically by reference to past experience. A 'rough and ready' general provision is not allowable.

16.1.10 Valuation of stock and work in progress

A trader's accounts should include his or her stock in hand at the accounts year end. Individual items of stock should be valued at the lower of cost or net realisable value. Cost should normally include a proportion of overheads.

Similarly, work in progress should be valued at the year end on the same basis. Where the accounts relate to a profession, the traditional view has been that it is not necessary to include in the cost the time value of work put in by the sole proprietor or partner, since this represents the proprietor's profit rather than a cost incurred in carrying on the profession. However, see below on UITF 40.

The treatment of long-term work in progress can involve complex issues and should be discussed with your accountant.

16.1.11 UITF 40

Where the accounts relate to a profession or other service provider, the traditional approach was changed by the ASB's guidance note on revenue recognition (UITF Abstract 40 published in March 2005), which required accountants to adopt a different method of revenue recognition for accounting periods ending on or after 22 June 2005. The traditional method was for work on unbilled services to be accounted for as work in progress (ie at the lower of cost or realisable value). Instead, UITF 40 generally requires that revenue be recognised as the services are provided and shown on the trader's balance sheet under the general heading of debtors. The difference between the two methods of accounting is that the UITF 40 method recognises profit earlier. The taxable profits of a business will normally be based on its accounting profit (subject to specific adjustments) and so the application of UITF 40 will generally mean that a business has higher taxable profits.

Changing the method of accounting gave rise to a large one-off profit in the first accounting period ending on or after 22 June 2005. The

Government recognised that taxing this in full might give rise to hardship and Schedule 15, FA 2006, contained provisions that allowed the additional tax to be spread over three to six years.

A business qualified for spreading relief if:

- it prepared accounts for the period after 22 June 2005 on the new UITF 40 basis; and
- previous accounts had been prepared on the basis of UK GAAP but did not follow the revenue recognition rules set out in UITF 40.

For details of the spreading provisions, see the 2008–09 *Tax Handbook*.

16.1.12 Withdrawal of 'cash basis' practice for professions

Until the late 1990s, relatively large businesses were able to prepare accounts purely on a cash receipts basis without taking into account income from unpaid invoices or the value of work in progress. The cash basis was widely used by barristers, solicitors, surveyors, actuaries, doctors and accountants, supported by a HMRC statement of practice that allowed such businesses to use this method subject to conditions that profits were computed on the earnings basis for the first three fiscal years and thereafter could be accounted on a purely cash basis. The cash basis also applied to expenses.

This cash basis was abolished by FA 1999. Businesses have had to use the earnings basis for accounting periods starting on or after 6 April 1999. Furthermore, there was a one-off catching-up charge based on the value of work in progress and debtors, net of creditors, at the start of the first accounting period affected.

The catching-up charge was payable over ten years of assessment, which started with the 2000–01 year of account. The amount chargeable in each year except the last was restricted to the smaller of:

(1) one-tenth of the total charge; and
(2) 10% of the 'normal' profit.

In the tenth year, 2009–10, the balance of the catching-up charge was taxed (for details, see the 2009–10 *Tax Handbook*). Barristers and advocates moving from the cash basis to GAAP may have had two different spreading adjustments: one for the cash basis and a subsequent one on adopting the principles of UITF 40, unless the change to GAAP was for a period of account ending sometime later than 22 June 2005, in which case there will be only one adjustment – that for the cash basis. The details will depend on the date on which the individual made the change of basis.

The total catching-up charge for partnerships was based on the first accounting period starting on or after 6 April 1999. The charge was spread over ten years as if there were annual instalments. The first year's instalment was allocated to the persons who were members of the partnership during that year, according to the way in which they shared profits. The same method was used for instalments taxed in the following nine years, with the instalments being allocated to individual partners according to the profit-sharing arrangements for the 12 months ending on the anniversary of the catching-up charge that fell into the tax year. This applied irrespective of any change in accounting date. The one-tenth and 10% limits operated at partnership level for the first nine years as they did for individuals. A partner remained liable for his or her share of the catching-up charge only for the period up to the date he or she left the partnership. Similarly, anyone joining the partnership during the ten-year spreading period became liable for his or her share of the charge in the future.

16.1.13 Other consequences of the catching-up charge

There were some relieving provisions:

- As the catching-up charge was taxed as 'miscellaneous income', it was not income for Class 4 NIC purposes.
- There was no charge in a loss-making year, unless it was the final year of the business.
- Losses arising from the same business could be set against the charge.

16.1.14 Cessation of trade

Where a business ceased, the ten-year spread of the charge continued but without the 10% profits cap because there were no longer any profits.

16.1.15 Barristers and advocates

Barristers (in Scotland, advocates) have always been regarded as a 'special case' (see 37.2).

16.1.16 Use of 'true and fair view' approach

The 'true and fair view' approach to computing taxable profits and losses is intended merely to ensure that profits are calculated in accordance with appropriate accounting standards and that time is not wasted on immaterial amounts. HMRC has confirmed that sole traders and partnerships do not need to have an audit even though their taxable profits must now be based on accounts that would comply with the true and fair view recognised for audited accounts.

Guidance on the application of accounting principles for traders who were formerly on the cash basis is contained in the Consultative Committee of Accountancy Bodies (CCAB) guidance note on the application of UITF 40, found on HMRC's website at www.hmrc.gov.uk/manuals/bimmanual/BIM74270.htm.

16.1.17 Miscellaneous matters

Own consumption

Any manufactured items or stock that is taken out of the business for the proprietor's own use, or for members of his or her family and friends, should be treated as sales at market value. The same also applies where the proprietor has provided business services to family and/or friends. See box 59 of the full self-employment form.

This rule was previously based on *Sharkey* v *Werhner* 936 TC 275, but was put on a statutory basis by FA 2008, in chapter 11A, ITTOIA 2005, with effect from 12 March 2008.

Payments under the Business Start-up Scheme

(s 207 ITTOIA 2005)

Where a trader has received a payment under a Business Start-up Scheme it should be included in his or her computation of trading profits, in box 29 of the short form or box 74 of the full self-employment form.

Class 4 NIC

No deduction is due for the trader's liability for Class 4 NIC (see 23.4) in arriving at the trader's taxable profits.

Gifts in kind to charities

(ss 70 and 108 ITTOIA 2005)

Relief can be claimed by traders who donate computers or other equipment to charities. Relief is also due for the employer costs of staff seconded to educational establishments.

16.2 CAPITAL ALLOWANCES

16.2.1 Introduction

A trader is entitled to capital allowances on plant and machinery used in the trade. Up to 2010–11, limited allowances were available on commercial buildings located in an enterprise zone, agricultural buildings, industrial buildings and hotels, although these allowances have been fully withdrawn from April 2011.

Allowances may also be claimed for expenditure on know-how and scientific research expenditure. All these are dealt with differently, and various rates of initial and annual allowances are given.

Capital allowances are treated like any other business expense. The allowances are computed on the current year basis, but once again with special rules for the first tax year. Allowances are due only if claimed within 12 months of the filing date for the relevant SA return.

As with much of UK tax law, successive Finance Acts have overlaid one another during the past 50 years and can make it difficult to see the wood for the trees. The main issues are addressed below.

16.2.2 What is plant and machinery?

Despite the introduction of specific legislation in 1994, the definition of 'plant and machinery' remains unclear. The statutory definition focuses mainly on what is *not* plant because it forms part of a building, and HMRC's practices and interpretation are still based largely on decisions handed down by the courts. The earliest judicial definition was provided in *Yarmouth* v *France* (1887) 19 QBD 647, in which Lindley LJ stated:

> … in its ordinary sense, it includes whatever apparatus is used by a businessman for carrying on his business – not his stock-in-trade, which he buys or makes for sale, but all goods or chattels, fixed or movable, live or dead, which he keeps for permanent employment in his business …

Some items are clearly within this definition (eg typewriters, dictating machines, telephone equipment, computers, manufacturing equipment, vans and other motor vehicles). What is less obvious is that a building may contain items that are plant and machinery. In some cases the plant will have become part of the building (eg a lift). Also, there may be structures that are items of plant (eg a dry dock or a grain silo, or a mezzanine floor put into a factory to create storage space). Capital allowances are also due on building work needed to enable plant and machinery to be installed (eg if a floor has to be strengthened to install a computer).

You should take professional advice if you acquire a building or adapt premises to meet the requirements of your trade to ensure that you obtain HMRC's agreement on the full amount eligible for capital allowances.

16.2.3 Expenditure treated as incurred in a period

(s 5 CAA 2001)

Expenditure is deemed to be incurred in a period if a trader enters into an unconditional contract; it is not necessary that the trader should actually have paid for the item or brought it into use by his or her year end. There is an exception for plant and machinery acquired under an HP contract where entitlement to allowances arises only when the plant is actually brought into use.

16.2.4 Assets brought into use part way through year

(s 56 CAA 2001)

An asset acquired towards the end of a trader's accounting period still attracts full writing down allowances at the appropriate rate, unless the trade has not been going for 12 months. In such a case, the allowance may be scaled down.

Example – Scaled down allowance

> U commences trading on 5 October 2011. On 5 April 2012 he acquires plant and machinery for £60,000. He makes up his first accounts for the six months ended 5 April 2012. Ignoring the annual investment allowance (see below), the capital allowances due to him for 2011–12 on this expenditure would be:
>
> $$\frac{6}{12} \times 20\% \times £60,000, \text{ ie } £6,000$$

16.2.5 Allowances for plant and machinery

The 'main pool'

(ss 11–15 CAA 2001)

Plant and machinery qualifies for a 20% writing-down allowance (25% before 2008–09; reducing to 18% from 2012–13). The allowance is based on the balance of the 'pool' of expenditure at the year end. The pool's opening balance represents the cost of plant brought forward from previous years, less capital allowances already received. A trader receives writing-down allowances based on the opening balance plus the cost of additional plant acquired during the year, less any disposal proceeds.

16.2.6 Small balances can be written off

(s 56A CAA 2001)

The pool may be fully written off if it goes down to £1,000 or less.

16.2.7 Annual investment allowance

From 6 April 2010 to 5 April 2012, the annual investment allowance (AIA) at 100% applies to the first £100,000 of expenditure on plant and machinery. This allowance was introduced in April 2008 with a limit of £50,000. From April 2012 it will reduce to £25,000.

Example – Writing-down allowances

S and *T* are in partnership. In their year to 31 March 2010 they had acquired plant and machinery at a cost of £30,000 and received capital allowances of £6,000. During their year ended 31 March 2011, they sell some of this plant for £2,000 and buy new plant for £20,000 (assume that this did not qualify for the AIA). In the year ended 31 March 2012, the partnership buys plant and machinery for £120,000. *S* and *T*'s pool would be as follows:

	£
Written-down value brought forward at 1 April 2010	24,000
Additions during year ended	
31 March 2011	20,000
	44,000
Less: disposal proceeds	(2,000)
	42,000
Writing-down allowances for 2010–11 (20%)	(8,400)
Written-down value carried forward	33,600
Additions during year ended 31 March 2012 (less 100% AIA)	20,000
	53,600
Writing down allowances for 2011–12 (20%)	(10,720)
Written-down value carried forward	42,880

Where qualifying expenditure in a period exceeds the AIA limit, a taxpayer may choose which expenditure to allocate the allowance against. Where some also qualifies for other 100% allowances (such as enhanced capital allowances for energy-efficient equipment), it makes sense to allocate the AIA against expenditure that qualifies for lower allowances, particularly integral features, which only attract allowances at 10%. Purchases are only relieved once.

Each individual business is eligible for relief. Where an individual owns more than one business, each business may be eligible for the AIA, although there are rules to prevent artificial fragmentation of businesses, abusive multiple claims and artificial use of unused allowances.

16.2.8 Temporary first-year allowances for 2009–10

In most cases, the first £50,000 of qualifying expenditure on general plant and machinery in 2009–10 already qualified for the 100% annual investment allowance. Expenditure in excess of that amount would normally be allocated to the main pool and qualify for a 20% writing down allowance. However, for the 2009–10 tax year such expenditure by companies, individuals and partnerships qualified for a temporary 40% first-year allowance.

16.2.9 Reduced rate of WDA for integral features

The 20% writing-down allowance is reduced to 10% for expenditure incurred after 5 April 2008 on plant consisting of fixtures that are integral to a building (unless the fixtures qualify as energy-saving or water-saving equipment, see 16.2.13 and 16.2.14 below). However, the 100% AIA for expenditure on plant (see 16.2.7 above) may be allocated against integral features.

Integral features (see s 33A(5) CAA 2001) include:

- electrical systems (including lighting systems);
- cold water systems;
- space or water heating systems, powered systems of ventilation, air cooling or air purification and any floor or ceiling comprised in such systems;
- lifts, escalators and moving walkways;
- external solar shading;

Post 5 April 2008 expenditure on integral features that does not attract the AIA is kept in a separate 10%, or 'special rate' pool. From April 2012, allowances on the main pool will be given at 18% and on the special rate pool at 8%.

Replacement/restoration expenditure

(s 33B CAA 2001)

Beware expenditure on replacement/restoration expenditure. Expenditure incurred over a 12-month period which represents more than 50% of the cost of replacing an integral feature will be capital and will fall into the 10% pool. Maintenance expenditure is normally treated as revenue expenditure, but s 33A(3) dictates that it is expenditure on an integral feature and not eligible as a revenue expense. A quote will need to be obtained for the replacement of a feature at the same time as getting it repaired.

16.2.10 Assets kept separate from the pool

Cars

Cars that cost £12,000 or more needed to be dealt with separately before 6 April 2009. The maximum annual writing-down allowance for such a car was £3,000, and a balancing allowance (or charge) arose on disposal.

Example – Writing-down allowances for cars

V operates an advertising business. She makes up her accounts to 30 April. On 1 May 2008 she bought a car that cost £30,000 and this was used by an employee. After two years, the car is sold for £10,000.

The car is deemed to be in a separate pool and the position is as follows:

		£
Year 1:	Cost	30,000
	Writing-down allowances	(3,000)
		27,000
Year 2:	Writing-down allowances	(3,000)
		24,000
Year 3:	Disposal proceeds	(10,000)
	Balancing allowance	14,000

The expensive car rules were abolished for expenditure incurred on or after 6 April 2009 for non-corporate businesses. Instead, all new qualifying expenditure on cars used exclusively for the business goes either into the main 20% pool or into the special rate 10% pool. This will be determined by the level of the car's carbon dioxide emissions. Cars with emissions over 160g/km will go into the special rate pool. Cars with an element of non-business use will continue not to be pooled but will attract only the 10% special rate of WDAs if their emissions exceed 160g/km. Expenditure incurred before 6 April 2009 on cars costing over £12,000 will continue to be subject to the previous rules for a transitional period of, broadly, five years. At the end of the transitional period, any remaining written-down value will be transferred to the main pool.

Other assets kept separate

Certain other assets are kept separate from the pool. One particular category is assets used partly for the purposes of the trade and partly for other purposes. For example, a van used by a sole trader for 40% business and 60% private motoring is deemed to form a separate pool. The trader is entitled to 'scaled down' allowances, ie he or she would receive 40% of the full writing-down allowance and 40% of any balancing allowance.

'Short-life' assets (see below) are also pooled separately.

'Long-life' assets (16.2.12), integral features (16.2.9) and expenditure on thermal insulation are also kept separate in the new 'special rate pool' from 6 April 2009, where the rate of writing down allowances is 10%, until 2012–13 when it will fall to 8%.

16.2.11 Short-life assets

(ss 83–84 CAA 2001)

Where no expenditure is added to the pool, the writing-down allowances that the trader receives are likely to get smaller and smaller. For example, a trader invests expenditure of £100,000 on plant in Year 1 (which is prior to 2011–12). He does not acquire any other plant and machinery for five years. His writing-down allowance in Year 1 will be £20,000 (ie 20% of £100,000); £16,000 in Year 2 (ie 20% of the residual £80,000); and so on. By the end of Year 5, the written-down value will be £32,768, but the equipment itself may be worn out and have a scrap value of only £2,000. To cover this type of situation, the legislation allows for a trader to designate certain assets as short-life assets. The cost of these assets is kept in a separate pool and a balancing allowance (or charge) arises on a sale within five years (ie the fourth anniversary of the end of the chargeable period in which the qualifying expenditure was incurred, or, if the qualifying expenditure was incurred in different chargeable periods, the first chargeable period in which any of the qualifying expenditure was incurred) or on the assets being scrapped by then. If an asset is not sold within that period, the asset's written-down value is transferred to the general pool. For expenditure incurred on or after 1 April 2011 (corporation tax) or 6 April 2011 (income tax) the cut-off period increases from four years to eight years from the end of the chargeable period in which the expenditure is incurred.

(1) In the above example, if the plant were actually scrapped at the start of Year 5 and the trader received no scrap value at all, he would receive a balancing allowance of £40,960.
(2) Again using the same basic facts, if the plant and machinery were still in use at the end of Year 5, the written-down value of £32,768 would be transferred to the trader's pool of other plant.

The following cannot be short-life assets:

● cars;
● assets used partly for non-trade purposes;
● assets originally acquired for non-trade purposes (eg assets acquired before the trade commenced);
● ships;
● certain assets leased out in the course of a trade.

An election must be made for an asset to be treated as a short-life asset. This needs to be submitted to HMRC within two years of the accounting period in which the asset is acquired. HMRC will require sufficient information to be able to identify the assets at a later stage (see SP1/86).

16.2.12 Long-life assets

(ss 90–104 CAA 2001)

FA 1997 introduced the concept of long-life assets (LLA). An LLA has an expected working life of 25 or more years. Where a trader incurs expenditure of more than £100,000 on an LLA, capital allowances are available at a rate of 10% (6% before 2008–09; reducing to 8% from 2012–13).

This rule affects assets purchased on or after 26 November 1996, but not those purchased before 1 January 2001 where the contract was entered into before 26 November 1996. Some categories of expenditure are specifically excluded from the general definition. Thus LLAs do not include any machinery or plant that is a fixture in, or is used in, a dwelling-house, retail shop, showroom, hotel or office or for ancillary purposes. Also, there are specific exclusions for motor or hire cars.

Expenditure on LLAs is segregated into the special rate pool, qualifying for writing-down allowances at 10%. This categorisation of an asset as being an LLA is irrevocable and it cannot later be reclassified as non-LLA, for instance when the remaining useful life drops below 25 years. The LLA rules do not apply where second-hand plant is purchased from a person who qualified for 20% writing-down allowances.

16.2.13 100% allowance for energy-saving and environmentally friendly equipment

(ss 45A–45E CAA 2001)

Expenditure after 31 March 2001 on designated energy-saving technologies and products qualifies for 100% first-year allowances. The qualifying items are set out in a list issued by the government (ss 45A–45C CAA 2001): see www.eca.gov.uk. The list of technologies covered by the scheme was revised and updated in October 2010.

A 100% FYA is also available for the purchase of a new, unused car with low CO_2 emissions of not more than 110g/km up to 31 March 2013, for expenditure on equipment for refuelling vehicles with natural gas or hydrogen fuel, and for a period of five years from April 2010, for expenditure on new, zero-emission goods vehicles.

16.2.14 Expenditure on water technologies

Since 1 April 2003, businesses have been able to claim 100% FYAs for expenditure on designated plant and machinery to reduce water use and improve water quality. The designated technology classes include:

- meters and monitoring equipment;
- flow controllers;
- leakage detection;

- efficient toilets;
- efficient taps.

Qualifying technologies and products can be found at www.eca.gov.uk.

16.2.15 100% capital allowances for refurbishing flats over shops

(ss 393A–393W CAA 2001)

Qualifying expenditure on flats over shops has attracted 100% allowances since 11 May 2001. This relief is due to be abolished during 2012, following a period of consultation. There are conditions:

- the expenditure must be incurred on the renovation or conversion of vacant or underused space above shops and other commercial premises;
- the property must have been built before 1980, have no more than five floors and all upper floors must have originally been constructed primarily for residential use;
- the upper floors must have been either unoccupied or used only for storage for at least one year before the conversion work is put in hand;
- the properties must be in traditional shopping areas and the whole or greater part of the ground floor must be 'authorised for business use', ie designated as such for business rates imposed by the local authority;
- the conversion must not be part of any scheme to extend the building;
- there must not be more than four rooms in each flat;
- each flat must have separate external access (ie not through the shop); and
- the flats must not have a notional weekly rent exceeding the following limits (which have remained unchanged since this relief was first introduced):

Number of rooms	Flats in Greater London	Elsewhere
1–2	£350	£150
3	£425	£225
4	£480	£300

No balancing charge will arise if the flats are retained for seven years and are either let or made available for letting throughout that period.

16.2.16 100% first year allowances for refurbishing business premises in disadvantaged areas

This relief applies to expenditure incurred in the five-year period between 11 April 2007 and 10 April 2012 and gives relief for the costs of renovating business property that has been empty for at least a year in designated 'disadvantaged areas'.

The capital costs of such renovations attract a 100% first year allowance. The FYA is subject to a clawback on a disposal within seven years. The allowance (also referred to as Business Premises Renovation Allowance or BPRA) is not available for premises used for

- farming;
- fisheries;
- aquaculture;
- manufacture of substitute milk products or synthetic fibres;
- shipbuilding;
- steel or coal industries.

It cannot be claimed for renovation expenditure on a residential property, nor for the costs of acquiring land, extending business premises or developing land next to the business premises.

16.2.17 Expenditure on landlord's fixtures

(s 172 CAA 2001)

Tenants are often required to install plant within a building, such as lifts and air conditioning. Where such items become part of a building they constitute landlord's fixtures. This means that the items of plant do not 'belong' to the tenant and as such would not qualify for capital allowances under the normal rules. The legislation deals with this potential anomaly by specifically providing that a tenant who incurs expenditure on such plant can receive allowances, but is subject to a balancing charge on the expiry or surrender of his or her lease, according to the plant's market value at that time. There are complex provisions dealing with situations where more than one person incurs expenditure on the same fixture or where expenditure is incurred by an equipment lessor.

As noted above, the rate of writing-down allowance on features integral to a building is reduced to 10% for expenditure incurred from April 2008 and will reduce to 8% from April 2012.

16.2.18 Acquisition of second-hand buildings

(ss 172–204 CAA 2001)

There are anti-avoidance provisions which:

- prevent allowances being given on fixtures as plant and machinery and under other categories such as enterprise zones or scientific research;
- limit allowances given on fixtures as plant in total to the fixtures' original cost (or, where capital allowances were claimed on the fixtures for periods before 24 July 1996, the cost price to the most recent claimant): this applies only where the disposal by the previous claimant took place on or after 24 July 1996;
- treat a fixture as sold at its tax written-down value if it is sold for less than that value to accelerate allowances (other than where the disposal is for good commercial reasons and is not part of a tax avoidance scheme).

16.2.19 Buildings located in an enterprise zone

(ss 298–299 CAA 2001)

Qualifying expenditure on a commercial building located in an enterprise zone could in the past qualify for a 100% initial allowance. A 'commercial building' was defined as a building or structure, other than an industrial building or hotel, used for the purposes of a trade, profession or vocation or as an office. The definition specifically excluded a building wholly or partly used as a dwelling-house. Certain conditions needed to be fulfilled, in that the building must:

- have been constructed under an unconditional contract entered into before the enterprise zone came to the end of its designated life; and
- been acquired unused or within two years of its having been let for the first time.

The part of the purchase price relating to the cost of the land did not qualify for capital allowances. Plant and machinery that had become an integral part of the building could also qualify for the 100% allowance. The initial allowance could be disclaimed, in whole or in part, and the remaining amount of qualifying expenditure was then available at 25% (enterprise zone allowances were not reduced to 20% in line with other WDAs). The 25% writing-down allowances were given on a straight-line basis over four years rather than on the reducing basis that applies for plant.

Example – Capital allowances on buildings in an enterprise zone

An enterprise zone building was acquired for £200,000. The land cost was £20,000, so £180,000 qualified for capital allowances. The purchaser disclaimed the whole of the initial allowance. He received annual allowances up to 2010–11 as follows:

Year of expenditure	£
Year 1	45,000
Year 2	45,000
Year 3	45,000
Year 4	45,000

If the purchaser had disclaimed only £80,000, the position would have been:

Year of expenditure	£
Initial allowance	100,000
Annual allowance	45,000
Year 1 total	145,000
Year 2	35,000

The point to note is that the annual allowances were based on the total qualifying costs, not on the balance left over after deducting the initial allowance.

Enterprise zone allowances were withdrawn from April 2011, but without the phasing out rules that applied to industrial and agricultural buildings allowances. The Government announced the creation of 21 new Enterprise Zones in the 2011 Budget. It has said that it will consider, in a limited number of cases, the scope for introducing enhanced capital allowances to support enterprise zones in those assisted areas, where there is a strong focus on high value manufacturing, so it is possible we will see some form of replacement relief in selected areas in future.

Sale of a relevant interest

Readers should take advice on a sale of an enterprise zone property because such a sale may still give rise to a balancing charge notwithstanding the general abolition of such charges from 21 March 2007.

16.2.20 Agricultural buildings allowances (ABAs)

(ss 361 and 372 CAA 2001)

The term 'agricultural buildings allowances' was misleading because the expenditure did not need to be used for a building. The allowances were given in respect of expenditure on farmhouses, farm or forestry buildings, cottages, fences, ditches, and drainage and sewerage works. The land must, however, have been used for agricultural purposes.

Rate of annual allowances

Expenditure on agricultural buildings previously qualified for a 4% annual allowance given on a straight-line basis. This was reduced to 3% for 2008–09, 2% for 2009–10 and 1% for 2010–11.

ABAs phased out

The available allowance is nil for 2011–12 and subsequent years.

Balancing charges and allowances

A balancing allowance or charge could arise on a disposal that took place before 21 March 2007 within 25 years of the expenditure having been incurred (but it was possible to make an election so that the asset passed across at tax written-down value). No charge or allowance arises on a disposal on or after 21 March 2007 unless the contract was entered into before that date.

16.2.21 Industrial building allowances (IBAs)

(s 271 CAA 2001)

An 'industrial building' is a building or structure used for the purpose of a trade consisting of:

(1) manufacturing or processing goods or materials; or
(2) maintaining or repairing goods or materials for customers; or
(3) maintaining or repairing goods or materials owned by the trader him or herself provided the relevant trade consists of manufacturing or processing goods or materials; or
(4) storage of:
  (a) raw materials for manufacture;
  (b) goods to be processed;
  (c) goods manufactured or processed, but not yet delivered to any purchaser;
  (d) goods on arrival by sea or air into the UK; or
(5) working mines, oil wells, etc or foreign plantations.

In addition, a sports pavilion provided for the welfare of workers employed in any trade qualified for industrial buildings allowances. Qualifying expenditure again excluded the land element in the purchase price.

Rate of allowances

Expenditure on an industrial building brought into use for a trade by the year end previously qualified for a 4% annual allowance, given on the straight-line basis. This was reduced to 3% for 2008–09, 2% for 2009–10 and 1% for 2010–11.

IBAs phased out

The available allowance is nil for 2011–12 and subsequent years.

Balancing charges and allowances

A balancing charge or allowance could arise on a disposal before 21 March 2007 within 25 years of the date that the expenditure was incurred. No such charge arises on a disposal on or after 21 March 2007 unless the contract was entered into before that date.

16.2.22 Hotels

(s 279 CAA 2001)

A qualifying hotel attracted allowances that are calculated in the same way as industrial buildings allowances (see 16.2.21).
A qualifying hotel was one that met the following conditions:

- Accommodation must have been provided in a building of a permanent nature.
- The hotel must have been open for at least four months during the period April to October.
- There must have been at least ten bedrooms available for letting to the public in general that were not normally be in the same occupation for more than a month.
- The services provided must normally have included the provision of breakfast and evening meals, making beds and cleaning rooms.

Once again, the allowances were phased out and are not available for 2011–12 and subsequent years . Balancing charges or allowances do not arise on disposals on or after 21 March 2007.

16.2.23 Expenditure on know-how

(s 452 CAA 2001)

Expenditure on acquiring know-how for use in a trade attracts capital allowances. 'Know-how' means any industrial information and techniques of assistance in manufacturing or processing goods or materials, or working or searching for mineral deposits, or that may be relevant to agricultural, forestry or fishing operations. Allowances are given on 'qualifying expenditure', which is the aggregate of any capital expenditure on know-how during the basis period, together with any unused balance of expenditure brought forward from the previous basis period and less any disposal value for know-how that has been sold.

Writing-down allowances are given at the rate of 25%.

16.2.24 Expenditure on research and development

(s 437 CAA 2001)

Certain capital expenditure incurred by a trader on research and development related to a trade attracts a 100% allowance. Research and development in relation to a trade includes research:

- that may lead to or facilitate an extension of trade; or
- of a medical nature that has a special relation to the welfare of workers employed in particular industries.

16.3 PRE-TRADING EXPENDITURE

(s 57 ITTOIA 2005)

A person may incur expenditure before starting to trade such as:

- rent for business premises;
- rates, insurance, heating and lighting;
- advertising, wages or other payments to employees;
- bank charges and interest;
- lease rentals on plant and machinery and office equipment;
- accountancy fees.

Expenditure qualifies for relief only if it is incurred within seven years of the date trade is commenced. The expense is treated as an ordinary trading expense incurred on the day the trader starts business.

Pre-trading capital expenditure that qualifies for capital allowances is also treated as having been incurred at the date trade is commenced.

16.4 POST-CESSATION RECEIPTS

(ss 242–243 ITTOIA 2005)

Where a person has been assessed on the cash basis (see 16.1.11), special rules apply if the trade or profession is discontinued. Subsequent receipts are normally taxed as income for the year in which they come in, although an election may be made for the post-cessation receipts to be treated as arising in the year of discontinuance.

Expenses may be deducted in so far as they were incurred wholly and exclusively for business and are not otherwise allowable. For example, a solicitor who had post-cessation receipts could deduct premiums paid on a professional indemnity policy where the cover related to the period after the solicitor had ceased to carry on his or her profession.

A similar charge may arise where a change occurs in the treatment of a trader's profits so that the cash basis ceases to apply and his or her profits are assessed on the earnings basis. Amounts received from customers that relate to invoices issued when the business was dealt with on the cash basis are treated as post-cessation receipts.

16.5 POST-CESSATION EXPENSES

(s 250 ITTOIA 2005)

Expenditure may qualify for tax relief if it is incurred within seven years of a business ceasing. The following types of expenditure may qualify for this relief:

- the costs of remedying defective work done, goods supplied, or services rendered while the trade or profession was continuing and damages paid by the taxpayer in respect of such defective work, goods or services whether awarded by a court or agreed during negotiations on a claim;
- insurance premiums paid to insure against the above costs;
- legal and other professional expenses incurred in connection with the above costs;
- debts owed to the business that have been taken into account in computing the profits or gains of the trade or profession before discontinuance but that have subsequently become bad;
- the costs of collecting debts that have been taken into account in computing the profits of the trade before discontinuance.

The amount of the relief will be reduced by any expense allowed as a deduction in the final accounting period that remains unpaid at the end of the year of assessment in which the new relief is given.

Expenditure that qualifies for the relief will be set against income and capital gains of the year of assessment in which the expense is paid. Where there is insufficient income or capital gains to cover the expenditure, the unrelieved expenditure of that year cannot be carried forward under the relief arrangements against future income or capital gains. However, the unrelieved expenditure will still be available to be carried forward under the existing rules and set against subsequent post-cessation receipts from the trade or profession.

Tax notes

The legislation requires a formal claim to be made within 22 months of the end of the year of assessment in which the expense is paid.

17

CAPITAL GAINS TAX AND BUSINESS TRANSACTIONS

This chapter focuses on the CGT aspects of various business transactions and contains the following sections:

(1) Loans to private businesses
(2) Losses on unquoted shares
(3) Relief for replacement of business assets
(4) Hold-over relief for gifts of business property
(5) Partnerships and capital gains
(6) Transfer of a business to a company
(7) Business taper relief
(8) Entrepreneurs' relief
(9) Earn-outs
(10) Sale of shares to all-employee share trusts
(11) Sales to certain employee trusts

17.1 LOANS TO PRIVATE BUSINESSES

A common type of transaction is a loan to a sole trader or partnership (an 'unincorporated business') or to a private company. Almost as common are situations where a person gives a guarantee to a bank, etc, that makes a loan to a business. This section deals with the CGT position if a loan becomes written off, or a person is required to make a payment under a bank guarantee that he or she has given.

17.1.1 Loans to unincorporated businesses

(s 253 TCGA 1992)

A CGT loss may be deemed to accrue to the lender if HMRC is satisfied that a loan has become irrecoverable. There are conditions that need to be fulfilled, ie the borrower must:

- not be the lender's spouse or civil partner;
- be resident in the UK;

- have used the loan wholly for the purposes of a trade carried on by him or her. The trade must not have consisted of (or included) the lending of money.

When a claim is submitted, HMRC must satisfy itself that any outstanding amount of the loan is irrecoverable and that the lender has not assigned or waived his or her right to recover the loan.

A claim must be made within four years of the end of the accounting period for a company, or tax year for an individual, in which the loan becomes irrecoverable (s 253(4A)).

The allowable loss is restricted to the amount of the loan that is irrecoverable, ie there is no indexation relief (only relevant if the lender is a company) in these circumstances.

Tax notes

A claim for a loss on a loan must be made within four years of the end of the tax year in which the loan becomes irrecoverable.

17.1.2 Loans to companies

(s 253 TCGA 1992)

Similar provisions apply where a person has made a loan to a company that proves to be irrecoverable. The principal conditions that need to be satisfied are:

- the company must be UK resident;
- it must be a trading company;
- the lender must not be a company that is a member of the same group of companies.

In all other respects, relief normally applies exactly as described in 17.1.1.

Loan notes and debentures

(s 254 TCGA 1992)

Another complication may apply to a loss on a loan that constitutes a 'debt on a security', which is a special type of loan. In broad terms, the loan is usually evidenced by a debenture deed and is transferable. A typical example is loan stock.

If a loan falls into this category, it is necessary to ascertain whether it also falls into another sub-class, ie a qualifying corporate bond (QCB, see 13.4.2). No loss relief is available on a disposal of a QCB. However, losses on other debts on securities continue to attract relief under the general principle that a debt is not a chargeable asset in the hands of the original creditor.

17.1.3 Payments under loan guarantees

(s 253(1)(c)TCGA 1992)

Instead of lending money to a relative or friend or his or her private company, a person might have given a guarantee to a bank, etc. Similarly, a company director might have had to give personal guarantees in respect of bank loans to his or her company.

Where the borrower cannot repay the loan, the bank will call on the guarantor to pay the amount due. In these circumstances, the guarantor may be able to claim a CGT loss as if he or she had made a loan that was irrecoverable. The following conditions must be satisfied for relief to be claimed:

- payment has been made under a guarantee;
- the payment arises from a formal calling in of the guarantee – a voluntary payment attracts no relief;
- the original loan met the requirements listed in 17.1.1;
- the amount paid under the guarantee cannot be recovered either from the borrower or from a co-guarantor.

17.2 LOSSES ON UNQUOTED SHARES

(Chapter 6, Part 4 ITA 2007)

From time to time, an individual may invest in a private company, either as a working director/shareholder or perhaps as a 'passive' investor with a minority shareholding. Investments may also be made in companies that, while they are technically public companies as defined by the Companies Act 2006, are not quoted companies.

17.2.1 Special relief for subscribers

A loss may arise on a disposal of shares in such a company. If the investor acquired existing shares by purchasing them, the loss is a normal CGT loss and the only way it can be relieved is as set out in 13.1.3. However, if he or she acquired the shares by subscribing for new shares, it may be possible to obtain income tax relief for the loss. Subject to certain conditions, the capital loss may be offset against his or her income for the year in which the loss is realised.

The following conditions must be satisfied:

(1) The loss must arise from one of the following:
   (a) a sale made at arm's length for full consideration (this rules out a sale to a connected person); or
   (b) a disposal that takes place when the company is wound up; or
   (c) a deemed disposal where the shares have become of negligible value.

(2) There are also conditions that attach to the company itself. In particular:

    (a) the company must not have been a quoted company at the date the individual subscribed for the shares and there must be no arrangements for the company to cease to be unquoted or to become a subsidiary of another company. If any class of shares in the company is quoted, this rules out relief even though the loss might have arisen on another class of share that was not quoted;

    (b) the company must be a trading company, or the holding company of a trading group, at the date of disposal or it must have ceased to have been a trading company not more than three years before the date of disposal and it must not have been an investment company, an excluded company or a non-trading company since the cessation;

    (c) the company's trade must not have consisted wholly or mainly of dealing in shares, securities, land, trades or commodity futures (further restrictions apply in relation to shares issued after 6 April 1998 so that the company must have met the conditions necessary to qualify for EIS relief: see 25.5);

    (d) the company's trade must have been carried out on a commercial basis.

17.2.2 Relief also available for subscriber's spouse

The spouse or civil partner of a person who subscribed for shares may also claim relief where he or she has acquired the shares in question through an *inter vivos* transfer from his or her spouse or civil partner. Shares acquired on a spouse's death do *not* entitle the survivor to relief on a subsequent disposal.

17.2.3 Nature of relief

The loss is calculated according to normal CGT principles. If the loss is eligible for relief, the individual may elect, by the first anniversary of the normal self-assessment filing date for the year of the loss, for it to be set against his or her taxable income for either the year of the loss or the preceding year. For example, if an individual realises an allowable loss in 2011–12, he or she has until 31 January 2014 to make the relevant claims. Either claim may be made independently of the other. Where he or she has losses that are available for relief and is also entitled to relief for trading losses, he or she can choose which losses should be relieved in priority to the others.

Any part of the capital loss that is not relieved can be carried forward for offset against future capital gains in the normal way.

17.2.4 Shares acquired by exercising a share option

If a person acquired shares by exercising a share option, and was taxed under the employment income legislation, his or her CGT acquisition cost may be much higher than anticipated (see 13.10.3). An unexpected CGT loss may therefore arise when the shares are disposed of. If the other conditions are satisfied, the person can get income tax relief (see Chapter 7).

17.3 RELIEF FOR REPLACEMENT OF BUSINESS ASSETS

(ss 152–160 TCGA 1992)

'Roll-over' relief may be available where a person sells an asset used by him or her in a trade (or in certain circumstances, by his or her family company) and reinvests in replacement assets used for business purposes.

17.3.1 Nature of roll-over relief

A gain is said to be rolled over in that it is not charged to tax, but is deducted from the person's acquisition cost of the new assets.

Example – Roll-over relief

> L sells a farm for £450,000. His capital gain is £200,000. He starts up a new business and invests £500,000 in a warehouse. By claiming roll-over relief, he avoids having to pay tax on the gain of £200,000 until the new asset is disposed of. The acquisition cost of his warehouse is reduced as follows:
>
> | | £ |
> | --- | --- |
> | Actual cost | 500,000 |
> | *Less*: rolled-over gain | (200,000) |
> | Deemed acquisition cost | 300,000 |
>
> The relief is really a form of deferment since a larger gain will arise on a subsequent disposal of the replacement asset.

17.3.2 Conditions that need to be satisfied

The asset disposed of must have been used in a business and must have fallen into one of the following categories:

- land and buildings;
- fixed plant and machinery;
- ships;
- goodwill (but not goodwill purchased by companies after 31 March 2002: see 18.6);
- milk and potato quotas;
- aircraft;
- hovercraft, satellites and spacecraft;

- Lloyd's syndicate rights ('capacity');
- ewe and suckler cow premium quotas and fish quota.

The replacement asset must also fall into one of these categories (but not necessarily the same category as the assets disposed of).

The replacement asset must normally be acquired within a period starting one year before and ending three years after the date of the disposal of the original asset. The time limit can be extended (at HMRC's discretion) if it was not possible to replace the original asset within three years because of circumstances outside the person's control.

Example – Full relief available only where all the sale proceeds are reinvested

s 152(3)–(11) TCGA 1992

> Using the same figures as in 17.3.1, *L* sells his farm for £450,000, making the same capital gain of £200,000. He starts up a business but invests only £400,000 in the new warehouse. The part of the £450,000 disposal consideration for the farm that is not applied in acquiring the warehouse is £50,000. This is less than the gain that arose on the disposal of the farm and therefore, only the balance of the gain may be rolled over. The warehouse's acquisition value is reduced by £150,000, with £50,000 becoming chargeable immediately.

17.3.3 Old assets not used for business throughout ownership

If the old asset was not used in the trading business throughout the period of ownership, s 152 applies to a proportionate part of the asset concerned.

Example – Old assets

> In March 2007, *M* sold a warehouse at a gain (before taper relief) of £50,000. It had originally been bought in March 1997 but had been used in his trade only since March 1999. The amount of gain that can be rolled over into the purchase of a new asset is calculated as follows:
>
> $$\text{Chargeable gain } £50,000 \times \frac{\text{Period of trading use of old asset}}{\text{Period of ownership}}$$
>
> This equals £50,000 × $\frac{8}{10}$, ie £40,000. The balance of £10,000 (£50,000 – £40,000) was a chargeable gain (before taper relief) of 2006–07.

17.3.4 Treatment where replacement assets are wasting assets

(s 154 TCGA 1992)

The roll-over relief is modified where the replacement expenditure consists of the purchase of a wasting asset (ie with an expected useful life of less than 50 years) or an asset that will become a wasting asset within ten years.

Plant and machinery is always considered to have a useful life of less than 50 years. Furthermore, the acquisition of a lease with less than 60 years to run also constitutes the acquisition of a wasting asset. Paradoxically, the goodwill of a business is not regarded as a wasting asset.

The capital gain in these circumstances is not deferred indefinitely, but becomes chargeable on the first of the following occasions:

- the disposal of the replacement asset; or
- the asset ceasing to be used in the business; or
- the expiry of ten years.

Examples – Roll-over relief on wasting assets

> (1) *N* sells a factory and reinvests in a 59-year lease of a warehouse that he uses in his business. In Year 6 the warehouse is let as an investment property. The rolled-over gain becomes chargeable in Year 6.
>
> (2) *O* also rolls over into a 59-year lease. He is still using the property after ten years, but because it has become a wasting asset within that period, the rolled-over gain becomes chargeable in Year 10.

17.3.5 Reinvestment in non-wasting assets

If the person acquires new non-wasting replacement assets during the ten years, the capital gain that was originally held over on the purchase of the wasting assets can be transferred and rolled over into the base cost of the new replacement assets. Assume in example (1) above that *N* had bought the goodwill of a business in Year 5. He could transfer his roll-over relief claim to the new asset. No gain would then become chargeable in Year 6 when he lets the warehouse.

17.3.6 Furnished holiday lettings

A property acquired for letting as furnished holiday accommodation (see 8.5) may qualify for roll-over relief; gains from the disposal of such properties may be rolled over.

17.3.7 Assets used by partnership

(SP D11)

Roll-over relief can be secured where the replacement assets are used by a partnership in which the owner is a partner.

17.3.8 Assets used by family company

(s 157 TCGA 1992)

Relief can be obtained where an individual disposes of a property, etc, used by his or her 'personal trading company', but only if the replacement asset is acquired by him or her and is used by the same company. A company is an individual's personal trading company if he or she personally owns at least 5% of the voting shares.

He or she need not be a director of the company – indeed, the person need not even be employed by it. Also, roll-over relief is not lost because he or she has charged the company rent.

17.3.9 Assets owned by employee or office-holder

An employee or office-holder may claim roll-over relief where he or she disposes of an asset used in the employment. This condition may apply to, for example, a sub-postmaster who has an 'office' for tax purposes, but who generally owns the sub-post office premises. For details, see SP 5/86.

There are circumstances where these provisions can mean that a director of a family company who has sold an asset used by one company and bought new assets used by another family company is entitled to roll-over relief: this is a difficult area where professional advice is essential.

In addition, ESC D22 provides that expenditure on improvements to existing assets may be treated as expenditure incurred in acquiring other assets for the purposes of the relief. ESC D24 provides that it is possible to ignore a delay in taking an asset into use, where this arises out of the completion of improvements to the asset, and ESC D25 provides that where the proceeds from the disposal of an 'old' asset are used in acquiring a further interest in an asset already in use in the trade, the further interest can be treated as a 'new' asset taken into use for the purposes of the trade.

17.4 HOLD-OVER RELIEF FOR GIFTS OF BUSINESS PROPERTY

(s 165 TCGA 1992)

17.4.1 Background and nature of hold-over relief

At one time, a UK-resident individual could transfer any asset to another UK-resident person on a no gain/no loss basis by claiming hold-over relief.

The relief was abolished for gifts of most types of assets but the same type of relief can still be claimed on gifts of business property to a UK-resident person.

17.4.2 Definition of 'business property'

Business property is defined for these purposes as:

- an asset used by the transferor in a trade, profession or vocation (this includes properties let as furnished holiday accommodation); or
- an asset used by the transferor's personal company in a trade; or
- an asset used for a trade by a member of a trading group of which the holding company is the transferor's personal company; or
- it consists of shares in a trading company, or holding company of a trading group, which does not to any substantial extent have investment activities and is either unlisted or the trading company or holding company is the transferor's personal company.

17.4.3 Situations where hold-over relief is not available

Hold-over relief cannot be claimed in respect of a gift of shares or securities to a UK company where the gift took place after 8 November 1999. The relief can, however, still be claimed on the gift to a company of an unincorporated business. Since 10 December 2003, hold-over relief has not been available for transfers to settlor-interested trusts.

If the company whose shares are being gifted has substantial investment activities no hold-over relief is available. There is no hard and fast rule as to what constitutes 'substantial investment activities'. HMRC's practice is to consider the income generated, assets used in, and management time devoted to, non-trading activities. Where, in the round, at least 20% of the company's activities are non-trading, it is considered not to be a trading company.

17.4.4 Claiming the relief

You should obtain a copy of Helpsheet IR295, which incorporates an election that needs to be signed by the donor and donee (see overleaf).

17.4.5 Relief clawed back if donee emigrates

Where an individual holds over a gain under s 165 and becomes either resident or not ordinarily resident within six years of the end of the tax year in which the asset was transferred, then the held-over gain is deemed to have accrued to the transferee immediately before the date of migration.

Claim for hold-over relief - Sections 165 and 260 TCGA 1992

	Transferor		Transferee
Name		Name	
Address		Address	
	Postcode		Postcode
Inland Revenue office		Inland Revenue office	
Tax reference		Tax reference	

Except in case of a gift in settlement, the claim must be made by both transferor and transferee. If the transferor or transferee has no Inland Revenue office or reference please explain why.

I/We hereby claim relief under Section 165/Section 260 TCGA 1992 in respect of the transfer of the asset specified below. The particulars given in this claim are correctly stated to the best of my/our information and belief.

Description of asset and date of disposal

√ one box

The gain held over is £   A calculation is attached ☐

We apply for deferment of valuations and have completed the second page of the claim form. ☐

We qualify for relief because:

√ one box

- the asset is used for the business of _____ ☐
  Please insert name of person

- the asset consists of unlisted shares or securities of a trading company or holding company of a trading group ☐

- the asset is agricultural land ☐

- the asset consists of listed shares or securities of the transferor's personal company or, where trustees are the transferors, a company in which they had 25% of the voting rights ☐

- the disposal was a chargeable transfer, but not a Potentially Exempt Transfer, for Inheritance Tax purposes ☐

- Capital Taxes Office reference number _____

- the disposal was exempt from Inheritance Tax under IHTA Section _____ ☐
  Please insert Section number

Signed _____ Signed _____

Date / / Date / /

17.5 PARTNERSHIPS AND CAPITAL GAINS

How CGT affects partnership transactions can at times be complex. Partners should familiarise themselves with SP D12 and take regular professional advice. The following section describes some key aspects.

17.5.1 Partnership's acquisition value

Although individual partners' entitlement to profits may vary over the years, the partnership's acquisition value for the firm's chargeable assets is not affected unless there are cash payments from one partner to another to acquire a greater interest in the firm, or unless assets are revalued as part of the arrangements for changes in profit-sharing.

17.5.2 Assets held by the firm at 31 March 1982

Where, after 5 April 2008, a partner disposes of an interest in a partnership asset which he or she held at 31 March 1982, his or her gain will normally be computed by reference to the value of the asset at 31 March 1982 (see 13.9.2).

Where partners have acquired interests in a partnership asset through changes in profit-sharing ratios between 31 March 1982 and 6 April 2008, they will generally have a cost computed by reference to the 31 March 1982 value plus any indexation allowance for the period from 31 March 1982 to the month in which the person making the disposal disposed of it or, if earlier, to April 1998.

See Revenue & Customs Brief 9/09.

17.5.3 Partnership gains divisible among partners

Where a partnership asset is sold at a capital gain (or loss), the gain is divided among the partners in accordance with their asset-sharing ratios. Each partner is personally assessable on his or her share of the gain.

The partner's actual CGT liability depends on his or her own situation, ie whether he or she has other gains for the year, has available losses, or can claim roll-over relief.

17.5.4 Revaluations and retirement and introduction of partners

Problems may arise where a partnership has substantial assets (that are chargeable assets for CGT purposes) worth more than their book value (ie the value at which they are shown in the firm's accounts). A revaluation to bring the assets' book value into line with their market value can produce a liability for individual partners if there is a reduction in their asset-sharing ratios. This commonly happens when existing partners retire or new partners are introduced.

Example – Retirement of partner

P is a partner in a five-partner firm and is entitled to 20% of the profits. He retires and his colleagues then share profits on the basis of 25% each. As part of the arrangements for his retirement, the book value of the firm's office block is increased from £150,000 to its current value of £750,000. The surplus is credited to each partner's account so that *P* is credited with £120,000.

P is treated as if he had realised a gain on the disposal of a one-fifth share of the building. This would be based on the £120,000 credited to his capital account. The remaining four partners are not treated as having made a disposal. Indeed, they each have made an acquisition of a 5% interest in the building for an outlay of £30,000.

Example – Introduction of partner

Q and *R* are partners. Their premises are included in their firm's balance sheet at £200,000 (original cost), but are actually worth £500,000. *Q* and *R* agree to admit *S* as an equal partner in return for his paying new capital into the firm of £700,000. They revalue the premises before admitting *S* as a partner, and the surplus of £300,000 is credited to their accounts. In this case, *Q* and *R* are each regarded as having made a disposal of a one-sixth interest in the premises. This is because *S*'s new capital will go into the firm as a whole. After coming in, he effectively owns one-third of all the assets (and is responsible for one-third of the liabilities).

The former partners' ownership of the premises has been reduced from 50% to a one-third interest.

17.5.5 Retirement and introduction of partners with no revaluation of assets

There is no such problem where partners leave or come in and there is no revaluation of assets. In such a case, the remaining or incoming partners normally take over the outgoing partners' acquisition values for the firm's asset.

Example – Change of partners with no revaluation of assets

> *T* and *U* are in partnership. They own premises that have a book value of £94,000 (equal to cost in 1980). *T* retires and is replaced by *V*. The premises are not revalued. After 5 April 2008, the premises are sold for £244,000. *U* and *V* are assessed on their share of the gain.
>
> The gain is computed by reference to the premises' market value at 31 March 1982, not their value at the time that *V* became a partner. This may not apply where the partners are connected persons (eg because they are relatives), or where cash payments are made to acquire an interest in the firm. In either of these categories you should seek specialist advice.

17.6 TRANSFER OF A BUSINESS TO A COMPANY

(s 162 TCGA 1992)

Where a person transfers a business to a company (ie he or she 'incorporates' the business), there is a disposal of the assets that are transferred to the company. Not all the assets necessarily become chargeable assets for CGT purposes, but a gain may arise on assets such as land, buildings and goodwill. Fortunately, there is a relief that may cover such situations.

17.6.1 Nature of relief

The main relief applies only where a business is transferred to a company in return for an issue of shares to the former proprietor(s) of the business. Where the necessary conditions are satisfied so that s 162 relief is available, the gains that would otherwise arise on the transfer of chargeable assets are rolled over into the cost of the shares issued.

Example – Transfer of a business to a company

> *W* transfers a business to B Ltd in return for shares worth £75,000. There are capital gains of £48,000 on the assets transferred to the company. If s 162 relief applies, *W* will not have any assessable capital gain, but her shares in B Ltd will be deemed to have an acquisition cost of £27,000 computed as follows:

	£
Market value	75,000
Less: rolled over gain	(48,000)
Base cost for CGT purposes	27,000

17.6.2 Conditions that must be satisfied

For s 162 relief to be available, all the business's assets, other than cash, must be transferred to the company. It is not acceptable for certain assets of the unincorporated business (eg trade debts) to be excluded, even though this might otherwise be advisable to save stamp duty.

Relief is available only in so far as shares are issued by the company instead of other forms of payment such as loan stock. The market value of the shares issued in return for the transfer of the business must be at least equal to the capital gains arising on the transfer of assets.

Tax notes

When transferring a business to a company, certain assets of the unincorporated business (eg trade debts) cannot be excluded, even though this might otherwise be advisable to save stamp duty.

Example – Limitations of s 162 relief

X transfers a business with a net value of £400,000 to C Ltd, a new company specially formed for the purpose. Shares in C Ltd are issued to him, and these have a value of £400,000. However, closer examination reveals that the business's value is depressed by heavy bank borrowings. Furthermore, capital gains totalling £490,000 arise on chargeable assets transferred as part of the business.

Section 162 relief would be limited to £400,000. The balance of £90,000 would be taxable in the normal way.

17.6.3 Conditions that are not required

(1) Relief is not confined to a transfer of a business to a company by a sole trader; the same relief is available where partners transfer a business currently carried on in partnership to a company.
(2) The shares that are issued need not be ordinary shares.

(3) Relief does not seem to be confined to a business that is classified as a trade. It is arguable that the relevant business might, for example, consist of letting a group of properties.

(4) There is no requirement that the company should be incorporated or resident in the UK. It can be both of these things, but relief is not prejudiced just because a foreign company is involved.

17.6.4 Relief may be due on proportion of capital gains

Some relief will still be available if the business is transferred to the company in return for a mixture of shares and loan stock, or shares and cash. The formula to be used is:

$$\text{Ch arg eable gain} \times \frac{\text{Value of shares received}}{\text{Value of whole consideration received}}$$

17.6.5 Election to disapply this relief

It is possible to elect for s 162 relief not to apply. This might be appropriate where the disposal of individual assets to the company would qualify for entrepreneurs' relief (ER) but the subsequent disposal of the shares would not (because, for example, the company has substantial non-trading activities). The election must be made by 31 January following the filing date for the year in question, eg the election has to be made by 31 January 2014 for a business incorporated during 2011–12.

17.7 BUSINESS TAPER RELIEF

Taper relief does not apply to a disposal after 5 April 2008. For information on this, see the 2008–09 *Tax Handbook* at 16.7.

17.8 ENTREPRENEURS' RELIEF

(Chapter 3, Part 5 TCGA 1992)

This relief was introduced from 6 April 2008 to remove a widespread sense of disillusionment on the introduction of the 18% flat rate and the abolition of taper relief. Many business people had come to regard the appropriate rate of CGT on the eventual sale of their business as 10%.

The relief between 6 April 2008 and 22 June 2010 was a reduction in qualifying capital gains of 4/9ths. If gains of £180,000 qualified, they were therefore reduced to £100,000. In summary, 18% of £100,000 = £18,000, ie an effective rate of 10% on £180,000.

The life-time limit of gains eligible for relief for disposals between 6 April 2008 and 5 April 2010 was £1m. The life-time limit was increased to £2m for disposals between 6 April 2010 and 22 June 2010. The relief was amended from 23 June 2010 so that up to £5m of gains on disposals of qualifying business assets are charged at 10% and was again increased from 6 April 2011 to £10m. The £10m remains a life-time allowance.

17.8.1 Conditions relating to the individual

ER is normally available only if the individual has been in business, as a sole trader or as a partner, or as an officer or employee of his or her personal trading company for at least 12 months ending on the date of the relevant disposal. It is necessary for the disposal to be a material disposal of all or part of his or her interest in the business or of shares in his personal trading company (see below).

17.8.2 Only some businesses qualify

Where a business is being disposed of, it must be a trading business and not an investment business. Furnished holiday accommodation should continue to qualify.

17.8.3 Personal trading company

A company qualifies as an individual's personal trading company only if:

- he or she owns at least 5% of the ordinary share capital and has at least 5% of the voting rights by virtue of that holding; and
- he or she is an officer (eg director) or employee of that company; and
- the company is a trading company or the holding company of a trading group and it does not exist to any substantial extent for any non-trading purpose (this is the same as the 20% test that applies for hold-over relief purposes, as described in 17.4).

17.8.4 Associated disposals

ER can also be claimed on gains arising from associated disposals. An associated disposal consists of the disposal by the individual of an asset he or she has owned personally but which has been used – throughout the 12 months ending on the date of the associated disposal (or the date of cessation of the business, if earlier and relevant) – in the business of a partnership of which the individual was a partner or a company that was the individual's personal trading company.

The associated disposal must take place within three years of the disposal by the individual of an interest in the partnership or company concerned (or cessation of the business of the partnership or company, whichever is the earlier). The associated disposal must also be related to the individual withdrawing from the business concerned. It is unclear precisely what this means although this condition will normally be met where the disposal takes place as part of the same arrangements under which the individual retires from the partnership or ceases to be involved in the company's business, either fully or partially.

Tax notes

The relief is available from 6 April 2008 for a gain on the sale of land or buildings used by a partnership or an individual's personal trading company but only where the individual owner had not charged the business a market rent throughout the full period of business usage since 6 April 2008. The level of any rent charged to the business for periods of business usage before 6 April 2008 is ignored.

17.8.5 Worked examples provided by HMRC

HMRC gave the following worked examples in its press release of 12 March 2008 (these have been updated, where appropriate, by the author for the increases in the life-time limit from 6 April 2011):

(1) Miss *S* sold her trading business in 2008–09 and realised gains of £250,000 on her factory premises and £300,000 on goodwill but a loss of £100,000 on her retail shop giving net gains of £450,000 (before ER). She had made no other claims to the relief and the whole of the gains were eligible for relief.

    Miss *S* claimed ER, meaning the gains of £450,000 were reduced by 4/9ths (so reduced by £200,000, resulting in a chargeable gain of £250,000). Miss S had no allowable losses and no other gains in that year so she deducted the annual exempt amount £9,600 (for 2008–09) giving an amount chargeable to CGT of £240,400. This amount was taxed at 18%, giving tax payable of £43,272.

(2) Mr *W* sold his shares in a trading company in May 2010 and realised a gain of £360,000. He owned 50% of the ordinary shares of the company, which gave him 50% of the voting rights, for several years, during which time he has been a director of the company. He therefore qualified for ER on the disposal of his shares.

    On making a claim, Mr *W*'s gain was reduced by 4/9ths, resulting in a chargeable gain of £200,000. He had no allowable losses or other chargeable gains, so after deduction of the annual exempt amount, £10,100 (for 2009-10 and 2010–11), the amount chargeable to CGT was £189,900. This amount was taxed at 18%, giving tax payable of £34,182.

(3) Mrs *L* sold her trading business in two transactions, as part of the same arrangements, in May and July 2010, and realised gains of £3.5m (before ER). She had made no other claims for the relief, and the whole of the gains were eligible for relief. She claimed ER.

The gain arising in May 2010 was £2.3m and in July 2010 £1.2m. For the May 2010 disposal, the maximum amount of gains on which ER could be claimed was £2m. So £2m of Mrs *L*'s gains was reduced by 4/9ths (to £1,111,110), and the balance (over the £2m) of £300,000 was chargeable in full, resulting in net chargeable gains of £1,411,110. She had no allowable losses or other chargeable gains, so after deduction of the annual exempt amount (£10,100) she had an amount chargeable to CGT of £1,401,010. This amount was taxed at 18%, giving tax payable of £252,181.80. The disposal in July took place after the increase in the life-time allowance to £5m. The gain of £1.2m was therefore chargeable at 10%. The unused balance of the life-time allowance carried forward up to 5 April 2011 was £1.8m. From 6 April 2011, the unused balance of the lifetime allowance available to use against future gains increased to £6.8m.

(4) Mrs *F* sold her trading business in 2008–09 and realised gains of £720,000. This amount qualified in full for ER, which she claimed, and the gain was reduced by 4/9ths, resulting in a chargeable gain (before any deduction of losses or annual exempt amount) of £400,000. From January 2009 to September 2013 Mrs *F* is a director of trading company P Ltd, and owns 15% of the ordinary share capital, which entitles her to exercise 15% of the votes. In September 2013 she sells her shares, realising a gain of £6m. She claims ER.

Mrs *F* will be able to claim ER on the full gain of £6m arising in 2013–14, assuming that the lifetime limit is still £10m at that time.

(5) In 1995 Mr *E* purchased a buy-to-let property for £100,000 that is let out on an assured short-hold tenancy. In October 2011 he sold the property for £250,000. The CGT due is calculated by deducting the purchase cost from the sale proceeds giving a gain of £150,000. This gain is not eligible for ER.

Mr *E* has no allowable losses or other capital gains in 2011–12 so he can deduct the full annual exempt amount of £10,600 giving an amount chargeable to CGT of £139,400. Mr *E* is a higher rate taxpayer. The gain is taxed at 28% giving tax payable of £39,032.

(6) Mr *R* has been a member of a trading partnership for several years. He leaves the partnership in 2011–12 and disposes of his interest in partnership assets to the other partners, realising gains of £125,000, all of which qualify for ER. He also sells the partnership office building which he owned outright, but let to the partnership, realising a gain of £37,000. The disposal of the office building is 'associated' with Mr *R*'s withdrawal from the partnership business, and the £37,000 gain therefore also qualifies for ER (assuming there is no restriction on the amount of the gain qualifying for relief as a result of non-qualifying use).

Mr *R* claims ER in respect of total gains of £162,000. This amount is chargeable at 10%. Mr *R* has no allowable losses or other gains, so after deduction of the annual exempt amount of £10,600 there is an amount chargeable to CGT of £151,400. This amount is taxed at 10%, giving tax payable of £15,140.

(7) Mrs *N* sold her business in 2009 and realised a gain of £99,000 that qualified for ER. She claimed the relief, but also made an investment of £80,000 in qualifying EIS shares and claimed to defer the gain.

Mrs *N*'s gain of £99,000 was reduced by 4/9ths, resulting in a chargeable gain of £55,000. The investment in EIS shares exceeded £55,000, so the whole of the chargeable gain of £55,000 was deferred. This amount will come into charge at some later time under the normal EIS rules for charging deferred gains (but see notes below, regarding anomalies arising when the deferred gain comes back into charge, and the removal of the ability to claim both deferral and ER for periods after 22 June 2010).

(8) Mr *C* sold his trading business in May 2006 and realised a gain of £270,000. He invested this amount in qualifying EIS shares in July 2011, so the gain was deferred. In September 2011 he sells the EIS shares and the deferred gain becomes chargeable to CGT.

Mr *C* can still claim ER in respect of the deferred gain under the transitional provisions applying to disposals after 22 June 2010, and the deferred gain will be charged at 10%, resulting in a CGT charge (in September 2011 when he disposes of the EIS shares) of £27,000 (ignoring any deduction for losses and annual exempt amount).

(9) Mrs *A* exchanged her shares in the trading company Y Ltd for qualifying corporate bonds (QCBs) in May 2010. For some years she had been an employee of Y Ltd, owning 10% of the ordinary shares, which entitled her to exercise 10% of the votes in the company. She therefore met the conditions for claiming ER in respect of her shares in Y Ltd. The normal rules for share exchanges apply and there was no immediate charge to CGT in 2010 when she exchanged the shares, but the gain that would have arisen on a disposal of those shares for full market value at the date of the exchange was calculated. The calculation resulted in a gross gain of £63,000, which would have been reduced by 4/9ths to £35,000 and then 'frozen' until such time as the QCBs are redeemed or otherwise disposed of.

Mrs *A*'s reduced gain of £35,000 will become chargeable to CGT at 18% or 28% when the QCBs are redeemed or she disposes of them in any other way.

(10) Mr *D* exchanged his shares in trading company Z Ltd for qualifying corporate bonds (QCBs) in 2007. Before the exchange he had, for several years, been a director of Z Ltd and owned 25% of its ordinary share capital, which entitled him to exercise 25% of the votes in the company. A gain of £315,000 was deferred as a result of the

exchange. In August 2010 the QCBs were redeemed, and the gain of £315,000 became chargeable.

At the time of the exchange Mr *D*'s gain would have qualified for ER if the relief had been available in 2007. So Mr D can claim the relief when the gain crystallises in August 2010, and will therefore be taxed at only 10%.

(11) In August 2010, Miss *K* exchanged her shares in the trading company X Ltd for shares issued by a new company, H plc. For some years she has been an employee of X Ltd, owning 40% of the ordinary shares, which entitled her to exercise 40% of the votes in the company. She therefore met the conditions for claiming ER in respect of her shares in X Ltd. But in the exchange she received shares amounting to only 2% of the ordinary shares of H plc. This is below the minimum 5% holding requirement, so Miss K will not be able to qualify for ER on a disposal of her new shares in H plc.

Under the normal rules for share exchanges Miss K would have been treated as making no disposal of her shares in X Ltd at the time of the exchange in August 2010 and there would have been no immediate charge to CGT then. These rules would therefore have meant she lost all possibility of claiming ER. To allow a claim to the relief she could have elected to disapply those normal rules. Disapplying the rules means that she would have been treated as disposing of the shares in X Ltd at the time of the exchange in August 2010. She could then have claimed ER on the gain arising on that disposal.

17.8.6 Transitional considerations

As a result of the changes to the ER regime in the short time since its introduction, there are anomalies surrounding the treatment of deferred gains. In particular, under the transitional provisions introduced on 23 June 2010, the entrepreneurs' relief limit is determined by the timing of the first relevant disposal. This event determines the ER cap for all subsequent encashments.

So, if for example following a sale, loan notes have been taken to defer the gain and the first tranche of loan notes is encashed between 6 April and 22 June 2010, the then lifetime limit of £2m will apply to all future disposals of those loan notes, even if those disposals take place after 6 April 2011 when the lifetime limit is £10m. Similarly, where the first disposal takes place between 23 June 2010 and 5 April 2011, the lifetime limit of £5m is 'locked in', irrespective of the lifetime allowance at the time of any future disposals and – if there had been an earlier chargeable event (ie during 2008–09 or 2009–10) triggering the assessment of part of the deferred gain – the £1m lifetime limit would have applied, limiting the relief available when the balance of the deferred gain was assessed.

This anomaly applies to any situation where there is a deferred gain (ie where there was a share-for-QCB transaction, or a gain was deferred by investing in EIS shares), limiting the available lifetime allowance (as it relates to that deferred gain) to the rate applying at the time of the first relevant disposal (ie the first disposal bringing part of the deferred gain into charge).

Where gains are deferred into EIS shares on or after 23 June 2010, it is no longer possible to claim both deferral and ER. If the gain is not deferred, and the applicable conditions are met, then ER can be claimed and a 10% tax rate will apply on gains up to the lifetime allowance. If the gain is deferred, then ER will not apply when it eventually comes into charge and it will be taxed at 28% (or the applicable rate at the time of disposal).

Tax notes

In view of this, it may be sensible in future to limit EIS deferral claims to situations where either the ER lifetime allowance has already been used, or where the original gain would not have qualified for ER in any event.

A similar problem arises with share-for QCB exchanges on or after 23 June 2010. It is necessary to choose between treating it as a transaction which creates an immediately taxable gain (ie electing to disapply the application of s 116(10)), so that the gain is taxed at 10%; or defer the full gain (without regard to ER) by applying s 116(10). Entrepreneurs' relief will only be available if the ER conditions are met when the deferred gain comes into charge. In most situations this will not be the case because the company issuing the loan notes will not be the taxpayer's personal company.

Tax notes

It is likely that it will be preferable to disapply s 116(10) and claim ER, despite the cash-flow disadvantage, to lock-in the 10% tax rate.

17.9 EARN-OUTS

An earn-out is where a person sells shares and part of the consideration is dependent on the company's subsequent performance. For example, an individual might sell his or her private company for £1m cash plus an amount based on the company achieving certain profit targets for the next three years.

The right to receive more cash if profit targets are achieved is a valuable one, but its value will not normally be the maximum sum: it depends on whether the targets are achieved. The case law *(Marren* v *Ingles)* indicates that a present (discounted) value should be ascertained and this should be included as part of the sale consideration that is taxable for the year in which the sale takes place. When the earn-out period is over, and the actual amount due under the earn-out is known, another capital gain (or loss) occurs for the year in which the entitlement is ascertained.

This has in the past meant that a person who is entitled to receive an earn-out could be taxed on sums that are never in fact received. Fortunately, the law has now changed. Provided the sale contract specifies that the earn-out consideration *must* be satisfied by the acquiring company issuing securities or debentures (eg loan notes) rather than paying cash, and provided the person entitled to the earn-out does not make an election under s 138A TCGA 1992, there is no question of anything being taxed in respect of the earn-out until the individual makes a disposal of the securities that are received in satisfaction of his or her earn-out rights.

Tax notes

Be especially careful with this. Until recently, the effect of making an election under s 138A was beneficial in that it postponed the date of disposal for CGT purposes until the individual disposed of the securities received from the earn-out. The situation has now been turned upside-down: you are now automatically treated in this way unless you positively elect under the revised version of s 138A to have a CGT assessment on the initial value of the earn-out. It is possible that such a CGT assessment could be beneficial in some circumstances and in these cases the s 138A election needs to be made within 22 months of the end of the tax year in which the disposal giving rise to the earn-out takes place.

17.9.1 CGT treatment for earn-outs since 2003

There is now also some relief for individuals who are entitled to an earn-out that can be taken in cash. Such individuals are liable to be taxed on the initial value of the earn-out but there is now a carry-back relief. This allows a vendor who has been taxed on a higher amount than is eventually received to carry back the difference as a loss. In other words, the end result is that CGT is paid only on the amount that is actually collected.

This relief applies only to earn-out rights disposed of after 9 April 2003.

17.9.2 Earn-outs and income tax

See also 6.7 regarding a possible income tax charge on certain earn-outs.

17.10 SALES OF SHARES TO ALL-EMPLOYEE SHARE TRUSTS

(Schedule 7C TCGA 1992)

Where an individual transfers unquoted shares to trustees who hold them for employees under an approved all-employee share scheme (see 6.4), the individual may roll over any capital gain arising from this transfer provided he or she reinvests in chargeable assets within six months. The all-employee trust must acquire at least a 10% interest in the company. The chargeable assets into which the individual's gain is rolled over cannot consist of shares in the company concerned or a property that is exempt as the individual's main residence.

> **Tax notes**
>
> You will need to take professional advice if you seek to rely on this relief. But if you qualify, the roll-over relief rules are quite generous.

17.11 SALES TO CERTAIN EMPLOYEE TRUSTS

(s 239 TCGA 1992)

In certain situations, a gift of an asset by an individual to an employee trust may be treated as a disposal at cost.

The conditions which need to be satisfied are as follows:

(1) The employee trust must be for the benefit of all or most of the employees of the company concerned.

(2) No employees who are participators owning 5% or more can be eligible to benefit under the trust except on the basis that any benefits received by them will be taxable income (or would be so but for the fact that the participator is resident outside the UK).

(3) No person who is connected to a participator who owns 5% or more may benefit except on the basis that any benefits received will be taxable income.

(4) Within 12 months of the individual making his or her gift, the trustees must hold more than one half of the ordinary share capital of the company.

> **Tax notes**
>
> When considering any transactions with employee trusts, bear in mind the new rules on disguised remuneration (see 5.1), which can apply even in innocent situations. You will need to take professional advice.

18

TAX AND COMPANIES

RICHARD JONES

This chapter looks at the taxation of companies under the following headings:

(1) Corporation tax
(2) Self-assessment
(3) How 'profits' are defined
(4) Accounting periods, rates and payment of tax
(5) Loan relationships
(6) Intangible assets
(7) Companies' capital gains
(8) Dividends
(9) Losses
(10) Overseas aspects
(11) Transfer pricing rules
(12) Groups of companies
(13) Investment companies
(14) Close companies
(15) Real Estate Investment Trusts (by Marios Gregori and Viran de Silva)
(16) Corporate venturing
(17) Research and development (R&D) tax relief
(18) ECA tax credits
(19) Sale of lessor companies: anti-avoidance
(20) iXBRL and online filing
(21) Claims, elections and penalties

18.1 CORPORATION TAX

18.1.1 Corporate tax road map

The corporate tax road map is the Government's plan to make the UK a more attractive home for international business by creating a competitive and stable corporate tax system. Its principles for reform include:

● lower tax rates but fewer tax reliefs;
● avoiding unnecessary changes (for simplicity and stability);
● keeping pace with modern business practice;
● a level playing field for businesses.

Reforms introduced as part of the road map will also be designed and implemented according to the Government's new procedures for making policy on tax. Proposals for these procedures (set out in the *Tax Policy Making* consultation document published with the Emergency Budget in June 2010) envisage extensive consultation with affected businesses before changes are made.

The Government has provided a timetable (Table18.1) showing the planned reforms and has confirmed that it does not intend to make any significant reforms in the first three years, other than those listed. It has, however, retained the option of introducing unplanned anti-avoidance legislation to prevent revenue losses if necessary.

Table 18.1 – Timetable for company tax reforms

2010	*Reform action*
Autumn	Published paper on reforming CFC rules Published paper covering IP, the patent box and R&D tax credits Published details on the CFC interim improvements and on chosen option for foreign branch reform
2011	
Spring	Introduced rate cuts in small companies' rate and the main rate to 26% Published details of new CFC rules for consultation Published details of the patent box for consultation
Finance Bill	Legislate for capital allowances reductions Legislate for CFC rules interim improvements and foreign branch reform
Autumn	Publish draft legislation on new CFC rules and the patent box
2012	
Spring	Introduce further cut in main rate to 25% and reductions to capital allowances
Finance Bill	Legislate on outcomes from consultation on new CFC rules and the patent box
2013	
Spring	Introduce further cut in main rate to 24% and the patent box
2014	
Spring	Introduce further cut in main rate to 23%

18.1.2 Who pays corporation tax?

(ss 8–11 CTA 2009)

Corporation tax is levied on the chargeable profits of companies resident in the UK for tax purposes. A company is generally defined as meaning any body corporate or unincorporated association, but does not include a partnership, local authority or local authority association. The definition extends to authorised unit trusts, detailed provisions for which are set out in s 616 CTA 2010.

Corporation tax also extends to non-resident companies carrying on a trade in the UK through a permanent establishment. Such companies are chargeable to tax on any income attributable to the permanent establishment and on any capital gains arising on the disposal of assets used in the UK trade of the permanent establishment. Any income of a non-resident company from sources within the UK that is not charged to corporation tax is liable to income tax.

A company that was incorporated in the UK is regarded as resident here regardless of where the directors exercise their management and control. Some of the double taxation conventions negotiated with other countries override this in practice and treat a dual resident company as if it were not UK-resident.

A company that was incorporated overseas may still be regarded as resident in the UK on the basis that its central management and control is exercised in the UK. Questions relating to a foreign incorporated company's residence status are usually determined by reference to the guidelines set out in SP1/90 dated 9 January 1990 (see www.hmrc.gov.uk/manuals/intmanual/INTM120140.htm).

18.2 SELF-ASSESSMENT

(ss 5, 6 and 8 CTA 2009; s 963 CTA 2010 and Schedule18 FA 1998)

Self-assessment has been in force since 1999. Corporation tax self-assessment is similar to the income tax self-assessment system for individuals and trustees.

Self-assessment for companies brings with it extensive record-keeping obligations.

A copy of the manual, *A Guide to Corporation Tax Self-assessment* can be obtained from HMRC's website at www.hmrc.gov.uk/ctsa/ctsaguide.pdf.

The CTSA system requires payments on account for certain companies. Where a 'large' company (as defined in 18.4.4) has taxable profits for an accounting period, and it also had such profits in the preceding year, it must make four payments on account of its expected corporation tax liability for the year. Online filing has been introduced for almost all companies from 1 April 2011 for accounting periods ending after 31 March 2010. See 18.19 for more on this.

18.3 HOW 'PROFITS' ARE DEFINED

18.3.1 Computation of profits

(ss 2–4 CTA 2009)

The income and chargeable gains of a company, collectively termed 'chargeable profits', are chargeable to corporation tax. The computation of chargeable profits can be a very complex process bearing in mind the detailed tax legislation and extensive case law. There is also a myriad of HMRC statements of practice, press releases and extra-statutory concessions that may need to be borne in mind when calculating chargeable profits on which corporation tax is payable.

18.3.2 Special computational rules for companies

Rental income

All income from UK rental activities is now treated as arising from one source and taxed along the same lines as trading profits. Any losses are relieved first against other income and gains of the same period, and any excess is available to carry forward against future property income, or may be surrendered as group relief (subject to certain restrictions).

Foreign exchange transactions

Special rules apply for foreign exchange profits and losses; professional advice should be taken if the company has significant foreign assets or borrowings in a foreign currency.

Loan relationships

Specific rules govern the treatment of loan relationships such as gilts and other fixed-interest investments. Basically, any profits on disposal of such assets are taxed as income and any losses are allowed against the company's income. If the company decides to revalue its loan relationships for accounts purposes in accordance with generally accepted accounting principles (GAAP), any increase compared with the market value at the start of the period (or the date of acquisition where the gilt, etc, was acquired during the course of the year) is taxable income; any reduction in value is an allowable loss (see 18.5).

Interest

FA 2009 introduced a regime called the worldwide debt cap that applies to all large groups for accounting periods beginning on or after 1 January 2010. A large group is defined as one having at least 250 employees or turnover of more than £50m and gross assets of more than £43m.

Under these rules, tax deductions for interest will be disallowed to UK members of the group to the extent that the 'tested amount' exceeds the 'available amount'.

The tested amount is the aggregate net finance expense of all relevant group companies (UK resident companies and non-resident companies with UK permanent establishments) that have net finance expenses for the period concerned, calculated under UK tax rules. The available amount is the worldwide group's gross consolidated finance expense (UK and non-UK). In other words, if the group's overall interest bill is £15m but UK companies have paid interest of £17.5m, broadly speaking £2.5m will be disallowed.

Capital allowances

Although depreciation is not regarded as an allowable expense for tax purposes, tax relief is given for expenditure on qualifying capital assets by means of capital allowances. The principles follow very closely those that apply to individuals (see 16.2) and therefore the main provisions are not covered in detail here. Capital allowances for a trade carried on by a company are regarded as trading expenses for the accounting period in which they arise. They are therefore taken into account in arriving at the chargeable profits or overall tax loss for the accounting period.

Capital allowances for non-trading activities are primarily deductible from the income arising from that source. Any surplus allowances may be carried forward against similar source income arising in later accounting periods or deducted from overall chargeable profits for the accounting period in which they arise.

Contributions to employee benefit trusts

Contributions attract tax relief only if an employee receives sums within nine months of the company's year end on which PAYE and NIC are charged. If this condition is not satisfied, the company receives a deduction only for the accounting period in which sums are paid out subject to PAYE and NIC. Following the introduction of new rules on disguised remuneration (see Chapter 5) from 6 April 2011, it is probable that a tax charge will arise at the time – or shortly after – a contribution has been made, if this is 'earmarked' for specific employees. Accordingly, ss 1290 to 1295 CTA 2009 have been amended to ensure that a deduction will be given in the employer's tax computation for any amounts that are subjected to tax under the new provisions in Part 7A ITEPA, for the period that the tax charge arises.

Intangible assets

The tax treatment for expenditure on, and gains from the sale of, intangible assets was introduced by FA 2002 (now in part 8 CTA 2009) (see 18.6).

Insurance policies

See 28.8 on life assurance policies held by companies.

Annual payments

(s189 CTA 2010)

Certain annual payments (termed 'charges on income') are deductible from a company's profits in arriving at the amount assessable to corporation tax. An example of such an annual payment is Gift Aid payments. The principle is that these charges on income are offset against the payer's total profits, not merely against a particular source of income with which the payment is connected.

A payment counts as a charge on income only if the following conditions are met:

- It has been made out of the company's profits brought into charge to corporation tax.
- It is a payment of money to a charity.
- It must not be in the nature of a dividend or distribution made by the company.

The basic rule is that payment must actually be made in the accounting period for it to count as a charge for that period. In certain restricted circumstances, some companies that are owned by charities are able to treat Gift Aid payments made within nine months of their year end as if they had been paid during the year.

Where the total profits for an accounting period are insufficient to absorb charges on income, excess charges in respect of payments made wholly and exclusively for the purposes of the company's trade may be carried forward and used against its future trading income. Non-trade charges may not be carried forward in this manner and no further relief is available.

Exemption for foreign dividends

Following a long period of consultation, FA 2009 introduced an exemption for foreign dividends received by a UK company on or after 1 July 2009. The dividends must satisfy one of a range of conditions. This exemption is not available to small companies unless the dividends are received from a company that is resident in a territory with which the

UK has a comprehensive double taxation agreement which includes a non-discrimination article. Anti-avoidance provisions apply to deny the exemption where one of a number of prescribed schemes has been used.

The availability of the exemption does not depend on the percentage holding in the company paying the dividend.

18.4 ACCOUNTING PERIODS, RATES AND PAYMENT OF TAX

18.4.1 Accounting periods for tax purposes

(ss 9–11 CTA 2009)

Companies pay corporation tax by reference to their accounting periods and the chargeable profit included is assessed on an actual or accruals basis. Financial years for corporation tax purposes run from 1 April to the following 31 March and tax rates are set for each financial year. The year to 31 March 2012 is called financial year 2011 and so on. Accounting periods may straddle the end of a financial year, in which case the chargeable profits are apportioned on a time basis for the purposes of determining the rate of tax to apply to the overall profit. This is only relevant, of course, if the rates of tax in the two financial years concerned are different.

An accounting period begins for corporation tax purposes when:

- the company comes within the charge to corporation tax either by becoming UK-resident or acquiring a source of income; or
- the company's previous accounting period ends without the company ceasing to be within the charge to corporation tax.

An accounting period runs on for a maximum of 12 months from its commencement. It will end earlier if the company's own accounting date falls within the 12 months and it will also end if the company:

- ceases to trade; or
- begins or ceases to be UK-resident; or
- ceases to be within the charge to corporation tax altogether.

Where accounts are made up for a period of more than 12 months, the income is usually apportioned on a time basis to the relevant accounting period. Where a more appropriate basis of apportionment is available, HMRC may apply that basis instead (see *Marshall Hus & Partners Ltd* v *Bolton* [1981] STC18). In some instances, the accounts year end may vary slightly for commercial reasons (eg where accounts are made up to the last Friday of a specified month). Provided the variation is not more than four days from the 'mean' date it is normally acceptable to treat each period of account as if it were a 12-month accounting period ending on the mean date.

18.4.2 **Corporation tax rate**

(s 3 CTA 2010)

The corporation tax rate is fixed for each financial year, which for these purposes starts on 1 April. The main rate of corporation tax was reduced to 30% from 1 April 1999 and was then reduced to 28% from 1 April 2008 to 31 March 2011. The rate is 26% for 2011, and will reduce further to 25% for 2012, 24% for 2013, and finally 23% for 2014.

18.4.3 **Small companies rates and associated companies**

(Part 3 CTA 2010)

A reduced corporation tax rate (known as the small companies' rate) applies to a company's profits if they do not exceed a minimum level. That level has been £300,000 for some years.

The small companies' rate was 20% for financial year 2007 (year to 31 March 2008). It was increased to 21% for financial years 2008 to 2010 and has been reduced to 20% for financial year 2011.

Where profits exceed the maximum profit limit for small companies' rate purposes, profits are charged at the full rate of corporation tax but an element of marginal relief is given for profits between £300,000 and £1.5m. Profits falling within this band are effectively taxed at a marginal rate of 27.5% from 1 April 2011.

The profit limits applicable to small companies' relief are restricted, based on the existence of any 'associated' companies that the company has during the accounting period concerned. For example, if a company has one associated company, the small companies profit limits are divided by two, ie one plus the number of associated companies.

A company is an associated company of another if they are under common control or one has control of the other. 'Control' for this purpose is defined as the ability to exercise direct or indirect control over the company's affairs and in particular:

- the possession or entitlement to acquire more than 50% of the share capital or voting rights in the company; or
- entitlement to receive the greater part of income distributed among the shareholders; or
- entitlement to receive the greater part of the company's assets in the event of a winding-up.

These rules are complex and can, in some circumstances, lead to companies being treated as associated where one is controlled by one person and the other is controlled by a different person who is connected in some way with him, her or it. Specialist advice should be sought, particularly in the case of family owned companies.

An associated company that has not carried on any trade or business at any time during the accounting period concerned is disregarded. On the other hand, a foreign company may be an associated company even though its profits are not subject to UK corporation tax.

Where a company's accounting period straddles more than one financial year and the marginal relief limits for each financial year differ, the 12-month period is treated as separate accounting periods for the purpose of calculating marginal relief.

18.4.4 Payment of tax

Corporation tax automatically becomes due and payable nine months and one day from the end of the accounting period. Large companies must pay corporation tax by instalments. For these purposes, a 'large' company is one that has taxable profits of over £10m in the year, or profits of £1.5m for the current year *and* the preceding year. Both the £10m and the £1.5m limits are divided by the number of associated companies, in the same way that the £300,000 limit is reduced in determining eligibility for the small companies' rate. The instalment payments commence 14 days after the first six months of the year in question, and are due in four equal quarterly instalments. A company with a year end of 31 December will pay on 14 July, 14 October, 14 January and 14 April. Where a company's accounting period is less than 12 months long, the £1.5m and £10m profit limits are reduced proportionally and there may be fewer than four quarterly instalment payments.

Interest is charged on any unpaid tax due and is an allowable deduction. Interest is payable to the company on any overpayments and this interest is taxable.

18.5 LOAN RELATIONSHIPS

In broad terms, the tax treatment of profits and losses from loan relationships follows the accounting treatment. Rules introduced in FA 1996 (now found in parts 5 and 6 of CTA 2009) govern the tax treatment of items such as interest received and paid, premiums and discounts.

18.5.1 Scope of legislation

The legislation applies to all UK-resident companies and UK permanent establishments of overseas resident companies.

18.5.2 'Loan relationships'

(ss 294 and 302 CTA 2009)

The legislation refers to 'loan relationships' rather than loans, and these can arise where:

- a company is a debtor or creditor in respect of a money debt, and this debt arose as a result of a transaction for the lending of money; or
- an instrument is issued for the purpose of representing security for, or the rights of a creditor in respect of, a money debt.

Loan relationships therefore include bank loans, director's loans, gilts, inter-company accounts and debentures. Even where a money debt does not fall within the definition (eg trade creditors and debtors), the interest charged on such debts and some other items in respect of the debt fall within the regime.

18.5.3 Tax treatment

(s 297 CTA 2009)

In general, income and expenditure is taxed or allowed in the year it is credited or debited to the profit and loss account or, if appropriate, reserves. The company's accounting treatment must comply with GAAP (which means either UK GAAP or IFRS).

Banks are permitted to use an authorised mark-to-market basis where a loan relationship is brought into account in each accounting period at the fair value.

18.5.4 Taxation of corporate debt

(s 298 CTA 2009)

The tax treatment of corporate debt depends on whether the item arose from the trade. Debits and credits arising in an accounting period from loan relationships entered into for the company's trade purposes are treated as forming part of its trading profits or losses, whereas any debits and credits arising from activities outside the company's trade (or any loan relationships of a company without a trade) are aggregated in arriving at a profit or loss on non-trading loan relationships.

Where any expenditure or income arises partly from trading and partly from non-trading, it is split pro rata.

Taxation of non-trading profits and losses

(Chapter 16, Part 5 CTA 2009)

Net profits from non-trading loan relationships are taxed as non-trading profits. If there are net losses, these may be:

- offset against the company's profits chargeable to corporation tax for that accounting period; or
- surrendered as group relief to other group companies; or
- carried back against total profits arising in the 12 months prior to the accounting period in which the loss arose; or
- carried forward against all profits, other than trading profits, of the next period.

Claims must be made within two years of the accounting period in which the loss arose for the first three relief methods. No claim is required for losses carried forward under the fourth.

18.5.5 Connected parties

(Chapter 5, Part 5 CTA 2009)

Special rules apply when the two parties to the loan relationship are connected companies. A company and another party are connected for these purposes if one controls the other at any time or they are under the control of the same person, in that accounting period. A person controls a company if he, she or it has the power to secure that the affairs of the company are conducted in accordance with the person's wishes. This could be achieved by holding shares or possessing voting power in the company or could be conferred under the articles of association or other document regulating the affairs of that company or any other company.

18.5.6 Late interest

(Chapter 8, Part 5 CTA 2009)

The legislation had provided that if two parties were connected (and in some other situations), then interest would only allowable when it was paid in the course of the year or within 12 months of the end of the accounting period unless the connected party was liable to UK corporation tax on the full amount of interest received.

This led to a general understanding that, if the connected party was an individual, trustee, non-resident company or exempt body such as a charity, the interest must actually be paid by the anniversary of the accounting reference date of the company to secure a deduction.

It has transpired that the denial of relief where interest is paid to a non-UK resident company is contrary to EU law. The anti-avoidance rule was suspended from 28 July 2008 whilst the Government took stock of the situation (see Revenue & Customs Brief 33/08).

The Government addressed this situation so that, for accounting periods beginning on or after 1 April 2009, the late interest rule will only apply – if the creditor is a company – where that creditor company is resident in a 'non-qualifying' territory. This is broadly one that does not have a double taxation agreement with the UK with a non-discrimination article. The rule continues to apply as it did previously where the creditor is not a company. Debtor companies can elect to continue applying the old rules for its first period beginning on or after 1 April 2009. The election has to be made in the corporation tax return for the accounting period in question.

18.5.7 Bad debts and waivers

(Chapter 6, Part 5 CTA 2009)

Generally, no tax relief is available for any losses arising from providing against or writing off bad debts on connected party loan relationships, and conversely no liability to tax arises on the borrower when such a debt is waived. However, tax relief may be available for bad debts on connected party loan relationships where the creditor company is in liquidation. This aspect of the legislation is extremely technical and specialist advice should be taken where material sums are involved.

From 22 April 2009, when a company formally releases another company from an outstanding trade debt, the loan relationship rules will apply to both the company that owes the debt (the debtor) and the company which is owed this amount (the creditor). Where the two companies are unconnected, the debtor will be taxed on the release and the creditor will be able to obtain tax relief for the bad debt expense. However, if the two companies are connected, no tax charge will arise on the debtor and, similarly, the creditor cannot claim tax relief for the bad debt expense incurred.

18.5.8 Income tax deduction at source

In the recent past, companies were required to deduct and account to HMRC for income tax on payments of annual interest and other charges on income, with the exception of annual interest paid to a UK bank. A return form CT61 had to be submitted each quarter, detailing payments made and computing the income tax payable to HMRC. In arriving at the income tax liability due, any income tax suffered on income received under deduction of tax could be offset. Where the income tax suffered on income received exceeded the income tax payable on annual charges, the surplus could be carried forward to the next quarterly return. If at the end of the accounting period it had not proved possible to obtain credit against income tax payable, credit could be obtained against the corporation tax liability for the accounting period (and if there was no or insufficient corporation tax liability to offset any income tax credit, a repayment could be obtained from HMRC).

These rules were substantially changed by FA 2001, with effect from 1 April 2001. There is no longer any requirement for a company paying interest, etc, to deduct income tax provided the recipient is a UK-resident company.

A company is still required to deduct basic rate income tax where the recipient is an individual or a non-resident company.

Sometimes a company pays interest by issuing funding bonds. Basic rate tax has to be accounted for on the market value of funding bonds issued to individuals or non-resident companies.

18.6 INTANGIBLE ASSETS

The tax regime for intangible assets that has applied since 1 April 2002 was designed to:

- provide tax relief to companies for the cost of acquired intangibles;
- give relief in line with the amortisation in the company's accounts;
- treat gains on the disposal of relevant intangibles as taxable income but allow for roll-over relief where the proceeds are reinvested in new intangibles;
- provide transitional provisions that preserved the previous regime for intangibles held on 31 March 2002.

The legislation applies to intangible fixed assets as recognised under UK GAAP or IFRS. It is specifically stated to apply to goodwill and intellectual property, which includes patents, trademarks, registered designs, copyright and design rights; licensing and similar rights are also included.

Assets representing rights over real property (ie land and buildings), tangible moveable property, oil licences and financial assets are among the categories of intangibles specifically excluded from the regime.

18.6.1 Key concepts

The structure of the legislation is similar to that relating to corporate debt in that it identifies tax-effective accounting debits and credits in respect of expenditure incurred after 31 March 2002 on intangible fixed assets.

Debits that attract tax relief for expenditure and losses include all expenditure on an intangible fixed asset that is charged to the profit and loss account. This includes the amortisation of capitalised costs (or, at the taxpayer's option, 4% annually of that cost) and even abortive expenditure of realisation of an intangible fixed asset. A loss on the sale of such an asset (compared against its tax written-down value) also qualifies for relief.

Taxable credits include all receipts in respect of intangible fixed assets credited to the profit and loss account, gains over the tax written down value on disposal of the asset and the total proceeds of realisation of intangible fixed assets not carried on the balance sheet.

18.6.2 How debits and credits are given effect

Debits and credits are brought into account for corporation tax purposes as follows:

- assets held for the purposes of a trade – treated as a trading expense or receipt;
- assets held for the purposes of a property business – treated as an expense or receipt of the business;
- any other assets – the debits and credits are described as giving rise to non-trading losses and gains and aggregated. Credits are taxed while debits may be relieved against total profits, carried forward or surrendered as group relief.

18.6.3 Roll-over relief

Where the proceeds of the realisation of a chargeable intangible fixed asset are reinvested in whole or in part in the purchase of other intangible fixed assets, the legislation provides for a form of roll-over relief. Entitlement to relief is subject to certain conditions. The amount of the relief is calculated as follows:

- If the expenditure on new assets exceeds the proceeds of old assets, relief is the excess of proceeds over the indexed cost of the old asset.
- If the expenditure on new assets is less than the proceeds of old assets, relief is the excess of expenditure over the indexed cost of the old asset.

18.6.4 Pre-commencement intangible assets

It was never intended that a company should secure the tax reliefs under the intangibles regime by buying intangible assets already in existence at 31 March 2002. Therefore, where a company acquires assets from a related party (which includes fellow group companies or, in the case of a close company, participators in that company) and the vendor held or created those assets before 1 April 2002, the assets remain outside the intangible fixed assets regime from the perspective of the purchaser. The tax treatment then depends on the nature of the asset concerned. Goodwill, for example, would fall within the capital gains rules as they apply to companies (see 18.7 below).

18.7 COMPANIES' CAPITAL GAINS

18.7.1 Computation of gains

Capital gains made by companies are included in their chargeable profits and are subject to corporation tax. CGT therefore does not apply to companies, although chargeable gains and losses are computed in accordance with the detailed provisions of CGT. The main differences between CGT and corporation tax on chargeable gains for companies are, first, that provisions that clearly apply only to individuals (eg the annual exemption) have no application as far as companies are concerned and, second, that computations of chargeable gains are prepared on an accounting period basis rather than by income tax years of assessment. Furthermore, companies remain entitled to indexation allowance. The total chargeable gains for an accounting period less a deduction for any allowable losses are brought into charge to corporation tax in the same way as any other source of income.

Capital losses can only be offset against chargeable gains; they cannot be offset against trading or other income. However, it is possible for another company in the group to treat a loss arising after 31 March 2000 as if it had realised that loss. That then allows it to offset the loss against its chargeable gains.

18.7.2 Roll-over relief

(ss 152–158 and 175 TCGA 1992)

Roll-over relief is available where the proceeds on the disposal of a qualifying asset are reinvested in other qualifying assets. It operates as a deferral of the corporation tax liability arising on the chargeable gain if the proceeds are fully reinvested in qualifying assets up to 12 months before or three years after the date of disposal.

Where the proceeds are only partly reinvested, a proportion of the gain is deferred or 'rolled over' and the balance (equivalent to the amount of proceeds not reinvested) is brought into charge. The element of gain deferred or rolled over is deducted from the new asset's base cost for capital gains purposes. This operates to increase the potential gain on the eventual sale of the new asset acquired, hence the term 'roll-over relief'.

Qualifying assets for this purpose are freehold and leasehold land and buildings, ships, aircraft and hovercraft, fixed plant and machinery, satellite space stations and spacecraft. Expenditure on an asset acquired from a group company (see 18.12) does not rank as qualifying expenditure for roll-over relief.

18.7.3 Disposals of substantial shareholdings

With effect from 1 April 2002, a gain accruing to a company on the disposal of a shareholding in another company is not taxable provided certain conditions are met. The exemption also applies to a disposal of an asset that derives its value from a substantial shareholding, including put or call options on the shares, securities that carry rights to acquire or dispose of the shares and interests in such securities.

The company making the disposal (the 'investing company') must have had a substantial shareholding in the company whose shares are being disposed of for a continuous 12-month period beginning not more than two years before the date of disposal.

A 'substantial shareholding' is one where the investing company is beneficially entitled to not less than 10% of:

- the ordinary share capital; and
- the profits available for distribution to equity holders of the company; and
- the assets available for distribution to equity holders of the company on a winding-up.

In addition, the following tests must be met throughout the period beginning with the start of the latest 12-month period by reference to which the substantial shareholdings test was met and ending immediately after the disposal.

(1) The investing company must have been a trading company or a member of a trading group. For this purpose, 'group' refers to a capital gains group but with a 51% ownership requirement. Non-trading activities must not be a substantial part of the vendor company/group's business. For this purpose, activities carried on by a group company that contribute to the trade of another member of the group qualify as trading. 'Substantial' is taken to be 20% or more.

(2) The company that has been invested in must have been a qualifying trading company. In practice this means that less than 20% of its assets consist of investments and less than 20% of its income is derived from non-trading activities.

Note that this exemption can apply to disposals of shares in foreign trading companies.

In the same way that gains are exempt, losses are not normally available for offset against other chargeable gains where the substantial shareholdings conditions are met.

See the flow charts in Figure 18.1 (overleaf) on the main conditions that need to be satisfied. However, this relief has complex provisions and professional advice should be taken. For example, some commentaries take the view that a company can never qualify if it is liquidated immediately after selling its only subsidiary but a contrary opinion is expressed in the leading textbook (*Bramwell on Corporation Tax*) and this interpretation is reflected in the flow charts. See also December 2002 *Tax Bulletin 62* and the HMRC manuals, CG 17953i–r, and CG 53113–53120 (www.hmrc.gov. uk/manuals/CG1manual/CG17895+.htm) for guidance generally.

18.7.4 Investment trusts and REITs

Approved investment trusts are exempt from tax on capital gains. A similar exemption applies for Real Estate Investment Trusts (REITs). Both need to be quoted companies to enjoy this status.

18.8 DIVIDENDS

18.8.1 Taxation of company distributions

Company distributions are defined as any dividends, and any other distribution out of the company's assets, paid by a company in respect of shares in the company. The main exception to this is that any repayment of share capital is not regarded as a distribution of assets.

No tax deduction is available to a UK company on its making a distribution.

UK recipients of the distribution are entitled to a tax credit. This aggregate amount is described as a 'franked' payment and, as far as individuals are concerned, represents the gross equivalent of the dividend received. This amount is taxable income, but the shareholder may set the tax credit against his or her tax liability on the 'grossed-up' amount.

In most cases, dividends received from another UK company are not taxed. However, the conditions set out in the dividend exemption rules must apply (see 18.3 for more details).

18.8.2 Advance corporation tax (abolished from 6 April 1999)

ACT was a tax that became payable when a company made distributions. This tax was then treated as a prepayment of the company's tax liability on its profits.

ACT was abolished with effect from 6 April 1999. However, it may be that a company which paid substantial dividends before that date, and which has not paid out a similar proportion of its post-1999 profits, may be able to claim relief for 'shadow ACT'. If you are dealing with such a case, you should refer to the 2007–08 edition of the *Tax Handbook*.

Figure 18.1 – Exemption for disposals of substantial shareholdings

Conditions to be satisfied by the vendor company

Figure 18.1 – Continued

Conditions regarding the shares which are being sold

18.9 LOSSES

In this section, we look first at rules on trading losses and we then cover relief for capital losses.

18.9.1 Trading losses arising in accounting period

(ss 37 and 44 CTA 2010)

When a company has a trading loss for an accounting period, it may claim that the loss arising may be offset against other profits including chargeable gains arising in that accounting period. A tax loss is computed in the same manner as taxable profits, but is restricted to losses arising from trading activities carried out on a commercial basis and with a view to realising profit.

18.9.2 Utilisation of loss relief

(ss 37 and 45 CTA 2010)

There are several ways in which a trading loss may be relieved for tax purposes apart from being offset against other profits arising in the accounting period. The loss can be carried forward to offset against trading profits from the same trade arising in succeeding accounting periods. Losses can be carried forward indefinitely in this manner for as long as the company carries on the trading activity that generated the loss. A loss may also be carried back.

Losses can be carried back and offset against profits in the 12 months immediately preceding the accounting period in which the loss was incurred.

Schedule 6, FA 2009 temporarily extended the period of carry-back to three years for trading losses arising in accounting periods ending between 24 November 2008 and 23 November 2010. The maximum amount that could be carried further back in this way was £50,000 for an accounting period ending between 24 November 2008 and 23 November 2009; and £50,000 for an accounting period ending between 24 November 2009 and 23 November 2010. It should be noted that should any such accounting period be for a period of less than 12 months then the maximum amount of £50,000 was reduced on a pro-rata basis.

Any trading losses carried back to a previous period can be set against any type of profits.

The company must have been carrying on the relevant trade in the earlier periods. Partial relief claims were not allowed, and relief was obtained for later years before earlier years. Relief must be obtained for the loss against other profits of the accounting period before computing the balance of the loss available for carry-back.

> **Tax notes**
>
> Losses can be carried back and offset against profits in the 12 months preceding the accounting period in which the loss was incurred.

18.9.3 Terminal losses

(ss 39 and 41 CTA 2010)

A trading loss arising in the accounting period in which the trade ceases may be carried back and offset against profits of the three years ending immediately before the commencement of the final period of trading.

Anti-avoidance provisions apply if the trade ceases as a result of its transfer to a person not subject to corporation tax and the transfer was part of arrangements the main purpose, or one of the main purposes, of which was to secure that terminal loss relief applied.

18.9.4 Changes in company ownership

(ss 673 to 676 CTA 2010)

There are anti-avoidance provisions designed to ensure that trading losses carried forward can only be used against future trading income from the trading activity that generated the losses. Losses may not be carried forward if:

- within any period of three years there is a change in the ownership of the company preceded or followed by a major change in the nature or conduct of the trade carried on by the company; or
- there is a change in ownership of the company at any time after the scale of activities in a trade carried on by the company has become small or negligible, and before any considerable revival in the trade.

A 'change in ownership' broadly means a change in more than 50% of the ownership of the ordinary share capital in the company. A 'major change in the nature or conduct of a trade' includes a major change in the type of property dealt in, or the services or facilities provided in the trade or in customers, outlets or markets. HMRC issued SP10/91 on some of the factors that are relevant in determining whether there has been a major change in the nature or conduct of a trade or business.

Similar anti-avoidance provisions apply for excess management expenses and other non-trading losses brought forward by a company with an investment business.

18.9.5 Foreign denominated losses

(ss 7–9 and 11–17 CTA 2010)

Where a company's primary economic activities are carried out in a currency other than sterling, it can produce its accounts and compute its profits for tax purposes in that other currency. The basic rule is that it then translates such foreign currency profits into sterling at the appropriate exchange rate for the period. If losses are carried forward or carried back, special rules apply so as to stop exchange rate fluctuations distorting loss relief claims. These rules broadly state that a loss will be converted into sterling at the rate used for conversion of the profits against which the losses are offset.

Most commonly, foreign currency losses are carried back or forward to utilise against profits in an accounting period where the profits have been calculated in the same foreign functional currency. In these circumstances the above rule will apply. However, where there has been a change in functional currency of the company so that the currency used for the period in which the loss arose is different from that used in the period the profits arose:

- the loss must first be translated at the spot rate of exchange between the two currencies;
- this loss is then translated into sterling at the rate used for conversion of the profits against which the losses are offset.

If the losses are being carried forward, the spot rate of exchange used is that operating on the first day of the period in which the functional currency changed. If the losses are being carried back the spot rate used is the one operating on the last day of the accounting period in which the old operational currency was used.

18.9.6 Capital losses

Capital losses, like capital gains, are computed in accordance with CGT rules, although the net capital gains are subject to corporation tax as part of the overall chargeable profits for the accounting period. Capital losses cannot be set against a company's other profits but they may be offset against capital gains in computing net chargeable gains. Capital losses that cannot be relieved in this way may be carried forward and offset against gains arising in subsequent accounting periods without limit. The carry-forward of capital losses is not dependent on whether the company continues to carry on its trading activity, and may be offset against gains arising on trade and non-trade assets.

18.10 OVERSEAS ASPECTS

(Part 2 TIOPA 2010)

Where a UK company has a shareholding in a foreign company, there are a number of tax provisions to be considered:

- transfer pricing (also applies to UK–UK transactions);
- controlled foreign company rules;
- double taxation relief;
- unremittable dividends;
- the regime for foreign dividends.

18.10.1 Transfer pricing

This is dealt with separately at 18.11.

18.10.2 Controlled foreign companies

A controlled foreign company or 'CFC' is one which:

- is not resident in the UK; and
- is controlled directly or indirectly by persons who are resident in the UK; and
- is subject to a 'lower level of taxation' in the territory in which it is resident.

A 40% test can be applied for determining that a company is controlled by UK resident persons, ie even if a foreign company would not otherwise be regarded as UK controlled, if a UK person (together with his, her or its associates) has 40%, the company will often fall within the definition of a CFC. If an individual who is connected with a UK company holds shares in a foreign company, his or her shares may be taken into account for the control test.

'Lower level of taxation' means less than 75% of the tax that would be payable if the foreign company had been UK resident.

Unless it can be shown that there are good commercial reasons for the CFC's existence, a UK company with an interest in the CFC may be charged tax on the proportion of the CFC's profits (but not capital gains) that matches its interest. Thus, a UK company holding 46% of the shares in a CFC might be taxed on 46% of the CFC's profits. An individual may not be taxed under the CFC rules but may be taxed instead under s 731 ITA 2007 (see 33.4). The Government abolished (in FA 2009) the exemption which previously applied for CFCs that followed an acceptable distribution policy.

The CFC rules are complex and are changing in both 2011 and 2012: readers should seek professional advice if they believe that they may be affected by them.

18.10.3 Major changes for controlled foreign companies in 2011 and 2012

The Government proposed, in a July 2010 consultation document, that it would reform the controlled foreign companies (CFC) legislation in two stages and details were provided in the Autumn Statement issued in November 2010. The two stages consist of:

- a set of interim improvements that have been included in schedule 12, Finance Act 2011; and
- a more fundamental reform of the regime to be implemented in 2012.

18.10.4 Interim improvements: accounting periods of CFCs beginning on or after 1 January 2011

The two key aims of the interim improvements are to provide exemption from the CFC rules for commercially justified activities that both business and HMRC agree do not erode the UK tax base and to help UK businesses to undertake overseas acquisitions and reorganisations.

To assist with the first aim, two exemptions have been enacted that will apply to intra-group trading activities and intellectual property (IP) exploitation where there is minimal connection with the UK. The conditions applicable to these two exemptions are broadly similar. For the intra-group activities test to apply, the CFC must:

- have a genuine business establishment in its territory of residence;
- carry out no, or only a small amount of, non-trading activities (a small amount is defined as no more than 10% of the company's activities);
- not receive more than an incidental amount of finance and IP income (defined as no more than 5% of the CFC's total income);
- not derive more than 10% of its business income or expenses from transactions with the UK (referred to as the company's 'connection with the UK'); and
- not derive more than 50% of its related party business expenditure from transactions connected with the UK (where the CFC is involved in a scheme or arrangement that has a main purpose of achieving a reduction in UK corporation tax or in a CFC tax charge).

If the CFC meets all of these tests in a particular period, it will be fully exempt for that period. If it fails one or more of these tests (and no other exemption is available) then a CFC charge may be applied, but can be reduced in certain circumstances on application by the company to HMRC. For example, if the CFC's combined finance and IP income exceeds 5% of total income, then the company could apply to have only the excess above 5% subject to the charge.

To assist with the second aim, there will be a 12-month extension to the period during which a company is exempt from the CFC rules when it comes within the scope of the regime for the first time following a reorganisation or change to UK ownership. The exemption will apply for two years (previously one) after the end of the accounting period in which the relevant acquisition takes place both to companies acquired from third parties (and vehicles set up to make such acquisitions) and certain types of group reorganisations.

The exemption will also apply to groups migrating into the UK. The period of exemption, however, will cease if there is an 'early termination event'.

Two other miscellaneous changes have been introduced. The first of these is an extension to the de minimis profits exemption. Under the existing exemption, a CFC's chargeable profits (calculated under UK tax principles) can be ignored if they do not exceed £50,000. Going forward, companies will have the choice of using this test or a de minimis profit level of £200,000 based on the company's accounting profits as calculated under GAAP but adjusted to exclude distributions treated as exempt under part 9A CTA 2009 and capital gains or losses and to include trust and partnership income. The result is also to be adjusted by applying the transfer pricing rules in relation to related party transactions, unless the amount of this adjustment to profit would be less than £50,000.

The second miscellaneous change is to extend for 12 months the transitional rules for superior and non-local holding companies that previously allowed them to remain exempt from the CFC rules until July 2011 (now to be July 2012). Unlike the rest of the changes, which have effect for accounting periods of CFCs beginning on or after 1 January 2011, this provision is treated as always having had effect.

18.10.5 Longer-term reforms

The Government proposes to make further fundamental changes to the CFC legislation in Finance Act 2012 so it is more consistent with a territorial basis of taxation. Its aims are to:

- focus CFC charges only on artificially diverted UK profits;
- exempt foreign profits where there is no erosion of the UK tax base; and
- not tax profits from genuine economic activities undertaken offshore.

At the time of writing, a consultation document was due to be published on more fundamental reforms to be introduced in Finance Bill 2012. It was proposed that the regime would be mainly entity-based but would only focus on the proportion of overseas profits that had been artificially diverted from the UK. The profits of finance companies caught under these rules would be taxed at a maximum of a quarter of the main corporation tax rate (ie an effective rate of 5.75% by 2014).

18.10.6 **Branch profits**

An opt-in exemption regime for UK companies with foreign branches has been introduced and is available for accounting periods commencing on or after the date of Royal Assent to Finance Bill 2011.

Once a company has made the necessary irrevocable election, profits arising in all of its current and future overseas branches will be permanently exempt from UK corporation tax. Should any of the branches make losses, those losses will not be available to offset against the company's profits. A transitional measure deals with those companies with branches that have realised losses in any of the six years before applying the exemption. Under this rule, a company's branch profits will become exempt as soon as the tax losses of those branches in the immediately preceding six years have been matched by profits. A special rule applies to very large losses (those over £50m).

The exemption applies to the trading profits, investment income and chargeable gains that are effectively connected to the branches concerned. Trading profits and chargeable gains are defined with reference to the relevant double tax treaty. Investment income must be genuinely connected to the business to qualify for the exemption. In other words, the economic ownership of the assets that generate the income should lie with the branch. However, the exemption will not be available to a company whose business is wholly or mainly investment business.

For branches in territories that have no tax treaty with the UK, the measure of exempt profits will be determined with reference to the OECD model treaty as released in July 2010. However, the exemption will not be available to small companies because of the perceived risk of loss of tax through diversion of personal income unless there is a 'full treaty' between the UK and the territory in which the branch was set up. A full treaty is one with a non-discrimination article.

Anti-avoidance measures have been introduced, along similar lines to the CFC rules, to prevent the diversion of profits for tax avoidance purposes. There will be exclusions from the anti-avoidance rules including a motive, lower level of taxation and de minimis level of profit test. When the CFC rules are amended in Finance Act 2012, the anti-avoidance rules applicable to the branch exemption may be re-written so that the same broad rules continue to apply to both subsidiaries and branches of UK companies. Companies will also be expected to minimise the profits that are subject to tax in the overseas jurisdiction, for example by taking full advantage of the extent to which the treaty limits that territory's taxing rights and claiming all possible reliefs and exemptions.

The branch exemption does not extend to international air transport and shipping as these activities are generally not taxable in the foreign jurisdiction under the relevant treaty and the OECD model.

18.10.7 **Patent box**

The Government has confirmed that a reduced 10% rate of corporation tax will be introduced from 1 April 2013 on profits arising from certain patents created after 29 November 2010. A consultation on the detail of the provisions closed on 22 February 2011, with second and third stage consultations to take place later in 2011, in time for the provisions to be enacted in Finance Act 2012. It is expected that:

- entry into the regime will be optional, to avoid placing a compliance burden on businesses that may only receive marginal benefit;
- the intention is that all patents first commercialised after 29 November 2010 will qualify for inclusion, subject to specific qualification and transitional rules;
- the patent box will be available for both royalty income and embedded income included in the price of the patented products;
- the intention is for the preferential rate to apply to net patent income after associated expenses (including pre-commercialisation expenses); and
- the relief will not incentivise the purely passive holding of IP.

The Government is also considering methods of preventing abuse, such as linking the amount of income that may be attributed to the patent box to the level of R&D or manufacturing activity, but does not intend to limit the benefit of the regime for any businesses genuinely engaged in patent development.

18.10.8 **Double taxation relief**

A UK resident company may claim a credit for foreign tax paid on income or capital gains arising from any overseas source. Credit is available against the corporation tax liability payable on the same income or gains. Relief may be due either under the provisions of a double taxation agreement between the UK and the overseas country concerned, or under the general rules for 'unilateral relief' as provided in s 2 *et seq.* TIOPA 2010. Where credit is due under a double taxation agreement, the relevant agreement takes precedence over UK domestic legislation.

For most types of income and gains, the full amount is brought into charge for the purpose of computing the corporation tax liability on chargeable profits for the accounting period. Any overseas tax suffered is then offset by way of credit against the corporation tax liability. The amount of credit available is limited to the corporation tax liability on the source of income or gain that has suffered overseas tax. No relief is due for the excess foreign tax paid.

Further relief may be available for dividends received. In addition to relief for withholding or other taxes suffered on payment of the dividend, relief may also be available for the foreign tax suffered on the profits out of which the dividend has been paid. This is known as 'underlying tax', for which relief is given automatically if the UK-recipient company controls

10% or more of the voting share capital in the overseas company paying the dividend. The dividend taxable in the UK is grossed up at the rate of underlying tax applicable to the profits out of which the dividend has been paid. This, together with any withholding and other taxes suffered on payment of the dividend, can then be offset against the corporation tax liability arising on the grossed up equivalent of the dividend received (subject to the restriction that underlying tax relief cannot exceed the corporation tax liability on the same income).

In the vast majority of cases, overseas dividends are not taxed in the UK due to the dividend exemption (section 18.3).

Where double tax relief would be lost (eg where no corporation tax liability arises for the accounting period) it is possible to obtain relief for overseas tax paid by treating the tax as an expense in computing profits of the company's trade.

18.10.9 DTR on dividends

FA 2009 retrospectively amended the double tax relief rules applicable to overseas dividends received by UK companies since 1 April 2008. These rules restrict the amount of relief available using a formula which makes reference to the corporation tax rate in force on the date the dividend is paid. Where the actual rate of UK tax paid by the recipient company is different (because, for example, the rate of corporation tax changes during the accounting period) this produces a mismatch. The new measure ensures that double tax relief is limited by reference to the actual corporation tax suffered on the dividend concerned.

18.10.10 Unremittable income

Where an overseas source of income is taxable on an arising basis but it is not possible to remit the income because of government actions in the overseas territory, it is possible to make a claim to defer the corporation tax liability until such time as sufficient funds are remitted to the UK to satisfy the liability. A claim under these circumstances may be made to HMRC at any time within four years of the end of the accounting period in which the income arises.

18.11 TRANSFER PRICING RULES

(Part 4 TIOPA 2010)

Transfer pricing tax rules are designed to prevent related parties that are subject to different levels of taxation from entering into uncommercial transactions which move profits into a lower level of taxation. The rules require corporation tax to be computed as if transactions had been carried out on arm's-length terms. This may result in a UK company having profits imputed to it which substantially exceed the actual profits.

The scope of the transfer pricing rules was extended from 1 April 2004 to include UK-to-UK related party transactions. Previously, these rules only applied to cross-border transactions.

The change was forced on the UK Government by European Court of Justice (ECJ) decisions. In a number of cases the ECJ decided that the UK rules were invalid because, by exempting UK-to-UK related party transactions, they were discriminatory under EC law.

This means that now, for tax purposes, all related party transactions that are not carried out on an arm's-length basis may trigger investigations and tax adjustments. However, for UK-to-UK transactions, HMRC allows a compensating reduction in the profits of the other party to the transaction (ie if costs are disallowed for one party, the corresponding income should not be taxed in the other).

18.11.1 Related parties

Related parties can be companies, individuals, partnerships and trusts where a control relationship exists (ie one party controls the other). A transaction can be anything from a normal sale of goods to the use of one party's assets or lending arrangements.

Fortunately, many small and medium-sized businesses are exempt from the rules. The exemption applies to all related parties in the same control relationship (including entities based outside the UK) and is based on their combined number of employees and turnover. Small groups, those that have not more than 50 employees and either total turnover or total assets of no more than £10m, will not need to self-assess.

Medium-sized groups, those with not more than 250 employees and either an annual turnover of less than £50m or net assets of less than £43m, should maintain records of relevant transactions. HMRC has the power to require any medium-sized business to apply an arm's-length price where there has been blatant manipulation of transaction prices leading to a significant loss of UK tax.

Businesses close to the limits should watch out for seasonal staffing increases because these count, pro rata, towards the annual limits. If staffing limits are breached at any point during an account year, transactions during the whole account year are subject to the rules and documentation requirements.

Neither exemption applies if the transaction is with a party resident outside the UK, unless they are in a country with which the UK has a double tax treaty that includes a non-discrimination article (visit www.hmrc.gov. uk/international/small-medium-ent.pdf to check the list of countries).

18.11.2 Keeping up to date

If your business carries out transactions with related parties, the first thing to establish is whether or not the small enterprise exemption applies. If not, then you will need to identify which related party transactions may not be on an arm's-length basis and assess what records should be maintained. Only a higher level review may be needed if the medium-sized exemption applies, but detailed records and analysis will be needed if your business is part of a larger group.

18.12 GROUPS OF COMPANIES

18.12.1 Group relationships

(Part 5 CTA 2010)

There are special rules that apply to groups of companies. For corporation tax purposes, a group relationship exists between two companies if one company holds not less than 75% of the other's ordinary share capital, or if both companies are 75% subsidiaries of a third company. At one time, such companies had to be UK-resident 75% subsidiaries of a UK-resident parent company, but the rules now allow UK-resident subsidiaries of non-resident companies to constitute a group for UK tax purposes.

The definition of a 75% subsidiary was amended by FA 2009 in order to ensure that companies do not fall outside of loss relief and capital gains groups as a result of issuing certain types of preference shares to external investors such as financial institutions. The changes apply to accounting periods beginning on or after 1 January 2008.

18.12.2 Use of losses

(ss 99–110 CTA 2010)

Where one company in a group makes a tax loss for an accounting period, it may 'surrender' that loss to a member of the group for offset against that company's taxable profits. For this purpose, losses available for surrender include charges on income to the extent that they exceed profits chargeable to corporation tax. Where the accounting periods of the surrendering and claimant companies do not coincide, the amount of loss to be surrendered is restricted on a time basis reflecting the length of the accounting periods common to both companies.

For group relief purposes, the requirement for a 75% shareholding relationship is extended so that the company owning the shares must also be beneficially entitled to 75% or more of the profits available for distribution to equity shareholders, and of assets available for distribution in a winding-up. This requirement prevents group relief being secured by the use of ordinary shares which carry limited rights to dividends, etc. See 18.12.1 on FA 2009 changes which are intended to ensure that the existence of certain types of preference shares do not create problems in this regard.

Group relief is not available for losses in an accounting period during which arrangements exist for the company to leave the group.

The legislation originally required that the company seeking to surrender a loss must be UK-resident but this requirement was successfully challenged by Marks and Spencer before the ECJ. FA 2006 introduced provisions that in theory allow group relief for a non UK-resident company's losses but such relief is dependent on various tests, which in practice are rarely satisfied. The UK's new legislation has been referred to the EC as a result and the outcome of this is awaited.

18.12.3 Capital gains

(ss 171 and 175 TCGA 1992)

For capital gains purposes, chargeable assets may be transferred from one group company to another without tax consequences. Such transfers are treated as if made on a no gain/no loss basis and the recipient company will take over the assets' capital gains base cost from the transferor company. A capital gains tax group exists where at least 75% of the ordinary share capital is beneficially owned (directly or indirectly) by the principal company. This is extended to 75% subsidiaries of subsidiaries provided the subsidiary company in question is an effective 51% subsidiary of the principal company.

For roll-over relief purposes, all the trades carried on by group companies are treated as a single trade and therefore it is possible to roll over a gain made on qualifying assets by one group member against qualifying expenditure incurred by another group member within the appropriate timescale. Roll-over relief is generally available only for trading companies within a group although, by concession, relief is also available for a property-holding company where the properties are used for trading purposes by the other group members.

TCGA 1992 does not allow losses of one company in a group to be set off against gains of another group company. However, since 1 April 2000, two members of a group may jointly elect for the gain or loss arising on the disposal of an asset outside the group by one of them to be attributed to the other company. Previously, the asset had to be actually transferred to the company that wished to make use of the gain or loss.

18.12.4 Transfer of a business within a group

Where a trading activity is transferred from one group company to another, relief is available under ss 939–953 CTA 2010, to ensure that the company transferring the trade does not suffer balancing charges on assets that have qualified for capital allowances. The successor company merely takes over the tax residue for capital allowances purposes relating to those assets. Generally, all unrelieved trade losses are also transferred with the trade to the successor company.

This relief also applies where a trade is transferred to another company that is under 75% common control, even though it is not a member of a group.

18.13 INVESTMENT COMPANIES

(ss 1217–1255 CTA 2009)

A company with an investment business is able to claim relief for management expenses. A company with an investment business is a company whose business consists wholly or partly of making investments. It is possible for a company be a 'hybrid company' which undertakes both trading and investment activity, thereby taking relief for both trading costs and management expenses. The expenses of managing a UK-resident company with an investment business are deductible in computing its total profits from that investment activity for corporation tax purposes. Where management expenses exceed the company's chargeable income and gains for an accounting period, the surplus may be carried forward and treated as management expenses incurred in the next succeeding accounting period, and may continue to be carried forward until relieved. Surplus management expenses may also be surrendered as group relief from one group company to another. Expenses brought forward from previous periods are not available for surrender as group relief.

18.14 CLOSE COMPANIES

(Part 10 CTA 2010)

18.14.1 Definition

(s 439 CTA 2010)

Companies that are under the control of five or fewer persons, or are under the control of their directors, are known as 'close companies'. There are special provisions designed to ensure that such individuals cannot take undue advantage of corporation tax legislation by virtue of their positions of influence over the company's affairs.

A person controls a company if, in fact, he or she is able to exercise control directly or indirectly over its affairs by owning the greater part of its share capital, voting capital, or other capital giving entitlement to more than half the assets on a winding-up. Shareholders and certain loan creditors in a close company are known as 'participators'.

18.14.2 Loans to participators

(ss 455–464 CTA 2010)

Where a close company makes a loan or advances any money to a participator, or an associate of a participator, there is a liability to account for an amount of tax equal to 25% of the loan.

This tax falls due on the normal corporation tax due dates of the company's accounting period in which the loan is made; no tax need be paid if the loan is repaid before the tax falls due. Where the loan is repaid after the tax falls due, the repayment of tax is not due until nine months and a day after the accounting period in which the loan is actually repaid.

Regardless of when the loan was originally made, if it is wholly or partly written off or released, the borrower is treated as receiving, as part of his or her total income, an amount equal to the amount so written off, grossed up at the lower rate of income tax. While no basic or lower rate tax liability arises, there may be a further liability to higher rate tax collected via the self-assessment regime. From 24 March 2010, it is specifically provided that companies cannot obtain a corporation tax deduction on the release of such a loan.

18.14.3 Close investment-holding companies

(s 34 CTA 2010)

These are close companies carrying on specific investment-holding activities. For this purpose, investment-holding activities do not include carrying on a trade on a commercial basis, property holding, or holding shares in companies carrying on either of these activities. An exception to this rule is a company that exists wholly or mainly for holding property rented to connected persons. A close investment-holding company does not qualify for the small companies' corporation tax rate.

18.15 REAL ESTATE INVESTMENT TRUSTS (REITs)

MARIOS GREGORI AND VIRAN DE SILVA

A REIT is a listed property company that has elected for REIT status in the UK. Similar reliefs have been available in other countries for a number of years (eg USA).

The broad rationale is that a REIT itself pays no corporation tax at the company level on qualifying activities. Instead, tax is payable by the shareholders on distributions received – this applies to both rental profits and capital gains.

However, a withholding tax of 20% applies to most distributions by a REIT to its investors. The main exceptions are where the investors are UK-resident companies or various exempt bodies.

Qualifying distributions received from a REIT are treated as rental income rather than dividends. This means that investors can use their personal allowances to mitigate any tax charge.

The legislation is aimed at companies that own property as a letting investment, rather than for property trading or development. There are detailed rules on this point, which split the business between qualifying and non-qualifying activities. Other rules for REITs are as follows:

- The shares in a REIT must be listed on a recognised stock exchange.
- There can be only one class of ordinary shares, and the only other permitted class of shares is non-participating fixed-rate preference shares.
- 75% of income and asset value must be attributed to the property letting business. The asset value test is calculated on the first day of each accounting period.
- 90% of all profits of the property rental business must be distributed before the filing date of the tax return of the company. Section 10 FA (No.3) 2010 made it clear that REITs will be able to issue stock dividends in lieu of cash dividends for the purpose of the distribution requirement with effect from 16 December 2010.
- A REIT must own at least three rental properties.
- No one property must account for more than 40% of the total value of the properties.
- A REIT must have interest cover of at least 1.25:1. The ratio compares the taxable profits of the business before financing costs and capital allowances to the financing costs. Failure to meet this test results in a tax charge.
- If any distribution is payable to a shareholder who owns more than 10% of a REIT, this will crystallise a tax charge in the REIT. This is to reflect the intention that any shareholders of a REIT should not own more than 10%.

Failure to meet these rules will result in a range of penalties, depending on which test has been failed. These penalties may include complete removal from the REIT regime at a later stage.

There is a tax charge on conversion of an existing company into a REIT. This is 2% of the market value of the properties at the time the company converts. It is possible to spread this charge over four years in instalments of 0.5%, 0.53%, 0.56% and 0.6%.

18.15.1 FA 2009 changes

Measures were introduced in FA 2009 to prevent artificial restructuring undertaken by groups to enable them to meet the REIT conditions and tests. These measures ensure that owner-occupied properties are excluded from the regime. In addition, an impediment that prevented potential REITs with tied premises from entering the regime has been removed.

The measures came into effect from 22 April 2009 and include:

- allowing a REIT to raise funds by issuing convertible preference shares;
- providing an accounting based definition for the 75% balance of business assets test;
- clarification on the application of the apportionment provisions where the proceeds of a sale arise from a property asset that is partly used for the property rental business and partly for non-rental purposes;
- uncoupling two of the REIT conditions for joining the regime, which previously provided an unfair barrier to some organisations where both conditions had to be satisfied.

18.15.2 Proposed FA 2012 changes

The Government commenced an informal consultation with industry and representative bodies on relaxations to the REITs legislation shortly after the 2011 Budget. Subject to the consultation, the Government intends to make changes both to reduce the barriers to entry and investment and to reduce the regulatory burden for existing and future REITs. The proposed legislation will be included in Finance Bill 2012. The consultation will seek views on:

- the introduction of a diverse ownership rule for institutional investors that would enable them to meet the non-close company rule. This would enable institutional investors to set up UK REITs;
- allowing cash to be a 'good' asset for the purpose of the REIT balance of business asset test. This would allow UK REITs to make investment decisions on a commercial basis;
- extending the time limit for complying with the distribution requirement in particular circumstances involving stock dividends. This would reduce the administrative burden on those REITs that pay out dividends every six months;

- redefining 'financing costs' for the REIT interest cover test to give certainty regarding this requirement;
- abolishing the conversion charge for companies joining the REIT regime;
- introducing a fixed grace period for new REITs to meet the non-close company requirement. This would enable start-up REITs to build sufficient reputation to attract shareholders;
- relaxing the requirement for a REIT to be listed on a recognised stock exchange. This would encourage entry into the REIT regime, particularly for start-up property investment companies; and
- making technical changes to the REIT legislation.

18.16 CORPORATE VENTURING

Companies that subscribe for new ordinary shares in EIS-type companies (see 25.5 and18.3.3) may qualify for tax relief at 20% on the sum invested. The rules for corporate investments do not mirror the changes for individual investors, which apply from 6 April 2011. This relief is dependent on the shares being retained for at least three years. The investment may also attract a capital gains deferral so that if the company invests £50,000 it may defer £50,000 of capital gains realised during the preceding three years or the following 12 months. These gains are then brought into charge as and when the company disposes of the shares or if the qualifying conditions are breached within a three-year period.

If all or part of the investment eventually has to be written off, the loss may be set against any of the company's profits for the year in which the loss is realised, or the preceding accounting period.

The company in which the investment is made must meet basically the same tests as apply under the EIS (see 25.5), ie its gross assets must not exceed £7m before the investing company subscribes for its shares, nor exceed £8m after that subscription.

The investing company must not have more than 30% of the equity. Furthermore, at least 20% of its shares must be held by individuals.

18.17 RESEARCH AND DEVELOPMENT (R&D) TAX RELIEF

DENISE ROBERTS

Research & development tax relief is available to all companies that incur expenditure on qualifying R&D activities. The relief works by increasing the companies' tax deductible R&D costs.

Up to 31 March 2010, tax relief was available to small and medium-sized enterprises (SMEs) at a rate of 175% for qualifying expenditure incurred on R&D projects. Larger companies are able to claim a 130% deduction for the same type of expenditure.

Subject to EU state aid approval, the rate of relief available to SMEs on qualifying expenditure increased to 200% for expenditure incurred from 1 April 2011. From 1 April 2012, again subject to EU state aid approval, the total rate of relief will increase to 225%.

However, the rate of relief available to SMEs for expenditure on vaccines research will be reduced from 140% to 120% from 1 April 2011, and enhanced relief will no longer be available to SMEs from 1 April 2012.

At present, a company is only eligible for R&D tax relief if it spends more than £10,000 on qualifying R&D expenditure in the year concerned. It is proposed that this de minimis limit will be abolished from 1 April 2012 for all companies. From the same date, changes are also anticipated to the rules governing relief for work done by subcontractors under the large company scheme.

In some cases, SMEs can choose to claim a tax credit by surrendering the tax relief available on qualifying expenditure. This is typically where the company is loss-making and therefore would otherwise have merely carried forward a trading loss enhanced by the uplifted tax relief. The credit is worth 14% of the surrenderable loss for the period. The value of the credit will be reduced to 12.5% to reflect the change in the R&D tax relief rate. The credit is currently limited to the company's PAYE and NIC liabilities for payment periods ending in the accounting period concerned. It is proposed that this limit will be abolished from 1 April 2012.

For SMEs, the relief is now 200% of the costs incurred. Accordingly, if the company eventually pays tax at the full 2011 26% rate of corporation tax, this amounts to relief at an effective rate of 52%. For those companies paying tax at the 2011 small companies' rate of 20% this is still relief at an attractive 40% effective rate.

An SME is defined for these purposes as a company with fewer than 500 employees and either turnover not exceeding £100m or a balance sheet total of not more than £86m. This data can be drawn from the company's statutory accounts. However, where a company is owned 25% or more by another company then a proportion of that company's data will need to be aggregated in assessing whether the limits are exceeded. There are exemptions to this rule where the ownership does not exceed 50% and is held by certain types of investors. Where the company is part of a group or under the control of another company then the consolidated data of the group needs to be taken into account.

In addition to being an SME enterprise as per the above definition, a company has also needed to meet all the following conditions:

- have qualifying R&D revenue expenditure of at least £10,000 in a 12-month accounting period (to be abolished for all companies from 1 April 2012);
- carry on a trade with its accounts prepared as a going concern;
- retain any intellectual property created as a result of the R&D.

The 2009 Pre-Budget Report announced that the qualification with regard to intellectual property was to be removed – and this change was finally enacted as s 13 FA (No.3) 2010 having effect for accounting periods ending after 9 December 2009.

18.17.1 Relief for companies that are not SMEs

Companies that do not meet the definition of an SME are able to claim R&D tax relief under the large company scheme, which provides 130% relief for costs incurred on qualifying R&D activities. Whilst a large company cannot make a claim to surrender losses in return for a cash sum, it is still able to carry the losses forward to set against future profits. Under the large company scheme, a company is still required to meet the going concern and minimum expenditure requirements but is not subject to the intellectual property restrictions.

18.17.2 Definition of research and development

The definition of R&D is set out in the *DTI Guidelines on the Meaning of Research and Development for Tax Purposes* dated 5 March 2004 and can be found on HMRC's website (www.hmrc.gov.uk/manuals/cirdmanual/cird81900.htm). The significant points covered in the guidelines are that:

● R&D for tax purposes takes place when a **project** seeks to achieve **an advance in science or technology** with activities that **directly contribute** to the **resolution of scientific or technological uncertainty.**
● Certain **indirect activities** related to a qualifying project also qualify.
● Activities other than qualifying indirect **activities that do not directly contribute** to the resolution of scientific or technological uncertainty in a project **do not qualify** as R&D.

The interpretation of certain areas of the DTI guidelines has been the subject of much debate between HMRC and tax advisers and in 2009 HMRC confirmed its view on production activities related to R&D whilst also announcing a change in its approach to indirect activities.

With regard to production activities it was confirmed that where the intention behind the activity is the manufacture or attempted manufacture of goods, or the delivery or attempted delivery of services, for customers, then the activity will not qualify as an R&D activity. However, where the manufacturing activity is undertaken solely to resolve technological uncertainties aimed at advancing technology then it may do so.

Indirect activities as listed in section 31 of the DTI guidelines have long been disputed by HMRC as qualifying for relief. However, in 2009 it relented and confirmed that as long as the activity was specifically identifiable as a particular part of the activity of an R&D project it could qualify. There is no effective date for this change so any corporation tax returns which are still open may be amended to reflect this.

18.17.3 Qualifying R&D costs

A claim for R&D tax relief may be made in respect of the following qualifying cost categories:

- staffing costs – including employers' NIC and pension costs but excluding benefits in kind;
- computer software;
- consumable or transformable materials;
- payments for externally provided workers – only where the payment is made to a company and the workers who are being provided are employees of that agency company;
- payments to the subjects of clinical trials;
- payments made in respect of subcontracting out an R&D activity.

Under the SME provisions, if any of the above costs are subsidised then they will not be eligible for R&D tax relief. If the subsidy is notified state aid, then the expenditure is treated as subsidised if it is or has been obtained in respect of the whole or part of the above expenditure or received in respect of any other expenditure associated with the same R&D project. Accordingly, any notified state aid subsidy in respect of the R&D project is capable of disqualifying all of the expenditure on that project.

Where the qualifying costs are met wholly or partly by a grant or subsidy which is not a notified state aid or by someone other than the company, then only the element that is subsidised will not be eligible for R&D and the remaining unsubsidised element will be eligible for R&D tax relief.

These restrictions do not apply to claims made under the large company relief provisions and therefore in such circumstances an SME may be able to make a claim under the provisions for those subsidised costs.

18.17.4 Vaccine Research Relief (VRR)

Take-up of VRR has been very low with reportedly only ten claims a year made through the scheme. The Government is considering whether VRR as currently operated is effective, or whether it would be more effective to deliver support through other mechanisms. Reflecting this is the withdrawal of relief for SMEs: it decreases from 140% to 120% of allowable costs for financial year 2011, with enhanced relief being removed completely from SMEs from financial year 2012. As matters stand, 140% relief will continue to be available to large companies that do not benefit from the enhanced R&D relief rates available to SMEs.

18.18 ECA TAX CREDITS

Loss-making companies carrying on a qualifying activity can surrender losses in exchange for a cash payment provided:

- the losses are attributable to 100% first-year allowances available on designated energy-saving or environmentally beneficial plant and machinery;
- the losses cannot be otherwise relieved by the company; and
- the qualifying expenditure was incurred on or after 1 April 2008.

The amount of the first-year tax credit that will be paid to the company is equal to 19% of the losses being surrendered, although it cannot exceed the greater of:

- the total of the company's PAYE and NIC for the chargeable period; or
- £250,000.

Any first-year tax credit will be clawed back if the qualifying plant and machinery is sold within four years of the end of the period in which the first-year tax credit was paid.

The lists for designated energy-saving or environmentally beneficial plant and machinery can be found at www.eca.gov.uk.

18.19 SALE OF LESSOR COMPANIES: ANTI-AVOIDANCE

Where there is a change in ownership of a company that carries on a business of leasing plant and machinery (either on its own or in partnership with other companies), a tax charge arises at the time of the sale on profits that have been earned but not yet taxed, because of the mismatch between recognition of leasing income for tax and accounting purposes. Changes have been made to these rules to make them more effective, including widening the scope of the types of companies that are subject to the charge.

An ability to opt out of the charge was introduced in December 2009 to deal with the exceptional circumstances arising in the financial crisis. However, it was thought that some companies were abusing the election to ensure that their profits were not fully taxed so this ability was withdrawn from 23 March 2011. For those companies that had already made the election, further changes will ensure that whenever any of the plant and machinery concerned is disposed of by the company, the full value of the asset will be taken into consideration when calculating the disposal value.

18.20 iXBRL AND ONLINE FILING

18.20.1 iXBRL only from 1 April 2011

Online filing is now mandatory for all corporation tax returns for accounting periods ending after 31 March 2010, filed after 31 March 2011. Paper returns will no longer be accepted, and online returns must (with very few exceptions) be filed using the iXBRL standard reporting language. Similarly, corporation tax must also be paid electronically from 1 April 2011.

A complete corporation tax return includes the tax computation and accounts alongside the return (CT600), so iXBRL tags in the correct form must be applied to each of these elements. These compulsory changes will be an administrative burden for companies. The extent of this will depend on how your tax returns and accounts are prepared, and by whom.

Companies that have – to date – prepared their accounts in a variety of formats may face problems with the requirements. If you plan to use your own accounts preparation software, you should check whether an upgrade to an iXBRL-enabled version will be available by the time you have to prepare your first set of tagged accounts. Remember that all accounts submitted after 31 March 2011 will need iXBRL tags unless they relate to an accounting period ending before 1 April 2010 being filed late (in which case it is likely that penalties will arise).

iXBRL tagging is complex, with thousands of possible tags (collectively termed the 'taxonomy' by HMRC). Any staff members who undertake it will need a good understanding of the taxonomy. In addition, if you submit your own corporation tax returns, you will need to use the facilities on the HMRC website (but these are very basic – see www.hmrc.gov.uk/ct-online/file-return/use-hmrc-software.htm#2) or use specialist tax software.

To avoid the need to maintain such software and expertise in-house, you could consider asking your accountant to produce your accounts and submit CT600 for you in the correct iXBRL format. Your accountant should be able to produce accounts using their standard template for a fixed (relatively low) additional fee, which should include the time spent reviewing the iXBRL file independently of the accounts. For customised accounts, tailored to your specific requirements, it is likely that fees will increase substantially. Your accountant will then ask you to review and approve the final iXBRL document that is to be submitted with your corporation tax return.

Most advisers will also accept iXBRL files prepared by your team for submission to HMRC, albeit they will not review the entries unless you request this additional service. Bear in mind that files rejected by HMRC's systems could result in increased costs for the submission of your tax return.

If you – or a third party – prepare your company's accounts in MS Word or Excel, they must be converted to a fully tagged iXBRL format for submission. Your adviser is likely to be able to do this for you, agreeing a fee for the work in advance. Please note, however, that any conversion service will be more time consuming than using accounts preparation software, and will require a greater level of review. The amount of work involved (and hence the cost) can vary greatly depending on the format and content of your accounts, how the accounts have been formatted in Word or Excel, and the terminology used.

It is understood that, during the introductory phase, HMRC plans to advise and support people and help them get iXBRL submissions right, rather than penalising them for getting it wrong. Therefore, it has not yet introduced penalties in relation to online filing, although the usual penalties will apply for late filing of returns, or errors in the tax declared, and HMRC will expect to see that you have made a 'good effort' at getting the filing right; ignoring these rules is not an option!

Sets of tags (taxonomies) have been created for accounts prepared using UK GAAP (around 5,300 tags) and for accounts prepared using IFRS (up to 3,800 tags). However, in the initial two years of iXBRL filing, HMRC plans to use a basic taxonomy consisting of up to 1,500 tags for all accounts submitted in iXBRL, although its online portal will also accept fully tagged accounts. HMRC will require full tagging of accounts only from 2013. To view the taxonomies online, as well as guidance on iXBRL and online filing generally, go to www.hmrc.gov.uk/thelibrary/ct-online.htm#4.

The first two years, when the reduced minimum tagging list can be used, is being referred to as a 'soft landing period'. During this time, HMRC plans to work with companies, agents and software providers to increase the accuracy of the tagging. It is aware that some of the anticipated software solutions are not yet available, and is therefore looking at ways that those submitting returns can advise HMRC if they are unable to file on time.

Submitted files may be rejected by HMRC, even after being apparently accepted by the HMRC online filing gateway at the time of submission, if there is a shortfall in the iXBRL tagging.

18.20.2 Companies House filing

Unlike HMRC, Companies House originally took the approach that filing company accounts in iXBRL format would not be compulsory but that it intended to be able to accept them in iXBRL from July 2011.

However, in November 2010 Companies House announced that it would *require* accounts to be filed in iXBRL format from March 2013. It intends to 'mandate electronic submission for all incorporations and for filings of annual returns, accounts and the main company changes for the standard company types and corporate entities'.

Although a consultation will take place and regulations will have to be passed by Parliament, once implemented, the change will move Companies House substantially towards becoming a fully electronic registry.

18.20.3 Charity returns concession

Charities required to prepare accounts under the Companies Act 2006 or the Friendly and Industrial and Provident Societies Act 1968 must file their company tax return and accounts and computations online from 1 April 2011 for any accounting period ending after 31 March 2010. However, HMRC has now recognised that the free software it will be providing for small companies may not be suitable for charities because of the accounting principles that smaller charities must use to prepare their accounts.

Therefore, as a transitional measure, HMRC will continue to accept accounts from smaller charities in PDF format although the tax computations must be filed in iXBRL format (because the free HMRC software can be used). Where no computation is required because all income and gains of the charity are exempt from tax (ie form CT600E is filed), a charity can simply attach a PDF of a letter stating so.

A smaller charity is defined as one where the combined income of the charity and any wholly owned subsidiaries does not exceed £6.5 million for the accounting period. In addition, unincorporated associations and charities that are incorporated by guarantee, shares or charter can also continue to submit accounts as a PDF with computations in iXBRL format. However, subsidiary companies of charities will be required to submit returns, accounts and computations in iXBRL format. Unincorporated charities are not required to file using iXBRL.

These transitional arrangements will end when HMRC is able to provide free online filing software that is suitable for charity returns.

18.21 CLAIMS, ELECTIONS AND PENALTIES

Throughout the Taxes Acts there are various claims for relief from corporation tax that must be lodged with HMRC and, in practice, are made to the tax office dealing with the company's affairs. From 1 April 2010, unless otherwise specified by legislation, claims must be made within four years of the end of the accounting period to which they relate. Previously, the time limit was six years. The most common claims and elections are set out below, together with the time limit by which the claim or election must be made. HMRC does not generally have discretion to accept claims made after the time limit has expired for a particular claim unless the legislation (or HMRC practice) allows otherwise.

In practice, most claims are normally made in the CTSA return form CT600.

Claim	Time limit for submission	Reference
Trading losses offset against other income of accounting period	2 years	s 37 CTA 2010
Trading losses carried back	2 years	s 37 CTA 2010
Terminal loss relief	2 years	s 39 CTA 2010
Capital allowances	2 years	s 3 CAA 2001
Group relief	2 years	Chapter 4, Part 5 CTA 2010
Roll-over relief	4 years	s 152 TCGA 1992

18.21.1 Error and mistake relief claims; recovery of overpaid tax

Relief may be claimed within four years against any over-assessment to corporation tax because of an error or mistake in, or an omission from, any return or statement. No relief is due where the information was not used to form the basis of an assessment, or where the assessment was made in accordance with practice generally prevailing at the time of issue. An error or mistake claim under para 51, Schedule18, FA 1998 (as amended by schedule 52, FA 2009) should be made to HMRC.

Amended schedule18 goes into much more prescriptive detail than its predecessor. The gist of the rules has, however, not changed, although prescribed circumstances are now listed at paras 51A to 51C where such claims will not be entertained. These include cases where the taxpayer knew (or ought to have known) that relief could have been claimed before a certain period expired (such as the tax return amendment window or the time limit to appeal against an assessment) but did not do so.

18.21.2 Penalties

- Failure to notify chargeability – for obligations arising on or after 1 April 2009, Schedule 41 FA 2008 introduced an amended penalty regime for failing to notify chargeability to tax, based on the same principles as those contained in Schedule 24 FA 2007 for penalising incorrect returns.
- Filing deadline – 12 months after accounting reference date – Schedule 55 FA 2009, contains details of changes to the penalty system, and has applied since 1 April 2011. In addition to the £100 penalty for submitting a return late, a penalty of £10 may be applied for each day that the failure continues during the period of 90 days beginning with the date specified in a notice given by HMRC. If a return is more than six months late, the penalty will be the higher of 5% of any liability to tax which would have been shown in the return in question, and £300. If the failure continues for more than 12 months and the taxpayer has deliberately withheld information that would enable HMRC to assess the tax due, this becomes the greater of 100% of any liability to tax which would have been shown in the return in question, and £300. If the withholding of the information is deliberate and concealed, the penalty is the greater of 100% of any liability to tax that would have been shown in the return in question, and £300. If the withholding of the information is deliberate but not concealed, the penalty is the greater of 70% of any liability to tax that would have been shown in the return, and £300. In any other case, the penalty will be the greater of 5% of any liability to tax which would have been shown in the return, and £300. Higher penalties (up to double the amount of tax due) can be charged where the withheld information concerns offshore matters.

- Error in return – tax-related penalty of between 30% and 100% of potential lost revenue.
- Failure to keep proper records – penalty currently up to £3,000.
- Failure to produce documents for an enquiry – penalty £300 plus a daily fine of up to £60.

19

FINANCING YOUR BUSINESS

This chapter sets out the tax consequences of various methods of financing a business. It deals with unincorporated business ventures (sole traders and partnerships, including limited liability partnerships) and incorporated (limited liability companies). Some of the areas covered in this chapter may be covered elsewhere in the book in greater detail, but this chapter consolidates these considerations under the following headings:

(1) Financing through own resources
(2) Financing through personal borrowing
(3) Issuing additional shares (with and without tax incentives)
(4) Borrowing through the business
(5) Financing assets
(6) Cash flow management

19.1 FINANCING THROUGH OWN RESOURCES

19.1.1 Separate funding

The establishment of a partnership or the incorporation of a limited liability company allows an individual to separate and invest funds to provide capital for a business. In the case of a partnership, funds can be made available through contributions to a partner's capital account or the subscription of quotas. In the case of limited liability companies, funding can be made through subscription to newly issued share capital. The purchase of shares in a company from an existing shareholder or a partnership interest from an existing partner does not provide additional liquid funds to the company or partnership. Further capital can be subscribed as necessary to fund the growth of the business, through additional contributions to the partner's capital account, or subscription to quotas or additional share issues.

In the case of a sole trader, funds may be put into a separate business bank account but there is no formal separation of assets between the business and its owner.

The capital accounts of partners can be either interest-bearing or free of interest. The decision lies with the partners and will be reflected in the partnership deed. The payment of interest by a partnership to partners is treated as an allocation of partnership income to the specific partner and will be included as partnership income of that partner for tax purposes.

Limited liability companies do not pay interest on funds that have been subscribed as share capital. Preference shares can be used to give a recurrent and fixed dividend on an equity base, with preference dividends paid out in priority to ordinary dividends. For UK tax on income and capital gains, preference dividends are treated in the same way as other dividends.

An individual who is a shareholder in a company can provide funds to the company by way of a loan as well as, or instead of, subscribing for shares. Such loan accounts fall within the loan relationship rules and the charge in the profit and loss account for any interest charged will normally be followed for tax purposes, subject to observing the conditions applicable to connected party transactions (see 18.5.5).

19.1.2 Losses on funding a sole trader's business

Because there is no effective separation of funds paid into the business, no specific relief is given for the loss of such funds. As with partnerships, relief for losses that have arisen and resulted in the failure of a business will be given under the various specific headings of the tax legislation (see 7.7).

19.1.3 Losses on capital investments in partnerships

No specific income tax relief is given for losses of capital invested in a partnership. A partner's share of trading losses can be relieved against his or her other income (see 7.7). A capital loss may arise on an individual retiring from the firm if payment has been made to acquire the partnership interest.

19.1.4 Loss on shares

(ss 131–133 ITA 2007)

If an individual acquires shares in a company through subscribing for the shares and realises a loss on those shares, then, subject to various conditions being satisfied, the loss can be set off against the income of the individual for the year in which the loss is suffered or for the previous year. The conditions placed on this relief are given at 17.2.

A qualifying loss is calculated according to CGT principles. A claim to set the loss off against income has to be made within one year from 31 January of the year following that in which the loss arose. A loss not so used can be carried forward as a loss for CGT purposes.

Normal CGT rules apply to losses on shares in companies when the shares have not been acquired through subscribing for the shares.

19.2 FINANCING THROUGH PERSONAL BORROWING

To be able to finance a business entirely from personal resources is a rare luxury; in most cases borrowing will be required. Such borrowing can be through the business itself (see 19.4), or drawn down personally by the individual. The form of security that has to be provided as a condition of the loan being made is not significant; whether the individual obtains tax relief on the interest depends on satisfying the conditions in the tax legislation.

19.2.1 Loans to invest in partnerships

(ss 398–400 ITA 2007)

An individual can claim relief against income for interest paid on eligible loans (see 11.4). Conditions are that the loan is used:

- to purchase a share in a partnership; or
- to contribute capital to a partnership or to make an advance to a partnership where the advance is used wholly for the purposes of the trade profession or vocation carried on by the partnership; or
- to pay off another qualifying loan.

The borrower:

- must be a member of the partnership throughout the period during which the interest expense arises;
- must not have recovered any capital from the partnership since the loan has been drawn down.

19.2.2 Interest on loans to invest in companies

(ss 392–395 ITA 2007)

An individual can claim relief against income for interest paid on eligible loans (see 11.5). Conditions are that:

- the loan is used to purchase shares in a close company; or
- the loan is used by a close company for its business purposes; or
- the loan is used to pay off another loan that would have qualified for relief;
- the individual alone or with associates owns a material interest in the close company (material interest being defined as more than 5% of the ordinary share capital of the company or the right to receive more than 5% of the assets of the company on a winding-up of the company); or
- the individual holds less than 5% of the ordinary share capital but works for the greater part of the time in the management or conduct of the company or an associated company;
- the company is a qualifying company.

Status as a qualifying company depends on the activity. The close company must exist wholly or mainly:

- to carry on a trade or trades on a commercial basis;
- to make investments in land or property let commercially to unconnected parties;
- to hold shares or securities or to make loans to qualifying companies or intermediate companies that are under the control of the company (qualifying meaning that the business of the company falls under one of the two headings immediately above);
- to co-ordinate the administration of two or more qualifying companies.

Relief for interest expense on a loan can continue if the company ceases to be close at a time after the loan has been drawn down provided that the other conditions continue to be satisfied.

19.2.3 Definitions

(ss 439–441 CTA 2009)

A close company is a company that is under the control of five or fewer persons (see 18.14.1). Interests of associates are taken into account when testing.

Ordinary share capital, for these purposes, comprises all shares other than those that can participate in distributions only at a fixed rate.

19.2.4 Loans to invest in employee-controlled companies

(ss 396–397 ITA 2007)

Interest on qualifying loans drawn down to acquire shares in companies controlled by employees can also qualify for relief. The excess of an individual's holding over 10% of the shares of the company is treated as being owned by a person who is not an employee of the company when testing whether the company is employee-controlled, so this relief is likely to be of limited use when financing a business. For the conditions to be met for a qualifying loan, see 11.6.

19.3 ISSUING ADDITIONAL SHARES (WITH AND WITHOUT TAX INCENTIVES)

A limited liability company can obtain funds through the issue of additional share capital in return for cash payments. If the additional shares are placed through a rights issue, in which the share allocation is proportional to existing shareholdings, the company will only receive additional funds to the extent that the shareholders make payment for the new shares. The share subscription can be structured as an issue to new or existing shareholders, without specific tax advantages, or to qualify as an investment under the Enterprise Investment Scheme, the Venture Capital Trust scheme or the Corporate Venturing Scheme.

In all cases, the effect of the share issue in diluting the ownership interests of existing shareholders will need to be considered.

19.3.1 Share issue without tax incentives

If the share issue is not to be structured to be a qualifying investment under a tax incentive scheme:

(1) The terms and conditions of the share issue and the amount of the issue are a decision for the owner and, if applicable, the other shareholders in the company.

(2) The shares taken up in return for the new investment will be an asset for CGT purposes with the gain or loss on disposal being calculated according to the normal rules of CGT.

(3) Tax relief for interest paid on qualifying loans will be available subject to the required conditions being met (see 19.2.1 above); otherwise the issue will not attract tax relief or incentives.

Share issues to venture capitalists may be structured through venture capital trusts; see 19.3.6 below, or as an issue that does not attract tax relief in which case the above three points will apply.

19.3.2 Enterprise Investment Scheme

(Part 5 ITA 2007)

The Enterprise Investment Scheme (EIS) provides tax incentives for individuals to encourage investment in shares in companies that meet certain conditions and carry on qualifying activities. It is intended to help small, higher risk, unquoted trading companies raise start-up and expansion finance by issuing ordinary shares.

Subject to state aid approval, the rate of tax relief and certain qualification thresholds will be increased over the next two years.

From 6 April 2011, individuals investing in companies qualifying under the EIS will be able to claim income tax relief at a rate of 30% (currently 20%) on the first £500,000 invested. The current qualification rules will remain unchanged from that date.

From 6 April 2012, certain thresholds will increase. The annual amount an individual can invest under the EIS on which he or she can claim income tax relief will increase to £1m (currently £500,000). The maximum annual amount that can be raised by an individual company from EIS or Venture Capital Trust investments will increase to £10m (currently £2m) and the maximum limit on gross assets held by the investee company before any investment will increase to £15m (currently £7m). In addition, the maximum permitted number of employees of the company will increase to fewer than 250 (currently fewer than 50).

The Government will also consult on removing some restrictions on qualifying shares and types of investor and will refocus the scheme on genuine risk capital investments. Feed-in tariff businesses will be added to the excluded activities list.

The increased rate of relief – and the proposed 2012 changes – are subject to EU state aid approval, so enhanced relief will not be given in practice until that has been granted. The investment may also qualify for CGT deferral relief.

This section provides a summary of the conditions that have to be met for the investment to qualify and continue to qualify during the required holding period (see 25.5 for a more detailed analysis). The trade-off for the current shareholder or shareholders in the company is between the ability to access funds through the share issue (investors may not be prepared to make an investment in the absence of tax relief) and the continuing commitments (which are likely to be legally enforceable through contractual obligations required by investors) for the company to continue to comply with the conditions.

19.3.3 EIS conditions relating to the company

(ss 172–188 ITA 2007)

For EIS to apply:

(1) The issue must be of new ordinary shares in the company; the shares cannot have preference features.

(2) The company cannot have assets of more than £7m (set to increase to £15m from 6 April 2012) before the share issue and £8m (it is assumed this limit will increase appropriately from 6 April 2012) after the issue.

(3) The company (or group of companies) must have fewer than 50 full-time employees or their equivalents (set to increase to fewer than 250 full time employees or their equivalents, from 6 April 2012) at the time the shares are issued.

(4) The company must have raised no more than £2m (set to increase to £10m from 6 April 2012) under EIS or the Corporate Venturing Scheme or as a qualifying holding for a Venture Capital Trust (see below) in the 12 months ending on the date on which the investment is made. If the limit is exceeded, none of the shares within the issue that causes the limit to be breached will qualify for EIS.

(5) The company must be unquoted (although the shares of the company can be listed on the AIM) and there must be no arrangements under which the company can become quoted.

(6) The company cannot be under the control of another company, or another company and associated persons and there must be no arrangements under which it can come under such control.

(7) The company must not control another company unless that second company is a qualifying subsidiary (see 25.5.5 for the definition) and there must be no arrangements under which such control can be established.

(8) The company must be carrying on a qualifying trade (see 19.3.4).

The company will be expected to issue certificate EIS 3 to investors claiming relief, confirming that conditions have been met in respect of the issued shares. The conditions summarised above should clearly fall within the knowledge of the company's existing shareholders and/or management who, in addition to the issue of the certificate, will be expected to give a warranty that the conditions have been met.

19.3.4 Qualifying trades

(s 192 ITA 2007)

Certain trades are excluded under s 192. The company's business must not consist to any substantial extent of any of the following:

(1) dealing in land, commodities or futures, or shares, securities or other financial instruments;

(2) dealing in goods otherwise than in the course of any ordinary trade of wholesale or retail distribution;

(3) banking, insurance (but not insurance broking), money-lending, debt-factoring, HP financing or other financial activities;

(4) oil extraction activities;

(5) leasing (except for certain short-term charters of ships) or receiving royalties or licence fees. A recent Special Commissioners case concerned a medical company called Optos, which developed eye test machines that it leased to opticians. It was held that the company was excluded from EIS relief because of this leasing;

(6) providing legal or accountancy services;

(7) providing services or facilities for any trade carried on by another person (other than a parent company) that consists to any substantial extent of activities within any of (1)–(6) above and in which a controlling interest is held by a person who also has a controlling interest in the trade carried on by the company;

(8) any of the following property-backed activities:
    (a) farming and market gardening;
    (b) forestry and timber production;
    (c) property development;
    (d) operating or managing hotels or guest houses; and
    (e) operating or managing nursing or residential care homes.

(9) Legislation will be introduced in Finance Bill 2012 providing that companies whose trade consists wholly or substantially in the receipt of feed-in tariffs or similar subsidies will only be eligible for the two schemes (EIS and VCT) where commercial electricity generation commences before 6 April 2012. Shares issued before 23 March 2011 will not be affected.

Wholesale and retail distribution trades

Wholesale and retail distribution trades qualify only if they are 'ordinary' trades. Section 193(5) states that a trade does not qualify as an ordinary trade of wholesale or retail distribution if:

- it consists to a substantial extent of dealing in goods of a kind that are collected or held as an investment; and
- a substantial proportion of those goods are held by the company for a period that is significantly longer than the period for which a vendor would reasonably be expected to hold them while endeavouring to dispose of them at their market value.

The following are taken as indications that a company's trade is a qualifying trade:

- The trader buys the goods in quantities larger than those in which he sells them.
- The trader buys and sells the goods in different markets.
- The company incurs expenses in the trade in addition to the costs of the goods, and employs people who are not connected with it.

The following are 'indications' that the trade is not a qualifying trade:

- There are purchases or sales from or to persons who are connected with the trader.
- Purchases are matched with forward sales or vice versa.
- The trader holds the goods for longer than is normal for such goods.
- The trade is carried on otherwise than at a place or places commonly used for the type of trade.
- The trader does not take physical possession of the goods.

The above are only indications and are not conclusive that a company's trade is or is not a qualifying trade, but it will be difficult to persuade HMRC that a trade qualifies if there are several indications to the contrary.

19.3.5 EIS conditions relating to the individual investor

(ss 162–171 ITA 2007)

EIS income tax relief is denied if the investor is connected with the company. This means that the individual alone or with associated parties possesses directly or indirectly more than 30% of:

- the share capital of the company or any of its subsidiaries;
- loan capital of the company or any of its subsidiaries;
- voting power in the company or any of its subsidiaries; or
- rights that would give entitlement to more than 30% of assets available for distribution to shareholders in the event of the company being wound up.

While the more-than-30% test can be monitored by the company in respect of investment or rights of an individual investor, knowledge of which persons are to be treated as associated may go beyond what the existing shareholders and/or management of the company might be expected to know.

EIS income tax relief is also denied if the individual has been previously connected with the company within the two years before the issue of the EIS shares. 'Connected' in this sense means an individual who is or was:

- a paid director of the company or any of its subsidiaries;
- an employee of the company or any of its subsidiaries;
- a partner of the company or any of its subsidiaries;
- an associate of a person falling into any of these categories.

Again, while the company can be expected to have knowledge of an individual falling into any of the categories, knowledge of the associated persons may go beyond what the existing shareholders and/or management of the company might be expected to know.

The First-tier Tribunal has held in a recent case (*Thomason, Godwin & Markham* v *HMRC* [2010] UKFTT 579 TC) that a management buy-out (MBO) team was entitled to EIS relief on shares it subscribed for in the acquisition company, despite the fact that the managers had previously worked for the company whose trade was taken over.

The three taxpayers were employed as line managers of Tufnol Ltd (Old Co) until 25 October 2004. Old Co went into administrative receivership on 13 September 2004. A newly incorporated company (New Co) was set up in which the taxpayers subscribed for initial subscriber shares and of which they became directors on 15 October 2004.

It was agreed that New Co would purchase most of the assets of Old Co. Some of the assets were left behind, principally the debtor and cash balances. However, it was generally agreed that the business had been transferred across as a going concern. The transfer took place on 25 October 2004.

A year later, New Co issued more shares to the taxpayers who claimed EIS relief both in respect of their original share subscriptions and this later share issue.

HMRC disputed the availability of EIS income tax relief on the basis that the three directors were connected with the issuing company at the time of the relevant share issues. This was because they had received remuneration as directors of the company (other than remuneration that is specifically allowed under the relevant tax legislation). However, a get-out was available if it could be shown that the directors had not previously been involved in carrying on the whole or any part of the trade of the company.

HMRC argued that, because the directors had been involved in running the trade when it was operated by Old Co, this meant that the get-out could not apply.

The taxpayers' case was largely built on the argument that the trade now being carried on by New Co was not the same as that previously carried out by Old Co. For example, they claimed that some of the rights held by Old Co were not transferred to New Co and could not have been because of restrictions and deficiencies set out in the sale and purchase agreement.

The tribunal did not accept the taxpayers' argument that the trade carried on by New Co was not the same as that previously carried on by Old Co. However, that was not important because, based on the tribunal's interpretation of the legislation, the taxpayers' previous involvement in the trade as employees of Old Co could be ignored – it was only their involvement in managing the trade after it had been transferred to New Co that was important. Since they had not taken up duties by the time of the first share subscription, this meant that the get-out applied in respect of that issue.

Another rule states that, where the get-out applies to a share subscription made by a company, any subsequent issues to the same individuals by the same company in the following three years would also be deemed to qualify for the get-out. Therefore, even though by the time of the subsequent share issue the directors had certainly been involved in managing the trade in New Co, the further share issue made by New Co in 2005 also qualified for EIS relief.

It is still possible that HMRC may appeal against this decision. However, based on the judgment reached by the tribunal, the lesson to be learned here is to always ensure that where an MBO of this kind is undertaken, any previous managers looking to take advantage of EIS relief should only be appointed as directors (and not employees) of New Co and should always be party to the initial share subscription if this takes place before the business of New Co commences.

19.3.6 EIS – withdrawal of relief

(ss 208–244 ITA 2007)

As detailed in 25.5, EIS relief is withdrawn where:

- The company redeems share capital.
- The investor receives value from the company.
- The company ceases to be a qualifying company.
- The investor becomes connected with the company (withdrawal of income tax relief).
- The investor disposes of the share within a three-year period (withdrawal of income tax relief).

With the exception of the last heading, the other grounds for the withdrawal of relief should lie within the knowledge of the company's existing shareholders and/or management.

19.3.7 Venture Capital Trusts

(Part 6, ITA 2007)

Venture Capital Trusts (VCTs) are companies that are quoted on the London Stock Exchange and derive value from investment in shares or securities. The requirements for qualification as a VCT are set out in 25.6.

Subject to EU state aid approval, legislation is to be introduced in Finance Bill 2012 making the following changes to VCTs, which will have effect on and after 6 April 2012:

- an increase in the threshold for the size of qualifying company for VCTs to fewer than 250 employees (currently fewer than 50) and to the company having no more than £15m (currently £7m) of gross assets before the investment;
- an increase in the annual amount that can be invested through EIS or VCTs in an individual company to £1m (currently £2m).

At least 70% by value of the investments made by a VCT must consist of shares or securities in qualifying holdings, defined as holdings in unquoted companies that exist wholly for the purpose of carrying on one or more qualifying trades, wholly or mainly in the UK. Cash proceeds from disposals are ignored for six months when applying the 70% test. Qualifying trade is defined as for the EIS. For 2011–12, the assets of the unquoted company must not exceed £7m before the share issue and £8m after the share issue and the company in which the investment is made must not have raised more than £2m under EIS, the VCT legislation or the Corporate Venturing Scheme in the 12 months ending on the date on which the investment is made. If the limit is exceeded, no part of the investment that causes the limit to be breached will count as a qualifying investment for a VCT.

An individual investor in a VCT obtains income tax relief at 30% on a subscription for new ordinary shares in the VCT not exceeding £200,000.

The investor also benefits from income tax relief on dividends paid on shares in a VCT to the extent that the shares acquired each year do not exceed £200,000 in value.

The minimum period for which VCT investors must hold their shares is five years.

The trade-off for the current shareholder or shareholders in the company seeking finance is between the ability to access funds through the share issue to the VCT (investors may not be prepared to make an investment in the absence of tax relief) and the continuing commitment (which is likely to be legally enforceable through contractual obligations) for the company to continue to comply with the conditions for the relief to be obtained.

19.3.8 Corporate Venturing Scheme

(s 63 and Schedule 15 FA 2000)

The Corporate Venturing Scheme (CVS) provides tax incentives for companies to encourage investment in shares in other companies meeting certain conditions and carrying on qualifying activities (see 18.16). Requirements for the investing company are that:

(1) It does not have a material interest in the issuing company at any time during the qualifying period (three years); a material interest is present if the investing company possesses directly or indirectly or is entitled to acquire more than 30% of the ordinary share capital of or voting power in the issuing company.
(2) It is not party to reciprocal arrangements with the issuing company.
(3) It does not control the issuing company at any time during the qualifying period.
(4) It is carrying on a non-financial trade.
(5) It holds the shares in the issuing company as a chargeable asset.
(6) The share issue is not tax avoidance.

At the time of issue, the issuing company must be unquoted and there can be no arrangements for it to become quoted. Gross assets of the issuing company must not exceed £7m before the issue and £8m immediately afterwards. The company in which the investment is made must not have raised more than £2m under EIS, the VCT legislation or the CVS in the 12 months ending on the date on which the investment is made. If the limit is exceeded, no part of the issue of shares that causes the limit to be broken will qualify under the CVS.

Requirements to be met during the qualifying period for the issuing company are that:

(1) It is independent in the sense of not being a 51% subsidiary of another company or under the control of another company.
(2) At least 20% of the share capital is owned by one or more independent individuals.
(3) It is not a member of a partnership or a joint venture.
(4) It has no subsidiaries that are not qualifying subsidiaries and no property management subsidiaries that are not at least 90% owned.
(5) It is carrying on a qualifying trade.

Qualifying trade is defined as for the EIS scheme (see 19.3.4).

The trade-off for the current shareholder or shareholders in the company seeking finance is between the ability to access funds through the CVS (investors may not be prepared to make an investment in the absence of tax relief) and the continuing commitment (which is likely to be legally enforceable through contractual obligations) for the company to continue to comply with the rules for the relief to be obtained.

19.4 BORROWING THROUGH THE BUSINESS

As a business develops, its actual and projected cash flows and the assets it owns may allow it to borrow funds in its own right. As with other forms of borrowings discussed in this chapter, the deductibility of the interest expense depends on satisfaction of the conditions in the tax legislation and not on the form of security given for the borrowings.

19.4.1 Loans to unincorporated businesses

Interest paid by a sole trader or partnership (as opposed to a partner in a personal capacity) and incurred wholly and exclusively for the purposes of the business can be claimed as a deduction in computing the profits of the business.

A deduction for tax is also available for costs of raising finance when these costs:

(1) were incurred wholly and exclusively for the purposes of obtaining loan finance, providing security or repaying a loan; and
(2) represented expenditure on professional fees, commissions, advertising, printing or other incidental expenses in relation to raising finance.

19.4.2 Corporate loan relationships

Since 1996, the treatment of interest expense incurred by companies for tax has depended on the loan relationship legislation (now found in Parts 5 and 6 of CTA 2009) (see 18.5). The legislation applies to all UK resident companies and UK permanent establishments of non-UK resident companies. Loan relationships arise when:

- a company is a debtor or creditor in respect of a money debt and the debt arose as a result of a transaction for the lending of money; or
- an instrument is issued for the purpose of representing security for, or the rights of a creditor in respect of, a money debt.

In general, the tax treatment follows the accounting treatment with the expenditure on interest being allowed in the year that it is charged to the profit and loss account of the company. The company's accounting treatment must comply with generally accepted accounting practice (GAAP) (which means either UK GAAP or IFRS).

If the interest is payable to a connected party, a deduction for interest accrued in the accounts is only allowed where the recipient is chargeable to UK tax on the interest income or the interest is paid within 12 months of the end of the accounting period. If the 12-month limit is not met, a new late interest rule, introduced in FA 2009, applies where a company owes interest to certain connected individuals or overseas companies and that interest remains unpaid 12 months after the end of the period. The rule denies relief to a company which is due to pay interest where interest is payable by the debtor company to:

- a participator in the company (if it is a close company); or
- a connected company; or
- a company where there is a 'major interest' relationship between the two companies concerned.

In the last two situations, the late interest rule will apply only if the creditor company is resident in a 'non-qualifying' territory.

19.5 FINANCING ASSETS

As a business expands, it usually will need access to more assets. Possibilities are that the assets are financed outside the business and made available to the business or that the business itself acquires the assets.

19.5.1 Loans to purchase assets

A decision to provide an asset to a business through personal funding may result from an individual having better access to credit than the business itself. There can also be efficiencies, for instance a building needed by the business but owned by an individual offers the possibility of long-term capital appreciation and, if so, the possibility of realisation with one layer of tax rather than two if the property were owned by a limited liability company. Entrepreneurs' relief may be available to reduce the eventual gain on disposal. A property may also be a suitable investment for a self-administered pension scheme.

An asset acquired personally and let or leased to a business may attract capital allowances, depending, according to the heading under which the allowances are claimed, on the nature of the asset and demonstrating that the asset is used for a qualifying activity. Capital allowances are first set off against the income generated from the asset.

As the investor and the business are likely to be connected, care must be taken to ensure that the terms of the transaction are justifiable as arm's length, defined as being the terms that would have been agreed in the absence of such a connection.

19.5.2 Interest on loan to acquire property

Generally, interest expense on a loan drawn down by an individual for the purchase of a property to be let to a business will attract tax relief, through set-off against the rental income received.

19.5.3 Loans drawn down by a partner

(ss 388–389 ITA 2007)

A partner can claim a deduction for interest paid on a loan drawn down to finance capital expenditure on the provision of plant and machinery for the purposes of the business of the partnership. The relief is available in the year in which the loan is drawn down and the following three years.

19.5.4 Purchase of assets by business

If the business draws down a loan to finance the purchase of an asset, interest deductibility will depend on the loan relationship legislation (see 19.4.2 and 18.5).

Depreciation on fixed assets charged in the profit and loss account of a business is disallowed and added back when calculating the taxable profit. If the asset qualifies, capital expenditure will qualify for capital allowances under various headings (see 16.2). The rates of capital allowances vary and not all fixed assets will qualify for capital allowances. For tax purposes, the deductions in respect of the purchase of intangible assets generally follow the charge in the accounts of the business.

19.5.5 Leasing of assets by business

Leasing is another method for a business to obtain assets. A substantial volume of asset leasing business is written annually. In many cases, leasing is provided by the manufacturers or suppliers of assets, for example office machinery such as computer equipment and copiers, but leasing possibilities also exist for major fixed assets. The lessor is often a subsidiary of a financial institution and the cost of the lease reflects the ability to reduce taxable profits of the company itself and through group relief the profits of associated companies by the capital allowances available.

The accounting treatment of leased assets varies as to whether the lease is an operating or a financial lease. An operating lease is for a period that is less that the asset's anticipated useful life; a financial lease is written for a period that effectively equates to the expected life of an asset. When testing to determine the category of the lease transaction, an arrangement in which the net present value of the rentals is 90% or greater than the value of the asset will be treated as a finance lease.

Lease rentals under an operating lease are charged to the profit and loss account as incurred and a corresponding deduction is given when calculating taxable income of the business.

To ensure that the accounts give an accurate picture of the resources and obligations of a business, a finance-lease transaction is capitalised on the balance sheet, entries reflecting the purchase of the rights to use and enjoy the asset and the requirement to make future payments. The rental payments are apportioned between a finance charge and a reduction of the obligation to make future payments. The tax deduction in respect of payments under a finance lease is normally the amount charged to the profit and loss account in that period in respect of the finance lease. However, the tax treatment of long funding leases entered into after 1 April 2006 has been changed and the lessee may now be entitled to capital allowances (see 16.1.6), but not in excess of the costs incurred (see s 33 Finance Act 2011).

If the lease is for a major asset, the lessee is usually required to enter into a contractual commitment to make good any reduction in the tax benefit to the lessor of the capital allowances on the leased asset through a change in tax legislation, including a reduction in the rates of tax.

19.5.6 Lease/buy analysis

When carrying out a lease/buy analysis to determine the optimum method of acquiring assets for the business, the cash flows under each of the two cases will have to be set out for the expected period of use of the asset, or a period of, say, five or ten years, if considered more appropriate to the circumstances and forecasting pattern of the business. The cash flows will include the tax effects, in the purchase case the reduction in tax for the interest costs and the capital allowances received on the asset and, in the lease case, the reduction in tax through the lease rental payments allowed for tax. Tax is only one consideration: the real point in preparing the cash flows is to ensure that the business will be able to meet the obligations under the chosen route. The effect on the profit and loss account of each route should also be determined so that a well informed decision can be taken.

19.5.7 **Sale and leaseback**

A business can seek to raise finance for current expenditure through selling an asset and leasing it back. This arrangement may be particularly useful if the business has an asset or series of assets that would fit within a specialist activity of the buyer. An example would be a business that sells a portfolio of properties to a pension fund or property company.

The tax effects of the disposal of the asset will need to be calculated in advance of the decision being taken. While the tax effect of the purchase is a matter for the purchaser, there are certain situations in which the capital allowances on the purchased asset will be restricted.

19.5.8 **Hire purchase**

When an asset is bought on hire purchase, the purchaser is entitled to capital allowances on the full purchase price from the beginning of the contract, although this sum is going to be paid by instalments. The interest element of the periodic payments charged to the profit and loss account is allowable as a tax deduction in the year when it is so charged.

19.6 CASH FLOW MANAGEMENT

Managing cash flow prudently for a growing business requires the owner/managers to avoid circumstances in which tax liabilities bear heavily on cash flow. It should also involve accelerating tax deductions wherever possible. Three points are worth noting.

19.6.1 **Cash basis for VAT**

Using the cash basis for VAT means that the output VAT due on invoices issued to customers does not have to be accounted for to HMRC before the money has been received from the customer. The business owner should review the turnover limits to determine whether the scheme will apply.

19.6.2 **Research and development**

There are specific incentives to encourage research and development (see 18.17). The business owner should review activity to determine whether these incentives will apply.

19.6.3 **Capital expenditure**

Capital expenditure incurred by the business should be reviewed to allocate as much as possible to assets qualifying for capital allowances. Although deferred tax may have to be provided on the difference between the written down values for book and tax, it is an accounting entry and not a cash movement.

20

SHOULD YOU OPERATE THROUGH A COMPANY?

There is no simple answer to this question. There are both advantages and disadvantages in carrying on business through a limited company rather than operating as an unincorporated business. Some of the considerations arise from commercial rather than tax aspects. Limited liability may be an important consideration, either for the business's proprietors or to attract finance from an outside investor. However, the apparent protection given by limited liability is often illusory because banks or other lending institutions normally require personal guarantees from directors for any bank loans made to the company. Furthermore, if limitation of liability is the main concern, you may find that having an LLP (limited liability partnership) gives you the best of both worlds.

This chapter contains the following sections:

(1) Tax advantages of having a company
(2) Possible disadvantages
(3) CGT and IHT considerations
(4) Limited liability partnerships (LLPs)
(5) Transferring an existing business to a company or LLP
(6) Having a company as member of a partnership

20.1 TAX ADVANTAGES OF HAVING A COMPANY

20.1.1 Lower rate of tax on profits

Having a company means that a lower rate of tax will apply to retained profits. The small companies' rate of 20% applies to profits up to £300,000 in financial year 2011 provided there are no associated companies. If there are associated companies, the threshold at which profits attract tax at either the normal 26% (for 2011) rate or the marginal small companies' rate is reduced. If there are no associated companies, the small companies' rate can produce a very substantial saving.

Example – Tax saving through incorporation in 2011–12

Unincorporated business	£
Profits	450,000
Tax and NIC	214,453
Incorporated business	£
Profits before director's remuneration	450,000
Less: director's remuneration and employers' NIC, say	(150,000)
	300,000
Corporation tax at 20%	60,000
Tax and total NIC on director's remuneration (no PA as gross > £114,950)	69,418
Total tax and NIC on profits of £450,000	129,418
Annual saving in tax through operating via a company	85,035

Of course, some of this saving may have to be handed back as and when the retained profits are extracted from the company as dividends, which attract higher rate tax.

The savings for some high earners are significantly greater in 2011–12 as a result of the continuing 50% top rate of income tax. It is clear that if profits of (say) £500,000 are earned and retained by a company owned by such an individual rather than paid out to him or her as remuneration, the company will retain £385,000 after corporation tax. If it used the £500,000 to pay remuneration, the position would be as follows:

	£
Available for remuneration and Employer's NIC	500,000
Employers' NIC	(59,775)
Tax and Employees' NIC (assuming no other income)	(210,282)
Retained by individual	229,943

In other words, the money available for reinvestment in the business will be increased by about 67%.

20.1.2 Other tax considerations

Timing difference

There is a useful timing difference where a business is carried on through a company in that remuneration can be deducted from the company's profits even though it is not paid (and is not taxable income of the individuals until the earlier of payment, or entitlement to receive payment, provided it does not trigger the anti-avoidance rules on disguised remuneration – see Chapter 5). Provided the remuneration is actually paid within nine months of the company's year end, the company is normally entitled to a deduction in arriving at its profits.

Example – Timing of tax payments

> If a company draws up accounts to 31 March 2012, it may secure a deduction for director's remuneration of £150,000 even though the remuneration is not paid until 31 December 2012, in which case PAYE does not have to be paid over until 19 January 2013. Contrast this with an unincorporated business where tax needs to be paid on account on 31 January 2012 and on 31 July 2012, with a balancing payment on the following 31 January.
>
> An even longer timing difference would arise if an individual takes his or her £150,000 out as a dividend on 31 December 2011. The company would have to pay corporation tax on 1 January 2012 and the individual will often not need to pay tax on his or her dividend until 31 January 2013.

Pension contributions

With the introduction of the new regime for registered pension schemes, there is more of a level playing field for proprietors of unincorporated businesses and companies. There is no longer any great advantage in having a company in terms of pension provision.

Payment of remuneration may prevent personal allowances going to waste

Where an unincorporated business operates at a loss, and the individual concerned has no other private income, the benefit of his or her personal allowance is lost forever. By trading through a company, it is possible to vote remuneration equal to the personal allowance and the remuneration voted in this way will increase the amount of the company's loss that can be carried forward and set against subsequent profits.

Certain reliefs are only available to companies

Companies can qualify for R&D and ECA tax credits (see 18.17 and 18.18) and get allowances for expenditure on intangibles (see 18.6). These reliefs are not available to unincorporated businesses.

20.2 POSSIBLE DISADVANTAGES

Possible disadvantages of operating through a company include the following:

20.2.1 Extra administration

There are more statutory requirements concerning book-keeping, filing annual accounts, audit (in some cases), iXBRL filing, disclosure, etc. An unincorporated business does not normally need to file annual accounts at all, whereas a company must file accounts with Companies House and make an annual return.

20.2.2 IR35 regulations

Some companies may be caught by IR35. Income received by personal service companies may still be taxed as if it were remuneration (see 21.3).

20.2.3 Admitting future partners

If profits are retained, this may make it increasingly difficult for individuals who come up through the business to become shareholder directors. For example, if a company has 100 £1 shares in issue and retains profits after tax of £15,000 pa for ten years, each share will be worth £1,500 more at the end of the ten years than at the start of the period. For an individual to acquire a 10% shareholding, he or she must find sufficient finance to purchase shares that reflect this. The problem does not arise in the case of a partnership, since the normal procedure is to allocate past profits to partners' capital accounts and then admit a partner on the basis that he or she would share in future profits at a specified percentage.

20.2.4 Tax savings may only be a deferment

The traditional analysis has been that tax generally becomes payable by the shareholders on their share of retained profits, either when they sell their shares and realise a capital gain, or as and when they extract retained profits by taking a dividend. On this analysis, the tax saving on retained profits is often little more than a deferment of tax. This is not really the end of the story as there can be a true saving because of the difference between the 28% CGT rate (or even 10% if entrepreneurs' relief applies) and the higher rates of tax payable on income. For example, an unincorporated trader will pay tax at an effective rate of 52% on his or her earnings in the additional rate band (50% income tax and 2% NIC) – say, £100,000 for the purposes of this illustration. If £100,000 accrued to a company that paid the full rate of corporation tax, the company would retain £74,000. If the trader eventually realised his or her shares, he or she might pay 28% CGT on this £74,000 and end up with around £53,300. Much of the overall saving can be dependent on the rate at which the company pays tax.

20.2.5 Increased liability for NIC

A company must pay Class 1 NIC at a single rate on all amounts above a certain level paid as remuneration. There is no reduced rate above the upper earnings limit such as applies to employees' contributions. This can give rise to a substantially increased burden for a company as compared with an unincorporated business. Comparing an unincorporated business owned by four equal partners with a company that has four 25% shareholders (and it is assumed that in both cases the individuals had income of £75,000 each), the NIC bill for 2011–12 is as follows:

	Partnership		*Company*
	£		£
Class 2	520	Employees' Class 1 (not-contracted-out)	19,529
Class 4	15,292	Employer's contributions	37,496
	15,812		57,025

While the benefits payable to employees are better than those received by the self-employed (a larger pension because of S2P and entitlement to unemployment benefit), the higher NIC cost can be a very expensive way of financing such benefits.

20.2.6 Work in progress

In principle, a professional firm should not include partner time in arriving at the cost of work in progress. This means the figure brought into account should be lower because of this. However, if a business is carried on by a company, time put in by a director should be included when valuing work in progress.

20.3 CGT AND IHT CONSIDERATIONS

20.3.1 Potential double charge for capital gains

Where a valuable asset is held within a company, a tax liability may arise at two stages before the shareholders can enjoy the sale proceeds. For example, if a company liable at the mainstream corporation tax rate of 26% acquired a property at a cost of £100,000, and it is sold five years later when it is worth £550,000 then there is a gain for the company of £450,000 (ignoring indexation). The company will pay tax on this capital gain at 26%. The company will have net funds available – after paying tax – of £333,000, as here:

	£
Profits for accounting purposes	450,000
Less: tax on gain (£450,000 at 26%)	117,000
	333,000

If the company is then wound up and the cash distributed to the shareholders, they are likely to have a personal CGT liability on the £333,000. The maximum CGT payable by the shareholders (ignoring the availability of entrepreneurs' relief, annual exemptions, losses, etc) would be £93,240 (ie £333,000 at 28%), giving an effective overall rate of 46.72% on the disposal and extraction of the gain.

While it is not generally good policy to have appreciating assets within a company, the extent of the extra tax payable is not as great as it was in the past. While some additional tax is likely to be payable if an appreciating asset is held within a company, this is not an argument in itself against a business operating through a company. Correctly analysed, the treatment of capital gains within a company is an argument in favour of shareholder directors holding such assets in their personal capacity rather than through a company.

20.3.2 **Property owned privately but used by a company**

Where a shareholder director owns a property used by his or her trading company, roll-over relief (see 17.3) should be available if he or she sells the property and buys another property for use by the same company.

If a shareholder director needs to take a loan to buy property, he or she can secure relief on the interest by charging rent. Doing this will not prejudice roll-over relief but it will mean that CGT entrepreneurs' relief may not be available on an eventual sale of the property (this relief is restricted if the individual has charged a market rent during any periods of business use after 6 April 2008).

20.3.3 **Inheritance tax**

Where a partner owns a property that is used by the firm, he or she will generally qualify for 50% business property relief.

Where a controlling shareholder owns a property that is used by a trading company, he or she will also qualify for 50% business property relief. But no BPR is available for non-controlling shareholders who own a property used by the company. From this point of view, it is better for the property to be owned by the company because 100% business property relief will generally be due for all holdings of unquoted shares in trading companies, controlling and non-controlling.

20.4 LIMITED LIABILITY PARTNERSHIPS (LLPs)

An option that should be borne in mind is to operate through an LLP (see 7.5). These are treated as companies for company law (and VAT) purposes but are taxed as partnerships (ie profits or losses, and gains, are attributed to each individual partner in proportion to his or her stake in the business, and taxed as his or her own income). Using an LLP means you can limit your personal liability towards customers, etc, while retaining the tax treatment that applies to partnerships.

20.5 TRANSFERRING AN EXISTING BUSINESS TO A COMPANY OR LLP

20.5.1 Transferring to a company

Some care is necessary when transferring a business to ensure that no CGT charge arises. Fortunately there is a special CGT relief intended to cover this (see 17.6). See also Chapter 39 on stamp duty. The VAT consequences should also be explored and this is an area where you will need to seek professional advice.

The timing of the transfer may be important. Bear in mind that if you were carrying on an unincorporated business, transferring it to a company may enable you to utilise your overlap relief (see 7.3.6). If your future employment income is expected to be much lower than your current self-employed profits, consider applying for a reduction in your payments on account (see 2.1.3).

If you have substantial qualifying loans used to put money into a partnership, you should take advice. But an HMRC concession will cover most situations (see 11.4.4).

See *Tax Bulletin 76,* April 2005 regarding the tax implications if HMRC challenges a sale of goodwill as being at an over-value. HMRC is likely to tax the over-value as a distribution (see 9.9.6).

20.5.2 Transferring to an LLP

Transferring an existing unincorporated business to an LLP does not normally involve a disposal for CGT purposes or a cessation of your self-employed business for income tax purposes. Remember to keep your VAT office advised and take advice on any VAT implications of the transfer.

20.6 HAVING A COMPANY AS A MEMBER OF A PARTNERSHIP

A possible way of fine-tuning the position may be for the members of a partnership or LLP to consist of individuals and a company that is owned by them. Provided that there is a commercial basis for the company being a member (it might, for example, employ the staff), this allows for some profits to be retained as working capital rather than forming part of the taxable income of the individual partners.

This is something that you should discuss with your tax adviser.

21

DEDUCTING TAX AT SOURCE AND PAYING IT OVER TO HMRC

ANNE-MARIE BODEN

This chapter outlines the requirements imposed by law on employers, etc, to collect tax on the Treasury's behalf. Employers are advised to take these obligations seriously, as the administrative burden can be onerous and the penalties for non-compliance severe.

The chapter contains the following sections:

(1) Employers
(2) Contractors in the construction industry
(3) IR35
(4) Managed service companies (MSCs)
(5) Non-resident landlord scheme
(6) Non-resident sportsmen and entertainers
(7) Other payments to non-UK resident persons

21.1 EMPLOYERS

An employer has an obligation to collect tax and national insurance contributions (NIC) and to operate the following schemes:

- Pay As You Earn (PAYE)/NIC;
- student loans;
- Construction Industry Scheme (CIS).

21.1.1 Payment of PAYE to HMRC

Employers are required to withhold tax under PAYE and deduct Class 1 primary (employees') and secondary (employers') NIC and pay them over to HMRC each month. If the total PAYE and NIC deductions do not normally exceed £1,500 pm, the employer can account for the tax and NIC deductions quarterly. The £1,500 pm is inclusive of sums collected under the Student Loans Scheme. At the end of the year, the employer must give employees form P60 (by 31 May) showing the tax and NIC withheld from their earnings.

21.1.2 Earnings subject to PAYE

The payment of earnings by a UK-resident employer to directors and employees is subject to PAYE.

Earnings, in relation to employment income means any salary, wages or fees, any gratuity or other profit or incidental benefit of any kind obtained by the employee if it is money's worth, or anything else that counts as income from the employment.

The following list provides some examples of payments that are earnings and are subject to PAYE:

- salary;
- wages;
- fees;
- overtime;
- bonus;
- commission;
- pension;
- honoraria;
- pay during sickness or other absence from work;
- holiday pay;
- Christmas gifts in cash;
- employee's income tax borne by his or her employer;
- payments for the cost of travelling between the employee's home and his or her normal place of employment;
- payments for time spent in travelling;
- cash payments for meals;
- payments in lieu of benefits-in-kind;
- certain lump sum payments made on retirement or removal from employment;
- gratuities or service charges paid out by the employer.

A far more exhaustive list can be found in HMRC booklet CWG2 *Employers' Further Guide to PAYE and NIC*.

There are however certain payments from which PAYE cannot be deducted even though they are regarded as taxable income of the employment. The most common of these is known as the pecuniary liability principle. This is where an employer discharges an employee's debt. An example of this is where the employer pays for an employee's home internet service. An employer cannot deduct PAYE when making a payment to a third party. The item should therefore be reported to HMRC on Form P9D or P11D.

It must be remembered however that such payments are still earnings and therefore both employees' and employers' Class 1 NIC must be deducted and paid over to HMRC in the normal pay period.

The PAYE regulations also require employers to account for PAYE when they pay staff using 'readily convertible assets' (RCAs). There are ten classes that fall within this category:

- an asset capable of being sold or otherwise realised on a recognised investment exchange;
- an asset capable of being sold or otherwise realised on the London Bullion Market;
- an asset capable of being sold or otherwise realised on the New York Stock Exchange;
- an asset capable of being sold or otherwise realised on a market for the time being specified in PAYE regulations;
- an asset consisting in the rights of an assignee, or any other rights, in respect of a money debt that is or may become due to the employer or any other person;
- an asset consisting in property that is subject to a warehousing regime, or any right in respect of property so subject;
- an asset consisting in anything that is likely (without anything being done by the employee) to give rise to, or to become, a right enabling a person to obtain an amount or total amount of money that is likely to be similar to the expense incurred in the provision of the asset;
- an asset for which trading arrangements are in existence, or are likely to come into existence in accordance with any arrangements of another description existing when the asset is provided;
- an asset for which trading arrangements are in existence, or are likely to come into existence in accordance with any understanding existing when the asset is provided;
- an asset consisting in securities, which is not a readily convertible asset under the above, is to be treated as a readily convertible asset unless the securities are shares that are corporation tax deductible.

PAYE may also have to be accounted for on gifts of shares in the employing company or profits realised in connection with the acquisition of employment-related securities or shares (see 6.3) or where a charge arises under Part 7A ITEPA (disguised remuneration – see Chapter 5).

National insurance contributions

The PAYE and NIC rules have been largely aligned since 6 April 1999 and it is now unusual for a payment or benefit to be taxable as employment income but not subject to NIC. See Chapter 23.

21.1.3 Anti-avoidance of PAYE and NIC

In 1997, the PAYE legislation was amended to deal with assignments of trade debts by employers to their employees. The legislation referred to 'tradeable assets' and treated such assets as if they were cash payments.

The term 'tradeable assets' was subsequently replaced by 'readily convertible assets': these include the assets listed above.

If an employee becomes liable to income tax on employment income on the exercise, assignment or release of an option for shares that are readily convertible assets, these provisions require the employer to operate PAYE. Similarly, PAYE will apply if the employee is rewarded by the enhancement of a readily convertible asset that he or she already owns. PAYE must be operated on a reasonable estimate of the amount likely to be charged to tax as employment income. Comparable rules were also introduced for NIC.

21.1.4 Failure to operate PAYE

An employer who fails to operate PAYE (and/or deduct NIC) takes a substantial risk. The primary liability to account for the tax rests with the employer and the scope of PAYE does not extend simply to deducting tax from an employee's gross pay and remitting it to HMRC. Instead, an employer must remember that PAYE can also apply to all forms of casual labour, which may or may not be paid through the payroll, and to individuals otherwise considered to be self-employed (see 7.2).

Another area frequently overlooked is expenses (see 4.4.1) that constitute part of an employee's income from employment and accordingly fall within the scope of PAYE. While genuine business expenses incurred wholly, exclusively and necessarily in the course of an employee's duties may qualify for a tax deduction, there remain several areas where employers are required to operate PAYE and deduct NIC. These include the payment of all round sum allowances that have not been approved by HMRC in the form of a dispensation, and the payment of unauthorised or unvouched expenses. Even the payment of travel expenses may not be permitted tax free in circumstances where the place visited is deemed to be the permanent place of work. As an example, an employee living in London and permanently working on a site in Aberdeen will be taxed on all his or her expenses for travel between London and Aberdeen. This shows that special attention must be paid to such payments and the circumstances surrounding them. HMRC's booklet 490, *Employee Travel – a Tax and NIC Guide for Employers*, provides more details on the rules.

HMRC is legally obliged to seek recovery of any underpaid tax from the employer in the first instance. In limited circumstances HMRC has discretion to issue a direction that underpaid tax may be recovered from the employee. The Regulations make it clear that such a direction will only be given if the employee received payments knowing that the employer wilfully failed to deduct the amount of tax that should have been deducted or an employee received a notional payment that was not taxed, the most obvious example of which would be employee shares.

All lump sum compensation payments should be considered carefully because of HMRC's approach to the taxation of termination payments. It is wrong to assume that the first £30,000 of **every** lump sum compensation payment is exempt from income tax. Basically, if there is any contractual obligation or expectation on the part of the employee to receive a sum then HMRC is likely to take the view that the employer should have deducted tax and Class 1 NIC. HMRC looks specifically at the habitual and automatic making of payments in lieu of notice (autopilons) – see HMRC's employment income manual at www.hmrc.gov.uk/manuals/eimanual/eim12800.htm.

Summary of year end deadlines and penalties

Due dates for submission of end of year and end of quarter returns

1	PAYE returns (**P14, P35, P38A, P38 (S)**)	**19 May**
2	Agreement of PAYE Settlement Agreement contracts	**5 July**
3	Expenses and benefit returns (**P9D, P11D, P11D(b)**)	**6 July**
4	Termination payment details, if in excess of £30,000	**6 July**
5	Benefits in excess of £100 provided to former employees, where not excluded from charge	**6 July**
6	**P46 (car)** – from April 2010 employers must submit these forms when an employee is provided with a company car or when the employee no longer has the company car. HMRC will no longer accept any replacement car information from employers (including via a form delivered electronically) Almost all employers are now required to file their Employer Annual Return (P35 and P14s) online, as well as in-year forms P45 and P46. The 2010–11 return must be filed by 19 May 2011. It is also possible (but not mandatory) to file the following forms online: P9D, P11D, P11D(b), P12, P37, P38A, P46 (Car), WNU (works number update) and CIS300 (verification request for the Construction Industry Scheme).	**5 July, 5 October, 5 January, 5 April**

Due dates for providing information to employees for tax year ended 5 April

1	**P60** (Pay and tax details)	**31 May**
2	Expenses and Benefit Returns (**P9D, P11D**)	**6 July**
3	Termination payment details, if in excess of £30,000	**6 July**

Due dates for payments (automatic interest applies if paid late for all categories from 6 April 2011)

		Paid by cheque (date reaches HMRC accounts office)	**Paid electronically** (cleared payment in HMRC's bank)
1	PAYE/NIC	19 April	22 April
2	Class 1A NIC	19 July	22 July
3	PAYE Settlement Agreement tax and Class 1B NIC	19 October	22 October
4	Monthly PAYE/NIC remittances	19th of each month	22nd each month
5	Quarterly PAYE/NIC remittances	19 July, 19 October, 19 January and 19 April	22 July, 22 October, 22 January and 22 April

It is mandatory for employers with 250 or more employees to make their payments electronically.

See www.hmrc.gov.uk/paye/file-or-pay/payments/deadlines.htm#1

Penalties for late payment

In April 2010, a new system of penalties was introduced for late payment of income tax, Class 1, 1A and 1B NIC and CIS and student loan deductions collected via PAYE. The first penalty notices will be issued from April 2011. There are two types of penalty. The first is based on the number of defaults (late payments) in the year as shown in Table 21.1 below. The additional penalty is independent and targets very late payments.

Table 21.1 – Late payment penalties

Number of times payments are late in the tax year	*Penalty percentage*	*Amount to which penalty percentages apply*
1	No penalty	
2–4	1%	Total amount that is paid late in the tax year (ignoring the first late payment in that tax year)
5–7	2%	
8–10	3%	
11 or more	4%	

Additional penalty		
Any number	5% penalty on each amount of tax paid more than 6 months late	Total amount that is paid late
Any number	Additional 5% penalty on each amount of tax paid more than 12 months late	

Table 21.2 – Return filing penalties

Return filing penalties	Late returns and late provision of information to employees	Failure to file online (in addition to late filing penalty)*	
		No. of employees	Penalty
1 PAYE returns and P11D(b)	Initial up to £1,200 per 50 employees, fixed monthly penalty of £100 per 50 employees or part thereof, up to 12 months, with an additional tax-geared penalty thereafter	50–249 250–399 400–499 500–599 600–699	£600 £900 £1,200 £1,500 £1,800
2 Expense and benefit returns (P11D)	Up to £300 per return **plus** up to £60 per day	700–799 800–899 900–999 1,000or more	£2,100 £2,400 £2,700 £3,000
* Note that submitting a return on paper (even if within the deadlines) will not be treated as filing a return as most employer returns have had to be filed online since 2009–10.			

Table 21.3 – Penalties for incorrect returns

Penalties for incorrect returns	
1 PAYE and Sub-contractor returns and P11D(b)	Up to the difference between the amounts payable on the incorrect and correct returns
2 Expense and Benefit Returns (P11D, P9D)	Up to £3,000 per return

Forms P11D and P9D

An employer must file forms P11D to report benefits and expenses for all employees earning at a rate of £8,500+ pa. Directors are automatically included in this category unless they:

- are full-time working directors or directors of a not-for-profit organisation; and
- earn less than £8,500 pa; and
- do not control directly or indirectly more than 5% of the company's ordinary share capital; and
- do not have directorships in other businesses under the same control.

All benefits and expenses payments (including business expenses) must be reported, except those covered by dispensations or PAYE Settlement Agreements. The amount is the cash equivalent (see 4.4–4.9 on taxation of benefits in general).

Except where special rules apply, the cash equivalent is normally the VAT-inclusive cost to the provider. Where the special rules apply, employers are responsible for calculating the cash equivalent and entering the appropriate amount on the P11D. HMRC can supply the following P11D Working Sheets to assist you:

- living accommodation and associated benefits
- car and fuel benefits
- vans available for private use
- interest-free and low interest loans
- relocation expenses
- mileage allowance and passenger payments.

If an arrangement has been made for someone else to provide benefits to an employer's employees, the cash equivalents must be reported on P11D as though the employer itself had provided the benefits. If the provider cannot or will not give details of the benefits to the employer, the employer must make a best estimate of the cash equivalent and notify HMRC of this. The affected arrangements are where an employer has guaranteed or facilitated provision of benefits, or the benefits were part of a reciprocal arrangement with another employer.

If a third party makes any expense payments or provides benefits to an employer's employees and the employer is not involved, the third party has an obligation to notify the employees of the cash equivalent of the expense payment paid or benefit provided. The third party does not have to submit a P11D for another employer's employee and many third party providers enter into arrangements to pay the tax due through a Taxed Award Scheme (TAS). These are dealt with by HMRC's Incentive Award Unit in Manchester and guidance is available in *The Employer's Further Guide to PAYE and NIC* at Chapter 2. Unlike awards covered by PAYE Settlement Agreements (PSAs), non-cash awards and the tax paid on them under TAS arrangements remain assessable on the employee. So the employee has to enter the grossed-up value of the award and the tax paid on it on his or her tax return. Normally no further tax is due from an employee unless the provider has only entered into a basic rate TAS and the recipient of the award is liable at the higher or additional rate.

P11D returns are due for submission to HMRC by 6 July following the end of the tax year. Filing an incorrect return can result in a penalty as detailed above.

Details of taxable benefits must be supplied to employees by 6 July. Forms P9D may also be required for benefits provided to employees earning less than £8,500 pa. The deadlines for submitting returns of Classes 1A and 1B NIC must also be borne in mind (see 23.1.7–23.1.8).

21.1.5 Pensions and benefits for former employees

A return must also be made of pensions and other payments to former employees, and 'relevant benefits' taxable under Part 4 and Schedule 36 FA 2004, and s 393B ITEPA 2003. See 4.16.6 on this.

21.1.6 Collection of student loans

Student loans are the main source of funding higher education. The Student Loans Company (SLC) administers the scheme but employers are responsible for making deductions from the former student's salary and for paying over the amounts deducted to HMRC.

The system is similar to that for working tax credits in that employers will receive start and stop notifications from HMRC. The employer is not responsible for identifying employees who are liable to make these repayments or for answering questions from the employee regarding the loan. Such queries should be referred to the SLC. Only questions about the operational aspects of the scheme should be referred to HMRC.

The calculation of student loan repayments is very similar to that for NIC. There is an annual limit of £15,000 pa (£1,250 pm or £288.46 pw) below which no deductions are made. This limit is non-cumulative as with NIC so an employee who earns £1,000 in one month and £2,000 in the next will only be liable to deduction in the second month. The deduction made would be as follows in respect of the latter case:

£2000 – £1,250	=	£750.00
Rate of deduction	=	9%
Student loan repaid	=	£67.50

The repayment percentage (currently 9%) is applied to those earnings subject to secondary Class 1 NIC.

An employer should only begin to make deductions when a start notice (form SL1) is received from HMRC. This gives at least six weeks' notice before deductions should commence. Deductions should begin on the first pay day after this date.

If a new employee hands over a P45 with a 'Y' in the SL box, it means the previous employer had received a start notice. In this situation, deductions should be made as soon as possible. If the P45 is received some time after the employee has started work, no attempt should be made to deduct any arrears. If the employee completes box D (student loans) of the new form P46, you should make deductions. The employer collects student loan repayments by making deductions from the borrower's pay either calculating the deduction (as above, or using the free tool on HMRC's employer CD), or by using the Student Loan Deduction Tables. These tables are available from the Employer's Orderline, on 08457 646 646. Further information is available in HMRC leaflet E17, which is available online at www.hmrc.gov.uk/helpsheets/e17.pdf.

21.2 CONTRACTORS IN THE CONSTRUCTION INDUSTRY

HMRC regards payments made by contractors to subcontractors as a high risk area because of cash payments and what it refers to as 'dubious practices'. It is an obvious area in which tax is being lost to the Treasury. Subcontract workers can now be paid:

- net after the deduction of PAYE/NIC as employees;
- net under deduction of the Construction Industry Scheme standard rate of 20%;
- net under deduction of the Construction Industry Scheme higher rate deduction of 30%;
- gross, if registered for Gross Payment under the New Construction Industry Scheme.

Agency workers

Construction workers supplied by employment agencies or other third parties were brought within the PAYE system by FA 1998. This aligned the tax and NIC treatment of such workers, who were in the past regarded as self-employed for tax purposes but as employees for NIC purposes.

Note that this does not only apply to agencies. Companies acting as 'in-house' agencies within the construction industry that supply labour to others, and anyone else who supplies construction workers to others, fall within the legislation.

21.2.1 Payments to subcontractors in the construction industry

Where a person carries on a business that includes construction work, payments to a subcontractor in respect of 'construction operations' may be subject to deduction of tax, as outlined above.

The contractor is normally the person making the payment for 'construction operations'. A contractor is a business or other concern that pays subcontractors for construction work. Contractors may be construction companies and building firms, but may also be government departments, local authorities, and many other businesses that are normally known in the industry as 'clients'. Non-construction businesses or other concerns that spend more than £1m a year (as an average over three years) on construction work, are treated as contractors and are also covered by the scheme.

Regulations that took effect on 6 April 2007 have the effect of excluding from the scheme most charities, provided that they are not 'mainstream contractors' (Regulation 24 SI 2005/2045); and deemed contractors in relation to expenditure on their own premises (Regulation 22). The exclusion does not apply to premises that are let or where there is significant use by third parties.

Construction operations

'Construction operations' are defined in law in s 74 FA 2004 and HMRC guidance can be found in Appendix B of the booklet CIS340 (see www. hmrc.gov.uk/forms/cis340.pdf). As a general guide, 'construction operations' cover almost any work that is done to a permanent or temporary building or structure, a civil engineering work or installation. The work can include site preparation, alterations, dismantling, construction, repairs, decorating and demolition. Some activities on construction sites are not regarded as construction operations under the scheme, including any activity that is clearly not construction work, such as the running of a canteen, a hostel, provision of medical or safety and security services and the provision of site facilities.

Where a single contract relates to a mixture of construction and non-construction operations, all payments due under the contract are within the scheme. This is the case even if only one of the jobs is regarded as a construction operation. A typical example is where a carpet fitter is engaged to 'finish' a house, laying carpet in some rooms and wood flooring in other rooms. Unless there is a separate contract for the carpet fitting, which is not a construction operation; the scheme would have to be applied to all the works.

21.2.2 Construction Industry Scheme

The current scheme was introduced on 6 April 2007. It was designed to remove some of the administrative burden of the old scheme and provide options to the paper-based processes of CIS.
The main differences are:

- There is no longer any need for CIS cards, certificates or vouchers.
- Contractors must check or 'verify' the payment status of new subcontractors with HMRC. This requires the contractor to provide

details of the subcontractor's name, national insurance number and unique tax reference number (UTR); company name and registration number if a company subcontractor and partnership name and UTR, if a partnership.

- Subcontractors will be normally be paid either net of 20% tax or gross, depending on their own circumstances, with HMRC advising on the rate of tax to be deducted.
- Three tests need to be satisfied before a subcontractor can be granted gross payment status:
  - The business test – an unincorporated business or company needs to show that it is carrying out construction work in the UK, or supplying labour, and the business is run through a bank account.
  - The turnover test is based on net turnover, ie gross income from construction work excluding VAT and the cost of materials. Individuals need a net construction turnover of at least £30,000 in the 12 months preceding their application for gross payment. Partnerships and companies need net turnover either of £200,000 or of £30,000 multiplied by the number of partners or directors.
  - The compliance test requires that in the 12 months to the date of application for gross payment the subcontractor's tax affairs have been up to date and payment of all tax due from the subcontractor and the business, including subcontractor deductions, PAYE, NIC and any business tax have been made on time. It extends to the partners' and directors' affairs, where appropriate. HMRC's CIS343 fact sheet provides guidance on applying.
- Unlike the old scheme, there are no renewal applications and HMRC will police compliance by reviewing gross paid subcontractors annually and removing gross payment status if there are any significant failings at the time of the review. This is an on-going process known as the Tax Treatment Qualification Test (TTQT), under which a subcontractor's compliance obligations are kept under constant review and errors in compliance identified. These might include for example, where monthly PAYE or CIS deductions are paid late or monthly CIS returns (whether a nil return or not) are either late, or not submitted at all. Under the TTQT a computer generated letter will be issued to the subcontractor. This letter will itemise compliance failures, and advise the subcontractor that its gross payment status will be withdrawn within 90 days from the date of the letter.
- Any subcontractor receiving this letter may appeal against the decision to withdraw gross payment status within 30 days. If no appeal is received by HMRC, then contractors who use the services of this subcontractor will be advised to withhold tax from future payments
- To appeal against the withdrawal of gross payment status, the subcontractor must have a 'reasonable excuse' as to why the compliance failures occurred. A 'reasonable excuse' can include:

- an unavoidable or unexpected absence close to a payment or return filing date because of business commitments or domestic emergencies;
- accidental destruction of records by fire or flood;
- exceptional postal delays as a result of industrial action or civil disturbance;
- sudden disruption to a business as a result of a break-in;
- the installation of a computer system or program for payroll accounting which has hit 'unexpected teething problems'.

- There is also a higher rate tax deduction of 30% if a subcontractor cannot be 'matched' on the HMRC system. This rate will continue to apply until the subcontractor contacts HMRC and registers or sorts out any matching problem.
- Contractors must make a return every month to HMRC showing payments made to all subcontractors. A late return gives rise to an automatic £100 penalty, followed by a further £200 penalty if the return is two months late. If the return is over six months late, there is a further penalty of £300 or 5% of the tax shown in the return, whichever is greater. If the failure continues after the end of the period of 12 months beginning with the penalty date, where, by failing to make the return, information which would enable or assist HMRC to assess the amount payable is withheld, the penalty is determined as follows:
  - If the withholding of the information is deliberate and concealed, the penalty is the greater of 100% of any liability which would have been shown in the return in question, and £3,000.
  - If the withholding of the information is deliberate but not concealed, the penalty is the greater of 70% of any liability which would have been shown in the return in question, and £1,500.
  - In any other case, the penalty is the greater of 5% of any liability which would have been shown in the return in question, and £300.
- If the return is incomplete or incorrect, the penalty rules in Schedule 24, FA 2007 will apply to determine the amount of further penalties which may be payable. Furthermore, repeated non-compliance could affect the contractor's own right to receive payments without tax being deducted.
- Contractors must declare on their return that none of the workers listed on the return is an employee. This is called a status declaration.
- Nil returns must be made when there are no payments in any month. These can be made over the telephone as well as online or on paper, but they must be made – there will be financial penalties for failure to submit a return.

The new penalty regime discussed above was introduced by Schedule 55, FA 2009, which has effect from 6 April 2011. The specific rules for CIS returns are in paragraphs 8 to 13.

21.2.3 'False self-employment' in the construction industry

The Government announced in the 2009 Budget that it would be consulting on 'false self-employment' in the construction industry. HMRC issued an update in October 2009, which indicated that basically the intention was to press on with the original proposals, broadly unchanged, despite a swathe of negative responses. It does beg the question: 'What is the point of consulting, if HMRC are not going to listen to the industry?'

HMRC wants to prevent construction workers 'falsely' claiming to be self-employed by establishing simple indicators of self-employment. Its favoured indicators are:

- the provision by the worker of the plant and equipment required to complete the job,
- the provision by the worker of the materials used in the job,
- the employment or provision of other workers.

Many respondents to the consultation told HMRC that genuinely self-employed workers would be caught by these basic tests even though they would be quite properly treated as self-employed under current case law, and indeed pointed to the existing body of case law which quite clearly defines when someone is or is not self-employed.

HMRC has said that those 'genuinely running their own businesses' will not be affected, but its track record on such issues is of concern. In recent years, the trend has been for HMRC to use the strictest possible interpretation wherever possible. This is bound to cause yet more disputes in what is already a complex area of tax law.

Using VAT registration as a further test of self-employment was roundly condemned by respondents to the consultation, but HMRC has still not ruled out this idea entirely. It states that 'further consideration needs to be given' to it and to other possible indicators such as the provision of own transport and public liability insurance, submission of invoices and working for only one engager. It has completely ignored the fact that such a test would unfairly discriminate against those businesses that are too small to be VAT registered.

In addition, those affected will have the worst of both worlds, as they will be treated as employees for tax and NIC purposes, but will not be entitled to the employment law rights that normally go with that status.

The intention is that the paying company will be responsible for operating PAYE and NIC for those classified as employees for tax purposes under the new rules. The Government has stated that these rules would be brought in as soon as the construction industry had 'recovered from the current economic downturn'. This initiative, which has been universally reviled by everyone except HMRC, will be implemented in the near future; a further consultation period in May 2011 and legislation is expected in FA 2012.

21.3 IR35

These rules use existing case law (see Chapter 7) to determine whether an individual performs services that would be taxed as employment income were it not for the fact that his or her services are provided through an intermediary such as a service company. Those caught by these rules will pay approximately the same PAYE and NIC as an individual who is an employee of the end customer.

Earlier this year, there was great excitement when it was announced that the OTS would review IR35 to see whether it could be simplified, improved, or even replaced. These hopes were however dashed in the 2011 Budget, when the Government stated that:

> ... following the publication of the OTS review of small business tax, the Government commits to making clear improvements in the way IR35 is administered. These improvements will include setting up a dedicated helpline staffed by specialists, publishing guidance on those types of cases HMRC views as outside the scope of IR35, targeting compliance activity by restricting reviews to high risk cases and setting up an IR35 Forum which will monitor HMRC's new approach. The Government has decided to retain IR35, as abolition would put substantial revenue at risk.

HMRC has set out a nine-point plan for determining the deemed employment income tax charge for a tax year (see Table 21.4):

- *Step 1* determines that the starting point for the calculation is the total amount received by the intermediary during the tax year from relevant engagements. This figure includes any benefits-in-kind provided to the intermediary in respect of those engagements. This total amount is then reduced by 5%, which is an allowance for the intermediary's running costs.
- *Step 2* adds in any payments or benefits-in-kind received by the worker or his or her family in respect of any relevant engagements from anyone other than the intermediary, which are not otherwise taxable as employment income, but which would have been so taxable had the worker been employed by the client.
- *Step 3* deducts any amounts spent by the intermediary that could have been claimed as expenses against income tax had the worker been the client's employee and met them him or herself.
- *Step 4* allows a deduction for any capital allowances that could have been claimed by the worker had he or she been the client's employee.
- *Step 5* deducts any contributions paid by the intermediary to an approved pension scheme for the worker's benefit.
- *Step 6* deducts any employers' NIC (Classes 1 and 1A) paid by the intermediary in respect of salary or benefits-in-kind provided to the worker during the year.
- *Step 7* deducts any amount of salary and benefits-in-kind provided by the intermediary to the worker during the year, which has already been

subject to income tax and Class 1 and 1A NIC (excluding any amounts that have already been deducted at Step 3). Note: if, after Step 7, the result is nil or a negative amount, there is no deemed employment income payment and no further tax or NIC is payable. If the result is positive, a deemed employment income payment must be calculated in accordance with Steps 8 and 9.

- *Step 8* allows for a deduction of the employers' NIC payable on the deemed payment. So Step 8 requires the calculation of the amount that, together with the employer's NIC due on it, equals the result of Step 7.
- *Step 9* states that the result after Step 8 is the amount of the deemed employment income payment.

Note that if the worker is within the Construction Industry Scheme (see above), it is the amount before deduction of tax under that scheme that must be brought in at Step 1 of the calculation.

Payment of tax

The tax and NIC calculated under IR35 regulations in respect of deemed payments is due for payment by 19 April following the end of the tax year. In some situations, HMRC believes that the P35 should be filed on the basis of estimates of the deemed payment and the tax and NIC due on it. See the advice published on www.hmrc.gov.uk/ir35.

21.4 MANAGED SERVICE COMPANIES (MSCs)

Payments received after 5 April 2007 by individuals who supply their services through a MSC are subject to PAYE. Furthermore, the cost of travel from the individual's home to place of work is not a tax-free expense for workers supplied by a MSC.
This is subject to the following exclusions:

- companies providing individuals who perform professional accountancy or legal services;
- 'normal employment agencies' that do not influence or control the way in which payments to individual workers are made.

Collection of tax from directors of the managed service company

From 6 August 2007, where PAYE and NIC cannot be recovered from a MSC, HMRC may enforce the debt personally against a director of the MSC or from a person who has provided the MSC. There are also wider provisions that came into force on 6 January 2008 allowing HMRC to transfer the debt to 'specified persons', ie people who 'encourage, facilitate or are otherwise actively involved in the provision of an individual's services' through a MSC.

Table 21.4 – Deemed calculation: HMRC template

Step 1	Enter in this box the amount of all payments and benefits received by your company or partnership in the year for contracts to which these rules apply	1
	Enter in this box 5% of the amount in box 1	2
Step 2	Enter in this box the amount of any payments and benefits received directly by you in the year for contracts to which the rules apply and which are not already taxable	3
Step 3	Enter in this box the amount of any expenses met by your company or partnership in the year which you could have claimed personally if the worker had been an employee of the client and had paid for them yourself	4
Step 4	Enter in this box the amount of any capital allowances for purchases made by your company or partnership which you could have claimed yourself if you had been employed by your client and had made the purchases yourself	5
Step 5	Enter in this box the amount of any contributions to an approved pension scheme made by your company or partnership for your personal benefit	6
Step 6	Enter in this box the amount of any employer's Class 1 and Class 1A NIC which your company or partnership paid in the year in respect of salary or non-cash benefits which it provided to you in the year	7
Step 7	Enter in this box the amount of any salary you received from your company or partnership in the year which is already taxable as employment income (this does not include anything for which a deduction has already been given at Step 3)	8
	Enter in this box any benefits in kind or expenses you received from your company or partnership in the year which are already taxable as employment income (this does not include anything for which a deduction has already been given at Step 3)	8a
	Add together the figures in boxes 1 and 3 and enter the total in this box	9
	Add together the figures in boxes 2, 4, 5, 6, 7, 8 and 8a and enter the total in this box	10
	Deduct the figures in box 10 from the figures in box 9 and enter the answer in this box	11
	If the answer in box 11 is nil or a negative number there is no deemed payment	
	If the answer in box 11 is a positive number you will need to process this figure to get the deemed payment and the employer's Class 1 NIC on that deemed payment	

Step 8	Multiply the figure in box 11 by 100 and enter the answer in this box	12
	Divide the figure in box 12 by (100 + 12.8) and enter the answer in this box (case a), unless the figure in box 8 is less than the secondary Class 1 NIC earnings threshold, in which case complete the steps below (case b). The final figure in box 13 is the deemed payment	
	Case b: subtract the figure in box 8 from the Class 1 NIC earnings threshold and enter in this box	13a
	Case b: subtract the figure in box 13a from the figure in box 11 and enter in this box	13b
	Case b: divide the figure in box 13c by (100+12.8) (see footnote 1) and enter the answer in this box	13d
	Case b: add the figure in box 13d to the figure in box 13a and enter the answer in box 13	
Step 9	Deduct the figure in box 13 from the figure in box 11 and enter the amount you are left with in this box. This amount is the amount of employer's Class 1 NIC due on the deemed payment	14
	Enter the figure from box 13 in this box. This amount is the deemed payment	

1. The employer's contribution rate can vary. Contracted-out or contracted-in rates are different. The figure you add to 100 at this stage should be the contributions rate that is applicable to you. See HMRC National Insurance tables CA38 and the Employer's Annual Pack for further details

Source: HMRC

21.5 NON-RESIDENT LANDLORD SCHEME

If you rent a property from a non-resident landlord, you have an obligation to withhold basic rate tax and pay this over to HMRC each quarter. There are two main exceptions to this rule, ie where:

- the rent paid is less than £100 pw; or
- you have received confirmation from HMRC that you may make the payment gross.

If you are paying rent to a non-resident landlord you should contact:

HMRC Centre for Non-Residents
St John's House
Merton Road
Bootle
Merseyside L69 9BB.

HMRC will forward you a form to complete within 30 days of the end of each quarter, explaining how the tax is calculated and how to make a payment to the Accounts Office.

Example – Calculation of quarterly payment

> Tax is calculated at the basic rate on the rent due in the quarter less allowable expenses. Therefore, if the rent due in the quarter to 31 December 2011 is £3,000 but during the quarter you have paid £300 out of this sum to repair a broken window, then the calculation would be as follows:
>
> | | £ |
> |---|---|
> | Rent | 3,000 |
> | *Less*: Allowable expenses | (300) |
> | | 2,700 |
> | Tax at 20% | 540 |

No later than 5 July following the end of each tax year you must provide a return including details of the rent paid, allowable expenses and tax deducted. Within the same time frame you should also supply the landlord with a certificate of the tax deducted. The payments are dealt with by the Centre for Non-Residents (previously FICO) at the address above.

Landlords can obtain exemption from these provisions by entering the Non-Resident Landlords Scheme. If they do so, in return for undertaking to account for tax on their rental income, they will be permitted to receive rental payments without the deduction of any tax at source.

In order to qualify, at least one of the following conditions must apply:

- the landlord's UK tax affairs are up to date; or
- he or she has not had any UK tax obligations prior to applying; or
- he or she does not expect to be liable to UK income tax for the year in which he or she applies; or
- he or she is not liable to pay UK tax because he or she is a sovereign immune (these are generally foreign heads of state, governments or government departments).

21.6 NON-RESIDENT SPORTSMEN AND ENTERTAINERS

Basic rate tax must be withheld from most payments made to non-UK resident sportsmen and women and entertainers for work performed in the UK. In addition, where benefits-in-kind are provided to them, the cost must be 'grossed up' for tax at the basic rate and accounted for. A tax voucher must be provided for each payment and the person making the payments must account for tax on a quarterly basis.

21.6.1 **Payments caught by this scheme**

Payments or benefits subject to these regulations include:

- prize money;
- appearance or performance fees;
- endorsement fees where the individual has appeared in the UK (whether or not his or her appearance is to promote the goods he or she is endorsing);
- payments that finance any of the above (eg commercial sponsorship).

Certain payments specifically excluded from the scheme are those:

- subject to deduction of tax;
- subject to PAYE;
- solely for the use of copyright in words or music;
- made to the Performing Rights Society;
- made to UK residents and ancillary to a performance (including the cost of hiring a venue and payments for the services of UK-resident performers appearing with a non-resident);
- that are royalties on the sale of records and tapes; and
- amounting to less than £1,000 in a tax year. This de minimis limit applies to all payments made in a tax year in connection with the same event. Furthermore, payments made by the same or connected persons must be aggregated and the £1,000 exemption applies only if the total is less than £1,000.

Schedule 20 FA (No.1) 2010 also provides that, subject to conditions, where an employee or contractor of an overseas team which competes in the 2011 Champions League final is neither UK resident nor UK ordinarily resident at the time of the final, then the duty to deduct income tax (s 966 ITA 2007) will not apply.

21.6.2 **Special arrangements**

It is possible for a payer to secure HMRC's agreement to a lower rate of withholding tax provided an application is made at least 30 days in advance. Such authorisation may be given provided that:

- the organiser can arrange that he or she is responsible for accounting for the tax; or
- the sponsor can apply for clearance on the grounds that the tax will be collected from someone else; or
- to reflect the fact that the non-resident will have certain allowable expenses or perhaps because only some members of a group are non-resident. Expenses which may be taken into account include general subsistence expenses, UK and international travelling expenses, commission, manager's and agent's fees.

21.6.3 Indirect payments also caught

The regulations provide that the withholding system should also apply to payments made to any person:

- who is under the control of the non-resident sportsman or woman or entertainer;
- who is
  - not resident in the UK; and
  - not liable to tax in a territory outside the UK where the rate of tax charged on profits exceeds 20%;
- who receives a connected payment or value transferred by a connected transfer where there is a contract or arrangement under which it is reasonable to suppose that the entertainer (or other person connected with him or her) is, will or may become entitled to receive amounts not substantially less than the amount paid.

The High Court held that the obligation to withhold tax applied to payments made by non-resident companies, to a company owned by Andre Agassi (see *Agassi* v *Robinson* (2004) STC 610). This ruling was overturned in the Court of Appeal but was then upheld in the House of Lords.

21.6.4 Further information

See HMRC booklet FEU 50 *A Guide to Paying Foreign Entertainers*. This has recently been of considerable concern to foreign entertainers, sportspeople and their advisers. HMRC has completely changed its view regarding the basis on which the income to be subjected to UK tax is calculated. Firstly, HMRC is no longer willing to accept that an element of endorsement deals relates to passive income, but even worse, HMRC's view on the calculation of the apportionment fraction to the UK has also changed.

Instead of looking at days spent competing and preparing to compete, training and preparation is completely ignored and HMRC instead considers 'worldwide playing days', ie the days on which performers actually compete or perform. This could have the effect of halving (or worse) the denominator for a top level sports star.

The change in interpretation becomes even more disadvantageous for an individual who may only compete or perform two or three times in a typical year. Where previously, the number of days training and preparing per annum might have been over 300, based on worldwide competition and performance days, under the new interpretation, the denominator in the fraction would be only two or three. This means that if an individual plays one concert in New York and one in London, albeit he or she spends the bulk of time outside the UK practising and preparing to perform, half of all endorsement deals would be subject to UK tax.

21.7 OTHER PAYMENTS TO NON-UK RESIDENT PERSONS

21.7.1 Interest paid to non-resident lender

Tax at 20% must normally be deducted where interest is paid by a UK-resident person and the lender is not UK-resident. It may be possible for the lender to make a claim under a double taxation agreement and where such a claim has been made, HMRC may authorise payment of interest without deduction of tax.

Section 934 ITA 2007 contains provisions that enable a member of a group of companies to pay interest to another member of the group without deduction of tax provided that the overseas company trades in the UK via a permanent establishment and the payment is required to be brought into account in calculating the profits (within the meaning of s 19 CTA 2009) subject to UK tax.

21.7.2 Patent royalties paid to non-residents

Patent royalties paid to a non-resident are normally subject to deduction of basic rate tax. Companies may pay royalties without deducting tax if the recipient is a person resident in a country for which the relevant double tax treaty contains an exemption from UK tax. If it turns out that the exemption was not in fact due, the company paying the royalty will have to account for the tax that should have been withheld.

21.7.3 Copyright royalties

Copyright royalties paid to a non-resident are also normally subject to deduction of tax. Where the payment is made via a commission agent, basic rate tax must be withheld for the net amount paid on to the non-resident. The obligation to withhold tax does not apply where copyright payments are made to rights owners who are resident abroad and are not within the charge to UK income tax or corporation tax (ss 906(1)(b), 906(2) ITA 2007).

23.7.4 Purchase of British patent rights

There is an obligation for basic rate tax to be withheld where a person sells all or part of his or her patent rights and the vendor is not UK-resident. Once again, the provisions of a double taxation agreement may override this, but a person making payment for such rights must deduct tax unless he or she is authorised not to do so by HMRC.

22

OUTLINE OF VAT

NICK WARNER AND SARAH HALSTED

Value Added Tax (VAT) was introduced by FA 1972 and became operational on 1 April 1973. In concept, it is a simple tax, although various exclusions from the VAT charge and increasing European influence have resulted in that simple concept becoming one of the most complicated and fast changing taxes we have.

This chapter covers some of the detail of VAT under the following sections:

(1) Introduction
(2) Legal authorities
(3) Liability to VAT
(4) Practical implications
(5) Anti-avoidance measures
(6) Special schemes
(7) Control and enforcement procedures
(8) Fraud
(9) Appeals

22.1 INTRODUCTION

The introduction of VAT was a precondition of the UK's acceptance into the then European Economic Community (EEC) which, as a result of the European Communities Act 1982, became the European Community (EC), now commonly referred to as the European Union (EU). Part of the single market philosophy is the harmonisation of taxes, particularly those that affect cross-border trading activities, a good example of this being customs duty, which is payable whenever goods enter the EU and is charged at the same rate when or wherever the goods enter the Community.

The harmonisation of VAT has been the subject of much discussion by the EC Commission, resulting in the introduction of transitional rules with effect from 1 January 1993 and commonly referred to as the Single Market legislation. The rules implement a degree of harmonisation on the VAT accounting requirements for the movement of goods between member states. Further harmonisation has been agreed in respect of invoicing and, with effect from 1 January 2010, the cross border supply of services.

Several EC directives are the ultimate legal authority for VAT, and they must be reflected in the national legislation of each member state. To that extent, directives have what is known as 'direct effect'. For example, if national law is not in accordance with a directive and thereby disadvantages the taxpayer, the taxpayer can argue his or her case, using the directive, in the national court, which must recognise the directive, and with the ultimate right of appeal to the European Court of Justice (ECJ).

The UK administration of VAT was given to HM Customs & Excise, which introduced a completely new system of tax enforcement to the majority of businesses and the accounting profession. Customs & Excise, which was steeped in the history of duty enforcement, brought with it its practical approach to controlling the taxpayer. For the first time, many businesses and their professional advisers had to justify, face to face with the VAT control officer, what had been declared in the VAT return and the amounts shown in the annual accounts. Customs & Excise merged with HM Inland Revenue in April 2005 to form a new government department, HM Revenue & Customs (HMRC). This chapter will refer to the administrative authority for VAT as HMRC.

VAT is not, in principle, a tax on profits but a tax on transactions. VAT is a tax on the consumer that is collected in stages throughout the business chain and, eventually, by the business supplying the consumer, whether that be an individual, or a business that is not registered for VAT.

A business must account for VAT on its supplies ('outputs') but can deduct VAT on its expenditure ('input tax') thereby adding tax to the 'value'.

If a business fails to charge and account for VAT correctly, it must account for both the VAT and any penalties from its own resources and thereby, by default, VAT becomes a charge on profits. Put simply, the business is a tax collector.

For VAT purposes, the UK consists of England, Scotland, Wales, Northern Ireland and the Isle of Man; the Channel Islands are not included.

22.2 LEGAL AUTHORITIES

No single piece of legislation covers the administration and collection of VAT. The VAT legislation is described briefly below.

22.2.1 The VAT Act 1994 (VATA 1994)

This consolidation Act brought together VATA 1983 and subsequent Finance Acts amending the original legislation. It deals with the administration of the tax and provides for certain aspects to be dealt with by delegated legislation.

22.2.2 **VAT Regulations 1995**

This consolidated 60 sets of existing regulations and amendments introduced since 1972. It deals with a wide range of administrative procedures that must be complied with, for example the detail to be shown on tax invoices, the method of recovering VAT when a VAT-registered person is not entitled to a full recovery of VAT paid to his or her suppliers, and special VAT accounting procedures for particular transactions.

22.2.3 **Treasury Orders**

Certain Treasury Orders describe among other things what is or is not chargeable to VAT, and give certain organisations legal authority to recover VAT that would otherwise not be recoverable. Treasury Orders are published in the *London Gazette*.

22.2.4 **Public Notices, leaflets and Information Sheets**

Generally, VAT public notices are not part of the law, although certain notices are published pursuant to VATA 1994 and the VAT Regulations 1995 and, thereby, become part of the law. As such they have the same status as Acts of Parliament and are legally binding on the taxpayer. For example, Notice 700 (General Guide) is principally HMRC's interpretation of the law, but the section dealing with values expressed in a foreign currency is part of the law, as is much of the Public Notice on the special VAT Retail Schemes (Notice 727).

HMRC's leaflets are not strictly part of the law, but certain leaflets explaining HMRC's requirements for particular types of transactions have legal force. This applies to relatively few of the leaflets, the vast majority being simply HMRC's interpretation of the law.

22.2.5 **EC directives**

All VAT law now has its roots in European Council Directive 2006/112 on the common system of value added tax, which is implemented in the UK and other EU countries through their respective national laws. This Directive replaced the Sixth VAT Directive, which dated from 1977, and consolidated other EC legislation. There are still other EC directives (the Thirteenth Directive and Directive 2008/9) dealing with traders' rights to recover VAT incurred in countries other than their own.

22.3 **LIABILITY TO VAT**

Unless excluded by zero rating or one of the exemptions, VAT is chargeable on transactions in the UK when the goods or services are supplied 'in the course or furtherance of any business'. Services supplied free of charge are not subject to VAT. Supplies made outside the UK are outside the scope of UK VAT. There are complex rules for determining the place of supply and the rules differ depending on whether the supply is one of goods or services.

With effect from 1 January 2010, the default position for the place of supply of services between businesses is the country where the customer belongs. There are however a number of exceptions to this rule and professional advice should be taken if you are unsure about the place of supply of a transaction.

22.3.1 Business

(s 94 VATA 1994)

'Business' is not defined in VAT legislation, but has been widely interpreted to cover all organisations that carry on an activity in a business-like way. This has resulted in a number of organisations that do not consider themselves to be carrying on a business (eg charities) having to conform to VAT legislation and, where appropriate, register and account for VAT on their business income. In addition, the VAT legislation provides that certain organisations are deemed to be businesses (eg clubs and associations). If it can be demonstrated that an activity is a hobby, there is no requirement to charge VAT on any resulting income.

An employee's services to an employer in return for a salary meets the definition of a supply of services, but the law specifically provides that they are not in the course or furtherance of a business and so are outside the scope of VAT.

Charities

There is no automatic relief from VAT for supplies either to or by charities. A charity carrying on a business activity must register and account for VAT on its business income the same as any commercial organisation.

Certain supplies to charities are zero-rated (see 22.3.2), but these are mainly in the health and welfare area, and new commercial property used wholly for charitable non-business activities, known as 'qualifying buildings'. HMRC allows zero rating by concession where there is a small amount of business use (up to 5%) by the charity concerned.

Zero rating was extended in FA 2000 to include supplies of advertising when made to charities and all costs incurred in producing the advertising material when supplied with advertising. This includes pay-per-click advertising services on internet search engines. In addition certain goods used in connection with collecting monetary donations became zero-rated by concession from 1 April 2000.

A more generous relief from VAT for fundraising by charities was also introduced by FA 2000. This allows charities, in certain circumstances, to treat fundraising income as exempt from VAT.

Clubs and associations

(s 94(2)(a) VATA 1994)

Many local clubs and associations, including those formed by local residents, consider they are not carrying on a business, but this is not correct. The law specifically provides that the provision of benefits to members in return for a subscription or other payment is a business activity.

Certain trade and professional organisations consider they either are not in business or qualify for exemption as professional associations, and consequently have no requirement to register for VAT. Yet because they generally provide other benefits to their members and possibly non-members that are not within the exemption, they may be liable to register.

To avoid the risk of penalties all clubs, associations and similar organisations should review their activities to ensure they meet their VAT obligations at the correct time.

Admission to premises

(s 94(2)(b) VATA 1994)

Admitting persons to any premises in return for a payment is a business activity. Anyone carrying on such an activity must register and account for VAT if the income exceeds the registration threshold.

Under s33A VATA 1994, several national museums and galleries granting free admissions are treated in the same way as local authorities and similar organisations covered. Thus, these museums and galleries can recover VAT on related costs. The museums and galleries eligible to recover VAT on costs are chosen by the Treasury. Normally free admission is a non-business activity and museums and galleries granting free admission cannot recover VAT on costs although, from December 2001, certain national museums are permitted VAT recovery. A similar arrangement is being introduced from 1 April 2011 for Academies (schools).

22.3.2 Supplies

The application of VAT differs depending on whether there is a supply of goods or a supply of services.

A supply of goods is where title to the goods is, or is to be, transferred to another person. This includes, for example, the transfer of title in land by means of a freehold sale or a lease exceeding 21 years.

Anything that is not a supply of goods and supplied for a consideration is a supply of services. The definition is deliberately wide. For VAT to be charged on a supply, it must be a taxable supply made in the UK. This means that the supply must not fall within any of the categories of exempt supply (22.4.7). A charge to VAT arises only where consideration is present, so a free supply of services is outside the scope of VAT. Care is required, because what may appear to be free is not necessarily so in real terms and a hidden VAT liability could arise.

Taxable supplies

These are supplies subject to VAT at either the zero, reduced (see below) or the standard rate. There is no list of standard-rated goods or services. If a particular supply is not relieved from VAT by lower rating, zero rating or exemption, and is not treated as outside the scope, then the supply is by default standard-rated.

The standard rate of VAT is currently 20%. Prior to 4 January 2011 it was 17.5% except when it was temporarily reduced from 17.5% to 15% from 1 December 2008 to 31 December 2009.

Zero-rated supplies

Zero-rated supplies include exports of goods to places outside the EU (s 30(6) VATA 1994). Supplies of goods to VAT registered customers in other member states are zero-rated (s 30(8) VATA 1994). Other categories of zero-rated supplies are listed in Schedule 8 VATA 1994. The current groups in Schedule 8 are:

(1) Food for human consumption and animal feeding stuffs.
(2) Sewerage services and water (but not bottled water).
(3) Books and newspapers, etc.
(4) Talking books and wireless sets for the blind.
(5) Construction and sales of new dwellings (including sales of non-residential buildings converted to dwellings).
(6) Approved alteration of listed residential buildings and listed buildings used by charities for non-business purposes.
(7) International services (ie making arrangements for the export of goods outside the EU or work on goods that have been imported from outside the EU for repair and will be re-exported afterwards).
(8) Transport.
(9) Caravans and houseboats.
(10) Gold.
(11) Bank notes.
(12) Drugs, medicines, aids for the handicapped, etc.
(13) Imports, exports, etc.
(14) *This group has been deleted – it was tax-free shops.*
(15) Charities (certain supplies to or by charities).
(16) Clothing and footwear (children's and protective).
(17) Emissions allowances.

Reduced-rate supplies

VAT is charged on certain supplies of goods and services at a reduced rate, currently 5%. The categories of goods and services to which the lower rate applies are set out in Schedule 7A VATA 1994:

- Supplies of domestic fuel and power.
- Installation of energy-saving materials.
- Grant funded installation of heating equipment or security goods or connection of gas supply.
- Women's sanitary products.
- Children's car seats.
- Residential conversions.
- Residential renovations and alterations.
- Contraceptive products.
- Welfare advice or information.
- Installation of mobility aids for the elderly.
- Smoking cessation products.

Care is required when determining whether the zero or reduced rate applies. Only the group headings are shown above and there is extensive detail to consider.

Exempt

These are supplies that are exempt from VAT by statute, ie those listed in Schedule 9 VATA 1994 (see 22.4.7). The exemption rules are, in theory, the same throughout the EU whereas zero rating is a derogation from normal EU rules. Exemption and zero rating must not be confused because the overall effect on a business is totally different. As discussed below, zero rating gives entitlement to recover VAT on underlying costs whereas exemption does not.

VAT-exempt goods and services are listed in Schedule 9 VATA 1994. The main headings are:

- Land (with a number of exceptions, and see above).
- Insurance.
- Postal services.
- Betting, gaming and lotteries.
- Finance.
- Education (when provided by eligible bodies, which include youth clubs).
- Health and welfare.
- Burial and cremation.
- Trade unions, professional bodies and other public interest bodies.
- Sports, sports competitions and physical education.
- Works of art, etc (in limited circumstances).

- Fundraising events by charities and other qualifying bodies.
- Cultural services.
- Supplies of goods where input tax cannot be recovered.
- Investment gold.

As the headings are a general description and the rules for exemption can be complex, it is advisable to take professional advice before exempting a particular transaction.

'Outside the scope'

Certain supplies or business activities are outside the scope of VAT. For example, the supply of goods situated outside the UK, or services where the place of supply is treated as being outside the UK. There are also sundry business transactions which are not subject to VAT (eg transactions between companies in the same VAT group (see 22.4.1)).

VAT is recoverable, subject to partial exemption rules, on costs relating to supplies outside the UK (and therefore outside the scope of UK VAT) which would be taxable supplies if made in the UK.

Non-business activities are outside the scope. VAT is irrecoverable on costs relating to non-business activities. Examples of non-business activities include free supplies of services, donations, free entry to museums, etc.

22.3.3 Exports

Goods which are exported to a place outside the EU are zero-rated. This includes goods exported to the Channel Islands but not to the Isle of Man. Usually, it is only the final exporter who is allowed to zero rate his or her supply, although in certain cases zero rating is allowed one stage back from the last supply in the UK. Details can be found in HMRC Notices 703 and 704.

Exporters must be able to satisfy HMRC that the goods have been exported. Detailed records of exports must be retained. HMRC requirements are contained in Notice 703, parts of which have the force of law.

22.3.4 Imports

VAT is normally charged on the importation of goods into the UK from outside the EC. Payment of VAT is due at the time of importation, but can be deferred until the 15th day of the month following importation provided a deferment number is obtained. The VAT payable can be recovered as input tax, subject to the normal rules. Security may be required for VAT and duty payable in the form of a bank guarantee. Since 1 December 2003, the duty deferment scheme has been relaxed. Approved importers no longer have to provide security for the full amount of VAT deferred. Customs duties must still be fully secured. Businesses can apply to HMRC for approved importer status which will reduce bank charges as the guarantee will be either cancelled or reduced (if goods are liable to Customs duty).

22.3.5 European Community

The terms 'acquisitions' and 'despatches' replace 'imports' and 'exports' respectively for transactions with other member states. It is not necessary to make an import declaration on an acquisition of goods from a supplier in another EC country. Provided the customer gives his or her VAT registration number to the supplier, the supplier will not charge local VAT. However, VAT has to be declared to HMRC on the acquisition of goods by calculating the VAT on the amount payable and declaring the VAT in box 2 of the VAT return. The self-generated 'acquisition' VAT charge can be recovered as input tax in box 4 of the VAT return subject to the normal rules.

Subject to certain conditions (eg showing the customer's VAT number on each invoice), despatches or supplies to a customer registered for VAT in another EC country can be zero-rated. UK VAT is chargeable if the conditions cannot be met.

UK VAT is chargeable on goods provided to non-registered customers in other member states. However, where the supplier is responsible for delivery (eg mail order businesses) then distance selling rules apply. The effect of the distance selling rules is that, subject to turnover limits, suppliers have to register in the relevant customer member state.

22.3.6 Commercial property

The sale of the freehold of a new commercial property ('new' meaning less than three years old) is subject to standard rate VAT. The standard rate applies to all sales of a property within three years of completion. The grant of the freehold of 'old' commercial property or the grant of a leasehold interest in new or old property is exempt from VAT, but the landlord has the right to elect to waive the exemption and charge VAT on the sale or on rental payments, commonly known as 'the option to tax'. The major advantage of making an option to tax is that a landlord can recover VAT on costs relating to an opted property. The tenant can recover VAT charged on rent provided he or she is using the property for taxable purposes.

The option to tax election is not available for certain supplies where, at the time the interest was granted, there is an intention or expectation that the land will become 'exempt land'. In broad terms, exempt land is land or buildings used wholly or mainly for non-VATable purposes. See 22.5.6.

The legislation relating to the option to tax land and/or buildings was rewritten with effect from 1 June 2008. The intention was to simplify the legislation. It is also now possible, for the first time, for taxpayers to revoke an option to tax after 20 years. A number of associated changes were also made. For example, it is now possible to revoke an option within six months after it was made (the 'cooling off period') in limited circumstances.

22.3.7 Transfers of going concerns (TOGC)

The sale of a business as a going concern is, subject to certain conditions, outside the scope of VAT. The conditions can be found in Article 5 of the VAT (Special Provisions) Order 1995 (SI 1995/1268). This area has been the subject of extensive litigation and, if there is any doubt as to whether or not a transfer of trade and/or assets qualifies as a TOGC, advice should be sought. There are also special rules when a TOGC includes property.

22.4 PRACTICAL IMPLICATIONS

The administration of VAT is by a system of VAT registration, the submission of regular VAT returns and control verification visits (known as 'assurance visits') by HMRC.

22.4.1 VAT registration

Compulsory registration

Registration is required where a business or any other organisation makes taxable supplies over a predetermined limit. The limits, which are based on gross turnover, are increased each year, generally in line with inflation.

It is the person who is registered, not the business activity. Once registered, all business activities must be reflected in the VAT accounting records; for example, a solicitor VAT-registered as a sole proprietor must also include his or her farming or writing income in his or her VAT accounts.

Currently, registration is required when one of the following two conditions is satisfied:

(1) When, at the end of any month, the gross taxable turnover during the previous 12 months, on a rolling basis, exceeds £73,000 (£70,000 prior to 1 April 2011). Liability to VAT registration must be notified within 30 days and registration is effective from the first of the month following the month in which a liability to notify arose. For example, where taxable turnover in the 12 months to 31 May 2011 is, say, £75,000, notification must be made within 30 days (by 30 June 2011) and registration is effective from 1 July 2011. There is no VAT liability on income received prior to the effective date of registration.

(2) As soon as there are reasonable grounds to believe the value of taxable supplies to be made within the following 30 days will exceed £73,000 notification has to be made immediately. This rule catches large transactions (eg property sales). Registration is effective from the first day of the month in which the large transaction will take place.

Only taxable turnover (ie goods or services liable to VAT at either the zero, reduced or standard rate) is taken into consideration when determining whether there is a liability to register for VAT. Income that is exempt or outside the scope of VAT is ignored.

Voluntary registration

There is an entitlement to voluntarily register for VAT where the taxable turnover of the business is below the VAT registration limits. This could be an advantage to a small or expanding business as VAT on costs is recoverable and, providing the VAT charge on supplies does not reduce demand for the product, will increase profitability. Businesses based in the UK that do not make any supplies in the UK but make what would be taxable supplies overseas are entitled to register and can thereby recover VAT on UK costs.

VAT groups

Incorporated companies under common control may register as a single unit – a VAT group. All supplies between the companies in the VAT group are disregarded for VAT purposes; ie no VAT charge arises. One company is nominated as the representative member and is responsible for submitting the VAT returns and accounting for VAT on all supplies to or received from persons outside the group. There is joint and several liability on all companies within a VAT group for any VAT due to HMRC. This means HMRC can recover a debt by a member of a VAT group from any other member of the group. HMRC has extensive powers to refuse to allow VAT grouping but in practice only uses its powers where it considers there is an avoidance motive to grouping (for further comment see 22.5.5).

The UK's practice of allowing 'non-taxable' companies to join VAT groups has been challenged by the European Commission and is expected to lead to infraction proceedings in the ECJ. This could result in additional restrictions to certain types of companies' eligibility to join a VAT group registration, particularly holding companies and dormant companies.

22.4.2 Tax invoices

A tax invoice containing specified details must be issued by a VAT-registered person in the following circumstances:

- when a standard- or reduced-rate supply is made to another taxable person;
- a supply, other than an exempt supply, is made to a person in another member state of the EU.

The details required are set out in Regulation 14 to the VAT (General) Regulations 1995. Issuing invoices by electronic means is permitted, provided the invoices are electronically signed and their authenticity and integrity can be guaranteed.

Where the value of a supply does not exceed £250, a document referred to as a 'less-detailed tax invoice' can be issued. In addition to the supplier's name, address and VAT registration number, the document need only include time of supply, description, total amount payable (including VAT) and the VAT rate in force.

22.4.3 Time of supply

VAT has to be accounted for in the VAT accounting period (22.4.4) in which the time of supply (or tax point) occurs.

The basic tax point is determined in accordance with rules set out in s 6 VATA 1994. These rules are different depending on whether the supply is goods or services (22.3.2). The basic tax point for goods is the date the goods are sent to or made available to the customer. For services, the basic tax point is the date the service is performed.

However, if an invoice is issued or any payment is received before the basic tax point, the date of issue or receipt creates a tax point that overrides the basic tax point date.

Another tax point rule allows for an invoice issued after the basic tax point to become the actual overriding tax point. This is provided the invoice is issued within 14 days of the basic tax point.

There are also rules for particular circumstances including continuous supplies of services. The tax point rules are complex and if in doubt professional advice should be sought.

22.4.4 VAT returns

Once a business is registered, VAT returns must be submitted on a regular basis. Each VAT-registered person is allocated a three-monthly VAT accounting period, but it is possible to request particular VAT periods (eg to coincide with the business's financial year). It is also possible to request monthly returns if the business regularly recovers VAT from HMRC.

Returns must be submitted, with full payment, by the end of the month following the end of the VAT accounting period. Failure to submit returns and make full payment by the due date is penalised by a default surcharge (see 22.7.2). There is an automatic seven-day extension to the due date for electronic payments. Payment of VAT by direct debit is also available (payment is taken ten days after the due date).

For VAT periods beginning on or after 1 April 2010, most businesses are obliged to submit their VAT returns online (this will apply for all businesses from 1 April 2012). The current exceptions are businesses already registered for VAT before this date whose annual turnover does not exceed £100,000, some insolvent businesses and those that can satisfy HMRC that they have a religious objection to the use of electronic communications.

The VAT chargeable on supplies made during the period (known as 'output tax') must be declared on the VAT return. Output tax is due on all tax invoices issued during the period, irrespective of whether they have been paid. Special schemes are available to ease this particular requirement for certain classes of business, as explained in 22.6. In addition, VAT is also due on all monies received for supplies made during the period and for which a tax invoice has not been issued, for example scrap sales, vending machine income, emptying phone boxes, staff canteen sales, and certain deductions from salaries for supplies to staff.

For businesses that do not issue tax invoices (eg retailers), VAT is due on the gross taxable income received during the VAT period.

Payments on account

Businesses that normally pay more than £2.3m annually to HMRC must make monthly payments on account with a balancing payment when the three-monthly VAT return is submitted; payments must be made by electronic means. Monthly payments on account are 1/24th of the annual VAT liability. Businesses have the option of paying their actual monthly VAT liability instead of the set amount. Unfortunately, payments on account are subject to the default surcharge (see 22.7.2) and the seven-day period of grace given to taxpayers who pay their VAT liability by electronic means does not extend to businesses that have to pay on account.

22.4.5 **VAT recovery**

VAT-registered businesses may offset any VAT paid to suppliers (known as 'input tax') against the output tax declared, subject to the following conditions:

- goods/services have been supplied to and have been, or will be, used by the business to make taxable supplies;
- documentary evidence of the supply received, ie a tax invoice, is obtained and retained.

If there is no tax invoice or other documentary evidence, HMRC will normally refuse claims for input tax. However, HMRC has discretion and may accept other evidence of VAT paid.

Supplies of zero-rated and reduced-rated goods or services are taxable supplies with an entitlement to recover VAT on related costs, whereas there is no such entitlement in respect of exempt supplies.

VAT is recoverable on the purchase of a motor car used wholly for business purposes. HMRC interprets 'wholly for business purposes' strictly, and in practice most businesses, with the exception of car leasing companies, cannot recover the VAT.

VAT is recoverable on buying road fuel for business purposes, but unless business mileage is logged, VAT on private use of the fuel has to be declared using the scale charges laid down. The amount of VAT to be declared depends on the engine size and type of vehicle. Since 1 May 2007, the VAT chargeable on private use of fuel has been based on the vehicle's CO_2 emissions.

The rules were amended with effect from 1 March 2000 to allow for the sale of items to be treated as exempt where input tax deduction on the purchase of the item had previously been blocked. This follows an ECJ decision against the Italian Government in favour of an appeal made by a taxpayer.

VAT is not recoverable on business entertainment expenses, although it is expected that changes will be made to allow some VAT on entertainment of overseas customers to be allowed from 1 May 2011. In addition, VAT on goods or services received by the VAT-registered person and used for either a non-business activity or private use is not recoverable as input tax. Many people believe that merely because a VAT-registered person pays an invoice, there is an automatic entitlement to recover the VAT shown on it. This belief is not correct and recovery of VAT that is not input tax may give rise to penalties. Where assets are purchased and used for both business and private (non-business) purposes, taxpayers should normally apportion input tax at source between business and non-business use. An alternative approach, known as *Lennartz* accounting, allows VAT to be recovered in full at the time of purchase, with output tax to be accounted for on non-business use over a set number of years, however recent EU case law has curtailed the use of this approach. *Lennartz* is no longer available for corporate bodies or charities and similar organisations and, with effect from 1 January 2011, can no longer be used to apportion VAT incurred on land and property purchases.

The recovery of VAT by businesses that make both taxable and exempt supplies is described in 22.4.7.

Bad debt relief

A claim for bad debt relief may be made for any debt that is more than six months old. A claimant used to have to notify VAT-registered debtors of his or her claim within seven days of making it. However, for supplies made after 1 January 2003 such notification is not required. Businesses that have not paid for supplies within six months of the due date for payment will have to repay the input tax to HMRC automatically and regardless of whether the supplier has made a bad debt relief claim.

Once a debt is six months old and providing the VAT has previously been accounted for to HMRC, the debt may be written off by being entered in a Refund for Bad Debt Account (ie not written off in the accounting sense, as for corporation tax). The VAT is recovered by including the sum in Box 4 (input tax recovery). Any payment received after the claim has been made is VAT inclusive and the VAT element must be repaid to HMRC. VAT bad debt relief is not available for businesses that use either a retail scheme or the cash accounting scheme; as such relief is automatically built into such schemes.

22.4.6 Time limit for refund claims

Claims for refunds of overpaid VAT are now limited to a period of four years. The time limit was three years until April 2009. HMRC's power to issue assessments for underdeclared VAT is also limited to the same period.

However, there is a 20-year limit in cases of fraud. It should be noted that there is currently a series of challenges to the way the three-year cap was introduced in 1996, ie relating to the lack of a proper transitional period following a decision from the ECJ in the case of *Marks & Spencer*. A number of recent cases have been won by taxpayers at both tribunal and court level and there could be a further reference to the European Court in future.

22.4.7 Partial exemption

A business that makes both exempt and taxable supplies is known as 'partly exempt' and is generally unable to recover all VAT paid to its suppliers. Partly exempt businesses have to adopt a method of calculating recoverable VAT. The only method which can be used without HMRC's written approval is the standard method. This method apportions VAT incurred in the ratio of taxable to total income, eg if 50% of income is taxable then 50% of VAT on costs which are not directly related to taxable or exempt supplies, ie general overheads, can be recovered.

Partial exemption calculations are normally carried out on a provisional basis on quarterly or monthly VAT returns, with a set annual adjustment taking place at the end of the partial exemption year, where the calculations from all four quarters (or twelve months) are consolidated, a percentage calculated for the year, and adjustments to input tax, either under or over, are accounted for on the VAT return.

If any other method of calculating recoverable VAT is required the method has to be negotiated with and agreed in writing by HMRC. Methods other than the standard method are known as special methods. Since 1 April 2007 businesses submitting applications for special methods have been required to declare that the proposed special method is fair and reasonable.

If the VAT on costs relating, directly and indirectly, to the exempt activities (known as 'exempt input tax') is below prescribed limits (known as 'de minimis limits'), all the VAT incurred is recoverable in full. The current limits are that the exempt input tax must not exceed £625 pm on average and 50% of the total input tax incurred. This means that a business can incur approximately £7,500 of VAT per annum on costs that relate to its exempt activities without having to restrict its recovery of input tax (provided the 50% qualification is not breached). Once the exempt input tax limit is exceeded in any VAT year (the VAT year ends in March, April or May depending on the business's VAT return period), all the relevant VAT is irrecoverable, ie the £625 pcm is not an automatic entitlement.

There are other minor limits that apply in particular circumstances. The rules are complex and it is advisable to obtain professional advice. Full details may be found in the VAT Regulations 1995 (SI No 2518), Regulations 99–111 and VAT Notice 706.

One situation where partial exemption can arise, which has been of particular significance recently, is where house builders let dwellings before selling them. Many house builders can recover all their input tax because the sale or first grant of a 'major interest' in a dwelling is standard-rated for VAT purposes. The letting of a dwelling, in contrast, is an exempt supply. HMRC VAT Information Sheet 07/08 (September 2008) explains the issues and implications.

22.4.8 Capital goods scheme

Certain capital expenditure used for partly exempt purposes and for non-business use is also subject to adjustments under the capital goods scheme. Under the scheme, adjustments are made to take account of any change in the extent to which the asset is put to a taxable use. All businesses are required to maintain records of any capital items described below.

The scheme applies to:

- the purchase of single items of computer equipment costing £50,000 or more (adjustments must be carried out over a period of five years);
- taxable land and property purchases, civil engineering works, property extensions and refurbishments, each where the value is at least £250,000 (adjustments must be carried out over a period of ten years);
- ships and aircraft costing £50,000 or more.

22.5 ANTI-AVOIDANCE MEASURES

Several anti-avoidance measures are available to HMRC. These include the following.

22.5.1 Business splitting

Where a business activity has been divided among a number of legal entities (eg a series of partnerships with a partner common to all) and the reason for splitting the business is to avoid accounting for VAT, HMRC may issue a direction informing all the businesses that they are registered as a single unit (see 22.4.1) and that VAT must be accounted for on all taxable income. The direction can only take effect from a current or future date.

HMRC is not obliged to prove the division was for VAT avoidance; it can treat connected businesses as one entity for VAT purposes, whether or not there is genuine commercial reason for the division.

22.5.2 Sales to connected parties

Where a VAT-registered business supplies goods or services at below market value to a connected party that is not entitled to a full recovery of input tax, HMRC may direct at any time, during the three years following the supply, that VAT is accounted for on the open market value.

22.5.3 Self supplies, etc

In certain circumstances, an output VAT charge will arise on normal business activities that are not supplies made to third parties, ie a VAT charge arises on business expenditure (usually referred to as 'self supplies'). The value of such supplies is taken into consideration when determining a liability to register for VAT; the more important ones are described below. The reasons behind such a liability are both anti-avoidance and to reduce possible trade distortion.

Reverse charges

Since 1 January 2010, the scope of reverse charges has been greatly widened and most B2B (business to business) services purchased from overseas persons give rise to an output tax liability on the recipient. The services are deemed to be both supplied and received by the UK organisation, ie there is an output tax liability, and the VAT may also be recovered under the normal rules (restricted if partly exempt). Exceptions to this general rule are listed in Schedule 4A VATA 1994 and include services related to land, passenger transport, restaurant and catering services, hire of goods, telecom and broadcasting services and, from 1 January 2011, cultural, artistic, sporting, scientific, educational and entertainment services, including fairs and exhibitions.

Services purchased from abroad on a B2C (business to non-business customer) basis are generally taxed in the country where the service provider belongs. Again, exceptions to this are listed in Schedule 4A VATA 1994.

HMRC has also obtained derogations to use the reverse charge as an anti-avoidance measure on certain B2B transactions, eg mobile phones, computer chips and trading in emissions allowances. This means suppliers will not charge VAT (customers will apply the reverse charge), thereby reducing the scope for VAT fraud.

Joint and several liability

The VAT legislation provides that VAT-registered purchasers of certain goods can be held jointly and severally liable for any VAT unpaid in the supply chain. This is provided the purchaser has reasonable grounds for suspecting VAT would be unpaid. This measure was first applied to mobile phones and computer chips but since 1 May 2007 has applied to electronic equipment used by individuals for leisure, amusement or entertainment purposes.

22.5.4 Transfer of a business to a partly exempt VAT group

Where the assets of a business are transferred to another person who intends to use them to carry on the same kind of business as the vendor, the transaction is not subject to a VAT charge (22.3.7). However, where a partly exempt VAT group (ie a VAT group that is not entitled to a full recovery of input tax) acquires assets in these circumstances, there is a deemed taxable supply by the VAT group and output tax must be accounted for on its VAT return. There are a number of conditions that may reduce the amount of this charge. This is a complex area, and professional advice should be sought. The corresponding input tax will be restricted by whatever method has been agreed with the local VAT office.

22.5.5 Group registration

HMRC can, in exceptional circumstances, direct that VAT be charged on intra-group supplies, which are normally disregarded for VAT purposes. In addition, it can treat an associated company as part of a VAT group retrospectively from a particular date or remove a VAT group member from that group with effect from a particular date.

These powers are used only where the group structure will result in a loss of tax revenue; they are designed to have effect only in cases involving VAT avoidance. HMRC consulted with professional bodies and issued a statement of practice (SP 6/1996) in May 1996. The statement of practice gives examples of proposed structures where the powers will be used.

HMRC is also able to remove companies that are no longer eligible from a VAT group and also has the power to remove companies where it appears to be necessary for the protection of the revenue.

Overseas companies are not eligible to be included in VAT groups unless they have a branch or substantial business establishment in the UK.

22.5.6 Option to tax commercial property

The option to tax the grant of freehold or leasehold interests in commercial property is not available in certain circumstances if the purchaser or tenant does not use the property wholly or mainly for taxable purposes. This is to counter avoidance by businesses which are not entitled to recover all or any of the input tax they incur on purchase or major construction work on land and property.

Landlords and vendors of commercial property must enquire about a tenant's or purchaser's legal relationship with the vendor, the financing arrangements and likely use of the property as, if the option is disapplied, this may affect the landlord's or vendor's right to recover VAT on related costs. Indemnity clauses may therefore need to be inserted into leases and agreements. A full discussion of these anti-avoidance provisions is beyond the scope of this book; those entering into property transactions should seek professional advice, as this is a complex area and the cost of 'getting it wrong' may be considerable.

22.5.7 Disclosure of VAT schemes

New rules were introduced with effect from 1 August 2004 requiring users of tax avoidance schemes designated by HMRC, to notify HMRC (on the relevant VAT return) that the scheme has been used in the period concerned. HMRC has published a list of the designated schemes which includes schemes relating to land and property, value shifting arrangements, various cash-flow saving schemes where goods are supplied on approval or sale or return, and credit card or cash handling services provided as an intermediary for a retailer. The list is updated from time to time, to include new arrangements that have come to HMRC's attention.

Smaller businesses will not need to report the use of designated schemes. Smaller businesses are those with a turnover below £600,000 in the year immediately preceding the VAT accounting period that triggers notification, or where the turnover in the immediately preceding VAT accounting period is less than £50,000 (monthly returns) or £150,000 (quarterly returns).

Businesses which have a turnover above £10m in the year immediately preceding the VAT accounting period that triggers notification, or where the turnover in the immediately preceding VAT accounting period is less than £833,334 (monthly returns) or £2.5m (quarterly returns) are required to report the use of any scheme where the main purpose is to save VAT and the scheme arrangements include a published list of specific provisions known as 'hallmarks'. These include agreements to share tax savings with another party or adviser, where contingency fees will be paid and where consideration for a supply is given by a loan or by subscription for shares between connected parties.

Businesses that are currently considering putting VAT saving arrangements in place should take professional advice and consider the most current list of designated schemes and hallmarks published by HMRC. Full details can be found in Public Notice 700/8.

22.6 SPECIAL SCHEMES

Several special schemes are either designed to simplify accounting for VAT or reduce the VAT liability.

22.6.1 Flat-rate scheme for small businesses

A flat-rate scheme for VAT-registered small businesses was introduced on 25 April 2002. The turnover test was simplified from April 2009. A business can use the scheme where its taxable turnover in the next year is expected to be £150,000 or less and its total business income is expected to be £187,500 or less. A business that elects to use the flat-rate scheme will simply account for VAT at a flat-rate percentage of its turnover rather than on every single transaction. The flat-rate percentage applied depends on the trade sector of the business concerned, and is calculated to include relief for input tax. It is not possible to use cash accounting (see 22.6.4) with a flat-rate scheme, but the flat-rate scheme in any case has its own cash basis. HMRC has published full details of the scheme in VAT Notice 733.

22.6.2 Retail schemes

These are special schemes used by retailers, ie businesses that sell, hire or repair goods direct to the general public rather than to other VAT-registered businesses and are in trade classification Groups 24 (Retail Division) and 28 (Miscellaneous Services). Generally the schemes are for those businesses which deal direct with the public on a cash basis and who do not normally issue tax invoices.

Use of retail schemes is however restricted. Taxpayers are only allowed to use a retail scheme when normal VAT accounting is not possible. Further information on specific schemes can be found in notices:

- 727/2 Bespoke retail schemes
- 727/3 How to work the Point of Sale scheme
- 727/4 How to work the Apportionment schemes
- 727/5 How to work the Direct Calculation schemes.

As retailers normally account for VAT on receipt of payment, retail schemes provide automatic bad debt relief, although retailers must account for VAT on all credit sales at the time of sale.

22.6.3 Second-hand schemes

The second-hand scheme allows suppliers to charge and account for VAT on the profit, if any, as opposed to the full selling price, provided the goods have not been acquired with VAT thereon. The scheme is currently available for sales of the following:

- supplies of works of art, antiques and collectors items;
- supplies of motor vehicles;
- supplies of second-hand goods;
- any supply of goods through an agent acting in his or her own name.

Special stock recording and records are required.

Dealers in low-value, high-volume goods have difficulty maintaining the detailed records required, so may use a simplified VAT accounting method, 'Global Accounting'. Under this method, 'eligible businesses' can account for VAT on the difference between total purchases and sales in each tax period rather than on individual items.

22.6.4 Cash accounting

The general principle is that VAT must be accounted for on all tax invoices issued, whether or not the customer/client has paid for the supply. Businesses that cannot use a retail scheme and have a turnover of less than £1.35m pa excluding VAT (since 1 April 2007; previously the limit was £600,000), may use the cash accounting scheme, provided certain conditions are satisfied. The conditions are laid down in regulations as described in HMRC Notice 731, which in this respect has the force of law. Output VAT is not due until payment has been received but, similarly, input tax on purchases/expenses cannot be recovered until the supplier has been paid and a receipt obtained. Once a business has joined the scheme it may continue to use it until the annual value of its taxable supplies (including the disposal of stock and capital assets, but excluding VAT), reaches £1.6m. If this figure is exceeded, the business will have to leave the scheme at the end of its current VAT period and use the normal method of accounting in future.

22.6.5 Annual accounting

To avoid having to submit returns quarterly, businesses with an annual turnover not exceeding £1.35m (excluding VAT) may be authorised, in writing, by HMRC to use the annual accounting scheme. Nine monthly payments or three quarterly payments, in either case based on the previous year's VAT liability, are made by direct debit and a final, balancing payment is made with the VAT return at the end of the second month following the allocated VAT year.

The annual accounting scheme can be combined with the flat-rate scheme, under which a business can account for VAT as a flat-rate percentage of its turnover. The applicable percentage depends on the business sector concerned. A business can apply to join the flat-rate scheme if its taxable turnover in the next year will be £150,000 or less and its total business income will be £187,500 or less.

22.6.6 Tour operators' margin scheme

This scheme must be used by any VAT-registered business that supplies packaged travel/accommodation services. As the name implies, VAT is accountable on the margin, if any, on the taxable element of the package. Special record keeping and an annual calculation are required.

22.6.7 Agricultural flat-rate scheme

This is a special scheme under which farmers and other agricultural businesses need not register and submit VAT returns in order to recover VAT on overhead expenses, etc. Instead, the farmer charges VAT at a nominal 4% on all his or her supplies that he or she retains (in lieu of input tax). The recipient is entitled to recover the charge as input tax under the normal rules. The scheme requires authorisation by HMRC and is not applicable to all farmers: farmers who would benefit by more than £3,000 pa compared with being VAT registered are not entitled to join the scheme.

22.7 CONTROL AND ENFORCEMENT PROCEDURES

22.7.1 VAT visits

HMRC officers regularly visit VAT-registered businesses to verify the returns submitted. Their powers are extensive and include the right to see any documents, accounts, etc relating to the business activities, and to inspect (but not search) the business premises. The frequency of visits depends on a number of factors such as business size, types of business activity and compliance history. Visits can range from half a day every few years for smaller business to several weeks a year for multinationals.

Where errors are discovered, the visiting officer will raise an assessment for any VAT previously underdeclared and, where appropriate, impose penalty and interest charges (see 22.7.2). It is therefore advisable to have all assessments independently reviewed.

22.7.2 Penalties

HMRC may impose a number of penalties, automatically and arbitrarily, for failure to comply with the many complex VAT regulations. The penalty provisions were introduced with a view to improving compliance and reducing the amount of VAT outstanding at any one time.

HMRC is currently in the process of modernising and harmonising its penalties for all taxes, including VAT. New provisions have recently been introduced in respect of late registration, incorrect VAT returns and voluntary disclosures, while further changes to the penalties affecting late VAT returns are expected in the near future.

Broadly speaking, the new penalties are based on behaviour and degrees of culpability. For the purposes of calculating a penalty, an error or failure is deemed to be:

- 'careless' if it is due to the taxpayer's failure to take reasonable care;
- 'deliberate but not concealed' if it was deliberate but the taxpayer does not make arrangements to conceal it;
- 'deliberate and concealed' if it is deliberate and the taxpayer makes arrangements to conceal it, eg by submitting false evidence to support an error or failure.

HMRC can waive penalties if the taxpayer can show that they had a reasonable excuse for failing to comply with the VAT rules. However, HMRC regards most errors as, at minimum, 'careless', so the potential for incurring a penalty is high.

Late registration

(Schedule 41 FA 2008)

A new penalty system for the belated notification of a liability to register for VAT was introduced with effect from 1 April 2010.

The standard penalties are as follows:

- a deliberate or concealed act or failure – up to 100% of the potential lost revenue;
- a deliberate but not concealed act or failure – up to 70% of the lost revenue;
- for other cases – up to 30% of the lost revenue.

Where the obligation to register arose before 1 April 2010, HMRC has the power under the previous legislation (s 67 VATA 1994) to impose a penalty of between 5% and 15% (depending on the length of the delay) of the net tax due between the date notification was required and the actual date of notification.

Late payments

(s 59 VATA 1994)

If one payment is submitted late in any 12-month period, HMRC issues a Surcharge Liability Notice to notify the VAT-registered person that payments submitted late during the following 12 months will be subject to a default surcharge of the specified percentage (see below) or £30, whichever is greater.

If a payment is submitted late during the 12-month surcharge period, a 2% penalty is imposed and the surcharge period extended for a further 12 months. The surcharge rises for each successive late payment during the surcharge period; for the second, to 5%; for the third, to 10%; and for the fourth and any further defaults, to the maximum of 15%. If payments have been submitted by the due dates for a full 12 months after the last penalty was imposed, the business is removed from the default surcharge regime and the cycle starts again.

Since December 2001, HMRC has waived the surcharge where it is assessable at the 2% or 5% rates and below a minimum amount of £400. However, the Surcharge Liability Notice period will be extended to 12 months from the date of the default, and any following defaults in that period remain liable to surcharges.

Businesses may appeal against the imposition of a surcharge on the grounds that they had a reasonable excuse for the default – either by asking HMRC to review the decision, or appealing to a tribunal.

In the 2010 *Enersys* case, a large energy company, operating non-standard tax periods, had misunderstood the due date of its VAT return and submitted the return and payment just one day late, resulting in a surcharge of over £130,000. The First-tier Tribunal ruled that the penalty should be withdrawn, stating that no reasonable court or tribunal would impose such a high penalty for an error of this kind. The *Enersys* decision does not, however, set out clearly quantifiable limits to decide where the line should be drawn between a fair surcharge and an excessive one.

This is the first time that a tribunal has quashed a default surcharge on the grounds of proportionality. However, HMRC has not changed its system following the decision. Despite this, a business that has incurred substantial surcharges in similar circumstances should consider asking HMRC to reconsider the surcharge in the light of the *Enersys* decision.

A new penalty regime, which is to replace the current surcharge system for late VAT returns, was announced in the 2010 Budget. So far, no firm implementation date has been announced, but the new system is expected to introduce separate penalties for late submission and late payment of VAT returns, plus additional penalties if the return remains outstanding at six or 12 months past its due date.

Penalties for incorrect returns or claims

(Schedule 24 FA 2007)

A new penalty regime, relating to incorrect returns for income tax, corporation tax, PAYE, NIC and VAT, came into force on 1 April 2008 in respect of documents relating to tax periods starting on or after that date. No-one will however be liable to a penalty under the new regime in respect of a tax period for which a return is required to be made before 1 April 2009.

Under the new regime the penalties are as follows:

- for careless action – up to 30% of the potential lost revenue;
- for deliberate but not concealed action – up to 70% of the potential lost revenue;
- for deliberate and concealed action – up to 100% of the potential lost revenue.

HMRC has the power to conditionally suspend a penalty for a careless error for up to two years.

Voluntary disclosures

Errors in VAT periods beginning on or after 1 July 2008 may be corrected on a subsequent VAT return, subject to the following limits:

- where the turnover in Box 6 of the VAT return is less than £5m, the greater of £10,000 or 1% of that turnover;
- where the turnover in Box 6 of the VAT return is £5m or more, £50,000.

Errors where the net tax exceeds these thresholds must be specifically disclosed to HMRC in writing. (The limit applicable to VAT periods beginning before 1 July 2008 was £2,000.) Where the error has resulted in an underpayment of VAT, HMRC may charge interest on this type of voluntary disclosure.

HMRC may decide not to impose a penalty, provided it is satisfied that the disclosure is voluntary and unprompted. HMRC also has the power to reduce penalties in the case of an unprompted disclosure of a deliberate error. Once an attempt to arrange an assurance visit is made by an officer, HMRC normally considers the point of voluntary disclosure to have passed.

Interest

(s 74 VATA 1994)

An interest charge is imposed on assessments for additional tax issued by VAT visiting officers. The interest rate is the prescribed rate as enacted by Treasury order and is not deductible for income or corporation tax. HMRC has stated that interest may not be imposed where there is no overall loss of revenue, for example where a supplier has failed to charge VAT to a customer who would have been entitled to recover the VAT charge. HMRC has indicated that each case will be decided on its merits, but that officers have been made aware of the need to consider whether there has been a loss of revenue.

It should be noted that, in some circumstances, interest is payable from HMRC to the taxpayer where VAT has been overpaid or under-recovered due to an official error. The legislation currently provides for the payment of simple interest only on sums refunded by HMRC. There are several (direct tax and indirect tax) cases currently going to appeal on the question of whether EU law requires compound interest to be paid. This is a very complex area, and an analysis of the relevant case law is worthy of a book of its own, so it will not be addressed further here.

Other penalties

There are other penalty provisions which may be levied for various failures and inaccuracies. A discussion of these is beyond the scope of this book: however, they include failure to keep or produce records, unauthorised issue of a tax invoice (by non-registered persons), failure to notify use of certain avoidance schemes, failure to comply with the duties of senior accounting officers, incorrect issue of certificates to support zero-rating and inaccuracies in or failure to submit EC Sales Lists.

22.8 FRAUD

There are two forms of fraud in VAT law: civil and criminal.

22.8.1 Civil

(s 60 VATA 1994)

The civil penalties for dishonesty under s 60 have been largely superseded by the new penalties for incorrect declarations and failure to comply with VAT obligations. These civil fraud provisions will, however, remain in effect with respect to dishonest conduct which does not relate to an inaccuracy in a document or a failure to notify HMRC of an underassessment by HMRC.

If, after an investigation, HMRC is satisfied there has been an element of dishonesty, it may seek to impose a civil fraud penalty of 100% of the tax involved. If there has been full co-operation by the taxpayer, HMRC, or (on appeal) a VAT tribunal, may reduce the penalty by whatever percentage is considered reasonable.

22.8.2 Criminal

(s 72 VATA 1994)

The more serious cases are dealt with under the criminal law with a fine or imprisonment, or both. In these cases HMRC must use the criminal rules of evidence, etc and prove beyond reasonable doubt that a fraud has been committed deliberately. HMRC may accept a financial settlement in lieu of criminal proceedings.

22.9 APPEALS

22.9.1 VAT tribunals

There is a right of appeal to an independent Tribunal on a number of matters, including:

- assessments considered to be incorrect or not issued to the Commissioners' best judgement;
- liability rulings by HMRC in respect of a specified supply;
- penalties, other than the interest charged for errors, if there is a reasonable excuse for the error. (The law does not define 'reasonable excuse' but does state that insufficiency of funds or reliance on another is not a reasonable excuse.)
- the amount of the reduction, if any, of a penalty for civil fraud where the taxpayer considers he or she has provided full co-operation with the investigating officers.

In April 2009 a single tax appeal system was introduced for VAT and direct taxes, comprising a First-tier Tribunal and an Upper Tribunal. The First-tier Tribunal will hear most tax appeals; the Upper Tribunal will hear appeals against the decisions of the First-tier tribunal and may also hear some first instance appeals.

The details of appeal procedures are outside the scope of this book. However, the procedure for lodging an appeal to a tribunal (which must be made within 30 days of the appealable decision) is straightforward. It is prudent to obtain professional advice before appealing and it is advisable to be represented at the tribunal hearing, which in many ways resembles a court hearing, although less formal.

A First-tier Tribunal decision may be appealed against to the Upper Tribunal on a point of law and, in some circumstances, an appeal may be referred to the ECJ for a ruling.

Where a dispute arises over an issue that does not constitute an appealable decision (eg unreasonable delays by HMRC or refusal to apply a concessionary VAT treatment), the taxpayer cannot appeal to the tribunal. The matter can however be pursued through one of the following channels:

- complaining to HMRC, either to the officer involved or the Regional Complaints Unit;
- complaining to the independent Adjudicator;
- complaining to a Member of Parliament;
- an application to the High Court for a judicial review.

22.9.2 Departmental reviews

(ss 83A–83G VATA 1994)

Many disputes are settled by negotiation with HMRC by formally requesting a departmental review of the disputed ruling/assessment within the 30-day time limit. This allows discussions to continue without the loss of the right to appeal to the tribunal.

The review is carried out by a review officer who was not previously involved in the disputed decision. Unless it agrees a longer review period with the taxpayer, HMRC must complete the review within 45 days. A review is not compulsory and the taxpayer is entitled to appeal to tribunal without requesting a departmental review first.

23

NATIONAL INSURANCE CONTRIBUTIONS

BRIAN LOVIE

This chapter covers the following topics:

(1) Class 1 contribution
(2) Class 2 contribution
(3) Class 3 contribution
(4) Class 4 contribution

Where rates are quoted, they are the 2011–12 rates; these and the 2010–11 rates can be found in Table 23.1 (see 23.4).

23.1 CLASS 1 CONTRIBUTION

23.1.1 Introduction

Employed individuals are liable for Class 1 NIC unless they are under 16 or have reached pensionable age. Secondary contributions are paid by employers (see 23.1.7).

No contribution is payable unless the employee earns £139+ pw, although entitlement to benefits starts for earnings in excess of £102. If he or she earns £139+, contributions are calculated at 12% on the excess amount over £139 on earnings between £139 and £817 pw (eg on weekly earnings of £155, the employee NIC due is £155 – £139 = £16 × 12% = £1.92). A lower rate of 10.4% contributions is payable on earnings below the upper earnings limit if the employee is contracted out of the State Second Pension (S2P).

An additional 2% charge is imposed on all earnings above the upper earnings limit. This increased on 6 April 2011 from the previous 1%.

Women who married on or before 6 April 1977 and have chosen to pay a reduced rate are subject to pay NIC at only 5.85%. This right is lost if the woman is divorced, but is not lost if she is widowed. Women in this situation still have to pay the 2% on earnings in excess of £817 pw.

Contributions are assessed by reference to the normal earnings period which will usually be either weekly or monthly. If the employee is paid on a different schedule (eg fortnightly), contributions are calculated on the corresponding figures for whatever other period is covered by the payment to him or her.

An individual's liability to NIC is not affected by a previous period of unemployment during the year. Each 'earnings period' is looked at in isolation and there is no principle that corresponds to the cumulative method used for income tax where a tax year is looked at as a whole. There is an exception to this for company directors (see 23.1.3), but this is basically an anti-avoidance provision.

HMRC's National Insurance Contributions Office (NICO) administers NIC, statutory sick pay (SSP) and statutory maternity pay (SMP).

Most NIC, SSP and SMP appeals can be heard by an independent tribunal in the same way as tax appeals. Note, however, that appeals on contracting-out pensions issues and Working Families' Tax Credits (WFTC) are not heard by the tax tribunals.

23.1.2 Deferment

An individual who has more than one job and total earnings likely to exceed the upper limit may apply for deferment. The result is that NICO can authorise certain employers not to withhold contributions from his or her remuneration (form CA 2700). The deferment application is made on form CA72A. Ideally, this form should be submitted before the start of a tax year for which deferment is sought. Deferment will not usually be granted for a tax year unless NICO has received the application form by 14 February before the start of the year. NICO is also reluctant to grant deferment for a year in which the individual will reach pensionable age. Where a deferment application is made, the individual cannot choose which earnings should be subject to deduction of NIC. In addition, NICO will always defer contributions at the non-contracted out rate if any of the employments is not contracted out.

The position is reviewed after the end of a tax year. If an individual has not had the anticipated level of earnings from a particular employment and thus the liability for the year has not been satisfied, NICO will apply for payment of the balance. This falls due for payment within 28 days of its making such a demand.

Where the employee's contributions exceed the maximum for the year, there is still an entitlement to a repayment of contributions withheld from the remuneration, even if the individual has not applied for deferment.

Where deferment is granted, the second employer should deduct 2% contributions from all earnings above the earnings threshold and not just the upper earnings limit. A similar principle applies if someone is employed and also has profits from self-employment. In this situation, there will generally be a residual 2% on all profits above the lower profits limit.

23.1.3 Company directors

Remuneration paid to a company director is normally assessed for NIC as if it arose on an annual basis. Therefore, a large lump sum payment of fees or a bonus early in the year could attract the maximum annual contributions, rather than just the contributions limit for one week or one month.

Example – Assessment on lump sum payments

A weekly paid company director received remuneration of £35,000 paid in a single sum. The liability for contributions is the liability for the year, ie

52 × £678 (ie £817 upper limit – £139 lower limit) × 12%	= £4,230.72 plus
(£35,000 – (52 × £817)) × 2%	= £149.68
Total	= £4,380.40
It is *not* simply the maximum for one week's earnings, ie	= £765.02 (£678 x 12%), plus 2% of the excess over £817.

Regulation 6A of the Social Security (Contributions) Regulations (SSCR) 1979 ensures that the earnings period is annual but it is possible to make payments on account. When the last payment is made to the director in the tax year, the employer is required to reassess the NIC due on the total earnings for the tax year on an annual, or pro rata annual, earnings period, as appropriate. To qualify for these arrangements, the following three conditions must be satisfied:

- the director agrees to NIC being assessed this way;
- he or she normally receives his or her earnings in a regular pattern; and
- those payments normally exceed the lower earnings limit for the pay period.

Directors (and officers) may also be held liable for secondary contributions where the employer has failed to pay NIC on time and the failure appears to be attributable to fraud or neglect by the culpable officers.

23.1.4 Definition of earnings

'Earnings' for NIC purposes includes all cash remuneration. Contributions are also payable on sick pay, holiday pay, etc. The NIC definition of 'earnings' is quite different from that used for income tax purposes. For example, NIC is assessed on an individual's pay before pension contributions and before any charitable donations made under a payroll deduction scheme. There are also special rules for tips, service charges and troncs.

Where an employer settles an employee's pecuniary liability, the sum paid is treated as earnings for NIC purposes even though it is not pay for PAYE purposes. Previously, only certain types of benefits-in-kind that could easily be converted into cash were liable to NIC. For example, premium bonds and National Savings Certificates are regarded as earnings for NIC purposes because they can be encashed if the holder surrenders them. From 6 April 2000 the definition of earnings for NIC purposes was extended to cover all benefits-in-kind that are taxed as employment income (see 23.1.8).

Non-cash vouchers are also treated as earnings with the following exceptions (see 4.4.7 and 4.4.8):

● transport vouchers where the employee earns less than £8,500;
● transport vouchers for the disabled;
● transport vouchers for the armed forces;
● vouchers exchangeable for the use of sports or recreational facilities;
● vouchers associated with long service awards;
● vouchers in respect of staff functions (less than £150 per person);
● vouchers exchangeable for meals provided on employer's premises or at a staff canteen;
● first 15p per working day of luncheon vouchers – until the exemption is abolished later in 2011–12 (maximum £1.05 pw);
● incentive awards up to £150 pa per donor;
● childcare vouchers for children up to age 16.

NIC was not previously due on employer's contributions to an EFRBS (employer funded retirement benefit scheme) established specifically for an individual director or employee, however, on introducing new Part 7A ITEPA 2003 dealing with 'disguised remuneration', the Government announced its intention to bring forward equivalent NIC provisions and these are expected to have force from 6 April 2011.

Share options

No NIC arises on the grant or exercise of approved share options, unless the shares are readily convertible assets and the event gives rise to an income tax charge, for example, where an EMI option is exercised at below the market value at the time of grant.

There is no NIC liability on the grant of an unapproved option.

The exercise of unapproved options over shares that are 'readily convertible assets' at that time attracts NIC if the option was granted on or after 6 April 1999. The charge arises on the same amount as is chargeable to tax (see 6.4.2), ie it is based on the amount the shares would realise if sold on the day the option is exercised less any sum paid for the grant of the option and/or its exercise. The definition of readily convertible assets was substantially widened by FA 2003 (see 21.1.3).

No NIC liability arises on the exercise of a non-approved option over shares that are not readily convertible assets at the time of exercise.

Employers and employees can jointly elect for employees to bear the employers' NIC or reimburse the employer for the NIC. The elections cover securities options, conditional awards such as long-term incentive plans, cash cancellation payments made to give up a security option or restricted and convertible securities and post-acquisition gains from restricted or convertible securities.

Income tax relief will be available to the employee equal to the amount of the secondary NIC borne by the employee under the terms of the election.

Dividends

In the normal course of business, NIC ought not to arise where a director receives a dividend, or interest on a loan made to the company, or rent for a property used by the company. However, following the tribunal decision in *PA Holdings Ltd* v *HMRC* [2009] UKFTT 95(TC), it was established that in certain circumstances, payments that are treated as distributions and not taxable as earnings can still be subject to NIC.

23.1.5 Problem areas

One major problem area concerns directors' drawings. NICO takes the view that where a director arranges for a personal liability to be settled by the employer and charged to his or her drawings account, the payment constitutes earnings for NIC purposes unless the drawings account is in credit.

Example – Directors' drawings

> A has a drawings account with his company which is £60 in credit. The company pays a personal bill for A of £100 and debits his drawings account with £100, thus turning the credit balance into an overdrawn balance of £40.
>
> NICO takes the view that £60 of the payment of the £100 bill is a repayment of a loan and attracts no NIC, but the balance of £40 is a payment of earnings and the grossed up amount is subject to NIC.

Another problem area surrounds tips paid to employees. Tips are exempt from Class 1 NIC if one of two conditions is satisfied:

- they are not paid, directly or indirectly, to the employee by the employer and do not comprise or represent monies previously paid to the employer by a customer;
- they are not allocated, directly or indirectly, to the employee by the employer.

Therefore, NIC is due on tips paid through a tronc if the employer decides, directly or indirectly through another person, who should receive what amount by way of tips. Thus, to avoid any charge, an independent troncmaster should be appointed who genuinely decides which employees are to receive a payment and the amount of such a payment. Only in this way is it possible to ensure that the employer does not allocate the payments.

23.1.6 Loans from the employer

Curiously, NICO takes the view that if an individual arranges for a loan from his or her employer that is used to settle a personal liability, there is no NIC liability unless (and until) the employer writes off the loan. Considerable care should be taken when dealing with any documentation and the structure of such arrangements to minimise liability.

23.1.7 Employer's NIC

In addition to the 'primary' contributions paid by the employee, employers are required to pay 'secondary' contributions. There is no ceiling on the amount of an employee's earnings that attracts secondary contributions. No liability for secondary contributions can arise unless there is a liability for primary contributions, except when an employee with other employments has a deferment form CA 2700 or is a pensioner (Table C or S).

An employee can agree to pay his or her employer's NIC on profits from the exercise of non-approved share options after 19 May 2000. The NIC borne by the employee is then deducted in arriving at his or her ITEPA 2003 income (see 6.2.2). HMRC has published model agreements under which an employee can agree to pay the employer's NIC on his or her share option (see www.hmrc.gov.uk/shareschemes/jointelectionsfaq.htm#3).

Employers are also liable for Class 1A NIC where the employee receives benefits-in-kind (see 23.1.8).

For company cars, the cash equivalent used for income tax purposes is treated as if it were additional earnings subject to secondary contributions. A further charge may arise if the employee is provided with fuel for private mileage, with the Class 1A charge again being based on the scale benefit used for income tax purposes.

The Class 1A NIC charge on cars also extends to unremunerated employees and directors. Where a director or employee is provided with a car which attracts a car benefit charge, but no other earnings are paid, the car itself is treated as a relevant payment of earnings for the purposes of identifying the secondary contributor.

NIC has been aligned with HMRC's treatment of income tax in the operation of PAYE Settlement Agreements (PSAs). This means that Class 1B NIC is payable on PSAs and is payable at the same time as the tax (19 October). Class 1B NIC is currently payable at 13.8% on the total value of:

- all items covered by the PSA that would give rise to a Class 1 or 1A liability, and
- the tax payable by the employer under the PSA.

23.1.8 Class 1A NIC

Class 1A NIC now applies to most benefits-in-kind. The payment date of Class 1A NIC is 19 July after the end of the year of assessment. The Class

1A liability is an employer's charge only and is a tax-deductible expense. The charge is not payable by employees or directors.

The amount of the charge is normally equivalent to the highest rate of employer's secondary Class 1 NIC, which is currently 13.8%.

Class 1A NIC is not charged if:

- Class 1 NIC is already due (eg on expense payments);
- the expense payment or benefit-in-kind is covered by a P11D dispensation, extra-statutory concession or specific exemption;
- the expenses payment or benefit-in-kind is included in a PSA (where Class 1B NIC will be payable instead); or
- the benefit-in-kind is provided to an employee earning at a rate (inclusive of benefits) of less than £8,500 pa.

To reduce reporting requirements, HMRC has announced an exemption from income tax and NIC for the following:

- tools and equipment provided for work use where there may be a small amount of private use in the home, workplace or elsewhere;
- qualifying beneficial loans;
- general welfare counselling (but not private medical treatment or consultation); and
- refreshments provided by employers.

Class 1A NIC reports are merged with the existing forms P11D.

23.2 CLASS 2 CONTRIBUTION

23.2.1 Introduction

A self-employed individual is liable to Class 2 NIC of £2.50 pw unless his or her earnings are less than £5,315 pa and he or she has applied for a Certificate of Exemption. A penalty can be charged if he or she has not notified NICO within three months of taking up self-employment.

The Class 2 NIC for share fishermen is £3.15 pw and for volunteer development workers is £5.10 pw.

23.2.2 Earnings from employment and self-employment

Where an individual has income from both employment and self-employment, both Class 1 and 2 NIC is payable unless he or she applies for deferment. The maximum he or she may pay for any year is an amount equal to the maximum Class 1 primary contributions on 53 weeks' earnings. A repayment may be claimed if he or she has paid a mixture of Class 1 and 2 NIC in excess of this amount. From April 2011, payments of Class 2 NIC will fall due on 31 January and 31 July, at the same time as the self-assessment tax payments.

23.2.3 Small earnings exemption

A person may avoid paying Class 2 NIC by applying in advance for the small earnings exemption. The limit for the small earnings exemption for 2011–12 is £5,315.

Earnings for this purpose are measured by reference to actual earnings for the tax year. For example, if a trader makes up accounts to 30 September, the small earnings exemption is available only if his or her earnings for 2011–12 are less than £5,315 when computed as follows:

6/12 × profits for the year ended 30 September 2011

6/12 × profits for the year ended 30 September 2012

An individual may apply for repayment if Class 2 NIC has been overpaid. The repayment claim must normally be made between 6 April and 31 January following the end of the tax year and thus the deadline for making a repayment claim for 2011–12 will be 31 January 2013.

A false economy?

In general, choosing not to pay Class 2 NIC could prove a false economy as entitlement to benefits such as pensions and sick pay may be affected.

23.3 CLASS 3 CONTRIBUTION

This is a type of voluntary contribution. A person who is neither employed nor self-employed (or whose earnings fall below the exemption) may pay voluntary Class 3 NIC to secure the state retirement pension and certain bereavement payments. The weekly rate is set at £12.60 for 2011–12.

23.4 CLASS 4 CONTRIBUTION

This is payable by self-employed individuals according to the level of their profits as determined for income tax purposes. For 2011–12, Class 4 NIC is levied at the rate of 9% of trading profits between £7,225 and £42,475. Earnings in excess of the upper profits limit attract Class 4 NIC at the rate of 2%.

Where an individual pays interest on a business loan or has suffered trading losses, such amounts may be set against his or her earnings for the purposes of assessing liability for Class 4 NIC. This situation applies even where the losses have been relieved for income tax purposes by way of offset against his or her other income.

International issues surrounding NIC are outside the scope of this book. However, you should be aware that new EC regulations came into force on 1 May 2010. HMRC has published guidance on this which can be found at www.hmrc.gov.uk/nic/work/new-rules.htm

Table 23.1 – National insurance contributions

Item	2009–10	2010–11	2011–12
Lower earnings limit, primary class 1	£95 per week	£97 per week	£102 per week
Upper earnings limit, primary class 1	£844 per week	£844 per week	£817 per week
Primary threshold	£110 per week	£110 per week	£139 per week
Secondary threshold	£110 per week	£110 per week	£136 per week
Employees' primary class 1 rate	11% of £110.01 to £844 per week; 1% above £844 per week	11% of £110.01 to £844 per week; 1% above £844 per week	12% of £139.01 to £817 per week; 2% above £817 per week
Employees' contracted-out rebate	1.6%	1.6%	1.6%
Married women's reduced rate	4.85% of £110.01 to £844 per week; 1% above £844	4.85% of £110.01 to £844 per week; 1% above £844	5.85% of £139.01 to £817 per week; 2% above £817
Employers' secondary Class 1 rate	12.8% on earnings above £110 per week	12.8% on earnings above £110 per week	13.8% on earnings above £136 per week
Employers' contracted-out rebate, salary-related schemes	3.7%	3.7%	3.7%
Employers' contracted-out rebate, money-purchase schemes	1.4%	1.4%	1.4%

Table 23.1 – Continued

Item	2009–10	2010–11	2011–12
Class 2 rate	£2.40 per week	£2.40 per week	£2.50 per week
Class 2 small earnings exception	£5,075 per year	£5,075 per year	£5,315 per year
Special Class 2 rate for share fishermen	£3.05 per week	£3.05 per week	£3.15 per week
Special Class 2 rate for volunteer development workers	£4.75 per week	£4.85 per week	£5.10 per week
Class 3 rate	£12.05 per week	£12.05 per week	£12.60 per week
Class 4 rate	8% of £5,715 to £43,875 per year; 1% above £43,875 per year	8% of £5,715 to £43,875 per year; 1% above £43,875 per year	9% of £7,225 to £42,475 per year; 2% above £42,475 per year
Class 4 lower profits limit	£5,715 per year	£5,715 per year	£7,225 per year
Class 4 upper profits limit	£43,875 per year	£43,875 per year	£42,475 per year

PART 3

WEALTH PLANNING

This part contains the following chapters:

These chapters (and especially chapters 24 to 28) have been prepared as a general guide. They are not a substitute for professional advice. They are designed to raise some topical issues, rather than to provide specific answers to particular circumstances.

Please remember that any decisions that affect your investments should only be taken after seeking expert advice from an Independent Financial Adviser and should take into account the impact of the proposed transactions on your investment strategy as well as any possible tax advantages.

24

WEALTH PLANNING BY MANAGING YOUR FINANCIAL AFFAIRS

RICHARD JONES AND JENNIFER GRASHAM-WHALLEY

This chapter addresses issues that are likely to come up in connection with your personal financial affairs and those of your immediate family. We all have objectives, needs and expectations that have financial implications. These may include the following:

- paying off a mortgage;
- getting married or entering into a civil partnership;
- providing for children's education;
- funding the costs of higher education;
- buying a second home;
- saving for retirement;
- children's marriages;
- providing for dependants;
- giving to charity;
- increasing spendable income in retirement;
- funding grandchildren's school fees;
- passing on capital to children;
- mitigating IHT.

Managing savings and investments should take account of these objectives. The management process should be flexible and continuous because different objectives may need to take priority as events unfold.

An important part of managing investments is making sure that particular types of investment are appropriate for your situation. A given investment's tax treatment is often a big factor in determining this, but the 'tax tail' should not wag the 'appropriate investment dog'!

This chapter contains the following sections:

(1) Your family and personal financial planning
(2) Managing your investments
(3) Tax-deductible investments
(4) Some special situations
(5) Planning for retirement
(6) Helping the next generation
(7) Estate planning

24.1 YOUR FAMILY AND PERSONAL FINANCIAL PLANNING

There are important personal financial planning issues to be addressed. These may include selecting a suitable type of mortgage, making sure you claim all that is due to you from child tax credits, tax implications of marriage and civil partnership (and separation and divorce), protecting your dependants by taking out life assurance, funding school and university education, providing help to elderly dependent relatives and assisting your children in buying their first home. Looking further ahead, there are longer-term matters that need to be kept in mind, for example the way in which your (and possibly your spouse or civil partner's) Will should be drawn up. IHT planning also needs to be considered.

24.1.1 House purchase

When you buy a home, there are several types of mortgage available. For interest-only loans take advice about which investment vehicle is utilised to pay the outstanding mortgage at the end of the term. For instance, an option is to open an ISA and use this type of tax privileged savings to build up capital so you can clear the mortgage in due course.

Some mortgages involve an offset arrangement so that an allowance is made for a credit balance on your current account and you are charged interest only on your net indebtedness to the bank. These offset mortgages can be a way of saving interest, which far exceeds the amounts that you would retain after tax if you had a conventional mortgage and earned interest on temporary cash surpluses and the money that you would otherwise put on deposit. You should, however, be aware of the danger of actually increasing your indebtedness if you overspend, especially if you are locked into a comparatively unfavourable interest rate.

If you are lucky, you may have a tracker mortgage where interest is currently being charged at comparatively low rates. Make the most of it because it will not last. Even if you have a normal mortgage, the rate of interest will often be very low compared with past years. Try to put the difference to one side rather than use it to cover your monthly outgoings as sooner or later interest rates may go back up.

24.1.2 Pay down debt before making long-term investments

If you receive a bonus, a gift or an inheritance, it will probably make more sense to use it to clear expensive debt than to make investments. For example, clearing credit card debt may save you from paying 15% interest – you would need to make 25% or maybe 30% pa on investments to get an equivalent return.

24.1.3 If you and your partner are not married

UK tax legislation does not currently recognise common law marriages, although the extension of some rights to long-term partners is under consideration. If your partner has not made a Will, you may have no rights under the intestacy rules. The tax legislation may also be stacked against you because the CGT exemption for transfers between spouses and civil partners will not be available and neither will the IHT exemption for transfers of assets to your partner. The absence of such relief could seriously damage your wealth if you and your partner have substantial assets.

If your partner is a foreign national, bear in mind that the intestacy rules that would apply on his or her death may be quite different from the rules that apply here.

All in all, there is a lot to be said in favour of marriage from a financial point of view. However, there may be other considerations (see below).

Tax notes

Tax legislation does not recognise common law marriages, so CGT exemption for transfers between spouses and civil partners is not available and neither is there an IHT exemption for transfers of assets to your partner.

24.1.4 Marriage

There are several important tax considerations that arise in connection with marriage.

Capital gains tax

Bear in mind that if, for instance, you transfer shares or other chargeable assets to your fiancé(e) at less than market value, you are deemed to have made a disposal at market value and a capital gain may therefore arise. From this point of view, it may be better to delay matters until after you marry as no capital gain arises on transfers between spouses or civil partners who are living together. However, if you are thinking of transferring an asset on which a capital *loss* would arise, it may be best to crystallise this loss by making the transfer before you marry.

Something else to bear in mind is the position if each of you already owns your own home. Basically, you have two years' grace to resolve the position, but at the end of that time only one property can qualify as your main residence (see 14.2.5). The property concerned may be a new home or one of you may move into the other's existing home.

Inheritance tax

No IHT arises on transfers of assets by one spouse to another unless the transferor is UK-domiciled and the transferee is not (see 30.5.1).

24.1.5 Civil partners

The Government changed the rules for same-sex relationships with the enactment of the Civil Partnership Act 2004, which came into effect on 5 December 2005.

The most notable benefits of the Act are that registered civil partners benefit from spouse exemption for IHT and CGT. These benefits are, however, tempered by the fact that civil partners will also be subject to the same anti-avoidance provisions that affect married couples (see 33.4 on transfers of assets overseas and 33.5 on the settlement provisions).

Couples affected by the change in legislation will generally need advice on the following:

- private residence (a couple can have only one main residence for CGT purposes);
- pension planning;
- IHT and estate planning.

Civil partners who own businesses or who have a significant shareholding in a company should talk to their tax and financial advisers before registering as civil partners.

24.1.6 Pre-nuptial agreements

Divorce lawyers say that there is no certainty that the UK courts will pay any attention to pre-nuptial agreements, although recent case law has indicated that these are increasingly being given weight provided that the wealthier spouse has made full disclosure of his or her assets and given the other party a proper opportunity to consider matters and take advice. Simply thrusting a bit of paper in front of your fiancé(e) the day before the marriage will not meet these tests.

Tax notes

Divorce lawyers say there is no guarantee that UK courts will pay any attention to pre-nuptial agreements in all cases.

24.1.7 Child tax credits

Remember you have to claim your entitlement, and you should bear in mind that claims cannot be backdated by more than three months (see 12.7.1).

24.1.8 Tax relief for having a nanny

The Government extended the working tax credits regime from April 2005 so that all, or more realistically, part of the cost of a nanny can be covered by a tax credit (see 12.7.2).

24.1.9 Life assurance

Income tax relief is not given for life assurance premiums on policies taken out after 13 March 1984.

You may well have some death in service cover through your employer's pension scheme, or your personal pension plan will produce a lump sum in the event of your untimely death. Remember, you will need to nominate a beneficiary, who will be paid at the discretion of the scheme trustees, in order to prevent the proceeds from falling into your estate.

However, this is unlikely to be sufficient if you have a young family. Consider taking out term insurance or family income cover, which provides a series of capital sums on death, if the death occurs during a specified period. The sums payable are known as 'family income benefit'. Remember to have the policies written in trust so they would not attract IHT if you and your spouse or civil partner were to die in quick succession.

24.1.10 Funding school fees and higher education

Your children's school may run a prepayment scheme that effectively gives you a tax-free return on money you deposit with the school. Ask the bursar about this.

If grandparents or other relatives are able to help, advantage could be taken of your children's tax allowances. One way is for your relatives to set up trusts, utilising part of their nil rate band for IHT, and for the trustees to distribute income to your children. This money could then be used to pay school fees.

Bear in mind that this will not work if you make a trust for your own children, as any income that is paid out before they attain age 18 will be treated as if it were your income.

Where relatives cannot assist, matters are more difficult but not necessarily impossible. You should start saving as early as possible and take full advantage of privileged investments such as ISAs and qualifying insurance policies. Take advice from a specialist.

If your son or daughter is over 18, you may be able to save tax by assigning insurance bonds for him or her to cash in and use to cover university costs. A gift of such a bond does not trigger a tax charge (see 28.3.1). No tax will be payable on encashment unless your son or daughter is liable for higher or additional rate tax at that time.

Investigate the possibility of buying a property for your son or daughter to occupy while at university. They may be able to let spare rooms to fellow students and the rent can then cover some of your costs. Remember that you will have to pay tax on any net rental income you receive. If the house or flat is bought in your children's name, they may be able to claim CGT main residence exemption when the property is sold (see 14.1).

Another approach would be to set up a trust to hold the property with the trustees making the property available to your adult child for them to use as their main residence (see 31.4.11) because the CGT exemption can also be available in these circumstances. If you are a trustee, you will have some measure of control over what happens to the property after that particular child has finished his or her course.

24.1.11 Saving for retirement

It's never too early to start making provision for retirement. A pension contribution that you make when you are 30 will benefit from tax free growth for 30 years, a contribution that you make when you are 62 will not grow to anything like the same extent.

We focus on planning for retirement at 25.5.

24.1.12 Separation and divorce

You may need to make the best of an event that you would rather had not arisen, the break-up of your marriage or civil partnership. First, there is only one situation in which any tax relief for maintenance payments is available: to qualify, you or your ex-spouse or former civil partner must have been born before 6 April 1935 and be separated or divorced or had your civil partnership dissolved and you must be making the payments under a court order.

The payments must be for the maintenance of your ex-spouse or former civil partner (provided he or she has not remarried or entered into a new civil partnership) or for your children who are aged under 21).

In these extremely limited circumstances, for the tax year 2011–12, relief for maintenance payments can reduce your tax bill by the lower of 10% of £2,800 (£280) (where you make maintenance payments of £2,800 pa or more) or 10% of the amount you have actually paid (where you make maintenance payments of less than £2,800 pa).

You cannot claim a tax reduction for any voluntary payments that you may make for a child, ex-spouse or former civil partner.

So far as CGT is concerned, you could find yourself in a Catch 22. The legislation provides that spouses or civil partners are connected persons for CGT purposes until the marriage comes to an end. The marriage comes to an end when there is a decree absolute, not a decree nisi. However, the exemption for transfers between spouses and civil partners applies only if you are living together. You may therefore find yourself in a situation where a CGT charge may arise because you are required to transfer assets to your spouse or civil partner as part of your divorce settlement.

It is possible to get round this problem if you plan ahead. The basic rule that transfers between spouses are not subject to CGT applies to transfers made during a tax year in which you have been living together at some time. Thus, if you and your spouse or civil partner separated on, say, 10 April 2011, a transfer of assets between you will not give rise to a CGT charge provided the transfer is made before 6 April 2012.

Tax notes

Taking financial and legal advice if you become separated is a difficult issue but, as in most situations, the earlier you seek expert advice the more likely it is that tax liabilities can be minimised – benefiting both parties when it comes to a financial settlement.

24.1.13 Buying a second home

There are some tax issues with buying a second home.

If you are going to let it out when you do not want to use it yourself, it might make sense to take out a mortgage because at least part of the interest that you pay will then attract income tax relief (by deduction when calculating your rental profit).

If you create a trust to hold your second home, you may be able to achieve a more flexible situation. In due course, when your children have grown up, the trustees might allow one of them to use the property as his or her main residence and this could save tax when the property is eventually sold as the trustees may then escape CGT on part of their capital gain because of the main residence exemption (see 31.4.11).

The property may be overseas. If so, think twice about having an overseas company own the property because this can, in some situations, expose you to an income tax charge (see 36.4.4). If lawyers or other professionals in the country concerned recommend that you buy through a local company, it may be best for the property to be registered in the name of the company but held by that company on trust for you and your spouse or civil partner – this is a matter where you need specialist advice, both in the UK and in the jurisdiction where the property is located.

24.1.14 Providing for dependants

Disabled children

You may have a disabled child or grandchild. If so, consider making provision for him or her; perhaps by creating a trust (see 31.7).

Elderly dependants

Many readers will be making a contribution towards the support of elderly parents or other relatives. Unfortunately, successive Chancellors have significantly reduced the scope for obtaining assistance towards these costs through tax relief: it was once possible to transfer income via a deed of covenant and claim an income tax allowance for dependent relatives, but these reliefs have been abolished.

One possibility for securing tax relief is where it is necessary to purchase a property that is used by the relative as his or her home. There is no tax relief for a mortgage taken out for this purpose and CGT exemption is not available if you own the property yourself (unless you owned it before 5 April 1988). It may, however, be possible to secure CGT exemption in due course if you follow a fairly involved route, using a trust. IHT could be a problem here if the property is worth more than £325,000 or if you have previously made chargeable transfers and a gift into trust takes you over the £325,000 nil rate band.

Talk this through with a specialist tax adviser to see if a trust would fit with your objectives and makes sense in your particular circumstances.

24.1.15 Helping your adult children to make investments

If you can afford it, it may make sense for you to give or lend your adult children the money so that they can use their quota of tax exempt and tax privileged investments such as ISAs or even pensions.

Another option offering more control to the parent is to set up a family investment company. Such companies can be used in a similar way to a family trust with the parents gifting some shares in the company but retaining large enough share holdings (over 50% combined) to keep control of it. This gives the parents control over the way the investments are managed and when cash distributions are made, while putting income in the hands of their children. It can also be a tax-efficient method of investing in equities for the long term as companies do not suffer tax on dividends received from other companies – allowing income to be accumulated and reinvested without an income tax or corporation tax charge.

A family investment company is a complex vehicle and using one should only be contemplated after taking expert advice.

24.1.16 Giving to charity

There are many ways of getting tax relief for gifts to charities. Gift Aid means that the charity will get a tax rebate of nearly one third of what you give and you will receive higher tax relief at your highest marginal rate (which could be 50%) (see 11.9).

If you have quoted securities that you bought for a fraction of the current price, it may be better to give these to charity rather than draw down on your cash – you will save the CGT that you would have paid if you had sold the shares and you will get income tax relief at your top rate. See 11.10–11.11 on the income tax reliefs for gifts of quoted securities and land, as well as the anti-avoidance measures that have recently been introduced.

Some readers may be able to set up charitable trusts of their own. This can make financial sense if you are prepared to put in capital of (say) £100,000 or make regular Gift Aid payments of £20,000 or £25,000 pa.

Watch out for the rules on 'tainted donations' though, where you enter into arrangements to obtain an advantage from a charity, as under the new rules it is the donor who will be penalised rather than the charity – see 38.1.21.

Notwithstanding this, as part of a wider package of measures to encourage charitable giving, the benefit limit for donations over £10,000 has been increased. The current rule that any benefits to the donor must not exceed 5% of the donation will remain but the upper limit has been increased from £500 to £2,500. This new measure will enable charities to thank their larger donors in a more generous way, without disqualifying the donation from Gift Aid and triggering the anti-avoidance rules.

Tax notes

If you have quoted securities that you bought for a fraction of the current price, it may be better to give these to charity to avoid paying the CGT – and get income tax relief.

24.1.17 Increasing disposable income in retirement

There are many ways of increasing your retirement income. For example, you can invest in an insurance bond and make 5% annual withdrawals (as a deemed return of capital) to use as income. No tax is charged on such withdrawals although they are taken into account in determining any tax charge on encashment of the policy. You may also invest in National Savings certificates, premium bonds and ISAs. See Chapter 24 on tax reliefs. If all else fails, you might consider using some of your capital to buy an annuity but hopefully you will be able to postpone such a radical step as it is by its nature irrevocable.

One issue to consider in this context is that income-producing investments can reduce the available age allowance. An investment bond does not produce regular income year on year, but when it is surrendered any gain accrued then counts as notional income, subject to a notional 20% tax credit for UK bonds, which should mean that basic rate taxpayers have no further tax to pay. There will be tax leakage within the fund though, which generally means growth is likely to be more limited than in unit trusts or open-ended investment company shares (OEICS). The term, tax rate and your attitude to risk will determine which is the most suitable option for you – this will often be a combination of investments.

Withdrawals from the bond are not assessed as income for age allowance purposes. In addition an income stream taken from ISAs and National Savings will not be taken into consideration when assessing eligibility for age allowance.

Another option is the use of the CGT annual exemption (£10,600 for 2011–12) to reduce tax liabilities and (if appropriate in terms of risk and performance) lower yield unit trusts or OEICS.

Remember not to look only at one tax. For example, a wealthy individual has pension income taxable at 40%. He puts all his shares into his (much younger) wife's name so that the dividends are declared on her return and do not attract higher rate tax. This works fine but when he dies she is left with a potential CGT charge if she sells the shares. It might have been better if they had stayed in his name so that most of the exposure to CGT would have disappeared on his death. Then again, the position may be quite different where the donor pays tax at 50% (42.5% on dividends) and his or her spouse would be taxed at only 10% on the dividend income, and 18/28% on any capital gain arising above the annual exemption.

24.1.18 Funding grandchildren's school and further education costs

If you are able to do so, you will make a tremendous contribution to your children's financial position by relieving them of some of the costs of educating your grandchildren.

Regular gifts out of surplus income qualify for IHT exemption (see 30.5.2).

Setting up a settlement for your grandchildren with funds less than the nil rate band (£325,000 until 2014–15) can still be tax-efficient. Putting capital into such a trust will be a chargeable transfer for IHT purposes, but the immediate tax charge will be nil and there should be no further IHT charge on your death provided you survive seven years (see 30.6 on this). In addition, there should be no IHT charges within the trust for the first ten years and on the ten-year anniversary, only if the value exceeds the nil rate band at the time. The trustees will have to pay income tax at 50% on income that they receive but part or all of this tax (probably most of it) can be reclaimed on behalf of your grandchildren as and when income is paid out for their benefit (see 31.5.7).

24.1.19 Passing on capital to children

If you are having a prosperous retirement, it may be that you should turn your attention to IHT planning. You should consider making PETs and chargeable transfers that are covered by your £325,000 nil rate band and utilising any other available IHT exemptions. This is covered in more detail at 24.7.

24.2 MANAGING YOUR INVESTMENTS

24.2.1 General strategy

All investments involve a degree of risk. Investments that are apparently risk-free, such as keeping money on deposit, run the risk that they will not keep up with inflation. The reality is that people who concentrate all their financial resources on any one investment automatically run some risks, albeit the nature of the risk varies according to the nature of the investments and the way they are funded.

Investments based on borrowings are inherently more risky: if you have taken a 100% mortgage to buy an investment property you are going to be under financial pressure if the tenant moves out and the property remains vacant. If you cannot cover the interest costs, you will have to liquidate your investment even though you would have preferred to wait until the property market had picked up.

There are probably higher short-term risks with stock market investments. Don't assume that past performance is a guarantee to what will happen in the future, especially in the near future. All markets fluctuate in value daily. Stock markets tend to overshoot. They are just as liable to respond to good news by surging ahead and becoming 'over bought' as to over react to bad news or a period of uncertainty.

If you have known financial commitments (eg a tax liability falling due for payment on 31 January 2012 or your mortgage has to be redeemed in two years' time) then you should set aside funds to cover these and invest the funds conservatively. Most sound investments will make money for you in the long term but it's much more risky to take a bet on the level of the stock market in 15 months' or two years' time. The long-term trend may be positive but the markets could give you a bumpy ride in between.

The same applies if there are things that could happen in the next few years, eg if you can foresee being made redundant.

As retirement approaches, you may need to be able to draw on savings in the foreseeable future. This means that you are less able to sit tight and ride out the fluctuations of the markets.

It is therefore important to keep tax planning in perspective. In general, investment considerations should dictate your investment policy. Naturally, these vary according to an individual's perspective, whether it be age, need for short-term and medium-term liquidity, income requirements, the degree of acceptable risk, expectations for future inflation levels, perception of the economic climate, etc. Tax planning must fit in around such considerations. However, there are some simple steps that can help you to reduce the tax payable on your investment income and gains.

24.2.2 Selecting investments that suit your requirements

Investments have varying tax treatments and this variation needs to be taken into account. For example, advisers often say that you should try to arrange matters so that both you and your spouse or civil partner use up your CGT annual exemption every year but as always it will depend on your individual circumstances. You should take independent financial advice.

Here are our thoughts on certain types of investment and the objectives they are likely to meet:

Objective	Type of investment
Tax-free returns	Certain index linked and fixed-interest National Savings certificates (see 25.3)
	ISAs (see 25.1)
	VCT investments (see 25.6) Solar panels for your home can generate tax-free income from the current feed-in tariff as well as giving you free electricity: in most cases, the overall return on this long-term investment currently exceeds the returns available on cash deposits.
Use annual exemptions and brought-forward CGT losses	Quoted shares
	Unit trusts/OEICs
	Investment trust shares
	Collective funds
Avoid internal tax*	Unit trusts/OEICs
	Investment trusts
	Offshore insurance bonds (see 28.4)
Avoid paying tax on switching between specialised funds	Insurance bonds (see 28.2)
Avoid paying tax until encashment	Roll-up funds (see 10.7) insurance bonds (28.2)
Deferring taxable income	Roll-up funds
	Insurance bonds
Avoid two-tier CGT**	Unit trusts/OEICs
	Investment trusts/shares
	REITs (see 27.6)
Reducing tax by making investments also known as 'tax reducers'	VCTs (see 25.6)
	EIS investments (see 25.5)
	Pension schemes (see 26.1)
IHT savings	Unquoted shares (see 30.8.2)
	AIM shares

* Investments are subject to internal tax where the fund is liable for tax (eg corporation tax) that is separate from the tax payable by the investor and which cannot be reclaimed by him or her.
** Investments attract a two-tier tax charge where tax is charged on income and gains realised by the fund and the investor is subject to a separate tax charge, usually on realising his or her investment.

Property investments

Chapter 26 looks at some of the differences in the tax treatment various types of property investments.

24.2.3 Further analysis

Selecting an appropriate investment involves a great deal more than just the 'tick box' approach that the above table may suggest. This is partly because some of the objectives run in opposite directions. For example, investing in a VCT may give you tax-free dividends but it is also a more risky investment.

Similarly, it may well be desirable (all other things being equal) to avoid a fund that is subject to an internal tax charge but this drawback may be less than it looks. If you hold shares and unit trusts that are likely to produce capital gains, and you are subject to 40% or 50% income tax, an investment in an insurance company may have its plus points.

A lot depends on circumstances. If you are giving £5,000 to be set aside for your newly arrived grandson to use when he gets to age 18, it may well be best to invest in a broadly based unit trust or other managed investment rather than, for example, using the money to buy shares in one particular company.

It is important to know what you are getting. If you are buying units in an offshore fund, you need to know whether it has reporting status because profits realised on the sale of reporting funds are taxed in a different way.

Similarly, if you invest in an investment vehicle known as a structured product issued by a bank that gives you (say) 75% of the increase in the FTSE100 index over the next five years or a minimum 10% return if the index goes down, you need to know how any profit will be taxed. The tax treatment of these bonds means the return may be taxed either as a gain or as income, depending on the structure, and it is important to know which will apply, and plan accordingly.

You should consult an IFA or other investment specialist on these types of issues.

24.2.4 Managing investments to take account of your personal situation

In the next section of this chapter, we look at ways in which you may be able to fine-tune your investments by taking full advantage of opportunities that arise from your own (and your family's) circumstances.

24.2.5 Take full advantage of tax-efficient investments

Investments in an ISA are not charged to tax in your hands (though charges can arise in some instances within the funds held) (see 25.1), so if possible you should open ISAs for yourself and your spouse or civil partner. National Savings certificates and Friendly Society tax exempt policies also offer a safe and tax-free return, albeit at a relatively low interest rate.

Also consider taking out a personal pension plan for a non-working spouse or partner.

24.2.6 Use all your family's allowances

There is generally scope for planning both in relation to income tax and CGT.

ISAs

The tax-free income and capital growth available through use of an ISA make it one of the most important vehicles for family investment. Ensuring that the annual ISA allowances of both spouses are used (£10,680 for 2011–12 of which up to £5,340 can be in the form of a cash deposit) is important and don't forget that adult children can also invest through an ISA. It may even make sense for you to lend cash to your adult children so that they can make tax-efficient investments in ISAs (see 25.1).

For children aged under 18, the Government proposes that a new junior ISA will be available from 1 November 2011 with an annual investment limit of £3,000, which can all be invested in stocks and shares or in a cash deposit. The invested funds will be locked in until the child reaches the age of 18 and both parents and other relatives can pay in funds but, unlike the child trust fund (CTF), the Government will make no contributions to the savings. Existing holders of a CTF will not be allowed to apply for a junior ISA, but the CTF investment limits will be increased from the present £1,200 to £3,000 a year.

Deposit interest

Spouses and civil partners each have their own personal allowances and each spouse or civil partner's income is taxed completely separately. If your spouse or civil partner has little or no income, or is liable only at 20% whereas you have to pay 40% or 50% tax, there may be advantages in transferring income to him or her. A fairly straightforward way of doing this is to hold bank deposit accounts and other investments in your joint names. The basic rule is that where investments are held in this way, half of the resulting income is taxed on each spouse or civil partner.

Sterling is exempt from CGT (and from the gift with reservation of benefit tracing rules see 30.7) so partners can gift cash of any amount. This will be a potentially exempt transfer for IHT purposes, chargeable if you die within seven years, but you may be able to use the annual and normal expenditure out of income exemptions to exempt much of the value of the gift.

If you open a bank account in your minor child's name, the interest is treated as your income for tax purposes only if the total income arising from such potential gifts exceeds £100 pa per child (see 33.5.4), so there may be some limited opportunity for achieving tax-free savings. Note that this rule will not apply to the proposed junior ISA (see above) making them particularly tax-efficient for parents.

Capital gains tax

Your spouse or civil partner will have his or her own £10,600 CGT annual exemption and you should look for ways of using this each year where your combined gains exceed a single allowance. This could be achieved by transferring investments (transfers between spouses and civil partners are deemed to take place on a no gain/no loss basis) in order to put your spouse or civil partner in a position to realise a gain on a sale to a third party which you would otherwise have had to pay tax on (see 29.1.1).

This is often appropriate where a gain has built up on quoted securities. A judicious transfer of stocks and shares that show a paper gain can save significant amounts of tax even if the transfer takes place shortly before the securities are sold. But take care: HMRC often looks very closely at the paperwork on such inter-spouse transfers and you must show that beneficial ownership of the securities actually passed to your spouse or civil partner before a firm of stockbrokers was instructed to sell the shares. All other things being equal (which they seldom are), it is generally best to allow at least a few days, but better still, a couple of months, to elapse between the transfer of the shares to your spouse or civil partner and the sale by him or her.

There may sometimes be scope for using your children's annual CGT exemption as the £100 limit for income tax purposes does not apply for capital gains. Bear in mind that this is more difficult since a gift of shares, etc, to anyone other than your spouse or civil partner is normally treated as a disposal that is deemed to take place for CGT purposes at market value. However, if you hold shares in unquoted trading companies and you can see an opportunity coming up whereby you could realise those shares at a large gain, it may be worth transferring part of your shareholding to your children. Because the shares are in unquoted trading companies, it may be possible to 'hold over' any capital gain so that your child (or other relation or friend) takes over the shares at your original acquisition value (see 17.5). This means that you will have no capital gain. The recipient will have a gain on disposal of the difference between your acquisition value and the sale proceeds, which may be covered in whole or in part by the annual exemption or losses available when the asset is disposed of.

When there is an opportunity to take up an attractive share issue, consideration should be given to subscribing in your child's name as well as your own.

For CGT planning generally, see Chapter 29.

Tax notes

When there is an opportunity to take up an attractive share issue, consideration should be given to subscribing in your child's name as well as your own.

Long-term planning

You may even take out a personal pension plan for a minor child and contribute up to £2,880 (£3,600 gross) pa – but bear in mind that this is a much more long-term savings plan. (Based on current legislation benefits cannot be taken before age 55.)

24.3 TAX-DEDUCTIBLE INVESTMENTS

There are three types of investment that attract income tax relief on investment; pension contributions; investments under the EIS; and investments in VCTs.

24.3.1 Pension contributions

We return to pension contributions because the tax situation is so attractive. There is no other type of investment where you can gain tax relief when you pay money in, enjoy the benefits of a fund that pays no tax on its income and gains and take part of the fund as a tax-free lump sum. The last aspect is one of the most important; contributions to pension schemes allow a person effectively to convert taxable income into a tax-free capital sum. Bear in mind, however, that there are restrictions on the amount that can be contributed to registered pension schemes and which can obtain tax relief (see 26.5 for details).

Personal pensions

An individual is allowed to make a payment of up to £3,600 pa even if he or she does not work and so has no earnings. If he or she is employed, this limit is reduced by any contributions into an occupational scheme. The pension payments are made net of basic rate tax even if the individual has no taxable income.

Pension contributions generally

If you have employment or trading income, you can make contributions to a registered pension scheme equal to those earnings (subject to a limit of £50,000 pa, plus any unused relief (up to £50,000 pa) in the preceding three tax years). Subject to the 'wholly and exclusively' rule your employer could (if it were so inclined) make contributions which exceed your earnings (subject to the same limits). See 26.1.4 on this. For individuals who own their own company, this is a particularly tax-efficient way to extract value from the company: it avoids an immediate income tax charge on the individual, avoids any national insurance contributions that would be payable by the individual and the company if the money was paid out as a salary and the company gets corporation tax relief on the contribution.

24.3.2 Investment in enterprise zone properties

A 100% allowance used to be available where a person invested in a commercial building located in an enterprise zone. Basically, the building must have been unused or you must have made your investment within two years of it having first been let. Enterprise zone allowances were abolished from April 2011.

Allowances given prior to 6 April 2011 may be clawed back if the person entitled to them receives capital value attributable to a subordinate interest in the building within seven years of acquiring the relevant interest. This could arise where, for example, a long lease is granted to a tenant in respect of the property.

New enterprise zones were announced in the 2011 Budget but the proposed advantages for businesses setting up in the new zones will only extend to reduced business rates, extra allowances for plant and machinery and some reductions in red tape.

24.3.3 Investments under the Enterprise Investment Scheme

Wealthy individuals should consider making selective investments under the EIS. It is now possible to invest up to £500,000 pa under this scheme (increasing to £1m from 6 April 2012). Investors are entitled to 30% income tax relief (from 6 April 2011, subject to EU state aid approval) and may also be able to claim CGT deferral relief (see 25.5). Any capital gain arising on a disposal of the EIS shares after three years is totally tax free, albeit deferred gains come back into charge when the EIS shares are disposed of.

The Government has also made the EIS more attractive in other ways. Many of the restrictions and anti-avoidance rules have been abolished. It is now possible for an investor to become a paid director and take a full part in the management of the company. If you have gains in excess of the entrepreneurs' relief allowance of £10m, or you have made gains in the last few years that you would like to 'roll over', you may be able to obtain CGT deferral relief by investing further amounts under the EIS. From 6 April 2012, the EIS rules for the qualifying company are also to be relaxed: the maximum limit on gross assets held by the investee company before any investment will increase to £15 million and the employee limit to fewer than 250. This should expand the range of EIS investment opportunities significantly.

Remember that one of the requirements for EIS investors to qualify for the 30% income tax relief is that they must not hold more than 30% of the equity, but you do not need to meet this rule if you are investing in an EIS company only in order to secure CGT deferral relief (see 25.5).

24.3.4 Venture Capital Trusts

An individual is allowed to invest up to £200,000 pa in VCTs – although note that these can be relatively high-risk investments. There are significant tax advantages in that if you subscribe for new VCT shares you are entitled to income tax relief at 30%, although there is no longer any CGT deferral relief. In addition, the dividends you receive from your investment and any capital gain when you eventually dispose of it (after the end of the five-year clawback period) can be tax free (see 25.6).

24.4 SOME SPECIAL SITUATIONS

24.4.1 Securing tax relief for losses on investments

If you are nursing losses on investments in shares and unit trusts (OEICs), and you have realised gains on other investments during the current tax year (eg on the sale of a property that you have been letting), it may make sense to crystallise the losses, unless you hope that the investments will in time recover much of their value and you do not want to dispose of them altogether. It is still possible to consider transfers between spouses or civil partners to crystallise loses, however s 16A TCGA 1992 is a targeted anti-avoidance rule aimed at restricting allowable losses for those realising capital losses, where tax avoidance is a motive, and it may enable HMRC to attack such sales as artificial transactions entered into solely for tax avoidance, especially if the purchasing spouse or civil partner subsequently transfers the shares to the original owner.

Basically, s 16A is very widely drafted and would appear to catch even completely innocent transactions. In effect, it will be up to HMRC whether it takes the point, on a case by case basis. As a general rule of thumb, if the parties genuinely suffer the economic consequences of the transactions they each enter into, then the rule is unlikely to apply.

If you are the main beneficiary under the Will of someone who has died in the past few months, it may be possible to reduce the IHT on your inheritance. If the executors sell quoted securities within 12 months of the death, and the proceeds are less than their value at the date of death ('probate value'), it may be possible to have the IHT recalculated so that it is charged only on the lower value (see 30.11.3).

24.4.2 Planning for specific situations

Your circumstances may be special because of your residence or domicile status or your plans for the future.

For example, it may be that you plan to work overseas for a few years and will therefore cease to be UK resident. In such a case, it makes sense to defer taxable income until after you have ceased to be resident as this means no tax will arise provided it is not UK source income, and is not 'deferred' employment income that relates to a year when you were UK resident. A possible way of doing this is to invest in offshore roll-up funds, rather than bank deposit accounts, with a view to cashing in the roll-up investments after you have ceased to be a resident.

If you are about to return to the UK, having been resident abroad, then you should take advice on any investment bonds and insurance policies issued by foreign insurance companies (see 28.4). If you have been non-resident for a minimum of five tax years there may be merit in realising capital gains before you resume UK residence (see 34.5.4).

Your circumstances may be special in another way: if you have suffered 'miscellaneous income' losses in the past, look out for ways of realising miscellaneous income. The point is that such losses brought forward from previous years may only be set against miscellaneous income but the income does not have to arise from the same source (see 10.8).

24.4.3 Property investments

Investments in real estate tend to be longer-term investments. For that reason, the tax planning considerations also tend to be long term in nature.

One planning point is relevant at the time you acquire an investment property. Interest on a qualifying loan may be set against any UK rental income. The planning point is therefore very simple: you should normally borrow at the outset unless you are quite sure that you will not need to borrow money to finance your property investments later on. Even if you do have sufficient capital, it may be best to borrow to make property investments and use your spare capital for other purposes. For example, it would not be good tax planning to use your capital to purchase an investment property and at the same time take a long-term non-qualifying loan to finance school fees.

Do not plan for one tax in isolation. If you let part of your home, or if you let your home for a period while you are living elsewhere, check on the CGT implications (see 14.4.3). There are reliefs and extra-statutory concessions, but you must be very careful not to put your extremely valuable main residence exemption into jeopardy.

If you do let part of your home, bear in mind the special rent-a-room relief (see 8.4) that may mean rental income of up to £4,250 is exempt from tax.

It may make sense to form a company to hold property investments. If this is your only company and its profits do not exceed £300,000, the company is currently only subject to corporation tax at 20% on its rental income. But once again take advice on the long-term implications if capital gains are likely to arise when properties are sold. The VAT implications of property investment are also complex (see 22.3.6). This is an area where you need to take professional advice as there are special rules (eg option to tax and capital goods scheme) that are not straightforward. There are opportunities to save VAT, but also numerous pitfalls.

Bear in mind SDLT, both on purchasing a property and on transferring it to a company (see Chapter 39).

24.4.4 Qualifying loans for company directors

If you work full time for a close company in a managerial capacity or hold more than 5% of the shares, and you wish to purchase more shares, you may be able to raise a qualifying loan (see 11.5). The interest attracts tax relief at your top rate and there is no upper limit.

24.4.5 Plan ahead when buying a private company

If you purchase the whole of the share capital of a private trading company and things do not go to plan, you are not normally due income tax relief for any loss. You may be able to get a loss allowed for CGT purposes, but capital losses may be set only against capital gains, not against income, and therefore it may be some years before you get effective relief.

There may be a way around this if you follow certain steps when you acquire the company. You should speak to your accountant, but basically what will be involved is for you to form a new company, subscribe cash for new shares in that company and have the company acquire the shares in the private trading company. At the end of the day, your position will be almost exactly the same, except that you will hold shares in a company with a wholly owned subsidiary rather than hold shares in the subsidiary itself. What is important is that by dealing with matters in this way, you will be entitled to relief under s131 ITA 2007 on any capital loss (see 17.2), ie you will be able to set the loss against your income for the year of loss or the preceding tax year.

If you need to raise equity from outside investors, see if you can structure your company in a way that qualifies under the Enterprise Investment Scheme if possible – see 25.5. Also consider Venture Capital Trusts as a potential source of equity investment (see 25.6).

If you are in the process of buying or setting up a business, we suggest that you read Chapter 19 as part of your preparation for a discussion with your professional advisers.

24.4.6 Long-term planning for foreign domiciliaries

There are planning possibilities if you have foreign domicile (see Chapter 35) or indeed if part of your family has always been based overseas.

24.5 PLANNING FOR RETIREMENT

We all need to put serious thought into providing for our retirement. There are many things to be considered and this section can only highlight possibilities and direct you to the relevant parts of this book.

The obvious way of planning for retirement is to make contributions to a registered pension scheme (see 26.1).

If you are employed by someone else, first find out if there is an occupational pension scheme that you can join; otherwise consider making contributions into a personal pension scheme. Take full advantage of approved share schemes in order to accumulate capital for your retirement (see 6.3.13 and 6.4–6.5).

If you own and run a trading company, you should ensure that the company sets up the most beneficial scheme possible for both you and your spouse or civil partner (assuming he or she also works for the company). There is also CGT to be considered. Putting money into an executive pension scheme may mean that you can effectively make investments in a wider class of assets without your company undertaking substantial investment activities in its own right.

If you run your own unincorporated business, there are several retirement planning opportunities available to you. These could include direct investments into commercial property, equities, fixed interest securities or contributions into a personal pension plan. You need to take professional advice on the options available to you, to find the best 'fit' for your circumstances.

If your spouse or civil partner does not work, fund a stakeholder pension scheme for him or her. Annual contributions can be made of £2,880 (£3,600 after the addition of tax relief).

Looking at another aspect of retirement planning: if your work requires you to occupy job-related accommodation, and you don't own a home of your own, you should probably buy a property and nominate it as your main residence for CGT purposes (see 14.3).

Tax notes

If your work requires you to occupy job-related accommodation and you don't own a home of your own, you should probably buy a property and nominate it as your main residence for CGT purposes.

24.6 HELPING THE NEXT GENERATION

Once again, the purpose of this part of the chapter is to get you thinking about possible issues and to refer you on to other parts of this book.

There are all sorts of ways in which you may help your children. These may include loans or gifts to help with house purchases. Why not investigate the possibility of having your spare after-tax income taken into account if your son or daughter has an offset mortgage (see 25.1.1)? They will still pay the same amount each month but by entering into this arrangement you could help them to clear their mortgage after 15 or 16 years rather than the full term, and if properly documented, the gift is likely to qualify for the IHT normal expenditure out of income exemption.

Another situation where you might help is by making gifts or loans to fund retraining if they embark on a new career. We have already covered tax aspects of helping your children by covering part of the costs of school fees, etc. Another way in which you may wish to assist the next generation is by setting them up in business or passing on your family business – see Chapter 32 on this.

If your children work for your family company, you will want to ensure that they can also benefit fully from your company pension scheme. If they work for an unincorporated family business, you should encourage them to make regular contributions to a pension scheme.

One very important way of helping the next generation is to establish one or more family settlements (see Chapter 31).

24.7 ESTATE PLANNING

Inheritance tax planning is a complex technical area (see Chapter 30), but in general a person should:

- make a Will as dying intestate will mean that the intestacy rules will govern the way that your estate will be distributed and these rules may not coincide with your wishes (see 30.14);
- if you already have a Will, get it reviewed if it has not been since the IHT changes in 2006 (see 30.5.1). It is in any case good practice to review your Will regularly, because your assets and aspirations will change over time;
- use the annual exemptions as far as possible (see 30.6);
- preserve and maximise business property and agricultural reliefs;
- if you receive an inheritance, consider making exempt transfers by a deed of variation;
- make potentially exempt transfers that escape IHT after the donor has survived seven years; and
- fund insurance policies written in trust so as to provide cash to meet IHT payable on death.

If you have entered into IHT saving schemes in the past, you need to take advice on whether you could be subject to the income tax charge on pre-owned assets that started in April 2005 (see 33.7).

Making a trust can be an excellent way of putting capital outside your estate without relinquishing all control over the way that the capital is used (especially if you appoint yourself as one of the trustees); see Chapter 31 on trusts in general. You need to bear in mind the GWR (gift with reservation) rules (see 30.7) but with appropriate planning these rules need not apply if you are a potential beneficiary of a trust created by your spouse. There is also an exception from the GWR rule where a person gives an interest in a property to someone who also occupies the property and certain other conditions are satisfied (see 30.7).

See Chapter 32 on passing on the family business.

25

TAX EFFICIENT INVESTMENT

RICHARD JONES AND JENNIFER GRASHAM-WHALLEY

There are a range of investments where the interest and any gains are exempt from tax, or the investment attracts tax relief. This chapter covers the following sections:

Investments providing a tax exempt return

(1) Individual savings accounts (ISAs)
(2) Personal equity plans (PEPs) – now withdrawn
(3) National Savings investments
(4) Friendly society investments

Investments qualifying for tax deductions

(5) Enterprise Investment Scheme (EIS)
(6) Venture Capital Trusts (VCTs)
(7) Enterprise zone trusts (EZTs) – *reliefs now withdrawn*
(8) Investment in film partnerships

INVESTMENTS PROVIDING A TAX EXEMPT RETURN

25.1 INDIVIDUAL SAVINGS ACCOUNTS (ISAs)

ISAs are tax efficient savings vehicles and can be held in either cash or stocks and shares. The tax efficient status of ISAs means that they should be the starting point for any individuals considering saving in a tax-free environment.

UK tax residents have, in recent years, been able to save up to £7,200 each year within ISAs. This limit increased to £10,200 for 2010–11, and to £10,680 for 2011–12 and will increase along with the consumer prices index in future years. The terms Maxi ISA and Mini ISA no longer apply and investors are now able to invest in either a cash ISA or a stocks and shares ISA.

25.1.1 Cash ISAs

Cash ISAs are offered by a large number of financial institutions including banks and building societies and should be considered as deposit based savings. Investors need to compare the interest rates of cash ISAs and these vary between different providers. The maximum allowance available to invest within a cash ISA in 2011–12 is £5,340.

Investors should also ensure that any existing cash ISAs from previous tax years are still earning a competitive interest rate. If this is not the case, it is possible to transfer previous cash ISAs to a new provider whilst maintaining the tax efficient status of these monies. The new provider will organise the administration of the transfer and it is important that the investor does not simply withdraw their cash ISA monies and reinvest as this will not maintain the tax efficient status of these monies.

25.1.2 Stocks and shares ISAs

Investors are allowed to invest up to £10,680 for this tax year (2011–12) within stocks and shares ISAs. Should the investor have also taken out a cash ISA this will reduce the corresponding amount allowed within the stocks and shares ISA, ie the maximum cash ISA investment of £5,340 will restrict the investment within a stocks and shares ISA to £5,340.

Stocks and shares ISAs are tax free: however investment in equities does not allow a reclaim of the 10% tax credit on dividend payments. There is no capital gains tax applicable on the sale of equities within a stocks and shares ISA.

Stocks and shares ISAs are offered by a number of different ISA managers including investment fund groups, fund platforms, banks and stockbrokers. The underlying investments can be collective investment vehicles such as open ended investment companies (OEICs) or unit trusts or individual shares.

The investment decision is the same as for making any longer term investment of this type and investors need to take into account their investment timeframe, their attitude to investment risk and their objectives prior to investing. The investment performance of different funds and stocks will also need to be considered and investors may need to seek financial advice in selecting an investment that is appropriate for them. Charges also vary widely between different investment offerings.

Stocks and shares ISAs can be transferred to different providers whilst maintaining their tax status; again investors need to ensure that this transfer is organised by the new ISA manager to ensure that the tax efficient status of the monies remains. In recent years many investors have sought to re-register previous stocks and shares ISA on a single platform. The advantages of the re-registration exercise are simplification of overall administration and the ability to realign the underlying investment strategy from a wide selection of investment managers.

On a transfer, the existing provider will sell the investments and the cash from the sale is transferred within the ISA wrapper to the new provider. Once the transfer is completed it is then possible for the investor to reinvest, but dealing charges may be incurred.

Re-registration (in specie transfer) occurs when the name of the account manager is changed from the current provider and re-registered with a new provider. This method avoids the process of selling the underlying investments and therefore no additional costs/charges should be incurred in relation to the underlying investments as the investor remains fully invested.

25.1.3 ISA Changes in FA 2011

FA (No.1) 2010 provided that the limits referred to above would increase with inflation from 2011 onwards, rounded up to the nearest £120. At the 2011 Budget, it was made clear that this increase would be in line with the consumer prices index, rather than the retail prices index, so the increases in the applicable limits are unlikely to be as generous as hoped.

The Government also introduced the concept of a 'junior ISA'. All UK resident children aged under the age of 18 who do not have a child trust fund (CTF) account will be eligible for a junior ISA. Junior ISAs will be tax-relieved and will have many features in common with existing ISA products. They will be available as cash and/or stocks and shares products, with an annual investment limit of £3,000. The investment limit for existing CTFs will be increased from £1,200 pa to £3,000 pa to ensure parity of treatment.

Junior ISAs have been introduced to fill the gap left when eligibility for new CTF accounts ceased from 3 January 2011. It is expected that junior ISAs will be available from 1 November 2011.

25.1.4 Transfers of shares into an ISA

It is possible to transfer shares received from an approved profit-sharing scheme (see 6.2) or from an approved savings-related share option scheme (see 6.4) into an ISA. The market value of shares transferred into the ISA counts towards the annual limit, but no CGT is payable on the transfer. The transfer must take place within three years of the shares being appropriated in the case of a profit-sharing scheme and within 90 days of acquisition under a savings-related share option scheme.

It is not possible to transfer other shares into an ISA, for example, shares acquired under a public offer or on a building society demutualisation.

25.1.5 Withdrawals

It is possible to make withdrawals from an ISA at any time without loss of tax relief, but it is not normally possible to return sums to an ISA. There was however a special exemption for savers who withdrew money from Northern Rock ISAs.

25.1.6 **Consequences if rules are broken**

If the rules are broken within a cash ISA, the provider must withhold 20% tax and the individual must include the interest on his or her self-assessment return and pay any higher rate tax due. An individual who has knowingly broken the rules may also be liable for a penalty.

Tax notes

ISAs were originally intended to have a ten-year life but now appear to be a permanent feature of the tax planning landscape.

25.2 **PERSONAL EQUITY PLANS (PEPs)**

PEPs were merged into the same category as ISA investments from 6 April 2008 and are now known as ISAs. This change was a simplification measure and the tax status of any remaining continued PEP investments will remain.

25.3 **NATIONAL SAVINGS INVESTMENTS**

25.3.1 **National Savings certificates**

(s 692 ITTOIA 2005)

These certificates pay an accumulating rate of interest over a two, three or five-year period. All returns are tax free. Index-linked certificates accumulate at a rate related to the RPI. A bonus is payable if they are held for either a three or five year period. Similar tax-free benefits can be obtained from premium bonds and children's bonus bonds.

25.4 **FRIENDLY SOCIETY INVESTMENTS**

Friendly societies issue qualifying insurance policies and there is no tax charge for investors when such policies mature. In this respect the position is no different from policies issued by insurance companies. The difference lies in the way friendly societies are treated favourably for tax purposes in that they are not normally subject to tax on life assurance business; this has generally enabled them to produce attractive returns.

Friendly society policies are essentially a long-term investment (minimum ten years). The maximum premiums are very low: the maximum permitted is £270 pa (or £300 if paid monthly). Some societies do permit a lump sum investment to be made to cover a full ten-year plan. Most of the larger friendly societies are governed by the same investment regulations as life assurance companies. All investment income and capital gains within the fund are free of all UK tax, which enhances the rate of return.

INVESTMENTS QUALIFYING FOR TAX DEDUCTION

25.5 ENTERPRISE INVESTMENT SCHEME (EIS)

(Part 5 ITA 2007)

The enterprise investment scheme (EIS) is intended to provide a targeted incentive for new equity investment in unquoted trading companies and to encourage outside investors to introduce finance and expertise to a company. The reliefs allow minority investors to secure 30% (from 6 April 2011, subject to EU State Aid approval) income tax relief in addition to CGT deferral relief, which could be worth up to another 28% of the amount invested (or more if the EIS investment is used to roll-over pre-6 April 2008 capital gains).

Individuals can secure EIS CGT deferral relief even if they do not qualify for the income tax relief (eg because they take a controlling stake in the company). Trustees can also use the EIS to secure CGT deferral relief but are not eligible for the income tax relief.

25.5.1 Summary of main aspects

Tax relief is due only if an individual subscribes for new shares in a qualifying company (see 25.5.3) which satisfies the gross asset test (see 25.5.6).

Income tax relief

Income tax relief may be given at 30% on the amount invested up to a maximum of £500,000 (this is due to increase next year – see below and 19.3.2); this relief is forfeited if there is a disposal within three years.

CGT reliefs

Shares that attract the 30% income tax relief are exempt from CGT, provided all the relvant qualifying conditions continue to be met throughout the relevant period.

Where EIS shares are sold at a loss, relief is available either against capital gains or against the individual's income by virtue of s 131 ITA 2007 (see 17.2) but this will not normally give additional relief where the investment has qualified for EIS CGT deferral relief.

Conditions to be satisfied

Income tax relief is not available if the individual has – or is entitled to acquire – an interest in the company that exceeds 30%, but CGT deferral relief may still be available in these circumstances.

Income tax relief is also not available to an individual who had such an interest in the company at any time in the two years prior to the issue of the shares. This does not prevent a connected investor from qualifying for the CGT deferral relief.

There is a ceiling for investment by individuals who qualify for income tax relief under the EIS of £500,000 per tax year. This is due to increase on 6 April 2012 to £1m, subject to EU State Aid approval. The ceiling does not apply for CGT deferral relief. An individual can make a claim to treat any EIS investment as having been made in the previous tax year, thereby allowing up to £1m (currently) of income tax relieved investment in EIS companies in any one tax year (eg half of the £1m would attract tax relief in the year of investment and half in the previous year).

Further details on the EIS can be found at www.hmrc.gov.uk/eis.

Certificate EIS 3

An investor must obtain a certificate EIS 3 from the company before claiming either type of EIS relief.

25.5.2 Conditions to be satisfied for relief to be available

Subscription for new shares in a qualifying company

Neither EIS income tax relief nor EIS CGT deferral relief are available unless an individual subscribes for shares. The shares must be ordinary shares with no preferential rights and a minimum investment of at least £500 is required. The company must be a qualifying company.

25.5.3 Qualifying companies

The monetary and employee limits for EIS (and VCT) qualifying companies are to be relaxed from 6 April 2012 – see 19.3.2 for details. A qualifying company can be a UK-resident or non-resident company, but it must be an unquoted company that:

(1) has a permanent establishment in the UK; and
(2) has a qualifying trade or be the parent of a group of companies where the business of the group does not consist, wholly or substantially, in the carrying on of non-qualifying activities. A qualifying trade is one which is conducted on a commercial basis with a view to the realisation of profits and does not consist wholly or substantially of one or more of the prescribed 'excluded' activities.

Groups

A group's activities must be considered as a whole, rather than on a company-by-company basis. HMRC has confirmed that relief will not be withdrawn where any non-qualifying activities do not form a substantial part of the group's activities as a whole. In practice, 'substantial' is understood to mean 20% or more.

Company must be unquoted

A company does not qualify if any of its shares or securities are dealt in on the London Stock Exchange. The fact that a company's shares are dealt in on AIM does not disqualify it, but the gross asset test will rule out many AIM companies (see 25.5.6).

Other conditions

There are other conditions, all of which need to be satisfied, if a company is to be a qualifying company:

- It must not control another company apart from a qualifying subsidiary, either on its own or together with a connected person, and there must not be any arrangements in place under which the issuing company can acquire such control.
- It must not itself be under the control of another company, or of another company and persons connected with it, and again there must be no arrangements in place whereby such a company may acquire control of the issuing company.
- There must be no arrangements for the company to become quoted.
- It must not be reasonable to assume that the company would be treated as an 'enterprise in difficulty' for the purposes of the European Commission's Rescue and Restructuring Guidelines.
- The company must have fewer than 50 full-time, or full-time equivalent, employees at the time the EIS shares are issued (this limit is due to increase to fewer than 250 from 6 April 2012).

25.5.4 Meaning of 'qualifying trade'

This is covered at 19.3.4. Certain asset-based or low-risk trades are excluded, as are investment businesses. Feed-in tariff businesses are also to be excluded (see 19.3.4).

25.5.5 Definition of 'qualifying subsidiary'

(s 191 ITA 2007)

A qualifying subsidiary is one in which the issuing company or one of its subsidiaries holds at least 51% of the share capital. In addition, the company must meet one of the following tests:

- it must be carrying on a qualifying trade; or
- it must exist to hold and manage a property used by the parent company, or by a fellow 51% subsidiary, for qualifying trade purposes; or
- it must be dormant.

However, a subsidiary needs to be a 90% subsidiary if it is to be the company that uses the EIS money.

25.5.6 Gross asset test

EIS reliefs are available only where the company has gross assets of less than £7m (increasing to £15m from 6 April 2012) before and no more than £8m (it is assumed this limit will also increase appropriately next year) after the EIS share issue.

25.5.7 Reliefs available to an EIS investor

There are two types of relief: income tax and CGT deferral relief (see 25.5.1). They are separate, and either can be claimed without the other. An individual who invests, say, £100,000 can claim both reliefs by reference to the same £100,000 invested. Trustees can only claim the CGT relief.

25.5.8 Income tax relief

An investor is entitled to the lower of the income tax payable by him or her and relief at the lower rate (30% from 6 April 2011) on the amount invested up to a limit of £500,000 for 2011–12 (£1m for 2012–13). For this purpose, his or her tax liability is calculated without regard to any reliefs given as a reduction expressed in terms of tax.

His or her tax liability is also computed without regard to double taxation credits and basic rate tax deducted at source on annual payments.

25.5.9 Other conditions for income tax relief

Individual must not be connected with the company

The legislation provides that an individual may be treated as connected with the issuing company, and therefore not entitled to EIS income tax relief, if he or she directly or indirectly possesses or is entitled to acquire more than 30% of the:

- issued ordinary share capital of the company, or any of its subsidiaries;
- loan capital and issued share capital of the company or any subsidiary; or
- voting power in the company or any subsidiary.

A connected individual can still be eligible for CGT deferral relief.

An individual is also regarded as being connected with the issuing company if he or she directly or indirectly possesses, or is entitled to acquire such rights as would, in the event of the winding-up of the company (or any of its subsidiaries), mean he or she is entitled to receive more than 30% of the assets available for distribution to the company's equity holders.

Rights of 'associates' need to be taken into account. For these purposes, 'associate' means business partner, spouse or civil partner, parent, grandparent, great-grandparent etc, child, grandchild, great-grandchild etc and certain family trusts. The necessity to take account of partners' interests was confirmed by the decision in *Cook* v *Billings & others*.

An individual is also regarded as connected with the company if he or she possesses any loan capital in a subsidiary of the company.

Finally, if an investor receives a loan from a third party that would not have been made but for the EIS investment, he or she is disqualified. This also applies where a bank makes a loan that is secured on the EIS shares.

An individual is also deemed to be connected with the company if he or she is:

- a paid director of the issuing company or any of its subsidiaries; or
- an employee of the issuing company or any of its subsidiaries; or
- a partner of the issuing company or any subsidiary; or
- an associate of someone who is a director, employee or partner of the issuing company, or any of its subsidiaries.

An individual is disqualified if he or she falls into any of the above categories during the two years prior to the date the EIS shares are issued. Furthermore, he or she will not qualify for EIS relief if he or she is connected with the issuing company at the time the shares are issued, unless the individual is a business angel who qualified for EIS relief on his or her original investment and is now acquiring additional shares and is connected only because he or she is a paid director.

FA 2004 legislation

FA 2004 introduced two changes. The first allowed shares to be issued to EIS investors at the same time as other investors (previously not allowed). The second made it possible for investors who had previously had loans repaid to them by the company to obtain income tax relief, provided the loan repayment was not deemed an 'arrangement'. Both of these provisions came into effect from 17 March 2004.

25.5.10 CGT deferral relief

(Schedule 5B TCGA 1992)

This relief involves a concept of deferred gain. Basically, an individual who has realised a gain may secure deferral relief if he or she invests in the EIS during the period beginning one year before and ending three years after the disposal giving rise to the chargeable gain. CGT deferral relief can be claimed even where the investor is 'connected' with the company (see 25.5.9).

However, the deferred gain is separately identified and will come back into charge when certain events happen (see 25.5.17).

Example – EIS CGT deferral relief

> *N* sold quoted shares for £65,000 in December 2011. The shares were originally purchased in January 2004 for £10,000. In July 2011, *N* invested £55,000 in ordinary shares in an EIS company. The CGT position for 2011–12 would then be as follows:
>
> | | £ |
> |---|---|
> | Proceeds | 65,000 |
> | *Less*: Cost | (10,000) |
> | Gain | 55,000 |
> | *Less*: EIS CGT deferral relief | 44,400 |
> | Net chargeable gain for 2011–12 | 10,600 |
>
> *Note*: Although *N* invested £55,000, it is possible for him to claim CGT deferral relief of only £44,400 so as to avoid wasting the annual exemption for 2011–12. See 17.8.5 regarding the interaction of EIS deferral and entrepreneurs' relief and transitional considerations.

25.5.11 Withdrawal of relief where company redeems share capital

All EIS investors lose a proportion of their relief if at any time during the investor's relevant period the company repays, redeems or repurchases any of its share capital which belongs to any member other than:

(1) the qualifying individual in question; or
(2) another EIS investor who thereby loses relief under the disposal of shares rule;
(3) the total relief withdrawn from EIS investors is the greater of:
    (a) the amount receivable by the non-EIS investor; or
    (b) the nominal value of the share capital in question.

The relief so lost is apportioned between the EIS investors in proportion to the amounts of the investments that have previously qualified for relief.

25.5.12 Withdrawal of relief where value is received from the company

Relief is withdrawn to the extent that an investor receives value from the company within three years of making his or her investment. An investor is regarded as having received value where the company:

- repays, redeems or repurchases any part of his or her holding of its share capital or securities, or makes any payment to him or her for the cancellation of rights;
- repays any debt to him or her (other than a debt incurred by the company on or after the date on which he or she subscribed for the shares that are the subject of EIS relief);
- pays him or her for the cancellation of any debt owed to him or her other than an ordinary trade debt, ie a debt incurred for a supply of goods or services on normal trade credit terms. The legislation specifically provides that normal trade credit does not allow for payment to be left outstanding for a period that exceeds six months; or
- releases or waives any liability of his or hers to the company (the liability is deemed to have been waived if the liability is outstanding for more than 12 months) or discharges or undertakes to discharge any liability of his or hers to a third person.

Further, he or she is regarded as having received value where the company:
- (a) makes a loan or advance to him or her if this includes the situation where the individual becomes indebted to the company other than by an ordinary trade debt;
- (b) provides a benefit or facility for him or her;
- (c) transfers an asset to him or her for no consideration or for consideration less than market value;
- (d) acquires an asset from him or her for consideration exceeding market value; or
- (e) makes any other payment to him or her except:
  - (i) one that represents payment or reimbursement of allowable expenditure;
  - (ii) interest at a commercial rate on a loan from the individual;
  - (iii) dividends representing a normal return on investment;
  - (iv) payment for a supply of goods by the individual to the company (provided the price does not exceed the goods' market value);
  - (v) reasonable and necessary remuneration for services rendered to the company where the income is taxed as trading income (this does not cover remuneration for secretarial or managerial services).

However, any receipt of insignificant value can be ignored. A receipt is of insignificant value if it is not more than £1,000 or, if more is insignificant in relation to the amount subscribed by the investor for the relevant shares.

25.5.13 Withdrawal of relief where company ceases to be a qualifying company

EIS relief is withdrawn completely where any of the following events occurs during the three-year relevant period:

- the company issues shares that are not fully paid up;
- the company ceases to exist wholly for a qualifying trade purpose;
- the company comes under the control of another company, or of another company and persons connected with it;
- arrangements come into being whereby another company could acquire control.

25.5.14 Clawback of income tax relief where investor becomes connected with the company

EIS income tax relief (but not CGT deferral relief) is withdrawn completely where an investor becomes connected with the company during his or her relevant period (three years from the date that his or her shares are issued).

Definition of 'connected'

An individual is regarded as becoming connected with the company if he or she is:

- the owner (directly or indirectly) of more than 30% of the company's voting shares, its issued ordinary share capital, or its loan capital and issued share capital taken together;
- the owner of rights entitling him or her to more than 30% of the company's assets available for distribution to equity holders;
- entitled to acquire more than 30% of the company's voting shares, its issued share capital, or its share and loan capital taken together;
- entitled to acquire rights entitling him or her to more than 30% of the company's assets available for distribution to the company's equity holders;
- the associate of a person who owns or is entitled to acquire more than a 30% interest;
- the owner of any loan capital in a subsidiary of the company;
- an employee of the company;
- a partner of the company;
- an associate of an employee or a partner of the company; or

- a director of the company – unless he or she receives only 'necessary and reasonable' remuneration; reimbursement of expenses incurred wholly and necessarily in the performance of his or her duties; normal commercial returns on funds lent or normal commercial dividends on shares held; reasonable and commercial rents from property occupied by the company; or payment for the supply of goods not exceeding market value.

25.5.15 Withdrawal of income tax relief on disposal within three years

If a disposal takes place within three years, and the disposal is not to the investor's spouse or civil partner, relief is withdrawn. If the disposal is anything other than a sale to an unconnected party at an arm's length price, EIS income tax relief is withdrawn completely. Where the disposal is on an arm's length basis, relief is withdrawn only on the sale consideration received by the investor, as a proportion of the original investment.

The grant of an option during the relevant period may be treated as a disposal, ie where the exercise of the option would bind the grantor to purchase any of the EIS shares, or the investor to sell any of the EIS shares.

25.5.16 Loss relief on arm's length disposal at less than cost

Where a loss arises on disposal or the company goes into liquidation within the three-year period, further income tax/CGT relief may be due to the investor. In a case where the investor receives no payment under the liquidation, the net amount of his or her investment may qualify as a capital loss.

Example – EIS income tax relief

> *O* invests £80,000 under the EIS. She receives income tax relief at 20% of £80,000, ie £16,000. If the entire investment has to be written off, she will be entitled to a capital loss of £64,000. This loss may be set against *O*'s income or relieved against capital gains.

25.5.17 Clawback of CGT deferral relief

A gain that has been deferred is brought back into charge if any of the following events happens:

(1) the investor disposes of the shares other than to his or her spouse or civil partner and the deferred gain is not rolled forward into a new EIS investment within one year before and three years after the sale;

(2) the investor (or, where there has been a transfer between spouses, his or her spouse or civil partner) ceases to be UK resident at any time within three years of the issue of the EIS shares;

(3) the company ceases to be a qualifying company for EIS purposes within three years of the issue of the shares, or within three years of the date that it starts trading if this happens later.

The rule in (2) above does not apply if an individual temporarily becomes non-resident because of his or her employment, and he or she returns to the UK within three years still owning the shares.

Example – Withdrawal of CGT deferral relief

> During the year 2009–10, *P* realised a capital gain of £60,000. She made an investment into an EIS company of £55,000 in August 2011. Her other income was sufficient to warrant full EIS relief.
>
> For 2011–12 *P* receives EIS relief of £55,000 × 30% = £16,500. She could also elect to defer her 2009–10 gains of £49,900 (£60,000 less the annual exemption £10,100). This would defer a potential CGT liability of £8,982.
>
> In May 2012 *P* decides to emigrate. This causes the deferred gain of £49,900 to be reinstated as if it were a 2012–13 capital gain.
>
> The gain is then taxed at 28% (assuming the rate does not change from current levels). If *P* was aware, in August 2011, that emigration in 2012 was an option, it would have been cheaper not to defer her 2009–10 gain, and pay CGT at only 18%.

25.5.18 Taper relief

Where a capital gain arising between 6 April 1998 and 5 April 2008 has been reduced by taper relief and the gain is deferred by an EIS investment, the gain clawed back on disposal is the original gain (ie there could be no further accrual of the taper relief holding period during the period the EIS shares are held).

25.5.19 Disposal after three years of shares that qualified for EIS income tax relief

Once shares that qualify for the 30% income tax relief have been held for three years, there is no clawback of relief on a disposal of the shares. Furthermore, these shares are an exempt asset for CGT purposes so that no CGT will be payable on any gain on the shares. However, a loss realised on the disposal of the shares after the three-year period may still attract either income tax or CGT relief. Again, the loss is calculated as the difference between the net of tax cost and the disposal proceeds (see 25.5.16).

CGT may still be payable on disposal to the extent that CGT deferral relief has been obtained (see 25.5.16), even though any capital gain arising on the EIS shares themselves may be exempt.

25.6 VENTURE CAPITAL TRUSTS (VCTs)

(Part 6 ITA 2007)

25.6.1 Qualifying trusts

Venture capital trusts (VCTs) are companies broadly similar to investment trusts. The monetary and employee limits for VCT (and EIS) qualifying companies are to be relaxed from 6 April 2012 – see 19.3.2 for details. The main conditions for approval are that, in its most recent accounting period, as well as the period in which application for approval is made, the VCT meets the following requirements:

- its ordinary share capital has been or will be admitted on any EU regulated market (prior to April 2010, the condition was that shares should be quoted on the London Stock Exchange);
- it has not, or will not, retain more than 15% of the income that it derived or derives from shares or securities;
- its income must be, or have been, derived wholly or mainly from shares or securities;
- at least 70% by value of its investments has been, or will be, represented by shares or securities in qualifying holdings (see below). Securities can include medium-term loans for a period of at least five years;
- up to 5 April 2011, at least 30% by value of its qualifying holdings is made up of ordinary shares. From 6 April 2011, the VCT's qualifying holdings must contain at least 70% eligible shares, but these may include shares which carry certain preferential rights to dividends; and
- no holding in any one company represents more than 15% of the VCT's investments.

A VCT may be given provisional approval if HMRC is satisfied that the 70% requirements will be met within three years and the other conditions will be met in the current or next accounting period. If the trust fails to meet the conditions within these time periods, provisional approval is withdrawn.

Qualifying holdings

'Qualifying holdings' are holdings in unquoted companies that exist wholly for the purpose of carrying on wholly or mainly in the UK one or more qualifying trades (defined as for the EIS).

VCTs may count annual investments of up to £1m in total in any one qualifying unquoted trading company as a qualifying holding. The unquoted company's gross assets must not exceed £7m (£15m from 6 April 2012) before and £8m (it is assumed this limit will increase appropriately from 6 April 2012) immediately after the VCT's investment.

If a VCT holds shares in a qualifying company which subsequently becomes quoted, any shares or securities in that company will continue to be treated as qualifying for a period of five years from the time at which the company became quoted.

The rules that govern the types of companies in which VCTs may invest are very similar to the EIS rules (see 25.5).

It is permissible for a VCT to exchange its shares in an unquoted company for shares in a new holding company where that holding company has a 100% interest in the original company and the share exchange is being carried out to facilitate a flotation. In broad terms, the VCT may treat its shares in the new holding company as a qualifying investment provided the VCT has the same interest in the holding company and the VCT's shares in the original company were a qualifying investment.

Similarly, where a VCT holds convertible loan stock or preference shares, and it exercises its conversion rights, the resulting shareholding can be a qualifying investment.

Mergers and liquidations

The legislation was amended by FA 2002 to enable a VCT to retain its approved status where it merged with another VCT. The rules were also relaxed to enable VCTs to maintain approved status during a winding-up. These changes mean that investors do not forfeit their tax reliefs simply because of a merger or the appointment of a liquidator.

25.6.2 Income tax reliefs

There are two kinds of income tax relief available for investments in VCTs:

(1) Individuals aged 18 or over are exempt from income tax on dividends from ordinary shares in VCTs to the extent that the shares acquired each year do not exceed £200,000 in value. This relief can be withheld if HMRC can show that the VCT shares were acquired in order to avoid tax (eg where they were acquired shortly before the VCT paid a dividend and sold shortly afterwards).
(2) Individuals aged 18 or over who subscribe for new ordinary shares in VCTs are, in addition, entitled to claim income tax relief at 30%, subject to a limit on the amount subscribed in any one year of £200,000. This relief on investment will be withdrawn unless the shares are held for at least five years.

25.6.3 CGT reliefs

At one time, there was a CGT deferral relief for investors but this was abolished from 6 April 2004.

25.7 ENTERPRISE ZONE TRUSTS (EZTs)

It was possible, prior to 6 April 2011, to invest in properties in enterprise zones through a syndicate or enterprise zone property trust (EZT). An individual who invested in the trust was treated as if he or she had incurred a proportion of the trust's expenditure on enterprise zone properties. Similarly, rents (and sometimes interest) received by the trust were apportioned among the investors, ie HMRC looked through the trust and treated the individual as if he or she had acquired an interest in the underlying properties.

Where an individual was treated as having acquired such an interest in an enterprise zone property, the allowances could be set against his or her other income (see 8.7.6). However, an individual who invested in such a trust was entitled to capital allowances only for the year in which the trust invested in enterprise zone properties. In some cases, there was be a delay in that the investor invested in a trust at the end of one tax year and became entitled to allowances only for the following year (because that is the year in which the trust acquired the relevant properties).

Note that enterprise zone allowances have been completely withdrawn from April 2011, but without the phasing out rules which applied to industrial and agricultural buildings allowances. If there is a chargeable period that crosses the cut-off date, the writing-down allowance for that chargeable period is apportioned. However, the individual can still have pre-2011–12 allowances clawed back if he or she receives capital value attributable to a subordinate interest in the building within seven years of having acquired the relevant interest. This could arise where, for example, a long lease has been granted to a tenant in respect of the property.

New enterprise zones were announced in the 2011 Budget but the proposed advantages for businesses setting up in the new zones will only extend to reduced business rates, extra allowances for plant and machinery and some reductions in red tape.

25.8 INVESTMENT IN FILM PARTNERSHIPS

A number of schemes over the years have been based on exploiting tax reliefs for films.

Films are a very specialised form of investment and, because of the amount of capital involved in making films, many of the schemes that evolved were Limited Partnerships. Under such schemes an individual could benefit from the opening year rules for new businesses (see 7.3.3) and losses might also be used under s 64 ITA 2007 (see 7.7.2). These partnerships were perceived to be abusive as the return for investors was generally not dependent in any way on whether the film was successful.

FA 2004 removed much of the scope for artificial tax-based schemes. Since 10 February 2004, individuals who devote less than ten hours a week to the partnership business are denied tax relief for losses in excess of the capital that they have contributed to the partnership (except in so far as the partnership has profits in later years). FA 2004 also introduced an income tax charge (now found in Chapter 5, Part 13 ITA 2007) on an individual ceasing to be a partner on an amount equal to the difference between the tax losses that he or she has enjoyed and the amount of his or her economic loss.

Yet more anti-avoidance provisions were introduced in successive Budgets. Legislation included in FA (No. 1) 2010 ensured that no tax relief will be due where there are arrangements where the main purpose, or one of the main purposes, is to obtain a reduction in a tax liability. This provision is essentially a 'mini-*Ramsay*' test.

26

PENSIONS

JENNIFER GRASHAM-WHALLY AND RICHARD JONES

Pension planning is one of the most important decisions you will make during your financial life and as such it no longer pays to be an innocent bystander while others make decisions that could have such a dramatic effect upon both you and your family.

Many people hold negative views of pensions and this is not surprising given their recent experiences, which include low incomes in retirement, complicated legislative changes and the collapse of a prominent life office. However, pensions remain highly tax efficient vehicles and with a suitable investment strategy future return expectations have a good chance of being achieved. Pensions should typically form the core long-term financial plan for most people in the UK.

There are broadly two types of pension schemes: money purchase and defined benefit arrangements. Defined benefit (final salary schemes) are employer-sponsored schemes where the pension benefits in retirement will be known beforehand and will be paid by the pension scheme.

Under a money purchase type arrangement the pension fund increases through contributions and from investment growth; whatever the size of the pension fund at retirement will determine the size of pension income that can be attained.

Money purchase schemes include stakeholder pensions, personal pensions and self-invested personal pensions (SIPPs). The investment choice within all these types of schemes is important and is a key factor when reviewing or considering pension planning.

This chapter contains the following sections:

Registered pension schemes

(1) The regime that came into force on 'A' Day
(2) Retirement benefits under the 'A' Day regime
(3) Pension scheme investments under the 'A' Day regime
(4) Tax relief for contributions
(5) 2011–12 changes and transitional arrangements for 2010–11
(6) Personal pension accounts and NEST

Other retirement benefit schemes

(7) Unapproved schemes
(8) Transfers from UK pension schemes into a QROPS

State benefits

(9) State pension benefits
(10) Contracting out

REGISTERED PENSION SCHEMES

26.1 THE REGIME THAT CAME INTO FORCE ON 'A' DAY

On 6 April 2006 ('A' Day), a new, unified pensions tax regime came into force replacing the existing pension tax regimes. The rules affect pension scheme savers in all types of pension schemes, employers and the pension industry, together with financial advisers.

26.1.1 Pension scheme registration

On 'A' Day the whole concept of approved pension schemes and discretionary approval was replaced with the concept of registration.

To benefit from all tax privileges, a pension scheme must be registered with HMRC. All schemes are automatically registered unless they elect to be non-registered. De-registration results in a tax charge of 40% on the value of the scheme assets with the lump sum payable at retirement no longer being tax-free.

No tax benefits can be enjoyed until a scheme is registered. This could be important for company year-end tax planning.

26.1.2 Statutory lifetime allowance (SLA)

Limits on retirement benefits were replaced by a single statutory lifetime allowance (SLA) covering the amount of tax-privileged pension saving. The SLA was set at £1.8m for 2010–11 and 2011–12, but is expected to reduce to £1.5m from 2012–13, as a corollary to the changes introduced by the coalition Government to replace the previous administration's torturously complex proposals for restricting pensions tax relief (see 26.5).

The value of pension benefits, whatever the type of pension scheme, is tested against the individual's lifetime allowance whenever a benefit crystallisation event (BCE) occurs. BCEs include vesting of a policy, taking a tax-free cash lump sum, death and purchase of an annuity.

Under a defined benefit scheme, the pension is valued for the purposes of the SLA on a 20:1 basis. If the pension started before 'A' Day and was already in payment then this is valued by a factor of 25:1. This is applied to the annual payment when the first BCE on or after 'A' Day occurs.

Where the income is related to a pension income drawdown arrangement in place prior to 6 April 2006 then the 25:1 factor is applied to the maximum permitted annual income at the most recent review of the member's fund.

Any excess over the SLA that is taken as income attracts a recovery charge of 25%. This is charged to the member and deducted by the scheme. The additional pension income arising from the excess is taxed at the marginal rates prevailing at the time. Alternatively, the excess can be taken as a lump sum in which case the recovery charge will be 55% (regardless of the member's tax position).

26.1.3 FURBS and UURBS

Both FURBS and UURBS have been permitted to continue (but see Chapter 5 and 26.4 below for more detail of new anti-avoidance provisions affecting these structures), subject to transitional provisions for arrangements already in place on 'A' Day. However, they have ceased to have any tax privileges (and will in many cases, now, be disadvantageous – see Chapter 5). They are now taxed as EFRBS, for which there are special tax rules.

The value of EFRBS are not currently taken into account for SLA purposes, however, the Government is closely monitoring the extent to which 'alternatives' to registered pensions are being used. Its stated objective is to ensure that 'contributions to unregistered pension schemes do not benefit from tax advantages on pension savings beyond the annual and lifetime allowances available in registered pensions schemes', accordingly, future action cannot be ruled out.

26.1.4 Annual allowance

There are no limits on pension contributions although there is an Annual Allowance (AA) – an effective cap on the amount which can qualify for tax relief.

The AA had increased to £255,000 for 2010–11 and was expected to remain at this level until 2015–16. However, the coalition Government was reluctant to implement the complex restrictions on pensions tax relief for high earners designed by the previous administration, that were to come into force on 6 April 2011 and instead reduced the annual allowance to £50,000 with effect from 6 April 2011 (but subject to transitional provisions which took effect from 14 October 2010).

Tax relief is currently available on a member's contributions of up to 100% of relevant earnings, or the annual allowance if lower, or £3,600 if earnings are less than £3,600.

In a defined benefit scheme, it is not the actual contributions paid into the scheme but is instead the capital value of the member's pension at the end of the pension input period (PIP) – the 'closing value' – *less* the value of the member's pension at the start of the PIP (the 'opening value') revalued by CPI that is tested against the AA. A factor of 16:1 (prior to 2011–12, 10:1) is applied to the increase in benefit – after allowing for CPI revaluation – in order to calculate the capital value. Therefore a member within a defined benefit scheme would be able to accrue additional benefits of up to £3,125 (£50,000 divided by 16) for 2011–12 (in addition to increases in line with CPI) without exceeding the annual allowance. This compares (rather unfavourably!) to the ability to accrue additional benefits of up to £25,500 (£255,000 divided by 10) for 2010–11.

Previously, in any year in which a member wholly crystallised all the benefits in a pension scheme) the amounts treated as contributed to that scheme in the tax year in which the benefits crystallised were not tested against the annual allowance, although sufficient earnings were still required for the member to have made a contribution above the AA for that tax year. This 'vesting' exemption, was removed from 6 April 2011 and replaced with a new exemption for a tax year in which an individual becomes entitled to a lump sum for serious ill health.

Both before and after 6 April 2011, an individual's inputs to a pension scheme are not tested against the annual allowance in the tax year in which he or she dies.

Pension input periods

The annual allowance is tested against the total level of pension contributions made in a particular pension input period (PIP) that ends in the relevant tax year. As input periods are not necessarily aligned to the timing of tax years the annual allowance is not (as one might intuitively expect) tested against the total pension contributions made in any particular tax year.

Pension schemes will have a scheme input period which will be specific to the particular type of scheme. Although a pension arrangement can have only one PIP ending in any given year. The starting period will typically begin either on the first payment after 'A' Day or for defined benefit schemes, the date that benefits start to accrue. The pension input period will end one year after the period started.

Input periods can be changed by the member, or the scheme administrator, within a money purchase scheme. Changing input periods within a money purchase scheme may represent a planning opportunity for some individuals to make higher pension contributions above the annual allowance in a short period of time. If an individual had changed his or her input period during tax year 2010–11, then with careful planning he or she could potentially contribute a maximum of £510,000 (£255,000 × 2). For 2011–12, the maximum that could be contributed on such a change would be only £100,000 (£50,000 x 2) plus any unused relief (capped at £50,000 pa) for 2008–09, 2009–10 and 2010–11.

Employer pension contributions and spreading

Corporation tax relief is potentially available without limit on all employer contributions provided that they meet the 'wholly and exclusively' test. HMRC will determine whether a payment is appropriate in each case.

Employers will also need to take into account the relevant annual allowance when considering making a larger contribution.

The employer's tax relief may have to be spread over a period of years if the contribution is over £500,000 (see 16.1.5).

26.1.5 Transitional rules

The 'A'day rules apply to all pension savings after 6 April 2006. However, under transitional provisions, all rights built up before April 2006 could be protected by electing for appropriate protection. This applied to pension benefits that exceeded the SLA at 6 April 2006, or could be expected to exceed it after 6 April 2006, and tax-free cash sums, which may be greater than 25% of the value of the pension fund. There were two ways to protect a member's pre-6 April 2006 fund.

Primary protection

Primary protection was only available to those individuals whose fund value at 6 April 2006 exceeded £1.5m. Future contributions could be made, and any growth on the fund up to the increase in the SLA each year was protected from tax charges. However, should the fund grow at a faster rate than the SLA, a tax charge would be payable on the funds over this level.

Those people who registered for primary protection were also able to protect any tax-free entitlement over £375,000 (£1.5m × 25%). They will be able to take the amount of their pre-6 April 2006 lump sum rights increased in line with the increase in the standard lifetime allowance.

Enhanced protection

This allowed protection of funds even if they were below the SLA at 6 April 2006. This protection effectively required the individual to stop funding his or her pension, and accruing further pensionable service. However, a small level of accrual was allowed and this is described within the 'relevant benefit accrual' rules.

Providing enhanced protection had been elected for and any benefit accrual is within the rules, any benefits coming in to payment after 5 April 2006 will normally be exempt from the SLA, whatever the value. For an occupational scheme member who elected for enhanced protection who has earmarked funds within the pension scheme, it will require the benefits to be tested within the scheme under the old rules. If a surplus exists in the fund then this must be returned to the company and taxed at 35%.

It was also possible to protect any tax-free cash entitlement in excess of £375,000, at 5 April 2006, through enhanced protection. Under this option, the tax-free cash is protected as a percentage of an individual's overall pension benefits. Therefore, unlike primary protection, the entitlement can increase at a faster rate than the SLA with no penalties being applied.

For individuals in defined benefit schemes who have opted for enhanced protection, while benefits accrued after 5 April 2012 will not trigger an end to protection, they may still trigger an AA charge if the deemed inputs in a year exceed the new £50,000 limit.

If enhanced protection was elected for and future pension contributions or accruals occur, then it is possible to revert to primary protection <u>only</u> if it has also been elected for, otherwise the position will automatically revert to 'no protection'. Protection from the recovery charge is determined by the pre-6 April 2006 pension value, or the prevailing SLA for those whose pension value, did not exceed £1.5m. The deadline for electing for transitional protection was 5 April 2009.

It is proposed that the new regime (ie the decrease in the SLA to £1.5m) from April 2012 will include a right for individuals to opt for protection ('fixed protection') of the £1.8m current lifetime limit in a similar way as enhanced protection operated from 'A' Day. Whilst fixed protection will not be available to any individual already holding enhanced or primary protection, those with primary protection will automatically benefit from the £1.8m SLA going forward.

Tax payment administration

In a defined contribution pension scheme, any tax charge which is payable on retirement will be paid to HMRC by the administrators of the scheme and the fund value reduced accordingly. The remaining fund value will then be used to provide benefits for the individual on retirement.

With defined benefit pension schemes, the situation is slightly different. The tax charge due at retirement is computed on the basis that the value of the pension rights is equal to 20 times the annual pension.

Tax notes

- It is not possible to switch from primary protection to enhanced protection – or vice versa – at any time, although those individuals who are registered for both are able to relinquish EP in order to benefit from PP.
- The deadline for applying for transitional protection expired on 5 April 2009.

26.2 RETIREMENT BENEFITS UNDER THE NEW REGIME

There is now a single set of rules governing the ways in which benefits can be drawn from a pension scheme.

26.2.1 Minimum retirement age

Schedule 16 Finance Act 2011 removes the effective requirement for members of a registered pension scheme to purchase an annuity by age 75. The tax-free cash lump sum can be taken at any time after age 55. An income can also be taken from age 55 but can be deferred:

- until age 77, for those reaching 75 on or after 22 June 2010 but before 6 April 2011;
- from 6 April 2011, the concepts of an unsecured pension arrangement (USP) and alternatively secured pension (ASP).

Those with certain existing contractual rights to draw a pension earlier than age 55 may have that right protected. There is special protection for members of those approved schemes in existence before April 2006 with low normal retirement ages, such as those for sports people. The minimum retirement age also does not apply to 'unregistered' arrangements such as EFRBS. In those cases, retirement will continue to be a question of fact.

It is not necessary for a member to leave employment in order to access an employer's occupational pension. Members of occupational pension schemes may, where the scheme rules allow it, continue working for the same employer whilst drawing retirement benefits.

26.2.2 Lump sums on death before benefits have been drawn

In the event of death before drawing benefits, the whole of the individual's pension fund is potentially available to provide death benefits (subject to the pension scheme rules for occupational schemes). There are no limits on the size of the resulting fund and the whole of the fund can be used to provide a lump sum and/or dependants' pensions.

This applies in the event that the member dies before taking the benefits, provided he or she has not reached age 75. However, if a lump sum is chosen, the fund value will need to be tested against the SLA, and a recovery charge of 55% will apply to the excess over the SLA. If the fund is used to provide a dependant's pension then no tax charge will be payable regardless of the pension fund value at that time. However, any dependants' pensions will be subject to income tax. FA 2007 contains provisions that prevent a personal pension policy from only providing life assurance benefits.

The position up to 2010–11

FA 2006 contains provisions that may impose IHT on the payment of a death benefit. However, the IHT treatment of a lump sum paid out in these circumstances will, as in the past, generally depend on the circumstances in which the benefits are paid. If it is held under an appropriate trust or paid out at the administrator's discretion in a contract based scheme, then it will normally be exempt from IHT. The exception where HMRC may seek to charge IHT is where it can be shown that the individual did not take a pension because his or her life expectancy was seriously impaired and this resulted in an enhanced death benefit being paid (see *Fryer & Ors (personal representatives of Arnold deceased)* v *R & C Commrs* [2010] UKFTT 87 (TC)). Even if these conditions are satisfied, no IHT will be payable if the lump sum is paid to a spouse, civil partner, financial dependant or a charity.

The position from 2011–12

Favourable IHT changes have also been introduced from 2011–12. Under the new rules, no IHT will be payable on lump sums paid out on a pensioner's death provided these are paid at the trustees' discretion. The 55% exit charge will continue to apply to individuals who die after age 75. This provides another planning option for high-income individuals.

Example

An individual who has a high personal income from investments (she is a 50% taxpayer) has a personal pension fund of £1m which she has yet to draw on as she does not need the income. To minimise her inheritance tax position, she could take her tax-free cash and a pension and then pass money over to her children now – lifetime gifts out of surplus income are exempt from inheritance tax. However, this will mean suffering 50% income tax on the pension element. Alternatively, she could simply take the tax-free cash now and leave the balance of her fund untouched until she dies but leave a letter of wishes to request that the pension trustees use their discretion to pay the remaining funds to her children. The funds will suffer tax at 55% on her death but, in the meantime, will grow in a tax-free environment. Such an option may prove to be beneficial if the pensioner does not wish to pass over funds currently for practical family reasons.

26.2.3 Tax-free lump sums

The maximum amount of pre-commencement lump sum (tax-free cash) that can be paid from all pension schemes – except those with either enhanced or primary protection – is now a quarter of the value of the benefits subject to an overall maximum of a quarter of the SLA (2012–13 on £1.5m × 25% = £375,000: 2010–11on £1.8m × 25% = £450,000). However, for members of occupational schemes before 6 April 2006, who were entitled to a tax-free lump sum of more than 25% in respect of their service before 'A' Day, it is possible for their entitlement to higher tax-free cash to be protected, provided they remain in the same pension scheme. However, any transfer away from the scheme (unless part of a bulk transfer) could result in the higher entitlement being lost.

Members of post-1987 AVC schemes, FSAVC schemes and appropriate personal pension plans can now also take tax-free cash from these arrangements. This has introduced an extra degree of flexibility, because previous rules did not allow this.

26.2.4 Trivial commutation

In cases when an individual has a small level of pension benefits the rules may allow them to be paid off as a lump sum as opposed to drawing a small pension for life – this is known as a trivial commutation lump sum.

Full commutation can be taken where all benefits are taken at the same time, and the total amount of all of the individual's pensions is not more than 1% of the SLA currently in force. One quarter can be paid tax-free with the rest paid as a lump sum, which is subject to income tax at the individual's marginal rate. The triviality rules cannot be used before age 60, or after age 75.

In addition to this basic form of trivial commutation there are two other methods that are available in specified circumstances.

The first is where a member holds benefits worth less than 1% of the SLA within a scheme that is winding up. Here the trustees can offer the member the option of a 'winding-up lump sum'. In order to be eligible the member must meet the following conditions:

- The member's benefits under the scheme are less than 1% of the SLA.
- The payment extinguishes the member's rights to benefits under the scheme.
- The employer is not making contributions on behalf of the member to any other registered pension scheme and undertakes not to do so for at least one year.

Note that there is no minimum age requirement to receive a winding-up lump sum.

The second circumstance is where an individual has an occupational pension scheme pot of less than £2,000 and is aged over 60.

In both the above circumstances, the commutation is taxed in the same way as for a trivial commutation lump sum.

26.2.5 Retirement income

There were previously three ways in which income could be paid to an individual on retirement: secured income; unsecured income; and alternatively secured pension. This changed from 2011–12, with unsecured and alternatively secured pensions in effect disappearing.

Secured income

A secured income is a pension income in retirement that is promised to be paid until death. There are two forms of secured pensions; annuities and scheme pensions; both types will be treated as income for tax purposes.

An annuity is an income stream purchased from an insurance provider using the pension fund at retirement. An annuity could be considered as longevity insurance as it will continue to be paid until death, whenever that may happen.

Where annuities are purchased via money purchase type pension plans, the individual should use the open market option. The annuity market is competitive and this option will help to ensure that the most competitive annuity is purchased for the individual's personal requirements.

Many features can be built into an annuity. These include payment frequency, payment increases, spouse or civil partner's pension and pension guarantees. Depending upon the level and whether an individual selects a spouse or civil partner's pension or guarantee, the options chosen will effectively determine the death benefit position of the annuity.

In a defined benefit pension a scheme pension will be provided. This can either be paid to the member out of the scheme assets or the scheme can purchase an annuity to secure the income for the member. Death benefit options may be determined by the pension scheme rules or may offer flexibility.

Unsecured income: to 2010–11

The alternative to securing benefits under secured income was to take income directly from the pension fund by means of income drawdown. Unsecured income could only continue until the age of 75, or 77 for those reaching 75 on or after 22 June 2010, and has effectively disappeared as an option from 6 April 2011. Alternatively, there were 'third way' products which are effectively temporary annuities offering end of term guarantees. Third way products are outside the scope of this book and are not discussed further here.

Annual income could be taken of up to a maximum of 120% of the annual income payable from a single level annuity rate determined by the Government Actuaries Department (GAD) table. There was no minimum level of income set. Income levels could vary up to the limit and had to be reviewed every five years.

If a member died before age 75 after taking unsecured income, the fund could either be used to provide a lump sum payment or to provide a survivor's pension. If a lump sum was provided, a special income tax charge applied, of 35% of the fund value. A survivor's pension could be provided by an annuity or income drawdown depending upon the individual's requirements; these pension payments will be taxed as income.

These rules were amended in relation to individuals who reached age 75 on or after 22 June 2010. These individuals are able to keep their unsecured pensions until their 77th birthday but cannot leave their funds uncrystallised beyond their 75th birthday. In other words, such funds stay as an unsecured pension fund and do not become an alternatively secured pension fund until the age of 77.

These requirements have been removed in relation to individuals reaching age 75 on or after 6 April 2011. See below for more details.

FA 2006 introduced provisions that could impose an IHT charge. However, IHT was not normally charged on a lump sum paid out in these circumstances unless:

- the member died within two years of taking income or within two years of a five yearly review; and
- the level of unsecured income had been kept low to enhance death benefits and the member's life expectancy was seriously impaired at the time he or she made this decision.

Even if these conditions were met, no IHT was charged if the lump sum was paid to a spouse, civil partner, dependant or charity.

Alternatively secured pension (ASP) – to 2010–11

Before April 2006, the main option for the majority of pensioners was to secure their income from age 75 using an annuity. The 2006 rules introduced the alternatively secured pension (ASP). This was an alternative to purchasing an annuity as it allowed unsecured income to be drawn from age 75 (or 77, if reaching age 75 on or after 22 June 2010 and before 6 April 2011), but with different rules from those that applied before age 75/77 (unsecured income).

Alternatively secured pensions could not start before age 75 (or 77, if reaching age 75 on or after 22 June 2010 but before 6 April 2011), and unless benefits were crystallised before age 75 into an unsecured pension arrangement, the tax-free lump sum was lost.

The income limits under ASP were different from the unsecured pension income rules:

- A minimum pension income requirement was introduced: 55% of the single life GAD rate at age 75.
- The maximum pension income requirement was increased to 90% of the single life GAD rate at age 75.

Once income withdrawal had commenced under ASP, the upper income limit had to be reviewed every year, although the pension was always calculated based on the individual being age 75, regardless of their actual age.

The death benefit rules while an individual was in ASP are as follows:

- Where an individual died with dependants, the remaining drawdown fund had to be used to provide survivors' pensions.
- If an individual died with no dependants, the remaining fund could be gifted to a charity tax-free.
- The payment of any remaining pension fund, other than to a charity, was classified as an unauthorised payment and therefore attracted unauthorised payment tax charges. In many cases the total reallocation charges amounted to 70% (40% unauthorised payment charge + 15% unauthorised payments surcharge + 15% scheme sanction charge).

Any reallocated pension funds also remained subject to IHT in the original member's estate and this combination produced a potential effective tax rate of 82%.

The definition of an ASP was amended so that one is not created until the age of 77 in the case of a member who has not reached the age of 75 before 22 June 2010. The 55% minimum and 90% maximum limits referred to above continued to apply to those receiving an alternatively secured pension. The concept of ASP was removed from 6 April 2011, those in ASP will move across to the new rules – see below for further details – at the start of the next pension year, although they can reduce their income to nil, or increase to 100% GAD, immediately after 6 April 2011.

Scheme pensions

Scheme pensions were another option for those aged 75 and over. These are normally (apart from defined benefit schemes) only offered by a SIPP or small, self-administered scheme (SSAS) and are effectively annuities paid out of scheme funds. The benefit was that more income could be drawn than with an ASP and the income level could be reviewed in line with actual mortality rates. This was a good option for those who did not want their pension to die with them or wished to use their pension income for IHT planning.

Changes to the annuities and drawdown rules from 6 April 2011

As pension annuity rates have declined, the requirement that individuals with personal or group personal pensions (defined contribution schemes) must buy an annuity or take an ASP at age 75 has increasingly been regarded as a disincentive to fund a pension. This is particularly the case as any unused part of the pension fund is liable to IHT should the individual die after age 75 but before an annuity is purchased (IHT can also apply on earlier deaths if an annuity was deliberately delayed).

As a short-term measure, the annuitisation age was increased to 77 in the Emergency Budget in June 2010 but the requirement has been removed altogether after 5 April 2011.

As explained above, since April 2006, individuals have already been able to take an unsecured pension (drawdown arrangement) up to age 75 and an alternatively secured pension (ASP) from age 75 rather than buy an annuity. The amount that an individual can draw down is based on a percentage of a single life conventional annuity that the fund would buy as calculated by the Government Actuary's Department (GAD). The current percentages and the proposed changes for a general drawdown regime are shown in Table 26.1.

The new rules introduce the concept of 'capped drawdown' and 'flexible drawdown'. Under capped drawdown the maximum income is still linked to GAD annuity rates, with maximum income being 100% of GAD (reduced from 120%). However, if an individual can show that he or she has annual pension income (a total of all pension income apart from drawdown amounts) in excess of £20,000, they can opt for flexible drawdown under this option. This will give significant flexibility to better funded pensioners although it should be noted that a requirement of flexible drawdown is that no pension contributions be paid in the year of moving to flexible drawdown. In addition, although it is possible to restart contributions in future tax years, contributions – or defined benefit accrual – will be subject to the annnual allowance tax charge. Under capped drawdown it should be noted that individuals aged under 75 who are already drawing down over 100% of GAD annuity rate income each year will have their pension income reduced from the first five-year review after 5 April 2011. Under the new rules, reviews determining maximum income drawdown (ie reflecting changes in annuity rates) are to be carried out every three years (currently every five years) up to age 75 and annually after age 75.

Table 26.1 – Current percentages and proposed changes

	To 5 April 2011		From 6 April 2011 (over age 55)	
	Aged 55–75 Unsecured	*Over 75/77 Alternatively secured*	*Under £20,000 non-drawdown annual pension income*	*Over £20,000 non-drawdown annual pension income*
Min income	0	55%	0	0
Max income	120%	90%	100%	Unlimited

Drawdown considerations

Those whose review period fell between the date the new legislation was announced and 5 April 2011 should have been able to ask for their maximum income to be reviewed under the then 120% limit instead of waiting for the limit to drop to 100% in 2011–12. Taking into consideration the date on which the next five-year review is planned, this may have allowed individuals to benefit from the 120% limit for a few years longer than they might previously have been able to.

Example

An individual was taking a drawdown income of 90% of GAD and her pension year ended on 31 March 2011. If she requested a review of her maximum income before 31 March (even if the last review took place less than five years ago), she could have had her drawdown income set to 120% of current GAD and this payment amount would have stayed fixed from 1 April 2011 to 31 March 2016.

Those individuals who are eligible for flexible drawdown (ie have more than £20,000 guaranteed pension income) may wish to apply immediately after 6 April 2011 even if they do not wish to utilise it now. This will remove any requirement to review their normal drawdown pension. Those individuals who are currently in ASP no longer need to take an income in the PIP, if this ends after 5 April 2011.

Example

> A newly retired bank manager will have annual income from a state pension and a final salary pension of £22,000. He also has a personal pension fund worth £200,000. After 6 April 2011, he can opt for flexible drawdown and take the entire £200,000 personal fund in one year. The first £50,000, the pension commencement lump sum, would be tax-free but the remaining £150,000 would be subject to tax as income in 2011–12 – so while this option is possible, it is probably not the most tax-efficient way to extract the funds.

For individuals who do not have a final salary pension, it may still be possible to become eligible for flexible drawdown by using part of a personal pension to buy an annuity income to supplement any state pension income. However, it should be remembered that although it will be possible under UK law for pension trustees to allow flexible drawdown, not all pension providers may offer this facility: so it may be necessary to transfer to a different provider to use this option and this will have costs attached.

Example

> A businesswoman retires when she reaches age 65 in May 2011. She expects to have a state pension of £5,000 in addition to a personal pension fund valued at £950,000. Assuming an annuity rate of 6% for a level annuity, she could use £250,000 of her fund to buy an annuity to increase her annual pension income to £15,000. The remaining £700,000 fund could then go into flexible drawdown (if her pension provider allows it), so that she can withdraw funds as she likes.

26.2.6 Recycling of lump sums

Where an individual takes a pre-commencement lump sum (tax-free lump sum) from a pension and then deliberately reinvests this within another pension scheme this may be considered as recycling and pension tax law has had specific rules in place to prevent this since April 2006.

Recycling applies when the reinvestment is pre-planned, and in the following circumstances:

- where the individual has received a pre-commencement lump sum (PCLS), which, when added to any other PCLS received in the previous 12-month period, exceeds 1% of the lifetime allowance; and
- because of the payment of the PCLS, the amount of the contribution paid to a pension scheme is significantly greater than would otherwise be the case. This is defined as where the amount of the additional

contributions are more than 30% of the contributions that might have been expected; and

- the cumulative amount of the additional contributions to the registered scheme must exceed 30% of the PCLS.

If recycling is deemed to apply, the PCLS will be considered an unauthorised payment and a tax charge of up to 55% of the lump sum payment will be applied.

26.3 PENSION SCHEME INVESTMENTS UNDER THE 'A' DAY REGIME

26.3.1 General rules for scheme investments

A single set of investment rules now applies to all registered pension schemes. This effectively means that, in theory, it is possible to invest in almost any kind of asset, including residential property and connected party transactions. However, to avoid investment abuse HMRC also introduced tax charges if pensions schemes invest in 'taxable property' (see 26.2.3). All investments must be made on a commercial basis. It is considered unlikely that all pension companies will accept the full range of investments in their schemes, and a wider choice of investments will only be made available by specialist pension companies operating either SIPP or SSAS arrangements.

Loans to members, people or other entities connected to members are unauthorised payments and will be taxed accordingly. From 'A' Day, any registered pension scheme is permitted to make a loan to an unconnected third party, or in the case of SSAS to the sponsoring employer, (scheme lending is limited to a maximum of 50% of the net SSAS fund).

There are specific rules applying to loans made to sponsoring employers:

- the loan must be secured through a first charge on an asset at least equivalent in value to the loan plus interest;
- the minimum interest rate must be no less than 1% above the base lending rates of the leading high street clearing banks;
- the loan term must not be longer than five years; and
- the loan must be repaid through regular, at least annual, instalments of capital and interest.

Any investment entered into before 'A' Day is normally subject to the rules then in force and is not affected by the new rules. However, where a change takes place after 5 April 2006 to the terms of a loan made by the scheme before 6 April 2006, the whole loan is subject to the new rules. Scheme borrowing is limited to 50% of the value of the scheme assets and must be secured.

26.3.2 Prohibited investments

FA 2006 contains provisions relating to 'taxable property' (ie assets previously described as 'prohibited assets').

Taxable property consists of any of the following:

- residential property (whether in the UK or overseas);
- chattels (ie tangible moveable property) other than gold bullion.

A registered pension scheme is not debarred from investing in taxable property but, where it does so, it and the members of the scheme are subject to punitive tax charges. In addition, the pension scheme could face de-registration if it invests in any prohibited investment, which in addition to the punitive tax charges applied, would also mean that the scheme loses all the tax privileges associated with a registered scheme, for all of its assets.

There are exceptions for certain types of residential property that might be acquired as an investment, eg a nursing home.

Great care should be taken before a scheme invests in property that may constitute residential property and advice from a specialist will be required.

26.3.3 Pension investment strategies

Pension strategies by their very nature are long-term and therefore even small enhancements can have a big effect at retirement.

Individuals with money purchase type arrangements (stakeholder, personal pensions, self-invested personal pensions) should carefully consider the underlying investment strategy employed within their pension plan. Future investment performance is a determinant of future fund value at retirement and individuals should seek to assess the suitability of their underlying strategy particularly in relation to their objectives and personal attitude to investment risk.

The investment choices for most money purchase pension plans will be linked to collective investment funds and typically the pension provider will offer a flexible range to suit different risk profiles. As with all investments some managers will perform more consistently than others and assessing the long-term consistency of performance of an underlying manager is an important consideration.

Individuals within money purchase type schemes should also seek to adjust their asset allocation to a more cautious position when approaching annuity purchase, particularly within five years. Any equity-focused investment strategy has the potential risk of a sudden fall in value within five years of retirement and therefore by adjusting the allocation to a more cautious position the value of the retirement fund can be protected. Those intending to take an unsecured pension will remain invested for a longer time – and possibly until death under the new rules, however if they are likely to purchase an annuity in the future they should still assess their likely investment term prior to annuity purchase to ensure they are not exposed to excess volatility.

Pension investors with a longer time frame until retirement should consider carefully before making major changes to the asset allocation of their fund as this may crystallise a loss by moving out of an asset class when prices are low. It is nevertheless still important to review the performance of individual investments to ensure investment managers are meeting expectations. Understanding your pension investment strategy is important and pension investors would be well advised to remind themselves of the longer-term principles of developing an appropriate pension investment strategy.

Tax notes

A registered pension scheme is not debarred from investing in taxable property but, where it does so, it and the members of the scheme are subject to punitive tax charges.

26.4 TAX RELIEF FOR CONTRIBUTIONS

Employer contributions are always paid gross.

Contributions by a member into a registered scheme will normally be net of basic rate tax, ie a payment to an insurance company of £1,000 is treated as a payment of £1,250 from which £250 has been deducted. The insurance company recovers this £250 from HMRC.

In many occupational schemes (but not group personal pensions), pension contributions are deducted in full from pay prior to income tax being applied. As a result the member receives relief at his or her highest marginal rate immediately.

There is one other situation where a member's contributions may still be made in full, which is where the payment is in respect of an old retirement annuity policy and the insurance company has not established an arrangement for payments to be made net of tax relief.

26.5 2011–12 CHANGES AND TRANSITIONAL ARRANGEMENTS FOR 2010–11

26.5.1 The main changes

The coalition Government has simplified the former Labour Government's planned restrictions to pension tax relief from 2011–12. However, for some simpler does not mean more generous: for many individuals, the options for making tax-efficient pension contributions will be much more restricted in future years. Anti-forestalling rules (see below) remained in place until 6 April 2011 and there are a number of transitional rules that could affect individuals who wished to maximise contributions before the end of 2010–11.

26.5.2 Tax relief on contributions from 2011–12

From 2011–12, the maximum amount that can be paid into an approved pension scheme by (or on behalf of) an individual in a tax year without penalty – the annual allowance (AA) – was reduced from £255,000 to £50,000 (subject to the usual limit of 100% of the individual's relevant earnings for the year if lower). Contributions made by or on behalf of individuals that are in excess of this amount will trigger an AA charge.

Tax relief on pension contributions continues to be available at the individual's marginal income tax rate. However, the charge arising if the AA is exceeded will be at the full marginal rate of relief that an individual would otherwise have benefitted from – ie no tax relief will be available on excess contributions.

26.5.3 Transitional rules for 2010–11

The calculation of pension contributions made by and on behalf of an individual in a particular tax year is determined with reference to the 'pension input period' (PIP). If a scheme's PIP ends in a particular tax year, any contributions made in that PIP are counted towards the contributions made by or on behalf of that individual for that tax year. The Government has decided not to force pension providers to align all PIPs with the tax year. This means that there will be pension schemes with a PIP which begins in 2010–11 but ends in 2011–12.

Transitional rules applied where a pension scheme's PIP began before 14 October 2010 and ends after 5 April 2011. This broadly requires only contributions made on or after 14 October 2010 to be tested against the new £50,000 AA. Total contributions in the PIP are, in addition, tested against the 2010–11 £255,000 allowance. These rules apply alongside the anti-forestalling rules for 2010–11.

The transitional provisions meant that, in certain circumstances, it was possible to trigger both a special annual allowance charge (SAAC) for 2010–11 and an AA charge for the 2011–12 tax year on the same payment giving a combined tax charge of up to 80% of the contribution!

Example

> A company executive had total income of £250,000 in 2010–11 (including her bonus) and is a member of a scheme with a PIP ending on 30 June. In past years, she has always contributed £50,000 to her pension scheme but in 2010–11 also wished to pay in her bonus in March to make an additional gross contribution of £90,000. Without remedial action, she would have incurred a SAAC at 30% (£27,000) on the contribution plus an AA charge at 50% on the contribution (£45,000).

Fortunately, in some circumstances, it is possible to amend PIP dates to ensure that you can take advantage of maximum funding and are not disadvantaged by a PIP that is not aligned with the tax year dates.

The one-off option for changing a PIP (see 26.1.4) would not be available as it is not possible to have two PIPs for the same pension scheme ending in the same tax year. However, for most personal pension schemes, provided the PIP had not been amended before, it should have been possible for the contributing individual to request that the PIP be aligned with the end of the tax year – ie to end on 5 April 2011. This election must have been made prior to 5 April 2011 and would then have applied retrospectively for all PIPs since 6 April 2006 so the impact on past contributions would need to be considered: for example there may be tax consequences if large contributions previously in separate PIPs now fall in the same one as a result of the change.

For group schemes and contributory employer schemes (whether money purchase or final salary) the provider may not have been able or willing to realign the PIP to suit one individual. It was therefore vital to know what your PIP was if you intended to make substantial contributions before 6 April 2011.

It is possible for an individual to be a member of several different pension schemes all of which have different PIPs. Therefore, a potential solution was to pay any new contributions before 6 April 2011 into a new plan with the PIP set to end before 6 April 2011 thereby securing the benefit of the £255,000 AA limit. However, it was important to remember that where the SAAC was relevant, the charge applied to all contributions made in a year – no matter which scheme or schemes the funds were paid into.

26.5.4 Taking advantage by 5 April 2011

Individuals who were not affected by the transitional rules because the PIP for their scheme is the same as the tax year will have had some scope to maximise their pension contributions in the 2010–11 tax year where the funds were available.

However, it is worth noting that while the 2010–11 AA was £255,000, tax relief was still only available on contributions of up to 100% of an individual's relevant earnings for the year. In addition, additional, single or irregular contributions (ie irregular contributions made less frequently than quarterly) may have been subject to the SAAC (limiting net tax relief to 20% on personal contributions or imposing a direct cost on contributions made via an employer) if the individual's relevant income for 2010–11 (or either of the two prior tax years) exceeded £130,000.

Example

> A solicitor with a trading profit of £300,000 taxable in 2010–11 could have made a net contribution of up to £204,000 (£255,000 gross) without incurring an AA charge at the 2010–11 40% rate. Even after the SAAC restricting net tax relief to 20% (ignoring the first £20,000 of the contribution), this would still have attracted a tax subsidy of £57,000. It would also have added a significant amount to the solicitor's pension pot in one year.

Example

> An individual has £80,000 pa relevant earnings and wanted to make a pension contribution of £60,000 in 2010–11. Although making the payment before 6 April 2011 avoids the new £50,000 AA limit, not all of it will trigger tax relief at 40%. However, splitting the payment so that half falls in 2010–11 and half in 2011–12 will ensure that tax relief at 40% is given on the whole contribution.

For individuals with annual income in excess of £130,000 for 2010–11 (or the previous two years) it was important to consider the impact of the anti-forestalling special annual allowance charge (SAAC). The purpose of this charge was to limit the tax relief on the contribution to 20%, so where you made the contribution yourself the charge simply balanced the higher rate tax relief you could claim. However, where a contribution was made on your behalf by your employer the SAAC would still have applied and, where it did, it imposed a one-off tax charge payable on 31 January 2012 – a real cash flow cost.

26.5.5 Company owners

Company owners who have private funds have an extra dimension to consider. They may wish to pay the contribution personally or opt for their companies to make the payments on their behalf. For higher or additional rate taxpayers, it will usually prove to be less expensive overall to make the payment personally from their own funds than for the company to pay it – taking into account the cost of the payment and the tax charges and reliefs due to both the individual and the company.

Example

> A company owner had income of £135,000 in 2010–11 and wanted to make a pension contribution of £80,000 for that year (payments of £50,000 a year are to be made from 2011–12 onwards). If he could have funded the contribution from his own savings, it would have been more tax-efficient for him to do so: a saving of over £30,000 compared to the company paying the premium. However, if he needed to extract a dividend from the company to have sufficient cash to pay the contribution, this would cost more in tax terms (nearly £20,000 more) than if the company made the payment and he suffered a SAAC charge on 31 January 2012.

The position is different depending on the level of income: basic rate taxpayers, for example, will usually be better off arranging for the payment to be made from their companies as they do not benefit from higher rate tax relief on their personal pension contributions.

26.5.6 Individuals aged over 55 by 6 April 2011

Individuals who reached age 55 before April 2011 had a one-off opportunity to make very large contributions to their pension fund without triggering an AA charge. As mentioned above, before 6 April 2011, the AA charge was not applied in any year in which an individual took the full benefits of his or her pension fund – this allowed for a large top-up of a person's pension fund just before he or she retired. Therefore, contributions in excess of 100% of relevant earnings and £255,000 (in theory up to £1.8m) could have been made by or on behalf of an individual before 6 April 2011 provided the individual crystalised their benefits in the same tax year. Although in these circumstances contributions are not caught by the AA a contribution by an individual is restricted to 100% of earnings. Remember, it is not necessary to actually cease working to be able to take your pension benefits; you just need to be aged 55 or more.

Although taking a pension early may seem like an odd move, in these circumstances, it would have allowed the individual to add a large sum to his or her pension fund in one go – an option that has been lost from 6 April 2011 onwards. It should be remembered that, if an individual did take the benefits of one pension scheme in 2010–11, it does not prevent him or her from starting a new scheme in a later year provided he or she continues to have relevant earnings. As mentioned above, company owners who took this option should remember that they may personally face a SAAC at up to 30% of the payment (with the tax payable by 31 January 2012). In addition, the company may not obtain a full corporation tax deduction for a large one-off contribution immediately (see 26.1.4).

Example

> An entrepreneur aged 59 intends to retire in summer 2012 and had established a pension fund of £400,000 (2010–11 value). His company had sufficient funds to allow a contribution of £500,000 to be made before 6 April 2011. Although the entrepreneur's relevant income for 2010–11 was 'only' £90,000, the company was able to make a larger payment on his behalf. A £500,000 contribution is clearly over the 2010–11 AA limit but if he took pension benefits (vested the fund) before 6 April 2011, no AA charge would have arisen. Later in 2011 and between April 2012 and his retirement, the entrepreneur's company can make two further pension contributions of £50,000 each to a new pension fund to take his total pension funds at retirement to £1m. In contrast, if the entrepreneur had simply kept the company contributions to the annual allowance limit, his pension pot would be only £755,000 at retirement.

26.5.7 Final salary schemes

Ever since the 'A' Day pension reforms in 2006, there have been special rules to identify the deemed pension contributions made by employers on behalf of members of defined benefit (final salary schemes). From 6 April

2011, to determine whether or not the £50,000 AA has been exceeded, deemed contributions to defined benefit schemes will be calculated using a flat factor of 16 times (previously 10 times) the increase in the annual pension benefit during the pension input period (plus the increase in value of the lump sum). The new legislation does, however, allow for an inflationary increase in salary to be ignored in determining the increase in the value of an active scheme member's pension fund.

Where individuals exceed the AA in a given year, unused allowances from the three previous tax years will be available to offset against the excess pension savings. Unused allowances in 2008–09, 2009–10 and 2010–11 will be available for carry forward into 2011–12 but on the assumption that the AA was only £50,000 in those earlier tax years. Please be aware, however, that this option is only available if an individual was a member of a registered pension scheme in the tax year from which the relief is to be carried forward, although they do not have to have made contributions.

For individuals fortunate enough to be a member of a defined benefit scheme the reduction in the AA could have an impact on their benefits as an increase in their annual pension benefits of more than £3,125 (plus inflation) will be sufficient to bring the tax charge into play. Therefore defined benefit scheme members who have a large increase in pension benefits in one year (typically when a significant promotion and pay rise occurs) may now find that their deemed pension inputs for the year (using the new multiplication factor of 16) takes them over the £50,000 limit.

Where an individual has contributed (or is deemed to have contributed) more than the AA into a particular pension scheme in a particular PIP, the pension provider will be required to advise the member of the amount of contributions within six months of the end of the tax year.

Information must also be provided regarding contributions in the previous three tax years, so that the individual can determine whether he or she is able to make use of the carry-forward mechanism. Employers will also be required to provide sufficient information to the providers of defined benefit schemes to allow them to calculate the increase in benefit arising under these schemes. Individuals with multiple pension schemes will have the right to request the necessary details of contributions made from an employer or pension provider.

26.5.8 Paying the annual allowance charge from your pension

As noted above, with the reduction in the AA to £50,000 for PIPs ending after 5 April 2011, it is likely that some members of defined benefit schemes will face an AA charge in future – particularly with the deemed contribution multiplier rising from 10 to 16. Such individuals may not have the funds to pay such a charge in cash and the Government has made provision (new ss 254(7A) and 254(7B) FA 2004) for scheme administrators to be able to pay the AA charge out of the accrued funds in some cases, where the AA charge exceeds £2,000 and the aggregate of the individual's pension input amounts for arrangements within that pension scheme exceed £50,000. The scheme provider is only required to pay an amount up to the amount by which the pension inputs for that scheme exceed the annual allowance, although may offer to do so where pension inputs are below the allowance. The scheme administrator must pay the tax by 31 December of the year following the end of the tax year in which the AA charge arises. So, for example, if an AA charge arises for 2012–13, the scheme administrator must account for the AA charge in the quarter ending 31 December 2013 (although for the first year of operation (2011–12), this deadline is extended to 31 March 2013. There is also provision for the individual's pension entitlement to be reduced by a just and reasonable amount to reflect this payment. The scheme administrator is not liable to make payments in respect of AA charges which would result in the individual's pension entitlement being reduced below the Guaranteed Minimum Pension level.

26.5.9 Looking ahead to 2012–13: lower lifetime allowance

Although the lifetime allowance (SLA) is not scheduled to reduce from the current £1.8m to £1.5m until April 2012, the Government wishes to finalise the legislation as soon as possible to allow for some transitional protection rules to be put in place.

When the SLA was introduced in April 2006, individuals with large pension pots were able to protect themselves from the excess charge on their pension funds. Individuals whose funds already exceeded the LTA could apply for 'primary' protection and individuals with smaller funds could opt for 'enhanced' protection on the basis that their fund would grow over time (even though they would be blocked from making new contributions to it). See 26.1.5 for more details.

These protections will continue after 5 April 2012. However, for individuals in defined benefit schemes who have opted for enhanced protection, while benefits accrued after 5 April 2012 (provided these benefits are not deemed to be relevant benefits accrual) would not trigger an end to protection, they may still trigger an AA charge if the deemed inputs in a year exceed the £50,000 limit as the protection which was in place until 5 April 2011 no longer applies.

It is proposed that the new regime from April 2012 will include a right for individuals to opt for protection ('fixed protection') of the £1.8m current lifetime limit in a similar way as enhanced protection operated from 'A day', ie:

- it is not necessary for an individual's fund to exceed £1.5m at 5 April 2012 for the fixed protection election to be made; but
- protection will end if further contributions are made by the individual after 5 April 2012 (including where individuals in defined benefit schemes accrue further pension benefits in the current scheme or under a new scheme in excess of the limits currently available to those claiming enhanced protection under the 'A day' rules).

Fixed protection will not be available to any individual already holding enhanced or primary protection. HMRC must receive the completed applications for fixed protection before 5 April 2012 (although the opening date for applications has yet to be confirmed and the application form is not yet available).

A charge under the SLA rules will continue to arise at the time the pension vests and will remain at 55% of the excess used for a lump sum entitlement and 25% of the excess used for the pension entitlement. The charge may also arise at other later 'benefit crystallisation events' for individuals who opt to take a drawdown pension – in particular on reaching age 75. Individuals with large pension pots should take advice on their personal options as there are likely to be many situations where opting for fixed protection will be a sensible way of protecting the future growth of pension funds from a possible charge.

Example

A businesswoman in her mid-60s is about to retire and will have pension income of around £25,000 from the state pension and a final salary scheme. The final salary scheme is valued at £500,000 for SLA purposes and she has a self-invested personal pension fund of £800,000. Although she can opt for flexible drawdown on the personal pension, she has no pressing need for the funds. She will make no further contributions to the SIPP but plans to pursue an aggressive growth strategy with the SIPP investments. Although her current funds are valued at less than £1.5m, it would be sensible for her to opt for fixed protection so that her SIPP funds can grow to £1.8m by the time she reaches age 75 without any risk of triggering a SLA charge at that time. If they do get close to that limit, she could draw down some of the funds to ensure that the limit is not breached.

26.5.10 Early access

On 13 December 2010, the Government published an initial discussion document on possible ways to encourage pension savings by allowing individuals to access their pension funds before age 55. This was very much the first stage of the process with the Government seeking views on whether or not some relaxation in the current access rules would increase overall net pension savings. The document asked for views on what access model would be most appropriate (eg loan-back, permanent withdrawal, access to tax-free lump sum only or a feeder fund system) and in which situations individuals should be allowed early access (eg financial hardship of individuals or their children). Following this consultation, HM Treasury issued a statement on 19 April 2011 which indicated that this idea would not be taken forward as proposed. Mark Hoban, Financial Secretary to the Treasury said:

'The Government is committed to encouraging saving and wants to give individuals greater flexibility in saving for retirement. While early access has some merits, there is insufficient evidence to suggest it would act as an incentive to save more into pensions. We will work with industry to develop workplace saving to supplement pension savings. In addition, we will explore other ways of making pension tax rules simpler and more flexible, for example by making it easier to deal with small pension pots.'

26.5.11 2009–10 and 2010–11: tax relief restrictions for those earning above £130,000

The introduction of 'Pensions Simplification' in April 2006 and its objective of establishing a single set of rules to unify the various regimes seemed a victory for common sense. Unfortunately, FA 2009 was a huge step backwards, taking the regime away from simplification and introducing a new level of complexity.

To prevent individuals from increasing their contributions before 6 April 2011 and taking advantage of continued higher rate relief, anti-forestalling rules were put in place for 2009–10 and 2010–11. From 22 April 2009, the anti-forestalling rules applied to anyone earning £130,000 or more (known as high income individuals) in the current tax year or in either of the two previous tax years (although the rules only affected contributions made on or after 9 December 2009 in respect of individuals with relevant income of between £130,000 and £149,999 (not including employer contributions)).

The anti-forestalling rules introduced a special annual allowance (SAA) of £20,000 which was the maximum amount that a 'high income individual' could contribute to a registered pension scheme and attract tax relief at his or her highest rate. The individual suffered a special annual allowance charge (SAAC) on any additional contributions to registered schemes, which effectively reduced the tax relief available on those contributions to 20%. However, the charge also applied to employer contributions, which meant that individuals also suffered a tax charge on these amounts.

The SAA was higher than £20,000 (up to a maximum of £30,000) where the individual had made 'infrequent contributions' in any of the three tax years to 5 April 2009 and the mean amount of such contributions was more than £20,000 per tax year. Infrequent contributions were defined as those being made less frequently than quarterly.

The SAAC did not apply to normal regular ongoing contributions although such contributions did use up the individual's special annual allowance. For money purchase schemes, normal contributions were defined as the continuation of contributions made prior to 22 April 2009 that were paid quarterly or more frequently and at a rate that did not increase. For defined benefit arrangements, the rules included increases in pension benefits arising under the rules existing at 22 April 2009, including increases due as a result of normal pay rises and progression.

Salary sacrifice arrangements entered into on or after 22 April 2009 (9 December 2009 for those earning £130,000 or more) reducing income below the relevant level were not effective at avoiding the anti-forestalling rules.

26.6 PERSONAL PENSION ACCOUNTS AND NEST

The Labour Government introduced stakeholder pensions in 2001 in an attempt to make it easier for individuals to save for their retirement. The introduction of stakeholder pensions has heralded a generally lower and more transparent charging system, however still too few people are saving for their retirement. The Labour administration's response to this was to introduce personal pension accounts (PPA) in the March 2010 Budget. This measure was then confirmed at the Emergency Budget in June 2010 and is due to take effect from April 2012.

Personal pension accounts will effectively be personal type pensions run on an occupational basis and administered by employers. All employees will automatically be enrolled into a personal account providing they are aged between 22 and the state pension age, earn more than the primary threshold, and their employer does not already offer an equivalent or better pension scheme.

The eventual intention is for employees to contribute 4% of their earnings, employers 3% and a further 1% via tax relief to give a total overall minimum contribution rate of 8%. This minimum level will be phased in over five years.

UK employers will be required to automatically enrol those employees aged between 22 and state pension age who earn more than £7,475 (for 2011–12) into a 'qualifying' workplace pension scheme from October 2012. If your current company scheme does not meet the qualifying criteria (or your employer does not operate one) then you will instead be enrolled into a simple, low-cost national pension scheme – the National Employment Savings Trust (NEST).

Starting with the largest employers in October 2012, the scheme will be rolled out to all employers by September 2016. The Regulator intends to write to all employers around 12 months before their start date so that they know when to automatically enrol their eligible employees. Three months before the employer's start date the Regulator will write again to remind them of their new duties and the need to register.

Employers with more than one payroll will start automatic enrolment for all their payrolls at the same time, on the start date of their largest payroll. In addition to the automatic enrolment of all eligible employees, employees aged between 16 and 22, and earning more than the threshold will be able to opt into the scheme, as will any employees earning less than the threshold.

Employees will need to pay a personal contribution on which tax relief (based on a percentage of qualifying earnings) will be given but they can opt out of the scheme: employers will be required to make a contribution. The minimum contributions for employees and employers are to be phased in as follows:

Date	Employee (including basic rate tax relief)	Employer
October 2012 to September 2016	2%	1%
October 2016 to September 2017	5%	2%
From October 2017	5%	3%

The introduction of PPAs will require a significant change for employers and they will need to be aware of these proposals. PPAs will be held as part of the NEST.

OTHER RETIREMENT BENEFIT SCHEMES

26.7 UNAPPROVED SCHEMES

Unapproved (now unregistered) occupational pension schemes were introduced to allow employers the flexibility to provide benefits for those employees who had earnings in excess of the salary cap. However, their use is not restricted to such employees and they may be used to provide benefits in excess of the normal two-thirds maximum pension benefit or to provide greater benefits for those with less than 20 years' service.

26.7.1 Eligibility

Any person in receipt of employment income is eligible for an unregistered scheme. There is no requirement that the employee is also a member of a registered scheme.

26.7.2 Types of plan

Such schemes may be funded (ie contributions set aside to fund the promised benefits) or unfunded (ie at retirement the benefits will be paid by the company out of current income or investments). A funded scheme was traditionally called a FURBS (funded unapproved retirement benefits scheme) but both funded and unfunded retirement benefit schemes are now known as EFRBS (employer funded retirement benefit schemes). There is no requirement that funded schemes are established under trust, but this is commonly the case.

26.7.3 **Contributions**

Where a scheme was funded, the employer used to obtain tax relief on the contributions as a normal business expense and the employee was taxed on such contributions as if they were earnings. This ceased to be the case from 'A' Day. Contributions between 6 April 2006 and 5 April 2011 attracted no tax relief for the employer until the employee drew his or her benefits and the employee paid no tax until he or she drew the benefits.

The landscape has now completely changed for funded schemes; the introduction of the disguised remuneration rules (see Chapter 5) has meant that, where an amount is 'earmarked' for an employee, or the employee is given a benefit such as a loan or the use of a trust asset, a tax charge will arise under Part 7A ITEPA 2003 and the employer will be able to claim a deduction in the accounts to the extent that sums have been subjected to a Part 7A charge. A tax charge could already have arisen between 9 December 2010 and 5 April 2011 under the transitional provisions in certain circumstances.

There are continuing protections for sums placed in trust prior to 6 April 2006 (which were taxed up-front), but generally, the Part 7A charge will take precedence over a charge under s 394 ITEPA, which will then only apply to any excess.

In an unfunded scheme, there has never been a charge to tax on any reserves set up to provide for future benefits. Equally, the employer will not obtain any tax relief until the funds are provided and benefits are actually paid. 'Quasi' unfunded schemes (ie where the employer has secured payment of the future liabilities under the scheme against an asset or has earmarked funds with which to pay future liabilities) will be caught by the new Part 7A charge. Genuinely unfunded schemes will not.

26.7.4 **Taxation of scheme investments**

Unapproved schemes do not benefit from 'gross roll-up'. In the past, the trustees of a FURBS paid tax only at basic rate on investment income. For onshore trusts, from 6 April 2006, income and capital gains became subject to the rate applicable to trusts, ie currently 50% (to 2009–10, 40%) on income other than dividends, and 42.5% (to 2009–10, 32.5%) on UK dividends. From 6 April 2008 to 22 June 2010, capital gains in a pre-'A' Day EFRBS were subject to 18% CGT. This increased to 28% from 23 June 2010. Offshore EFRBS are taxed according to the normal rules for offshore trusts.

There are transitional rules in paras 56–58, schedule 36 FA 2004 which continue the existing treatment for FURBS where no new contributions have been made after 5 April 2006, and which ensure that where the contributions were taxed on the employee when they were made, they are not also taxed when benefits are paid from the scheme under the post-'A' Day EFRBS rules. If contributions have been made post- 6 April 2006, tax charges will arise on the part of the fund relating to the post- 'A' day contributions. The Part 7A provisions make similar allowance for pre-6 April 2006 amounts.

26.7.5 Benefits

The scheme must be set up to provide relevant benefits, but there are no set limits on the benefits that can be provided. Pensions from unregistered schemes, whether funded or unfunded, are subject to income tax as earned income.

Where a scheme with UK resident trustees was funded before 'A' Day, that part of the fund may be used to provide a tax-free lump sum on retirement. Where an offshore scheme was funded prior to 'A' Day, the tax-free amount will usually be the aggregate of the employer contributions before 6 April 2006. Any lump sum in excess of these limits is taxable in the normal way.

Tax notes

Where a scheme with UK resident trustees was funded before 'A' Day, that part of the fund may be taken as a tax-free lump sum on retirement.

In the March 2010 Budget, the then Chancellor announced that anti-avoidance was to be introduced from 6 April 2011 to prevent tax avoidance using 'employee trusts'. This was reiterated in the June Budget and the Chancellor made it clear that the planned anti-avoidance legislation would apply to both EBTs and EFRBS. It became clear, when the draft legislation on disguised remuneration was released on 9 December 2010 that these rules will cause these structures to become very much less attractive.

26.8 TRANSFERS FROM UK PENSION SCHEMES INTO A QROPS

For individuals who are working abroad and/or are going to retire overseas, transferring into a qualifying recognised overseas pension scheme (QROPS) can have advantages once the individuals have established five complete tax years of non-residence in the UK. However, such an early switch carries high risks for individuals since if the QROPS ceases to qualify (see below), there will be penalty tax charges that could add up to 104% of the fund value. One must also remember the increasing difficulty of establishing non-UK residence, reflected by current case law. Until such time as a statutory residence test is introduced, uncertainty will remain the order of the day, unless the individual has clearly made a complete and total break with the UK.

26.8.1 Advantages once you have completed five tax years of non-UK residence

One of the key advantages of a QROPS once you have completed five tax years of non-UK residence is that the fund can grow beyond the statutory lifetime limit imposed in the UK (£1.8m for 2010–11 to2011–12; £1.5m from 2012–13) without a tax penalty.

HMRC has recently made it clear that it believes any payment or investments that would be unauthorised under a UK scheme would also be liable to charges under a QROPS, regardless of whether the five-year limit is passed. It should therefore be assumed that benefits and allowable investments will broadly mirror UK rules and expert tax and financial advice should be sought in all cases.

When it comes to taking benefits, the advantages of a QROPS will vary depending on the jurisdiction in which it is established but might include:

- the opportunity to take 30% of the whole pension fund in cash (compared to 25% of the statutory lifetime limit for UK pensions)
- income limits in draw down are determined by the QROPS jurisdiction and scheme rules, so could be significantly more attractive than the limits applied to UK schemes;
- the lump sum death benefit where the individual dies in drawdown before age 75 (or 77, if reaching age 75 on or after 22 June 2010) may be far higher than the 65% imposed under UK rules;
- lump sum death benefits may be taxed at lower rates if the country the individual has retired to does not tax such benefits or only taxes them at low rates;
- depending on the local tax rules in the country to which the individual has retired, there may also be scope for trust planning to pass pension wealth down to the next generation rather than to a surviving spouse or civil partner.

26.8.2 Qualifying rules

Firstly, the scheme must be either an occupational pension scheme or personal pension scheme regulated by the appropriate government regulator in the country in which the scheme is administered (this need not be the same country to which the individual retires). Secondly, the scheme must be open to persons resident in the country in which it is established and:

- tax relief is not available on contributions made by the employee and/ or employer; or
- it is liable to tax on income and gains; or
- all or most of the benefits paid out are subject to taxation.

In addition, the scheme must be established in the EU, Norway, Iceland, Liechtenstein or one of the many countries with which the UK has a double taxation treaty. This requirement means that HMRC should be able to impose tax penalties on the fund via the local tax authorities for any breach of the qualifying rules.

The other limits on QROPS are that at least 70% of funds must be used to provide pension income and that retirement benefits cannot be paid earlier than under a UK registered scheme. These requirements do not fall away after five years' non-UK residence.

In addition to these rules, if the QROPS makes any payments or investments while the individual is resident in the UK or before five complete tax years of non-UK residence have been established that would breach the standard UK pension scheme rules, it must report them to the UK authorities and the relevant UK tax penalty charges will be applied. For this reason, QROPS providers effectively operate two types of fund, one that mirrors the UK rules for the first five tax years and, once the five years of non-UK residence have been established, another that follows the more advantageous investment rules of the local jurisdiction.

HMRC regularly updates a list of overseas pension schemes that meet the QROPS tests (available on its website) but not all approved schemes are listed, as scheme operators can choose whether or not to appear on the list. HMRC also regularly reviews jurisdictions to decide whether abuse is occurring; it famously dis-approved all the schemes in Singapore in 2010, and recently, anti-avoidance has been included in Finance Act 2011 to prevent a potential abuse of the treaty between the UK and Hong Kong, which would have meant that no tax was payable on the QROPS pension.

26.8.3 Retiring abroad

In practice, it is best to regard a QROPS as a conduit to switch a UK pension into a more flexible overseas vehicle after the individual has left the UK for good. Given the five-year rule and the fact that a person's intentions may change after retirement (many expats return to the UK after spending some time in retirement overseas), transferring into a QROPS before leaving the UK or in the early years after leaving could prove to be an expensive mistake in the longer term. It should also be remembered that, particularly on retirement, it can be difficult to establish non-UK residence so great care should be taken to confirm the five year non-UK residence test has been met before the advantages of a QROPS can be realised.

Even then, the long arm of HMRC could still impose penalties (via the local tax authorities). So, although a QROPS can have advantages, it will never provide a route to total flexibility. If you are considering such a transfer, it is vital that you seek advice from an independent financial adviser.

STATE BENEFITS

26.9 STATE PENSION BENEFITS

The state provides a number of pension benefits with a range of eligibility conditions and contribution requirements. There are also additional means-tested benefits payable in retirement, which are beyond the scope of this book. The main state pension benefits are as follows.

26.9.1 The basic state pension

The basic state pension is the first part of the Government's pension provision. Individuals will be eligible for all or a part, providing they have a sufficient national insurance contribution record. Individuals with earnings above or equal to the lower earnings level (LEL) in any year will be credited with a year's qualifying record for the purposes of the basic state pension. There are also special dispensations for carers (home responsibilities protection).

With effect from 6 April 2010, both men and women have needed 30 years of qualifying national insurance records to be entitled to the full basic state pension.

The state pension age is presently 65 for a man and 60 for a woman. This has started to equalise (from April 2010) in stages and by 2019–20 the state retirement age will be 65 for both sexes. The state pension age for both men and women will then rise from 65 to 66 by April 2020. The Government is looking into a new automatic mechanism for future increases in the state pension age, based on regular independent reviews.

As a result of a recent case, the Government has abolished the statutory retirement age, so that employers cannot automatically dismiss employees on attaining age 65;

The value of the basic state pension has in the past been linked to increases in inflation (RPI) each year in April. This level of increases has not been considered fair by many pensioners as average wages have typically risen at a higher rate and therefore the long-term value of the basic state pension has been gradually eroded. The Government has confirmed that it will re-link pensions to average earnings from April 2011. Old age pensions will also be protected by a new 'triple lock' which will guarantee every year a rise in the basic state pension in line with earnings, prices or a 2.5% increase, whichever is greater. The triple lock does not apply to SERPS or S2P.

26.9.2 State Earnings Related Pension Scheme (SERPS)

SERPS was introduced in 1978 and provides a pension that is based on earnings between the lower and upper earnings limits (for 2011–12, £7,225 and £42,475 pa, respectively). The earnings between these two figures are often called 'band earnings'. People who are self-employed have neither contributed towards, nor will benefit from, SERPS.

Benefit accrual under SERPS ended in April 2002 with the introduction of the state second pension (S2P).

SERPS provides a pension at state retirement age expressed as a percentage of band earnings. For those retiring in 2009–10 or later the percentage is currently 20%, with those retiring before then receiving a higher percentage up to a maximum of 25% of band earnings. Band earnings are based on an average over the whole of your working life.

The main benefit from the state scheme is a lifelong pension for the individual, but SERPS can also, in certain circumstances, provide a widow's pension, which will be of a reduced amount unless the widow is aged over 40 and has dependent children (or over 50 with no dependent children).

Accrual of SERPS benefits ceased from 6 April 2002, but benefits already accrued continue to be calculated in accordance with the rules at that date.

26.9.3 State Second Pension

S2P was introduced on 6 April 2002. Like SERPS, which it replaced, S2P is based on NI contributions made by employers and employees. However, S2P provides better benefits than SERPS for low and moderate earners.

To achieve this, earnings are divided into three bands rather than the single 'band earnings' used to calculate SERPS. In addition to the lower and upper earnings limits, there is a 'low earnings threshold' broadly equal to half of national average earnings (£14,400 for 2011–12) and a second earnings threshold (£32,592for 2011–12).

The rate of accrual for the lowest band (ie for earnings between the lower earnings limit and the lower earnings threshold) is double that of the highest band and four times that of the middle band.

In addition to the improved benefits for low and moderate earners, S2P also provides coverage for some carers and people with long-term disabilities or illness. In these cases, it is possible to build up an entitlement to S2P for periods where individuals are unable to work.

The Chancellor has proposed simplifying the state pension system into a new flat-rate pension based on contributions, at an estimated rate of £140pw. This new system will not however apply to existing pensioners at the date of introduction (which is as yet unknown).

State pension forecast

To obtain an illustration of potential state pension benefits and state second pension entitlement at state pension age individuals should obtain a forecast by completing the Department of Work and Pensions form BR19 or an online application directly on the DWP website (www.thepensionservice.gov.uk).

26.10 CONTRACTING OUT

Individuals are able to leave the state second pension by 'contracting out'. For any year where the individual has been contracted out they will forgo their second state pension benefits at retirement for that particular tax year. Individuals were also previously able to contract out of SERPS.

There are three ways in which an employee can be contracted out. These are:

- contracting out via a personal type pension;
- membership of a contracted-out money purchase pension scheme (COMPS); or
- membership of an occupational scheme providing guaranteed minimum pension (GMP – not available since 6 April 1997) or an occupational scheme that satisfies a 'Reference Scheme' test.

It is possible to leave S2P provided appropriate provision is made to replace the S2P benefits with a suitable approved alternative. To encourage this, individuals and employers who contract out in this way receive benefits in the form of reduced NIC charges and/or a direct payment into an individual personal pension scheme.

26.10.1 Contracting out via a personal type pension

Individuals are able to contract out via a personal type pension (including stakeholder and personal pension plans). This requires no employer involvement and is open to all employees who are not contracted out by another scheme, even those who are also members of an occupational scheme. To contract out, the employee and the chosen personal pension plan provider must complete a joint notice (Form APP1), which is submitted to HMRC. An individual can use only one APP1 to contract out at any time and must contract out for a complete tax year.

Once the joint notice is accepted by HMRC, payments are made once a year typically in September or October following the end of the tax year. These payments are called protected rights contributions and consist of the national insurance rebate, but both the employee and employer continue to pay the full rate of NIC. A system of age-related rebates applies.

Although the tax rules allow a tax-free lump sum of up to 25% of the protected rights fund to be taken, the remainder of the fund built up by protected rights contributions must be used to provide a pension benefit at state retirement age, or a surviving spouse, civil partner or dependant's pension or a lump sum on death.

The contracting out decision is not straightforward and each individual should assess his or her own personal situation and objectives when considering the contracting out position, and take independent financial advice if he or she is uncertain.

26.10.2 Contracted-out money purchase scheme

A COMPS is an occupational pension plan where the employer takes the initial decision to contract out, although the employer may then allow individuals the choice of whether to contract out or not.

Both the employer and employee pay a reduced rate of NIC (albeit both will pay more NIC from 6 April 2012, due to a planned decrease in the contracted-out rebates), but this saving is balanced by the protected rights contributions that the employer must ensure are paid into the pension scheme monthly. Normally, both the employer and the employee will contribute their respective shares of the protected rights contributions. In addition to the basic flat-rate rebates, the DWP pays an additional age-related payment after the end of the tax year.

The protected rights contributions must be used to provide benefits in the same way as those provided through a personal type pension.

26.10.3 Guaranteed minimum pension

This method of contracting out involved an occupational pension scheme providing a guaranteed minimum level of pension equivalent to that provided by SERPS. Both the employer and the employee benefited from a reduced level of NIC, but the employer had to be prepared to provide the pension scheme with sufficient funds to enable it to meet the guarantee. No further GMPs can accrue for periods after 5 April 1997.

Since then, occupational schemes can be contracted out either on a money purchase basis (ie a COMPS) or by satisfying the 'Reference Scheme test'. The latter involves the scheme's actuary certifying that the pension benefits from the scheme are 'broadly equivalent' to the pension benefits of a standard Reference Scheme.

The future of contracting out

The Pensions Act 2008 will bring an end to contracting out both through contracted out money purchase schemes and via personal type pensions (stakeholder and personal pension) from April 2012.

27

INVESTING IN REAL ESTATE

MARIOS GREGORI AND VIRAN DE SILVA

The choice of investment vehicle, whether direct or via a company, will affect the tax arising on rental income and capital gains. The CGT position is now more straightforward in that capital gains are normally taxed at 18% or 28%. Properties that are let to quoted companies, Government departments or charities are taxed at the same rate. The one situation where gains may still be taxed at 10% is where entrepreneurs' relief is available for the sale of a property used by the individual's personal trading company (see 17.8.3).

This chapter contains the following sections:

(1) 'Buy to let' investments
(2) Private investment companies
(3) Limited liability partnerships (LLPs)
(4) Investing surplus funds within a trading company
(5) Buying overseas property
(6) Quoted property companies
(7) Property funds offered by insurance companies
(8) Pension funds

27.1 'BUY TO LET' INVESTMENTS

The subject of rental property is covered in general in Chapter 8.

The attraction of buying properties for letting is that the business should produce a reasonable return provided that the gearing (financing by loans) is not excessive, void periods are kept to a minimum and the properties are properly maintained. Problems arise from unexpectedly long periods without a tenant and the fact that it is often necessary to refurbish the property substantially after a tenant moves out. It may be time-consuming and difficult to manage a portfolio of investment properties, particularly if they are let on short leases or the properties require a lot of maintenance and are a long way from one another. Letting properties can require a lot of business and management skills and the ability to think ahead.

27.1.1 Relief for interest

The decision whether to borrow and invest in a second property involves two factors: interest rates and tax relief. A loan to invest in a rental property will attract tax relief but most financial institutions will then charge a significantly higher rate of interest. A loan to purchase your main residence or a remortgage of your main residence does not normally attract tax relief but will attract a competitive interest rate from the bank or building society. However, relief for interest is governed by the way that the borrowed money is used, not by the way the loan is secured. Relief should therefore be available for interest on a loan that is secured by way of a remortgage of your home but is used to buy an investment property.

Tax notes

When considering any investment, you need to look at how you will fund the transaction and what you think you will gain at the end of that transaction. Borrowing money to buy investment properties makes no sense if the interest charges are likely to exceed the rental income and future capital gains on the disposal of the properties. But if you can get tax relief for the interest, it is more likely that the benefits will outweigh the costs.

27.1.2 Increasing your gearing

It is not always necessary to take loans out when you purchase properties. We have explained at 8.2.12 that it may be possible to obtain tax relief for interest if you take fresh loans later on that are used to fund your property business.

27.1.3 No IHT business property relief

Letting properties is a business but it is not normally the sort of business which will qualify for business property relief (other than some furnished holiday lets – see 30.8).

27.2 PRIVATE INVESTMENT COMPANIES

In this section, we look at UK and foreign investment companies.

27.2.1 UK investment companies

A UK investment company has certain pros and cons.

Pros

- An individual can raise qualifying loans if the borrowings are used to finance the purchase of shares or the making of a loan to a UK close company that exists to manage property investments. It is necessary that the individual holds a material interest in the company (either on his or her own or in conjunction with his or her associates) – see 11.5. Usually, where the individual and his or her immediate family hold all the shares and this condition is clearly satisfied, interest on such a loan may be set against the individual's general income. Relief is not confined to income from the company but may be restricted if the individual 'recovers' capital from the company (see 11.5.5).
- The investment company may pay corporation tax at only 20% (21% for 2010) – or at the full rate of 26% if it lets to connected parties – whereas an individual who lets properties may well be subject to 40% or 50% tax because of the level of his or her other income.
- It will be easier for an individual to either put shares into his or her children's names from the outset, or to transfer shares to his or her children later on, than it would be if he or she needed to transfer a part interest in an investment property owned personally.
- When the company sells the properties, it will be liable for corporation tax on its gains (ie potentially 20% or 26% as opposed to 28%). Also, these gains are computed with relief for indexation (see 13.12).

Cons

- When the individual draws money from the company, this will generally involve his or her taking remuneration or interest or a dividend. The receipt of such income may attract higher rate tax.
- When the shareholders realise a capital gain on disposing of their shares (on a sale or a winding-up), they will also be liable for CGT (in addition to the corporation tax liability the company may have on any property disposal gain – the 'two tier CGT charge').

Tax notes

In general, before you put any property in a company, consider the exit route. A buyer will be interested in the asset, ie the house, but may not be so keen to buy shares in a private company.

In general, the two tier CGT charge means that it is not likely to be beneficial for most landlords to operate through an investment company. Nevertheless, if you have an existing investment company and it has unrelieved losses, it may make sense for you to put an investment property into the company to generate more rental income and so use up these losses.

Putting investment properties into a company will normally result in an SDLT charge (see 39.3).

27.2.2 Foreign investment companies

A UK individual cannot raise a qualifying loan to finance the purchase of shares or in the making of a loan to a non-UK resident company.

A non-UK resident company that receives rents from UK properties will generally be subject to basic rate income tax.

It will not be subject to tax on capital gains but the shareholders may be taxed under s 13 TCGA 1992 (see 33.16) where the company would be a close company if it were UK resident and the shareholder and his or her associates hold an interest in the company that amounts to at least 10%. This charge now also applies to foreign domiciled individuals.

In practice, it may be difficult to show that an investment company owned by UK-resident individuals is not resident here for tax purposes (see 35.15.1).

27.3 LIMITED LIABILITY PARTNERSHIPS (LLPS)

An LLP is a type of body corporate (company) that has a transparent tax treatment for some purposes. For property investment LLPs, this is subject to the proviso that the properties are used in the commercial letting business of the LLP.

There is no relief where an individual borrows personally to finance the purchase of an interest in an investment LLP (see 11.4). However, interest on borrowings taken by the LLP is an expense in computing the LLP's rental income for tax purposes.

An individual member's share of the income received by an LLP (computed in the normal way and after deducting loan interest) is taxed as if he or she had received that income personally.

When an investment property is sold by an LLP, the gain is divided among the members. Those members who are individuals or trustees may enjoy the benefit of the annual exemption. Non-resident members are not subject to UK CGT on their share of the LLP's capital gains.

No further income tax or capital gains tax is payable when members withdraw profits or the LLP is wound up.

A member's share in an LLP that carries on a property letting business will not qualify for IHT business property relief.

Tax notes

Both LLPs and UK limited companies have annual Companies House filing obligations, which need to be met to keep the entity in good standing. More information can be found at the Companies House website (www.companieshouse.gov.uk) or by calling 0303 1234 500.

27.4 INVESTING SURPLUS FUNDS WITHIN A TRADING COMPANY

Many people operate a business through a limited company and, as the business prospers, start to make investments by using the company's surplus funds. This may involve direct investment in real estate or indirect investment via the purchase of quoted shares or other investments.

This may have adverse tax consequences in the long-term. See 17.8.3 on the way in which HMRC can withhold entrepreneurs' relief where a company has substantial investment activities. Entitlement to business property relief (see 30.8) will also be affected.

27.5 BUYING PROPERTY OVERSEAS

There are several aspects to be considered here.

27.5.1 Holiday homes

Many people buy a holiday home with a view to letting it out for a few weeks and occupying it themselves for the rest of the year. A proportion of the interest on a loan used to buy the property can be claimed as a deduction in arriving at your taxable income from such lettings.

The Government has recently relaxed the rules on benefits in kind (see 4.8.6) but there are still many traps for the unwary in holding such investments through a company.

27.5.2 Furnished holiday lettings

If you buy an investment property in the European Economic Area, and it qualifies as furnished holiday accommodation (see 8.5.1), you may be able to set any loss against other income from 2009–10 onwards. Subject to the normal time limits, you may also be able to claim such relief for past years. You may also claim roll-over relief (see 17.3).

While furnished holiday lettings (FHL) in the UK and other EEA countries will continue to qualify for the special tax reliefs available for FHL, the qualifying conditions have altered from April 2011 onwards.

In particular, it is now more difficult for a property to qualify as a holiday letting – it will have to be available for commercial letting as holiday accommodation for 210 days a year (previously 140 days) and actually let for 105 days (previously 70 days). However, to cater for fluctuations in lettings from year to year, it will be possible for owners to elect for continuation of a qualifying holiday letting to cover a break of one or two years where the letting thresholds are not reached.

FHL owners who may struggle to meet the new letting thresholds will have to decide whether or not to retain the property for personal use and/or hold it as an investment or take steps to ensure that the property is available and actually let for the appropriate periods (by advertising more widely etc).

27.5.3 Relief for financing costs

A UK individual may create a special purpose vehicle (SPV) to acquire overseas investment properties, eg by forming a UK limited company to make investments in overseas property. If the company is a close company, as will normally be the case, and the individual has a material interest (see 11.5), he or she can raise a qualifying loan to finance the investment by either subscribing for shares or making loans to the close company. The interest on such loans can be relieved against the individual's other income.

27.5.4 The company will be liable for tax on capital gains

Holding overseas property in this way will mean that the UK company may have a tax liability as and when it eventually realises the investment. There may then be a further CGT charge on getting money out of the company. However, there may be ways of minimising this if you plan sufficiently far ahead. One possibility is to hold each overseas investment in a separate SPV with a view to eventually selling shares in that company rather than having the company sell its property. It is not quite as simple as this because you may well need to be able to deal with a possible objection by a UK purchaser that this will leave him or her with a latent tax liability if he or she ever wishes to take the property out of the company. There are ways of squaring the circle and you should consult a specialist at the outset rather than only as and when you are ready to divest.

27.5.5 Using an overseas company

An overseas company may often be treated in the same way as a UK company. If the company is centrally managed and controlled in the UK it will be treated as resident here (see 18.1). Even if you manage to surmount this obstacle, you may still suffer tax on a disposal of the property if s13 TCGA 1992 applies (see 33.17).

27.5.6 Make the SPV a limited liability partnership instead?

Another way of organising matters is to form a limited liability partnership to hold overseas property. The LLP could be a UK LLP or, if you were acquiring a US property, a Delaware LLP. The tax treatment is likely to be as follows:

- Interest relief against rental income provided that the borrowings are taken out by the LLP.
- Capital gains on a disposal of a property (but only a single charge, not a two-tier charge as described at 27.2.1 above).

27.6 QUOTED PROPERTY COMPANIES

27.6.1 UK quoted shares

Shares in a quoted UK property company have the following tax treatment:

- No relief for interest on loans used to buy shares unless, exceptionally, the quoted company is a close company and the individual either has a material interest or works full-time in the management of the company's business (see 11.5).
- The company pays corporation tax on rental income and capital gains.
- A shareholder pays tax in the normal way on dividends (see 9.8).
- An individual who realises a capital gain on a disposal of shares is subject to CGT if he or she is resident in the UK.

27.6.2 Real estate investment trusts

REITs are quoted collective vehicles for investment in rental property. They have been available in other countries for a number of years. The legislation on UK REITs took effect from 1 January 2007.

Investments into REITs are broadly the same as making direct property investments. No tax is charged at the company level. Tax is instead payable by the shareholders – this applies to both rental profits and capital gains.

However, a withholding tax of 20% will apply to most distributions by a REIT to its investors. The main exceptions are UK-resident companies and various exempt bodies.

Qualifying distributions received from a REIT are treated as rental income rather than dividends. They are known as Property Income Distributions (PIDs).

27.6.3 Non-resident companies

Where a company is not resident in the UK (even though it may be quoted in London), the tax treatment is as follows:

- UK rental income is subject to tax at basic rate;
- capital gains are not normally taxed at the company level;
- distributions of income are taxed as dividends: these may attract a 10% credit (see 9.10);
- a shareholder will not normally be subject to tax on the company's capital gains: the only circumstance where this can apply is where the foreign company is a close company and the UK resident individual has a 10% or greater interest;
- a capital gain may arise for a UK shareholder on realising his or her investment.

27.7 PROPERTY FUNDS OFFERED BY INSURANCE COMPANIES

Most insurance companies offer unitised funds that include funds invested in property. These funds pay corporation tax at 20% on rental income and realised capital gains.

The tax treatment of individuals who take out investment bonds that are invested in such funds is set out at 28.2.

27.8 PENSION FUNDS

See 26.3.2 on the fact that residential property investments are a taxable asset for pension schemes, ie what were formerly called 'prohibited assets'.

Other property investments and, in particular, investments in quoted property companies and REITs are regarded as normal investments.

28

LIFE ASSURANCE

GRAHAM YEATMAN AND JENNIFER GRASHAM-WHALLEY

This chapter covers the tax treatment of life assurance and contains the following sections:

28.1 INTRODUCTION

A life assurance policy is simply the evidence of a contract between the individual policyholder and the life assurance company. The general principle is that the company is the collecting house for pooled investments and mortality risks, offering benefits directly to policyholders based on personal contracts. Life assurance policies can be used for a variety of purposes ranging from pure self protection to a tax-advantaged way to invest.

Life assurance policies can be classified in a number of ways, but the most common practical classification reflects the nature of the benefits provided under the policy and the periods for which they are provided. Types of policy are:

- whole of life policies, where the sum assured is payable on the death of the life assured, whenever that occurs;
- term policies, where the sum assured is payable on death during the policy term only; and
- endowment policies, where the underlying investment value is payable at the end of the policy term and the sum assured is paid out on death during the term.

Each type of policy has its own characteristics in terms of the blend of life assurance protection and potential investment return. Term policies for a relatively short period are most likely to offer the highest sum assured for each pound of premium while, towards the other end of the spectrum, an endowment policy will have a greater investment element.

An important characteristic of life assurance policies is that they do not produce income as such, but are essentially medium- or long-term accumulators. While a policy is held intact, the income and gains arising from the underlying investments held by the life company are taxed in the hands of the life company itself at 20%. In general, a tax liability only arises for the policyholder when he or she receives payment under the policy.

This chapter deals with the tax consequences of the policyholder paying premiums or receiving benefits under a life assurance policy issued by a UK company or a foreign insurer operating through a branch in the UK (although foreign life policies are covered briefly at 28.4).

Over the years many changes have been made to this complex and technical area.

28.1.1 The company's tax position

The taxation of life companies is complex, but broadly speaking, in respect of their life assurance business, companies are generally taxed on the excess of their investment income and realised capital gains over management expenses (the 'I-E' basis). For proprietary companies there is a formula to determine the proportions of the company's income and gains that should be allocated to policyholders and shareholders, respectively. Since 1 April 2003, the tax rate charged on the policyholder share of all life fund income has been 20%. The company's profits attributable to shareholders are, on the other hand, chargeable to corporation tax at the main rate (currently 26%).

To enable UK life companies to compete more equally for the business of residents of other European Union states, companies are currently able to write such business in an 'overseas' life fund, broadly on a gross roll-up basis with no UK tax on the income and gains, but with no relief for expenses.

A technical note, *Solvency II and the Taxation of Insurance Companies* was published on 23 March 2011, to announce the outline of a new life insurance tax regime, to take effect from 1 January 2013. The new regime is expected to deal with essential adjustments arising from Solvency II and, at the same time, deliver significant changes to create a simpler and more stable tax basis better aligned with the taxation of companies generally. The Government will be consulting further on this measure. It issued a consultation document in April 2011 and there will be further detailed discussions with stakeholders with a view to introducing legislation in Finance Bill 2012.

Changes will also be made to the way in which life insurance companies are taxed on certain long-term business. The 'I-E' basis mentioned above, used to calculate the profits on those life insurance policies which primarily provide protection in the event of death, will not apply to policies written after 31 December 2012. Instead the life insurance companies will be taxed on a trading profits basis. This change is also outlined in *Solvency II and the Taxation of Insurance Companies*.

Registered friendly societies are in a different position, being exempt from corporation tax in respect of tax-exempt life or endowment business. This is life 'and endowment business where total premiums under contracts do not exceed £270 pa, or £300 if paid monthly (a limit unchanged since 6 April 1995). Policies that can be written on the tax-exempt basis are generally qualifying policies provided they satisfy a 'minimum sum assured' test. Such policies can give tax-free proceeds even to higher rate taxpayers (see 25.4), but non-qualifying friendly society policies are taxable at basic and higher rates. The remainder of this chapter does not deal specifically with friendly society business.

28.2 QUALIFYING AND NON-QUALIFYING POLICIES

Although there is no differentiation between qualifying and non-qualifying policies in respect of taxation of the income and gains from the underlying assets in the life company's hands, the distinction does have a major impact on the tax position of the individual policyholder. Each of the three types of policy already identified (whole of life, endowment and term assurance) is capable of being a qualifying or non-qualifying policy depending on its initial design and the way in which it is dealt with once in force.

28.2.1 Qualifying policies

These are policies that satisfy the conditions set out in Schedule 15 ICTA 1988, and do not fall foul of the various anti-avoidance provisions. The main features of the qualifying rules are as follows.

Premiums

- must be payable for a period of ten years or more (though term assurances may be written for shorter periods) and must be payable annually or more frequently; and
- must be fairly evenly spread so that premiums payable in any one period of 12 months are neither more than twice the amount of premiums paid in any other 12-month period, nor more than one-eighth of the total amount of premiums payable over the first ten years (in the case of whole of life policies) or over the term of the policy (in the case of an endowment).

Premiums payable for an exceptional risk of death are left out of account for these purposes as are premiums payable for exceptional risk of a critical illness (see 28.3.8). However, these premium rules mean that 'single premium' policies used for lump sum investments are not qualifying policies (see 28.2.2).

The sum assured

- for an endowment policy, must not be less than 75% of the total premiums payable during the term of the policy. This percentage is reduced by 2% for each year by which the insured individual's age exceeds 55 years at the issue of the policy;
- for a whole of life policy, must not be less than 75% of the total premiums payable if death were to occur at age 75;
- for a term policy that has no surrender value and ends before the insured individual's 75th birthday, need not satisfy any minimum requirement.

Benefits

- may include the right to participate in profits, the right to benefits arising because of disability or the right to a return of premiums on death under a certain specified age (not exceeding 16 years); but
- may not include any other benefits of a capital nature.

The rules for certain special types of policy may vary from those referred to above, for example, mortgage protection policies, family income policies and industrial assurances.

Life assurers usually submit standard policy wordings to HMRC so that they can be certified as satisfying the qualifying rules (pre-certification). Policies in those standard forms can then be marketed as 'qualifying'.

Where a policy contains options by which the policyholder may, for example, increase the sum assured or the premium, or extend the policy term, these options are tested at the outset to ensure that, however any options are exercised, the policy will still satisfy the qualifying rules.

28.2.2 Insurance bonds and other non-qualifying policies

Non-qualifying policies are all other life policies not satisfying the qualifying rules, and those that, although they might have satisfied the qualifying rules at the outset, have been changed in some way such that they no longer satisfy those rules.

The most significant category of policies that are non-qualifying is single premium investment contracts (usually referred to as insurance or investment 'bonds'). These are written as whole of life contracts and provide for only a small amount of life cover, being primarily investment vehicles.

28.2.3 Taxation of premiums

(ss 266 et seq and Schedule 14 ICTA 1988)

No specific tax relief is available to an individual in respect of premiums paid under a non-qualifying life assurance policy. Similarly, there is no specific relief for premiums paid under qualifying policies issued in respect of contracts made after 13 March 1984. However, where qualifying policies issued before that date are still in force, Life Assurance Premium Relief (LAPR) is still available where the policy was issued on the life of the payer of the premium (or the payer's spouse) and where the payer is UK-resident at the time premiums are paid (albeit this is to be abolished – following the OTS review of reliefs – after a period of consultation).

Relief is given currently at the rate of 12.5% on premiums up to the greater of £1,500 or one-sixth of total income, and is usually obtained by deducting the tax relief from the premiums payable to the life company. Relief is lost if the policy becomes non-qualifying or if the benefits secured by the policy are increased, or its term extended, after 13 March 1984. Where an individual receives the benefit of LAPR but, in effect, recoups the outlay in premiums by withdrawing money from the policy, there is a process by which some or all of the LAPR is 'clawed back' by deduction from the amount withdrawn.

28.3 TAXATION OF LIFE POLICY PROCEEDS

(ss 461–546 ITTOIA 2005)

In view of life policies' position as income accumulators, where liability for gains and income in respect of the underlying assets is dealt with by taxing the life company, the usual income tax principles are inappropriate to life policy taxation. Accordingly, the tax regime that applies to the individual policyholder has been specifically constructed for the purpose. It caters separately for qualifying and non-qualifying policies and for mortality and investment profits realised from policies.

It is first necessary to determine if any particular action constitutes a 'chargeable event' in respect of the policy. If it does not, no income tax consequence arises under the life policy regime from that action. If it does, it is then necessary to calculate the 'gain', to determine the rate of tax applicable to the gain and to determine who is liable to pay the resulting tax.

Despite references to 'chargeable events' and 'gains', it is the income tax regime that applies to life policies (for the CGT position, see 28.3.10). For the taxation of personal portfolio bonds, see 28.3.11.

28.3.1 Chargeable events

Non-qualifying policy

(s 484 ITTOIA 2005)

For a non-qualifying policy such as an insurance bond, the chargeable events are broadly:

- the death of the life assured;
- the maturity of the policy;
- the total surrender of the policy;
- the assignment of the policy for money or money's worth; and
- excesses arising on partial surrenders or partial assignments in any policy year.

No chargeable event occurs where an assignment takes place by way of security for a debt (or on the discharge of the security). Similarly, an assignment between spouses or civil partners who are living together is not a chargeable event.

Qualifying policy

For qualifying policies, there are exemptions from the rules on chargeable events so that:

- death or maturity are only chargeable events if the policy has previously been made paid-up (ie premiums have ceased but the policy has remained in force) within the first ten years (or three-quarters of the term of an endowment policy, if shorter);
- surrender, assignment for money or money's worth or an excess will only be a chargeable event if it occurs before the expiry of ten years (or three-quarters of the term of an endowment policy, if shorter) or if the policy was made paid-up within that period.

Three consequences of the chargeable event rules are that:

(i)   the gift (ie assignment of the whole policy with no consideration) of qualifying or non-qualifying policies is not a chargeable event and so triggers no income tax consequences;

(ii) there is no chargeable event on the death of the life assured under, or on the maturity of, a qualifying policy where all due premiums were paid prior to the event in question;

(iii) there is no chargeable event on the assignment for value or surrender (in whole or part) of a qualifying policy where premiums have been paid for the first ten years (or three-quarters of the term for an endowment policy).

Where there is no chargeable event in respect of a life policy, there is no income tax charge under the specific life policy tax regime, irrespective of the tax position of the individual policyholder. In particular, points (ii) and (iii) above illustrate the main current advantage of qualifying policies – ie their ability to provide tax-free proceeds to individual policyholders.

28.3.2 Calculating life policy gains

(s 491 ITTOIA 2005)

Broadly speaking, where the chargeable event is either a maturity, total surrender or an assignment for consideration, the chargeable gain is the investment profit made under the policy. This is calculated by reference to the value of the benefits being received as a result of the chargeable event, plus the amount of any relevant capital payments previously received under the policy (ie any sum or other benefit of a capital nature, other than one paid as a result of an individual's disability), less the amount paid by way of premiums and any taxable gains as a result of previous partial surrenders.

This principle of charging tax only on investment gains also applies where the chargeable event is the death of the life assured. The exclusion of mortality profit from the taxable gain is achieved by using the policy's surrender value immediately before death instead of the value of the benefits being received under the policy.

A policy capable of paying benefits on more than one death could have the considerable disadvantage that, on a death, lump sums paid on previous deaths were taken into account when calculating the 'investment gain' under the policy. This result was not intended and FA 2003 confirmed this to be the case (both for the future and the past), subject to certain conditions.

See 10.9 regarding commission rebates.

28.3.3 Partial surrenders

(ss 498–508 ITTOIA 2005)

A chargeable event occurs when a policyholder surrenders part of the policy (often referred to as making 'withdrawals' from the policy). Partial surrenders include the surrender of a right to a bonus. They also include loans to a policyholder made by (or by arrangement with) the insurance company, unless the policyholder's policy is a qualifying policy and the loan bears a commercial rate of interest, or the loan is made to a full-time employee of the insurer for the purposes of a house purchase or improvement.

At the end of each policy year, the policy attracts an allowable payment of 5% of the total premium then paid under the policy. This allowance is then set against the value of any partial surrenders made up to that date. If the value of those partial surrenders exceeds the current cumulative net total of allowable payments, a chargeable event occurs; if the net total of allowable payments is equal to or exceeds cumulative withdrawals, no chargeable event occurs. Allowable payments are given up to 100% of the total premiums paid so that, for a single premium investment bond, the allowances are given at the rate of 5% for 20 years, ie a policyholder can take his or her allowable payment tax free every year for a 20-year period or in separate years spread over a longer period, so long as the cumulative allowable payments total for the relevant policy year is not exceeded. For instance, a policyholder who withdrew nothing in years one and two could withdraw up to 15% in year three.

Once an 'excess' (ie an occasion on which the cumulative partial surrenders exceed the cumulative allowances) has occurred, the cumulative withdrawals and allowances up to that date are considered to have been used and the process of accumulating allowances and withdrawals starts afresh (subject to the '100% of premiums' limit that applies to the allowances).

Example – Cumulation of allowances and withdrawals

X invests £10,000 in a single premium investment bond; £1,200 is withdrawn after four policy years, a further £4,500 after six policy years and £1,000 after eight policy years.

Policy years	A Cumulative allowable payments	B Partial surrender (C − A)	C Cumulative surrender between	D Taxable gain
	£	£	£	£
1	500 (1× 500)	0	0	0
2	1,000 (2× 500)	0	0	0
3	1,500 (3× 500)	0	0	0
4	2,000 (4× 500)	1,200	1,200	0
5	2,500 (5× 500)	0	1,200	0
6	3,000 (6× 500)	4,500	5,700	2,700
7	500 (1× 500)	0	0	0
8	1,000 (2× 500)	1,000	1,000	0
9	1,500 (3× 500)	0	1,000	0
10	2,000 (4× 500)	0	1,000	0

Note: (1)   A chargeable event occurs only when C exceeds A.
         (2)   The value of the policy is irrelevant to these calculations so that it is possible to have a taxable gain under a policy at a time when the policy itself is worth less than the premiums paid.

When the final chargeable event occurs under the policy (ie death, maturity, final surrender or assignment for value), the total profit on the policy is brought into account. The profit is the final proceeds (excluding any mortality profit where the event is death), plus previous partial surrenders, less premiums paid and any taxable gains from previous partial withdrawals.

Example – Total surrender after partial surrenders

> Using the example immediately above, if the policy were totally surrendered at the end of the tenth policy year for £10,400, the taxable gain on that final encashment would be as follows:
>
> £10,400 + £1,200 + £4,500 + £1,000 – (£10,000 + £2,700) = £4,400
>
> Note: If, on final termination, the 'gain' calculated in this way is a negative figure, it may be deducted from taxable income for the purposes of higher rate tax only (see 28.3.4).

Partial assignments of policies

FA 2001 clarified the position on partial assignments of policies (eg where spouses or civil partners jointly own a policy and want to transfer it to one of them only, such as on divorce) so that:

(1) partial assignments for no consideration are not chargeable events (but note that HMRC believes that assignment on divorce will almost invariably be for consideration); and

(2) any tax liability will fall on the person whose interest in the policy is reducing.

28.3.4 Taxing gains on chargeable events

(s 491 ITTOIA 2005)

In the majority of cases where the policyholder owns the policy for his or her own absolute benefit, the gain is treated as the top slice of his or her income and is taxed appropriately.

However, because the income and gains attributable to the policy's underlying assets have already been taxed in the hands of the life company, life policy gains are not chargeable to income tax at the basic rate. This applies to both qualifying and non-qualifying policies. Despite the fact that the gain is treated as having already suffered tax as if it were income from savings, there is no grossing up of the gain for higher rate tax purposes.

Accordingly, for an individual paying tax at the additional rate, the maximum rate of tax payable on life policy gains at present is 30% (50% less 20%). An individual whose income (including the gain) is taxable at the basic rate only will have no further income tax liability on the policy gain. Non-taxpayers will not be able to make any reclaim in respect of the notional credit for tax paid by the life company.

If the individual realises a loss under the policy, that loss is only available as a deduction from taxable income for the purposes of higher rate tax. Furthermore, the loss is only eligible for such relief to the extent of amounts charged as income in respect of previous chargeable events. FA 2004 contained anti-avoidance legislation that prevents loss relief for deficiencies on 'second-hand' insurance bonds.

Top-slicing

In view of the fact that the gain will have arisen over a period of years, the legislation recognises that it would be harsh to treat the total gain as part of the taxpayer's income in the year of receipt. A measure of relief is afforded by a process known as 'top-slicing'.

Top-slicing first requires calculation of the 'appropriate fraction' of the gain, more usually referred to as the 'slice'. Where the chargeable event in question is death, maturity, total encashment or assignment for value, the slice is calculated by dividing the gain by the number of complete policy years for which the policy has been in force. Where the chargeable event is caused by a partial surrender, the gain is divided by the number of complete policy years since the last excess caused by a partial surrender (or by the number of years for which the policy has been in force where the chargeable event is the first excess).

The slice (and not the whole of the gain) is treated as the top part of the policyholder's income, and the average rate of tax applicable to the slice (less the basic rate) is calculated. That tax rate will then apply to the whole of the gain to determine the total income tax liability on the gain. The result is that relief is given to individuals whose other income would mean that they pay tax at no more than the basic rate, but who would be taken into the higher rates of tax if the whole of the gain were added to their income.

Example – No tax on the gain

A invests £20,000 in a single premium investment bond in May 2011 and cashes it in after five years for £27,500. The gain is therefore £7,500 and the 'slice' is £1,500 (£7,500 divided by five).

	£
Taxable income (excluding policy gain)	25,000
'Slice'	1,500
Taxable income	26,500

The tax rate applicable to the 'slice' is therefore 20% less 20% = 0%.

Example – Slice falling into basic and higher rate bands

> *B* invests £12,000 in a single premium investment bond in May 2011. After five years she cashes it in for £17,000. The gain is £5,000 and the slice is £1,000 (£5,000 divided by five). In that year her other taxable income after reliefs is £34,200.
>
> | Tax calculation on gain: | £ |
> |---|---|
> | Taxable income + 'slice' | 38,000 |
> | Tax applicable to slice | |
> | On £800 (ie £34,200 to £35,000) at 0% (20% – 20%) | Nil |
> | On £200 (ie £35,001 to £35,200) at 20% (40% – 20%) | 40 |
> | Total tax on slice | 40 |
>
> Average rate on slice
>
> $$\frac{40}{1000} \times 100 = 4\%$$
>
> The tax payable is £5,000 × 4% = £200.
>
> To illustrate the effect of top-slicing, if it had not been available the calculations would have been:
>
> | Tax applicable to the gain | £ |
> |---|---|
> | On £800 at 0% (20%) | Nil |
> | On £4,200 at 20% (40% – 20%) | 840 |
> | Tax payable | 840 |
>
> *Notes*:
>
> (1) The whole gain (without top-slicing) is counted as income in determining whether any age allowance or entitlement to children's tax credit should be reduced.
> (2) There is no top-slicing where the taxpayer is a company.
> (3) For top-slicing purposes, total income is computed without reference to amounts chargeable in respect of loss of office or lease premiums chargeable as rent.
> (4) The examples given in this chapter assume no reliefs or amounts as mentioned in (3).

Age allowance for over 65s

If an individual is entitled to the age allowance, the gain on a life policy can reduce (or even eliminate) that additional allowance. Top-slicing relief does not apply in respect of this reduction of the additional allowance. See 12.2.1 for an example of how age related allowances can be reduced.

Tax credits

The gain on a life policy can affect entitlement to tax credits and, as for age allowance, top-slicing relief does not apply.

28.3.5 Two policy gains in one tax year

Where an individual has two policies with chargeable gains in a tax year, tax is calculated as if the gains arose under only one policy, with a slice equal to the sum of the individual slices. Thus, if two policies are surrendered in the same tax year, one with a gain of £10,000 (having been in force for five years) and one with a gain of £24,000 (having been in force for eight years), tax on the gains is calculated as if one policy had been surrendered, yielding a gain of £34,000 and with a slice of £5,000 (£10,000/5 + £24,000/8).

This approach can have the effect of increasing or decreasing the total tax payable (compared with disposing of the policies in separate tax years) depending on the individual's tax position and the performance of the relevant policies.

28.3.6 Persons liable for the charge

Where a policy is held by an individual for his or her own benefit, the tax charge falls on that individual. The same applies to an individual where the policy is held as security for a debt owed by the individual.

If the policy is held in trust, the charge falls on the settlor, who can recover the tax paid from the trustees. If a policy is held by a trust created by a settlor who has since died, it is possible that gains realised by trustees in these circumstances may escape tax altogether in view of the impossibility of taxing somebody who has not been alive in the appropriate year of assessment. Although somewhat anomalous, this has been very useful where an individual owned a policy that would not come to an end on his or her death (eg a joint life policy paying out on the second death). By declaring a suitable trust of the policy in his or her Will, the individual might have been able to put future gains realised under the policy outside the income tax net.

FA 1998 included provisions to counter this by enabling the trustees, or perhaps even the trust's beneficiaries, to be taxed where the settlor is dead (or not UK-resident at the time of the chargeable event). These rules do not apply where the settlor died before 17 March 1998 and the policy is not 'enhanced' after that date.

HMRC has recently clarified that where a policy is held on a bare trust for a minor, any chargeable event is taxed as arising to the minor. For example, if a grandparent assigns a policy to a grandchild but it has to be held by the parents until the child reaches age 18, any chargeable event gain would be taxable on the minor. However, where parents gift policies to their own minor children, the normal settlement rules apply and the parent would be taxable on any chargeable event gain arising before the child reaches age 18.

Where the policy is held by a company, or on a trust created by – or as security for a debt owed by – a company, the charge falls on the company (the company has the right to recover the tax paid from the trustees where the policy is held on trust). If a policy is assigned by way of gift, chargeable excesses arising during that policy year, but prior to the assignment are taxed on the assignor. Future gains are taxed on the new beneficial owner. This can allow some scope for tax planning, eg where one spouse assigns a policy to the other spouse or civil partner, who is subject to a lower rate of tax, and he or she then surrenders the policy.

28.3.7 Timing of the taxation of gains

Where the chargeable event is death, maturity, total surrender or assignment for value, the gain is treated as arising at the time of that event.

Excesses arising from partial surrenders, on the other hand, are generally only regarded as arising at the end of the policy year in which the excess occurs. Accordingly, if the policy was taken out in June 2006 and an excess occurs as a result of a partial surrender in February 2012, the gain resulting from that partial surrender is treated as arising in June 2012 and so is taxable in 2012–13.

28.3.8 Critical illness policies

For a number of years it has been possible to include critical illness or 'dread disease' benefits in a variety of policies. In general, such a benefit pays a capital sum if the insured individual is diagnosed as suffering from any of the specified 'dread diseases or events'. The diseases or events specified vary from company to company, but usually include heart attack, stroke, cancer and heart by-pass surgery.

It is understood that HMRC accepts that the payment of a benefit on the happening of a dread disease is not a chargeable event, so that this benefit is paid free of tax under the life policy tax regime. With critical illness plans, you have to survive a number of days before benefits are payable (the industry average is 28 days) also known as 'survival plans'.

28.3.9 Chargeable event certificates

(s 552 ICTA 1988)

When a chargeable event occurs, the life assurance company is required to provide HMRC with a chargeable event certificate that gives the policyholder's name and address, the nature and date of the chargeable event and information required for computing the gain, where the gain exceeds a threshold (set at half the basic rate tax band). Life companies also have to supply policyholders with chargeable event certificates to enable them to include the gains in their SA returns. The certificates also have to include information about the chargeable event and the gain produced.

28.3.10 Capital gains tax and life policies

(s 210 TCGA 1992)

If the policy is disposed of by a person who is not the original beneficial owner, and the policy at any time prior to that disposal changed hands for money or money's worth, the policy will be an asset potentially liable to CGT. The potential for double taxation (income tax and CGT) is resolved by s 37 TCGA 1992, which provides, broadly, that money or money's worth charged to income tax will be taken into account and excluded from the CGT calculations.

FA (No.1) 2010 included anti-avoidance which prevents capital losses arising in addition to income tax losses as a result of the interaction of these provisions.

Where a life policy is subject to the CGT regime, the occasion of the payment of the sum(s) assured and the surrender of the policy are treated as disposals.

28.3.11 Personal portfolio bonds

These are policies usually, but not exclusively, written offshore where the benefits due under the policy are (or may be) closely linked with the value of a portfolio of assets personal to the policyholder.

Since 6 April 1999 such policies have suffered a specific additional charge on a deemed gain of 15% of the total premiums paid to the end of each policy year and deemed gains from previous policy years. This charge does not apply to 'managed portfolio bonds', ie those that do not allow personalisation by restricting the policy investment to pooled assets generally available to investors.

28.4 FOREIGN LIFE POLICIES

(s 476 ITTOIA 2005)

In general, policies issued in respect of contracts made after 17 November 1983 cannot be 'qualifying' unless they are issued by a UK insurance company or the UK branch of a foreign insurer. Before that date, foreign policies could be qualifying policies if they satisfied the normal qualifying rules.

Other ways in which the life policy tax regime gives a different tax treatment for foreign policies are as follows:

(1) The gain calculated on a chargeable event is reduced by reference to the amount of time, during the life of the policy, that the policyholder was not UK resident.

(2) In calculating the 'appropriate fraction' for top-slicing purposes, any complete years during which the policyholder was not UK resident are excluded.

(3) Taxable gains arising under such policies are charged to basic rate as well as higher rate tax, as appropriate, as the life company has paid no underlying tax to 'frank' a notional tax credit. An exception to this applies where the insurer is taxed on the investment income and gains accruing for the policyholder's benefit at a rate of not less than 20%. In such cases, the policy gains will not be liable to basic rate UK income tax. This exception will apply only to policies issued by EU or EEA insurers.

FA 1998 included a framework requiring certain categories of foreign life companies to appoint a fiscal representative in the UK to be responsible for reporting gains on life policies to HMRC in accordance with s 552 ICTA 1988 (see 28.3.9).

At one time there was an advantage in holding offshore insurance bonds through a non-UK resident company but FA 2006 contained provisions that enabled HMRC to tax profits from the surrender of such policies under s 721 ITA 2007 (see 33.4) from 5 December 2005.

Gains arising from foreign policies are taxed as miscellaneous income. This means that a UK resident policyholder is taxed on the arising basis even if he or she is domiciled overseas (the remittance basis does not apply).

28.5 ANNUITIES

(ss 422–426 ITTOIA 2005)

An annuity is an arrangement under which one person agrees to pay another a sum of money for a known period, or a period to be determined by some specified contingency.

Annuities may be immediate (ie the payment will start straightaway) or deferred (where payments will start at some predetermined point in the future). Many annuities are established to continue for the lifetime of the annuitant, but temporary annuities cease at the end of a fixed period or on the annuitant's death, whichever comes earlier. Annuities may be effected on the lives of two or more individuals and, for example, continue until the death of the survivor. Annuities may be paid monthly, quarterly or annually, and may be of a fixed amount or subject to some sort of index-linking. Annuities may also be written with a guaranteed minimum period so as to reduce the loss that might otherwise be suffered by an individual who dies shortly after purchasing an annuity.

There are four main types of annuity:

(1) Purchased life annuities, where an individual pays a lump sum to an insurance company in return for the annuity.
(2) Annuities received as a gift (eg at one time it was common for testators to direct that annuities be paid out of their estates).
(3) Annuities paid as part of the purchase price of a business or by continuing members of a partnership to a former partner who has retired.
(4) Compulsory purchase annuities, for example, those purchased out of pension funds.

For the annuitant, a purchased life annuity attracts a special relief in that amounts received are treated in part as a return of the money paid for by the annuity (the capital element) and in part as interest on that purchase price. The capital element of each payment is calculated by reference to actuarial tables and is not taxable. This tax exemption applies even where the annuitant lives long enough for the capital element of the annuity payments he or she has received to exceed the original purchase price of the annuity. Other types of annuity do not receive this favourable treatment in respect of the capital element of annuity payments.

Purchased life annuities are also subject to an income tax regime similar to that applying to life policies (see 28.3.4). Chargeable events for life annuities are total surrender, assignment for money or money's worth and 'excesses' (calculated in much the same way as for life policy partial surrenders).

Where a gain arises on a chargeable event, the gain is not charged to basic rate tax where the company offering the annuity has been taxed in the UK. A notional tax credit is given in respect of tax paid by the life company on the income and gains of its general annuity fund.

For CGT purposes, deferred annuities are also treated in a similar way to life policies, with the effect that no chargeable gain accrues on the disposal of such a contract except where the person making the disposal is not the original beneficial owner and the annuity at any time changed hands for money or money's worth.

28.6 INCOME PROTECTION

28.6.1 Introduction

Income protection insurance plans (also known as permanent health insurance) provide a replacement income for an individual who is unable to work through illness or disability. Contracts are usually available to those aged between 16 and 60 but terminate on the insured individual reaching his or her normal retirement date.

Once the disability or illness arises, benefits commence on expiry of a deferred period, typically between one and 12 months, selected by the policyholder. The longer the deferred period, the fewer claims the insurer will expect to pay and so the lower the premium will be per £ of benefit.

Income protection contracts can be written as life assurance policies – typically as non-qualifying policies to avoid the provision of substantial sums assured payable on death. If structured as a life policy, payment of disability benefits is not treated as a surrender of rights for the purposes of life policy taxation.

28.6.2 Tax consequences

If an individual effects an income protection contract for him or herself, premiums are not deductible for tax purposes. If an employer effects a policy on an employee to enable the employer to continue to pay the employee's salary during a period of disability or illness, or if the policy covers a revenue loss during such a period, the employer may be able to claim the premiums as a business expense.

Benefits from most individually owned income protection policies are tax-free.

If the contract is effected by an employer to maintain the employee's salary during the period of illness or disability, the income is taxable in the individual's hands, in the same way as salary would have been.

28.7 PRE-OWNED ASSETS CHARGE

A problem may arise where individuals have taken out a policy that is written in trust so the proceeds on death would be paid to their business partners/fellow shareholders but the individual remains entitled to the amount paid out on the maturity of the policy. This type of arrangement may be wholly commercial and yet still be caught by the FA 2004 legislation (see 33.7), which imposes a charge on an annual benefit that will normally be a rate equal to the official rate at the valuation date, currently 4% of the capital involved (in this context, the surrender value of the policy).

The pre-owned assets legislation is extremely complex and this is an area where you should seek advice from a specialist.

28.8 LIFE POLICIES EFFECTED BY COMPANIES

There are circumstances in which a company can effect a life policy. For example, it may do so on the life of a director or other key executive to provide the company with compensation for the death of that individual. Similarly, policies may be effected to provide funds to repay loans.

In general, if a company buys term assurance for a short period (usually not more than five years), which does not acquire a surrender value and is used solely to provide protection against the loss of profits resulting from the death of a key person, the premiums are tax deductible and the proceeds taxable in the hands of the company.

If, on the other hand, the policy is for a longer term, may acquire a surrender value, is effected for a capital purpose, or where the life assured has a material shareholding in the company, the premiums are not tax-deductible but the proceeds are unlikely to be charged to corporation tax in the company's hands, other than by virtue of the life assurance chargeable event rules.

Since 14 March 1989 policies owned by companies (or held on trusts created by a company, or held as security for a debt owed by the company) cannot be qualifying policies – irrespective of their compliance with the qualifying rules. The only exception to this denial of qualifying status is where policies are used to secure company debts incurred in purchasing land to be occupied by the company for the purposes of its trade (or in constructing, extending or improving buildings occupied in that way). Broadly speaking, provided the policy has been used for this purpose since its inception, the chargeable gain will only be the amount by which the policy proceeds exceed the lowest amount of the loan that has been secured by the policy.

28.9 LIFE POLICIES IN TRUST AFFECTED BY THE FA 2006 IHT CHANGES

The 2006 Budget changed the way in which many trusts are taxed. The main change was bringing the IHT treatment of most interest in possession trusts into line with the regime that was previously confined to discretionary trusts. This means the creation of such trusts will normally be taxed as a chargeable lifetime transfer whereas such gifts were previously treated as potentially exempt transfers (PETs), which attracted IHT only if the donor died within seven years.

Interest in possession trusts had historically been used for protection policies written in trust, principally because of the flexibility that this type of trust provides. However, the change in rules means a more complex and potentially more highly taxed regime for policies now written in these types of trust.

For any protection plan written in an interest in possession trust after 22 March 2006, the premiums will potentially be subject to an immediate IHT tax charge of 20% (taxed as a chargeable lifetime transfer, see 29.2). The trust itself will be subject to a periodic charge on the value of the trust assets every 10 years (maximum 6%) and there will also be an exit charge on any capital distributions from the trust (see 31.4.23).

However, most regular premium plans written into interest in possession trusts should escape these tax charges. If the premiums are below £3,000 pa, they will be exempted by the annual IHT exemption. For premiums above this level, providing they are regular and meet the relevant conditions (see 30.5.2), they should be exempted from the tax charge, as 'normal expenditure out of income'. Where neither of these situations arises there will be no immediate tax charge provided they (together with other transfers made by the settlor in the previous seven years) do not exceed the IHT nil rate band (currently £325,000).

Protection policies established in trust before 22 March 2006 will not normally be caught by the new IHT regime, however care should be taken when any changes are made to these policies.

Absolute trusts or, to use their proper name, bare trusts, continue to fall within the PET rules and therefore do not attract tax as a chargeable lifetime transfer. Clearly, there will now be a temptation to write more policies under bare trusts. However, the disadvantage of these types of trust is that, by definition, it is extremely difficult to change the beneficiary and, should an individual's personal circumstances change in the future, they may be left with a policy written in trust that is no longer appropriate.

28.10 DISCOUNTED GIFT SCHEMES

A discounted gift scheme involves a gift of an investment bond (see 28.2.2) where certain rights are retained, typically the right to take annual withdrawals. For example, a couple aged 70 may give a bond valued at £100,000 to their children whilst retaining the right to take 5% pa for the rest of their lives. In such a situation, the gift is not £100,000 but the discounted value of the right to receive what value is left in the bond when the couple have both died.

HMRC published a technical note on discounted gift schemes on 1 May 2007 (although it should be noted that the valuation rate of interest has changed since then). See also the decision in *Executors of Mrs Marjorie Bower* v *HMRC*.

29

CAPITAL GAINS TAX PLANNING

GRAHAM YEATMAN

The simplest way to save on capital gains tax is to invest through tax exempt wrappers such as an individual savings account or into exempt assets such as shares of companies which qualify under the enterprise investment scheme or venture capital trust rules. However, planning ahead in this way is not always possible or desirable and it is often the case that it is only when an asset is about to be sold that the issue of CGT planning is actively considered.

Most capital gains typically arise from an exceptional or 'one-off' transaction. Instead of being spread evenly over the whole period of ownership, the capital growth on an investment that might have been held for many years falls entirely into the tax year in which the disposal takes place. This can often mean that a large amount of tax is involved. However, it is important to remember that, when it comes to capital gains tax, having a problem generally means you have made (or are about to make) a profit on your investment. It is important that you do not let tax considerations dominate to the exclusion of investment decisions.

There are ways of mitigating tax and it is usually a good idea to take professional advice before you commit to a transaction. This chapter focuses on the following planning points:

(1) Make use of annual exemptions for both spouses/civil partners
(2) Realise gains to avoid wasting the annual exemption
(3) Make sure you get relief for capital losses
(4) Use the basic rate band
(5) Save tax by making gifts to relatives
(6) Reinvestment relief
(7) Claim roll-over relief on furnished holiday accommodation
(8) Make the most of entrepreneurs' relief
(9) Selling the family company

29.1 MAKE USE OF ANNUAL EXEMPTIONS FOR BOTH SPOUSES/CIVIL PARTNERS

29.1.1 Inter-spouse transfers can be a way of saving tax

Each individual is allowed to realise capital gains of £10,600 in 2011–12 before he or she becomes liable for CGT. This applies to both spouses and civil partners (FA 2005 put the CGT treatment of married couples and civil partners on to the same footing from 5 December 2005) – each partner is entitled to his or her own annual exemption. However, there are no provisions under which any unused amount may be transferred to the other spouse or partner.

Example – Inter-spouse/civil partner transfers

If A has gains of £8,000 and his wife B has gains of £12,200, the position is as follows:

	A	B
	£	
Gains	8,000	13,200
Less: exemption	(10,600)	(10,600)
Taxable	Nil	2,600

There is often a way of avoiding this type of mismatch. If B had transferred* assets to A and he then sold them, she could effectively transfer her gain to him. A transfer between spouses does not count as a disposal for tax purposes and A would take over B's base cost. So, with a little forethought, the position could have been:

	A	B
	£	
Gains	10,600	10,600
Less: exemption	(10,600)	(10,600)
Taxable	Nil	Nil

* It is important to ensure that any such transfer is genuine, outright and unconditional.

29.2 REALISE GAINS TO AVOID WASTING THE ANNUAL EXEMPTION

Any unused annual exemption cannot be carried forward for use in a future tax year. Dealing costs may be a disincentive but, provided you expect to sell shares, etc, at some time, it can make sense to 'top up' any net gains to make full use of the exemption each year.

The rules for matching sales and purchases within a 30-day period before and after a transaction mean that 'bed and breakfast' transactions will not achieve this. However, you may be able to realise gains and then have your ISA buy the same shares (ie 'bed and ISA'). Alternatively, your spouse, civil partner or family trust could buy the shares.

29.3 MAKE SURE YOU GET RELIEF FOR CAPITAL LOSSES

Capital losses for previous years attach to each spouse or civil partner separately and can be set only against that spouse or civil partner's gain. However, it may be possible to save tax by transferring an asset between spouses or civil partners before it is sold to an outsider. Again, it is important to ensure that any such transfer is outright and unconditional so that the individual receiving the asset has complete freedom to sell or retain the asset as he or she sees fit.

Example – Relief for capital losses

If C's wife D has losses of £35,000 and C has an asset that has appreciated by £50,400, it will make sense for him to transfer it to D so that she can then choose to sell it. Instead of the position being like this:

	£
C's gains	50,400
Less: exemption	(10,600)
Taxable	39,800

the position could be:

	£
D's gains	50,400
Less: capital losses	(35,000)
	15,400
Less: exemption	(10,600)
Taxable	4,800

Of course, the ideal position would be achieved by *C* transferring part of the asset to *D*, so that they eventually make a joint disposal, use *D*'s losses and take full advantage of both of their annual exemptions.

29.3.1 Negligible value claims

You may have made an investment in the past that has gone badly. Indeed, you may have written it off in your own mind but, if you have not sold it, the loss is normally only a paper loss that is not allowable for CGT purposes. There is however an exception to this rule: you may be able to establish an allowable loss even though there has been no disposal. If HMRC can be persuaded that the asset has become of 'negligible value' (ie virtually worthless), you can claim a loss (see 13.5.9). In practice, HMRC issues lists of quoted shares that have been suspended and are recognised to be of negligible value: you can view the list online at www.hmrc.gov.uk/cgt/negvalist.htm. It may also be possible to establish losses on unquoted shares and other investments, by negotiation with HMRC.

In some situations, it may be best to defer making a negligible value claim. If you have made capital gains that are covered by the annual exemption you will waste part of your CGT loss by making a negligible value claim for that year.

29.3.2 Review your holdings

If you find yourself holding shares that have failed to live up to your expectations when you purchased them, or worse, made a loss, consider selling these shares to crystallise a loss to offset against your capital gains. By taking positive action before the end of the tax year, you may be able to save on your CGT bill and recoup in part the loss you suffered on a disappointing investment. However, if you have already made capital gains in the same tax year that are covered by the annual exemption there will be no point in crystallising a loss, only to see it wasted.

An experienced stockbroker, IFA or investment adviser working in conjunction with a good accountant should be able to more than cover their professional fees with proactive advice.

29.4 USE THE BASIC RATE BAND

Remember that where a taxable gain falls within an individual's basic rate band for the year it is liable to tax at 18% rather than 28% (which is charged once the band is exceeded) – see 13.1.4. It should also be remembered that it is the extended basic rate band that is taken into account for these purposes – see Chapter 15 for illustrations of when the basic rate band is extended. So, for example, an individual making taxable capital gains that take him or her over the basic rate band for the year, may wish to make additional pension contributions in that year or an additional Gift Aid payment to obtain further tax relief.

Example

Jane has an annual income of £30,000 for 2011–12 and realises chargeable gains of £25,000 in the year. Her capital gains tax position would be as follows:

Gain	£25,000
Less annual exemption	£10,600
Taxable gain	£14,400
Tax at 18% (£35,000 – £30,000)	£5,000 x 18% = £900
Tax at 28%	£9,400 x 28% = £2,632
Total	= £3,532

However, if Jane were to make a personal pension contribution in the year of £7, 520 this would reduce her tax liability as follows:

Basic rate band extended by grossed up contribution:

(£7,520 x 100/80 = £9,400 + £35,000 = £44,400)

Taxable gain £14,400

Tax at 18% (£44,400 – £30,000) £14,400 x 18% = £2,592

The tax saving to Jane is £940. The net result is that a total contribution to her pension fund (including the basic rate tax relief added by the Government) is £9,400 but this has only effectively cost Jane £6,580 (£7,520 – £940) giving her 30% tax relief on the gross contribution.

For married couples, where one spouse or civil partner is a basic rate taxpayer and the other a higher rate taxpayer, and it is clear that total chargeable gains for a year will exceed both annual exemptions, it makes sense for transfers of assets to be made such that the taxable gains arise in the hands of the basic rate taxpayer. This will save the couple 10% on the taxable gain up to the limit of the lower income spouse or civil partner's basic rate band for the year.

29.5 SAVE TAX BY MAKING GIFTS TO RELATIVES

If you are planning to sell shares in unquoted companies it may be possible to save tax.

Example – Sale of unquoted shares

G who is an additional rate taxpayer holds all the shares in a private trading company. He has reached broad agreement with a potential purchaser to sell his shares for £1,000 each in October 2011, which will produce a gain of £750 per share.

If *G* so wishes, he could transfer some shares to his son *H* (a higher rate taxpayer) to enable him to use his annual exemption, ie *G* could give *H* 15 shares in the company and claim hold-over relief. No capital gain need arise for *G* on his gift to *H* who would then dispose of the shares to the ultimate purchaser. *H*'s capital gain would then be as follows:

	£
Capital gain: 15 × £750 =	11,250
Less: annual exemption	(10,600)
Taxable at 28%	650

The overall effect is that *G*'s family saves tax of £2,968.

If *G* had four children, he could make similar gifts to all of them and save up to £11,872. As always, it is important to ensure that any such transfer is genuine, outright and unconditional.

Gifts of listed shares and securities

It is sometimes possible to achieve a similar saving by transferring shares that do not attract s 165 hold-over relief, for example shares in a quoted trading company where the owner has less than 5% of the voting shares, or shares in a private investment company. But you have to plan some way ahead.

It is also possible to claim hold-over relief under a different part of the legislation where you make a chargeable transfer for IHT purposes, normally on your putting assets into a trust (see 13.6, 31.4.23 and 31.5). (Bear in mind that neither s 165 or s 260 relief is available if the trust is a settlor-interested trust, see 33.5.) If the trustees subsequently appoint property in favour of the trust beneficiaries (eg your children, grandchildren, etc), they can make a similar hold-over election to avoid any CGT charge on them. The overall effect will be that the trust beneficiaries will have taken the property that you put into trust at a value equal to your original acquisition cost.

You will need to take professional advice. In particular, bear in mind that if transfers into trusts take your cumulative transfers over the nil rate band (at present £325,000), you may have to pay IHT at the rate of 20% on the excess (see 30.2, 30.10 and 31.4.23). And do not try to do all this in rapid succession because HMRC may well attack the transactions as a preordained scheme (see 33.19 on *Ramsay*).

29.6 REINVESTMENT RELIEF

Relief from CGT is available where disposal proceeds are reinvested in a company qualifying for the EIS. The original gain is frozen until the EIS shares are sold. Any further gain made on the qualifying EIS shares is exempt provided they have been held for a minimum period of three years and certain qualifying conditions continue to be met. Income tax relief is also available on such investments. Although EIS investments remain higher risk than many other investment choices, there are now a wide range of sector options available in this maturing market.

Remember that any decisions that affect your investments and realising gains and losses should only be taken after seeking expert advice from an Independent Financial Adviser and should take into account the impact of the proposed transactions on your investment strategy as well as any possible tax advantages.

29.7 CLAIM ROLL-OVER RELIEF ON FURNISHED HOLIDAY ACCOMMODATION

Where a person has realised a capital gain on the disposal of a business, or has sold a property used by a firm in which they are a partner, the gain may be rolled-over (see 17.3). This normally involves the person continuing to be in business. However, if the individual does not wish to carry on trading, roll-over relief may still be available. A particular type of property investment qualifies in this way because where a property is acquired for letting as furnished holiday accommodation and is let sufficiently as furnished holiday accommodation to meet the qualifying tests, the owner is deemed to have acquired an asset for a trade and roll-over relief may therefore be obtained. For 2009–10 and following years, this relief may also be obtained where the holiday property is an overseas property provided that it is in the EEA (see 8.5.1).

Two points are of particular interest:

- The property does not need be located at the seaside. A property in, for example, Central London could qualify provided it is let for at least part of the year on a short-term basis (see 8.5 and 17.3.6).
- Roll-over relief may be obtained provided the property has been let as furnished holiday accommodation for a period. If the property is subsequently let for a longer-term or used for some other purpose (eg as a second home) the relief is not normally withdrawn. The one exception to this is if the owner had acquired a leasehold interest in the property and the lease had less than 60 years to run at the time it was acquired. Taking such a property out of use as furnished holiday accommodation means that the deferred gain would become chargeable (see 17.3.4).

29.8 MAKE THE MOST OF ENTREPRENEURS' RELIEF

Entrepreneurs' relief is available on capital gains of up to a lifetime limit of £10m of gains (£1m for gains between 6 April 2008 and 5 April 2010; £2m between 6 April and 22 June 2010; £5m between 23 June 2010 and 5 April 2011). The tax rate is 10% rather than 18% or 28% so the relief is potentially worth a maximum of £1.8m. Where part of an individual's limit was used prior to 5 April 2011, the current £10m limit, less any amounts used on previous sales between 6 April 2008 and 5 April 2011, can be used against further sales of qualifying assets in later tax years. In principle, both spouses or civil partners, and other family members, can each qualify for relief on up to £10m of gains.

A gain on the sale of a property let as furnished holiday accommodation should, in principle, qualify for entrepreneurs' relief.

Conditions

The following conditions must be satisfied for the 12 months ending with the date of sale:

- The vendor must either be an individual who is employed by his or her personal trading company or, in certain circumstances, the trustees of a life interest trust where the life tenant is employed by the company and personally holds at least 5% of the shares in the company. This means that an individual who has retired completely may not qualify.
- A company is an individual's personal trading company only if he or she holds at least 5% of the shares and those shares give him or her at least 5% of the voting rights. Relief is therefore not available if the individual holds only 4.999% of the ordinary shares, even if he or she has more than 5% of the voting rights due to other holdings.

A gain on an associated disposal may also attract relief. Such a disposal may include the sale of a property used by the individual's personal company but the relief will be restricted where he or she has charged the company rent post-6 April 2008 (see 17.8.4).

29.9 SELLING THE FAMILY COMPANY

The sale of a family company may involve complex tax issues. Much will depend on the facts and circumstances. However, the vendors' advisers should generally address the following points.

29.9.1 Get clearance or you may end up paying income tax rather than CGT

It is advisable to obtain advance clearance from HMRC that it accepts that s 682 ITA 2007 does not apply in relation to the sale (see 33.3). If s 682 were applicable, the vendors might have to pay higher rate income tax rather than 28% CGT (or 10% where entrepreneurs' relief is available). This is even more crucial from 2010–11 onwards with the top rate of income tax at 50%.

Another situation where vendors may have to pay income tax rather than capital gains tax is where they hold employment-related securities (see 6.6). Bear in mind that the tax liability will often then fall on the company (see 21.1.4) but if the company obtains a deduction under Chapter 2, Part 12, CTA 2009 (see 18.3.2) the extra tax cost in 2011–12 may be rather less than one would expect.

29.9.2 Checklist

Relevant questions include:

(1) Should the company make large pension contributions for the benefit of shareholder directors? This will lead to a reduction in the sale price and to a corresponding reduction in CGT. However, be careful: there is a subtle difference between having your company pay pension contributions and requiring the purchaser to make such contributions. See *HMRC* v *Collins* [2009] EWHC 284 on this. It is also important for the individual to consider whether such contributions will cause him or her to exceed the £50,000 annual allowance, and the effect an annual allowance charge will have on the owner's overall tax position.

(2) Should shareholder directors receive termination payments (possibly exempt up to £30,000)? Again, this will lead to a reduction both in the sale price and the shareholders' CGT.

(3) If the purchaser really wants some specific parts of the company's business, would it make better sense for the company to sell those business operations rather than for the shareholders to sell their shares? Could the company secure roll-over relief (see 18.7.2)?

(4) If the company is a holding company, would it make better sense for it to sell its trading subsidiary? A crucially important aspect here is whether such a sale would qualify for the Substantial Shareholding Exemption (see 18.7.3).

(5) Does any member of the shareholder's family have substantial unrelieved capital losses? If so, consider gifts of shares to him or her before the sale.

(6) Are any of the shareholders long term non-UK resident? Look for ways of taking full advantage of their not being liable for CGT.

(7) Are any of the shareholders themselves companies? If so, a pre-sale dividend may be attractive.

(8) Will the purchaser want to acquire premises that are used by the company but owned by some of the shareholders in their personal capacity? What are the CGT implications? Those shareholders may not be able to secure roll-over relief in the future as the relief is limited to situations where the old and new assets are used by the same company (see 17.3.8). However, it may be that shareholders who are directors or employees are able to claim roll-over relief under a different head by reinvesting in assets to be used by another personal trading company (see 17.3.9).

(9) Will entrepreneurs' relief be available for some or all of the shareholders?

(10) If there is a 'mix' of types of consideration on offer (eg cash, loan notes, preference shares, ordinary shares, warrants, rights to an earn-out, etc), is it more appropriate for some vendors to take their entitlement in a particular form?

    (a) For example, if loan notes are offered, this can allow can CGT be deferred by shareholders simply by not selling them or seeking an early redemption (but see 29.7.4 on loan note issues).

    (b) Alternatively, an ambitious shareholder who has been offered a senior position by the purchaser might accept a share for share exchange if this will mean that he or she has a 5% stake in the acquiring company and should therefore qualify for entrepreneurs' relief on a future sale. This would especially make sense where the sale of the shares in the existing company would not use up a substantial part of the £10m relief.

    (c) Conversely, elderly shareholders may take loan notes on the basis that they intend to retain them for the rest of their lives (in which case the potential CGT liability will disappear) or they may take preference shares in the acquiring company on the grounds that these shares should continue to attract business property relief.

(11) To what extent is it practical for the vendors to plough their proceeds back into a new company and defer tax using the CGT deferral relief available for investments in companies qualifying under the Enterprise Investment Scheme?

29.9.3 Vendors temporarily non-UK resident

If you are selling your shares while you are non-UK resident but you expect to resume residence in the UK within five years of your departure, you may end up being liable for capital gains tax (see 13.3.2). A person who is in this position may be better off from a UK tax perspective in taking a pre-sale dividend because the five-year rule does not apply for income tax purposes. A non-UK resident who receives such a dividend will have no UK tax to pay at all. However, the shareholder will need to check on the tax treatment of the dividend in the jurisdiction in which he or she is resident.

29.9.4 Treatment of loan notes

Questions regularly arise concerning the tax treatment of loan notes issued by a company that takes over a family company.

The first point to bear in mind is that the vendor's advisers should seek clearance under s 138 TCGA 1992 to ensure the exchange of shares in company A for loan notes issued by company B will not be a disposal for CGT purposes. HMRC will normally give such clearance provided it is satisfied that the transaction is being entered into for bona fide commercial reasons and is not part of a CGT avoidance scheme. This in turn means that no CGT charge will normally arise until the loan note holder disposes of his or her loan notes, either by redeeming them or by selling or giving them away.

A second issue concerns the tax treatment of loan notes that are qualifying corporate bonds (QCBs) which are eventually realised at less than their face value. This can leave the loan note holders with a tax charge based on the value of the loan notes at the time of the share exchange. In practice, vendors of private companies should think hard about accepting loan notes unless they are guaranteed by a bank. You should seek professional advice if you hold loan notes that are QCBs and the company that issued them is likely to default on its obligations.

Finally, bear in mind that it may be possible to secure s 165 hold-over relief on gifts of loan notes that are not QCBs. This may allow you to achieve similar savings after the sale to those that can arise from gifts of shares before a sale of the family company (see 29.4 above). Section 165 relief is available where the securities (ie the loan notes in the purchasing company) are not quoted and the relief can therefore apply even though the shares of the company are quoted (provided it is a trading company).

30

INHERITANCE TAX AND INDIVIDUALS

HILARY SHARPE

Inheritance tax (IHT) is a combined gift tax and death duty. It was introduced in 1974 under the name 'capital transfer tax'. Much of the legislation dates back to that time and is now reproduced in Inheritance Tax Act (IHTA) 1984. It applies to gifts and deemed gifts made during a person's lifetime and to his or her estate on death. Close companies and trusts are also subject to IHT charges.

FA 1986 introduced updated legislation to counter 'gifts with reservation of benefit' (GWR), and Schedule 15, FA 2004 saw the introduction of pre-owned assets tax – an income tax charge imposed to counter avoidance of the GWR regime. Later, FA 2006 made some radical changes in relation to the tax treatment of interest in possession and accumulation and maintenance trusts.

There is a nil rate band for IHT (see 30.1), which is currently £325,000 and is expected to remain at that level until at least 2014–15. Cumulative transfers in excess of this amount, taking place either at or within seven years of death, are taxed at 40% (though the overall impact may be reduced on transfers that take place more than three years before death). On all other occasions when IHT is payable by individuals, the rate is 20%.

This chapter contains the following sections:

(1) Who is subject to IHT?
(2) When may a charge arise?
(3) Transfers of value
(4) Certain gifts are not transfers of value
(5) Exempt transfers
(6) Potentially exempt transfers
(7) Reservation of benefit
(8) Business property
(9) Agricultural property and woodlands
(10) Computation of tax payable on lifetime transfers
(11) Tax payable on death
(12) Life assurance and pension policies
(13) Heritage property
(14) Planning: the first step

30.1 WHO IS SUBJECT TO IHT?

As a general principle, a UK-domiciled individual is subject to IHT on all property owned by him or her, whether located in the UK or overseas. By contrast, a person of foreign domicile is subject to IHT only on property sited in the UK. There are however various specific exceptions to this. For example, UK unit trusts and open-ended investment companies (OEICs) held by non-UK domiciled individuals are excluded from any IHT charge. Also, transfers of exempt gilts are excluded from any IHT charge if the transferor is not resident or ordinarily resident in the UK even though he or she may be domiciled in the UK. (See Chapters 33 and 34 on domicile, residence, etc.)

Section 267 IHTA 1984 contains a special rule that applies for IHT purposes whereby an individual will be deemed to be UK-domiciled for a tax year if he or she has been resident in the UK during 17 out of the 20 tax years that end with the current tax year. Because residence for an entire tax year is not required, only residence *in* a tax year, this period can be as little as 15 years and 2 days.

Example – Deemed domicile

A became UK resident on 5 April 2001 and resides in the UK continuously thereafter. He will become deemed domiciled for IHT purposes on 7 April 2017.

He could however leave the UK on 5 April 2016 and avoid becoming deemed domiciled, provided he remains outside of the UK for four complete years of assessment, ie he could not return until 6 April 2020. If he did return then and resided again in the UK continuously, he would be deemed to be domiciled here for IHT purposes with effect from 6 April 2021.

Acquisition of deemed domicile in the UK for IHT purposes does not impact on domicile status under general law for other tax purposes.

This rule also applies so that a deemed domiciled, long-term UK resident will be treated as retaining his or her deemed domicile for IHT for three calendar years after leaving the UK for good.

Example – Deemed domicile

B is domiciled in Australia, but has resided in the UK for the past 30 years. If she decides to return home to Australia permanently on 9 December 2011, her UK deemed domicile for IHT purposes will persist until 8 December 2014.

The deemed domicile rule may in some circumstances be overruled by provisions contained in a few of the UK's older double taxation agreements, dating back to Estate Duty days, ie pre-1974 (basically, those with India,

Pakistan, Italy and France). The exemption generally only applies on death, not to chargeable lifetime transfers.

30.1.1 Nil rate band

The first £325,000 of chargeable transfers (the nil rate band) is free of IHT. The nil rate band is expected to remain at £325,000 until 5 April 2015.

There are circumstances where an additional amount can be claimed in respect of a spouse's unused nil rate band (see 30.11.7).

30.2 WHEN MAY A CHARGE ARISE?

IHT can apply in the following circumstances:

- on a chargeable lifetime transfer (CLT), ie a gift to anyone other than an individual, including gifts to most trusts;
- on an individual's death (including further tax to pay on chargeable or potentially exempt lifetime transfers made within the preceding seven years).

A lifetime gift to an individual or to some favoured trusts is regarded as a potentially exempt transfer (PET), unless exempt under some specific provision such as the spouse exemption, gifts on the occasion of marriage, etc. Gifts into most trusts, to a company, and some transfers by close companies and trustees are all chargeable transfers.

Trusts post-FA 2006

A person who had an interest in possession under a trust or settlement at 22 March 2006 is normally regarded as if he or she were entitled to the capital. When the beneficiary dies, the trust property's full value is treated as part of his or her estate for IHT purposes (see 30.4.15). The position is quite different where an individual first acquired his or her interest in possession after that date (see 30.4.17). In general, the capital in such trusts will not be subject to IHT on the death of the individual who has the interest in possession but instead the trust will be subject to the ten-year periodic charge applicable to relevant property trusts (see 30.5.15). There are, however, special rules that cover an individual who acquires an interest in possession on the death of his or her spouse or civil partner at any time after 22 March 2006, or where the interest in possession arose before 6 October 2008 and replaced an interest in possession held by someone else at 22 March 2006 and, in those cases, the trust property is still treated as forming part of the beneficiary's estate on death.

Figure 30.1 indicates the circumstances under which a gift may be a chargeable transfer for IHT purposes.

Figure 30.1 – Is a gift a chargeable transfer?

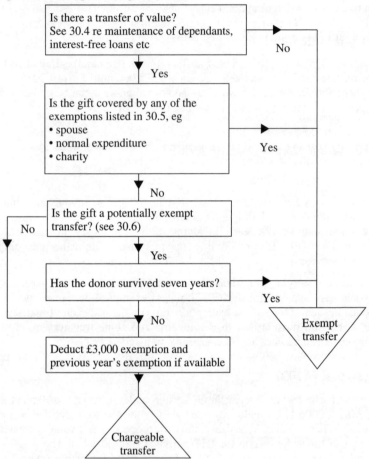

30.3 TRANSFERS OF VALUE

30.3.1 Not all transfers are gifts

(s 3 IHTA 1984)

The legislation refers to transfers and dispositions rather than gifts. The reason for this is that all gifts are transfers of value, but not all transfers of value are gifts. For example, where an individual deliberately sells an asset at less than market value he or she may not be making a gift, but he or she is certainly making a transfer of value. Similarly, deliberately omitting to exercise a right can be a transfer of value, but this is not a gift in the normal sense of the word. To give a third example, a transfer can even involve property not owned by the person since the IHT legislation deems a person to make a gift for IHT purposes if his or her 'qualifying' (ie treated as forming part of his or her estate) interest in possession under a trust comes to an end.

30.3.2 **There must be gratuitous intent**

(s 10 IHTA 1984)

IHT does not normally apply to a gift unless there is an element of 'bounty', ie there is a deliberate intention to make a gift. An unintentional loss of value (eg a loss made on a bad business deal) is not subject to IHT because there was no intention to pass value to another person.

30.3.3 **How a transfer is measured**

(s 3 IHTA 1984)

The amount of any transfer of value is determined by the reduction in value of the donor's wealth. This is not necessarily the same as the increase in the recipient's wealth.

Example

C owns 51 out of 100 shares in a company. He has control because he has the majority of the shares. If he were to give two shares to his son, he would relinquish control of the company and his remaining 49 shares might be worth considerably less because of this. The two shares given to his son might not be worth very much in isolation, and the son might not have acquired a very valuable asset, but C's estate would have decreased in value by the difference between the value of a 51% shareholding and that of a 49% shareholding, which could be a substantial amount.

30.4 CERTAIN GIFTS ARE NOT TRANSFERS OF VALUE

Certain gifts and other transactions are not regarded as transfers of value, so the issue of whether they are chargeable transfers simply does not arise. These include:

- maintenance of dependants, family, etc;
- waivers of dividends;
- waivers of remuneration;
- interest-free loans;
- disclaimers of legacies;
- deeds of variation;
- transfers involving trusts where the settlor has retained powers of appointment.

30.4.1 Maintenance of dependants, family, etc

(s 11 IHTA 1984)

The legislation specifically provides that the following lifetime payments are not transfers of value:

- payments for the maintenance of a current or former spouse or civil partner;
- payments for the maintenance, education or training of a child or stepchild under age 18;
- payments made to maintain a child aged over 18 who is in full-time education or training;
- reasonable provision for the care or maintenance of a dependent relative, ie the individual's relative who is incapacitated by old age or infirmity from maintaining him or herself, or the individual's mother or father, or his or her spouse or civil partner's mother or father.

30.4.2 Waivers of dividends

(s 15 IHTA 1984)

A waiver of a dividend by a company or an individual is not regarded as a transfer of value provided certain conditions are satisfied:

- The dividend must be waived by deed.
- The deed must not be executed more than 12 months before the right to the dividend has accrued.
- The deed waiving the dividend must be executed before any legal entitlement to the dividend arises.

The relief applies only to the waiver of dividends on shares and not to any other form of receipt such as debenture interest. The position is slightly different for interim and final dividends as the point in time at which entitlement may arise can be different.

Interim dividends

A shareholder has no enforceable right to payment before the date on which a board resolution has declared that a dividend shall be payable. However, the directors can declare an interim dividend that is payable immediately without having to first seek shareholders' approval. Therefore, a deed waiving a dividend should be executed in good time before any board resolution is passed.

Final dividends

A company may declare a dividend without stipulating any date for payment. In such circumstances, the declaration of the dividend creates an immediate debt and it is therefore too late to execute a waiver.

In other cases where a final dividend is declared as being payable at a later date, a shareholder may waive his or her entitlement provided he or she does so before the due date for payment.

In practice, a final dividend will require the shareholders' approval and an individual shareholder may therefore waive a dividend provided the deed is executed within 12 months before the company's annual meeting.

30.4.3 Waivers of remuneration

(s 14 IHTA 1984)

There is a specific provision whereby a waiver of remuneration does not constitute a transfer of value. Remuneration for these purposes does not include pensions. In practice, HMRC accept that remuneration is not subject to income tax if it is formally waived and the employer's assessable profits are adjusted accordingly to disallow a deduction for the sum waived.

It would be advisable to check in advance with HMRC that this treatment will apply in your particular circumstances, especially where substantial amounts are involved.

30.4.4 Interest-free loans

The grant of an interest-free loan repayable on demand is not a transfer of value (because the loan can be called in at any time and thus there is no discounting of the value of the right to repayment in the lender's estate). This is the position that HMRC adopts in practice. Prior to 6 April 1981, a different treatment applied and s 29(4) relieved the potential charge, where the transfer was a normal one on the part of the donor, and the donor was left with sufficient income to maintain his or her usual standard of living.

This treatment does not apply in a situation where a loan is made for a specific period, with the lender having no legal right to call for repayment before that time. The grant of such a loan might well be a transfer of value, with HMRC seeking to assess the transfer as the difference between the loan amount and its present market value if it were to be assigned. For loans between individuals, this is only an issue if the lender dies whilst the loan is outstanding, or if he or she dies within seven years of making the loan. The transfer of value on making the loan will be a PET. If the full value has been repaid to the donor's estate prior to death within seven years, you may be left with a 'failed PET' (the original loan) in the cumulation, which the double charges regulations fail to relieve.

30.4.5 Disclaimer of legacies

(s 142(1) IHTA 1984)

If a person becomes entitled to property under a Will or an intestacy or under a trust (eg on a life tenant's death), he or she may disclaim entitlement. Such a disclaimer is normally effective for IHT purposes and is not treated as a transfer of value provided that:

- no payment or other consideration is given for the disclaimer; and
- the person has not already accepted his or her entitlement, either expressly or by implication.

30.4.6 Deeds of variation

(s 142(2) IHTA 1984)

A deed of variation may be entered into where a person has died leaving property to his or her beneficiaries, and the beneficiaries (for whatever reason; generally to distribute the estate among the family in the most tax efficient manner) elect to vary the legacies, the effect being to redirect property. Where the necessary conditions are fulfilled, the revised disposition is treated as having taken place on the deceased person's death. Once again, a person who gives up an entitlement is not treated as making a transfer of value.

The following conditions need to be satisfied:

- The deed of variation must be executed within two years of the death
- It must be in writing and must specifically refer to the provisions of the Will, etc that are to be varied
- It must be signed by the person who would otherwise have, and anyone else who might have, benefited (in practice, this may cause issues where the Will contains legacies for minor beneficiaries, as their interests must be protected)
- Only one deed of variation in respect of each particular piece of property can be effective for IHT purposes
- No payment or other consideration may pass between beneficiaries to induce them to enter into the deed of variation (except that a variation is permitted that consists of an exchange of inheritances and a cash adjustment)
- For deeds executed since 1 August 2002, where the deed refers to the relevant legislation, there is no need for a formal election to be submitted to HMRC.

For further information, see www.hmrc.gov.uk/manuals/ihtmanual/IHTM 35000.htm

30.4.7 Powers of appointment over settled property

(ss 5(2), 47A, 55A, 272 IHTA 1984)

Powers of appointment are not treated as being part of an individual's estate for IHT purposes.

The applicable legislation was introduced following the decision in *IRC v Melville* CA [2001] STC 1297. This case concerned an individual who transferred property to a new discretionary settlement but had power to direct the trustees to return the property to him after three months. The Court of Appeal held that the chargeable transfer was only a modest amount as the settlor had retained a valuable right. Although this worked to the advantage of the taxpayer in *Melville*, it had caused concern for settlors who had retained such powers, particularly individuals who had created settlements while domiciled abroad (see 34.15.2). However, if the settlor retains an interest – rather than merely a power of appointment – in the trust, this will constitute a gift with reservation (see 30.7).

30.5 EXEMPT TRANSFERS

Even if a transfer takes place, it will not attract IHT if it is an exempt transfer. The full list of exempt transfers is as follows:

- gifts to spouse or civil partner (s 18);
- normal expenditure out of income (s 21);
- £250 small gifts exemption (s 20);
- annual £3,000 exemption (s 19);
- gifts in consideration of marriage or civil partnership (s 22);
- gifts to charities or registered clubs (s 23);
- gifts for national purposes (s 25, Schedule 3);
- gifts to political parties (s 24);
- gifts to housing associations (s 24A);
- certain transfers to employee trusts (ss 13, 28);
- compensation paid to former prisoners of war and Holocaust victims (ESC F20 and s 64 FA 2006);
- maintenance funds for historic buildings (s 27, Schedule 4);
- death on active service (s 154).

30.5.1 Gifts to spouse or civil partner

(s 18 IHTA 1984)

There is normally an unlimited exemption for transfers between spouses or civil partners. For this purpose, a couple is regarded as married or in civil partnership until a decree absolute has been obtained. The exemption covers outright gifts, legacies and a transfer of property on death to a trust under which the survivor has an interest in possession.

The exemption is restricted where a UK-domiciled spouse makes transfers to a foreign domiciled spouse. In this situation, the exemption is limited to £55,000. However, the 'deemed domicile' rule (see 30.1) applies for all IHT purposes except where expressly excluded. Consequently, a gift by a UK-domiciled individual to a spouse who has a foreign domicile, but who is treated as UK-domiciled for IHT purposes under the 17-year rule, qualifies for the unlimited exemption. Gifts from a non-UK domiciliary to a UK domiciled spouse or civil partner attract unlimited exemption, as do gifts of UK situs assets between two non-UK domiciled spouses or civil partners (non-UK situs assets of such individuals are excluded property).

In the past, the exemption has also applied to settled property in which a surviving spouse has an interest in possession. This could arise in one of two situations. First, the deceased might have been the life tenant of a settlement and his or her spouse might have been entitled to a succeeding life interest on his or her death. Alternatively, the deceased might have drawn his or her Will so as to create a Will trust under which the surviving spouse had an interest in possession.

Spouse exemption applies in both cases where the deceased died before 22 March 2006. For an individual who died on or after that date, the spouse exemption is still available in respect of a transfer under a Will trust. But where the trust is a lifetime trust, spouse exemption is now generally available only where the deceased either held a transitional serial interest (TSI) with a general power to appoint the interest to the survivor by Will (creating an immediate post-death interest), or held his or her interest at 22 March 2006 and the survivor takes a life interest on his or her spouse's death.

30.5.2 Normal expenditure out of income

(s 21 IHTA 1984)

A lifetime gift is exempt if it is shown that the gift was made as part of the donor's normal expenditure and is made out of surplus income. The legislation requires that the gift should be normal, ie the donor had a habit of making such gifts. The legislation also requires that taking one year with another, taking into account all normal transfers of value made by the donor, the gifts must have left the donor with sufficient income to maintain his or her normal standard of living.

Gifts that take the form of payments under deed of covenant or the payment of premiums on life assurance policies written in trust frequently qualify as exempt because of this rule. However, there is specific anti-avoidance rule to prevent abuse where the payment of the premiums is an associated operation with the purchase of an annuity by the donor. The capital repayment portion of any annuity payment the donor receives is not included as income for these purposes; however, surplus income which has been held on deposit may be.

30.5.3 £250 small gifts exemption

(s 20 IHTA 1984)

Any number of individual gifts of up to £250 in any one tax year are exempt. If an individual wished to, he or she could make 100 separate gifts of £250 at a time. However, if more than £250 was paid to any one person over the course of the tax year, it would need to be brought into account in full, subject to the availability of the £3,000 annual exemption. It is however important to remember that it is not possible to claim both exemptions. Where a payment of (say) £3,250 (or even of £300) was made to an individual in a year, then in that case, the £250 exemption would not be available at all and only the £3,000 annual exemption could be set against the payment.

30.5.4 Annual £3,000 exemption

(s 19 IHTA 1984)

This exemption is available to cover part of a larger gift. The exemption is £3,000 for each tax year. Furthermore, each spouse or civil partner has separate annual exemptions. There are detailed rules prescribed in s 19 setting out the order in which the exemption is to be used where a number of transfers take place on the same day and where a potentially exempt transfer becomes chargeable on death within seven years. However, HMRC now regards s 19(3A) as overridden by s 3A(1)(b), and will allocate the IHT annual exemption to transfers of value in chronological order, irrespective of whether the transfers would, disregarding the annual exemption, be immediately chargeable or potentially exempt. This means that if a potentially exempt transfer precedes an immediately chargeable transfer in the same tax year, the available annual exemption will be allocated to the potentially exempt transfer in priority to the immediately chargeable transfers, and unless the transferor dies within seven years of a potentially exempt transfer any annual exemption allocated to it will be wasted.

If the full £3,000 is not used in a given year, the balance can be carried forward for one year only and is then allowable only if the exemption for the second year is fully utilised.

Example – Carry forward

Situation 1	£	£
Gifts made in Year 1		1,000
Balance of exemption carried forward to Year 2		2,000
Gifts made in Year 2		4,000
Annual exemption for Year 2	3,000	
Part of unused exemption for Year 1	1,000	(4,000)
Chargeable gifts		Nil

The balance of exemption from Year 1 of £1,000 is lost completely if it cannot be used in Year 2.

Situation 2	£	£
Year 1 as in Situation 1 – unused exemption		2,000
Exemption for Year 2	3,000	
Gifts in Year 2	2,000	
Balance of Year 2 exemption to be carried forward to Year 3	1,000	

The balance of the Year 1 exemption of £2,000 is lost completely and may not be carried forward to Year 3.

30.5.5 Gifts in consideration of marriage

(s 22 IHTA 1984)

Gifts made to the bride or groom in consideration of their marriage or civil partnership, are exempt up to the following amounts:

Gifts made by:	Maximum exemption
Each parent	£5,000
Grandparents (or great grandparents)	£2,500
Bride or groom	£2,500
Any other person	£1,000

Parents may make gifts to either party to the marriage: their exemption is not restricted to gifts made to their own child but covers gifts made to both parties rather than £5,000 total for each recipient. This means that in relation to the groom, for example, the bride's parents may each give up to £5,000. Gifts should be made so that they are conditional upon the marriage taking place.

30.5.6 Gifts to charities and registered clubs

(s 23 IHTA 1984)

Gifts to charities established in the UK are exempt regardless of the amount. A charity may be established or registered in the UK even though it carries out its work overseas, and the exemption covers gifts to such charities. It has previously been the case that donations made to a foreign charity established abroad do not qualify but following the 2009 ECJ decision in *Persche*, Finance Act (No.1) 2010 extends the relief to charities established in the EU, Norway and Iceland.

Registered clubs were added to this exemption with effect from 1 April 2010 for companies and 6 April 2010 for other businesses and individuals. In the case of any property which is given to a registered club, the relief will not apply if any part of the gifted property may be used other than for:

- the purposes of the club in question;
- the purposes of another registered club;
- the purposes of the governing body of an eligible sport for the purposes of which the club in question exists; or
- charitable purposes.

A reduced rate of IHT is to apply for deaths occurring on or after 6 April 2012 where 10% or more of a deceased's net estate (after the deduction of all IHT exemptions, reliefs and the nil rate band) is left to charity. In such cases, the current rate of 40% will be reduced to 36%.

30.5.7 Gifts for national purposes

(s 25 IHTA 1984)

Gifts to certain national bodies are totally exempt. These include colleges and universities, the National Trust, the National Gallery, the British Museum and other galleries and museums run by local authorities or universities.

30.5.8 Gifts to political parties

(s 24 IHTA 1984)

Gifts to 'qualifying political parties' are exempt only if certain conditions are satisfied. A political party qualifies if it had at least two MPs returned at the last general election, or if it had at least one MP and more than 150,000 votes were cast for its candidates.

30.5.9 Gifts to housing associations

(s 24A IHTA 1984)

Gifts of UK land to registered housing associations are exempt.

30.5.10 Certain transfers to employee trusts

(ss 13, 28 IHTA 1984)

Transfers by a close company to an employee trust, or where an individual transfers shares in a company to an employee trust may be exempt provided the following conditions are satisfied:

(1) The trust's beneficiaries include all or most of the persons employed by, or holding office with, the company.
(2) The trust deed must not permit any of the trust property to be applied at any time for the benefit of:
   (a) a participator in the company (ie a person who holds a 5% or greater interest);
   (b) any person who has been a participator at any time during the ten years prior to the transfer;
   (c) any person connected with a participator or former participator.

The exclusions above do not apply if a participator, etc, can only receive benefits on which income tax will be charged (or would be charged if the participator was UK resident).

A further restriction applies where an individual makes a transfer of shares to an employee trust.

Within one year of the transfer:

(a) the trustees must hold more than 50% of the company's ordinary share capital and have voting control on all questions that affect the company as a whole; and
(b) the trustees' control must not be fettered by some other provision or agreement between the shareholders.

30.5.11 *Ex-gratia* payments to POWs

There is an exemption for compensation and *ex-gratia* payments made to former prisoners of war by the Japanese Government. This has recently been extended to cover compensation received by prisoners of war from the German Government. Ask for a copy of ESC F20.

30.5.12 **Holocaust compensation**

(s 64 FA 2006)

Compensation paid to Holocaust victims or their families is exempt.

30.6 POTENTIALLY EXEMPT TRANSFERS

(s 3A IHTA 1984)

30.6.1 **Definition of potentially exempt transfer (PET)**

Irrevocable gifts made during an individual's lifetime may, provided certain conditions are satisfied, be PETs. These gifts become exempt only if the donor survives seven years. If he or she dies during that period, the PET becomes a chargeable transfer. The tax payable depends on the IHT rates in force at the date of death. The donee is liable to pay the tax.

The main conditions to be satisfied for a gift to be a PET are that the gift is made to:

- an individual; or
- (for transfers up to 21 March 2006) a trust under which an individual has an interest in possession (see 30.4.18); or
- a trust for the disabled (see 30.7); or
- a trust for a bereaved minor out of an immediate post-death interest (see 30.6). Note that from 22 March 2006, a lifetime trust qualifies as an accumulation and maintenance trust only if it existed at 21 March 2006 and the beneficiaries will become absolutely entitled to the trust capital on attaining age 18 – this is a new condition and transfers to trusts before that date might well have constituted PETs even though the beneficiaries did not have an entitlement to anything other than income before age 25.

A gift that is subject to a reservation of benefit (see 30.7) cannot be a PET. Furthermore, a gift to a discretionary or (after 21 March 2006) an interest in possession trust is a CLT.

There is a quirk in the operation of the legislation where a PET is made between a chargeable transfer and death more than seven years later, for example:

2005: gift into discretionary trust equal to nil rate-band
2007: potentially exempt transfer on establishing an A&M trust
2013: death of donor.

If the potentially exempt transfer (PET) had not been made, the nil rate-band would have been available in full on death as death occurs more than seven years after the chargeable transfer. However, the PET was made and becomes chargeable on the donor's death within seven years of making it. In looking at the amount of IHT chargeable on the PET, it is necessary to take into account the fact that the nil-rate band was used on the chargeable transfer made within the previous seven years.

This means that the review period in seeking to establish the history of chargeable transfers can be extended back as far as 14 years.

30.6.2 Taper relief

(s 7 IHTA 1984)

Where an individual makes a PET or CLT and dies within the seven-year period, taper relief may reduce the amount of tax payable. The tax payable on the transfer that has become chargeable is reduced so that only a proportion is charged. The proportion is as follows:

Years between gift and death	Percentage of full charge
Three to four	80
Four to five	60
Five to six	40
Six to seven	20
Taper relief cannot reduce the tax on a lifetime chargeable transfer below the tax payable at the time the transfer was made. If a gift falls within the nil rate band, the taper relief is of no real benefit and does not reduce the tax that arises on other property that passes on the donor's death.	

30.7 RESERVATION OF BENEFIT

(ss 102, 102ZA, 102A, 102B, 102C and Schedule 20 FA 1986)

30.7.1 Introduction

Property that has been given away may still be deemed to form part of a deceased person's estate unless:

- possession and enjoyment of the property was bona fide assumed by the donee; and
- the property was enjoyed virtually to the entire exclusion of the donor and of any benefit to him or her by contract or otherwise.

The reference to the property being enjoyed 'virtually to the entire exclusion' of the donor means that for all practical purposes this is an 'all or nothing' test. HMRC's view is that the exception is intended to cover trivial benefits such as might arise where, for example, the donor of a picture enjoyed the chance to view it when making occasional visits to the donee's home. HMRC has provided guidance on benefits it considers to be de minimis – see www.hmrc.gov.uk/bulletins/tb9.htm#anchor551568. The later pre-owned asset tax rules on de minimis benefits are broadly the same.

The Act refers to a benefit reserved 'by contract or otherwise' and this is meant to refer to arrangements that are not legally binding but amount to an honourable understanding. This may arise where a person gifts away a house but remains in occupation. A reservation of benefit would arise even if there were no legal tenancy and the donee could, in law, require the donor to vacate the property at any time.

For the purposes of the GWR legislation, property includes property bought with the proceeds of the original gift. However, HMRC has confirmed that there is no such tracing where the original gift was cash (unless the cash is settled, in which case the tracing provisions in para 5, Schedule 20 may take precedence).

30.7.2 Start date

The GWR rules apply to gifts made on or after 18 March 1986. Where a gift or transfer was made before that date, and the donor reserved a benefit, the gift is effective for IHT purposes and the capital does not form part of that person's estate.

30.7.3 Two cases where the taxpayer succeeded (and the Government changed the rules)

The rules on gifts of land and buildings were tightened up in FA 1999 to block the type of arrangements upheld by the House of Lords in *IRC* v *Ingram* [1999] STC 37. Here, the late Lady Ingram carved out a 20-year lease that entitled her to occupy the property rent free and then gave away the freehold. It was decided that this did not constitute a gift with reservation, but the law was amended with effect from 9 March 1999 to block this loophole.

The Court of Appeal held in *IRC* v *Eversden* [2003] STC 822 that the reservation of benefit rules did not apply where a wife transferred property into a trust under which her husband had an interest in possession even though that interest subsequently came to an end and the settlor was then able to benefit. The point was that the original transfer (gift into settlement) was covered by the spouse exemption and the GWR rules were therefore not applicable. The subsequent termination of the spouse's interest in possession was not caught by the GWR rules because it was a transfer of value and not a gift (the GWR legislation applies only to gifts). However, this loophole was closed with effect from 20 June 2003.

30.7.4 Retrospective legislation

FA 2004 contained legislation on pre-owned assets that imposed an income tax liability from 6 April 2005 on many people who had used (entirely lawful) ways of sidestepping the GWR rules in the past. If Lady Ingram were still alive, she might well be caught by this legislation. These provisions can catch transactions that took place as long ago as 18 March 1986. See 33.7 for more details.

30.7.5 Three specific exemptions to the GWR rule

Donor pays a market rent

FA 1986 specifically provides that occupation of property or use of chattels does not count as a benefit provided the donor pays a market rent.

Benefit enjoyed after major change in circumstances

The legislation also provides that a benefit enjoyed by a donor occupying property can be ignored where there is an unforeseen change in the donor's circumstances, financial or otherwise, after the gift has been made and the occupation represents 'reasonable provision' by the donee for the care and maintenance of the donor.

Co-ownership

FA 1999 introduced a further exemption whereby an individual who transfers an interest in a residence to another individual who also occupies the property is not regarded as reserving a benefit provided that he or she continues to meet his or her share of all the expenses and outgoings. This can be a very important let-out where, for example, parents wish to give a half-share in the family home to children who live with them. However, relief is not limited to situations where only a half share has been gifted. A donor can give (say) a 60% or 70% interest in the property to a donee who then owns only (say) 30% or 40% of the property provided the donor meets at least his or her share of the normal property expenses and outgoings. It could however cause problems if in future a co-owner marries (for instance) and sets up home with his or her new spouse. Once the donee no longer occupies the property, if the original donor is still in occupation, then there will be a GWR at that point.

You should take expert advice before taking action that relies on this let-out, as the tax cost of getting it wrong may be severe.

30.7.6 Position where reservation of benefit ceases

Where a person makes a gift and initially reserves a benefit, but then relinquishes that reservation, he or she is normally treated as making a PET at the time he or she gives up the reserved benefit. The amount of the PET is governed by the donated property's market value at that time.

Example – Giving up reservation of benefit

> A gave away property worth £150,000 in July 2001 but reserved a benefit. The benefit was relinquished in July 2010 when the property was worth £220,000. A dies in October 2012.
>
> If no benefit had been reserved, the gift would have been completely exempt by August 2008 (ie seven years after the gift), but because a benefit was retained until July 2010 the seven-year period starts only from that date. The full £220,000 (ie the value at July 2010 when the reservation of benefit was released) would form part of A's estate for IHT purposes, with no tapering of the IHT charge, since death occurred less than three years afterwards.

30.7.7 Settlements and trusts

The same applies where a person has sought to reserve only the possibility of a benefit, for example, where he or she has created a settlement and he or she is a potential beneficiary. It is HMRC's opinion that a benefit is reserved where the settlor creates a discretionary trust and is a member of the class of potential beneficiaries. This would also apply where the trust clauses are such that the settlor may later be added to the class of potential beneficiaries during his or her lifetime.

Unless para 7, Schedule 20 FA 1986 applies, it will be a question of fact whether enjoyment, by or benefit to, the donor's spouse or civil partner is a benefit to the donor. Where spouses or civil partners are living together it will be difficult to avoid any benefit received or actual enjoyment of property, by the spouse or civil partner, from being shared by the donor, and thus being a GWR in relation to the donor, particularly as benefits by associated operations can be taken into account.

In contrast to this, HMRC has confirmed that no reservation of benefit arises where a person creates a settlement and is a contingent or default beneficiary. This may apply, for example, where property is put into trust for the settlor's children but the property would revert to the settlor in the event of the children dying or becoming bankrupt.

HMRC has confirmed that a settlor may be a trustee of a settlement created by him or herself without this constituting a reservation of benefit. Care should be taken over charging for the settlor's services as a trustee though, and it is recommended that professional advice is obtained for all matters where the GWR rules might apply, as they are notoriously complex. Where the settled property includes shares in a family company, the settlor/ trustee may also be a director of the company and may be permitted under the trust deed to retain his or her remuneration provided it is reasonable in relation to the services rendered.

30.8 BUSINESS PROPERTY

(ss 103–114 IHTA 1984)

30.8.1 Basic requirements

A special deduction is given against the value of business property where the following conditions are satisfied:

(1) The property must have been owned during the previous two years or have been inherited from a spouse or civil partner and, when the spouse's period of ownership is taken into account, the combined period of ownership of the property, or any replacement property, exceeds two years out of the last five.
(2) The property must not be subject to a binding contract for sale.

Where replacement property has been acquired, relief is limited to that which would have been available on the original qualifying property. (See 30.11.11 on replacement property.)

30.8.2 Rates of business property relief (BPR)

(s 103 IHTA 1984)

Unincorporated businesses

A sole proprietor's interest in his or her business qualifies for a 100% deduction, as does a partner's interest in his or her firm.

A 50% deduction is available for an asset owned personally by a partner but used by his or her firm.

Shares and debentures

Business relief is available on shares only where the company concerned is a trading company or the holding company of a trading group. The 100% relief is available on:

- unquoted ordinary or preference shares in a trading company; and
- debentures in an unquoted company where the donor has control of the company.

AIM shares are treated as unquoted.

Where a company's shares are quoted, 50% relief is due if (and only if) the person making the capital transfer had voting control before the transfer.

A 50% deduction is available where a controlling shareholder transfers an asset used by his or her trading company, or where such an asset passes on his or her death.

Figure 30.2 – Is there reservation of benefit?

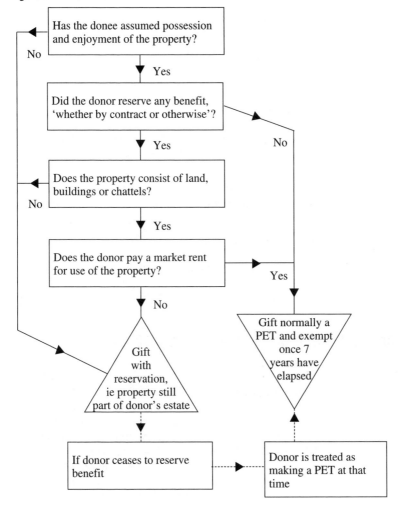

30.8.3 Businesses that do not qualify

Business relief is not normally available where the business carried on consists wholly or mainly of dealing in securities, stocks or shares, land or buildings or in holding or making investments.

Furnished holiday properties

HMRC has recently changed its stance on properties which are let as furnished holiday lettings. BPR will only be given where HMRC is satisfied that the owner or his or her agent provided substantial services to holidaymakers 'on and off the premises'. (See 8.5 for an update on furnished holiday lettings.)

Excepted assets

Where a transfer involves shares, business relief may be restricted if the company owns investments. The legislation refers to such investments as 'excepted assets', which are defined as assets that are neither:

- used wholly or mainly for the purposes of the business, nor
- required for the future use of the business.

Where a company has subsidiaries, it is necessary to look at the group situation (ie shares in subsidiaries may have to be treated as excepted assets if the subsidiaries are investment companies).

Other examples of assets that may be excepted assets are cash balances in excess of monies required to fund working capital and property used personally by the shareholders.

30.9 AGRICULTURAL PROPERTY AND WOODLANDS

(ss 115–124B IHTA 1984)

Agricultural property relief (APR) has historically been available on the agricultural value of farmland in the UK, Channel Islands or Isle of Man. From 22 April 2009, it also became available for land in other countries which belong to the European Economic Area. Furthermore, a claim could be made – during 2009–10 – for a refund where IHT had been paid on such land during the preceding six years. If you have yet to make the applicable claim, you are now limited to four years from the end of the relevant tax year from 1 April 2010 onwards, so that if IHT was paid in 2007–08 for which a refund is due as a result of this change, a claim must be made by 5 April 2012; if it was paid in 2006–07 or earlier, the chance has now been lost.

30.9.1 Land occupied by the transferor

A 100% deduction is available where the individual has occupied farmland for the two years prior to the transfer date. Where a farm has been sold and another acquired, the replacement farm normally qualifies for APR provided the owner has occupied the two farms for a combined period of at least two years in the last five years. APR is also available for land owned by an individual but occupied by a firm of which he or she is a partner or a company of which he or she is the controlling shareholder for the two years preceding the transfer date, or two out of the preceding five years where replacement property is involved. Where replacement property has been acquired, relief is limited to that which would have been available on the original qualifying property. (See 30.11.11 on replacement property.)

30.9.2 Relief for other land

A 100% deduction is also available on land not occupied by the owner provided he or she has (or had) the legal right to regain vacant possession within a period not exceeding 12 months. To qualify under this head, the individual must normally have owned the land for at least seven years.

30.9.3 Relief for tenanted farmland

A 100% deduction is available for farmland let on a tenancy granted on or after 1 September 1995 where the owner cannot obtain vacant possession within 12 months. This would generally be the case where the land is let under an agricultural tenancy. Once again, the land must normally have been owned for seven years.

The 100% deduction is also available for a tenancy over property in Scotland acquired on or after 1 September 1995 by right of succession.

A 50% deduction is available for land which is let under a tenancy granted before 1 September 1995.

30.9.4 Woodlands

(ss 125–130 IHTA 1984)

The tax treatment of UK woodlands is largely beneficial as business relief is normally available after two years of ownership. In very unusual circumstances where business relief is not available, alternative relief may be due under s 125 after five years of ownership.

30.10 COMPUTATION OF TAX PAYABLE ON LIFETIME TRANSFERS

In practice, IHT is likely only to be paid during a person's lifetime for chargeable transfers made by him or her to a trust. The tax payable is calculated as follows:

Initial calculation

Chargeable transfers made during the preceding seven years		A
Add	Amount of chargeable transfer	B
		C
Deduct	Nil rate band	D
		E
	IHT thereon at 20%	X
Deduct	IHT on a notional transfer of A minus D as if it took place at the same time	Y
	IHT payable in respect of the chargeable transfer	Z

Position if the donor dies within three years

Chargeable transfers made during the previous seven years		A
Add	PETs caught by the seven-year rule	B
		C
Add	amount of chargeable transfer	D
		E
Deduct	Nil rate band	F
		G
	IHT thereon at 40%	H
Deduct	IHT at 40% on a notional transfer of C minus F	I
		J

The donee is liable to pay additional IHT of J minus the amount Z above already paid.

Position if the donor dies during years 4–7

The above will be liable for additional IHT computed as J above, but subject to the IHT on PETs caught by the seven-year rule being reduced by taper relief (see 30.6.2).

30.11 TAX PAYABLE ON DEATH

30.11.1 Normal basis of computation

The charge on death is normally computed as shown in the flowchart in Figure 30.3. The IHT will be the tax on the figure in Box 6 minus the tax payable on a normal transfer equal to the amount in Box 4 as if the notional transfer took place immediately before the death. Some taper relief may be due on the PETs caught by the seven-year rule (see 30.6.2). Lifetime transfers use up the nil rate band first, with any balance being deducted from the chargeable transfer on death. However, special reliefs may be available.

30.11.2 Death on active service

(s 154 IHTA 1984)

Since World War II, death duty legislation has contained an exemption for a person who dies from wounds suffered while on active service. The exemption applies to the estates of those killed in the Falklands conflict and the Gulf War, and of members of the RUC killed by terrorists in Northern Ireland. The relief can only be granted by HMRC on receipt of a certificate from the appropriate MoD issuing department; the family of the deceased will need to apply to the MoD and the certificate is then forwarded direct to HMRC. HMRC has no discretion in operating this relief and can only do so once it is in possession of the appropriate certificate.

The exemption may well apply more often than people think. Death does not have to be immediate, nor need the wound be the only cause of death. The High Court held in 1978 that the exemption was owed to the estate of the fourth Duke of Westminster because serious wounds that he had suffered in 1944 contributed to his death in 1967.

30.11.3 Sales of quoted securities at a loss

(ss 178–189 IHTA 1984)

Relief is given where quoted securities or unit trusts are sold at a loss within 12 months of death. Where shares are suspended, s 186B permits similar relief to be claimed by reference to the shares' value when they return from suspension. If the shares are cancelled, s 186A treats them as having been disposed of for a nominal value of £1, enabling a claim to be made. It is not possible to pick and choose: the relief is confined to the amount of any overall loss. Executors must, in effect, elect that the total proceeds of any sales should be substituted for the value at date of death. The time limit for making a claim under this section is due to be reduced to four years from the end of the 12 months following the date of death (para 9, Schedule 51, FA 2009), but the date for this change is yet to be appointed.

Figure 30.3 – Charge on death computation

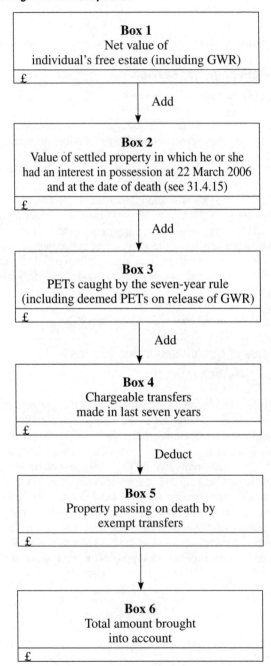

Example – Sale of quoted securities at a loss

> B died on 1 October 2011. His estate included a portfolio worth £70,000. The executors have to sell all of the securities in December 2011 and realise an overall loss of £25,000. The estate can be reduced by this amount so that, in effect, only £45,000 is taken into account.
>
> The overall loss of £25,000 may have been made up of a gain of £5,000 and losses of £30,000. Relief is, however, limited to the net figure.

30.11.4 Relief restricted where executors purchase quoted securities

Furthermore, the relief is restricted where at any time during the period beginning on the date of the death in question and ending two months after the date of the last sale is made, the executors repurchase quoted securities.

Example – Restriction of relief on quoted securities

> C died on 2 January 2011. His executors also sell securities for £45,000 in December 2011 at a £25,000 loss. On 10 January 2012, they reinvest £10,000 in new securities. The £25,000 loss cannot be claimed in full, it has to be reduced by
>
> $$\frac{10,000}{45,000} \times £25,000 = £5,556$$

30.11.5 Sales of land at a loss

(ss190–198 IHTA 1984)

Section 197A extends the relief from three years to the fourth year after the date of death. Relief is due where land and buildings are sold at a loss – within four years of death – provided the loss is at least £1,000 or 5% of probate value (whichever is less). The net proceeds are substituted for the value at the date of death and the IHT is recomputed. This relief will be denied where the property is sold to a beneficiary (or his or her spouse, civil partner, child or remoter issue) where the interest sold is the same as the beneficiary's original interest. The relief does, however, apply if the purchaser's entitlement is less than the interest sold (eg the sale of the whole property to a beneficiary, who was entitled to only a half share of the property).

Again, it is not possible to pick and choose: the relief is confined to the amount of any overall loss. Executors must, in effect, elect that the total proceeds of any sales should be substituted for the value at date of death. The only sales not taken into account in this way are sales in the fourth year for more than the date of death value, and sales excluded from the relief.

Note that there is no equivalent relief where the deceased held shares in a company that owned land which was subsequently sold at a lower value.

30.11.6 Debts that may be disallowed

(s 103 FA 1986)

There is a general rule that debts are not deductible where the deceased has made a capital transfer to a person who subsequently made a loan back to the deceased. This rule applies only to loans made after 18 March 1986, but there is no such time limit on the capital transfers. A debt may be disallowed because the deceased had made a capital transfer to the lender even though that capital transfer took place long before 18 March 1986. It is also of no help that the loan was made on normal commercial terms and a market rate of interest was payable.

This legislation was successfully invoked by HMRC to deny a deduction for a debt incurred by a widower where the debt arose from his buying an interest in the matrimonial home from his late wife's executors. He had given his wife her interest in the property eight years before her death – see *Phizackerley* v *HMRC* (SpC 591). This seems a very harsh decision, especially as s 103 would not have been in point if Mr Phizackerley had died first and his wife had incurred a similar debt in buying a similar interest in the property from his executors.

30.11.7 Using the balance of the nil rate band of a former spouse or civil partner

Section 8A provides that where an individual dies on or after 9 October 2007, he or she may also be entitled to an additional nil rate band amount based on the proportion of his or her spouse or civil partner's nil rate band which remained unused on the earlier death of that spouse or civil partner.

The additional relief has to be claimed.

The maximum relief is an amount equal to the full nil rate band at the rate in force at the time of the second death (in other words, a person who has been bereaved twice cannot claim the full unused nil rate band in respect of both his or her previous spouses or civil partners).

There is no time limit and the relief may therefore be claimed for cases where the spouse had died as much as 37 years ago, in fact right back to the introduction of IHT on 26 March 1974.

There is also no restriction by reference to the size of the spouse's estate or domicile status. In principle, the additional nil rate band can be claimed in respect of a spouse or civil partner who had no assets at all on his or her death. Even the situation where both spouses are non-UK domiciled may attract this relief, where there is a UK chargeable estate (ie UK situs assets). There would be a restriction if a UK domiciled spouse or civil partner died before his or her non-UK domiciled spouse, because only £55,000 of the transfer of value on the death would be exempt with the balance being chargeable; the relief would therefore be limited to the proportion of the nil rate band unused on the first death.

Care needs to be taken if the Will contains a survivorship clause as this may prevent the nil rate band from being transferred. Advice should always be taken when drafting Wills to ensure they are tax efficient.

30.11.8 Legitim: special rules for Scotland

(s 147 IHTA 1984)

Scottish law provides that a person must leave a set part of his or her moveable estate to his or her children: their entitlement is called 'legitim'. If a person makes a Will that does not take account of this, the children can have it set aside. In practice, children often decide to renounce their right to legitim; especially where a person's Will bequeaths all his or her property to the surviving spouse or civil partner. The legislation provides that children who renounce their entitlement within two years of the death are not treated as making a chargeable transfer and the property is treated as passing to the survivor in accordance with the Will.

The deed renouncing the rights must satisfy the provisions as to variations: see 30.4.6.

Practical problems arise where minor children are involved. The IHT legislation provides that children under age 18 (at the date of death) may renounce their entitlement within two years of attaining age 18 without this constituting a chargeable transfer by them. The property is then treated (for IHT purposes) as passing to the survivor in accordance with the Will. As a child under age 18 does not have the legal capacity to renounce his or her entitlement, the executors have a difficult choice: they can either account for IHT on the basis that the child takes his or her entitlement or on the assumption that the child will renounce his or her rights on reaching age 18.

Position where executors assume legitim rights are taken

IHT will have to be paid to the extent that the property that passes to the children exceeds the nil rate band. When each child attains 18, he or she may elect to renounce his or her rights so that the surviving spouse or civil partner benefits. The spouse exemption will then mean that no tax should have been paid. HMRC will then repay the IHT paid and pay repayment interest.

Position where executors assume that legitim will be renounced

No IHT will be paid in the first instance. However, if it turns out that one of the children decides not to renounce his or her entitlement, IHT on the death is recomputed and the tax payable attracts interest from the date it should have been paid.

30.11.9 **Quick succession relief**

(s 141 IHTA 1984)

Suppose a person has recently inherited property from someone else. If he or she was to die and the full rate of IHT applied, the same property would have been subject to IHT twice within a relatively short period of time.

Quick succession relief is intended to alleviate this. The relief works by giving credit for a proportion of the tax charged on the first occasion against the tax payable on the second death. The proportion is set out below:

Both deaths occur:	Proportion
within one year	100%
within two years	80%
within three years	60%
within four years	40%
within five years	20%

Example – Quick succession relief

> *D* inherited property worth £150,000 in October 2008. IHT was paid on that estate at an average rate of 25%, so the grossed-up amount was £200,000 (£150,000 × 100/75) and the tax suffered was £50,000. *D* dies in August 2011. The maximum amount on which quick succession relief can be claimed is:
>
> $$\frac{150,000}{200,000} \times £50,000 = £37,500$$
>
> This has to be reduced to 60% of £37,500 (ie £22,500) as three complete years have elapsed. The relief is not affected by the fact that property has been sold or given away before the second death takes place.

30.11.10 **Treatment of gifts caught by seven-year rule**

(s 113A IHTA 1984)

Tax on a PET that becomes a chargeable transfer because of the transferor's death is payable by the recipient of the gift. Business relief is available on a PET that becomes a chargeable transfer only if the conditions in 30.8 are satisfied both at the time of the gift and at the time of death.

Examples – Business relief on PETs

---

(1) *E* owns all the shares in a family company. He gives his son *F* a 24% shareholding. Three years later, the company is sold and F receives cash for his shares. One year after that *E* dies.

Business relief will not normally be available as the necessary conditions are not satisfied by the donee at the time of *E*'s death. If *F* had reinvested the proceeds in another private company, business relief might have been available after all.

(2) The basic position is as in (1) (ie *E*'s gift to *F* of a 24% shareholding). This time, *F* retains his shares, but by the time *E* dies the shares are quoted. No relief is due as *F* does not control the company and his shares are quoted shares.

(3) The basic position is as in (1), but *F* retains the shares and they are still unquoted at the time of *E*'s death. The shares attract the 100% relief and this is not lost even if *F* disposes of the shares shortly after *E*'s death.

30.11.11 Replacement property

(s 107 IHTA 1984)

Where a donee has disposed of business property, but acquires replacement property, the PET may still attract business relief provided the replacement property is acquired within three years of the disposal. Similar rules apply for agricultural property.

30.11.12 Reduction in value

Where the value at the date of death of property transferred within the previous seven years by a PET is lower than the value at date of gift, the chargeable transfer is based on the value at death.

30.11.13 Acceptance of property in lieu of IHT

HMRC has power to accept certain types of property in satisfaction of IHT liabilities. Such property includes pictures, prints, books, manuscripts, works of art, scientific objects and other items regarded as being of national, scientific, artistic and historic interest. HMRC has to clear such arrangements with Heritage ministers and in practice only property regarded as of 'pre-eminent interest' is accepted, for example the 2003 acquisition of Titian's *Venus Anadyomene*.

Taxpayers who own such items, that have been acknowledged as being first rate, can find out more about these arrangements by obtaining a copy of IR 67; *Capital Taxation and The National Heritage* from:

The Revenue Reference Room
Room 8, New Wing
Somerset House
London WC2R 1LB

30.11.14 Double taxation agreements

The UK has only a handful of tax treaties that cover inheritance tax. There are treaties with France, India, Italy, Netherlands, Pakistan, Ireland, South Africa, Sweden, Switzerland and the USA.

Where no double taxation arrangement exists, unilateral relief will normally be available by way of a foreign tax credit against the UK IHT charge.

30.11.15 Payment of IHT by instalments

It is possible to defer payment of IHT on certain types of property. IHT on assets that attract 50% BPR or APR, or IHT payable on other business/agricultural property because the two-year period of ownership is not satisfied, can be paid by instalments over ten years, with interest being charged only on instalments that are paid late. IHT on other land and buildings can also be paid by instalments but interest is charged from the normal due date.

Outstanding instalments generally become payable as and when the property is sold.

30.12 LIFE ASSURANCE AND PENSION POLICIES

30.12.1 Life assurance

Life assurance is one of the best ways of providing for the payment of IHT, but the tax treatment of policies needs to be watched carefully. The following is only a summary of a complex area and is not intended to be a substitute for taking independent professional advice.

30.12.2 Death of policyholder

A life assurance policy beneficially owned by the deceased is property subject to IHT in the same way as any other property owned by him or her.

30.12.3 Gifts of policies

Gifts of policies may generally be made in two ways:

- writing the policy in trust or making a subsequent declaration of trust;
- assignment of the policy.

In either case, subsequent premiums may be paid:

- by the donor direct;
- by the beneficiary out of cash gifts from the donor;
- by the beneficiary out of his or her own resources;
- by a combination of the above.

In general, if the gift is an outright gift to an individual or a trust for the disabled, it will constitute a PET and will only be taxable if the donor dies within seven years of making the gift. Gifts to other trusts such as discretionary trusts may attract lifetime IHT.

If any of the usual IHT exemptions applies (see 30.5), neither the gift of the policy nor any gifts of premiums that have been made will be taxable, for example:

(1) The gift of the premium or policy falls within the annual exemption – currently £3,000 (note that if the policy is a qualifying policy and premiums are payable net of life assurance relief, it is the net premium that constitutes the gift; if the premiums are paid gross, it is the gross premium that constitutes the gift).

(2) The premiums come within the donor's normal expenditure out of income exemption (note that this applies to payment of premiums, not to the gift of an existing policy).

(3) The gifts fall within the marriage settlement exemption.

(4) The gifts fall within the small gifts exemption – outright gifts of not more than £250 per donee (eg a premium on a policy written in trust for the absolute benefit of a child).

(5) Policies written by either spouse or civil partner for the absolute benefit of the other.

If none of the exemptions applies, IHT may be payable in respect of the gift of the policy or the payment of subsequent premiums (unless they fall within the nil rate band). However, payment of premiums on policies written under interest in possession trusts before 22 March 2006 will often constitute PETs under transitional provisions contained in FA 2006, provided there are no increases in premiums paid after that date which were not allowed for within the policy terms as they then stood.

If IHT is payable, the chargeable transfers are the premiums paid by the donor; or, if a gift of an existing policy is made by assignment or declaration of trust, the chargeable transfer is generally the greater of the total gross premiums paid or the policy's market value (usually the surrender value).

If cash gifts have been made to enable the premiums to be paid by the beneficiary, the amount of the cash gifts will usually be PETs. The proceeds of the policy on death, maturity or surrender will not be subject to IHT in the hands of the recipient of the assignment or a beneficiary having an interest in possession in the trusts.

30.12.4 Life of another policies ('pur autre vie')

On the death of the life assured the proceeds are totally free of IHT. Clearly they do not form part of the life assured's estate, as the policy is not owned by him or her. The surrender value will, however, be potentially chargeable in the policyholder's estate if he or she dies before the life assured.

If the donor makes cash gifts to the policyholder to help him or her pay the premiums, the cash gifts will be taxable for the donor, unless the exemptions mentioned above apply, but the proceeds will be free of IHT in the policyholder's hands, provided he or she survives the life assured.

30.12.5 Use of policies

Life assurance policies can be used in two main ways in IHT planning:

- as a vehicle for making gifts to beneficiaries; and
- to create a fund for the eventual payment of the tax.

Thus they may help to both minimise the amount of tax payable and offer a means of paying any unavoidable liability whenever it arises.

30.12.6 IHT and pension plans

Although the legislation does not permit a policyholder to alienate his or her right to a retirement pension, it is possible to assign any death benefits provided under retirement annuity or personal pension plans, whether provided as a sum assured or as a return of the retirement fund. The IHT rules are broadly similar to those applicable to life policy assignments except that:

- discretionary trusts of these assignable benefits will not be subject to the usual IHT charging regime of ten-yearly and exit charges provided the benefits are distributed within two years of the individual's death;
- the right to a pension is not treated as giving rise to an interest in possession in the pension fund;
- the gift of a 'return of fund' death benefit will usually be regarded as having no value, provided the individual is in good health at the time of the gift. Similarly, subsequent contributions to the pension will be treated as being attributable to the provision of the pension benefits and not the death benefit, provided the individual is in good health at the time the contribution is made.
- an IHT charge no longer arises on the death after age 75 (or 77; if the age of 75 is reached on or after 22 June 2010 and before 6 April 2011) of a person who has an alternatively secured pension, as these rules have now been abolished (see 25.2.5). Instead a pensions tax charge of 55% will arise.

Occupational schemes are usually written under discretionary trusts and also achieve the same IHT exemptions on payment of contributions and distribution of benefits.

30.13 HERITAGE PROPERTY

It is possible to claim exemption for transfers of qualifying heritage assets, for example chattels of museum quality, land of outstanding natural beauty or of historic or scientific interest, and buildings and amenity land deemed to be of outstanding historic or architectural interest. The exemption is currently conditional on the new owner undertaking to maintain and preserve the asset and to provide reasonable public access to it. It is no longer possible to restrict access by requiring an appointment with the asset's owner.

The rules for defining qualifying chattels have also been made more restrictive by FA 1998. There used to be no time limit for claiming heritage tax exemptions, but for tax charges arising after 16 March 1998 a claim for exemption normally has to be made within two years of the date of the relevant chargeable event. In addition, transfers made after 16 March 1998 no longer qualify for the special exemption previously available for gifts and bequests to certain non-profit making bodies.

30.14 PLANNING: THE FIRST STEP

Planning for IHT is something that many people would rather not think about. The first step should be to sit down and work out the value of your estate: it is something that your next of kin may already have done if you've ever argued! If the net value of your estate is close to the IHT threshold, then perhaps the time has come to talk with your financial or tax adviser to discuss ways in which you can ensure the people you would like to benefit from your estate are provided for.

If you do not have a Will, this should be the starting point for any planning. Bear in mind that if you do not have a Will, your assets will pass as set out in Figure 30.4. Do not assume all your assets will automatically pass to your spouse or civil partner. They will not, unless you have written a Will to provide that they do.

The Office of Tax Simplification, in its March 2011 report, recommended a major overhaul of inheritance tax, including the rules for trusts, and the main reliefs. Whilst this did not appear to be developed as a theme in the 2011 Budget and the Government's stated plans for 2012, there are no guarantees that we will not see a repeat of the 2006 fiasco next year. If you do have a Will, you should review it regularly and ensure that you have taken advantage of all available IHT reliefs; especially given the changes introduced by FA 2006 (see 30.2, 30.5.1 and 30.6.1) and the possibility of future legislative change.

Figure 30.4 – What happens if a person dies without making a valid Will?

When a person dies without making a valid Will, he or she is said to have died 'intestate'. His or her estate then passes as follows:

If he or she was married or in a civil partnership and had children
- Spouse or civil partner gets everything up to £250,000 and all personal chattels.
- Anything over and above this (the 'residue') is divided into two:
  - half in trust for children to get on attaining age 18, or on their marriage if earlier;
  - half in trust so that the spouse or civil partner has a life interest in income – on the spouse's death, the children inherit.

If he or she was married or in a civil partnership but had no children and there are parents or brothers or sisters (not half-brothers or half-sisters) or nephews or nieces:
- Spouse or civil partner gets everything up to £450,000 and personal chattels.
- Any residue is divided in two, half goes to spouse or civil partner, the other half goes to the parent(s). If no parent is living at the date of death, the other half is divided between the deceased person's siblings and offspring of a brother or sister who has died.

If he or she was married or in a civil partnership but no parents or siblings or nephews or nieces
- Spouse or civil partner takes whole estate.

If he or she was not married or in a civil partnership, and had children
- Estate goes to children at age 18 or on their earlier marriage. If a child has predeceased and had children, those children take his or her share *per stirpes*.

Note
A person who was dependent on the deceased may make a claim for provision out of an estate even though he or she is not a named beneficiary under a Will or is not entitled to benefit under the intestacy provisions.

31

THE TAXATION OF TRUSTS

MARK FRANCIS

This chapter covers the taxation of trusts under the following headings:

(1) When are trustees liable to pay income tax?
(2) When are trustees liable for UK capital gains tax (CGT)?
(3) Bare trusts
(4) Fixed-interest trusts
(5) Discretionary trusts
(6) Accumulation and maintenance trusts
(7) Trusts for the disabled
(8) Protective trusts
(9) Trusts for the most vulnerable
(10) Charitable trusts
(11) Miscellaneous aspects
(12) Executors and personal representatives
(13) Some planning points

31.1 WHEN ARE TRUSTEES LIABLE TO PAY INCOME TAX?

(ss 474, 475 and 812 ITA 2007)

31.1.1 General rules

UK resident trusts are liable to pay income tax on both UK and overseas income; trusts that are not UK resident are liable only in respect of UK source income.

In the main, trustees are liable for tax at the basic or lower rate, of 20%. Trustees of discretionary and accumulation trusts are subject to additional tax. From 2004–05 to 2009–10 the rate applicable to trusts was 40%. From 2010–11, this rose to 50% for non-dividend income and 42.5% for dividend income. A 'basic rate band' has also applied since 6 April 2005. This increased from £500 to £1,000 on 6 April 2006 and is split pro rata among existing settlements made by the same settlor since 1978 (see 31.5.2).

A non-resident trust is subject to tax on UK income under s 812 ITA 2007.

The offshore trustees will be subject to UK tax on UK trust income on the arising basis. Trustees are not entitled to personal allowances.

Where the settlor or his or her spouse, or civil partner, or unmarried, minor children can benefit, the trust income will be deemed to be that of the settlor for tax purposes (see 33.5) but any income received by the trustees still needs to be reported in the trust return.

If an offshore trust is settlor interested, the income is treated as that of the settlor for all purposes of the taxes acts, subject to the settlor's right of recovery as against the trustees. The remittance basis (under s 648 ITTOIA 2005) will be available to the settlor for non-UK income, subject to a clawback charge if funds are later remitted to the UK whether to the settlor or any other beneficiary.

31.1.2 Trusts and self-assessment

The same general rules apply to trustees as they do to individuals under self-assessment (SA). If a trust has UK chargeable income and gains, then the trustees have to file a self-assessment form (Form SA900) by 31 October for paper returns or 31 January for online filing (HMRC does not provide software to file form SA900 online, so proprietary software will be needed), following the relevant tax year.

31.1.3 Rules for determining the residence status of a trust

A single set of rules has applied since 6 April 2007 for determining the income tax and CGT residence of a trust:

- If all the trustees are UK resident, the trust is UK resident.
- If none of the trustees is UK resident, the trust is not UK resident.
- If only some of the trustees are UK resident, and the settlor was not domiciled or ordinarily resident or resident in the UK at the time that the trust was created, the trust is not UK resident.

Where a non-UK resident trustee acts as a trustee in the course of a business carried on through a branch, agency or permanent establishment in the UK, he, she or it will be treated as UK resident. (There were different criteria before 2007–08, and the residence status of a trust for income tax could be different from that for capital gains tax purposes. See the 2006–07 edition of the *Tax Handbook* at 32.1.1 and 32.2.1.)

31.2 WHEN ARE TRUSTEES LIABLE FOR UK CAPITAL GAINS TAX (CGT)?

(ss 2 and 69 TCGA 1992)

31.2.1 General rules

Trustees are subject to CGT only if the trust is resident in the UK, or if they realise capital gains from the disposal of assets used by them in carrying on a business in the UK through a branch or permanent establishment. In general, therefore, trustees are responsible for reporting gains and paying tax.

From 2008–09, gains realised by a UK resident settlement are taxed as the trustees' gains even where the settlor has retained an interest. This means that losses realised by the settlor cannot be set against the trustees' capital gains. For the treatment of settlor-interested trust gains for 2007–08 and earlier years, refer to the 2007–08 *Tax Handbook* at 30.2).

31.2.2 Annual exemption

(Schedule 1 TCGA 1992)

For a number of years the annual CGT exemption available to trustees has been half the individual amount, for example for 2011–12, the exemption is £5,300 (half of £10,600).

Where a settlor has created a number of settlements since 6 June 1978, the annual exemption is shared equally between them. The minimum annual exemption for each settlement is currently £1,060 (ie one-tenth of the individual annual exemption). An unused part of the exemption for one settlement cannot be used by another settlement.

Consequently, if a person created three trusts in 1975 and four in 1989, the 2011–12 exemption for the 1975 trusts would be £5,300 each, and the four trusts created after 6 June 1978 would each have an exemption of £1,325. If all seven trusts had been created after 6 June 1978, each would have an annual exemption of £1,060.

31.2.3 Entrepreneurs' relief

Entrepreneurs' relief (ER) against chargeable gains is a lifetime allowance. From 6 April 2008 to 5 April 2010 it was £1m. It increased to £2m from 6 April 2010 to 22 June 2010, and again to £5m from 23 June 2010 to 5 April 2011. It then increased to £10m from 6 April 2011. In most cases, entrepreneurs who have used the maximum relief under the previous threshold are able to take advantage of the increase to make further gains up to the new limit, which will be charged at only 10%, however, this is not always the case where deferred gains are involved – see 17.8. ER means that gains within the £10m lifetime limit are taxed only at 10% (up to 22 June 2010, the calculation involved taxing only 5/9^{ths} of the gain at the flat rate of 18%).

Where an individual has not used up his or her maximum relief, trustees of a trust in which he or she is a life tenant can use the balance of the ER lifetime allowance to cover gains realised from the trustees' sale of all or part of the life tenant's trust interest in an unincorporated business or trust holding of shares in the life tenant's personal trading company (ie a company where the life tenant is a director and he or she holds at least 5% of the shares and voting rights in his or her own right). It is necessary for the trustees to have owned the asset for at least 12 months.

The trustees may also be able to claim ER on gains realised from associated disposals, ie sales by the trustees of land and buildings that were used by the unincorporated business or by the life tenant's personal trading company. Relief will not normally be available where the trustees have charged a full market rent for periods after 5 April 2008.

31.3 BARE TRUSTS

A bare trust is one where trustees hold property on behalf of a beneficiary who is absolutely entitled to that property, or would be absolutely entitled if he or she were not a minor and therefore unable to give a valid receipt. Income and capital gains received by trustees of a bare trust belong to the beneficiary and he or she is required to report income and gains in his or her own return and to account to HMRC for the full amount of tax due

The trustees normally have no liability to tax and no requirement to complete trust tax returns.

Under self-assessment, bare trustees cannot deduct tax from income arising to them. Any income received gross by the trustees must be paid gross to the beneficiaries. The only exception to this rule is that UK resident trustees may be required, under the non-resident landlord scheme, to deduct and account for tax on the rental income of beneficiaries whose usual place of abode is outside the UK (see 33.6).

See 32.5.4 on the position where a parent gives money to a bare trust for his or her minor child.

31.4 FIXED-INTEREST TRUSTS

A fixed interest trust is one where a beneficiary is entitled to receive income as it arises, either during his or her lifetime or for a specific period. A simple type of fixed interest trust would be where the beneficiary (the life tenant) is entitled to receive all the income during his or her lifetime with the trust coming to an end on his or her death, perhaps with the capital then passing to his or her children absolutely.

There may also be a situation where a life tenant is entitled to receive a proportion of the trust income, say half, with the other half being held on different types of trust. It is also possible to have an entitlement to income (an interest in possession) for a specific period, so that a trust under which someone had a right to all of the income for a fixed period of ten years would be a fixed interest trust until the end of that period.

31.4.1 Settlor-interested settlements are subject to a special tax treatment

The following analysis is on the basis that the settlor, and his or her spouse or civil partner, or minor unmarried children are excluded from benefiting. See 33.5.2 on the tax position where the settlor can benefit.

A previously non-settlor interested trust can become settlor-interested where the settlor marries, enters a civil partnership, or has children and such relatives have not been excluded from benefiting under the terms of the trust, because in the past there have been no such persons.

31.4.2 Income tax

For 2011–12 (as in previous years), where property is held on fixed interest trusts, income tax is charged on the trustees at the following rates:

● dividend income at 10%;
● all other income at 20% (basic/lower rate).

As mentioned above there is no deduction for personal allowances, but if a trust owns investment properties on which an entitlement to capital allowances arises, such allowances may be set against the trustees' income in the same way as for individuals. Similarly, if the trustees carry on a trade, any losses arising may be relieved against other income. Subject to this, the trustees will either suffer tax at source or be assessed to tax on all untaxed income arising to them.

31.4.3 Ascertaining the beneficiary's income

It will not generally be possible for the trustees to pay over to a beneficiary with a fixed interest the full amount of the income left after tax. Inevitably, there will be some expenses (eg bank charges, interest, professional fees, etc) that are properly charged to income, and there may also be the trustees' own fees. Such expenses may not be deducted in arriving at the trustees' taxable income, but they need to be taken into account in determining the amount of the beneficiary's income. See 31.11.2 regarding an HMRC statement on expenses that may be taken into account in this way.

In broad terms, the proper procedure is to ascertain the trustees' taxable income for the year. The tax paid by the trustees for the year should then be deducted, and a further deduction made for expenses that are properly charged against income. The net amount must then be 'grossed up' at the appropriate rate and this is the amount the beneficiary will need to declare on his or her tax return.

Example – Tax treatment of income from a fixed interest trust

The trustees of a fixed interest trust have taxable deposit interest of £20,000 for 2011–12. They pay tax of £4,000 (20%). There are expenses of £1,700 that are properly chargeable against the income. The balance belongs to the life tenant, whose gross income will be ascertained as follows:

	£
Trustees' taxable income	20,000
Less: basic rate tax	(4,000)
	16,000
Less: expenses	(1,700)
	14,300
£14,300 grossed up at the lower rate (20%)	17,875

This income forms part of the life tenant's income for the year whether or not it is actually paid out to him or her. If the life tenant is subject to higher rate tax, he or she must pay the difference between his or her highest rate and the rate paid by the trustees.

31.4.4 Dividend income

(ss13, 481 ITA 2007)

It is necessary to distinguish UK dividends from income from other sources. Dividend income is taxable at 10% as opposed to the 20% charge on other income. Trustees' expenses are set first against UK dividend income, so as to minimise the restriction of the tax deemed to be withheld from the trust income.

31.4.5 Tax deduction certificates

For fixed interest trusts a tax deduction certificate (Form R185 (trust income)) should be completed by the trustees or their professional advisers, showing the appropriate gross, tax and net figures in respect of the beneficiary's income. It is necessary to show the different types of income separately on the certificate. If the trust has received foreign dividends it will also be necessary to advise the beneficiary (or his or her tax adviser) of the overseas tax deducted on those dividends.

31.4.6 Income mandated to a beneficiary

Trustees sometimes take the view that it is simpler to mandate dividends and other income to the beneficiary so that such income does not pass through the trustees' hands. This does not alter the fact that the trustees are still the legal owners of the assets that produce the income.

Although this income can be entered directly in the beneficiary's personal tax return, care should be taken to ensure that it is entered in the correct section for trust income so as to avoid any confusion with the beneficiary's personal income. Where this is done, HMRC will assess the beneficiary rather than the trustees.

If the trustees incur expenses, these may not be deducted (as in 31.4.2); this applies even where the beneficiary reimburses the trustees for such expenses later on.

Tax notes

Since 22 March 2006, trusts can be life interest trusts for income and capital gains purposes, but relevant property trusts for inheritance tax purposes. Accordingly, it may be sensible to appoint a flexible or revocable life interest from an existing discretionary trust, with no IHT impact, and mandate the relevant income to the beneficiary, in order for the income to be treated as that of the beneficiary and taxed at their marginal rates, rather than at the rate applicable to trusts, which increased to 42.5% (dividends) and 50% (other income) from 6 April 2010.

31.4.7 Beneficiary's exempt income

It is sometimes possible for UK-resident trustees to take advantage of a beneficiary's tax exemption to avoid paying tax that he or she would then have to claim back. For example, where a beneficiary is entitled to all the income of the trust and he or she is resident outside the UK, the trustees can agree with HMRC that the income that arises outside the UK (and any other income that is exempt for a non-resident, for example, interest from exempt gilts: see 34.6.3) should not be taxed in the trustees' hands.

This treatment is not normally available where a non-resident beneficiary is entitled to only a proportion of the trustees' income.

Tax notes

Where, under the terms of a settlement, income from foreign dividends belongs to, and is paid to, a beneficiary resident and domiciled abroad, that income cannot be assessed on trustees who are resident in the UK (*Williams* v *Singer* [1921] 1 AC 65; 7 TC 387 HL). If however there is no identifiable beneficiary in respect of income arising and accumulated abroad, a UK resident trustee is assessable in respect of that income (*Kelly* v *Rogers* [1935] 2 KB 446; 19 TC 692, CA).

Where a beneficiary is entitled to all the income of the trust and is resident outside the UK, the trustees can agree with HMRC that the income that arises outside the UK should not be taxed in the trustees' hands.

31.4.8 Where taxable income is not income for trust purposes

Difficulties can arise where the trustees receive something that constitutes income for tax, but not for trust, purposes. For example, if trustees of a fixed-interest trust receive a lump sum premium that is taxable income from property (see 8.3); this is not income that belongs to the life tenant. Similarly, a distribution such as may arise on a company buying back its own shares may be income for income tax purposes (see 9.9.7), but is capital for trust purposes. In both these situations, the trustees must pay tax on such deemed income at the trust rates, and the amounts must be excluded when calculating the life tenant's income for tax purposes.

FA 2006 contained new provisions that apply in relation to 2006–07 and subsequent years, now reproduced in s 482 ITA 2007. The effect of these provisions is that trustees of fixed interest trusts are now subject to the trust rate on any amounts that are taxed as if they were income but are not income of the life tenant for trust purposes. These provisions, however, still do not mean that the income is deemed to be that of the life tenant. The types of payment which are taxable at the trust rates are as follows:

(1) A payment which is made to the trustees or to which the trustees are entitled, and which is made by way of qualifying distribution by a company on the redemption, repayment or purchase of shares in the company or on the purchase of rights to acquire such shares.

(2) Accrued income profits treated as made by the trustees under ss 628(5) or 630(2) ITA 2007.

(3) Income treated as arising to the trustees under regulation 17 of the Offshore Funds (Tax) Regulations 2009 (SI 2009/3001).

(4) Income which the trustees are treated as receiving under ss 68(2) or 71(4) FA 1989 (which relate to employee share ownership trusts).

(5) A sum to which Chapter 4, Part 3, ITTOIA 2005 (which provides for certain amounts to be treated as receipts of a property business) applies.

(6) A profit in relation to which the trustees are liable for income tax under s 429 ITTOIA 2005 (profits from deeply discounted securities).

(7) A gain in relation to which the trustees are liable for income, tax under s 467 ITTOIA 2005 (gains from contracts for life insurance etc), other than a gain to which subsection (7) of that section applies.

(8) A profit or gain in relation to which the trustees are liable for income tax under s 554 ITTOIA 2005 (transactions in deposits).

(9) A profit or gain in relation to which the trustees are liable for income tax under s 557 ITTOIA 2005 (disposals of futures and options), and which does not meet any of conditions A to C in s 568 ITTOIA 2005.

(10) Proceeds in relation to which the trustees are liable for income tax under s 573 ITTOIA 2005 (sales of foreign dividend coupons).

(11) Income treated as arising to the trustees under Chapter 3 of Part 13 of ITA 2007 (tax avoidance: transactions in land).

31.4.9 Exempt receipts that are income for trust purposes

The converse may happen. For example, a trustee may receive income in the form of a tax repayment supplement that is exempt. This will still constitute income for trust law purposes and the life tenant will generally be entitled to receive the full amount, but it is not taxable income of the beneficiary.

The treatment of dividends arising from demergers (see 9.8.8) also gave rise to concern, but a test case involving the ICI demerger established that such receipts by trustees were generally capital rather than income from the point of view of trust law, so in this particular case the treatment for trust law and taxation will normally be the same. It is important to take professional advice where significant sums of money are involved as HMRC distinguishes between different types of demergers (see www.hmrc.gov.uk/manuals/cg2manual/cg33900+.htm).

31.4.10 Capital gains tax

From 6 April 2008 to 22 June 2010, trustees of UK resident fixed-interest trusts were subject to tax at 18% on any capital gains (after deducting ER where applicable). No further CGT (or income tax) liability normally arose on the trustees distributing cash to a beneficiary after they had realised a capital gain by selling an asset. Since 23 June 2010, trust gains have been chargeable at a flat rate of 28% (subject to the availability of ER).

31.4.11 Exemption for property occupied by a beneficiary

(s 225 TCGA 1992)

There is an exemption for trustees in respect of a property owned by them, but occupied by a beneficiary as his or her main residence (provided he or she is entitled to do so under the terms of the trust deed). The beneficiary may not also claim exemption for a property owned by him or her personally. Where an individual has more than one residence, and it is desired to elect that a property owned by trustees be treated as his or her main residence, a joint notice must be given by the trustees and that individual.

Anti-avoidance legislation, which came into force from December 2003 (see 33.13), restricts the availability of holdover relief for settlor interested trusts where the main residence exemption is to be claimed.

31.4.12 Disposals of business assets

Although taper relief is no longer available, ER may be claimed for gains arising from the sale of an interest in an unincorporated business or from the sale of shares in the eligible beneficiary's personal company. ER may also be claimed on gains arising from disposals of assets used by the business/personal company where the disposal is associated with a disposal of an interest in an unincorporated business or of shares in the beneficiary's personal company. (See further at 31.2.3.)

31.4.13 Liability may also arise on deemed disposals

A capital gain may arise on a deemed disposal such as where the trustees distribute assets to a beneficiary, or where a beneficiary becomes absolutely entitled to capital under the terms of a trust. Hold-over relief is only available in a pre-22 March 2006 (or other 'qualifying') fixed interest trust if the disposal involves business property (see 17.4).

31.4.14 Transfer of capital losses to a trust beneficiary

Where a beneficiary becomes absolutely entitled to settled property, losses realised in the past by the trustees do not pass across. Furthermore, if a loss arises for the trustees on an asset passing across to the beneficiary, he or she may use this only against a capital gain that he or she may subsequently realise on a disposal of that asset.

31.4.15 Death of the life tenant

(s 73 TCGA 1992)

There is one type of deemed disposal that does not give rise to a CGT charge. Where an interest in possession ceases on a death, the assets are treated as having been disposed of and reacquired at their value at that date, but there is no chargeable gain for the trustees. This does not apply where the trustees hold assets that were subject to a hold-over claim by the settlor at the time he or she transferred the assets to the trustees.

31.4.16 Inheritance tax

(s 49 IHTA 1984)

Where a beneficiary has an interest in possession, and he or she had that interest at 22 March 2006, or it is a transitional serial interest (TSI) or an immediate post-death interest (IPDI) (collectively referred to in this text as 'qualifying' interests in possession), he or she is treated for IHT purposes as if he or she owned the trust capital. On death, the value of the trust capital is brought into account as part of the individual's estate and IHT is charged accordingly. The trustees are, however, responsible for paying the IHT on the proportion of the tax attributable to the trust property.

Example – IHT liability on a pre-22 March 2006 fixed interest trust

A dies on 1 May 2012 owning property in his personal capacity worth £205,000 (this is called his 'free estate') and he was also the life tenant of a trust that had a capital value of £350,000. The total IHT payable is:

	£
Free estate	205,000
Trust	350,000
	555,000
Less: nil rate band for 2012–13*	(325,000)
	230,000
IHT thereon at 40%	92,000

* The nil rate band is expected to remain at £325,000 until at least 2014–15

IHT is payable as follows:

$$\text{Executore} \ \frac{205,000}{555,000} \times 92,000 = 33,982$$

$$\text{Trustees} \ \frac{350,000}{555,000} \times 92,000 = 58,018$$

31.4.17 Fixed interest trusts where the interest in possession did not exist at 22 March 2006

FA 2006 introduced a new IHT regime for such trusts (see 31.4.23). An IHT charge will not normally arise on the death of the life tenant but the trustees will be subject to a periodic charge.

31.4.18 Exemption where settled property reverts to settlor

(s 54 IHTA 1984)

The treatment described in 31.4.16 does not apply where the trust assets pass back to the settlor on the death of the life tenant who held his or her interest at 22 March 2006. No IHT charge arises on the property that reverts to the settlor. There is a similar exemption where property reverts to the settlor's spouse or his or her civil partner, but this is conditional on the spouse or civil partner being domiciled in the UK.

For post-22 March 2006 interests, the reverter to settlor exemption only applies if the trust is a disabled person's trust or a TSI and the property reverts to the settlor or his or her spouse or civil partner. If the trust is an IPDI, the exemption may be available if the property reverts to the settlor's UK domiciled spouse.

The reverter to settlor exemption does not apply if the settlor (or his or her spouse or civil partner) has purchased a reversionary interest.

31.4.19 Exempt pre-13 November 1974 Will trusts

(Para 2, Schedule 6 IHTA 1984)

These are trusts created by the Will of a person who died before 13 November 1974 and left property in trust on the following terms:

- his or her surviving spouse was entitled to an interest in possession;
- the surviving spouse was not entitled to demand that the capital should be paid out to him or her.

These trusts are exempt from the normal charge that arises when the surviving spouse's interest in possession comes to an end. The reason for this is that before 13 November 1974, estate duty was levied on an individual's death even if he or she left property in trust for his or her spouse. However, the estate duty legislation then provided an exemption on the death of the surviving spouse and this has been carried over to IHT.

Will trusts that came into being after 12 November 1974 are treated differently because of the exemption that applies for IHT purposes where property passes to a surviving spouse. Property held in a post-12 November 1974 Will trust is subject to IHT on the life tenant's death.

31.4.20 No charge where life tenant of qualifying settlement becomes absolutely entitled to trust property

(s 53(2) IHTA 1984)

There are no IHT implications where a life tenant (or any other beneficiary entitled to an interest in possession) who held his or her interest at 22 March 2006 (or is entitled to a post-22 March 2006 qualifying life interest) becomes absolutely entitled to the trust property. This is because the beneficiary is already regarded for IHT purposes as if he or she owns the capital concerned. All that has happened is that the beneficiary's interest has been enlarged and, while this may have CGT consequences, it does not give rise to an IHT charge.

Prior to 12 March 2008, no tax charge arose where a person's qualifying interest in possession ended and he or she became entitled to another interest in possession in the trust property, so long as the new interest was in the whole of the capital in which the first interest subsisted. From 12 March 2008, this exemption is restricted so that it only applies where the individual's new interest is a disabled person's interest or a transitional serial interest, ie in very limited circumstances.

Tax notes

There are no IHT implications where a life tenant who held his or her interest at 22 March 2006 (or is entitled to a post-22 March 2006 qualifying life interest) becomes absolutely entitled to the trust property because he or she is already regarded for IHT purposes as owning the capital concerned. However, if the value of the new interest is less than the value of the old interest (for instance, if a beneficiary with an entitlement to the whole of the income from a £1m fund becomes absolutely entitled to £500,000 of capital on attaining (say) age 35, with another beneficiary gaining absolute entitlement to the remaining £500,000) then tax will be chargeable on the difference.

31.4.21 If interest in possession ends during a person's lifetime

(ss 3A, 23 and 52 IHTA 1984)

Where a beneficiary's interest in possession comes to an end during his or her lifetime, and it was either a qualifying interest in possession (an IPDI, TSI or disabled person's interest) or was an interest within s 5(1B) (ie an IIP to which a UK domiciled individual became beneficially entitled on or after 9 December 2009 as a result of a disposition within s 10 IHTA) and he or she does not personally become entitled to the trust property, he or she is treated as making a transfer of value. The transfer is normally either a PET (see 30.6) or a chargeable lifetime transfer (CLT), according to what happens as a result of the interest in possession coming to an end. If, however, an individual's spouse or civil partner becomes absolutely entitled on the termination of his or her interest in possession, the transfer will normally be an exempt transfer because of the spouse exemption (see 30.5.1).

Section 5(1B) was inserted by s 53 FA (No.1) 2010 as an anti-avoidance provision to prevent planning whereby an individual A, paid the settlor full value to create the settlement (so that s 10 applied and neither the settlor nor the life tenant had made a transfer of value) with a life interest to A and remainder to B (a family member). B would also have had to pay full value for his or her interest and then the trust capital could have passed to B tax free on A's death. Section 5(1B) prevents this from working by treating such interests owned by UK domiciliaries as qualifying interests in possession, which means that the value of the trust fund would be treated as forming part of A's estate on his or her death, with IHT charges arising accordingly.

Until 5 October 2008, spouse exemption was also available if the spouse or civil partner acquired an interest in possession following the lifetime termination of a pre-22 March 2006 interest in possession, as opposed to acquiring the trust property absolutely. The interest thus created was a TSI and the trust property will be treated as being part of the spouse or civil partner's estate on his or her death.

Potentially exempt transfers (PETs)

If the effect of the beneficiary's interest coming to an end is that:

- another individual becomes entitled to an interest in possession; or
- another person becomes absolutely entitled to the trust property; or
- the trust becomes a disabled person's trust, or
- the trust becomes a trust for a bereaved minor when an IPDI ends,

then the person whose interest in possession has terminated is treated as having made a PET. In such instances, IHT is charged if (and only if) the person dies within the following seven years. If this should happen, the trustees are liable to pay the IHT unless the settled property passes to a beneficiary through his or her becoming absolutely entitled on the termination of the interest in possession. In such a situation the person who becomes absolutely entitled is liable to pay any such IHT.

Exempt transfers

Occasionally, the effect of a person's interest in possession coming to an end is that his or her spouse becomes entitled to an interest in possession. Where this happens, the person whose interest in possession has come to an end is treated as having made an exempt transfer. This treatment also applies if a trust becomes a charitable trust as a result of a beneficiary's interest in possession coming to an end.

Chargeable lifetime transfers (CLTs)

Where a person's interest in possession comes to an end and the trust thereby becomes a relevant property trust, he or she is treated as having made a CLT. If his or her cumulative CLTs bring him or her over the nil rate band, IHT is payable right away at the lifetime rate of 20%. If he or she should then die within three years, the rate increases to 40% (see 31.11); with tapering if death occurs in years four to seven.

31.4.22 How a transfer of value is computed on lifetime transfers

The legislation contains an anomaly. Where an individual makes a gift in his or her personal capacity, the transfer of value is deemed to be the amount by which his or her estate is reduced in value (see 30.6.2). This rule does not apply where a person's interest in possession comes to an end because, in this case, the amount of the transfer of value is taken as the value of the property in which the interest in possession has terminated.

Example – Calculation of value of lifetime transfer

> *B* owns 90% of a company in his personal capacity and is the life tenant of a trust that owns the remaining 10%. The value of a 100% shareholding in the company is worth £500,000. The value of a 90% shareholding is £450,000, but a 10% shareholding valued in isolation is worth only £20,000. If *B* had made a gift of 10% out of his personal shareholding, his transfer of value would be taken to be:
>
> | | £ |
> |---|---|
> | Value of a 100% shareholding | 500,000 |
> | *Less*: value of remaining 90% shareholding | |
> | (taking his own shares and the trust together) | (450,000) |
> | Reduction in value of his estate | 50,000 |
>
> However, if *B* surrenders his life interest in the trust so that his interest in possession comes to an end, the value transferred is taken as £20,000.

31.4.23 New regime for fixed interest trusts

FA 2006 introduced a new regime for lifetime trusts where an interest in possession came into existence on or after 22 March 2006. The rules do not apply where before 6 October 2008 a new interest in possession replaced an interest in possession held at 22 March 2006 (see 31.4.24 below).

New fixed interest trusts and existing trusts where an interest in possession has been created on or after 22 March 2006 are normally subject to the IHT regime that was formerly confined to discretionary trusts (see 31.5 below), ie the creation of such a trust will be a CLT for IHT and the trust will be subject to the periodic charge (see 31.5.13) and the exit charge (see 31.5.19). On the other hand, no IHT charge will normally arise on the termination of an interest in possession, whether on death or during the beneficiary's lifetime (contrast the treatment of qualifying trusts and interests within s 5(1B) described in 31.4.21 above).

Where a fixed interest trust is caught by the FA 2006 provisions, there will not be a CGT disposal and re-acquisition at the date of the life tenant's death (see 31.4.15). On the other hand, CGT hold-over relief may be available under s 260 TCGA 1992 (see 31.6.2) when property is put into a UK trust or comes out of the trust to a UK resident beneficiary.

31.4.24 Some situations where the pre-22 March 2006 treatment continues to apply

The regime does not apply where:

- An individual acquired an interest in possession before 6 October 2008 that replaced an interest in possession held by another individual at 22 March 2006 (the previous 5 April 2008 deadline was extended by six months by FA 2008).
- The trust is created as part of arrangements dealing with a relationship breakdown.
- An interest in possession trust was in being at 22 March 2006 to hold life policies and money is only added to the trust by additional premiums being paid.
- The trust is for the benefit of a disabled person (see 31.7 for definition). In this case, the let-out can apply both to lifetime trusts and trusts created on death.
- An individual who is in the early stages of a degenerative disease creates a settlement under which he or she has a life interest.
- A trust is created on death (by Will or intestacy) for the benefit of the deceased's minor child and the child will become absolutely entitled at age 18.
- Life interest trusts are created on death (by Will or intestacy).
- The life tenant is the deceased's widow or widower – spouse exemption is available (see 30.5.1).

31.5 DISCRETIONARY TRUSTS

In contrast to a fixed interest trust, a discretionary trust is one where the trustees can control the way in which income and capital are used. In most cases, the trustees have power to accumulate income, in which case it may be retained by them either with a view to its being paid out in later years or as an addition to the trust capital.

In other cases, the trustees have no legal right to accumulate income, but the trust is regarded as discretionary because no beneficiary has a fixed entitlement (ie the trustees must distribute the income, but they can choose how it is distributed and which particular beneficiary should receive it).

31.5.1 Special tax treatment for certain trusts

The following analysis is on the basis that the settlor and spouse are excluded from benefiting under the settlement. The tax treatment where a settlor can benefit is covered in more detail at 33.14 but it should be noted that trustees of discretionary trusts are currently liable for 50% tax on non-dividend income, and 42.5% tax on dividend income (subject to the £1,000 nil rate band). Since 23 June 2010, all onshore trusts have been liable to CGT at a flat rate of 28% (18% between 6 April 2008 and 22 June 2010). If the settlor is able to reclaim tax, because of allowances or reliefs he or she would otherwise not have been able to access, or because his or her effective tax rate is lower than that of the trustees, the repayment belongs to the trustees. Currently, a settlor has a right to reclaim tax due to be paid on trust income from the trustees but conversely, if he or she receives a repayment of tax in respect of an 'allowance or relief' in relation to trust income, this must be repaid to the trustees. Section 7 FA (No.3) 2010 amends s 646 ITTOIA 2005 so that it requires that any tax repayment received by a settlor, in relation to trust income, must be repaid to the trustees, including where the settlor's marginal tax rate is lower than that of the trust, but the Government has confirmed that such payments to the trustees will be disregarded for IHT purposes. Employee share ownership trusts may be exempt from the rate applicable to trusts (see 31.5.2 below) on certain types of income.

31.5.2 Rate applicable to trusts

(ss 9, 479 ITA 2007)

Subject to the £1,000 basic rate band (see below), trustees of discretionary trusts are liable for tax on income that is not dividend income at 50%. (This is called 'the rate applicable to trusts' although, as we have seen, it is not applicable to all trusts.) The rate increased from 40% to 50% with effect from 6 April 2010.

Where part of the trust income is subject to a fixed-interest trust and the balance is held on a discretionary trust, the 50% rate is charged only on the income held on discretionary trusts.

Exception for the first £1,000 of trust income (basic rate band)

(ss 491 and 492 ITA 2007)

There is an exception for the first £1,000 of the trustees' income subject to the rate applicable to trusts, which instead is taxable at the basic rate (currently 20%) or the dividend ordinary rate (10%) and only the balance over the threshold is taxed at the rate applicable to trusts. The relief is set against income bearing a higher rate of tax in priority to that bearing a lower rate, so dividends will be treated as the highest part of trust income for these purposes. Any income which is already charged at reduced rates (eg because it is covered by trust expenses) is not included in the first £1,000 for the purpose of this relief. So income which is received net of tax, and falls within this band, does not bear any further tax.

The band is modified if the settlor of the relevant settlement has made one or more other current (ie in existence at the date of measurement) settlements.

In that case, references to £1,000 are to be read as references to either £200, or if greater, 'the settlor's threshold amount'. The settlor's threshold amount is the amount calculated by dividing £1,000 by the number of current settlements (including the relevant settlement) made by the settlor. If there is more than one settlor, the fraction of the £1,000 is taken in relation to the settlor who has made the most settlements. The restriction applies irrespective of when the settlements were made or where they may be resident.

Calculation of the tax payable

In most cases, the trustees suffer basic rate tax at source and then pay additional tax to bring the total up to the required amount.

Notional income

Certain types of income are capital profits under trust law, for example:

- premiums treated as rent (see 8.3);
- profits on sale of certificates of deposit (see 10.6);
- gains from disposals of offshore funds (see 10.7).

Income which falls into one of the above categories is still subject to the rate applicable to trusts (ie 50%).

Accrued income scheme

Income taxed under the accrued income scheme is also taxed at the rate applicable to trusts (regardless of whether the trust is a fixed-interest or discretionary trust).

31.5.3 Computing the trustees' liability to the rate applicable to trusts

The trustees' liability for basic and lower rate taxes on income from savings is calculated in exactly the same way as for trustees of fixed interest trusts. A separate computation is then required for the purposes of the rates applicable to trusts (also called the 'special trust rates').

Expenses paid out of net income are 'grossed up' at the appropriate lower or dividend rate and the resulting amount is then deducted. Expenses are allowable expenses if they are expenses of the trustees, properly chargeable to income (ignoring the express terms of the settlement). Examples of such expenses are:

- bank charges;
- interest that does not qualify for tax relief;
- the costs of administering the trust;
- charges made by professional trustees;
- deficits on properties where the deficiency cannot be relieved against other UK property income.

Costs such as premiums on an insurance policy (excluding fire insurance), or property expenses such as the cost of maintenance or insurance of a property or charges made for collecting rents, cannot be included directly as a deduction in computing liability for additional rate tax. Expenses are set off first against basic rate/savings income with any balance being set against dividend income.

Example – Calculating the additional tax on discretionary trusts for 2011–12

A discretionary trust receives income from savings of £15,000 in 2011–12. It has no other income. Expenses that are not allowable in computing income for basic rate tax purposes, but are properly chargeable to income, amount to £960. The trustees' liability for tax at the 50% rate is computed as follows:

	£
Income from savings	15,000
Less: expenses – grossed up: £960 × $^{100}/_{80}$	(1,200)
	13,800
Less amount not subject to the rate applicable to trusts	(1,000)
	12,800
Tax at additional 30%	3,840

31.5.4 Special rate on dividend income

Trustees of discretionary trusts are taxed on dividend income at 42.5%. The applicable rate was 32.5% prior to 6 April 2010. Dividends received from UK companies carry a 10% tax credit.

Example – Calculating the additional tax on dividend income for 2011–12

A discretionary trust receives cash dividend income of £9,000 in a tax year. The trustees' tax liability on that income is computed is follows:

	£
Cash dividend received	9,000
Tax credit (10/90)	1,000
Taxable income	10,000
Rate applicable to trusts (42.5%)	4,250
Less: tax credit	(1,000)
Tax payable	3,250

Furthermore, when the trustees distribute income to beneficiaries, they will be required to pay additional tax unless the distribution can be shown to have come out of a 'pool' that has suffered the rate applicable to trusts.

Example – Situation where dividend income distributed between beneficiaries

---

In the above example, the trustees had dividend income of £9,000 on which they paid tax of £3,250, leaving them with £5,750. If they distribute the whole of this income to the beneficiaries, the trustees will have to pay further tax. The calculation is complicated and is as follows:

	£
Maximum distribution	4,500
Tax thereon (£9,000 × 50%)	4,500
Gross income for beneficiary	9,000

This income is regarded as having suffered 50% tax. The trustees then pay tax of £1,250 over to HMRC so that they have paid a total of £4,500, ie:

	£
Tax payable on the dividend	3,250
Tax payable on the distribution to bring payment up to tax of 50% of £9,000	1,250
	4,500

Tax Bulletin 71 (June 2004), covers all this in detail (albeit at historic rates), as does HMRC's Trusts manual (www.hmrc.gov.uk/manuals/tsemmanual/TSEM3010.htm).

31.5.5 Income distributions in excess of trustees' taxable income
(ss 493 and 494 ITA 2007)

There may be situations where trustees make distributions in excess of their taxable income. Such distributions also give rise to a liability for the trustees to account for tax at the rate applicable to trusts. There are several situations in which such a liability can arise:

- A trust may have income on which income tax does not have to be paid. If such income is paid out to a beneficiary as an income distribution, the trustees must account for tax at the rate applicable to trusts.
- Similarly, trustees may make a payment of an income nature that is subject to tax as income in the hands of the beneficiary even though it comes out of the trust capital. In practice, HMRC would not normally assess such distributions unless they were made regularly.

If the income is fully distributed each year and foreign securities are held, there will be an additional liability to tax when the foreign income is distributed to beneficiaries. The liability is equal to the credit allowed against basic rate tax for double taxation relief.

31.5.6 Tax returns

One tax return (form SA900) is now completed whether the trust is fixed-interest or discretionary. There are supplementary forms to be completed for various types of income, for capital gains, and where the trust is a non-resident or charitable trust.

> **Tax notes**
>
> HMRC provides a tax calculation guide for trusts and estates, but as the calculation layout is Byzantine in its complexity, the form is generally not used.

Tax deduction certificates

Where payments are made to beneficiaries during a particular tax year, a tax deduction certificate form R185 should be completed by the trustees or their professional advisers, showing the appropriate gross, tax and net figures.

31.5.7 The beneficiary's position

A beneficiary needs to include on his or her tax return the grossed up amount of any income distributed to him or her by the trustees during the tax year. Since the trustees are subject to the additional rate, the beneficiary's income is treated as net of tax withheld at the rate applicable to trusts.

31.5.8 Accumulated income subsequently distributed as capital

A distribution of capital that represents income that has been accumulated is not normally taxable income for the beneficiary. Such a distribution is treated as a capital distribution, although this presupposes that the trustees have power to accumulate income. In cases where they have no such power, any distributions will remain as income.

31.5.9 Capital gains tax

From 6 April 2008 to 22 June 2010, the rate of capital gains tax was 18% for both individuals and trustees. Since 23 June 2010, the rate for trustees and personal representatives has been 28%.

As with a fixed-interest trust, no further CGT (or income tax) liability will normally arise when trustees of a UK resident trust distribute cash to a beneficiary, after they have realised a capital gain by selling an asset, albeit an IHT liability may arise.

31.5.10 Exemption for property occupied by beneficiary

(s 225 TCGA 1992)

The courts have held that trustees of discretionary trusts are entitled to this exemption where they permit a beneficiary to occupy a property as his or her main residence under the terms of the trust, even though the trust deed did not confer a right for him or her to require the trustees to provide such a property (but see SP 10/79). HMRC will resist allowing this exemption where the trustees do not have a power to allow a beneficiary to occupy a property. However such a power need not be contained in the trust deed, for example it may be a power given to the trustees under the Trustee Act 2000. The anti-avoidance provisions in ss 169B–169G TCGA 1992 may apply where hold-over relief is claimed on a transfer of a property to the trustees (see 33.13).

31.5.11 Entrepreneurs' relief

This relief is not available to trustees of discretionary settlements unless there is an interest in possession in part of the trust property, in which case the rules for such interests will apply in relation to that part of the fund.

31.5.12 Deemed disposals/hold-over relief

(s 71 TCGA 1992)

A capital gain may arise on a deemed disposal such as where the trustees distribute assets to a beneficiary, or where a beneficiary becomes absolutely entitled to capital under the terms of a trust. Hold-over relief is normally available under s 260 TCGA 1992 where a disposal of the property arises on a capital distribution to a UK resident beneficiary (see 13.6 on s 260 relief).

31.5.13 Inheritance tax

(ss 64 and 65 IHTA 1984)

By definition, no beneficiary has an interest in possession in a discretionary trust and it follows that the trust capital is not treated as forming part of his or her estate. Therefore, no IHT charge arises on his or her death.

To make up for the absence of such a charge, the legislation imposes a lower charge every ten years (the periodic charge). The theory is that a generation is approximately 30 years and the tax charged on three separate occasions by reason of the periodic charge will approximate to the tax payable on property passing down to the next generation.

There is also an exit charge that applies where property leaves a discretionary trust. Until 22 March 2006, the exit charge also arose if the trust became a fixed interest trust. There are different rules for discretionary trusts created before and after 26 March 1974.

31.5.14 Trusts created after 26 March 1974

Periodic charge (ss 64–69 IHTA 1984)

The periodic charge arises on the tenth anniversary of the creation of the trust and on every subsequent tenth anniversary. The maximum rate is currently 6% (ie 0.6% pa), computed as follows:

Tax payable at lifetime rate (20%) × 30%.

The computation is actually more complex and involves the following process:

Amount of CLTs made by settlor in the seven years prior to creation of the trust	A
Value of trust property at tenth anniversary	B
Add A and B	C
Deduct nil rate band at date of charge	(D)
	E

The next step is to compute the IHT payable on E and on A – D. The tax payable by the trustees on the periodic charge is 30% of the difference.

Example – Periodic charge

C created a discretionary trust in June 2002. She had previously made CLTs of £194,000. In June 2012 the trust is worth £160,000. The periodic charge is therefore computed as follows:

		£
Amount of previous CLTs	(A)	194,000
Value of trust property in June 2012	(B)	160,000
	(C)	354,000
Deduct 2012–13 nil rate band*	(D)	325,000
	(E)	29,000
IHT on E		5,800
Less: IHT at lifetime rates on A–D		Nil
		5,800

The periodic charge is 30% of £5,800, ie £1,740.

* The nil rate band is expected to remain at £325,000 until at least 2014–15

31.5.15 Trusts created before 26 March 1974

This type of trust is simpler in that there cannot have been any CLTs made by the settlor before the creation of the trust. The computation is therefore:

Value of trust property at tenth anniversary	X
Deduct nil rate band	(Y)
	Z
IHT at lifetime rates on Z	w

The periodic charge is 30% of this amount.

31.5.16 Position where trustees have made capital distributions during the preceding ten years

Where the trustees have made a capital distribution within the previous ten years or property has otherwise ceased to be held upon discretionary trusts (eg by reason of a beneficiary becoming entitled to an interest in possession), the capital distribution value must also be brought into account in arriving at the periodic charge. The computation is as follows:

The sum of any CLTs made by the settlor in the seven years prior to creation of the trust and capital distributions since last periodic charge	A
Value of trust property at tenth anniversary	B
Add A and B	C
Deduct current nil rate band	(D)
	E

The next step is to compute the IHT payable on E and on A – D. The tax payable by the trustees on the period charge is 30% of the difference.

31.5.17 Treatment of undistributed income

HMRC accepts that undistributed income that has not been accumulated should be excluded in arriving at the value of the trust capital at the tenth anniversary. The reason for this is that such income remains income held for the benefit of beneficiaries and is not capital.

Where income has been formally accumulated, it must be brought into account for the purposes of the periodic charge. However, such accumulated income is treated as if it were additional capital added to the trust at the date the trustees resolved to accumulate it.

31.5.18 The exit charge (also known as the 'proportionate charge')

The way in which the exit charge is computed varies according to whether capital leaves a discretionary trust within the first ten years or only after there has been a periodic charge.

31.5.19 Exit charge during first ten years

(s 68 IHTA 1984)

The position here is that a notional rate of tax should be computed. This is the average rate of IHT that would have been payable had the settlor made a CLT at the time he or she created the trust equal to the trust property's value at that time.

Example – Exit charge during the first ten years

D created a trust in February 2002 and the original trust property was worth £500,000. A capital distribution is made in December 2011. The notional entry charge would be computed as follows:

	£
Value of trust property in February 2002	500,000
Less: nil rate band at time of distribution	(325,000)
	175,000
£175,000 at 20% =	£35,000

Effective rate $= \dfrac{35,000}{500,000} = 7\%$

The recalculated entry charge would therefore be taken as 7% and the tax payable is a proportion of this rate. The proportion is determined by the number of complete quarters during which the property has been relevant property before ceasing to be so. In this case, the exit charge occurred after the trust had existed for nine years and eight months, the charge would therefore be at the rate of:

$7\% \times \dfrac{39}{40} \times 30\% = 2.0475\%$

31.5.20 Exit charge after a periodic charge

(s 69 IHTA 1984)

The position here is that the charge applies only to the property that leaves the discretionary trust, with the proportion being determined by the following formula:

$$\frac{\text{Number of complete quarters since the last periodic charge}}{40}$$

A distribution during the first quarter following the ten-year charge is entirely free of IHT. The tax rate charged is normally fixed by the effective rate charged on the previous periodic charge. Once again, however, the effective rate is calculated by using the rates (including the nil rate band) in force at the time the exit charge arises. Thus, the notional effective rate may be slightly lower than the effective rate of IHT that actually applied on the last periodic charge.

31.6 ACCUMULATION AND MAINTENANCE TRUSTS

(ss 71, 71A–71H IHTA 1984)

An accumulation and maintenance trust is a special form of discretionary trust that has been set up for a stated class of beneficiaries. The following conditions needed to be satisfied up to 22 March 2006:

(1) One or more beneficiaries would become entitled to an interest in possession in the trust property on attaining a specified age that could not exceed age 25.
(2) Until one of the beneficiaries became beneficially entitled, the trust income had to be held on a discretionary basis with income being applied only for the maintenance, education or benefit of the beneficiaries or accumulated for their benefit.
(3) The trust could have a life of not more than 25 years or it had to be a trust for the benefit of grandchildren of a common grandparent.

From 22 March 2006, a trust can normally be an accumulation and maintenance trust only if the trust existed at 21 March 2006 and the beneficiaries will become absolutely entitled to the settled property at age 18. The trustees had until 5 April 2008 to vary an existing trust so that it satisfied this condition. If the trust is a Will trust for bereaved minor children of the deceased (s 71A IHTA 1984), it can qualify as a favoured trust provided that the beneficiaries will become absolutely entitled by the time they attain age 18. Grandparents can no longer settle tax favoured accumulation settlements for their grandchildren.

'18–25' (s 71D IHTA 1984) trusts provide a half-way house for families concerned that children should not have access to capital at age 18. It is possible to restrict access to capital until age 25, but with an IHT cost (maximum 4.2%) between ages 18 and 25.

If existing accumulation and maintenance settlements were not varied before 6 April 2008, and did not fall within either the s 71A or s 71D rules, then they will have become relevant property (ie discretionary) trusts on that date.

31.6.1 Taxation

The same rules apply, and the same returns and certificates need to be completed, for income tax and CGT as for discretionary trusts. There are, however, different rules for CGT hold-over relief and IHT.

31.6.2 Hold-over relief for trustees

(s 260 TCGA 1992)

Where trustees dispose of assets to a beneficiary, there may be a CGT charge. Section 260 hold-over relief will now generally be available. There is however an anomaly where the trustees hold indivisible assets: the case of *Crowe* v *Appleby* concerned a situation where beneficiaries became entitled to an undivided share in trust property on the deaths of the initial beneficiaries. The Court of Appeal decided that since the trust fund was realty, the beneficiaries could not direct the trustees how to deal with it nor could they call for the immediate payment of their respective shares or interfere with the due exercise by the trustees of their power to postpone sale, and thus could not be said to have become absolutely entitled to their shares. This is thought also to be the case where the trustees hold other indivisible assets, such as paintings or antiques or shares in private companies.

The principle in *Crowe* v *Appleby* has been applied in connection with the Schedule 20, FA 2006 trust changes to deny holdover where for instance there are several minor beneficiaries, who each become absolutely entitled to their share of the trust assets on reaching (say) the age of 18. For CGT purposes only, where a trust fund consists of land held in undivided shares under a single settlement, and those shares vest absolutely in different beneficiaries on different dates, none of the beneficiaries becomes absolutely entitled for CGT purposes to his or her share until all the shares have vested absolutely, except where there is an earlier sale of the land or earlier appropriation of specific property to an absolutely vested share. The rule in *Crowe* v *Appleby* does not however apply to IHT, so there is in that circumstance, no coterminous CGT and IHT event on which to claim holdover until the final child attains age 18.

31.6.3 **IHT privileges**

An accumulation and maintenance, or bereaved minors', trust that satisfies the conditions imposed by FA 2006 (ie the beneficiaries become absolutely entitled on attaining age 18) is not subject to the periodic charge described at 31.5.14. Furthermore, there is no exit charge on a beneficiary becoming entitled to an interest in possession under the trust or becoming absolutely entitled to trust property.

Pre-22 March 2006 trusts that do not meet the FA 2006 rules, but were modified prior to 5 April 2008 so that they fall within s 71D IHTA 1984, attract an IHT exit charge when the beneficiaries become absolutely entitled at age 25. However, provided that the beneficiaries become absolutely entitled no later than at age 25, this charge is limited to seven-tenths of the exit charge that would otherwise arise, ie the maximum rate of the exit charge is 4.2%. The charge did not arise at all on beneficiaries who became absolutely entitled before 6 April 2008, and only took effect from 6 April 2008, meaning that beneficiaries between 18 and 25 years old at that time will not incur the full seven years' charge. For example, L is the beneficiary of an '18–25' trust. She was 21 on 26 March 2008, and becomes entitled to trust capital on attaining age 25. The IHT charge will only apply between 6 April 2008 and 26 March 2012, ie for 15 complete quarters and so will be a maximum 2.25%.

Example – An accumulation and maintenance trust coming to an end in 2011

An accumulation and maintenance settlement set up on 9 April 2001 came to an end on 9 April 2011 on the beneficiary attaining age 25. Prior to 5 April 2008, the trustees altered the terms of the trust such that it fell within s 71D. The settlement was worth £400,000.

The basic rate of the exit charge is ascertained as follows:

- Take the tax rate as described in 31.5.15 (maximum rate is 6%).
- Reduce this rate for the part of the ten-year period ending in April 2011 that falls before 6 April 2008, ie 28/40^{ths}: this reduces the maximum rate on exit to 1.8%.

31.7 TRUSTS FOR THE DISABLED

(Schedule 1 TCGA 1992; ss 74 and 89, 89A, 89B IHTA 1984)

A trust for a disabled person is a type of discretionary trust that enjoys certain tax privileges. The trustees are entitled to the full 2011–12 CGT exemption of £10,600 for individuals and there is no liability for IHT periodic and exit charges.

Under ss 89 and 89A there is special treatment for trusts for disabled people, where there is no interest in possession (IIP), but which meet certain income and capital conditions (not the same as s 34 FA 2005 dealing with 'vulnerable beneficiaries'). Where the conditions are met, the disabled beneficiary is deemed to have an IIP. The test is the condition of the disabled person when the property is settled.

Section 89A extends this to self-settlements where the disabled person can satisfy HMRC that he or she has a condition likely to lead to serious disability. Broadly speaking the trusts must ensure that during his or her lifetime, the disabled person is the only beneficiary able to receive benefits from the trust; ie the conditions are narrower than those of s 89.

Sections 89(5) and (6) extended the definition of disabled person with regarded to property provided after 22 March 2006 to persons who would be entitled to the statutory allowances but for being in certain accommodation or being not resident in the UK.

Section 89B defines a 'disabled person's interest' as including not merely the deemed IIP in ss 89 and 89A, but also where a severely disabled person becomes beneficially entitled to an actual IIP on or after 22 March 2006. It is also considered to extend to actual IIPs where the trust would meet the tests but for the existence of the IIP. Where an actual IIP subsists, s 72 TCGA 1992 also applies, giving a tax-free uplift on the death of the beneficiary.

A disabled person is one who, at the time the trust was created, was:

- incapable by reason of mental disorder within the meaning of the Mental Health Act 1983 of administering his or her property or managing his or her affairs; or
- in receipt of an attendance allowance under s 64 Social Security Contributions and Benefits Act 1992; or
- in receipt of a disability living allowance under s 71 of the 1992 Act.

The two conditions that need to be satisfied are as follows:

- not less than half of the property within the trust should be applied for the benefit of the beneficiary concerned; and
- the person should be entitled to not less than 50% of the income arising from the trust property (this condition is regarded as satisfied where the trust provides that no income may be applied for the benefit of any other person).

Income is deemed to be applied for the benefit of a person where it is held by the trustees for that person on protective trusts.

31.8 PROTECTIVE TRUSTS

(s 88 IHTA 1984)

This is a term under s 33 Trustee Act 1925. A protective trust is one under which a person (known as the principal beneficiary) is entitled to an IIP in the trust unless he or she forfeits his or her interest, for example, by assigning it or by becoming bankrupt. Protective trusts are normally worded so that if a principal beneficiary forfeits his or her interest, the trust property is held on discretionary trusts for a class of beneficiaries that includes the principal beneficiary.

31.8.1 IHT position where principal beneficiary dies

The periodic charge does not apply while property is held on protective trusts just because the principal beneficiary has forfeited his or her interest under a trust where he or she had an interest in possession before 22 March 2006 or which met one of the conditions set out in 31.4.24. However, an IHT charge arises on the beneficiary's death. The charge varies according to whether he or she forfeited his or her interest before or after 12 April 1978. Where the interest was forfeited before 12 April 1978, the calculation of the tax on his or her eventual death was governed by ss 70(3)–70(10) IHTA 1984.

Where the interest is forfeited after that date, the trustees are subject to a charge on the principal beneficiary's death as if he or she had an interest in possession at the date of his or her death.

31.9 TRUSTS FOR THE MOST VULNERABLE

(ss 34 and 35 FA 2005)

This special tax regime has applied since 6 April 2004.

A trust can qualify for this treatment only if it has either:

- a disabled beneficiary and; if any of the property is applied:
- for the benefit of a beneficiary, it is applied: for the benefit of the disabled person, and either:
  - the disabled person is entitled to all the income (if there is any) arising from the trust property or
  - no such income may be applied for the benefit of any other person; or
- it has beneficiaries who are under 18 and have lost at least one of their parents, or who are incapable of managing their affairs because of mental disorder, or who are in receipt of attendance allowance or of a disability living allowance at the middle or highest rate.

The trustees must make an election (by 31 January 2013 for 2011–12). Once the election has been made, it applies until the beneficiary ceases to be a vulnerable person (eg by attaining age 18), or the trustees no longer hold the settled property for the benefit of that individual, or the trust is wound-up. The broad effect of the relief is that the tax on the trustees' income and gains is limited to the tax that would have been payable if those income and gains had been personal income and gains of the vulnerable person.

31.10 CHARITABLE TRUSTS

Provided property is held for charitable purposes only, income and capital gains received by the trustees are normally exempt from tax.

Exemption from income tax

(Part 10 ITA 2007)

There is total exemption from income tax for all income other than trading profits. The exemption is dependent on income being applied for charitable purposes.

Exemption from CGT

(s 256 TCGA 1992)

There is also total exemption from CGT provided the charitable trust applies the capital gains for charitable purposes.

31.10.1 Application for charitable purposes

(s 540 ITA 2007)

A charity's exemption from tax may be restricted where income is not applied for charitable purposes. A charitable trust's non-exempt amount for any tax year is the lesser of its 'non-charitable expenditure' for that year; and its 'attributable income and gains'. This is the sum of the income for the tax year which would otherwise be exempt from income tax as a result of any exemptions and the capital gains which would otherwise be exempt under s 256 TCGA 1992.

'Qualifying expenditure' for these purposes means expenditure actually made during the year for charitable purposes and commitments for such expenditure entered into during the year.

Payments made to bodies outside the UK count as qualifying expenditure only to the extent that the charity can show that it has taken such steps that are reasonable in the circumstances to ensure the payments will be applied for charitable purposes. Expenditure for charitable purposes also includes reasonable administrative and fund-raising expenses.

Non-qualifying expenditure includes, for example, political activities, trading expenses and excessive administration costs. Furthermore, the legislation specifically mentions certain types of investments or loans that are to be regarded as not being qualifying expenditure. This is intended to catch investments in a company controlled by a connected person (eg the settlor) or loans to such a company. Indirect arrangements may also be caught such as where a charity makes loans or investments used as security for borrowings by a connected person. Where a charitable trust makes a payment to another connected charitable trust, this does not count as application of the income for charitable purposes unless the trust that receives the payment actually applies it for charitable purposes.

31.10.2 IHT position

Property held on charitable trusts is exempt from periodic and exit charges. If the property is held on temporary charitable trusts, a charge arises on those charitable trusts coming to an end with tax being charged under s 70 IHTA 1984.

31.11 MISCELLANEOUS ASPECTS

31.11.1 Trusts with sub funds

Where a trust has a number of separate sub funds, it may be possible for the trustees to elect that a sub fund should be treated as if it were a separate trust. This could be advantageous if a sub fund has trustees who are not resident in the UK. It is necessary that the sub fund's beneficiaries are not beneficiaries under the rest of the trust. An election will need to be made by 31 January 2012 for a sub fund to be treated as a separate trust for 2009–10 and by 31 January 2013 for 2010–11. Making the election will mean that the trust will be treated as if it had made a CGT disposal of the assets held within the sub fund on the first day of the year in which the election takes effect.

31.11.2 Trust management expenses (TMEs)

HMRC has published a statement of practice, which indicates that many expenses incurred by trustees should be charged against capital rather than income. HMRC guidance on TMEs was issued on 31 January 2006 and is incorporated into the trusts manual at TSEM8000–8920. The professional bodies raised a number of issues with the guidance and some aspects were called into question by *Trustees of the Peter Clay Discretionary Trust* v *HMRC*. As a result, HMRC has had to substantially rewrite its guidance in the TSEM (see update on 31 March 2011 and www.hmrc.gov.uk/trusts/income-tax/reliefs-deductions.htm – also the tax return helpsheet HS392).

31.12 EXECUTORS AND PERSONAL REPRESENTATIVES

31.12.1 Being a personal representative

When a person dies leaving a valid Will, his or her assets vest in his or her executors. If he or she does not leave a Will, and so dies intestate, it is normally necessary for letters of administration to be obtained and the person who acts in this way (the 'administrator' or 'administratrix' if female) is treated for most legal purposes as if he or she or she were an executor. The term 'personal representative' covers both executors and administrators.

Personal representatives (PRs) of a deceased person are treated as a single body of persons so that there is no tax implication if an executor retires or dies. The estate is treated as a single entity for tax purposes. You may find it useful to access HMRC's guide dealing with a number of issues for the newly bereaved at www.hmrc.gov.uk/bereavement/index.htm. Also, see the Capital Taxes Office's glossary (www.hmrc.gov.uk/cto/glossary.htm).

See 31.12.7 where the deceased was not domiciled in the UK, or was not resident in the UK, at the date of death.

Tax notes

HMRC publishes a useful guide for the newly bereaved on its website at www.hmrc.gov.uk/bereavement/index.htm. There is also an online glossary at www.hmrc.gov.uk/cto/glossary.htm.

31.12.2 Income tax

(s 40 TMA 1970)

The deceased's PRs are liable to pay tax on income received by the deceased up to the date of his or her death.

The tax is assessed in exactly the same way as if the individual were still alive, ie all the normal allowances and reliefs are due. The only difference is that the PRs are responsible for settling the tax (they are also entitled to any repayments). PRs are subject to the normal time limits from 1 April 2010, ie four years after the end of the tax year concerned.

Quite separately, PRs are also charged to tax on income received by them following the death. No personal allowances are given. During the administration period, dividends are taxed at 10%, and other income at the basic rate. There is no higher rate or RAT liability for the PRs. Although there are instances where income has to be apportioned pre- and post-death for legal purposes, for tax purposes any income received after a person's death is treated as income of the estate.

Where assets devolve on trust, under the terms of the Will, the executors become trustees upon the completion of the administration period. Depending on the type of trust, the trustees may become chargeable to additional rate income tax first on the balance of accumulated income at that date and secondly on receipt of subsequent income. There is no date fixed by law to determine the completion of the administration period, but it is generally agreed that it is the date on which the residue is ascertained.

31.12.3 Beneficiary's position

(Chapter 6, Part 6 ITTOIA 2005)

A beneficiary of a Will may receive an annuity. This income is taxable for the year in which it is payable unless, as a matter of fact, the annuity is paid out of capital in which case it is income for the year in which it is paid. Beneficiaries of specific legacies are normally entitled from the date of death to the income that arises on the property they have inherited. Other beneficiaries will be entitled to the residue, either through a limited interest (eg a life tenant entitled to income arising from the residuary estate) or by an absolute entitlement. During the administration period, sums paid to a beneficiary are normally treated as income for the year of payment.

Where income that has accrued to the date of death is treated as capital of the estate for IHT purposes and as residuary income, there is higher rate tax relief available to beneficiaries. (See SA107, page TN5 'special situations'.)

31.12.4 Capital gains tax

(ss 3, 62 TCGA 1992)

PRs were liable to CGT at 18% from 6 April 2008 to 22 June 2010. Since 23 June 2010 they have been liable at 28%. They are entitled to the full annual exemption due to an individual for the year of death and the following two tax years.

In computing capital gains, assets held by the deceased at the date of his or her death are deemed to be acquired by the PRs at their market value at that date (the probate value). The probate value may need to be adjusted where securities are sold at a loss within 12 months of the death and relief from IHT has been claimed (see 30.11.3). A similar rule applies where land is sold within four years of death at a loss and the sale proceeds are substituted for the probate value. Assets transferred to beneficiaries, either during the course of or on the completion of the administration period of an estate, do not give rise to a chargeable gain because the beneficiary is regarded as having acquired the asset him or herself, at the date of the person's death and at the probate value.

Certain expenses incurred by the PRs in establishing legal title to assets are allowed in computing gains on the sale of the assets (see SP2/04).

The PRs of an estate in the course of administration are not entitled to an annual exemption if they realise capital gains after two full tax years have elapsed since the date of death. If, however, upon completion of the administration period, the assets devolve upon a Will trust, the trustees will then become entitled to their own CGT exemption.

Losses made by the PRs during the administration period, and not used, are not available to be transferred to residuary beneficiaries with absolute interests or trustees of a trust established by the Will that takes effect on the administration of the estate being completed.

31.12.5 Property owned by the estate, but used by beneficiary as main residence

HMRC treats the beneficiary's main residence exemption (see 31.4.11) as applying where PRs dispose of a property that has been used by a beneficiary of the estate as his or her only or main residence both before and after the deceased's death and he or she is entitled to at least 75% of the proceeds when the estate has been administered (see ESC D5 and HMRC capital gains manual, CG65470).

31.12.6 Deeds of variation

Where the terms of a Will have been varied by a deed of variation (also known as a deed of family arrangement), there are important consequences so far as IHT is concerned (see 30.4.6). Basically, the revised way in which property passes to beneficiaries is read back into the Will and effectively treated as something done by the testator so far as IHT is concerned. However, the House of Lords held in *Marshall* v *Kerr* [1994] STC 813 that where the variation creates a trust, the person(s) who relinquish their original entitlement under the Will are treated as the settlor(s) for CGT purposes.

The income tax treatment is also less favourable than the IHT treatment. Even where the deed specifically provides that all income is to be paid to a beneficiary named in the deed, this has no effect for income tax purposes for income that arose before the deed's execution. If payments have been made to the original beneficiary or beneficiaries named in the Will, they remain liable for any higher rate tax on such income that arose at a time when they were entitled to it. Furthermore, a person who gives up an entitlement under a Will by executing such a deed is treated as a settlor for income tax purposes.

Section 472 ITA 2007 and s 68C TCGA 1992 put the income tax and CGT position described above onto a statutory basis.

Tax notes

A person who gives up an entitlement under a Will by executing a deed of variation is treated as a settlor for income tax and CGT purposes.

31.12.7 Acting as a personal representative for a foreign person

(s 834 ITA 2007 and s 62(3) TCGA 1992)

The fact that one or more of the PRs is UK resident can mean that the estate is subject to UK tax. However, they are not subject to income tax on non-UK income if the deceased person was not domiciled in the UK. Furthermore, they are not subject to capital gains tax if the deceased was neither resident nor ordinarily resident in the UK at the date of death (except to the extent that capital gains are realised from disposals of UK assets that had been used in a trade which the deceased had carried on in this country). Even where neither of these exemptions applies, the PRs may not be regarded as UK resident where the deceased was not resident, ordinarily resident or domiciled in the UK at the time of his or her death.

31.13 SOME PLANNING POINTS

The following are just some of the important tax planning points that arise regularly in relation to trusts and estates.

31.13.1 Settlor-interested trusts

Would there be a significant income tax saving if steps were taken to ensure that the trust was no longer regarded as a settlor-interested trust? It might be, for example, that the trust deed provides for income to be paid to A but that income is treated as taxable income of the settlor (B) because he or she has a reversionary interest. If A is not subject to higher rate tax, there would be an immediate saving if the trust were varied or B took some other action to disclaim his or her reversionary interest (eg he or she could settle that reversionary interest on trust for his or her adult children).

31.13.2 Is it better to create a discretionary or a fixed interest trust?

It all depends! A discretionary trust has often been more appropriate where there are elderly beneficiaries as the settled property does not form part of their estate on death. The IHT exposure under the regime for discretionary trusts (see 31.5.13–31.5.20) has always been much less than it would be for a fixed interest trust. The differences are now less given the changes brought about by FA 2006 and where the fixed interest trust was created on or after 22 March 2006, the IHT treatment will now generally be the same as that which applies to a discretionary trust (see 31.4.23). For new trusts, the deciding factors are really the settlor's wish (or otherwise) to provide a beneficiary with a fixed right to income.

The CGT position is that the settlor can generally secure hold-over relief (see 13.6) for gains on transferring assets to the trustees of most fixed interest trusts created on or after 22 March 2006 and discretionary settlements. Exceptions where hold-over relief is not available are where a fixed interest trust is not caught by the FA 2006 changes (see 31.4.24) or where the trust is a settlor-interested trust or the trust is not resident in the UK.

From an income tax point of view, the position is largely neutral. A discretionary trust currently pays tax at 50% and 42.5% (see 31.5.2) but, if the trustees make distributions to beneficiaries who are not liable for tax or who are basic rate taxpayers, the beneficiaries can make repayment claims. A fixed interest trust pays income tax at 10% on dividends and at the 20% basic rate on other income but the life tenant has to include this income on his or her tax return and, if he or she is a higher or additional rate taxpayer, pay further tax, which brings the combined tax rate up to 40% or 50% (and 32.5% or 42.5% for dividends).

From the point of view of filling in forms, life is much more straightforward for the trustees of a fixed interest trust.

31.13.3 Would it save tax if a discretionary trust were converted into a fixed interest trust?

From an income tax perspective, the important thing is that income is regularly distributed to beneficiaries who are able to recover some or all of the tax. Creating an interest in possession could have a similar effect in that the trustees would not be required to pay tax at the rate applicable to trusts so that less tax would be withheld in the first place.

Tax notes

Now the rate of income tax applicable to trusts has increased to 50%, it will probably make sense to convert smaller discretionary trusts into fixed interest trusts ('smaller' in this context meaning a trust with less than £20,000 income).

31.13.4 Should assets be transferred to beneficiaries on a no gain/no loss basis?

This may be a good idea if the beneficiaries are able to use their annual exemptions to cover gains arising on the sale of the assets, or if they can utilise capital losses, or indeed if they plan to retain the assets. However, trustees need to be careful as they can be liable for tax on a held-over gain which becomes a chargeable gain if the beneficiary ceases to be resident (see 13.6).

Up to 22 June 2010, where trustees made a holdover election, and were entitled to ER, the 4/9ths reduction was deducted in arriving at the gain which was held over. This contrasted with the position for roll-over reliefs, where the gain is rolled over into the base cost of the new asset and ER may or may not apply on the eventual disposal of the new asset depending whether the conditions are met at that time. From 23 June 2010, entitlement to ER effectively means that a tax rate of 10% will apply to that portion of the gain.

31.13.5 Should a UK trust be exported?

Making a UK trust into a non-resident trust can precipitate a CGT exit charge (see 33.15). Also, it may not achieve very much if the settlor is going to be taxed on capital gains made by the non-resident trustees in the future (see 32.17). It may, however, make sense if the settlor has died or is elderly.

31.13.6 Should a discretionary trust be converted into a fixed interest trust before or after the IHT ten-year periodic charge?

It makes no difference. The changes in FA 2006 mean that there will be an exit charge only if capital is distributed outright as opposed to the trustees creating an interest in possession. Where the trustees create an interest in possession on or after 22 March 2006, the trust remains subject to the relevant property regime (see 31.5.13).

31.13.7 Should a discretionary trust make capital distributions before or after the ten-year charge?

There is no general rule here but the way in which the exit charge is computed means that the time that assets cease to be held on discretionary trusts can make a significant difference to the total tax payable (see 31.5.18–31.5.20).

31.13.8 Executors should take care

Suppose that the residuary legatees include a non-resident beneficiary or a charity that is exempt from CGT. If the executors sell a property they will be liable for CGT on any increase in value over probate value and the beneficiaries will receive their share of the amount left after tax. The beneficiaries cannot reclaim that tax. If the executors appropriate the property to the beneficiaries, the executors will have no capital gain. The beneficiaries will then be deemed to have acquired the property at probate value. Any gain on a sale will then be their gain, ie a non-taxable gain if the beneficiary is not subject to CGT.

32

PASSING ON YOUR FAMILY BUSINESS

There are many ways of passing on a share in a business, or transferring part of a business, to the next generation. And there are many tax aspects to be borne in mind, eg preserving relief for past trading losses, capital gains tax, inheritance tax and so on. Above all, the practical aspects need to be handled carefully. A factor for many proprietors is that they do not wish to relinquish control. This is why trusts often have an important role in enabling a person to hand over a business to his or her children.

This chapter contains the following sections:

(1) Basic strategy
(2) Setting up adult children in business
(3) Bringing an adult child into partnership
(4) Bringing an adult child into the family company
(5) Outright gifts of shares
(6) Why trusts are still often a suitable vehicle
(7) Demergers

32.1 BASIC STRATEGY

The most appropriate strategy will depend on your personal circumstances, objectives and the way that your assets are comprised. However, some principles recur time and time again when advising clients:

- The proper use of insurance policies and pension schemes can help to protect the family from any IHT charge that may arise in the short to medium term.
- Maximise the benefit of business property relief (BPR) and the facility to pay tax by instalments. Think twice about taking any action that would jeopardise these valuable reliefs.
- Draw up a Will in the most tax efficient way that is compatible with what the individual wishes to happen to his or her assets on death.
- The individual should take steps to secure his or her financial independence before making any substantial gifts.
- It may be better not to make outright gifts, especially while the individual is still making up his or her mind how to pass on the business. In some cases, the individual may prefer to set up his or her

children in business on their own account, possibly by lending them money. In other cases he or she may prefer to bring them into the business as partners.

- Look for ways of making gifts that will not involve substantial CGT liabilities.
- All other things being equal, it is best for the individual to make gifts sooner rather than later, especially if the business is growing in value.
- The individual will generally wish to retain some measure of control.

32.1.1 Proper use of insurance policies and pension schemes

For an individual in his or her 40s, who is still building up a business, it may be advisable to take out substantial joint survivor life insurance, which would pay out on the second death. Such policies should be written in trust so that the proceeds will not form part of the estate (see 30.12.3). Similarly, it will normally be advisable for the death benefits payable under a pension scheme to be subject to discretionary trusts so that they do not form part of the estate and no IHT charge is payable on them. The maximum amount payable as a death in service benefit from a company scheme is generally four times final remuneration and this would provide the family with the necessary liquidity in the event of an untimely death.

32.1.2 Maximise the benefit of BPR

Provided that it has been owned for at least two years, a trading business carried on by an individual as a sole trader or as a partner attracts 100% BPR. This relief is also due on shares in an unquoted trading company. There are also situations where 100% agricultural property relief is due on property that does not qualify for BPR. See 30.8 and 30.9 on BPR and agricultural property relief generally.

There are many situations where these reliefs can be lost or restricted. For example, giving shares in an unquoted trading company to a spouse or civil partner means that the person receiving the shares will have to hold them for two years before he or she qualifies for BPR (the position is different if he or she inherits the shares). Similarly, if an individual were to secure a bank loan by giving a charge against his or her shares, BPR will normally be due only on the net value after the loan has been deducted. Instead, consider securing borrowings against non-relieved assets, to reduce the value of the chargeable estate.

Bear in mind that 50% BPR is available to a controlling shareholder who owns a property that is used by his or her trading company, but no relief is due to minority shareholders. Once again, this rule means that BPR could be lost if a 51% shareholder were to transfer 2% of his or her shares to a spouse or civil partner.

Another potential trap applies if the individual has entered into buy/sell agreements with other shareholders. By entering into such an agreement, BPR may be forfeited because the shares will be subject to a binding contract for sale (see 30.8.1). Cross options are a better way of achieving the same commercial objectives without losing BPR.

Certain businesses do not qualify for either BPR or APR, eg a property investment business (see 30.8.3). However, such a business may still qualify for payment of IHT by instalments over ten years (see 30.11.14).

32.1.3 Draw up a Will in a tax-efficient way

Property left to a spouse or civil partner is exempt from IHT (unless the donor is domiciled in the UK and the donee spouse or civil partner is non-UK domiciled where only the limited £55,000 exemption applies). This exemption applies both to property passing to the survivor absolutely and to property left in a Will trust under which he or she has an interest in possession.

It would make sense from a tax perspective for assets that do not qualify for BPR to be left in a Will in such a way that the spouse/civil partner exemption applies. For example, the individual may have investment properties that do not qualify for BPR. One possibility would be for such assets to be left to the survivor and for him or her to then make gifts to the next generation. These may be outright gifts to individuals or gifts to a trust for bereaved minors given that gifts to other trusts may involve a lifetime IHT charge (see 31.4.23) although gifts that are covered by the survivor's nil rate band are still a viable option. Please note that there must be no arrangements or expectation that the survivor will make such gifts (s 29A IHTA 1984). No IHT will be payable on the survivor's death provided he or she does not die within seven years of making the gifts.

Where an individual owns assets that qualify for BPR, such as shares in a family company, it may be more appropriate for them to pass into a discretionary Will trust. This is because the assets will not then form part of the survivor's estate and so be vulnerable to IHT on his or her death if the business assets have been sold and the proceeds reinvested in other assets.

Tax notes

There can even be situations where a family can benefit from BPR twice. In many cases where shares in a family company have been left to a Will trust, it will pay for the survivor to buy the shares from the trustees, perhaps borrowing against other (non-relieved) assets to do so. You should consult a specialist on this but if you can arrange matters properly the survivor will qualify for BPR once he or she has owned the property for two years and the IHT exposure on other assets will be reduced by the borrowings secured against them.

32.1.4 Securing financial independence before making substantial gifts

A person who owns a business or shares in a private trading company would be well advised to create or ensure a separate source of income before giving away part of that business, etc. The creation and funding of a pension scheme should be a priority. Moreover, the fact that the company's profits are reduced by pension contributions may be a helpful factor in agreeing a low value for shares that are subsequently given away by the individual.

32.1.5 Would a loan be a better idea?

When the next generation are still in their 20s, parents may prefer to set them up in business on their own account rather than bringing them into the family firm. This may involve the individual making loans in a personal capacity, which will be entirely appropriate from a personal perspective but not particularly attractive from a tax point of view. Loans will not attract BPR if the lender were to die. Additionally, if the loan goes bad, the lender will not be entitled to income tax relief (but may qualify for CGT relief (see 17.1)).

Another possibility is for the family company to make a loan to the children but this may have income tax or corporation tax consequences (see for example 18.14.2 and s 455 CTA 2010). A half-way house that could work well in the right circumstances would be for the family company to inject working capital by subscribing for preference shares in a company formed by the child to carry on a business venture.

Yet another compromise is for the family company to establish a subsidiary that will carry on the son or daughter's new business. We go into these issues in more detail at 32.2.

32.1.6 Gifts that do not involve CGT

It does not make sense to give away assets to save IHT if the gift creates a substantial liability to CGT at 28%. It is therefore necessary to be selective about what is given to the next generation. There may be certain assets that would not give rise to a substantial CGT charge if given away, perhaps because they have been acquired relatively recently or are not standing at a substantial gain. Alternatively, it may be possible to rely on s 165 hold-over relief to avoid CGT being payable on gifts of business property and shares in unquoted trading companies. See 17.4 on hold-over relief.

32.1.7 Make gifts sooner rather than later

For many people, it is a question of competing priorities. They are anxious not to give away control of the business too early. This is understandable given the way in which the economic climate, personal relationships and the income and capital that they need can change so quickly. On the other hand, the sooner wealth is passed down to the next generation, the greater the potential saving in IHT. One reason for this is the seven-year rule for IHT (see 30.6). Also, in many cases the value of the business is likely to take off (perhaps a stock market flotation is planned in the next two or three years) and the amount taxed on a PET becoming a chargeable transfer on the donor's death is limited to the market value at the date of the gift.

32.1.8 Now may be a good time to make gifts

Given that company values are generally depressed in the current economic climate, now could prove to be an especially good time to make gifts, ie whilst values are low. If you can afford to make gifts now, the recovery in value which is expected to take place in the future will not form part of your estate for IHT purposes.

32.2 SETTING UP ADULT CHILDREN IN BUSINESS

As we have already touched upon, this may or may not involve bringing your son or daughter into the family firm. There are many situations where a son or daughter's business skills and mind-set mean that it makes more sense for him or her to set up his or her own business. But time and again, the problem is that he or she needs working capital.

32.2.1 Financing the child's unincorporated business

We have already covered the implications of a wealthy individual making a personal loan (see 32.1.5).

An alternative, which has much to commend it from a tax point of view, is for the adult child to form an LLP (see 7.5) and transfer his or her business to it. The parent could then become a member of the LLP in return for injecting capital. The parent need not be given any involvement in the management of the business or, indeed, in any share of the profits except for an amount corresponding to the interest that he or she would have received from making a loan.

The parent's interest in the LLP should rank as business property for IHT.

If the child's venture is unsuccessful, the parent's share of the LLP's trading losses can be set against his or her other taxable income (see 7.7), subject to the limitation on loss relief for non-active partners.

32.2.2 Financing the child's limited company

It may be that the child has already established a company. The business may have gone well to start with but now needs more substantial working capital.

One possibility is for a parent to give a bank guarantee for the company's borrowings. From a personal perspective, this seems to be the easiest option but often gives rise to major problems if and when the bank calls on the father or mother to honour the guarantee. This simply reflects the fact that most people who give guarantees never really face up to the possibility of having to part with money until it actually happens.

Where a person gives such a guarantee, is required to pay up and has lost the money, he or she can qualify for CGT relief (see 17.1). However, this is of no real benefit unless the person has capital gains.

In many cases, a more appropriate way of structuring the transactions would be for the parent to subscribe for new ordinary shares in his or her child's company (these can be non-voting shares if required, but remember, in that case, no entrepreneurs' relief would be due on an eventual sale). If the company's business fails, the parent will then be able to claim a capital loss on his or her shares and will generally be able to use this loss by setting it against his or her taxable income (see 17.2).

32.3 BRINGING AN ADULT CHILD INTO PARTNERSHIP

Moving on to another situation, suppose that the parent wishes to admit his or her son or daughter into partnership.

The section in Chapter 17 on partnerships and CGT (17.5) will be required reading in such a situation. However, the CGT aspects are manageable, especially as any deemed disposal of assets by the parent can normally be held-over under s 165 TCGA 1992 (see 17.4).

From a non-tax point of view, it may be a good idea for the new partnership to be an LLP as this will give the parties the benefit of limited liability given that a new and less experienced partner may make misjudgements that could damage the business.

It may also be advisable for certain assets (eg property) to be excluded from the partnership or LLP, with the parent continuing to own them in his or her personal capacity. Assets retained by a partner but used in the business will then attract only 50% BPR but it may be preferable to accept a lower rate of BPR rather than put those assets at risk.

32.4 BRINGING AN ADULT CHILD INTO THE FAMILY COMPANY

A child can become a director of the company without becoming a substantial shareholder (indeed, subject to the company's articles of association, he or she may not need to hold any shares at all).

In some situations, it may be advisable for the child to be a director of a subsidiary, especially where he or she is mainly involved in running the business of that subsidiary. He or she can always be appointed to the board of the parent company later, when it has become clear that the business relationship is going to work out as expected.

32.5 OUTRIGHT GIFTS OF SHARES

Sooner or later, the issue is likely to arise that the next generation who are involved in the business feel that they should own some of the equity.

The transfer of shares to the adult child ought not to fall within the employment related securities provisions (see Chapter 6) but the relevant legislation is drafted in such wide terms that the possibility should not be ignored. It is therefore always advisable to take professional advice in this situation.

If a parent transfers shares, he or she will be making a disposal for CGT purposes but hold-over relief should cover this (see 17.4) provided that the company does not have substantial investment activities.

32.6 WHY TRUSTS ARE STILL OFTEN A SUITABLE VEHICLE

32.6.1 Practical considerations

As we have already mentioned, many proprietors do not wish to relinquish control. This is one area where trusts are especially useful, particularly where the nil rate band or business property relief mean that little or no IHT is payable on their creation. For example, suppose that a parent who owns all the shares in a company wishes to give a 30% stake to each of his son and daughter. Making an outright gift will mean that he or she will then be a minority shareholder and his or her children will be able to outvote him or her on important business decisions. If he or she instead puts 60% of the shares into a trust for the benefit of the adult children, and he or she and/or his or her professional advisers are the trustees, the children can be given the desired stake in the equity without ceding control to them.

Trusts can also have important non-tax benefits. Suppose you and your son are in a partnership but you own the premises. You are planning to retire. You also have a daughter. You want to treat the children equally but you are not completely sure about your new son-in-law. You may therefore decide to put the premises into a trust for your two children so that your daughter may have an income without this affecting your son's security of tenure. This may be a more satisfactory compromise than giving the premises to your two children at the present time. This might, for example, lead to conflict if your daughter wishes to sell her half-share and your son cannot raise the capital to buy her out. Problems could also arise on an outright gift if your daughter goes through a divorce. Of course, the really important thing is to choose the right trustees.

Another situation where a trust comes into its own is if you want to divest yourself of shares, and so start the seven-year period running, but you are not sure how your children will work out. Perhaps your eldest son works in the company and you want to see how he shapes up before passing over control. Putting shares into a discretionary trust may be a very good way of reconciling conflicting objectives.

32.6.2 Tax issues around trusts

It is important to bear in mind the gifts with reservation legislation (see 30.7). Putting shares or other property into trust will not start the seven-year period running unless you are wholly excluded from benefiting under the trust.

An IHT charge may arise on a gift of shares into a trust if the property gifted does not qualify for business property relief (see 30.8) and the settlor's cumulative chargeable transfers exceed the nil rate band (see 30.10). On the other hand, CGT hold-over relief will generally be available, provided that the settlor, his or her spouse or civil partner, and the settlor's minor, unmarried children are excluded from benefiting under the trust (see 13.6).

32.6.3 An alternative to trusts

Some wealthy families are forming family limited partnerships or family investment companies. Typically, these structures allow older family members to retain control whilst the next generation participate in income and capital growth. There can be complications with using a partnership structure because of the FSA legislation which requires investment managers to be authorised. Going down this route may well be appropriate if your family's business assets do not qualify for IHT business property relief but you need to take specialist advice on this as it is very much a 'bespoke solution'. Another option is to use a family investment company (see 24.1.15) – once again, this is a bespoke solution and you will need to take professional advice to ensure that it meets your needs and fits your specific family circumstances.

32.7 DEMERGERS

It quite often happens that the founder's children carve out a niche for themselves in a particular section of the business. For example, a company may consist of three hotels and a daughter may run one of those hotels and have little to do with the others. It is possible for the daughter to carry out a demerger (see 9.8.8). This will involve the daughter in an exchange of her shares in the present company for 100% of the shares in a new company, which will own the hotel that she runs.

Another way of facilitating a parting of the ways may be for your company to buy back some of its shares (see 9.9.8).

The detailed aspects of such transactions are beyond the scope of this book. You should consult an accountant or solicitor if you wish to break up your family business in this way and pass part of that business down to the next generation.

PART 4

ANTI-AVOIDANCE LEGISLATION

This part contains the following chapter:

Each of the topics covered in this chapter is worthy of a book (or three) in its own right. Not only is the legislation complex, but over the years, a significant body of case law has built up in these areas. Of necessity, the treatment here is a quick overview, and not an in depth exploration of the subject matter; it should however hopefully highlight potential problem areas for which professional advice or further research – or both – is warranted.

33

ANTI-AVOIDANCE

Lord Clyde commented, in 1929, that:

> No man in this country is under the smallest obligation, moral or other, so to arrange his legal relations to his business or to his property as to enable the Inland Revenue to put the largest possible shovel into his stores. The Inland Revenue is not slow – and quite rightly – to take every advantage which is open to it under the taxing statutes for the purpose of depleting the taxpayer's pocket. And the taxpayer is, in like manner, entitled to be astute to prevent, so far as he honestly can, the depletion of his means by the Inland Revenue.

Seven years later, Lord Tomlin's dictum in the *Duke of Westminster* case made it clear that in his view, taxpayers were under no obligation to arrange their tax affairs in such a way that they maximised their tax liability:

> Every man is entitled if he can so order his affairs so that the tax attaching to them … is less than it otherwise would be. If he succeeds in ordering them so as to secure this result, then however unappreciative the Commissioners of the Inland Revenue or his fellow taxpayers may be of his ingenuity, he cannot be compelled to pay an increased tax.

Some 74 years later, the case law in this area has developed substantially. The courts have drawn a distinction between acceptable tax planning and unacceptably artificial avoidance, applying a purposive rather than the previous more restrictive, literal, interpretation of anti-avoidance legislation and in doing so, have sought to give effect to the assumption that Parliament – when deciding on new anti-avoidance measures – fully intends to catch a wide variety of avoidance devices.

Successive administrations have taken the view that the answer is more and more anti-avoidance legislation. Hence the fact that more than half of all UK tax legislation consists of specific anti-avoidance provisions. These anti-avoidance provisions must be borne in mind, especially when a tax planning exercise is being carried out. They are generally intended to ensure that a person cannot reduce his or her tax liability by carrying out a given transaction in a roundabout way.

The last Labour administration considered introducing a general anti-avoidance rule (GAAR), ie a rule that anything done purely for tax avoidance should be set aside by the courts, but drew back from this extreme remedy, due to the perceived complexity and doubts as to whether a GAAR has actually been helpful in the jurisdictions (such as Australia and Canada) that have implemented one. This vexed topic is however about to make a come-back (see below).

It should be remembered that, in any event, the courts have effectively introduced a kind of GAAR of their own, the *Ramsay* doctrine, and this must also be taken into account. Another weapon used by recent Governments is retrospective and retroactive legislation, ie moving the goal posts after the game has started.

Tackling tax avoidance

Tackling avoidance is very much at the forefront of people's minds in the current economic climate: in fact, the subject probably has a wider audience than ever before. It is therefore not surprising that a document was produced alongside the 2011 Budget setting out the future approach of HMRC and HM Treasury in tackling tax avoidance. It indicates that reviews will be undertaken of certain areas of the tax code which have seen repeated avoidance attacks over recent years. The first two areas to be reviewed, beginning in the summer of 2011, are income tax losses (and their relief against current and prior year income) and unauthorised unit trusts.

It is also proposed that action is taken to tackle the cash flow benefits that taxpayers can gain from using high-risk avoidance schemes despite the fact that HMRC may consider that the scheme does not work. The Government intends to bring forward proposals to list specific schemes through regulations. The users of those schemes will then be 'encouraged' to pay the disputed tax earlier than is currently required or will face an additional charge for late payment of the tax when it is found to be due. That is not however the end of it...

The coalition Government first floated the idea of implementing a GAAR in the UK in the June 2010 Budget. The Government's objectives for a GAAR are stated to be to:

- provide an effective means of deterring and countering tax avoidance;
- ensure that the rules work fairly without making the UK less attractive to international businesses;
- provide certainty about the tax treatment of transactions without undue costs for taxpayers or HMRC.

In December 2010, the Treasury announced the creation of a formal study group on the issue, headed by an eminent QC, which is to be tasked with preparing a report for the Treasury by the end of October 2011. The group will consider the scope and design of a possible GAAR so that it can be considered as part of the 2012 Budget process. However, there is to be further public consultation before any GAAR is introduced so any new rules are unlikely to take effect before 2013.

Of necessity, the discussion group will have to tackle many difficult and complex questions; for instance, should there be one over-arching GAAR, or should there be a mini-GAAR for each specific tax? If the latter, is this, or will this be, any different to the targeted anti-avoidance that already exists? Will existing anti-avoidance legislation be repealed, on the basis that the new GAAR adequately deals with avoidance activity in a particular area, thus simplifying the tax legislation (a laudable aim)? If not, is the complexity of different 'layers' of anti-avoidance such that there can be no realistic certainty as to the tax liability? For instance, could you meet the existing tests for a relief to apply (including not triggering any existing targeted avoidance measures) and still be susceptible to an over-arching GAAR? Is that a fair result, effectively giving HMRC two bites at the anti-avoidance cherry? Finally, and probably most telling from HMRC's point of view, will there be a fast, effective, pre-transaction clearance procedure, available to all taxpayers, and if so, how is this to be resourced?

Finally, you will notice that this chapter does not seek to discuss the new rules on disguised remuneration. These are sufficiently complex and wide-reaching to require a chapter of their own and details can be found in Chapter 5.

This chapter contains the following sections:

Income tax

(1) Interest income
(2) Transactions in land
(3) Transactions in securities
(4) Transfer of assets abroad
(5) Trust income taxed on the settlor
(6) Transactions involving loans or credit
(7) Pre-owned assets

Capital gains tax

(8) Bed and breakfast transactions
(9) Disposals by a series of transactions
(10) Transfers to a connected person
(11) Qualifying corporate bonds
(12) Value shifting
(13) Trusts and main residence exemption
(14) UK-resident settlements where the settlor has retained an interest
(15) Deemed disposal when a trust ceases to be resident
(16) Offshore companies
(17) Non-resident trusts

Inheritance tax

(18) Purchased interests in excluded property settlements

General

(19) *Ramsay* principle
(20) Disclosure of tax avoidance schemes
(21) Specific income tax avoidance schemes that have been blocked

INCOME TAX

33.1 INTEREST INCOME

33.1.1 Background

The Taxes Acts contain extensive legislation that is designed to prevent the conversion of taxable income into capital.

33.1.2 Sale of loan stock with right to purchase

(ss 581, 922, 923, 925 ITA 2007)

At one time it was possible to enjoy the benefit of income in a capital form that was not subject to tax by selling loan stock or other interest-bearing securities and retaining a right to repurchase them. For example, a person holding £1m 3½% War Loan stock could sell the stock to a charity for £400,000 cum-interest while retaining the right to repurchase the stock once it had gone ex-interest for, say, £385,000 – an overall profit of £15,000. He or she had to forgo the income of £17,500 but that was taxable and worth less than £15,000. The charity, meanwhile, got the income free of tax.

There is now specific legislation designed to catch such arrangements. Using the above example, the legislation on repo contracts means that the person would be subject to income tax on the £15,000 profit or 'differential'.

33.1.3 Sale of right to income

(ss 443–452G ITTOIA 2005)

A variation on the above scheme worked for a number of years. It was common for individuals to sell to a charity or other exempt body the right to receive interest payments for a specified period of time, while retaining legal ownership of the securities themselves. This is now caught by ss 443–452G ITTOIA 2005. If the loan stock is a UK security, the arising income is assessed on the vendor. If it is a foreign loan stock, the sale proceeds are assessable as if they were income.

33.1.4 Manufactured dividends

Manufactured payments arise during a stock loan or repo transaction. They involve the person who currently holds the securities paying over to the original owner an amount equal to dividends or interest received. Individuals could deduct such payments from their total income for tax purposes. FA 2002 introduced anti-avoidance provisions, now in ss 573–577 ITA 2007, to counter perceived abuses. This is a specialised area and those affected will no doubt already be aware of the changes and should have taken professional advice.

33.2 TRANSACTIONS IN LAND

(s 756 ITA 2007)

33.2.1 Introduction

Section 756 is intended to prevent tax avoidance by persons concerned with land or development of land. It may apply where a capital gain is realised and one of the following conditions applies:

(1) The gain arises from UK land (or some other asset deriving its value from land) and the land was acquired with the sole or main object of realising a gain.
(2) The gain arises from the disposal of UK land held as trading stock.
(3) The gain arises from a disposal of UK land that has been developed with the sole or main object of realising a gain on its disposal.

Where s 756 applies, all or part of the capital gain is charged as income.

The definition of land includes buildings and assets deriving their value from land (eg options). Consequently, s 756 could apply if a person received a lump sum for assigning the benefit of an option.

33.2.2 Exemption

There is an exemption from s 756 for gains that arise on the disposal of an individual's principal private residence. This exemption continues to be available even where the CGT exemption is not due because the property was acquired with a view to realising a gain (see 14.2.3).

33.2.3 Sales of shares

Section 756 may also apply where a person disposes of shares in a land-owning company. If a non-resident individual were to dispose of, say, a controlling shareholding in a company that itself owned a valuable UK property, he or she might be subject to income tax on the whole of his or her capital gain.

There is a let-out in the case of a land-owning company that holds land as trading stock (ie a company that is a builder or developer or deals in land as a trade). No liability arises under s 756 on a sale of shares in such a company, provided the land held by the company is disposed of in the normal course of its trade and a full commercial profit from that land is received by the company.

Despite this let-out, s 756 may still be a problem on a sale of a land-owning company since the company may be an investment company (in which case it will not hold the land as trading stock).

33.2.4 Clearance procedure

It is possible to apply for advance clearance from HMRC that s 756 will not apply to a particular disposal. This clearance may be sought either for a sale of land or of shares in a land-owning company. The legislation requires the applicant to supply full written particulars to HMRC who must then give a decision within 30 days. Once clearance is given, HMRC cannot subsequently charge tax under s 756 unless the clearance application was invalid because it did not accurately set out all the facts.

33.3 TRANSACTIONS IN SECURITIES

(ss 682–713 ITA 2007; ss 731–751 CTA 2010)

33.3.1 Introduction

Legislation was introduced in 1960 to enable HMRC to counteract tax advantages obtained by transactions in securities. At the time, CGT did not exist, and following its introduction in 1965, the differential between rates of tax on income and rates of tax on gains was considerable (as it is today), therefore supplying a huge incentive for taxpayers to seek to realise gains rather than income. The legislation was often applied by HMRC to prevent tax savings being achieved because a right to income has been converted into a capital gain. The provisions were less frequently used during periods when the incentive to realise gains was less, but in recent years, there have been four cases involving individuals, demonstrating that HMRC is taking a new interest in these rules as a tool in its arsenal. An example of the type of transaction that may be caught in this way is where a person sells shares with a right to repurchase them for a lower amount after a dividend has been received by the purchaser. The legislation also applies to more devious types of transactions where the tax advantage is less obvious at first sight.

33.3.2 Conditions to be satisfied before legislation can apply

The rules changed in FA (No.1) 2010 for transactions in securities on or after 24 March 2010, but it will still be necessary to consider transactions which occurred under the previous rules for some time to come.

For s 682 (s 731 for companies) to apply, the following conditions need be satisfied:

- there must be one or more transactions in securities to which the person is a party; and
- a person must have obtained, or be in a position to obtain, a tax advantage; and
- one of the prescribed circumstances set out in s 685 must have occurred.

If the legislation does apply, an income tax (or corporation tax) assessment may be made to counteract the tax advantage.

33.3.3 The term 'transactions in securities'

This term is widely defined to include transactions of whatever description relating to securities. It includes in particular:

- the purchase, sale or exchange of securities;
- the issuing of new securities;
- alteration of rights attaching to securities.

'Securities' is, in turn, defined as including shares and loan stock.

33.3.4 Tax advantage

In general, a tax advantage is deemed to arise if there is any increased relief, or repayment of tax, arising from transactions in securities, or if the transactions result in a reduction in the amount of tax that would otherwise be assessed. The courts have taken the view that a tax advantage may arise wherever HMRC can show that an amount received in a non-taxable form could have been received in a way that would have given rise to an income tax liability. Going back to the example given in 33.3.1, HMRC would say that a tax advantage arises when a person sells shares and has a right to buy back at a lower price after a dividend has been paid because he or she could simply have retained the shares and received the dividend.

> **Tax notes**
>
> A tax advantage is deemed to arise if a transaction in securities results in a reduction in the amount of tax that would otherwise be assessed.

See the recent case of *Trevor G Lloyd* v *HMRC* SpC 672 on the meaning of 'tax advantage'. Other relevant, recent, cases include *Snell* (2008 – SpC 699), *Ebsworth* (2009 – TC 00152) and *Grogan* (2009 –TC 00187).

33.3.5 The 'old' rules

Prior to FA 2008, s 684 listed five circumstances, of which at least one had to apply before HMRC could invoke s 682. These were:

- circumstance A: abnormal dividends used for exemptions or reliefs – s 686;
- circumstance B: entitlement to deduction in computing profits by reason of fall in value of securities resulting from the payment of a dividend – repealed by FA 2008;
- circumstance C: receipt of consideration representing company's assets, future receipts or trading stock – s 688;
- circumstance D: receipt of consideration in connection with relevant company distribution – s 689; and
- circumstance E: receipt of assets of relevant company – s 690.

Circumstances A and E are special situations that are outside the scope of this book; circumstance B was removed by FA 2008. The remaining two are as follows.

Section 688 ITA 2007 – circumstance C

This applied where a person received consideration without paying income tax on it as a result of a transaction whereby another person subsequently received an abnormal amount by way of dividend. The consideration received must have represented:

- the value of assets available for distribution by way of dividends; or
- future receipts of the company; or
- the value of trading stock of the company.

Section 689 ITA 2007 – circumstance D

This subsection applied where a person received consideration that was not subject to tax and represented:

- the value of assets available for distribution by way of dividends; or
- future receipts of the company; or
- the value of the trading stock of the company.

Section 689 could apply only to transactions involving specified companies, ie:

- companies that were under the control of not more than five persons; or
- transactions involving any other unquoted company.

33.3.6 The 'new' rules

FA (No.1) 2010 fundamentally rewrote the transactions in securities rules for circumstances C, D and E (and removed circumstance A), substituting new ss 682–687 for the old ss 682–694 ITA 2007. In addition, minor modifications were made to s 695 *et seq.*, albeit the procedural aspects remain broadly similar.

On 3 March 2010, CTA 2010 (which contains the equivalent provisions relating to companies at ss 733–751) was enacted, with provisions relating to circumstances C (s 736), D (s 737) and E (s 738) imported from s 704 ICTA 1988, which had been modified following the enactment of ITA 2007 so that it applied only to companies. Circumstance A (s 735) was repealed for companies with effect from 24 March 2010.

The new legislation for individuals is a targeted anti-avoidance provision aimed at transactions in securities of close companies, which are made with the intention of obtaining a tax advantage. In addition, the updated legislation applies to non-UK resident companies that would have been close if they had been UK resident (s 713). The rules do not apply where, as a result of the transaction, there has been a fundamental change (at least 75%) in ownership.

Section 682 ITA 2007 (s 731 for companies) now provides an overview of the chapter. Section 683 (s 732 for companies) explains what each of the following sections deals with. Section 684 identifies the individuals (s 733 for companies) liable to counteraction of a tax advantage, where the person is a party to a transaction where the circumstances are covered by s 685 but not excluded by s 686. For companies, the foregoing analysis of circumstances C and D (see the 'old' rules above) remains relevant.

Section 685 sets out new conditions where a person is in receipt of consideration in connection with a distribution by, or assets of, a close company:

- Condition A is that, as a result of the transaction in securities or any one or more of the transactions in securities, the person receives relevant consideration in connection with the distribution, transfer or realisation of assets of a close company, or the application of assets of a close company in discharge of liabilities, or the direct or indirect transfer of assets of one close company to another close company, and does not pay or bear income tax on the consideration (apart from under these provisions).
- Condition B is that the person receives relevant consideration in connection with the transaction in securities or any one or more of the transactions in securities, or two or more close companies are involved in the transaction or transactions in securities concerned, and the person does not pay or bear income tax on the consideration (apart from under these provisions).

'Relevant consideration' means consideration which:

- is or represents the value of assets that are available for distribution by way of dividend by the company, or
- is or represents the value of assets which would have been so available apart from anything done by the company, or
- is received in respect of future receipts of the company, or
- is or represents the value of trading stock of the company.

33.3.7 Exemption for fundamental changes in ownership

A person is not caught by these rules if, immediately before the transaction in securities, the person holds shares or an interest in shares in the close company, and there is a fundamental change of ownership of the close company.

There is a fundamental change of ownership of the close company if as a result of the transaction in securities, the following conditions are met, and continue to be met for a period of two years.

Condition A is that at least 75% of the ordinary share capital of the close company is held beneficially by a person who is not connected with the original owner and has not been so connected within the period of two years ending with the day on which the transaction in securities takes place, or persons none of whom is so connected or has been so connected within that period.

Condition B is that shares in the close company held by that person or persons carry an entitlement to at least 75% of the distributions which may be made by the company.

Condition C is that shares so held carry at least 75% of the total voting rights in the close company.

33.3.8 Exemption for bona fide commercial transactions

Previously, if there was a transaction in securities and the prescribed circumstances applied, a taxpayer might still have avoided assessment if he, she or it could show that the transactions were carried out for bona fide commercial reasons or in the ordinary course of making or managing investments, and that none of them had as one of their main objects the obtaining of a tax advantage. This provision has been removed for individuals, as a result of the FA (No.1) 2010 changes, but is retained for companies in s 734 CTA 2010.

33.3.9 Clearances

Section 701 ITA 2007 (s 748 for companies; see also SP3/80) provides a procedure whereby a person can give details of the proposed transactions to HMRC and request clearance that the Board will not apply s 682.

Once a written application has been made under s 701, HMRC has 30 days in which to request more particulars, which must then be provided within 30 days.

HMRC must give a decision either within 30 days of receiving the original application or within 30 days of receiving the further particulars.

Where HMRC has notified someone that it is satisfied that s 682 should not apply, it may not subsequently change its mind. Where information given in the application is incomplete or inaccurate, any clearance given by HMRC may be void.

33.3.10 Situations where clearance should be sought

It is standard practice for vendors or their advisers to seek clearance under s 701 where a private company is being sold for a substantial amount. Quite apart from anything else, the vendor would otherwise be at the mercy of the purchaser who might extract an abnormal dividend and thus bring s 682 into consideration.

It is also advisable to seek clearance under s 701 where a company is liquidated, the reserves are extracted in a capital form and it is intended that the company's business should be carried on by a new company owned by the current shareholders.

33.4 TRANSFER OF ASSETS ABROAD

Legislation was introduced in 1936 to prevent tax savings for UK-resident and ordinarily resident individuals arising from their transferring assets overseas. The legislation refers to avoidance of income tax. Capital tax avoidance is not subject to counteraction by ss 714–723 ITA 2007, although separate anti-avoidance legislation also exists for CGT (see 33.21).

33.4.1 Where the individual or spouse can benefit

Section 714 applies where a UK-resident has made a transfer of assets and either he or she or his or her spouse or civil partner may benefit as a result of it. He or she is deemed to meet this test if he or she has 'power to enjoy' income that arises overseas. Power to enjoy income exists in the following circumstances:

- The income accrues for his or her benefit.
- The receipt of the income increases the value to him or her of any assets held by him or her or for his or her benefit.
- He or she may become entitled to enjoy the income in the future.
- He or she is able in any way whatsoever, and whether directly or indirectly, to control the way the income is used.

Where s 714 applies, the transferor or his or her spouse or civil partner is assessed on the income as it arises, even if it is not actually paid out to them.

33.4.2 Exemption for bona fide transactions

Section 737 ITA 2007 contains a clearance procedure. Under the original rules, the individual used to have to show to HMRC's satisfaction that:

- the purpose of avoiding tax was not one of the purposes for which the transfer of assets was carried out; or
- the transfer of assets, and any associated operations, were bona fide commercial transactions and not designed for tax avoidance.

In *Carvill* v *IRC* SpC 233, the Special Commissioners held that the test was a subjective, and not an objective, one. The taxpayer also succeeded in the case of *Beneficiary* v *IRC* where a Japanese individual who was not resident in the UK established an offshore trust for the benefit of his daughter who was not capable of managing her own finances (this was a case where HMRC sought tax under s 732 ITA 2007 (see 33.4.5 below) rather than s 714).

Unfortunately, many of the successes achieved by taxpayers have been reversed by legislation introduced in FA 2006. The requirements for exemption have been reinforced in relation to income arising on or after 5 December 2005 and the exemption is now dependent upon HMRC or, on appeal, the First-tier Tribunal, being satisfied that one of two conditions are satisfied. These conditions are:

- it would not be reasonable to infer from all the circumstances of the case that avoiding tax was the purpose, or one of the purposes, for which the relevant transactions were effected;
- all the relevant transactions were genuine commercial transactions and it would not be reasonable to infer from all the circumstances of the case that any one or more of those transactions was more than incidentally designed for the purpose of avoiding tax.

A relevant transaction is a commercial transaction only if it is effected in the course of a trade or business or with a view to setting up a business.

A transaction is commercial only if it is made on arm's length terms and is a transaction that would have been entered into by independent persons dealing at arm's length, eg a loan will not be commercial even if it carries a commercial rate of interest if no arm's length lender would have made a loan of that amount.

Section 737 ITA 2007 specifies that the intentions and purposes of professional advisers may be taken into account as well as the transferor's own objectives. This is likely to make the test more 'objective', ie it is not sufficient to look at the transferor's intentions in a subjective way.

In practice, it is always going to be extremely difficult to satisfy HMRC that the re-stated conditions are satisfied.

33.4.3 Transfer of assets by non-residents

HMRC's view has always been that s 714 ITA 2007 could apply to income arising from a transfer of assets made by an individual at a time when he or she was not UK-resident. The House of Lords found against HMRC on this in *IRC* v *Willoughby* [1997] STC 995, but FA 1997 restored the position to what HMRC always believed to be the case in relation to income arising on or after 26 November 1996.

33.4.4 Assessment of income caught by s 714 ITA 2007

Income caught by s 714 is normally taxed as miscellaneous investment income. Where it is UK dividend income or other income that has borne tax at source, relief is given for such tax and the assessment will be for higher rate tax purposes only.

33.4.5 Liability of non-transferors

(s 732 ITA 2007)

A person may not be assessed under s 714 unless he or she, or his or her spouse or civil partner, has made a transfer of assets. However, a UK-ordinarily resident individual may be assessed under s 732 if he or she receives a benefit from a transfer made by another person. This applies particularly to beneficiaries of non-resident settlements created by someone other than the individual and/or his or her spouse or civil partner. It is also arguable that s 732 might apply to a person who had made a transfer of assets but was not 'caught' by s 714, perhaps because he or she was not resident at the time of the transfer.

In contrast to s 714, a liability may arise under s 732 only when the individual concerned receives a benefit. 'Benefit' is not specifically defined, although the legislation states it includes a payment of any kind. It is understood that HMRC regards an interest-free loan or the provision of accommodation as constituting a benefit.

This is an area where professional advice is essential.

33.4.6 Matching income with benefits

The legislation allows benefits to be matched with income received in either earlier or later years.

Example – Matching benefits

> An overseas trust receives income of £10,000 in 1994–95. In 2002–03 a capital payment of £100,000 is made to a UK-resident and ordinarily resident individual. In the year 2011–12, the trustees received further income of £120,000. If s 732 applies, the individual will be taxed as follows:
>
> | | £ |
> |---|---|
> | 2002–03 | 10,000 |
> | 2011–12 | 90,000 |

33.4.7 An interest-free loan may constitute a benefit

The High Court decided in January 2000 in *Billingham* v *Cooper* [2000] STC 122 that an interest-free loan that was repayable on demand gave rise to a benefit equal to interest at the 'official rate'.

33.4.8 Assessment under s 732

Where income is taxed under s 732, there is no credit for any UK tax suffered at source. This can give rise to double taxation. Thus, going back to the previous example, if the trustees' income represented interest from UK companies, the total tax suffered would really be as follows:

	£
Tax at source on interest: £100,000 × $^{20}/_{80}$ =	25,000
Tax charged on beneficiary under s 732 =	40,000
	65,000

33.4.9 Clearances

Once again, it is possible to obtain clearance from HMRC that s 732 should not apply because the transfer of assets concerned was not carried out for tax avoidance purposes.

33.4.10 Foreign domiciliaries

Where the income arising to the non-resident trust or company is foreign source income, no liability arises for a foreign-domiciled individual who elects for the remittance basis to apply, except to the extent that he or she remits such income to the UK (see 35.10). However, the individual may need to pay a £30,000 (or in some cases, from 2012, £50,000) remittance basis charge to obtain the benefit of the remittance basis (see 35.2).

33.4.11 Reporting income taxable under s 714 or s 732

Question 5 on page 2 of the tax return asks, among other things:

Have you, or could you have, received (directly or indirectly) income, or received a capital payment or benefit, from a person abroad as a result of any transfer of assets?

If you tick the 'yes box', you will be required to complete the Foreign pages.

Other overseas income and gains

41	Gains on disposals of holdings in offshore funds (excluding the amounts entered in box 13) and discretionary income from non-resident trusts – *enter the amount of the gain or payment*		44	Number of years
	£			
			45	Tax treated as paid – *read page FN 17 of the notes*
42	If you have received a benefit from a person abroad, enter the value or payment received – *if you are omitting income from this section because you are claiming an exemption, see box 46*			£
			46	If you have omitted income from boxes 11, 13 and 42 because you are claiming an exemption in relation to a transfer of assets, enter the total amount omitted (and give full details in the 'Any other information' box on your tax return)
	£			
43	Gains on foreign life insurance policies, etc. (excluding the amounts entered in box 13) – *enter the amount of the gain*			£
	£			

Extracts from HMRC notes to the tax return

The notes to the Foreign pages state:

Where:

● you have transferred, or taken any part in the transfer of assets, as a result of which income has become payable to a person abroad, or
● someone else has transferred, or taken any part in the transfer of assets, as a result of which income has become payable to a person abroad, and you have received a benefit as a result of the relevant transactions
● then Help Sheet 262 will help you decide if any income should be included on the *foreign pages*. A person abroad includes an individual, the trustees of a settlement, a company, or any other person.

(In notes to previous years' tax returns, HMRC stated that 'benefits' include, for example, loans at less than a commercial rate of interest and the occupation or use of property at less than a commercial rent, the value of the benefit being the difference between the commercial rate of interest or rental and any amount actually paid by you.)

HS262: How do you qualify for an exemption from charge on income or benefits?

Income or benefits may be excluded from charge under these provisions if you can show from all the circumstances of the case that the purpose of avoiding liability to taxation was not the purpose, or one of the purposes, for which the relevant transactions, or any of them, were effected. But if you omit income for this reason from boxes 11, 13 and 42, you must enter the total amount of income you have omitted in box 46, and provide relevant details and an explanation in the 'Any other information' box on your tax return, including details of the assets transferred and any associated operations, the persons abroad concerned, the circumstances of the relevant transactions and the basis of your claim to exclusion.

Source: HMRC

33.5   TRUST INCOME TAXED ON THE SETTLOR

33.5.1 Introduction

There are several provisions under which income on property that belongs to trustees may be taxed as if it were income that belonged to the settlor.

33.5.2 Trust where settlor may benefit

(s 624 ITTOIA 2005)

Legislation may catch income that arises to a trust under which the settlor or his or her spouse or civil partner may benefit (a 'settlor-interested trust'). The legislation provides that the settlor should be treated as capable of benefiting where he or she may benefit in any circumstances whatsoever except in one of the following exceptional cases:

- The bankruptcy of a person who is beneficially entitled under the settlement.
- The death under age 25 of a person who would be beneficially entitled to the trust property on attaining that age.
- In the case of a marriage settlement, the death of both parties to the marriage and of all or any of the children of the marriage.

HMRC interprets this legislation rather literally. For example, if a person creates a trust for the benefit of his or her son, and the trust deed states that the property should revert to the settlor if the son dies before age 35, HMRC takes the view that s 624 applies because the let-out applies only where property reverts on the death of someone before he or she attains age 25.

Sometimes the trust deed is silent on a matter. For example, a person creates a trust for the benefit of his or her three children and the deed makes no reference to the capital coming back to the settlor. In such circumstances, HMRC is apt to say that the property could revert to the settlor if all his or her children died and they left no children of their own. To avoid this kind of argument, it is normal for a trust to contain a clause that provides the capital shall in no circumstances whatsoever come back to the settlor but shall be held for the benefit of, say, a charity in the event that all the named beneficiaries die before the capital is distributed (the charity is often referred to as the 'longstop' beneficiary).

HMRC does not take the view that a person has reserved the benefit simply because his or her spouse or civil partner may benefit after his or her death as his or her survivor. On the other hand, cases have actually arisen where the settlor and his or her spouse were excluded but HMRC said that s 624 should apply because the settlor's current marriage might come to an end and he or she might marry or enter into civil partnership with someone who *could* benefit. Once again, it is best to make sure that the trust deed excludes such an interpretation by expressly providing that any present or future spouse or civil partner of the settlor should be excluded from all benefit, except after the settlor's death.

Where a settlor's spouse or civil partner can benefit, during the settlor's lifetime, the settlor is assessed on the trust income.

FA 2000 introduced a concession, now in s 628 ITTOIA 2005, for UK settlements. Where a settlor is not totally excluded but one of the beneficiaries under the trust is a charity, income arising after 5 April 2000 that is actually paid out to the charity will not be assessable on the settlor under s 624.

33.5.3 Settlements where the property given is just a right to income

(s 624 ITTOIA 2005)

The legislation contains a very wide definition of 'settlement'. It can even apply to an outright gift where the property given is 'wholly or substantially' a right to income. It can also apply where there is no gift at all but there are arrangements that amount to a settlement, such as might apply where an individual lets someone else subscribe for shares in a new company.

HMRC's arguments do seem to have a certain 'seasonality'. In the early 1990s, Inspectors often tried to apply these provisions where an individual had admitted his or her spouse into partnership. The argument was that this was uncommercial and the partnership's profits should be assessed on the spouse who contributed most to the business (and invariably paid tax at a higher rate). But as HMRC met dogged resistance from tax accountants these arguments largely ceased, albeit without HMRC ever conceding that the principle was incorrect.

In 2003, these arguments resurfaced in the context of small companies. HMRC argued that where one spouse was the main contributor to the company's profits, s 624 allowed HMRC to treat dividends paid to the other spouse as the first spouse's income. HMRC said tax avoidance arose from 'income-splitting'.

HMRC set out its views in the April 2003 and February 2004 editions of *Tax Bulletin (nos. 64 and 69 – see also IRInt.258)*. The February 2004 edition contains examples of circumstances where HMRC believed that s 624 was applicable. HMRC initially succeeded before the High Court in *Jones* v *Garnett* (often referred to as the *Arctic Systems Limited* case) but lost before the Court of Appeal and the House of Lords. The Government intended to reverse the decision of the House of Lords by bringing in specific legislation to counter 'income-splitting'. This was to feature in FA 2009 and take effect from 2009–10, but this proposal was deferred indefinitely following representations by professional bodies, accountants and advisers and it remains to be seen to what extent it will be revived under the new administration.

Also, bear in mind s 624 if you are entering into a dividend waiver. Again, see the *Tax Bulletin* articles for guidance on HMRC's position.

Section 836 ITA 2007 contains a specific provision regarding jointly-owned shares in private companies. The gist of this provision is that if s 624 were considered applicable, the normal rule that governs dividends from shares which are jointly owned by husband and wife is disapplied.

33.5.4 Settlements on minor children

(s 629 ITTOIA 2005)

Where a person gives capital to his or her minor children, the resulting income may be taxed as if it belonged to the parent. This treatment applies where the following three conditions are satisfied:

- The child is a minor.
- The child is unmarried (and not in a registered civil partnership).
- The income exceeds £100 per tax year for each child.

Similarly when a person makes a settlement under which his or her minor children may benefit, income distributed to the children before they attain age 18 is treated as the settlor's income (subject to the £100 *de minimis* exemption). This applies even where he or she is separated or divorced and the children live with his or her former spouse or civil partner.

For s 629 purposes, 'child' includes an adopted child and an illegitimate child. Again, HMRC interprets this legislation strictly and has even been known to tax a grandfather who set up a trust for his daughter's (illegitimate) child whom he subsequently adopted and brought up as his own.

There are two circumstances where s 629 does not apply:

- where the child has married;
- where the settlor is not resident in the UK.

The legislation does not stop here. Any capital payments made to the children are also caught so far as the capital payments may be matched with accumulated income within the trust. Since the trustees will normally pay tax at 50% (42.5% on dividends), this may mean that the settlor can claim a tax refund. However amendments to s 646 ITTOIA 2005 in FA (No.1) 2010 mean that the settlor must repay any tax repaid to him or her by HMRC, to the trustees.

Tax notes

HMRC has been known to tax a grandfather who set up a trust for his daughter's (illegitimate) child whom he subsequently adopted and brought up as his own.

Roll-up funds

A way that remains open for achieving a tax saving may be for a parent to give capital to a minor child, with the money being invested in a roll-up fund or some other investment that does not produce taxable income. If the roll-up fund is cashed in shortly after the child's 18th birthday, the income counts as the child's income, and not the parent's. This may be a good strategy where a child is unlikely to have much income in his or her own right, perhaps because he or she will be in full-time education during the year in which he or she attains age 18.

Insurance bonds

Another way of achieving a tax saving is for a parent to invest in single-premium insurance bonds.

Tax notes

One way of saving tax may be for a parent to give capital to a minor child, with the money being invested in a roll-up fund or some other investment that does not produce taxable income.

33.5.5 Capital payments to settlor

(s 633 ITTOIA 2005)

Section 633 may apply to enable HMRC to charge tax on income received by the trustees of the settlement under which the settlor and his or her spouse or civil partner are totally excluded from benefit, in situations where the trustees of the settlement have accumulated income and make a capital payment to the settlor. The capital payment is then treated as if it were income for the year in which the payment was made provided there is sufficient undistributed income.

If only part of the capital payment can be 'matched', the balance is matched with income for subsequent years (up to a maximum of ten), and amounts matched in this way are then taxable on the settlor for those years.

Example – Matching of capital payments

In 2003–04 *A* received a capital payment of £50,000. The trustees had undistributed income for that year of £20,000. The trustees made no further capital repayments but in 2006–07 and 2012–13 they have undistributed income of £10,000 and £8,000 (after tax). The following amounts are taxable under s 633:

			£
1999–00	£18,000 grossed up	=	27,272
2003–04	£32,000[1] grossed up	=	48,484
2006–07	£10,000[2] grossed up	=	16,667
2012–13	£8,000[3] grossed up	=	16,000

[1] including the balance of the undistributed income available at the end of 1999–00 grossed up for 34% tax.

[2] grossed up for 40% tax

[3] grossed up for 50% tax

Section 633 can also apply to capital payments from non-resident trusts. The tax payable may be greater in such cases because the undistributed income might not have suffered tax at the rate applicable to trusts.

33.5.6 Income may be matched with capital payments made in previous 12 years

Undistributed income can be identified with past capital payments for up to 12 years. The only way to get round this is for the whole of the capital sum to be repaid by the settlor, but even doing this does not affect the position for past years and the year in which the capital sum is repaid.

33.5.7 Loans may also be caught

A loan from the trustees to the settlor or spouse may be treated under s 633 as if it were a capital payment. Furthermore, the repayment of a loan made by the settlor to the trust can also be treated as a capital payment.

Example – treatment of loans

> In 1999–00 B made a £150,000 loan to a trust she had created. The trustees repaid the loan in full during 2006–07. At that time, the trustees had undistributed income of £45,000 (ie this was the net income retained after 40% tax). B was taxed under s 677 ICTA 1988 (now s 633) on £45,000 grossed up at 40%, ie £75,000.
>
> If the trustees had undistributed income of £30,000 for 2008–09 and £85,000 for 2012–13 (in both cases after tax), assessments would be made on £30,000 grossed up for 2008–09 and £75,000 grossed up for the year 2012–13.

33.5.8 Payments by companies connected with trustees

A liability could also arise under s 633 if a company connected with the trustees makes a capital payment to the settlor. Three conditions must be met:

(1) The trustees must have undistributed income.
(2) There must be 'associated payments' by the trustees to the company. An associated payment may include a capital payment (eg a subscription for shares) or the transfer of assets at an undervalue by the trustees to the company.
(3) The company must make a capital payment to the settlor, or make a loan to him or her or repay a loan made by the settlor to the company. For loans, this must occur within five years of the associated payment taking place.

33.6 TRANSACTIONS INVOLVING LOANS OR CREDIT

(ss 809CZA–809CZC ITA 2007 for individuals; ss 777–779 CTA 2010
for companies)

Specific legislation exists to prevent any tax avoidance that could otherwise arise if a person who was liable to pay non-allowable interest found a way of converting his, her or its liability to pay interest into some other payment that was tax deductible. Sections 809CZA–809CZC and ss 777–779 may apply where a transaction is effected with reference to money-lending. It can apply whether the transaction is between the lender and borrower or involves other persons connected with them.

(1) Section 809CZB (s 778 for companies) states that if the transaction provides for payment of any annuity or other annual payment it shall be treated as interest for all purposes of the Taxes Acts.

(2) Section 809CZC (s 779 for companies) states that if the borrower agrees to sell or transfer to the lender any securities or other property carrying a right to income, the borrower may be charged income tax on an amount equal to the income that arises from the property before the borrower repays the loan.

(3) Section 809CZC(4) (s 779(4) for companies) refers to income being assigned, surrendered, waived or forgone and states that the person who has assigned, surrendered, etc may be charged to tax on the amount of income assigned, surrendered, etc.

In theory, ss 809CZA–809CZC and ss 777–779 could apply to interest-free loans. HMRC has given some degree of comfort in that it has said that in the straightforward situation where one person lends money to another and then waives the interest, and there is no further transaction linked in any way to the arrangements, this anti-avoidance will not be invoked. There has been some concern in the past that these rules could apply where, for example, a client deposited a large lump sum with his, her or its accountant on the basis that the accountant would not pay interest but would reduce his or her accountancy fees by the amount of interest that would have been paid at commercial rates on the client's deposit. It is possible to read s 809CZC(5) (or s 779(5)) as permitting HMRC to make an assessment in this way even though the type of transactions described are somewhat different from those envisaged when the legislation was enacted.

33.7 PRE-OWNED ASSETS

The Government announced in December 2003 that it proposed to impose an annual income tax charge from 2005–06 where individuals had transferred assets but continued to enjoy benefits. It justified this charge as being aimed at individuals who had used artificial schemes to avoid the IHT legislation that catches gifts with reservation of benefit (see Chapter 30). The relevant Press Release stated that the effect of these artificial structures was that 'people have been removing assets from their taxable estates but continuing to enjoy all the benefits of ownership'. In practice, most of these schemes were intended to save IHT on the family home.

The legislation is in Schedule 15, FA 2004. A number of representations were made on the unfairness of such a charge where the transactions were entered into many years ago. The Government took some (but in reality very few) of these representations on board. After considerable discussion with professional bodies and advisers, HMRC also issued detailed guidance, which can be found at M05/2006 and www.hmrc.gov.uk/poa/poa_guidance.htm.

The charge does not apply in any of the following situations where:

- the benefit enjoyed by the donor is worth less than £5,000 a year;
- the benefit enjoyed by the donor is 'consistent with' an interest retained by him or her (eg where an individual gives a 50% interest in his or her home to a child living with him or her, and continues to pay – as a minimum – the expenses relating to the property retained, so in this example, at least 50%);
- the transfer was a gift that took place before 18 March 1986 (the date that the GWR rule for IHT was introduced);
- the property has been transferred to the donor's spouse;
- the transfer was a sale at market value and the purchase price has been paid in full;
- the transfer was effected by a deed of variation as permitted under the IHT legislation;
- any enjoyment of the property that has been given away is no more than incidental (HMRC has said that it regards 'incidental' enjoyment to fall within the same guidelines as that for GWR, which can be found in IRInt1001 (*Tax Bulletin 9*, November 1993));
- the asset given away is an intangible asset (eg an insurance policy) and the benefits retained by the donor are of a very limited nature;
- the donor was not domiciled in the UK (or deemed to be domiciled under the 17-year rule) at the time that he or she made the transfer and the property concerned is foreign property.

Furthermore, it was possible to make a special election by 31 January following the year of assessment in which the charge would first apply whereby the donor would renounce the IHT benefits in return for being exempt from the income tax charge. Where this election has been made, the property concerned will be treated as caught by the GWR rule.

33.7.1 Charge on occupation of a property

The charge may apply whenever a person occupies land and buildings that he or she does not own. The essential test is whether or not he or she owned the property or provided funds for its purchase, directly or otherwise, after 17 March 1986. If none of the reliefs and exemptions applies (see above) the calculation of the tax payable will be based on the rental value of the property.

33.7.2 Charge on use of chattels

Very similar rules can apply in respect of chattels (eg, works of art, cars, boats, etc). In this case the charge will be calculated by reference to the value of the chattel using a notional interest rate.

33.7.3 **Trusts**

The above charging provisions do not apply if land or chattels have been placed in an interest-in-possession trust for the benefit of either the taxpayer or his or her or her spouse or civil partner. However, there are separate rules for settlements where the settlor retains an interest in the property of the settlement and s 624 ITTOIA 2005 would apply (but not if it applies merely by reason of his or her spouse or civil partner retaining an interest under the trust). The charge is calculated by applying a notional interest rate to the value of settlement property in which the taxpayer has retained an interest.

Where the settlor suffers a capital gains or income tax charge under the existing settlement rules, the tax paid can be offset against this new liability. Nevertheless, there will be many circumstances were the taxpayer is being taxed twice in respect of the same source.

The pre-owned asset rules and their interaction with the GWR provisions are extremely complex, and a full discussion is outside the scope of this book. In October 2010, HMRC updated section 5 of its pre-owned assets guidance in relation to lifetime 'double trust/home loan' plans, adding the following note:

> Where the loan is only repayable at a time after the life tenant's death, HMRC is now of the view that these schemes are also caught as gifts with reservation. Further guidance, including the consequences for the pre-owned assets charge, will be issued shortly.

Unfortunately, the promised further guidance has not yet been issued.

Currently, all 'double trust' cases where the original owner of the house has died are being held pending a test case, but in the meantime, where significant sums are at stake, HMRC's view should be resisted as there are a number of technical reasons why HMRC's new stance may prove incorrect.

This is an area where professional advice is essential, not least because the charge generally applies because you have previously undertaken some form of IHT planning, which may need to be unwound or at least revisited, in order to keep the tax bill to a minimum.

CAPITAL GAINS TAX

33.8 BED AND BREAKFAST TRANSACTIONS

For disposals of shares by individuals or trustees on or after 17 March 1998, any shares of the same class and in the same company that are sold and then repurchased within a 30-day period will be matched so that the gain or loss that would otherwise have arisen by reference to shares already held will not be realised. This blocks a widely used way in which individuals used to realise losses and then buy back the same shares on the following day. It would appear that, in some circumstances, it is still possible to circumvent this rule by one spouse or civil partner selling and the other purchasing the same securities, provided s 16A TCGA 1992 is not triggered (see below).

33.8.1 Capital losses targeted anti-avoidance

Section 16A TCGA 1992 is a targeted anti-avoidance rule aimed restricting allowable losses for those realising capital losses, where tax avoidance is a motive, and it may enable HMRC to attack such sales as artificial transactions entered into solely for tax avoidance, especially if the purchasing spouse subsequently transfers the shares to the original owner. Basically, s 16A is very widely drafted and would appear to catch even completely innocent transactions. This legislation was one of the first rules to instigate a furore about 'taxing by legislation and un-taxing by concession' which has attended so much of the tax legislation introduced by the recent Labour administration. In effect, it will be up to HMRC whether it takes the point, on a case by case basis. This is clearly unsatisfactory, but as a general rule of thumb, if the parties genuinely suffer the economic consequences of the transactions they each enter into, then the rule is unlikely to apply.

33.8.2 Companies: capital losses after a change in ownership

At present, there are two sets of rules which apply to restrict the availability of capital losses of a company after it has been acquired by, and entered into, a capital gains group (the so-called 'pre-entry loss' rules). The rules apply to both realised and unrealised losses.

The older of these two sets of rules broadly states that a company's pre-entry losses can only be set against gains arising on assets that were owned by that company, or a member of the group that the company is entering, before the company's entrance into that group (change in ownership). Such losses can also be used against gains realised on assets that are used in a trade of the acquired company both before and after the change in ownership. This latter facility is to be widened slightly such that the asset on which the gain arose could have been used in any form of business, not specifically a trade. Furthermore, that business could be carried on by any member of the group, not just the newly acquired company. The new rules will apply to the deduction, on or after the date of Royal Assent to the Finance Bill 2011, of any loss that has accrued before a company joined a group.

The newer of the current rules is a targeted provision that prevents the use of pre-entry losses in circumstances where there are tax-avoidance arrangements. This rule will be amended so that it only applies in situations which are not already caught by other legislative provisions.

33.9 DISPOSALS BY A SERIES OF TRANSACTIONS

33.9.1 Basic principle behind the legislation

(s 19 TCGA 1992)

There are certain assets that are worth more in total than the sum of their various parts. For example, a 55% shareholding in a private company will almost always be worth a great deal more than five times the value of an 11% shareholding since a 55% shareholder has control of the company. It follows from this that if there were not specific anti-avoidance legislation, a person could reduce his or her exposure to CGT on a gift to a friend or relative by transferring the asset in stages.

In fact, in certain circumstances, HMRC may look at the value transferred by a series of transactions and assess that value by each separate transaction according to an appropriate part of the total value transferred.

> **Tax notes**
>
> In cases where a person has reduced his or her exposure to CGT on a gift by transferring an asset in stages, HMRC may assess the value of each separate transaction as an appropriate part of the total value transferred.

33.9.2 Legislation may have wide application

The legislation can also apply in unexpected ways. Thus, if an individual with a 75% shareholding in an investment company decided to give 25% to each of his or her brother's three children and even arranged to make the gifts over a period of two (or more) years, HMRC could still apply s 19 to catch the total value transferred.

33.9.3 Circumstances that cause s 19 to apply

The following circumstances may result in HMRC applying s 19:

(1) A person disposes of assets to another person (or other persons) who falls within the definition of a connected person.
(2) There are 'linked transactions' that fall within a period of six years.
(3) The disposals have all taken place since 19 March 1985.
(4) The aggregate value transferred by the series of linked transactions is greater than the total of the values transferred by the individual transactions.

A transaction may be caught by s 19 even if it is a sale rather than a gift.

33.9.4 Section 19 can result in retrospective adjustments

If HMRC invokes s 19, it may result in assessments for previous years being reopened. For example, *C* may have made a gift to her father in 2007–08 of a 10% shareholding in X Ltd and the shares' value may have been agreed with HMRC as, say, £20,000. If *C* made a further gift to her brother in 2011–12 of a 70% shareholding, the position might have to be reopened. If HMRC establishes that an 80% shareholding is worth £800,000 at the time of the gift to *C*'s brother, the effect of applying s 19 will be:

Deemed disposal proceeds on the 2007–08 gift	£100,000
Deemed disposal proceeds on the 2011–12 gift	£700,000

33.9.5 Hold-over relief may cover the position

In some circumstances, the donor may not have to pay extra tax because he or she, together with the donee, has agreed that the hold-over provisions should apply (see 13.6 and 17.4). However, hold-over relief will not always be available since the asset will not always fall within the definition of business property or the donee may not be UK-resident or a trust (see 13.6 and 17.4.3).

Professional advice is clearly essential where a person is contemplating making a series of gifts to connected persons.

33.10 TRANSFERS TO A CONNECTED PERSON

Another potential pitfall arises from special rules that govern the way market value is to be determined when assessing a gain on a transaction between connected persons (whether the transaction is a gift or a sale).

33.10.1 Some restrictions may be taken into account

(s 18 TCGA 1992)

A gift or sale at undervalue to a connected person may involve an asset over which the acquirer already has certain rights. Thus, *D* may own the freehold of a building and his daughter, *E*, may have valuable rights as a tenant. Suppose the freehold is worth £230,000 with vacant possession, but is worth only £180,000 if *E*'s lease is taken into account. When *D* sells the freehold to *E*, will the market value be taken as £230,000 or £180,000? The legislation states that the market value shall be taken to be the asset's market value less the lower of:

- the value of the interest held by the connected person who acquires the asset; or
- the amount by which the transferor's asset would increase in value if the connected person's rights did not exist.

Consequently, *D* would be deemed to make a disposal of an asset worth £180,000.

33.10.2 Some restrictions are ignored

(s 18(7) TCGA 1992)

Certain valuable rights may have to be left out of account. One example of this is an option. Suppose the facts set out in 33.10.1 had been slightly different so that *D* had vacant possession of a property worth £230,000, but his daughter had an option under which she could acquire it for £180,000. If *D* sells the property to *E* or if she exercises her option he will receive only £180,000, but he may be assessed as if he had received £230,000.

This is because the legislation requires options to be ignored or left out of account when computing an asset's market value. Similarly, legal rights that, if exercised, would effectively destroy or impair the asset also have to be ignored. Market value is determined as if such rights did not exist.

Tax notes

Options are ignored when computing an asset's market value. Similarly, legal rights that, if exercised, would effectively destroy or impair the asset also have to be ignored.

33.11 QUALIFYING CORPORATE BONDS

(ss 116–117A TCGA 1992)

Anti-avoidance provisions took effect from 26 November 1996 concerning situations where an individual or groups of individuals disposed of their private company shares and took loan stock issued by the acquiring company as part of the sale consideration (referred to as 'rolling over' into loan stock since no capital gain normally arises until the loan stock is sold). Since 1984, legislation has made specific provision for the situation where a person received qualifying corporate bonds (QCBs) in exchange for shares. The capital gain that would have arisen had he or she taken cash rather than QCBs is calculated but held over until such time as he or she disposes of the bonds. The legislation did not however make express provision for the situation where the vendor received loan notes that were not QCBs at the time of acquisition but subsequently become QCBs before a disposal takes place. As QCBs are normally an exempt asset for CGT purposes, the legislation seemed to allow a capital gain to escape a charge altogether, which gave rise to the term 'disappearing trick'.

HMRC was sceptical that these arrangements succeeded in their objective. However, and without prejudice to litigation on past transactions, FA 1997 clarified the position.

The CGT legislation was amended so that when a loan stock has changed from a non-QCB into a QCB after 25 November 2006, the change is treated as a conversion of securities. This ensures that any gain that has been rolled over on an exchange of shares for loan stock is preserved and does not escape charge.

33.12 VALUE SHIFTING

(s 29 TCGA 1992)

The legislation contains provisions that are intended to ensure that disguised gifts are assessed as a disposal at market value.

33.12.1 Type of transaction that may be caught

A controlling shareholder might exercise his or her control over a company to transfer value in an indirect way.

Example – Value shifting

> F owns all the shares in Y Ltd. The company has 1,000 £1 ordinary shares in issue. Assume that the value of these shares is £300,000. If F allowed his son G to be issued with 2,000 £1 shares at par, he would not have made a disposal of his own shares. However, G would have acquired a valuable asset in that his 2,000 shares will probably be worth in excess of £200,000 compared with the £2,000 that he had paid to acquire them. Furthermore, F's 1,000 shares will have gone down in value since he will have become a minority shareholder.
>
> Where HMRC can apply s 29, the person who has transferred value (in this example, F) is treated as if he or she had disposed of an asset.

The value shifting rules are designed to prevent value being stripped out of companies in a tax-free form before they are sold so as to reduce the size of any taxable gain arising. These provisions are to be replaced with a new targeted anti-avoidance rule which has the same aim but will be less mechanistic and will operate based on the purpose for which transactions have been entered into.

There will be a specific exclusion for reductions in value attributable to the payment of an exempt distribution of profits. The new rules will have effect from the date of Royal Assent to thhe Finance Bill 2011. Section 30 charges may however continue to arise in respect of disposals that take place prior to Royal Assent.

A separate set of provisions (known as the depreciatory transactions rules), ss 176 to 177A TCGA 1992, apply in tandem with the value shifting rules and are designed to prevent value from being stripped out of a company prior to a sale by way of dividend payments so as to create a capital loss on the disposal of the company. These rules will continue to apply going forward but will only apply to transactions taking place up to six years before the sale of the company.

33.12.2 Omission to exercise a right

There can be circumstances where s 29 is relevant because a person has failed to exercise a right. For example, if H and his grandson J were 50:50 shareholders in Z Ltd and the company announced a rights issue of three new shares for every one share already held and the amount payable for each share was £1 (par), s 29 would come into operation if H chose not to exercise his entitlement to the rights issue, as this omission would mean that after the rights issue the shares in Z Ltd would be owned as to:

H 20%

J 80%

Control would have thereby passed to J.

33.13 TRUSTS AND MAIN RESIDENCE EXEMPTION

(ss 169B–169G and 260 TCGA 1992)

Anti-avoidance legislation was introduced by FA 2004 and took effect from 10 December 2003.

33.13.1 No main residence relief for a property that has been transferred under a hold-over election

Where a property is given to a settlor-interested trust and the donor's gain is held over (see 13.6) the trustees are not able to claim exemption under s 225 TCGA 1992 (main residence exemption where a property is occupied by a beneficiary of a trust). PPR relief is also denied where the residence was acquired by the trustees subject to a hold-over election under s 260 TCGA 1992 (s 226A) and later transferred to a beneficiary who occupies the property as his or her main residence.

There is no equivalent provision preventing trustees from making a holdover election on transferring assets out of the trust to beneficiaries.

33.13.2 **Transitional rules**

These provisions also apply to cases where an asset was transferred to a trust under a hold-over election before 10 December 2003. However, in this situation the trustees may be able to claim the main residence exemption for part of their gain, this being calculated on a time-apportionment basis with the proportion of the gain relating to the period up to 10 December 2003 being exempt.

Example – Claiming main residence exemption

A owned a second property. On 10 December 2002, it was worth £360,000. *A* transferred the property to a settlor-interested discretionary trust on that date and made a claim for hold-over relief under s 260 TCGA 1992. Assume that the gain held over amounted to £200,000.

The property was then occupied as the main residence of one of the beneficiaries of the trust. The property is eventually sold for £400,000 on 10 December 2011.

The trustees' gain will be calculated as follows:

Proceeds		400,000
Less cost	360,000	
Held over gain	(200,000)	
		160,000
		240,000

The trustees held the property for nine years. The period of ownership up to 10 December 2003 was exactly one year.

The trustees would be entitled to main residence exemption on one ninth of the gain, ie £26,667.

33.14 UK-RESIDENT SETTLEMENTS WHERE SETTLOR HAS RETAINED AN INTEREST

33.14.1 **Introduction**

(s 77 TCGA 1992, abolished for disposals after 5 April 2008)

Capital gains realised by trustees of a UK-resident settlement before 6 April 2008 were taxed under s 77 as if they were the settlor's own gains if he or she was deemed to have retained an interest in the trust. The gains were simply added to his or her personal gains and he or she was responsible for paying the CGT. He or she could, however, reclaim the tax from the trustees. This treatment did not apply unless the settlor was UK-resident or ordinarily resident for the tax year concerned.

33.14.2 Section 77 abolished from 2008–09 onwards

A settlor is no longer taxed under s 77 even if he or she has retained an interest. This is because the rate payable by the trustees is the same 18% (to 22 June 2010) rate that is payable by individuals. From 23 June 2010, a flat rate of 28% applies to trustees' gains, which is the same as the rate for individuals taxed at the higher and additional rates.

33.15 DEEMED DISPOSAL WHEN A TRUST CEASES TO BE UK RESIDENT

A trust is regarded as resident or non-resident in the UK for an entire tax year, there is no 'split year' concept for trusts.

A UK resident trust can cease to be resident if non-resident trustees are appointed and the ordinary administration of the trust is then carried out overseas.

In such a case, there is a deemed disposal for CGT purposes at the time that the trust ceases to be UK resident with market value being taken as the deemed disposal proceeds. As regards subsequent disposals, the trustees are deemed to have re-acquired all of their assets at market value. There is a question mark over whether such 'exit charges' are consistent with taxpayers' Community rights and free movement of capital, but as yet, no-one has been willing to fund a case on this important principle.

33.16 OFFSHORE COMPANIES

(s 13 TCGA 1992)

A person who is resident and ordinarily resident in the UK (see 34.2) may be liable for a proportion of capital gains realised by a non-resident company in which he or she has a shareholding.

Example – Possible liability for capital gains

> *K* owns all the shares in X Ltd, a company incorporated and resident in Bermuda. The company realises a capital gain by disposing of a US property that it owns. The legislation enables HMRC to assess *K* as if he made the capital gain himself. However, certain conditions need to be satisfied before HMRC can assess a capital gain in this way (see 33.16.1).

33.16.1 Conditions that need to be satisfied

First, the company must be controlled by five or fewer shareholders, or shareholder directors must between them own more than 50% of the company's shares.

Second, the individual must be resident (or ordinarily resident) and, for years up to 2007–08, domiciled in the UK (see 35.1 and 35.14). For 2008–09 onwards, s 13 can apply to individuals who are resident or ordinarily resident but not domiciled in the UK.

Third, he or she, together with any persons connected with him or her for this purpose, must between them have an interest in the company of at least 10%.

33.16.2 Certain gains not assessable under s 13

The legislation is really intended to catch gains on investment assets held through an offshore company. There is therefore an exemption under s 13(5) for gains arising:

- on the disposal of foreign currency where the currency represents money in use for a trade carried on by the company outside the UK;
- from the disposal of 'tangible property' used for the purposes of a trade carried on by the company outside the UK;
- from disposals of assets used by a UK permanent establishment of the company.

The application of s 13 can be complex, particularly the reliefs available where there have been distributions in the period prior to the gain accruing and it is recommended that professional advice is taken where this legislation may be in point

33.17 NON-RESIDENT TRUSTS

(ss 86, 87 and Schedule 5 TCGA 1992)

33.17.1 Introduction

The trustees of a trust may be resident outside the UK and the administration of the trust may be carried out overseas. Provided both these conditions are satisfied, the trust is not resident and there will not normally be any liability for the trustees so far as UK CGT is concerned. There may be a liability for either the settlor (ie the person who set up the trust) or the beneficiaries (who may include the settlor).

33.17.2 'Qualifying' trusts

(s 86 and Schedule 5 TCGA 1992)

The legislation refers to 'qualifying settlements'. In fact, they qualify for an adverse CGT treatment in that the trustees' gains are deemed to be the settlor's personal capital gains subject to the proviso that the settlor's annual exemption and any personal losses are set first against personal gains and only any excess set against the 'attributed gains'. The amount attributed to the settlor is the amount remaining after the deduction of losses. If the computation itself produces a loss, this cannot be transferred to the settlor. Unlike the s 87 charge on beneficiaries, the s 86 charge was not extended by FA 2008 to include non-UK domiciled settlors.

33.17.3 Attribution of gains – conditions

The conditions under which the trust's capital gains will be treated in this way are as follows:

(1) The settlor must be UK resident or ordinarily resident for the year concerned.
(2) The settlor must be domiciled in the UK for the year in which the trustees realise capital gains.
(3) He or she must not have died during the course of the year.
(4) The people who benefit from the trust include one of the following:
    (a)   the settlor;
    (b)   the settlor's spouse or civil partner;
    (c)   any child (including step-children) of the settlor or of the settlor's spouse or civil partner;
    (d)   the spouse or civil partner of any such child;
    (e)   any grandchild of the settlor or of the settlor's spouse or civil partner;
    (f)   the spouse or civil partner of any such grandchild;
    (g)   a company controlled by a person or persons falling within (a) to (f) above;
    (h)   a company associated with a company falling within (g) above.

33.17.4 Relief for the settlor's personal losses

It is possible for an individual who would be taxed on capital gains under s 86 to set off his or her personal CGT losses against these attributed gains, but only after setting these (and the annual exemption) against personal gains.

33.17.5 Interaction with entrepreneurs' relief

Where trustees make a disposal of qualifying business assets and a beneficiary ('the qualifying beneficiary') has an interest in possession in the whole, or the part of the trust fund comprising those assets, then entrepreneurs' relief (ER) may be due. A further condition must be met in relation to the qualifying beneficiary's personal interest in the business assets or shares concerned. See 31.2.3 for more details.

Trustees are not themselves entitled to a £10m (£5m between 23 June 2010 and 5 April 2011) ER allowance in the same way as individuals. Any relief given to trustees is treated as having been given to the qualifying beneficiary and serves to reduce his or her entitlement for future disposals.

Where there are two qualifying disposals made on the same day, one by the trustees and the other by an individual who is also a qualifying beneficiary of that trust, the trustees' disposal is treated as having occurred after the one made by the individual.

The effect of these provisions is to restrict an individual's relief threshold by the relief granted to trustees of a settlement of which he or she is a qualifying beneficiary.

In calculating the ER due on a disposal, up to 22 June 2010, 'relevant' gains and losses were aggregated, and the resulting total was reduced by 4/9ths. Since 23 June 2010 a 10% tax rate has applied to gains qualifying for the relief. For non-UK resident trusts, the resulting gain is attributed to the settlor (who may not be the qualifying beneficiary), and he or she can use his or her personal losses or excess annual exemption against this attributed gain in the normal way. This may have the odd effect that the qualifying beneficiary's lifetime entitlement to ER is reduced by the relief claimed by the trustees, but the gain after ER is itself is taxed on the settlor. A claim to ER, however, must be made jointly by the trustees and the qualifying beneficiary and so it is not possible to utilise the qualifying beneficiary's lifetime limit without his or her consent.

33.17.6 Stockpiled gains in pre-March 1991 trusts

(s 97(1) TCGA 1992)

Provided the trust did not become a qualifying settlement (see 33.17.2), there was no CGT liability for beneficiaries for years up to 1998–99 until such time as 'capital payments' were received.

UK-resident (and domiciled, for years to 2007–08) beneficiaries may now be assessed for CGT purposes under s 87 TCGA 1992 on a proportion of the trustees' pre 1998–99 capital gains ('stockpiled gains') that can be 'matched' with capital payments received.

The receipt of a benefit may count as a deemed capital payment (the rules are virtually the same as under s 732: see 33.4).

Example – Pre-19 March 1991 offshore trusts

> Trustees of an offshore trust make capital gains in 1989–90 of £200,000. In
> 1989–90 to 1991–92 the trustees distribute income, but their doing this does
> not have any CGT consequences. In 2011–12 they make a capital payment
> of £50,000 to *L*, who is UK-resident.
>
> *L* would be assessed as if she had personally made capital gains of £50,000
> for 2011–12. The tax actually payable will depend on whether she has made
> other capital gains, whether she has capital losses available for offset and
> her rate of tax.

33.17.7 UK-resident beneficiaries of settlements not caught by s 86

(ss 87, 87A–87C TCGA 1992)

Where a UK resident beneficiary receives a capital payment from a
settlement that is not caught by s 86 (eg where the settlor has died, or
none of the persons defined at 33.17.3 can benefit), he or she may be
taxed under s 87 on stockpiled capital gains that can be matched with the
capital payment. This rule has been in place since 1981 as far as settlements
created by UK domiciliaries are concerned.

33.17.8 Supplementary charge

A supplementary charge may be made of 10% of the tax for each complete
year between 1 December following the year in which the trustees realised
the gain and the time the trustees make the capital distribution. The
supplementary charge cannot exceed 60%. Since 6 April 2008, gains are
matched on a LIFO basis. Prior to that, matching was on a FIFO basis.
With the increase in the tax rate from 18% to 28% for trusts, the potential
maximum rate on offshore trust gains has increased from 28.8% to 44.8%.

33.17.9 Settlements created by foreign domiciliaries

UK domiciliaries were made liable to tax on capital payments from trusts
created by foreign domiciliaries by FA 1998. With effect from 17 March
1998, UK-resident and domiciled beneficiaries could be assessed where they
received capital payments from a non-resident trust created by a foreign
domiciled settlor; this applied only where payments made after 16 March
1998 could be matched with gains realised by the trustees after that date.
With effect from 6 April 2008, the charge was extended to non-UK domiciled
beneficiaries, the only proviso being that they were resident in the UK.

33.17.10 Beneficiary's capital losses

It is not possible for a beneficiary to offset personal CGT losses against gains attributed to him or her under s 87 TCGA 1992.

33.17.11 Finance Act 2008 changes

FA 2008 brought foreign domiciliaries within the scope of s 87 in relation to capital gains realised by the trustees on or after 6 April 2008. However, there is a key difference in that if the beneficiary is a remittance basis user he or she will be subject to tax under s 87 only if he or she brings the capital payment into the UK (depending upon his or her circumstances, the foreign domiciliary may need to pay the £30,000 special charge to obtain the benefit of the remittance basis (see 35.2)). Furthermore, the trustees can elect for all gains to be computed as if the market value of the asset at 5 April 2008 were the cost.

The FA 2008 changes are wide-reaching and this is a complex area where professional advice is essential.

33.17.12 Sale of trust interest by beneficiary

(s 76 TCGA 1992)

A disposal of an interest in a non-resident trust has been a disposal of a chargeable asset for CGT purposes since 1981. On the other hand, a disposal of an interest in a UK resident trust has not normally been subject to CGT, unless it is for consideration (see Schedule 4A).

FA 1998 introduced a further rule so that if beneficiaries of UK-resident trusts dispose of their interests, and the trust has been non-resident in the past, the beneficiaries' disposal is subject to CGT.

A double tax charge is prevented where the disposal of the interest is not exempt under s 76(1) TCGA 1992, and the disposal also triggers a deemed disposal under Schedule 4A. The broad effect is to maximise the net chargeable gain or, if there is no net gain, to minimise the net allowable loss, by securing that the provision which would maximise the gain (or minimise the loss) has effect and that the other does not.

33.17.13 Flip-flop arrangements

(ss 76A, 76B and schedules 4B and 4C)

It used to be considered possible to avoid s 87 by arranging for a trust to borrow and to use the borrowed funds to make a gift to another settlement. The terms of the original trust were varied so that no UK person could benefit and any gains subsequently realised within that trust were not taxable under s 86. The settlement receiving the transfer had no capital gains and could therefore make a capital appointment to UK beneficiaries without their being liable under s 87. Legislators have made several attempts to block all such loopholes, most recently in FA 2003, with amendments to Schedules 4B and 4C.

The decision in *West* v *Trennery* and others [2005 STC 138] has indicated that many flip-flop schemes may in any event be caught by the courts interpreting the legislation in accordance with principles established in the *Ramsay* case (see 33.19).

INHERITANCE TAX

33.18 PURCHASED INTERESTS IN EXCLUDED PROPERTY SETTLEMENTS

A trust created by an individual of foreign domicile settling foreign situs assets is excluded property for IHT purposes (see 35.16).

The last Labour Government discovered that this has been used for avoidance by UK domiciliaries who purchased interests under such settlements as a form of 'death-bed planning'. The definition of excluded property now excludes interests in such trusts where the interest was purchased on or after 5 December 2005 (whether the purchase was by the individual who owns the interest or by someone else).

33.18.1 Reversionary interests in relevant property

(s 81A IHTA 1984)

Section 81A, which was inserted in IHTA by FA (No.1) 2010, applies where an individual transfers property into a trust in which he or she or his or her spouse or civil partner retains a future interest. The rule also applies where an individual purchases a future interest in a trust on or after 9 December 2009.

It provides that there will be a chargeable event for IHT purposes when the future interest comes to an end and the person becomes entitled to an actual interest under the trust. If that future interest is given away before the person becomes entitled to an actual interest, it may be immediately chargeable to IHT.

32.18.2 Purchased interests in possession

Section 5(1B) IHTA 1984 (see 31.4.21) was inserted by s 53 FA (No.1) 2010. This means that where an individual purchases an interest in possession in a trust at full value, such an interest will be treated as part of the his or her estate for IHT purposes (ie as a 'qualifying' IIP). If the interest comes to an end during the purchaser's lifetime, there may be an immediate charge to IHT. This legislation has effect for interests purchased on or after 9 December 2009.

GENERAL

33.19 *RAMSAY* PRINCIPLE

This chapter has concentrated so far on anti-avoidance legislation. There is another factor, ie case law, which has been developed by the courts that HMRC can use in much the same way as anti-avoidance legislation to counter tax avoidance schemes.

The House of Lords decided in the *Ramsay case* (*IRC* v *W T Ramsay Limited* [1981] STC 174) that it should determine the tax consequences of a 'composite transaction' (ie a series of interlinked transactions) by looking at the overall effect. Furthermore, artificial steps that had been introduced only for tax avoidance purposes could be disregarded.

In another famous case, *Furniss* v *Dawson* 1984 STC 153, taxpayers sought to avoid CGT by exchanging their shares in a UK company for shares in an Isle of Man company which on the same day (in fact immediately after lunch) sold its shares in the UK company to a third party purchaser. The House of Lords held that the interpolation of the Isle of Man company was an artificial step that could be disregarded and the UK vendors were therefore treated as if they had sold their UK company directly to the ultimate purchaser.

Broadly, the *Ramsay* doctrine was summarised in another House of Lords case as applying only in the following circumstances:

- There was a pre-ordained series of transactions in mind from the outset that were intended to produce a given result.
- Certain transactions within that series of transactions had no purpose other than tax avoidance.
- At the time that the transactions were carried out, there was no practical likelihood that the pre-planned series of transactions would not take place in the order ordained. In that sense, some of the intermediate transactions were not contemplated as having a life independent from the pre-ordained series of transactions.
- The pre-ordained events did in fact take place.

Note that the courts have attached a great deal of importance to transactions being pre-ordained. This is not quite the same thing as pre-conceived. An individual might carry out a series of transactions with a view to ultimately selling a company to a third party. That series of transactions would be pre-conceived but would be pre-ordained only if the series of transactions were carried out with a particular purchaser in view. In one particular case, steps had been carried out with a view to a sale to a particular purchaser. That transaction fell through and the vendors eventually sold to a different person. It was held that a series of transactions started with the original purchaser in mind was not a single composite transaction and *Ramsay* therefore did not enable HMRC to strike out those individual steps that secured a tax advantage for the vendor.

The likely application of the *Ramsay* doctrine to specific transactions carried out with tax savings in mind is fraught with uncertainty. There have been several recent court decisions. At one stage, it appeared that a distinction was being drawn between commercial concepts and legal concepts, with purely legal concepts being less susceptible to *Ramsay*. However, this appears to have been a misunderstanding and recent decisions in the *Arrowtown* and *Carreras* cases indicate a very wide interpretation of the *Ramsay* doctrine.

The House of Lords has held that conditions put into contracts merely to create some uncertainty as to the final outcome should be ignored. Their Lordships held that the creation of uncertainty by the insertion of such conditions did not prevent the final outcome from being preordained. Tax statutes generally will be construed purposively, unless it is obvious that they should not be so construed (for instance in the case of a purely 'mechanical' section, stating how the gain or loss on a certain transaction is to be calculated).

The ECJ has held that a VAT avoidance scheme failed because it amounted to an 'abuse of rights'. It remains to be seen whether this will be invoked by HMRC in areas other than VAT (*Halifax plc & others* v *C&E Commissioners 2006* 2 WLR 905).

Tax notes

Any taxpayer undertaking an artificial tax scheme should bear in mind that HMRC may well attack it by invoking the *Ramsay* doctrine and that the courts have become increasingly sympathetic to such arguments.

33.20 DISCLOSURE OF TAX AVOIDANCE SCHEMES

The disclosure regime was introduced with effect from 1 August 2004 and was limited in scope to tax arrangements concerning employment or certain financial products. This was widened with effect from 1 August 2006 to the whole of income tax, corporation tax and capital gains tax.

A tax arrangement must be disclosed when:

- it will, or might be expected to, enable any person to obtain a tax advantage;

- that tax advantage is, or might be expected to be, the main benefit or one of the main benefits of the arrangement; and
- it is a tax arrangement that falls within any description ('hallmarks') prescribed in the relevant regulations.

In most situations where a disclosure is required it must be made by the scheme 'promoter' within five days of it being made available. However, the scheme user may need to make the disclosure where:

- the promoter is based outside the UK;
- the promoter is a lawyer and legal privilege applies; or
- there is no promoter.

The hallmarks are:

- wishing to keep the arrangements confidential from a competitor;
- wishing to keep the arrangements confidential from HMRC;
- arrangements for which a premium fee could reasonably be obtained;
- arrangements that include off market terms (to be removed in 2010);
- arrangements that are standardised tax products;
- arrangements that are loss schemes;
- arrangements that are certain leasing arrangements.

Upon receiving the disclosure under the disclosure regime, HMRC issues the promoter with an eight-digit scheme reference number for the disclosed scheme. By law the promoter must provide this number to each client that uses the scheme, who in turn must include the number on his or her return or form AAG4. A person who designs and implements their own scheme must disclose it within 30 days of it being implemented. The registration does not imply any judgment on the technical merits of the scheme.

The disclosure regime was extended in 2005 to include tax arrangements relating to SDLT where the subject matter of the arrangements is commercial property with a market value of at least £5m and further in 2008 to include residential property with a value in excess of £1m.

The main differences compared with the disclosure regime for income tax, corporation tax and capital gains tax are:

- the hallmarks are not applied to limit what is required to be disclosed, however there is a 'white list' of arrangements that are not required to be disclosed;
- promoters are not obliged to provide reference numbers to scheme users;
- some minor differences in the time limits for making disclosure.

The disclosure regime was extended again from 1 May 2007 to include arrangements relating to NIC. Again the rules broadly mirror those for income tax, corporation tax and capital gains tax, except that the last two hallmarks do not apply.

VAT is subject to a separate disclosure regime.

There have been further updates since August 2006, one of which was the introduction of a hallmark relating to avoidance of the pensions special annual allowance charge, which had effect from 1 September 2009 to 5 April 2011. Further changes were introduced in FA (No.1) 2010:

- A change in the trigger point for disclosure – this will now be when a scheme is first marketed, rather than when it is made available for implementation.
- 'Introducers' to disclose details of promoters – advisers who are approached by promoters of schemes with a view to introducing them to their clients will be required, on production of a notice by HMRC, to provide details of the promoters that have approached them.
- Enhanced penalties – the maximum penalty has previously been £5,000 plus £600 a day for continuing failures. It is recognised that this is not a sufficient deterrent, so the penalty will be fixed with regard to the fees potentially earned from the arrangement, subject to a maximum of £1m.
- Promoters to provide periodic lists of clients – promoters of tax schemes will be required to provide quarterly lists of clients to whom they should have issued a scheme reference number. The first returns under this provision fell due on 30 April 2011, for the quarter ended 31 March 2011.
- Changes to existing hallmarks – minor changes to the hallmarks, including the abolition of the 'off-market terms' hallmark, and a change from '**the** main purpose [of the arrangements]' to '**a** main purpose […]' for the 'standardised tax products' and 'loss schemes' hallmarks.
- Three new hallmarks have also been proposed covering:
  - employment schemes;
  - income into capital schemes;
  - offshoring schemes.

The disclosure regime was also extended to encompass the avoidance of IHT on making transfers to trusts from 6 April 2011, subject to 'grandfathering' for IHT planning techniques already in use prior to the start date.

See also the HMRC guidance at www.hmrc.gov.uk/aiu/, which is regularly updated.

Tax notes

Since 1 August 2006 it has been necessary to disclose all arrangements that seek to avoid income tax, corporation tax and CGT which contain certain 'hallmarks'.

33.21 SPECIFIC INCOME TAX AVOIDANCE SCHEMES THAT HAVE BEEN BLOCKED

The last nine Finance Acts (there were of course three in 2010!) have contained provisions that blocked certain income tax avoidance schemes. These include the following:

- Schemes and arrangements involving special shares and securities. Almost every Finance Act has dealt with this area of abuse. This culminated with FA 2006 amending s 420 ITEPA 2003 retrospectively with effect from 1 December 2004.
- Schemes involving the creation of a relevant discounted security (now deeply discounted security) and its subsequent sale to an unconnected party – now in ss 453–456 ITTOIA 2005, applicable from 27 March 2003.
- Schemes involving the abuse of reliefs for deficiencies on non-qualifying insurance policies – now in s 541 ITTOIA 2005, applicable from 3 March 2004.
- Schemes involving stripped gilts and gilt futures – now in ss 447–451 and 460 ITTOIA 2005, applicable from dates between 15 January and 17 March 2004.
- Schemes involving repos and/or 'manufactured dividends' – now in Part 11 ITA 2007, applicable from 17 March 2004.
- Schemes that sought to take advantage of the relief for gifts of quoted securities to charities – now in Chapter 3, Part 8 ITA 2007, applicable from 2 July 2004.
- Schemes involving an abuse of the reliefs due for films – applicable from 10 February 2004 with further legislation in both FA 2005 and FA 2006.
- SDLT anti-avoidance provisions aimed at schemes involving foreign unit trusts – Schedule 24 FA 2006.
- An investor who holds 10% or more of a unit trust could be subject to an annual tax charge in future (this legislation seems to be directed at 'private unit trusts') – FA (No. 2) 2005.
- Restrictions on trade loss relief for individuals, non-working partners or limited partnerships – these prevent sideways relief for losses against other income in so far as such losses exceed £25,000 pa or the capital contributed, if less. This legislation has been updated in each subsequent year – now in ss 74ZA–82 and 102–116 ITA 2007, with the most recent Written Ministerial Statement introducing changes made in Schedule 3 FA (No.1) 2010, which took effect from 21 October 2009.
- CGT relief is not available for artificial losses realised on or after 6 December 2006 (s 16A TCGA 1992).
- Legislation contained in FA 2008 – now in ss 858 ITTOIA 2005 and 59 TCGA 1992 – seeks to prevent the abuse of double taxation agreements for UK resident beneficiaries of trusts that participate in partnerships controlled in the overseas territory concerned.

- FA 2009 contained provisions aimed at artificial schemes which exploited relief for interest payments (now s 384A ITA 2007), avoidance using life insurance policies (s 152(8) ITA 2007) and schemes which exploited aspects of the employment income legislation (now ss 346 and 556A ITEPA 2003, s 128 ITA 2007).
- Similarly, FAs (No.1) and (No.3) 2010 contained a number of anti-avoidance measures amongst which are:
  - New s 74ZA ITA 2007, which applies where an individual makes a loss from a relevant activity, and the loss arises in consequence of, or in connection with, relevant tax-avoidance arrangements. In those circumstances, no sideways relief or capital gains relief will be given for the loss (unless it relates to qualifying film expenditure within s 74D).
  - New s 127A ITTOIA 2005 prevents the use of losses arising from the annual investment allowance where they are connected with a tax-avoidance motive.
- New Part 7A ITEPA 2003 was added by Schedule 2, Finance Act 2011, dealing with disguised remuneration (see Chapter 5). This will completely change the treatment of EBTs, EFRBS and other deferred remuneration arrangements. In addition, FA 2011 contains sweeping changes to the rules for CFCs (see 18.10.2) and foreign branches, as well as changes to the rules on value shifting and depreciatory transactions.
- Similar legislation will be introduced from time to time as HMRC continues to learn about schemes at an earlier stage through the registration of schemes (see 33.20). Much of this legislation may in future be overtaken by a GAAR, which will necessitate a complete re-evaluation of the tax planning landscape.

PART 5

RESIDENCE, DOMICILE AND INTERNATIONAL MATTERS

This part contains the following chapters:

34

RESIDENCE STATUS

This chapter contains the following sections:

(1) Consequences of residence in the UK
(2) Various criteria for determining residence status
(3) Individuals who are resident but not ordinarily resident
(4) Basis on which individuals are regarded as ordinarily resident
(5) Ceasing to be resident in the UK
(6) UK income and capital gains received by non-residents
(7) Non-resident investment companies
(8) When tax should be withheld from payments to non-residents

34.1 CONSEQUENCES OF RESIDENCE IN THE UK

The basic principle of UK taxation is that an individual may be charged tax on worldwide income and capital gains if he or she is resident in the UK. If not so resident, he or she is still liable for tax on income that arises in the UK, but not for tax on income that arises overseas, or on any capital gains wherever arising (subject to the provisions relating to temporary non-UK residence).

There is an exception to this in that an individual who is UK resident but not ordinarily resident and/or not domiciled in the UK, may only have to pay tax on UK income and overseas income which is brought to (or 'remitted' to) the UK. The concept of domicile is different from residence (see 35.1) and this chapter proceeds on the basis that an individual has a domicile within the UK. (Strictly speaking, an individual's domicile will be within a specific country, ie England, Wales, Scotland or Northern Ireland. For the sake of expediency, this is referred to throughout this book as 'domicile within the UK', 'UK domicile', etc).

34.2 VARIOUS CRITERIA FOR DETERMINING RESIDENCE STATUS

34.2.1 Introduction

For UK taxation purposes, 'the UK' means England, Scotland, Wales and Northern Ireland. It does not include the Republic of Ireland, the Channel Islands or the Isle of Man. A person may be resident in more than one country so the fact that he or she is treated as resident in, for example, the US or South Africa does not necessarily mean that he or she is not resident in the UK.

A person is usually resident or not resident for an entire tax year. A person may also be ordinarily resident if he or she is habitually resident in the UK as opposed to simply being resident for one year in isolation.

Somewhat surprisingly the word 'resident' is not defined in the Taxes Acts, albeit there are ongoing calls for a statutory residence test to be introduced (which would, one assumes provide an absolute definition). The Government has announced its intention to include such a test in FA 2012. In addition, HMRC's non-statutory guidance on residence, *IR 20*, has now been replaced by *HMRC 6*, which arguably takes a far stricter view on what constitutes residence in the UK. This has led to considerable confusion for taxpayers and agents. The guidance is however non-statutory and the current position is wholly determined by the considerable case law on residence: the position is summarised below.

34.2.2 Two tests

An individual will always be treated as UK-resident for a tax year if he or she is caught under either of the following tests:

- The six-month rule, ie he or she is present in the UK for 183 days or more during the tax year (s 831 ITA 2007).
- The three-month average rule, ie he or she is present in the UK for an average of 91 days or more per annum measured over a period of four tax years (non-statutory, see *HMRC6* and *IR20* (now obsolete for years after 2008–09)).

Relevant case law on residence and ordinary residence

> *R (on the application of Davies & Anor)* v *Revenue and Customs Commissioners*
>
> *R (on the application of Gaines-Cooper)* v *Revenue and Customs Commissioners* [2010] EWCA Civ 83
>
> *Philip George Turberville* v *Revenue & Customs* [2010] UKFTT 69 (TC); TC00381
>
> *R (on the application of Hankinson)* v *Revenue and Customs Commissioners* [2009] UKFTT 384 (TC); TC00319

Genovese v *R & C Commrs* (2009) SpC 741

Grace v *Revenue and Customs Commissioners* [2009] EWCA Civ 1082

Gaines-Cooper v *Revenue and Customs* [2007] EWHC 2617 (Ch)

Gaines-Cooper v *Revenue & Customs Rev* 2 [2006] UK SpC SPC00568

Gaines-Cooper v *Revenue and Customs* [2008] EWCA Civ 1502

Barrett v *R & C Commrs* (2007) SpC 639

Shepherd v *Revenue and Customs Commissioners* [2006] EWHC 1512 (Ch)

Carstairs (HMIT) v *Sykes* [2000] STC 1103

Goodwin v *Curtis (Inspector of Taxes)* [1998] STC 475

R v *Barnet LBC, ex parte Shah* [1983] 2 AC 309

Reed (HMIT) v *Clark* [1985] 58 TC 528

Lysaght v *IR Commrs* (1928) 13 TC 511

Levene v *IR Commrs* (1928) 13 TC 486

In one case decided some years ago, fractions of a day were taken into account in applying the 183-day test. HMRC later introduced a practice whereby days of arrival and departure were normally left out of account for these tests but this was not a universal rule. In a 2006 case (*Gaines-Cooper*), the Special Commissioners did take such days into account because, they said, omitting such days would have distorted the position. The High Court and Court of Appeal subsequently approved this treatment. ITA 2007 now contains specific rules covering part days (see 34.2.3 below).

Mobile workers may also be treated differently: *Tax Bulletin 52* April 2001 sets out HMRC's view that individuals whose home and settled domestic life are in the UK may be regarded as remaining UK resident despite frequent and regular trips abroad. See *Shepherd* v *HMRC*, for a case where HMRC successfully argued this. A key factor in this decision was that Mr Shepherd spent a lot of time at the family home in Wokingham and his Cyprus home was more in the nature of a holiday home than a main residence. Furthermore, in *Grace* v *HMRC* [2008] EWHC 2708, the taxpayer who was also an airline pilot retained a small flat near Gatwick and had his main home in Cape Town but was still held to be resident and ordinarily resident in the UK. In *Grace*, Lewison J commented that the Special Commissioner's analysis of the current case law on residence in *Shepherd* had been 'impeccable'.

> **Tax notes**
>
> An individual will be treated as UK-resident if (a) he or she is present in the UK for 183 days or more during the tax year, or (b) for an average of 91 days or more per annum over a period of four tax years. But there are also situations where a person who has spent fewer days in the UK may nevertheless be regarded as resident.

34.2.3 Days that are counted as UK days

Sections 831(1A) and 831(1B) ITA 2007 provide that from 6 April 2008 onwards, any day in which an individual is present in the UK at midnight is counted as a day in the UK. However, days spent in transit will not count as UK days even if the individual is present in the UK at midnight, provided that the individual does not engage in activities that are inconsistent with merely being in transit.

34.2.4 Existing UK residents

So far as a person who has been resident in the UK for a number of years is concerned, he or she is likely to continue to be regarded as UK resident despite temporary periods of absence from the UK unless the following conditions are satisfied:

- he or she works full-time abroad, and the period spent overseas includes a complete tax year, or
- he or she has no accommodation in the UK and lives abroad for at least one full tax year.

The treatment of UK residents who move overseas is covered at 34.5.

34.2.5 Foreign nationals coming to the UK

The residence status of individuals who come to the UK is now governed by the statutory six month and non-statutory three month rules set out in 34.2.2. Individuals who regularly visit the UK, and are therefore caught by the three-month rule, are normally treated as ordinarily resident only from the beginning of the fourth year after arrival. However, an individual may be regarded as ordinarily resident from the date of arrival if it is clear at the outset that he or she intended to spend an average of three months a year in this country.

34.2.6 Double taxation agreements

The UK has entered into many double taxation agreements (also known as double tax treaties) with other countries. The provisions of such an agreement may override UK tax law. Specifically, the agreement may provide exemption for certain income received by a person resident overseas even though the income arises in the UK. For example, most double taxation agreements provide that a resident of the foreign country concerned may claim exemption from UK tax in connection with interest income arising in the UK.

Most double taxation agreements also make provision for the situation where an individual is resident in both the foreign country and the UK. They usually contain a clause along the following lines:

(1) If the individual has a permanent home in only one country, he or she is deemed to be resident there.
(2) If the position has not been resolved by (1), he or she is treated as resident where he or she has the centre of his or her personal and economic interests.
(3) If the above tests do not resolve the position, he or she is treated as resident in the country where he or she has a 'habitual abode'.
(4) If he or she has a habitual abode in both countries, he or she is deemed to be a resident of the country of which he or she is a national.
(5) If he or she is a national of both countries or he or she is not a national of either country; the revenue authorities of the UK and the foreign country may settle the matter by mutual agreement.

These provisions apply only for the purposes of determining residence under the agreement. They are deeming provisions and, under UK law, an individual might still be regarded as UK resident even though he or she might be treated as resident in the foreign country for the purposes of the double taxation agreement. However, the terms of a double taxation agreement override UK tax law and, if an individual is deemed to be resident in a foreign country under the agreement, his or her liability to UK tax is then computed in accordance with the other provisions of the agreement.

34.3 INDIVIDUALS WHO ARE RESIDENT BUT NOT ORDINARILY RESIDENT

An individual who is resident but not ordinarily resident in the UK has certain tax privileges.

34.3.1 Employment income

Earnings from duties performed outside the UK may be taxed on the remittance basis. This applies even where the employment relates to a mixture of UK and overseas duties or where the employer is UK resident (contrast foreign earnings where the employer must be non-resident).

Section 690 ITEPA 2003 allows an employer to require a direction from HMRC as to how much of a not ordinarily resident employee's remuneration should be subject to PAYE deductions.

Table 34.1 – Basis for assessment for employment income

	Services performed			
	Wholly in UK	*Partly in UK*	*Partly abroad*	*Wholly abroad*
Non-resident	All	That part	None	None
Resident but not ordinarily resident	All	That part	Remittances*	Remittances*
Resident and ordinarily resident	All	All	All	All

* From 6 April 2008, all employment income will be taxable on the arising basis unless a remittance basis claim is made.

Remuneration from a mixed employment (ie duties performed both within and outside the UK) is normally allocated on a working day basis. It is HMRC's practice to work to the nearest half day.

See SP1/09 on the various conditions which need to be satisfied in order that remittances to the UK out of an offshore account which contains only the income from a single employment. Interest and currency gains thereon can be matched primarily with remuneration for duties performed in the UK.

See also 35.6 on tax free subsistence and accommodation allowances which may be paid to employees who are seconded to the UK for periods not exceeding 24 months.

34.3.2 Overseas investment income

This was automatically taxable under the remittance basis, up to 5 April 2008. From 6 April 2008, it is taxable on an arising basis unless a claim for the remittance basis is made. Moreover, offshore income gains from sales of non-distributor funds are always taxed on the arising basis unless the taxpayer is foreign domiciled and claiming the remittance basis.

34.4 BASIS ON WHICH INDIVIDUALS ARE REGARDED AS ORDINARILY RESIDENT

34.4.1 Intention to make a permanent home in the UK

Where an individual arrives with the intention of staying in the UK for at least three years (apart from holidays and short business trips), he or she is regarded as ordinarily resident from the outset. If he or she arrives with no definite intention but stays in the UK he or she will be regarded as becoming ordinarily resident for the tax year in which the third anniversary of his or her arrival falls (unless he or she decides to stay in the UK on a longer term basis during the first three years in which case he or she will become ordinarily resident from the start of the tax year in which he or she makes such a decision). If an individual owns or acquires accommodation on a long-term lease in the year he or she arrives, this is likely to be taken as evidence that he or she intends to remain in the UK and is ordinarily resident here from the date of acquisition, or if it is the first year, the date of arrival. However, if the property is sold and the person leaves the UK within three years of arrival, the ownership of the property will no longer be a relevant factor. This is an extremely complex area and it is recommended that professionals should read the recent case law and refer to *HMRC 6*, and that, if you are unrepresented, you should seek professional advice.

Different rules apply to an individual who spends a significant part of his or her time overseas (see below).

34.4.2 Accommodation in the UK

Where an individual does not spend all his or her time in the UK but has UK accommodation available for his or her use, he or she is normally regarded as ordinarily resident as well as resident. The individual does not have to own the accommodation; it is sufficient if it is made available to him or her. Accommodation is regarded as available if it is kept in a permanent state of readiness for his or her occupation. Rented accommodation is ignored if the lease is for a period of less than 12 months (unfurnished) or for a period of less than two years (furnished).

34.4.3 Regular visitors

An individual who comes to the UK with the intention of spending at least 91 days a year in the UK over a period of four tax years is regarded as taxable from the date of arrival. An individual who comes without any such clear intention becomes ordinarily resident from the start of the fourth tax year after arrival, although in limited cases it may be possible to remain not ordinarily resident for a further 12 months. However, where he or she forms a definite intention to stay (or acquires accommodation on a long-term basis) during the intervening years, he or she would become ordinarily resident from 6 April of the year in which he or she acquires the accommodation or decides to reside in the UK for at least four tax years.

34.4.4 Visits for education

A person who comes to the UK for a period of study or education expected to last more than four years is regarded as resident and ordinarily resident from the date of his or her arrival. If the period is not expected to exceed four years, he or she may be treated as not ordinarily resident, but this depends on whether he or she:

- has accommodation available in the UK, or
- intends to remain in the UK when his or her education is complete, or
- proposes to visit the UK in future years for average periods of three months or more per tax year.

If, despite originally intending not to do so, a student remains in the UK for more than four years, he or she is usually treated in any event as ordinarily resident from the beginning of the fourth year of his or her stay. This applies to both a person who comes to the UK for his or her own education or a parent or guardian of a child who comes in connection with the child's education.

34.5 CEASING TO BE RESIDENT IN THE UK

34.5.1 Working abroad

Up to 1992–93 there was an important distinction between individuals who worked full-time abroad and others who lived overseas in that the legislation provided specifically that, where an individual worked full-time abroad, the fact that he or she had accommodation available for his or her use was not regarded as a relevant factor in determining his or her residence status. From 6 April 1993, this distinction became less important as the legislation now provides that if an individual is in the UK for some temporary purpose only and with no view to establishing residence here, he or she will not be regarded as resident just because he or she has available accommodation in the UK (s 831 ITA 2007). Nevertheless, it is still easier to establish non-UK resident status if you are working overseas.

HMRC 6 (which has effect from 6 April 2009) at 8.5 states that:

If you are leaving the UK to work abroad full-time, you will only become not resident and not ordinarily resident from the day after the day of your departure, as long as:

- you are leaving to work abroad under a contract of employment for at least a whole tax year
- you have actually physically left the UK to begin your employment abroad and not, for example, to have a holiday until you begin your employment
- you will be absent from the UK for at least a whole tax year

- your visits to the UK after you have left to begin your overseas employment will
  - total less than 183 days in any tax year, and
  - average less than 91 days a tax year. This average is taken over the period of absence up to a maximum of four years.

Any days you spend in the UK because of exceptional circumstances beyond your control, for example an illness which prevents you from travelling, are not normally counted for this purpose. If you do not meet all of these conditions, you will remain resident and ordinarily resident in the UK unless you are leaving the UK permanently or indefinitely.

If these conditions are met, the individual is normally regarded as not resident and not ordinarily resident in the UK on the day following the date of his or her departure until the day preceding the date of his or her return. On his or her return, he or she is regarded as a new permanent resident.

The treatment whereby a person is treated as not resident for part of a tax year is called the 'split year' concession. The last edition of *IR20* indicated that this concession would also apply to self-employed people who left the UK to work full time in a trade, profession or vocation providing they were able to meet conditions similar to those set out above. *HMRC 6* states (at 8.8) that 'if you are leaving the UK to work abroad for yourself in a trade, profession or vocation, then as long as your working circumstances are similar to those outlined in paragraph 8.5 (above), you will be taxed in the same way'.

34.5.2 **Involuntary residence**

(SP2/91)

HMRC accepts that where individuals are forced to spend time in the UK because of exceptional circumstances outside their control, for example, someone who was working in Libya in 2011, but who had to return to the UK prematurely following advice from the Government, would not be regarded as spending time in the UK when it was unsafe to remain in Libya. This applied to both the 91-day average test and the 183-day test. Similarly, where an individual spends days in the UK because he or she became ill while in the UK, these may be left out of account.

These concessions do not apply where an individual returns to the UK because his or her employer has prematurely terminated his or her employment contract. Also, and more fundamentally, HMRC's concession does not affect the statutory rule that an individual is automatically treated as UK-resident if he or she spends 183 days or more in the UK during a particular tax year.

> ### Tax notes
>
> Concessions on residence status do not apply where an individual returns to the UK because the employer has prematurely terminated an employment contract.

34.5.3 Other individuals who live abroad

Different rules apply where a person does not work full-time abroad (eg where an individual moves to a foreign country on retirement), or where he or she works overseas but continues to perform duties in the UK that are not incidental to the work carried out abroad. A person who falls into this category continues to be treated as resident where he or she spends an average of three months a year in the UK over a four-year period and/or has not shown a 'complete break' with the UK.

Just before the end of 2010–11, after considerable agonising, HMRC announced its new interpretation of the rules relating to those who cease to be resident because they are taking up full-time employment overseas. This typically relates to employees who are initially posted overseas for two or three years.

In HMRC's view, if someone spends ten or more days working in the UK in any tax year, ignoring incidental duties, he or she is likely to remain UK resident in that tax year. However, if it is still believed that the individual has made the necessary break and is no longer UK resident, his or her circumstances will need to be considered by HMRC on a case by case basis.

34.5.4 Temporary non-residence

An individual who leaves the UK on or after 17 March 1998 and who:

- has been tax resident in the UK for any part of at least four out of the seven tax years immediately preceding the year of departure; and
- becomes not resident and not ordinarily resident for a period of less than five tax years; and
- owns assets before he or she leaves the UK, remains liable to tax on any gains arising on those assets after departure from the UK. Gains made by him or her in the year of assessment in which he or she leaves the UK are chargeable for that year. Gains made after that year are chargeable in the year of assessment in which he or she resumes residence in the UK at the rates prevailing in that year. Losses are allowable on the same basis as gains are chargeable. Gains of non-resident trusts and companies may also be taxed if they would have been taxable had the individual been resident here (see 33.17).

Any gains made in the intervening years (ie between the tax years of departure and of return) on assets acquired by the taxpayer after becoming tax resident abroad are exempt from the charge. This exemption will not apply to assets held in a non-resident trust or closely controlled non-resident company. Special rules prevent gains on assets held before departure from escaping the charge, where gains are rolled over or otherwise deferred on the acquisition of assets during the period of absence.

It was at one point believed that certain double taxation agreements might protect a temporary non-resident from the five-year rule. Statements by HMRC cast doubt on this and the matter was put beyond doubt in FA 2005.

A similar rule was introduced in FA 2008 (now in s 832A ITTOIA 2005) in respect of relevant foreign income of temporary non-residents remitted to the UK during periods of temporary non-UK residence.

34.6 UK INCOME AND CAPITAL GAINS RECEIVED BY NON-RESIDENTS

A person who is not UK resident for a tax year may still be subject to tax on UK source income, but is not liable to tax on income that arises abroad. The following types of income are deemed to arise within the UK and are therefore subject to tax even where the individual is not resident there:

- employment income that relates to duties performed in the UK;
- trading profits from a branch or permanent establishment in the UK;
- rents from UK properties;
- dividends from UK companies;
- interest paid by a person who is UK-resident;
- 'annual payments' made by a UK-resident person.

Tax charged on investment income of a non-resident individual is normally limited to the tax deducted at source (s 811 ITA 2007). This does not apply to income from property in the UK or from trading in the UK through a broker or investment manager. UK investment income of non-resident trustees is specifically excluded from this limitation to tax deducted at source (s 812 ITA 2007).

The provisions of a double tax agreement or extra statutory concession may also limit the tax charged on a non-resident individual.

34.6.1 Earned income

Where an individual is non-resident, profits from a trade carried on outside the UK are not subject to UK tax. Where such a person has a branch or permanent establishment in the UK, a liability to UK tax may arise on profits earned from that UK presence. Double taxation agreement provisions may govern what type of presence in the UK is deemed to constitute a branch or permanent establishment.

Earnings from an employment will attract UK tax where the duties are performed in the UK unless exemption is available under a double taxation agreement (see 34.6.5).

Where an individual works full-time abroad under a contract of employment, the resulting income is not subject to UK tax even though the employer may be a UK company. However, a Crown employee or a member of the Armed Forces is regarded as performing the duties of his or her employment in the UK and he or she may therefore be subject to UK tax even though he or she performs all his or her duties overseas and is not resident in the UK.

Problems have arisen in recent years where an individual was granted a non-approved share option at a time when he or she was UK-resident and subject to tax under s 15 ITEPA 2003, with the option subsequently exercised after he or she ceased to be UK resident. HMRC's view is that a liability arises in these circumstances even if he or she is no longer employed by the company concerned (see *Tax Bulletin 60* (as well as articles in *Bulletins 46, 55* and *56*) October 2002 on HMRC's views on treaty relief). However, any lingering doubts were put to rest in FA 2008 with effect from 6 April 2008. The amount taxable will usually be calculated by reference to the proportion of UK residence during the option vesting period.

Pensions paid by UK providers to non-UK residents are subject to tax unless the recipient can claim the benefit of a double taxation agreement (see 34.6.5).

34.6.2 Concession for bank and building society interest

In practice, certain income arising from a UK source is not subject to UK tax. In particular, bank deposit interest is not subject to deduction of UK tax at source provided the non-resident certifies he or she is not ordinarily resident in the UK (s 858 ITA 2007). HMRC will not assess such income unless the account is managed or controlled by a UK-resident agent. This also applies to interest or dividends paid gross by a building society, discounts (eg on deep discount bonds), gains on deep gain securities and interest on certificates of tax deposit.

34.6.3 Exempt gilts

Interest paid on all British Government securities is exempt from UK tax where the person who owns the security is not UK-resident (unless the interest forms part of the profits of a trade carried on in the UK).

34.6.4 Income from property

Rental income received by an individual from a UK property is subject to UK tax even if he or she is not UK-resident. A tenant who pays rent exceeding £100 pw direct to a non-resident landlord should withhold basic rate tax at source unless HMRC has authorised the tenant to pay the rent gross under the non-resident landlord scheme. Where rent is paid to a UK agent, the tenant should pay the rent without deduction, but the agent must then deduct tax from the net rental income.

HMRC will authorise a tenant or agent to make gross payments if the landlord has registered for self-assessment and his or her tax affairs are up to date. See www.hmrc.gov.uk/cnr/nr_landlords.htm.

Tax notes

Rental income received by an individual from a UK property is subject to UK tax even if he or she is not UK-resident.

34.6.5 Double taxation agreements

Where a non-UK resident individual is resident in a foreign country that has a double taxation agreement with the UK, it may be possible for certain income that would normally suffer UK tax at source to be exempted from UK tax, or subjected only to a lower rate.

Remuneration for work performed in the UK

Most double taxation agreements provide an exemption from UK tax for employment income, provided the following conditions are satisfied:

- the person who is entitled to the remuneration is present in the UK for a period not exceeding 183 days in aggregate in the tax year concerned; and
- the remuneration is paid by, or on behalf of, an employer who is not UK resident; and
- the remuneration is not borne by a permanent establishment or a fixed base that the employer has in the UK.

In practice, employers can agree with their tax office not to apply PAYE for employees on short-term business visits to the UK if all the following conditions are met:

- the employee is resident in a country with which the UK has a double taxation agreement which contains the standard article that exempts short-term earnings in the UK;
- he or she is coming to the UK to work for a UK company or the UK branch of an overseas company;
- he or she is expected to be in the UK for no more than 183 days in any 12-month period.
- the UK company or branch is not going to bear the cost of the employee's remuneration.

See HMRC's PAYE online manual; www.hmrc.gov.uk/manuals/
pommanual/PAYE82000.htm.

Pensions

Double taxation agreements generally provide for exemption from UK tax
in respect of a pension paid by a UK company or pension scheme, although
such a pension is normally subject to tax in the foreign country concerned.

Interest

In general, most double taxation agreements provide for a person resident
in the foreign country concerned to be exempt from UK tax on interest.
The company, etc that pays the interest can be given authorisation to pay it
gross. In cases where tax has been withheld at source, the individual may
be entitled to a repayment.

Dividends

A double taxation agreement usually includes a provision that a person
who receives a dividend from a UK company is entitled to the benefit of a
reduced tax credit and any balance should be repaid.

Royalties

Most double taxation agreements provide that where a royalty is received
by a person resident in the foreign country concerned, the royalties shall be
free from UK tax.

34.6.6 Allowances and reliefs

A British subject, or Commonwealth citizen, was previously entitled to full
personal allowances for a tax year, even if he or she was not a UK resident.
This entitlement was withdrawn for Commonwealth citizens from 6 April
2010, unless available under the provisions of a double taxation agreement.

Nationals of EU countries have been entitled to a full personal allowance
since 1996–97. This also applies to nationals of Iceland, Norway and
Liechtenstein. Allowances may also be available to residents or citizens of
other countries under the terms of a double taxation agreement (eg Japan).

A non-resident person is not generally entitled to repayment supplement
so it is normally important that tax should not be overpaid where this can
be avoided. However, EU nationals may be entitled to such a supplement
even though they are not UK-resident.

Limit on tax liability of non-residents

Chapter 1, Part 14 ITA 2007 limits the extent of the UK tax liability on non-residents so that, in general terms, it does not exceed:

- the tax due on total income less excluded income, but without relief for personal allowances, plus
- the tax deducted at source from the excluded income.

For the purposes of this section excluded income is:

- interest from UK sources (see Chapter 9);
- dividend income from UK companies (see 9.8);
- profits on the disposal of certificates of deposit (see 10.6);
- certain Social Security benefits including state pensions (see
- Chapter 40);
- other trading income carried out by brokers and investments managers as defined by s 817, but not Lloyd's underwriting income (see 37.7); and
- any other income so designated by the Treasury.

Example – Alternative calculations

Mr and Mrs *M* live in Spain and are treated as not resident in the UK for the tax year ended 5 April 2012. They have the following UK income arising in the tax year:

	Mr M	Mrs M
Source	£	£
Rental income	3,000	8,000
Bank interest paid gross	10,000	500
Dividends and tax credits	4,000	0
Total taxable income	17,000	8,500
UK tax liability for 2011–12		
Income	17,000	8,500
Less: Personal allowances	7,475	7,475
Taxable UK income	9,525	1,025
Tax calculation		
Interest £2,560/£500 at 10%	256.00	50.00
Interest/Rents £2,965/£525 at 20%	593.00	105.00
Dividends £4,000/0 at 10%	400.00	0.00
Total	1,249.00	155.00
Less: Tax credits	400.00	0.00
Balance payable	849.00	155.00

The s 811 calculation produces the following results:

Source	Mr M £	Mrs M £
Total UK income	17,000	8,500
Less: Excluded income under s 813		
Bank interest	10,000	500
Dividends and tax credits	4,000	0
Net taxable UK income	3,000	8,000
Tax calculation		
Rent £3,000/£8,000 at 20%	600.00	1,600.00
Total	600.00	1,600.00
Normal tax liability (see above calculation)	849.00	155.00
Tax advantage/(disadvantage) of s 811	249.00	(1,445.00)

In this example, Mr *M* would consider using the alternative calculation and Mrs *M* would not as it is obviously not to her advantage.

HMRC Helpsheet IR300 (www.hmrc.gov.uk/helpsheets/hs300.pdf) deals with this subject.

Bank interest

If bank interest suffers tax at source (usually because the individual has not declared his or her non-resident status to the bank) it is not exempt.

Section 811 ITA 2007 merely limits the UK tax on such income to the amount of tax which has been withheld. Unless you can make a claim under a double taxation agreement, you will be stuck.

Tax notes

If you are not resident in the UK, notify your bank so that interest need not be withheld at source. If tax is deducted, you may not be able to reclaim it.

34.6.7 Capital gains

A non-UK resident is not normally subject to CGT except where capital gains arise from the disposal of assets used by a branch or permanent establishment of a business carried on by him or her in the UK (but see 34.5.4 on the taxation of gains realised by former UK residents who are non-resident for less than five complete tax years and s 10(4) TCGA 1992 where temporary non-residents seek to rely on DTA exemption).

34.7 NON-RESIDENT INVESTMENT COMPANIES

A non-UK resident who has significant investment income arising within the UK may take certain steps to minimise his or her UK tax liability. In particular, where he or she cannot claim the benefit of a double taxation agreement, it may be advisable for UK assets such as real estate to be held through a non-UK resident company. This means that any tax liability is confined to basic rate tax and there is no question of any higher rate liability. Care must be taken to ensure the company is not centrally managed and controlled in the UK; otherwise it will be taxed as a UK resident.

In such a case, it would still be sensible for some portfolio investments to be retained in his or her own name if he or she is a British subject or is otherwise entitled to claim a personal allowance. Sufficient personal income should arise to use such an allowance as this will be wasted if all the income arises within an offshore company.

In some cases, a non-resident landlord should form an offshore company to acquire UK properties already owned and let by him or her. The offshore company can raise a qualifying loan to purchase the properties from the individual concerned and interest payable on the loan may then be offset against the non-resident company's rental income. This is a way in which an individual who already owns a property that is not subject to a mortgage may create a situation where interest is payable on a qualifying loan that is deductible in computing UK property income.

Tax notes

Where a non-UK resident cannot claim the benefit of a double taxation agreement, it may be advisable for UK assets such as real estate to be held through a non-UK resident company.

34.8 WHEN TAX SHOULD BE WITHHELD FROM PAYMENTS TO NON-RESIDENTS

34.8.1 Non-resident sportsmen and entertainers

A person paying a non-UK resident sportsman or entertainer for work carried out in the UK is liable to withhold tax at basic rate and pay this over to HMRC (see 21.6), although it may be possible to agree an alternative withholding rate with HMRC.

Olympic Games 2012

Legislation has been introduced (ss 65 to 68 FA 2006) in respect of the 2012 Olympic Games to be held in London. One of the measures introduced effectively takes non-UK resident Olympic athletes and their entourages out of the foreign entertainer rules and consequently out of the scope of UK tax.

Similar rules in schedule 20, FA (No.1) 2010 applied to employees or contractors of overseas teams which compete in the 2011 Champions League final and were neither UK resident nor ordinarily UK resident at the time of the final.

34.8.2 Rent payable to non-resident landlord

A person who pays rent to a non-resident landlord must withhold tax at the basic rate and account for this to HMRC unless he or she has been authorised to pay gross (see 34.6.4). This obligation arises whether the payment is made within the UK or by payment out of a bank account held overseas.

Where a UK resident pays a premium to a non-resident landlord, the same requirement to withhold tax arises.

Where a tenant has failed to withhold tax, he or she could be required to account for it to HMRC. In such circumstances, he or she may withhold sums from subsequent payments of rent to cover the amounts paid over to HMRC.

The obligation to withhold tax does not arise where the tenant pays rent to an agent in the UK. Also, HMRC would not normally pursue a tenant who had failed to deduct tax where he or she could not have known that the landlord was non-resident and nothing had happened to put him or her on notice. For more details, see 21.5.

34.8.3 Interest

A person paying interest to a non-resident individual or trust should withhold tax at the basic rate and account for this to HMRC.

34.9 DO NOT RELY ON IR20

From 6 April 2009, HMRC has started again from scratch. The department does not consider itself to be bound by anything in *IR20*. Its practice and interpretation of the law on residence and domicile is now set out in guidance published on its website in *HMRC 6*. See www.hmrc.gov.uk/crn/hmrc6.pdf

35

THE INCOME AND CAPITAL GAINS OF FOREIGN DOMICILIARIES

This chapter deals with the tax treatment of individuals who are resident but not domiciled in the UK. As this is a complex and constantly developing area it is recommended that professional advice is sought prior to taking any significant action. This chapter contains the following sections:

General principles

Earned income

Investment income

Capital gains tax

Inheritance tax

GENERAL PRINCIPLES

35.1 MEANING OF 'DOMICILE'

Domicile is a fundamentally different concept from residence and ordinary residence. It is not a tax concept at all, but a concept arising out of general law. It is not the same as nationality, although an individual's nationality may be one relevant factor in determining his or her domicile. The basic concept is that a person is domiciled in the country he or she regards as his or her real home. The fact that he or she may be prevented from living in that country or may need to live elsewhere because of temporary reasons (eg business and/or employment) does not necessarily mean he or she is domiciled in the country in which he or she currently resides. Under English law, an individual normally acquires his or her father's domicile at birth and retains it unless his or her father changes his own domicile before the child attains age 16. The mother's domicile will usually apply instead where a child is illegitimate or the parents divorce. The domicile acquired in this way is called the individual's 'domicile of origin'.

An individual may change his or her domicile to a 'domicile of choice'. Normally this would occur when he or she leaves his or her country of origin and takes up permanent residence abroad with no intention of returning permanently to live in the country of origin. The domicile of origin will revive if these intentions alter and he or she decides not to make a permanent home in the new country after all. This is a question of fact; see *Allen & another (exors of Johnston)* v *HMRC*, 2006 SpC 481, where a woman who had acquired a Spanish domicile of choice was held to have retained this even though she returned to the UK to be cared for by a relative.

35.1.1 Married women

A woman married before 1 January 1974 generally acquired her husband's domicile (referred to as a 'domicile of dependency'), which continued after divorce or the husband's death, although it is possible to discard her domicile of dependency and gain a new domicile of choice (which might or might not be the same as her domicile of origin). A domicile of dependency in a jurisdiction may be discarded by a woman establishing that she no longer intends to remain permanently in that country and by her ceasing to be resident there. The mere intention is not itself sufficient: an Australian woman who had acquired a domicile of dependency in England was held to be domiciled here, despite her intention to return to Australia, because she had not ceased to be resident in England.

The law is somewhat different for women married after 31 December 1973. Since then the Domicile and Matrimonial Proceedings Act 1973 allows a woman to retain an independent domicile on her marriage.

There may be exceptions to this rule imposed by a taxation treaty with the other state. For example, the treaty with the US treats wives as if they were married after 31 December 1973, regardless of the actual date of marriage.

35.1.2 Registration as an overseas elector

Section 835B ITA 2007 provides that where an individual registers as an overseas elector to vote in UK elections, this is not to be taken into account in determining his or her domicile status for tax purposes.

35.1.3 Remittance basis

The remittance basis means that an individual pays tax on foreign income and capital gains by reference to amounts brought into the UK. Foreign domiciliaries are eligible for this tax treatment but they have to make a claim to be taxed in this way. Up to 5 April 2008 it was only necessary to make a claim in respect of overseas investment income, as overseas earnings and capital gains were automatically taxed on a remittance basis. From 6 April 2008 the claim must cover all overseas income and capital gains, but there is a cost involved in making this claim, as personal allowances and the annual capital gains tax exemption will be forfeited. There may also be an additional £30,000 (or from 2012–13, £50,000) charge for longer term residents (see 35.2 below).

35.2 £30,000 SPECIAL CHARGE FOR SOME REMITTANCE BASIS USERS FROM 2008–09

A special £30,000 charge applies from 2008–09 where a non-UK domiciled individual over the age of 18 elects for the remittance basis and

- he or she has been resident in the UK for seven of the preceding nine tax years; and
- his or her unremitted overseas income and capital gains are £2,000 or more.

The special charge does not apply to minors, but years of UK residence accrue during an individual's minority, such that the remittance basis charge may apply immediately on attaining age 18, if the remittance basis is claimed.

If an individual does not elect for the remittance basis he or she will be liable for UK tax on his or her worldwide income and capital gains (see Figure 35.1).

It is open for an individual to choose the remittance basis for some tax years and not others. If the individual pays the £30,000 to HMRC directly from an overseas bank account, doing so will not constitute a remittance.

But if money is transferred into the individual's UK account to pay it this will be a remittance even if he or she then uses that money to pay the £30,000 special charge.

Ideally, an individual who chooses to pay the £30,000 should have a small source of overseas income or gains and should nominate income from this source so that the £30,000 covers UK tax on it if and when he or she makes remittances to the UK from his or her other overseas sources. Individuals should at all costs avoid remitting nominated funds to the UK. The income from that source need not be very much (but should be at least £1); it is not necessary that the UK tax on the nominated income should actually amount to £30,000.

Figure 35.1 – New rules for non-doms from 2008–09

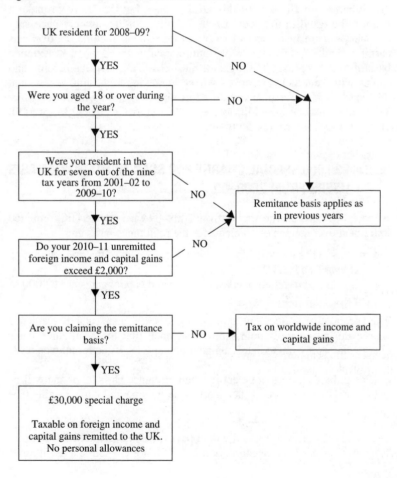

If the individual does not nominate the income to which the £30,000 relates, subsequent remittances may be treated as remittances of income on a most unfavourable basis (see 35.3.8).

35.3 £50,000 SPECIAL CHARGE FOR SOME REMITTANCE BASIS USERS FROM 2012–13 AND LIMITED RELAXATION OF CHARGE

At the June Budget 2010, the Government confirmed that it intended to review the taxation of non-UK domiciled individuals. It has done so, and announced the following changes in the 2011 Budget.

The Govenment intends to increase the existing £30,000 annual charge to £50,000 for non-UK domiciliaries who have been UK resident for 12 or more years and who wish to retain access to the remittance basis, with effect from 6 April 2012.

The £30,000 charge will be retained for those who have been resident here for at least seven of the past nine tax years but fewer than 12 years. It is expected that the new charge will work in much the same way as the existing RBC, as regards minor children, nomination, etc.

The Government considered that the fact that foreign income and gains are taxed if they are brought to the UK is a disincentive to inward investment. Accordingly, it intends to remove the tax charge when non-UK domiciliaries remit foreign income or capital gains to the UK for the purpose of commercial investment in UK businesses. It also wishes to simplify some aspects of the current tax rules to remove undue administrative burdens. The Government will issue a consultation document in June 2011. It has however promised that there will be no other substantive changes to these rules for the remainder of this Parliament.

35.4 WHAT CONSTITUTES A REMITTANCE?

35.4.1 General principles

A remittance arises where an individual brings money into the UK, either in cash or by transferring money to a UK bank account, or by using overseas funds to purchase an asset or a service in the UK, even if the funds themselves are paid abroad.

Overseas income and capital gains are also remitted if they are brought into the UK or enjoyed there. For example, payment of disposal proceeds into a UK bank account counts as a remittance, as does a payment into a UK bank account from an overseas bank account containing such proceeds. Less obviously, the income will be enjoyed in the UK if an individual has a large deposit account outside the UK and he or she formally secures a

UK bank loan against this deposit account. However, if the money is spent outside the UK, and is not used directly or indirectly in the UK for the benefit of a relevant person, it is not deemed to have been remitted.

Payment of disposal proceeds into a bank account in the Channel Islands or Isle of Man does not constitute a remittance to the UK. An outright gift that takes place outside the UK will not normally be a remittance provided the cheque, etc is paid into an overseas bank account for the recipient. However, if the recipient is a relevant person and the funds are used in the UK for his or her benefit, or a 'gift recipient', and funds are used in the UK for the benefit of a relevant person, then a remittance will arise.

35.4.2 Constructive remittances

(ss 831–834 and 839 ITTOIA 2005)

The legislation deals with constructive remittances and states that a remittance is deemed to have occurred if an individual applies overseas income towards the satisfaction of:

- a debt (or interest thereon) for money lent to him or her in the UK;
- a debt for money lent to him or her abroad and brought to the UK;
- a loan incurred to satisfy such debts.

However, these rules were substantially amended for 2008–09 and subsequent years, see 35.4.4.

Case law also indicates that a constructive remittance is deemed to have occurred if an individual borrows from a UK bank but had his or her borrowings formally secured against money held in an overseas bank account.

The courts have held that a complex arrangement whereby money was transmitted between two South African companies, with the individual receiving a loan from one of them, constituted a constructive remittance of income because the individual had never really relinquished control of the money as it passed through various intermediaries. Since the courts are increasingly having regard for the overall consequences of a series of transactions, it would be unwise to rely on an artificial scheme that enabled an individual to enjoy sums in the UK that could be matched with overseas income.

35.4.3 Unauthorised remittances

In the Duchess of Roxburgh's case, a bank remitted untaxed overseas income by mistake. Because the bank acted contrary to its customer's instructions, it was held there was no liability under the remittance basis. HMRC has confirmed that it will continue to apply this treatment after 6 April 2008 (using its discretionary powers) to allow the individual to undo his or her mistake, by reversing the transfer without unreasonable delay and in any event before the end of the tax year, for example by paying the income or gains back to the original account, so that the ordering rules at ss 809I and 809J ITA 2007 will not apply. HMRC will only use its discretion in such situations as long as there have been no relevant transactions or other benefits conferred on a relevant person in the interim. Otherwise the normal ordering rules will apply.

To take an example from HMRC's residence, domicile and remittances manual: if £20,000 is transferred in error from an overseas bank to a UK bank account and two weeks later the account owner realises the mistake and immediately transfers that £20,000 directly back to the overseas bank account, HMRC will accept that s 809I and s 809J do not apply. However if, for example, the £20,000 was spent in the UK and then £20,000 from another UK account was transferred back to the overseas account then a remittance will have occurred – s 809I and s 809J do apply.

35.4.4 Extension of the definition of 'remittance' for 2008–09 onwards

The definition of 'remittance' has been extended to include bringing into the UK property that has been purchased out of overseas unremitted income. However, this does not apply to certain assets owned on 11 March 2008 or to assets acquired after that date but which were brought into the UK before 6 April 2008, or to any of the following:

- artwork brought into the UK for public display;
- personal effects, eg clothes, shoes, jewellery and watches;
- assets costing less than £1,000;
- assets brought into the UK for restoration;
- assets which are physically in the UK for less than 275 days.

A remittance may also be deemed to have occurred when a loan from a non-UK institution has been advanced in the UK and interest has been paid out of unremitted overseas income. However, this charge will not apply to mortgages already in existence on 11 March 2008 until 6 April 2028 (or the remaining period of the loan, if shorter) provided that the terms of the loan are not varied and no advances are made on or after 12 March 2008.

Tax notes

Be careful not to change the terms of an offshore mortgage in place on 11 March 2008 or using overseas income to pay the interest may in future count as a remittance.

35.4.5 Five-year rule

If a foreign domiciled individual ceases to be resident in the UK but resumes residence within five tax years, remittances made to the UK in years during which he or she was not resident may be taxed as if they were remittances made in the year that he or she returns to the UK.

35.4.6 Gifts of unremitted income after 5 April 2008

Another extension of the concept of remittance may bite where income or gains have been alienated after 5 April 2008, ie given to another person. If that person then brings the money into the UK and it is enjoyed by a relevant person, he or she is deemed to have made a remittance. Relevant persons in respect of remittances of foreign income accruing after 5 April 2008 are:

- the individual;
- the individual's spouse;
- the individual's civil partner;
- a child or grandchild of a person falling within any of the bullets above, if the child or grandchild has not reached the age of 18;
- a close company in which a person falling within any other paragraph of s 809M(2) is a participator or a company which is a 51% subsidiary of such a close company;
- a company in which a person falling within any other paragraph of s 809M(2) is a participator, and which would be a close company if it were resident in the UK, or a company which is a 51% subsidiary of such a company;
- the trustees of a settlement of which a person falling within any other paragraph of s 809M(2) is a beneficiary; or
- a body connected with such a settlement.

For these purposes, a man and woman living together as husband and wife are treated as if they were husband and wife and two people of the same sex living together as if they were civil partners of each other are treated as if they were civil partners of each other.

35.4.7 Remittances – conditions A to D

From 6 April 2008, there is a remittance of funds to the UK if either conditions A *and* B, or condition C, or condition D in s 809L ITA 2007 are met.

Condition A, (s 809L(2)) is that money or other property is brought to, or received or used in, the UK by or for the benefit of a relevant person, or a service is provided in the UK to or for the benefit of a relevant person.

Condition B is that the property, service or consideration for the service, is (wholly or in part) the income or chargeable gains, or the property, service or consideration derives (wholly or in part, and directly or indirectly) from the income or chargeable gains, and in the case of property or consideration, is property of – or consideration given by – a relevant person.

Condition B also applies where the income or chargeable gains are used outside the UK (directly or indirectly) in respect of a relevant debt, or anything deriving (wholly or in part, and directly or indirectly) from the income or chargeable gains is used outside the UK (directly or indirectly) in respect of a relevant debt.

If either condition A or condition B is not satisfied then conditions A and B together cannot be satisfied so we then have to consider conditions C (s 809L(1)(b)) and D (s 809L(1)(c)).

Turning to condition C, this requires that qualifying property of a 'gift recipient':

- is brought to, or received or used in, the UK, and is enjoyed by a relevant person;
- is consideration for a service that is enjoyed in the UK by a relevant person; or
- is used outside the UK (directly or indirectly) in respect of a relevant debt.

A gift recipient is a person, other than a relevant person, to whom the individual makes a gift of money or other property that is either income or chargeable gains of the individual, or derives (wholly or in part, and directly or indirectly) from income or chargeable gains of the individual. If a person to whom a gift is made subsequently becomes a relevant person, that person ceases to be a gift recipient.

Condition D is that property of a person other than a relevant person (apart from qualifying property of a gift recipient) is brought to, or received or used in, the UK, and is enjoyed by a relevant person, or is consideration for a service that is enjoyed in the UK by a relevant person, or is used outside the UK (directly or indirectly) in respect of a relevant debt, in circumstances where there is a connected operation. The scope of the term 'connected operation' is very wide.

35.4.8 Remittances made out of mixed funds

An individual may have a 'mixed fund', eg a bank account where the money has come from a number of sources. Section 809R ITA 2007 provides that where a mixed fund was built up out of monies from different types of income and gains, remittances of income and gains accruing post-5 April 2008 (income and gains which accrued before 6 April 2008 are still subject to the previous – non-statutory – mixed fund rules) are matched on a LIFO (last in-first out) basis with those types of income and gains in the following order:

(1) employment income;
(2) foreign self-employed earnings not subject to foreign tax;
(3) relevant foreign earnings that have not suffered foreign tax;
(4) foreign investment income that has not suffered foreign tax;
(5) foreign capital gains that have not suffered foreign tax;
(6) foreign self-employed earnings that have been subject to foreign tax;
(7) relevant foreign earnings that have suffered foreign tax;
(8) foreign investment income subject to foreign tax;
(9) foreign capital gains on which foreign tax has been charged;
(10) other income or capital.

EARNED INCOME

35.5 FOREIGN EARNINGS

35.5.1 Introduction

Someone resident and ordinarily resident in the UK but domiciled elsewhere who is employed by a UK resident employer is usually treated in the same way as a UK domiciled individual in a similar position. The earnings from such an employment are taxed in full on the arising basis under ITEPA 2003 (for the taxation of such earnings, see Chapter 4).

Where a person domiciled outside the UK is employed by a non-UK resident employer, and he or she claims the remittance basis, the tax treatment can be fundamentally different but only if none of the duties of employment are carried out in the UK. Earnings from such an employment are called 'foreign earnings'. The tax treatment of such earnings is as set out in Table 35.1.

Table 35.1 – Tax treatment of earnings under ITEPA 2003

UK domicile status	UK residence status	Arising basis (AB) or remittance basis (RB) claimed	Employment duties performed wholly or partly in the UK		Employment duties performed wholly outside the UK
			Duties performed in UK	Duties performed outside UK	
Domiciled within UK	R / OR	AB	Liable	Liable	Liable
	R / NOR	AB	Liable	Liable	Liable
		RB	Liable	Liable on remittance	Liable on remittance
	NR / NOR	AB	Liable	Not liable	Not liable
Domiciled outside UK	R / OR	AB	Liable	Liable	Liable
		RB	Liable (on AB)	Liable (on AB)	See below
	R / NOR	AB	Liable	Liable	Liable
		RB	Liable	Liable on remittance	Liable on remittance
	NR	AB	Liable	Not liable	Not liable

Notes

This table is subject to any different treatment provided for under the terms of the relevant article in a double taxation agreement.

(1)   Indicates the individual is liable to pay UK tax unless subject to the Seafarers Earnings Deduction.

(2)   For individuals not resident in the UK, the arising basis is limited to liability to UK tax on income arising in the UK.

(3)   If the individual is resident and ordinarily resident but not domiciled in the UK the remittance basis operates differently from the way in which it works for individuals who are resident but not ordinarily resident in the UK. The individual will be liable to UK tax on the arising basis for any earned income where the duties are performed wholly or partly in the UK. The liability to UK tax on income earned wholly outside the UK will depend on the residence status of the employer:

(a)   when the employer is non UK/foreign resident – liable on remittance basis

(b)   when the employer is UK resident – employment earnings are liable on arising basis.

Source: HMRC: *HMRC 6*, 10.10

35.5.2 Employer's residence status need not be same as individual's domicile

It is not necessary that the employer should be resident in the same country as that in which the individual is domiciled (although this is often the case). An individual domiciled in, for example, Switzerland and employed by a company resident in the US still has foreign earnings.

35.5.3 Earnings from employer resident in the Republic of Ireland

(s 22 ITEPA 2003)

Prior to 5 April 2008, there was one exception to the general rule that foreign earnings arise from the employment of a person not domiciled in the UK in an office or employment with a non-UK resident employer. Where the employer was resident in the Republic of Ireland, the earnings were not regarded as foreign earnings. However, with effect from 6 April 2008 foreign earnings will include earnings from an employer resident in the Republic of Ireland.

35.5.4 Earnings of person not ordinarily resident in UK

Where an individual is resident in the UK, but not ordinarily resident (see 34.2.1 for meaning of ordinary residence), it may be necessary to divide their earnings between those that derive from duties performed in the UK and those performed overseas. The remuneration referable to the UK duties is always taxed on an arising basis under ITEPA 2003 but the remuneration for duties performed overseas can be taxed on the remittance basis under s 26 ITEPA 2003, if a remittance claim has been made. Typically, the earnings would be split pro rata on a time basis.

35.5.5 Split contract needed for person not domiciled in UK

A different rule applies when a non-UK domiciled individual is both resident and ordinarily resident in the UK. The earnings from an employment with a foreign employer are all subject to tax in the UK on an arising basis where any of the duties are performed there. There are no provisions whereby remuneration can be split between earnings relating to work done in the UK and work performed overseas. However, if a foreign-domiciled individual has a separate contract of employment under which all of the duties are performed outside the UK, the earnings are taxed on the remittance basis under s 26 ITEPA 2003 providing that a remittance claim has been made.

An individual can take advantage of this treatment by having two separate contracts of employment, one covering duties performed in the UK and the other covering duties performed overseas. However, HMRC has announced that it will be considering dual contracts very carefully to ensure that in practice they really do relate to separate employments, and are not merely a single employment dressed up as two.

For these purposes, there have to be separate employments with distinct duties. It is not good enough merely to have contracts for carrying out the same duties in different geographical locations.

Where a foreign national is given a right to tax equalisation in his or her service contract, the amount charged from the UK employment may be carefully scrutinised by HMRC. This is an area where you should take advice from a specialist.

> **Tax notes**
>
> HMRC has said that it will be considering dual contracts of employment much more carefully in future to ensure that they do indeed represent separate employments, and are not merely an artificial split of a single contract.

35.6   TRAVELLING EXPENSES

(ss 373–375 ITEPA 2003)

There are special provisions that apply to individuals of foreign domicile. Certain travel expenses paid or reimbursed by an employer are not assessable income where all the following conditions are satisfied:

- The expenses must be paid during the five-year period that begins with the date of arrival in the UK.
- The expenses must relate to a journey between the individual's usual place of abode and the place in the UK where he or she works.
- The expenses must relate to journeys made by the employee, unless he or she is in the UK for a continuous period of 60 days or more for the purposes of performing duties. In this event, the expenses of a visit by his or her spouse, civil partner or minor child will also be allowable, although there is a limit of two return journeys by any such person in a tax year.

To secure this exemption it is also necessary that the employee must not have been resident in the UK in either of the two tax years that precede the year in which he or she took up UK employment.

35.7 SUBSISTENCE ALLOWANCES FOR EMPLOYEES SECONDED TO THE UK

HMRC accepts that an employer may bear certain costs where an employee is seconded to the UK for a period where it is 'reasonable to assume' that this will not exceed 24 months.

The costs that may not be taxed under this 'detached duties relief' can include travel, subsistence and accommodation costs.

An article in *Tax Bulletin 50,* December 2000 analyses what is meant by 'secondment' and outlines circumstances in which an employee of an overseas company may actually be coming to the UK to take up a new office or employment rather than working there under a continuation of his or her existing employment contract.

The article explains that if the employer provides, for example, a flat for the seconded employee to use instead of hotels, the expenditure is not regarded as a taxable benefit provided 'the total cost of the accommodation is appropriate to the business need and is reasonable and not excessive'. Examples are given of what might not be regarded as reasonable.

35.8 'CORRESPONDING PAYMENTS'

(s 355 ITEPA 2003)

Certain payments made by an individual out of foreign earnings qualify for tax relief where they are made 'in circumstances corresponding to those in which the payments would have reduced his or her liability to income tax' had they been paid in the UK. The main type of payment that can be relieved under this heading is a contribution to an overseas pension fund (see below).

35.9 OVERSEAS PENSION FUNDS

An overseas pension fund will not normally qualify as a registered pension scheme for UK tax purposes. However, where the benefits provided by an overseas pension fund are broadly similar to those that arise from UK registered pension schemes, HMRC may regard the employer's contributions as not constituting remuneration for ITEPA 2003 purposes and any contributions made by the employee may be deducted as corresponding payments (see above). In some situations, HMRC will accord this treatment only where the individual's rights under his or her overseas pension scheme are adapted or restricted. For example, a US national who has an individual retirement plan may be required to give notice to the US administrators so as to waive his or her ability to take a lump sum in circumstances where this would not be permitted under the rules that govern UK-approved retirement benefit schemes. Some double taxation treaties (eg UK/US) also provide for relief to be given for foreign pension contributions.

35.10   SELF-EMPLOYMENT

Where an individual is resident in the UK, any earnings from a business carried on as a sole trader are taxed as self-employment income on the arising basis. This even applies in a situation where all the work is actually performed overseas. The basis for this interpretation by the courts is that a business is deemed to be carried on from where it is controlled and, in the case of a sole trader, control is located where the proprietor is resident.

A foreign-domiciled individual who is self-employed and performs a substantial amount of work overseas might wish to consider forming an offshore company which is managed and controlled overseas. In particular, if an overseas company were to be formed, employed the individual and supplied his or her services outside the UK to customers, the earnings from that employment would constitute foreign earnings. Provided no work is performed in the UK under the employment contract, interposing an offshore company in this way would mean that he or she could take full advantage of the remittance basis for earnings taxable under ss 22–26 ITEPA 2003. As always, care should be taken over where the company is centrally managed and controlled, because it will be UK resident if it is controlled here.

> **Tax notes**
>
> A foreign-domiciled individual who carries on self-employment and who performs a substantial amount of work overseas should consider forming an offshore company.

35.11   PARTNERSHIPS CONTROLLED OUTSIDE THE UK

Where a UK-resident but foreign domiciled individual is a partner in a firm controlled outside the UK, his or her earnings from that firm are taxed as follows:

- profits from a UK branch: as trading income on the arising basis;
- overseas profits: as foreign trading income under the remittance basis.

35.12 PENSION BENEFITS

35.12.1 Lump sums paid under overseas pension schemes
(ESC A10)

Income tax is not charged on lump sum benefits received by an employee (or by his or her personal representatives or any dependant) from an overseas retirement benefit scheme or overseas provident fund where the employee's overseas service comprises:

- not less than 75% of his or her total service in the employment concerned; or
- the whole of the last ten years of his or her service in that employment (subject to the total service exceeding ten years); or
- not less than 50% of his or her total service in that employment, including any ten of the last 20 years, provided the total service exceeds 20 years.

If the employee's overseas service does not meet these requirements, relief from income tax is given by reducing the amount of the lump sum that would otherwise be chargeable by the same proportion as the overseas service bears to the employee's total service in that employment.

For payments from overseas EFRBS and s 615 schemes, charges can still arise. Although ESC A10 is being partially withdrawn from 6 April 2011, HMRC will continue to apply it to payments of lump sum relevant benefits from overseas EFRBS and s 615 ICTA 1988 schemes, where the rights to receive the benefit accrued to the employee before 6 April 2011, whenever the lump sum is paid. See Chapter 5 for the interaction of new Part 7A ITEPA with lump sum payments from overseas pensions.

35.12.2 Pensions

A non-domiciled individual who receives a pension paid by a non-UK resident person may be subject to tax under the remittance basis if this is claimed. There is no similar reduction such as that which exists for UK-domiciled individuals (see ss 573–575 ITEPA 2003), who may be taxed on only 90% of overseas pensions. If the whole pension is remitted, tax is charged on the full amount.

INVESTMENT INCOME

35.13   THE REMITTANCE BASIS FOR INVESTMENT INCOME

35.13.1   Remittance basis

Individuals who are not ordinarily resident or not domiciled in the UK can make a claim for their assessable income to be based on the amount of overseas income remitted to the UK (subject to paying the £30,000 – or £50,000 – remittance basis charge, see 35.2–35.3).

35.13.2   Income arising within the Republic of Ireland

(s 269 ITTOIA 2005)

For years up to 2007–08, where a foreign-domiciled individual had income that arose within the Republic of Ireland, it was always taxed as it arose and not on the remittance basis. It was taxed on the current year basis. This distinction was abolished by FA 2008 so that Irish income can constitute overseas income and be taxed on the remittance basis.

This brings the treatment of a foreign domiciliary's Irish income into line with the treatment of capital gains arising in Ireland, which have always been taxed on a remittance basis.

35.13.3   Individual ceasing to have source of income

For years up to 2007–08, an assessment on the remittance basis could be made for a tax year only if the source of the income still existed during that year. This rule was abolished by FA 2008 with effect from 6 April 2008. This means that previously 'source-ceased' income is potentially chargeable whenever it arose. This has caused considerable concern among clients and their advisers, as many non-UK domiciliaries have accounts which, under the old rules, contained clean capital (including source-ceased income), but which under the new rules are mixed funds.

35.13.4   Relief for foreign tax

(s 18 TIOPA 2010)

Where overseas income has borne foreign tax, credit may be claimed for this against the UK tax assessed on the same income. Relief for foreign tax paid will, however, be restricted to the UK tax payable on the same income, and will only take into account the maximum foreign tax rate permitted under the terms of a double taxation treaty.

35.14 POSITION IF FOREIGN DOMICILIARY ACQUIRES UK DOMICILE

It used to be the case that where an individual who was assessable under the remittance basis acquired a UK domicile of choice, the remittance basis ceased to apply for income tax purposes and his or her overseas income was thereafter taxable only on the arising basis. No tax liability arose if he or she then remitted money that would formerly have given rise to an income tax liability under the remittance basis. The Special Commissioners held that this rule did not apply for CGT purposes and gains that were remitted after the individual acquired a UK domicile continued to attract a tax liability.

In any event, this rule ceased to apply, from 6 April 2008. Where a person has been on the remittance basis, but is taxed in a year on the arising basis, he or she now remains subject to tax on bringing past years' income into the UK during a period when he or she is taxed on the arising basis, irrespective of whether or not he or she has in the meantime acquired a UK domicile.

35.15 MANAGING THE REMITTANCE BASIS

35.15.1 Maintaining separate bank accounts

Where a foreign-domiciled individual has substantial overseas income, it is normal for arrangements to be put in place so that remittances to the UK may be identified, as far as possible, with capital. The way this is normally dealt with is by arranging for him or her to have a minimum of four (but realistically, often more) separate bank accounts, as follows:

(1) The first account is capital, ie the cash actually held by the individual at the time he or she took up residence in the UK. It is normal for further sums to be paid into this bank account where the cash relates to the sale proceeds of assets sold at a loss for CGT purposes or the proceeds arise from sales of exempt assets. The bank should be instructed that any interest on this bank account should not be credited to the account, but paid to a separate income account (see below).

(2) The second account should contain the sale proceeds of assets that give rise to non-UK capital gains.

(3) A third account should be kept for income, including interest on the capital account and the capital gains account.

(4) At least one account containing a nominal amount of income or gains should be kept completely separately, and used as the 'nominated' account from which the £30,000 remittance basis charge is derived. In theory, this account may contain as little as £1 of income or gains, but funds from this account must not be remitted to the UK until *all* other offshore funds have been remitted.

HMRC's residence, domicile and remittances manual sets out the information required when nominating a source of income or gains on which the £30,000 remittance basis charge is to be paid. The manual states that HMRC requires the following information:

- the precise amounts of income and gains that have been nominated, (this should include the country of origin and the type and source of the income);
- the computation of the gain (if applicable);
- the exchange rates used;
- the calculation of the tax due in relation to the nominated income and gains;
- if there have been deductions for expenses or losses from either foreign income or foreign gains in arriving at the final taxable amount, full details of the amounts and nature of those expenses or losses must also be provided.

In many cases, identifying the nominated source will be simply a matter of identifying 'my bank account with XYZ Bank in Guernsey', however, there are concerns that where a client has a number of accounts with the same bank, within the same jurisdiction, stating 'my bank account with XYZ Bank in Guernsey' is not sufficient information to separately identify which account is meant, and there is a risk of 'tainting' the other accounts held at that branch so that a remittance from one of those other accounts might be treated as a remittance of nominated income or gains.

Therefore, if you have more than one account with the same bank in the same jurisdiction, when making the nomination on the SA return, you should also give sufficient information to identify the specific account, whether that is an account 'name' (eg high interest deposit account with XYZ Bank) or an account number, or some other unique identifying feature, to distinguish it from the others held with the same bank in the same territory. This does not sit well with a statement by Dave Hartnett, permanent secretary for tax, on 12 February 2008 that 'the intention is that those using the remittance basis will not be required to disclose the source of those remittances'.

Clearly, in practice, an individual may minimise his or her liability under the remittance basis by taking remittances from the capital account in (1).

In some situations, it may be sensible to go one stage further and keep two income accounts with one containing income that has not borne tax at source (eg overseas bank deposit interest) and the other income that has borne foreign tax. By organising matters in this way, remittances of income can come out of the account that contains income that has suffered foreign tax, and this will further minimise any UK tax liability.

There may also be CGT savings from having different capital gains accounts.

35.15.2 Use overseas income accounts to fund expenditure outside UK

A foreign-domiciled individual should, where possible, arrange that all possible expenditure outside the UK is funded from the income account and, where relevant, one containing income that has not borne any foreign tax at source.

CAPITAL GAINS TAX

35.16 REMITTANCE BASIS FOR CAPITAL GAINS ON FOREIGN ASSETS

35.16.1 Introduction

(ss 12 and 275 TCGA 1992)

A foreign domiciliary may be subject to CGT if he or she is either resident or ordinarily resident in the UK. Gains on UK assets are charged in the same way as gains realised by UK domiciled individuals. Gains realised on assets situated overseas by foreign domiciled remittance basis users are subject to UK CGT only if the proceeds are remitted to the UK (however the foreign domiciliary may need to pay the £30,000 remittance basis charge, see 35.2–35.3).

The following rules determine whether an asset is deemed to be situated in the UK or abroad:

- Real estate and rights over such property are situated in the country where the real estate is located.
- Tangible movable property and rights over such property are situated in the country where the property is located.
- Debts are normally situated in the country where the creditor is resident.
- Stocks, shares and securities are generally situated in the country where the company maintains its principal register. Bearer shares and securities issued by a UK incorporated company were brought within the definition of UK situs assets by FA 2005.
- Goodwill is treated as situated where the trade or business is carried on.
- Patents, trademarks and designs are situated in the country where they are registered.

> **Tax notes**
>
> If the remittance basis has been claimed, gains realised on assets situated overseas are subject to UK CGT only if the proceeds are remitted to the UK.

35.16.2 Losses not generally allowable

(s 16(4) TCGA 1992)

For 2007–08 and earlier years, where a loss arose on an overseas asset, a person of foreign domicile could not claim a capital loss. In some situations this could give rise to hardship.

This restriction was amended, from 6 April 2008. However, if a foreign domiciliary wishes to claim such losses he or she must make an irrevocable claim under s 16ZA TCGA 1992 for the first tax year after 2007–08 that incorporates a claim for the remittance basis. Moreover, choosing this relief comes at a cost as claiming losses on overseas assets means that losses on UK assets cannot be set against past years' capital gains which are assessed on the remittance basis.

There has been confusion over the time limit for making claims. The consensus among advisers is that this is governed by s 43 TMA 1970, meaning that the time limit for making a claim for the 2011–12 tax year will be four years after the end of that year, ie by 5 April 2016. However, there is an argument that ss 42(2) and (5) reinstate the self-assessment time limit of 22 months for s 8 TMA 1970 cases (ie where a notice to complete a return has been issued).

HMRC states in the residence, domicile and remittances manual that 'The election should be made for the first year for which the remittance basis is claimed, irrespective of whether the individual has any foreign chargeable gains or overseas losses in that year. The election will usually be expected to be made within the white space in the capital gains supplementary pages of the same SA Return as the first remittance basis claim is made.' This certainly indicates that HMRC believes that where a s 8 TMA 1970 notice has been given, ss 42(2) and (5) do override the longer period in s 43(1). Therefore it would be prudent to work on the basis that this is the limit.

Tax notes

Foreign domiciliaries will need to consider whether to make a claim for loss relief on disposals of non-UK assets when the tax return for the first year in which a remittance basis claim is made post-6 April 2008 is submitted. You should seek professional advice on this.

35.16.3 Rate of CGT for foreign domiciliaries

Any UK resident non-UK domiciliary paying the remittance basis charge for a particular tax year is subject to CGT on any gains chargeable in that tax year at a rate of 28% (or 10% if the gain qualifies for entrepreneurs' relief). This is because the £30,000 charge is deemed to be the income tax or CGT payable on income or gains taxable on the arising basis, which therefore automatically exceeds the basic rate limit for the year.

35.16.4 Remittances from mixed funds

Where an individual was subject to the 'order of remittances' rules in s 809J ITA 2007 in 2010–11 (because he or she was a foreign domiciliary claiming the remittance basis of taxation), any gains are deemed to have arisen before 23 June 2010 such that the 18% CGT flat rate applies to the gains.

In all other cases where a non-UK domiciliary is being taxed on the remittance basis, the tax rate applicable to a remitted gain is that in force on the date of remittance (but see above regarding the rate of tax on post-22 June 2010 remittances where the £30,000 charge is paid).

35.16.5 Gains arising in non-resident trusts

Chargeable gains treated as accruing to settlors of non-resident or dual resident settlements under s 86(4)(a) TCGA 1992 in the tax year 2010–11 were deemed to accrue before 23 June 2010 and therefore the 18% CGT flat rate applied to them.

There are some situations where chargeable gains are treated as accruing to beneficiaries of settlements where they have been matched with capital payments. In the tax year 2010–11, where the capital payments concerned were received before 23 June 2010, the gains were deemed to have accrued before that date. Where the capital payments were received on or after that date, the gains were deemed to have accrued on or after that date such that the new rates of CGT apply to them. This has resulted in unfairness in some situations as the true position is considerably more complex, but it is seen as a pragmatic solution to the numerous possible variants on matching gains with capital payments. The new rates of CGT (ie 18% or 28% – see above) apply to capital payments from 2011–12.

Table 35.2 – Effect of in-year CGT changes in 2010–11

Individual's situation	6 April to 22 June 2010	On or after 23 June 2010
Taxed on arising basis	Gains arising are taxed at 18% (4/9ths reduction where qualifying for ER).	Gains arising taxed at 18% and/or 28% dependent on availability of basic rate band (10% where qualifying for ER).
Taxed on remittance basis but no remittance basis charge (RBC) paid	Gains remitted are taxed at 18% (4/9ths reduction where qualifying for ER).	Gains remitted taxed at 18% and or 28% dependent on availability of basic rate band (10% where qualifying for ER).
Taxed on remittance basis and RBC paid	Gains remitted are taxed at 18% (4/9ths reduction where qualifying for ER).	Gains remitted taxed 28% (10% where qualifying for ER) – RBC is decmed to be a payment of tax on income or gains taxable on the arising basis which therefore exceed the individual's basic rate band for the year.
Mixed funds rules (s 809J ITA 2007) apply to a remittance in 2010–11 (regardless of whether or not the RBC is paid)	Taxed at 18%.	Treated as if remitted before 23 June 2010 and taxed at 18%.
Mixed funds rules (s 809J ITA 2007) apply to a remittance in 2011–12 and later years	N/A	CGT rate applicable for tax year in which gain remitted – but basic rate band will not be available where RBC is paid as RBC is deemed to be a payment of tax on income or gains taxable on the arising basis which therefore exceed the individual's basic rate band for the year.

Accordingly (and not to be confused with the deeming provision for 2010–11 remittances from mixed funds, referred to above) where non-UK gains were made between 6 April and 22 June 2010, foreign domiciliaries will need to consider carefully whether or not to make a remittance basis claim for 2010–11 (and pay the £30,000 RBC) and be taxed on the gain only when it is remitted, or to be taxed on the arising basis for 2010–11, to lock in the 18% rate on the gain. The claim will need to be made on the 2010–11 tax return form, ie by 31 January 2012.

35.16.6 How to take full advantage of the remittance basis

In some cases there may be no likelihood of the individual needing to bring the proceeds of a sale of foreign assets into the UK. In such a situation the payment of CGT is a matter of choice since he or she can control the amount of his or her chargeable gains. Where it is going to be necessary to bring money into the UK at some stage in the future, it is advisable to keep separate bank accounts as detailed above. Remitting funds to the UK and managing offshore accounts is an area where professional advice is essential, as the consequences of 'getting it wrong' can be very costly.

One account should receive the proceeds of assets that have been sold at a loss when measured for UK CGT purposes. This account may be used to fund remittances to the UK that are not going to give rise to a CGT liability. A second account should contain the sale proceeds of assets subject to foreign CGT. Remittances out of this account will give rise to a CGT assessment, but double tax relief will be due in respect of the foreign CGT that has been paid. Other sales of assets that have produced a gain, but have not been taxed in the foreign jurisdiction, should be kept in a third account, and should be remitted only as a last resort.

35.17 USE OF OFFSHORE COMPANIES AND TRUSTS

35.17.1 Offshore companies

The anti-avoidance legislation contained in s 13 TCGA 1992 (see 33.13) now applies to foreign-domiciled individuals who hold 10% or more of the share capital in overseas companies that would be close if they were UK resident. Provided that the individual is not caught by the IHT deemed domicile rule (see 30.1), it may well be advisable for him or her to create a non-resident trust and transfer shares in an existing offshore investment company to the trustees. This will create an excluded property trust, and prevent any personal tax liability arising under s 13 on the offshore company disposing of its investments.

It is also dangerous for the individual to occupy a property owned by an offshore company as HMRC may seek to assess him or her as a 'shadow director' if the provisions of ss 100A–100B ITEPA 2003 do not apply. If a trust is used to hold shares in an offshore company, which owns a UK residential property, which the non-domiciliary is to occupy, the impact of the pre-owned assets rules must also be considered

---

Tax notes

It is risky for an individual to occupy a UK property owned by an offshore company as HMRC may seek to assess him or her as a 'shadow director', unless ss 100A–100B ITEPA 2003 apply, or in some cases the pre-owned assets provisions may be triggered.

35.17.2 Offshore trusts

The formidable anti-avoidance provisions relating to offshore trusts (covered in Chapter 33) do not have the same effect where a foreign-domiciled individual is concerned.

Offshore or non-resident trusts can still be extremely tax-efficient where non-UK domiciled individuals are concerned. A settlement established by a non-UK domiciled individual after 18 March 1991 cannot be a 'qualifying settlement', however the provisions of s 86 TCGA 1992 (which charge a settlor to tax on gains realised by the trustees of his or her non-resident settlement) do not apply to non-UK domiciled settlors. The exemption from the s 86 charge applies even where the individual does not have the benefit of the remittance basis (see 35.2–35.3) for that year.

The provisions of s 87 TCGA 1992, which charge UK resident beneficiaries to tax when they receive capital payments from an offshore trust, which have been matched with gains, do apply to non-UK domiciliaries but are moderated where the beneficiary is a remittance basis user. Such an individual is taxed on capital payments only if he or she brings them into the UK (see 33.17.9).

See Figure 35.2 and Figure 35.3.

Figure 35.2 – Implications for a UK-resident user of the remittance basis having a shareholding in an offshore company

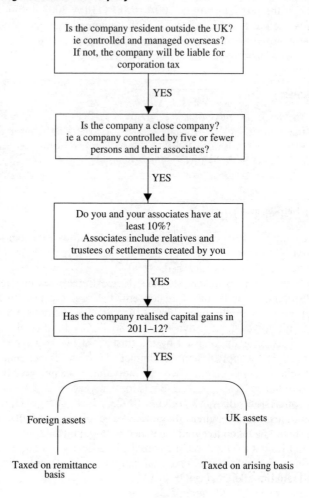

Figure 35.3 – CGT implications for a remittance basis user benefiting under an offshore trust

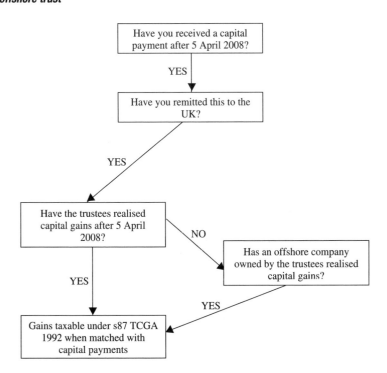

The provisions relating to offshore trusts, and their interaction with the remittance basis for non-UK domiciliaries are complex. Professional advice should be taken to avoid the many potential pitfalls.

INHERITANCE TAX

35.18   UK AND FOREIGN SITUS PROPERTY

IHT may be charged on the death of an individual who is not deemed to be domiciled in the UK, but only to the extent that his or her estate consists of property situated there. No charge arises on foreign situs property as this is classified as 'excluded property'. Table 35.3 indicates the types of property that are regarded as situated in the UK.

There is a special rule for IHT whereby an individual may be deemed to be domiciled in the UK if he or she has been resident here in 17 of the 20 tax years ending with the current year. However, foreign situs assets settled by a foreign domiciliary remain excluded property even if the individual is subsequently caught by the deemed domicile rule.

Table 35.3 – Assets chargeable to IHT

	Not chargeable	Chargeable
Channel Island property	✓	
Isle of Man property	✓	
Other foreign property	✓	
UK property	✓	✓
Bank deposits outside the UK	✓	
UK sterling bank deposits	✓	✓
UK foreign currency deposits	chargeable only if the owner is resident in the UK	
Shares in UK companies		✓
UK unit trusts and OEICs	✓	
Registered shares in foreign companies	✓	
Bearer securities	depends where the bearer certificates are held	
Debts owed by a UK resident person		(normally)
Debts owed by foreign resident person	✓	

36

BEING SUBJECT TO TWO TAX REGIMES

GERALD MOWLES, TONY FOREMAN AND MIKE WILKES

Increasingly, UK resident individuals find themselves spending significant amounts of time working in another country and may even become resident in that country as well as in the UK. There are also people who are subject to two tax regimes because their country of origin will not let them go. An example of this is the USA, where a UK resident who is a US citizen or who has a 'green card' has a continuing requirement to file a US tax return and pay US tax.

We focus here on US citizens because this is one of the more extreme examples of the tax complications that arise from having a tax footing in two regimes or 'jurisdictions'.

Another common situation is for a UK resident to have a second home in another country. Some people even have a foothold in three jurisdictions, for example someone might be UK resident, of French or Swedish domicile and have a second home in Portugal. If his or her spouse is a US national, they could end up reporting to four different revenue authorities! And it is not uncommon for such people to be beneficiaries of trusts that are administered in yet another country.

This chapter covers the following sections:

(1) General principles
(2) Working abroad
(3) US citizens living in the UK
(4) UK nationals with second homes overseas
(5) Exchange of information

36.1 GENERAL PRINCIPLES

As will become apparent, part of the art of managing all this is to recognise that there are aspects where no general rules apply.

36.1.1 Don't make assumptions

It is important to bear in mind that each country can have a tax system that is logically coherent but which does not fit another country's set of tax rules. For example, the UK draws a distinction between employment income and self-employment income. Directors are taxed on the basis that they have employment income. But in some countries the dividing line would be drawn at a different point and directors who were not full-time officers might be treated as independent contractors (ie, as if they were self-employed).

The UK system gives a 10% tax credit for UK dividends but a Jersey or Guernsey resident may have to pay 20% tax on the dividend.

There are also different rules for capital gains. Some countries do not tax capital gains unless they are closely connected with a business (countries as diverse as Belgium, New Zealand and Singapore fall into this category). Other countries are like the UK in having a comprehensive capital gains tax regime but calculate the gain very differently – if you were to take up residence in Australia or Canada the value of an asset at the date of your arrival is treated as your 'cost' for the relevant country's CGT purposes. UK legislation does not normally tax non-residents' capital gains (unless they arise from a permanent establishment in the UK); many other countries charge CGT on gains from real estate realised by non-residents and Australia for instance has reserved the right to assess non-residents on capital gains from sales of shares in Australian companies.

Just to make things even more confusing, countries call completely different taxes by the same name. Everywhere else in the EU, inheritance tax means a tax charged on a person who receives an inheritance rather than, as in the UK, a tax based on the circumstances of the person who leaves a legacy to someone else. And in these EU member states, the rate of inheritance tax payable generally depends on how closely you are related to the deceased. Many EU member states also have forced heirship rules, ie legislation that governs the way in which property must pass on death. Wills that do not accord with these rules are effectively over-ridden. Albeit a number of countries are signatories to the Hague convention on trusts, many countries' legal systems do not even contain the concept of a trust, let alone provide for the way in which trusts will be taxed.

Several EU member states also have taxes that are completely different from UK taxes, for example, France and Spain have an annual net wealth tax. Most other EU member states have a much higher rate of stamp duty on property purchases.

UK IHT gives a complete exemption where an individual leaves property to their spouse or civil partner (unless the donor is UK domiciled and the recipient is domiciled outside the UK, when the exemption is limited to £55,000). The USA allows an exemption for bequests to a non-US spouse only if the property is put into a Qualifying Domestic Trust (QDoT).

The discrepancies between different tax systems are more obvious in relation to personal taxes but they also exist in business taxes. Take VAT – just because the EU has a common VAT Directive this does not mean that each country applies VAT consistently. The UK is unusual in that it zero-rates sales of books. The threshold for registration in the UK is annual turnover of £73,000 (for 2011–12) but some other member states have no threshold at all.

To sum up, tax is often worked out very differently in other countries. You need to ascertain the principles which apply to you in any other country with which you are connected and (equally important) the way in which its taxes are administered. You will also need expert advice on how the two tax regimes interact, ie which country has primary taxing rights, and the consequences of a given transaction or series of transactions in each country. If you are a beneficiary of a trust in the foreign country, you probably need to find out how this will affect your taxable income in the UK.

36.1.2 One country will not recognise another's tax incentives

Bear in mind that if you become subject to Australian or US tax, you will not be exempt for interest earned within an ISA (see 25.1). In fact, UK tax-exempt investments such as life policies or pension schemes may not attract any special tax treatment abroad, especially if the framework in which such investments are set up is unfamiliar to the overseas system.

A stock option can qualify for tax exempt status in the USA but this treatment does not govern the UK treatment. The boot can just as easily be on the other foot – an Internal Revenue Service (IRS) official will not be over-impressed when he or she hears that a profit has been realised from the exercise of an EMI option by a US national working in the UK.

The IRS may tax a UK-resident US national on the sale of his or her London home even though it is an exempt asset for UK CGT purposes. The US system does not have a main residence exemption as such, instead it has an exclusion from charge on gains of $250,000 ($500,000 for joint filers), where the property qualified as the taxpayer's private residence for two of the last five years.

Donations to overseas charities that are not registered in the UK did not normally attract Gift Aid relief in previous years. Finance Act (No.1) 2010 has however extended UK charitable tax reliefs to certain organisations in the EU, Norway and Iceland providing the overseas organisations meet the definition of a charity under English and Welsh law as set out in the Charities Act 2006 and are regulated by an equivalent body to the Charity Commission in the UK. Gifts and legacies to charities outside these territories will be potentially subject to IHT. Likewise gifts to non-US charities will not qualify as a deduction on the US form.

Tax notes

The US system does not have a main residence exemption as such, instead it has an exclusion from charge on gains of $250,000 ($500,000 for joint filers).

36.1.3 Business entities may be taxed differently

The UK has a special tax treatment for LLPs but a foreign tax inspector will probably treat an LLP just like any other UK company. The same can apply the other way round. The US system accords a special tax treatment for Limited Liability Corporations so that the members are treated as if they were partners. HMRC will not adopt a similar treatment.

36.1.4 Double taxation agreements

Where the UK tax legislation (our 'domestic legislation') is in conflict with the provisions of a double taxation agreement, the UK domestic legislation gives way. This is not always the case with other countries!

The UK's network of double taxation agreements mean that an individual who is resident in both countries will be treated as if he or she were resident only in one country (see 36.3.9). This does not mean that the other country can impose no tax, it normally means that the country in which the individual is treated as resident can impose tax on his or her worldwide income whilst the other country can tax only income and gains arising in that country.

The UK also has some double taxation agreements for IHT. These can have some unexpected results: for example, an individual who dies domiciled in India is not subject to the normal UK rule, which deems an individual to be UK domiciled for IHT purposes if he or she has been resident in the UK in 17 of the last 20 tax years (see 30.1).

The UK has taken some measures to reduce what it would perceive as an abuse of tax treaties. For example, FA 2005 introduced measures aimed at stopping individuals who became temporarily non-resident for UK tax purposes from avoiding UK CGT by taking advantage of treaty relief with a country that has a low or nil rate of capital gains tax.

36.1.5 The EU dimension

There are very few Articles in the EC Treaty (the most important source of EU law) that cover direct taxes. Each member state has responsibility for setting its own domestic direct tax rules. However, these rules must not contravene fundamental principles of EU law. The EU is meant to be one large single market and any tax provisions that act as a disproportionate obstacle to the movement of workers, capital and the right for companies and individuals to establish themselves in different EU states have been held to contravene these principles.

Over the past ten years the European Court of Justice (ECJ) has heard a number of cases where aggrieved taxpayers have argued that legislation in particular member states does not accord with EU law. We have seen the repercussions of this in the UK where certain reliefs for UK property have had to be extended to cover property situated elsewhere in the European Economic Area (see 10.1 and 30.9).

Provisions that treat non-residents less favourably than residents have also been challenged as contrary to the EC Treaty. This has recently happened with a court case brought by the European Commission in Spain. Individuals who were not resident in Spain had been charged CGT at a flat rate of 35% whereas Spanish residents who sold after having owned the asset for 12 months paid tax at only 15%. UK residents who have sold Spanish holiday homes, etc and have been subject to the 35% rate may therefore be able to claim a refund.

Another ECJ case raised questions over the validity of exit charges imposed by UK domestic tax legislation. In the case of *Hughes du Lasteyrie du Saillant* v *Ministere de L'Ecomomie de Finances et de L' Industrie*, a French individual emigrated to Belgium and was subject to French tax on the unrealised gains on the shares a French company that he took with him. On 11 March 2004, the ECJ stated that such a charge was an impediment to the 'freedom of establishment' enshrined within the EU Treaty. It ruled that France could have asked the Belgian tax authorities for assistance in collecting the tax on any gains once the shares were sold and hence the exit charge was a disproportionate measure for collecting tax.

The UK applies an exit charge in a limited number of situations:

- when a UK individual emigrates and in the last six years he or she has received an asset on which the donor's capital gain has been held-over (see 13.6 and 17.4.5);
- when a UK resident trust becomes non-resident (see 33.15);
- when a company ceases to be UK resident;
- when assets of non-resident cease to be chargeable assets by virtue of a person ceasing to carry on a trade in the UK

It is arguable that this and other ECJ decisions mean that these exit charges are contrary to EU law. The Dutch and German tax authorities have already announced changes to their own exit charge rules as a result of this case. The UK may have to follow suit.

Individuals who have suffered exit charges should take professional advice on whether tax repayment claims could now be made.

Tax notes

People who have suffered exit charges on leaving a European country should take professional advice on whether tax repayment claims could now be made under EU law.

36.1.6 Enforcement of foreign taxes

Until recently, UK courts have not been prepared to enforce taxes imposed by other countries, however FA 2002 gave other EU countries the right to take out legal proceedings in the UK to collect unpaid taxes. Other countries have a more practical approach in that you may not be permitted to leave the country unless you have a 'tax clearance' certificate.

36.2 WORKING ABROAD

Bear in mind that the UK provides no exemption for UK residents' earnings from overseas employments. Unless you are domiciled abroad, or are treated as not ordinarily resident in the UK, and have foreign earnings (see 35.2 and 35.3), you will be taxable in full, regardless of whether these earnings are remitted to the UK or not.

We cover the rules on residence and non-residence in Chapter 34.

If you spend sufficient time in another country, you may become a resident of that state as well as a UK resident. See 34.2 regarding provisions in the UK's double tax agreements that provide for a dual resident to be treated as being resident in only one country.

Some EU countries (eg, the Netherlands and Belgium) sometimes exempt tax investment income arising in another country where an individual is newly arrived and is expected to remain there for less than five years.

Take advice if you are being seconded overseas and you have share options that you intend to exercise while you are abroad (see 6.3).

See 14.4 regarding the tax treatment if you retain your UK home but let it while you are working overseas.

36.3 US CITIZENS LIVING IN THE UK

36.3.1 US taxation

A US citizen, permanent resident or green card holder is liable to US taxation regardless of where in the world this income is paid, earned or received, so it can be said that a US citizen continues to be taxed on his or her passport. Relief is available in respect of foreign-earned income and housing credits. This section deals in brief with these allowances and some of the filing requirements that apply to a US citizen living and working in the UK.

The examples quoted are in respect of the 2010 US calendar year, but the general principles hold true for the current year, 2011.

36.3.2   Filing requirements

The filing date for the US federal return for the calendar year to 31 December 2010 was 17 April 2011. There is an automatic extension until 15 June to the filing date, though not to pay taxes, for a US individual working outside the USA who fulfils either the foreign residence or physical residence test (see 36.3.4). Care needs to be taken with the assumption that the automatic extension will apply as where federal tax has been deducted at source during the relevant calendar year normal filing dates and extensions will apply.

Table 36.1 shows the requirements for each filing status for the last three years. If your income was below the income limit for your filing status, you are not required to file a US federal income tax return for that year.

Filing status

When filing a US tax return, the taxpayer must first determine their filing status. This will decide the appropriate standard deduction and tax rates to apply. The choices are:

- single;
- head of household;
- married filing jointly;
- married filing separately;
- qualifying widow(er) with dependent child.

Filing extensions

If a US individual cannot file a return by the normal due date, he or she can file for an extension using the IRS Form 4868. This form should be filed by the due date of the return together with a 'good faith' estimate of the tax due.

The filing date is automatically extended by two months for US individuals living and working outside the USA or Puerto Rico on the date the return is due, ie for 2010 the normal filing date for those qualifying was 15 June 2011. Individuals relying upon this automatic extension do not need to file the extension but should reference that it applies when filing the Form 1040. For an additional four-month extension to this filing date, Form 4868 should have been filed by 15 June 2011 together with an estimated payment of the tax due.

Table 36.1 – Requirements in USA for each filing status

IF your filing status is:	AND at the end of the year you were	THEN file a return if your gross income for 2008 was at least:	THEN file a return if your gross income for 2009 was at least:	THEN file a return if your gross income for 2010 was at least:
Single	Under 65	$8,950	$9,350	$9,350
	65 or older	$10,300	$10,750	$10,750
Head of household	Under 65	$11,500	$12,000	$12,050
	65 or older	$12,850	$13,400	$13,450
Married filing jointly	Under 65 (both spouses)	$17,900	$18,700	$18,700
	65 or older (one spouse)	$18,950	$19,800	$19,800
	65 or older (both spouses)	$20,000	$20,900	$20,900
Married filing separately	Any age	$3,500	$3,650	$3,650
Qualifying widow(er) with dependent child	Under 65	$14,400	$15,050	$15,050
	65 or older	$15,450	$16,150	$16,150

Notes: This table refers to 'gross income', which means all income received in the form of money, goods, property and services that is not exempt from tax. *This includes any income from sources outside the USA, even if you may exclude part or all of it.* Foreign currencies must be converted to US dollars. Do not include social security benefits unless you are married filing a separate return and you lived with your spouse at any time in 2010. If you were born on 1 January 1946 you are considered to be 65 at the end of 2010.
Source: Based on IRS data

36.3.3 Foreign earnings exclusion

A US citizen or green card holder living outside the USA may elect to exclude up to $91,500 of foreign earned income. The exclusion can only be claimed if the tax home is outside the USA and the individual meets either the foreign residence or physical presence test. If only part of the qualifying period falls within the tax year, the amount of exclusion available is scaled down proportionally.

36.3.4 The foreign residence and physical presence test

The bona fide foreign residence test applies to US citizens only and requires that a US citizen is physically present in any one or a number of foreign countries for a period that includes a complete US tax year. The physical presence test extends to resident aliens as well as US citizens and to qualify the individual must be physically present in any one or a number of foreign countries for 330 days during any consecutive 12-month period.

36.3.5 Housing costs

A US citizen can elect to exclude from his or her US taxable income the excess of reasonable unreimbursed housing expenses. The housing exclusion is claimed on Form 2555.

36.3.6 Foreign tax credit

A US citizen can elect to claim tax paid on his or her non-US earnings as a credit as opposed to a deduction. The credit is limited to the ratio of foreign source taxable income to worldwide taxable income multiplied by the US tax. The foreign tax credit available will also be scaled down if he or she uses the foreign earned income exclusion.

Excess credits may be carried back one year and carried forward ten years.

36.3.7 Coming to work in the UK

A US individual coming to work in the UK should review his or her residence position as discussed in Chapter 34. If he or she is on secondment to the UK for two years or less, all reasonable subsistence accommodation expenses can be paid tax-free. Split contracts for non-UK duties are a way of mitigating UK, but not US, tax. There are also NIC (and other) exemptions from UK tax included in the US/UK double taxation treaty and the reciprocal social security agreement.

Alternative Minimum Tax (AMT)

To counteract the tax savings that legislative changes have created over the years, the US Congress enacted the Alternative Minimum Tax (AMT). In brief, the AMT ensures that where a taxpayer takes legitimate advantage of the tax reliefs available to him or her in the tax code, the IRS claws back part of this by use of the AMT calculation. In the past, overseas taxpayers who offset their US income tax with a substantial foreign tax credit often became liable for AMT, and the resulting calculations can be extremely complex. AMT is computed using IRS Form 6251. In effect, individuals with incomes that are offset by large deductions have those deductions and exemptions either reduced or eliminated. The remaining income is taxed at 28%.

Exchange rate

The IRS, via its website, publishes an unofficial exchange rate to assist individuals with their tax filing. For 2010, this rate was $1.54 to £1.

36.3.8 Forms and publications

The following forms and guidance notes can be found on the IRS website www.irs.gov or via the US Embassy website for London.

Form 1040 – US Individual Return and supporting schedules

Form 1116 – Foreign Tax Credit

Form 4868 – Application for Automatic Extension of Time to File US Individual Income Tax Return

Form 5471 – Information Return of US Persons With Respect To Certain Foreign Corporations

Form W7 – Application for IRS Individual Taxpayer Identification Number by non-US individuals

W8-Ben – Certificate of foreign status of beneficial owner for United States Tax Withholding.

Publn 54 – Tax Guide for US Citizens and Resident Aliens Abroad

36.3.9 Double taxation agreement

The current UK/US double taxation treaty was ratified on 21 March 2003. The treaty took effect at various times between 1 April 2003 and 1 January 2004. However it is important to appreciate that all US double taxation agreements contain a 'saving' clause which prevents US citizens from claiming exemption from US tax under the terms of a treaty. In order to prevent double taxation, US source income and gains may have to be re-sourced in the US to allow for credit to be given for UK tax paid on such income or gains.

To coincide with the introduction of the treaty, HMRC released a special *Tax Bulletin*, see www.hmrc.gov.uk/bulletins/tbse6.pdf.

Non-resident alien

A US non-resident alien in the past needed to file a US tax form if he or she had earnings that were effectively connected with a US business or trade. This requirement is effectively lifted where the amount is less than the personal exemption ($3,650 for 2010).

A non-resident alien is defined in the negative as an individual who is neither a US citizen nor green card holder and who is not resident in the USA.

36.3.10 Death duties

Under normal circumstances, the estate of a US citizen will be subject to US federal estate taxes, based on the value of the worldwide assets held on the date of death. The estate may also be chargeable to US local state estate taxes, depending on the deceased's connections with, and the property held, in that state.

However, UK situs assets may also be chargeable to UK IHT, although if the individual concerned had acquired a 'deemed domicile' in the UK at the date of death the potential charge to IHT is extended to the value of his or her worldwide assets.

For IHT purposes only, a deemed UK domicile can be acquired if the deceased had been resident in the UK in at least 17 out of the last 20 tax years before his or her death (see 30.1). This can lead to some complicated situations, but fortunately the double taxation estate treaty between the UK and the USA goes some way towards solving some of the problems. In particular, the treaty restricts the charge on the value of moveable assets to the country of domicile, and where the deceased was domiciled in both countries under domestic rules, a series of tie-breaker clauses set out to determine the country of domicile to be used for the purposes of applying the treaty.

Unfortunately, the treaty does not prevent a double charge on any immoveable real estate, and this will be subject to tax both in the country of domicile, and the country where the property is located. In these circumstances, credit for tax payable in the country where the property is located will be given in the country of domicile. This credit will, however, be limited if the rate of tax is more than in the country of domicile, and the overall rate of tax payable on real property will therefore always be at the highest rate of the two countries.

36.3.11 Potential conflict of laws

Further difficulties can arise where inter-spouse transfers take place, due to the slightly different way in which the usual inter-spouse exemption is applied in the UK and the USA. In the USA, the exemption is based on citizenship, whereas in the UK it is based on domicile, or deemed domicile.

For example, the estate of a US citizen husband, who has a deemed UK domicile because of his period of UK residence, will qualify for the full IHT spouse exemption in the UK if it passes to his UK domiciled British citizen wife. However, because the estate will not be passing to a US citizen spouse, it will not qualify for the surviving spouse marital deduction in the USA.

Similarly, the estate of US citizen husband, who has a deemed UK domicile because of his period of UK residence, which passes to a US citizen wife who does not have a deemed UK domicile will only qualify for a £55,000 IHT spouse exemption, even though the full surviving spouse marital deduction will be available in the USA.

Similar issues may arise with civil partnerships. These are recognised throughout the UK for tax purposes as being equivalent in all respects to marriage (Civil Partnership Act 2004), but they are only performed and recognised within certain US states, and US spouse exemptions or reliefs will not generally be extended to civil partners.

36.3.12 Useful contact details

Internal Revenue Service

The IRS in the UK can be contacted in the UK at:

United States Embassy/IRS
24/31 Grosvenor Square
London W1A 1AE
Tel: + (44) 207 408 8077 (9 am to 12 noon Monday to Friday)
Fax: + (44) 207 495 4224
www.irs.ustreas.gov

Overseas filers

Overseas taxpayers filing individual tax returns should mail them to the Austin Service Center:

Internal Revenue Service Center
Austin, Texas 73301-0215
USA

For private courier services (such as DHL, FedEx, or UPS) only, the following address should be used:

Internal Revenue Service
3651 South Interregional Hwy 35
Austin, Texas 78741
USA
Attention: Darryl Krebs
Telephone: 001 512-460-7944

National Association of Enrolled Agents (EAs)

The IRS licenses and regulates tax preparers who have either passed exams or have experience with the IRS as Enrolled Agents. You can get details of Enrolled Agents practising in your area from:

The National Association of Enrolled Agents
1120 Connecticut Avenue, NW Suite 460
Washington, DC 20036
Fax: 001 202-822-6270
E-mail: info@naeahq.org
Website: www.naea.org

36.4 UK NATIONALS WITH SECOND HOMES OVERSEAS

It is becoming more and more common for UK residents to have a second property located outside the UK. It is beyond the scope of this book to cover this subject in depth but the following should be considered by anyone buying such a property.

36.4.1 Income tax on rental income

You may let the property when you are not using it. The tax treatment of rental income is dealt with in Chapter 9. The income will be reported on the foreign pages of your tax return. Take your obligations in the foreign country seriously – it is not worth cutting corners here. For example, a person who lets a property in Eire is required to register as a landlord. If he or she or she fails to do this, he or she forfeits the ability to offset mortgage interest against the rental income.

> **Tax notes**
>
> Anyone who lets a property in Eire is required to register as a landlord. Failure to do so leads to the loss of the ability to offset mortgage interest against the rental income.

36.4.2 Capital gains tax

Capital gains tax (CGT) will apply on the disposal of a foreign property in the same way that it would apply on the disposal of an investment property in the UK. In some cases, the foreign property may be treated as your main residence for CGT purposes (see 14.1). Remember, you will also need to report any exchange gains.

36.4.3 Stamp duty

The purchase of a foreign property will not be subject to UK stamp duty. However, it is likely that the overseas country will impose local stamp duties.

36.4.4 Use of offshore companies to hold the property

There are often local tax reasons why it is considered advantageous for a UK purchaser to form an offshore company to hold the property. However, the UK tax aspects of this need to be very carefully considered. For example, in the past HMRC might well have argued that the owner's occupation of the property was a benefit in kind, which gave rise to a UK tax liability as employment income (see 4.8). Even where the UK owner was not a director of the offshore company, HMRC often argued that he or she was a 'shadow director' who could be treated as if he or she were a director. HMRC received some support for this from the Court of Appeal decision in the criminal case of *Dimsey* v *Allen* (2001 STC 1520).

> **Tax notes**
>
> Finance Act 2008 has partially addressed the problem of owning a foreign property via a company by removing the potential benefit-in-kind earnings charge in many circumstances. Furthermore, this relaxation is retrospective. However, the let-out applies only where the company was solely designed for the holding, maintenance and letting of a property and the company is owned and funded by an individual. This will not cover all situations (eg where the offshore company is owned by trustees).

The capital gains tax position on sale needs to be carefully considered. A sale of the property by an offshore company will generally give rise to a liability for a UK resident owner under s 13 TCGA 1992 (see 33.16).

Another strategy is for the property to be held in a UK LLP because the employment income issue will then not arise. If you are obliged to have a local company, investigate whether you can have the company as an undisclosed agent, which holds the property on trust for you and your wife but with this relationship being kept private. An employment income charge cannot arise in relation to property held by a company on trust in this way and it should be at least neutral for CGT. Remember however to check how such companies are dealt with for local tax purposes; some jurisdictions have sought to introduce punitive tax rates for foreign companies holding real property in the jurisdiction. Local wealth and 'council' type taxes should also be considered.

36.4.5 Will you become subject to local taxes?

If you acquire a second home overseas, you should take professional advice as to the circumstances in which you may become liable to taxes in the foreign country (eg net wealth tax).

36.4.6 Inheritance tax

The property will form part of your UK estate, but normally will generally also be subject to a charge in the country in which the property is situated. Your heirs should not suffer a double charge to IHT and foreign death duties as relief should be available, either under a double tax treaty or by virtue of the IHT provisions for unilateral relief. However, you would be well advised to make proper provisions for both UK and foreign taxes by taking professional advice in both jurisdictions and ensuring that your Will is recognised in both the UK and the other country. It may be advisable to have a UK Will governing your UK estate, and a Will in the jurisdiction concerned governing your property in that jurisdiction, especially if it is a 'forced heirship' territory and you will need to take professional advice on this.

Figure 36.1 – Flow of tax information

36.5 EXCHANGE OF INFORMATION

Not so long ago, providing information to a taxman was like confessing to a priest. The sinner would clear his or her conscience, a penance would be demanded but, where possible, the matter would be kept confidential. Now, HMRC cannot help but share its concerns, not just with other UK Government departments, but also with other countries. It also works the other way round. Figure 36.1 shows just how freely tax information can flow.

(1) All EU member states are bound by the Mutual Assistance Directive, which requires states to exchange information, either on request or spontaneously.

(2) Many parts of UK domestic legislation allow HMRC to share information with other agencies (and vice versa), in the continuing battle against crime. For example, the National Criminal Intelligence Service (NCIS) receives a huge amount of intelligence on money laundering (including the proceeds of tax evasion) and it will pass this information on to HMRC.

(3) The Anti Terrorism Crime and Security Act 2001 provides for a worldwide information gateway between tax authorities. HMRC says it will pass on information spontaneously.

(4) HMRC has the power to require third parties to provide information regarding specific or unnamed taxpayers. For example, in 2005 HMRC asked credit card companies to provide details of UK individuals who had been issued with credit cards funded by offshore bank accounts and this request was upheld by the Special Commissioners. More recently, HMRC has had more requests for information upheld so that UK banks are now being required to divulge information about their customers who have accounts with their overseas branches. In any event, since 1 July 2005 the European Savings Directive has required banks in any EU member state to either provide details of cross-border interest payments made to EU individuals or deduct 'retention tax'.

(5) Double taxation agreements between two countries usually include an 'exchange of information' article. Increasingly, in the UK's agreements, this article requires information to be exchanged to assist in preventing taxation fraud and avoidance. HMRC and the US IRS are particularly active in exchanging information. Similar agreements for the provision of information have recently been concluded with Bermuda, Guernsey and Jersey.

(6) Tax information exchange agreements (TIEAs) have been negotiated with a number of territories.

PART 6

OTHER TAXPAYERS AND TAXES

This part contains the following chapters:

37

SOME SPECIAL TYPES OF TAXPAYER

This chapter gathers together special tax provisions and HMRC practices that are relevant only to specific occupations. We also look at the tax treatment of Crown servants who are working overseas and the way that Irish nationals are taxed if they live in the UK.

The chapter contains the following sections:

Specific occupations and trades

(1) Creative artists
(2) Barristers and advocates
(3) Doctors
(4) Dentists
(5) Farmers
(6) Independent financial advisers (IFAs) and insurance agents
(7) Lloyd's underwriters ('Names')
(8) Ministers of religion
(9) Members of Parliament
(10) University lecturers
(11) Venture capitalists and participants in MBOs
(12) Seafarers
(13) Entertainers
(14) HMRC's Tactical and Information Packages

Specific rules for certain types of individuals

(15) Crown servants working overseas
(16) Irish nationals living in the UK

SPECIFIC OCCUPATIONS AND TRADES

37.1   CREATIVE ARTISTS

37.1.1   Averaging profits

(ss 221–225 ITTOIA 2005)

'Creative artists' (and farmers! see 37.5.7) are allowed to average the profits from creative works (literary, dramatic, musical or artistic works, or designs) – or farm income – of two consecutive tax years provided the profits of the lower year are less than 75% of those for the higher year. Where the profits of one year are no more than 70% of the other year's profits, the results of the two years are simply averaged. Where the profits of the lower year are between 71% and 75% of the profits for higher year, a specific averaging calculation is carried out (see 37.5.7).

37.2   BARRISTERS

37.2.1   General information

Since 1999, barristers have been required to produce accounts on an earnings (accruals) basis (see also 16.1.2).

Readers may refer to a Bar Council publication, *Taxation and Retirement Benefits Handbook*, available at www.barcouncil.org.uk. Among other things, this handbook gives detailed guidance on the amounts to be included in respect of disputed fees.

37.2.2   Accounts on a cash basis

(s 160 ITTOIA 2005)

Whereas a person carrying on a profession must normally submit accounts on an accruals basis, and include work-in-progress (see 16.1.12), barristers going into practice are allowed to remain on the cash basis until the seventh anniversary of the start of their practice. They then have to change to the earnings basis and meet the catch-up charge (Chapter 17, Part 2 ITTOIA 2005) at that time (or elect to spread the catch up charge over the following ten years).

It is possible for a barrister to change to preparing accounts on the accruals basis, including work-in-progress, during the initial seven-year period, but he or she cannot then change his or her mind and revert to the cash basis, and must prepare accounts on the accruals basis thereafter. This decision will depend on a number of factors, including his or her marginal rate of income tax and the reliability of future profit projections.

37.3 DOCTORS

Medical practices are independent contractors to the NHS, and proprietors (GPs and non-GPs) are treated for tax and national insurance purposes as self-employed individuals, either in business on their own, or in partnership.

37.3.1 Practice expenses claims

GPs and non-GP proprietors are entitled to make annual claims for income tax purposes in respect of any expenditure that has been incurred personally (ie not reimbursed by the practice) and is incurred wholly and exclusively for the purpose of the medical practice. The claims should be based on the accounting year-end of the partnership accounts.

These claims usually include the following items:

- motor expenses;
- home and mobile telephone;
- use of home/study allowance;
- employment costs of spouse or civil partner;
- courses and conferences;
- books and journals;
- computer costs;
- locum insurance premiums;
- professional subscriptions.

Capital allowances can also be claimed on any capital items such as cars, computers, medical equipment and surgery fittings.

37.3.2 Tax relief on personal loans

(ss 398–399 ITA 2007)

Interest paid on personal loans taken out by GPs to introduce capital into the partnership either to purchase a share in the partnership; to contribute money to the partnership, used wholly for the purposes of the trade or profession carried on by the partnership; to advance money to the partnership that is so used, and repaying a previous loan which qualified for this relief, attracts tax relief when claimed on the GP's personal tax return.

37.3.3 Surgery premises

It was previously possible to claim capital allowances on the cost of plant and machinery comprised within the surgery building. However, many of the items previously qualifying for capital allowances will now fall into the integral features category (s 33A CAA 2001) and join the '10% special rate pool' (see 16.2.9). The integral features listed are:

- lifts, escalators and moving walkways;
- electrical and cold water systems;
- space or water heating systems;
- powered systems of ventilation;
- air cooling or air purification (including any floors or ceilings comprised in the system);
- external solar shading.

37.3.4 Capital gains issues

Often, a GP will dispose of his or her share of the surgery premises to an incoming partner when reducing his or her commitment to the practice ahead of retirement; before actually leaving. However, one of the conditions of entrepreneurs' relief is that it is only available when leaving the practice. This will therefore affect many a GP who – when reducing his or her commitment to the practice – may now need to retain his or her full share of the surgery premises until actually leaving the practice to ensure entitlement to entrepreneurs' relief. It should also be remembered that the individual must have been engaged in the business throughout the 12-month period before sale to qualify for the relief. So temporary 'retirements' (eg related to pension entitlements) may be problematic.

> **Tax notes**
>
> Where a GP has a surgery attached to his or her main residence, the surgery is not normally covered by the principal private residence exemption when it is sold.

37.4 DENTISTS

Relief is due in respect of insurance premiums paid to secure locum cover (see 37.3.1).

The big issue for dentists is whether to take advantage of a recent change in the rules and transfer all or part of their business to a limited company. Doing this could involve a disposal of goodwill and the considerations set out in 17.6 are therefore relevant here.

37.5 FARMERS

There are several tax provisions that are specific to farmers.

37.5.1 All farming a single trade

(s 9 ITTOIA 2005)

The legislation specifically provides that all farming activities carried on by an individual within the UK are treated as a single trade. However, where an individual is a sole trader and also a partner in a farming partnership, the two activities are regarded as separate and distinct trades for tax purposes.

37.5.2 What counts as farming income?

'Farming' is defined within the statute. For tax purposes, it can be said to be the occupation of land in the UK wholly or mainly for the purposes of husbandry. Although there has always been the inclusion of items that should strictly not be taxed as farm income, HMRC has generally not sought to tax small amounts separately. Wayleaves, income from grazing and income from coppice cultivation are examples of types of income that would generally be included as farming income.

Where farmers engage in ancillary activities (eg providing B&B accommodation or self-catering facilities for holidaymakers), HMRC normally regards the resulting profits as forming part of a separate business unless they are relatively modest, in which case they may be included in the profits of the farming business for administrative convenience.

37.5.3 Farmhouse

It was normal practice for many years to claim that one-third of the farmhouse expenses were an allowable expense in computing the farm's trading profits. HMRC has since moved away from this practice and has emphasised that regard should be had to the actual usage of the farmhouse (see HMRC business income manual at BIM55250).

37.5.4 Valuation of stock

As with any business, an annual stock take and valuation exercise is required. If you are involved with the accounts for a farming business then the HMRC helpsheet IR232 sets out the principles to be applied and provides some guidance.

37.5.5 Herd basis

(Chapter 8, Part 2 ITTOIA 2005)

The effect of a herd basis election is that the herd is treated as a fixed asset. The original cost of the herd and any additions are excluded in arriving at the farm's profit for tax purposes. If the whole herd (or a substantial part of it) is disposed of, the proceeds are not treated as a trading receipt. Advice should be sought from an accountant about the mechanics of the herd basis and the potential effect of compensation payments for compulsory slaughter of animals for disease control purposes.

37.5.6 Single payment system

Many farm production subsidies were replaced by the single payment system from 2005 onwards. Rather than focusing on production subsidies, the single payment system is based on the farming land available to the farmer which triggers a 'payment entitlement'. All payments are chargeable to income tax but the basis of charge will depend on the circumstances under which they are received. For example, while it is usual for active farmers to be taxed on the payment as part of their farming income, a landowner does not have to actively farm the land to receive a payment under the scheme: payments are made where the land is simply kept in good agricultural and environmental condition. In such circumstances, this is still treated as trading income unless it is clear that the land is being used for leisure purposes (keeping pets, horses, etc): in the latter case any payment received is taxed as non-trading miscellaneous income.

37.5.7 Averaging

(ss 221–225 ITTOIA 2005)

It is possible for a farmer to make a claim under which his or her profits of two consecutive years of assessment are averaged. This election cannot be made where the profits of the lower year exceed three-quarters of the other year's profits.

Where the profits of the lower year are no more than 70% of the higher year's profits, the results of the two years are simply averaged. Where the profits of the lower year are between 71% and 75% of the higher year, averaging is done as follows:

Take three times the difference between the two years' profits	A
Deduct 75% of the profits for the higher year	(B)
	C

The resulting figure (C) is taken away from the taxable profits for the higher year and added to the profits for the lower year, to give the assessable profit for each year.

37.5.8 Farming losses

Restrictions in s 67 ITA 2007 may apply to losses suffered by farmers. The legislation may prevent a farming loss being set against the individual's other income where he or she has suffered losses for each of the preceding five tax years. This period may be extended to 11 years for thoroughbred horse breeders (see *Taxline* 1991/71) – this concession (which dates from a 1982 meeting of the then Inland Revenue and the Thoroughbred Breeders Association) applies to breeding of all thoroughbred horses (not just racehorses). The restriction will also not be applied where it can be shown that no reasonably competent farmer would have expected to have made a profit until after the period end. It should be noted that the loss position is considered before being adjusted for capital allowances.

When dealing with a farming business being carried through a partnership the losses available to a non-active partner are restricted by s 26 ITA 2007.

37.6 INDEPENDENT FINANCIAL ADVISERS (IFAs) AND INSURANCE AGENTS

IFAs and insurance agents will either be employed or self-employed. As such there are no special rules outside of those outlined in Chapters 4 and 6, and it is outside the scope of this book to examine why certain individuals in the insurance business are treated as self-employed while others in apparently similar positions are employed. The following areas have received comment from HMRC in regard to this anomaly.

37.6.1 Commissions

The time at which commission is brought into account depends on the terms of the contract. If the agent has carried out the majority of his or her work when the policy is sold, the full amount of the initial commission receivable should be charged in the tax period in which the policy is sold. In such circumstances a specific provision will be allowed, to take into account the contingent liability to repay the commission, should the policy lapse. *IRC* v *Gardner Mountain and D'Ambrumenil* 29 TC 69 and *Owen* v *Southern Railway of Peru* 36 TC 602 give some guidance, but specialist advice should be taken.

37.6.2 Agent's book

Agents may have a financial interest in their business, known as a 'book'. The book is a single asset for tax purposes and will give rise to a CGT charge on a material disposal. HMRC has issued guidance on how such a disposal may be treated. A test case, heard by the Special Commissioners, considered the purchase of an IFA's practice by an insurance company: HMRC unsuccessfully argued that the amount paid was a post-cessation receipt taxable as trading income. See *Rafferty* v *IRC* 2005 Sp Com 484.

37.7   LLOYD'S UNDERWRITERS ('NAMES')

It is beyond the remit of this book to cover the taxation of underwriters in any depth and Lloyd's has ceased to accept new individuals in an unlimited capacity. The following sections act as a general guide.

37.7.1   General principles

An individual who is a Name at Lloyd's is deemed to carry on a trade. All underwriting profits (including syndicate and other Lloyd's investment income and syndicate capital appreciation) are treated as earned income. Class 2 NIC is payable by all Names unless they are already paying the maximum NIC on other sources of earned income or are over retirement age.

Lloyd's profits are assessed for the year of assessment in which the results are declared and not for the year in which they arose (eg 2008 profits will be assessed in 2011–12).

37.7.2   Allowable deductions

A deduction may be claimed for the following personal expenses borne by the Name strictly on a calendar year cash basis:

(1) Premiums for insurance policies (known as 'Personal Stop Loss' policies) paid to minimise a Name's exposure to underwriting losses. The premiums are allowable as a deduction for the calendar year in which they are paid. Any recovery from the insurance company will in turn be treated as additional underwriting income for the year of the loss to which the recovery relates.

(2) The annual cost of maintaining a letter of credit or bank guarantee.

(3) Interest on a loan raised to finance an underwriting loss and on money borrowed to fund the Lloyd's deposit and personal reserves (and Lloyd's expenses).

(4) Personal accountancy fees. HMRC takes the view that only fees relating to the agreement of income tax assessments or to the earning or calculation of profits for the Name are allowable (and, therefore, those relating to the computation of transfers to the special reserve fund or the submission of loss claims are not). The deduction is on a cash basis.

(5) Premiums paid to an estate protection plan (an insurance arrangement intended to facilitate the winding-up of a Name's estate following death).

(6) Subscriptions to the Association of Lloyd's Members and certain expenses of attending meetings.

(7) Purchase of Lloyd's 'blue book' (annual listing of syndicate members), Chatset tables (Lloyd's league tables) and certain other publications.

(8) Subscriptions to Names' Action Groups (eg, Lime Street Action Group).

(9)   Central Fund payments, Members Agency fees and commissions and personal run-off contract premiums.

(10) Payment for exeat policies.

37.7.3   The special reserve fund

(Schedule 20 FA 1993)

The purpose of the special reserve fund is to enable Names to set aside some of their Lloyd's income, free of tax, as a reserve against future liabilities. Subject to the rules set out below, the amount transferred (if any) is entirely at the Name's discretion.

Transfers to the special reserve fund

The fund operates as follows:

(1)   Transfers into and withdrawals from the fund are made gross rather than net of tax at basic rate.

(2)   Payments into the fund are deducted as a trading expense and withdrawals are taxed as trading receipts.

(3)   A transfer into the fund is permitted of up to 50% of the profits for an underwriting year provided the fund's value at the end of the year does not exceed 50% of the Name's overall premium limit.

(4)   Transfers are voluntary and must be made by the earlier of:
      (a)   the date in which the balance of the Name's profit is paid to him or her; or
      (b)   31 October of the year of distribution.

(5)   Income and gains on the investments in the fund are exempt from income tax and CGT.

(6)   If an underwriting loss is sustained, a withdrawal must be made from the fund of the lower of the loss and the amount of the fund.

(7)   If a cash call is made, a withdrawal must be made of the lower of the cash call and the amount of the fund and, if the cash call is greater than the ultimate loss, the excess must be transferred back.

(8)   The fund is valued each year at 31 December and if the fund's value exceeds 50% of the premium limit for that year, the excess must be withdrawn.

(9)   When a Name ceases to underwrite, the fund's balance is repaid to him or her or his or her estate. This repayment may take the form of money or money's worth. Where assets are transferred, the Name (or his or her personal representatives) acquires the assets at market value for CGT purposes.

(10) The fund managers can claim repayment of tax suffered by deduction and payment of tax credit, because it is a gross fund.

(11) Although funds accumulate tax free in the fund, there is a potential tax liability on withdrawal and this is on the fund's full value.

(12) If a withdrawal is made when a Name ceases to underwrite, the payment is treated as a trading receipt received immediately after the end of the year preceding the one in which his or her Lloyd's deposit is repaid, ie normally a receipt of his or her final year of underwriting.

37.7.4 Payment of tax

The 2007 Account was declared in 2010 and will form the basis of assessment for the tax year ended 5 April 2011. Names or their agents will receive form CTA1 and CTA2 to help them complete the relevant pages of the SA form and the Lloyd's Members' Service Unit includes numbers on these forms that correspond with the boxes on the SA form. For further information see www.hmrc.gov.uk/worksheets/sa103l-notes.pdf.

37.7.5 Treatment of underwriting losses for UK taxation purposes

(ss 64,72 and 89 ITA 2007; ss 261B and 261C TCGA 1992)

Losses for an underwriting year arise where a Name's total syndicate net claims and expenses (including reinsurance costs and personal allowable expenses) exceed his or her total syndicate income from premiums, investments, capital gains and personal Lloyd's income (including stop loss recoveries). A formal claim for the relief of such losses must be made by the Name to HMRC, not later than 31 January following the end of the tax year after the year of the loss, and would normally be incorporated in the SA tax return. Thus a loss arising from the 2007 underwriting account (ie a loss for the tax year 2010–11) must be claimed by 31 January 2012.

37.7.6 Capital gains tax

A Name may have several sources of capital gains as a result of his or her participation in Lloyd's, and it is necessary to distinguish between each type to determine the correct tax treatment. Capital gains or losses that arise within each of the syndicates in which a Name participates are not subject to CGT, but are charged or allowed as Lloyd's syndicate income or expenses. They form part of a Name's Lloyd's trading income for the year of account in which the disposal takes place.

Capital gains or losses that arise within the Lloyd's special reserve fund are free of all taxes while in the fund, but are in effect taxed on withdrawal as trading income.

By contrast, capital gains or losses that arise from the disposals of assets held in a Name's Lloyd's deposit or personal reserves (other than the special reserve fund) are treated as personal gains or losses for the tax year in which the disposal takes place. They are therefore added to any other personal gains or losses arising during the same fiscal year.

Similarly, the sale or transfer of syndicate capacity is treated as a personal disposal and any gain or loss arising must be included with other capital gains or losses for the tax year in which the disposal takes place. Some Names write insurance through Members' Agent Pooling Arrangements (MAPAs), which allows them to buy into a preselected portfolio of syndicates, rather than participate directly in a much smaller number of syndicates. This enables them to spread the risk of their underwriting activities. MAPA is treated as a single asset for CGT purposes. Effectively, a CGT liability will only arise when there is a distribution from the MAPA manager of surplus funds (normally at the time of the annual auctions) or if the MAPA Name withdraws from the MAPA.

The classes of assets that qualify for roll-over relief include syndicate capacity whether held directly or through a MAPA.

37.7.7 Inheritance tax

The value of a Name's underwriting interests at Lloyd's is potentially chargeable to IHT when transferred on death. The valuation of these interests is normally based on the insolvency statement for the underwriting account ending with the calendar year preceding that in which the death occurs, and includes the value of investments held as funds at Lloyd's, underwriting profits or losses for open and running off accounts, and undistributed profits or losses for closed accounts.

Normally, underwriting interests qualify for business property relief (currently at 100%), but the Capital Taxes Office investigates all claims for relief, and may seek to reduce the relief where it believes a Name's combined reserves are excessive in relation to the amount and nature of the underwriting activities.

37.8 MINISTERS OF RELIGION

37.8.1 Ministers treated as office holders

For tax purposes, a minister of religion (which includes include vicars, reverends, priests, rabbis, imams or any other titles given to religious leaders) is generally treated as an employed person unless his or her remuneration does not consist wholly or mainly of stipend or salary. However, different rules can apply for NIC purposes (eg Elim Pentecostal ministers and Roman Catholic priests can be regarded as self-employed because of the absence of a right to remuneration).

37.8.2 No tax on rent-free accommodation

A minister of religion is not normally liable for tax in respect of his or her occupation of a vicarage or other living accommodation provided by the church, charity or ecclesiastical body (references to a 'church' include a mosque, synagogue, temple and so on; 'vicarage' includes any building in which the minister lives and from which the duties of the ministry are performed) for carrying out his or her duties (ss 99, 290 and 351 ITEPA 2003).

Sections 290A and 290B also provide exemption for payment or reimbursement of heating, lighting, cleaning and gardening expenses. This does not apply if the minister of religion is a P11D employee because his or her earnings exceed £8,500 pa (see 4.4.1).

Where the minister's earnings exceed £8,500, any tax charge on such 'service benefits' in respect of his or her vicarage or manse is limited to 10% of the net earnings (after deducting expenses).

If the minister pays his or her spouse wages for cleaning the part of the house used for official duties, this may be treated as a tax deductible expense.

37.8.3 Allowable expenses

The following expenses commonly incurred by clergy are allowable deductions under s 336 ITEPA:

- stationery, postage and use of telephone for clerical duties;
- secretarial costs (including wages paid to the minister's spouse for providing such assistance provided this is separate and distinct from work he or she performs as an active member of the church);
- travelling in the course of his or her duties (including 20p a mile for 'business use' of a bicycle);
- cost of repair or replacement of robes;
- communion expenses;
- cost of providing a locum;
- reasonable entertainment on official functions.

White v *Higgingbottom* [1983] STC 143 decided that a clergyman was not entitled to allowances for an overhead projector and screen that he paid for personally.

37.8.4 Capital gains tax

Where a minister of religion buys a property, he or she can often nominate it as his or her main residence for CGT purposes on the grounds that his or her work requires him or her to live elsewhere (see 14.3).

For further background information, *The Taxation of Ministers of Religion: A Rough Guide* can be downloaded from the Churches' Legislation Advisory Service at www.churcheslegislation.org.uk/publications.

37.9 MEMBERS OF PARLIAMENT

As one would expect, there are special rules that apply to MPs, Members of the Scottish Parliament (MSPs) and Members of the Welsh Assembly (AMs). MPs are dealt with by a central HMRC office in Cardiff. They complete a supplementary form SA102(MP), which is available on HMRC's website, together with help notes. HMRC also publishes a leaflet, *MPs, Ministers and Tax* (www.hmrc.gov.uk/freedom/mps-leaflet.pdf).

37.9.1 Salary and allowances

MPs have been paid an annual salary of £65,738 (since 1 April 2010) and, as is now widely known, they currently receive allowances for the costs of running an office, having homes both near Westminster and in their constituency, and travelling between both. Members of the cabinet, the Prime Minister and other Ministers of State receive additional amounts, on top of the basic MP's salary, although a number of Ministers have volunteered to cap these amounts in the current economic conditions.

Responsibility for paying MPs' expenses was passed to the Independent Parliamentary Standards Agency (IPSA) from 7 May 2010. This body will eventually take responsibility for MPs' pay and pensions also, when the Constitutional Reform and Governance Act 2010 comes into force. Details of the current guidance for MPs allowances can be accessed via the IPSA website (note the spaces in the PDF file name): www.parliamentarystandards.org.uk/IPSAMPs/Schemeold/schemedownload/Download scheme/MPs expenses third edition +Guidance.pdf.

FA (No. 2) 2010 includes a provision to exempt certain expenses (paid under the new rules) of MPs from tax. This broadly maintains the previous tax treatment of similar expenses paid under the 'old' rules.

Tax notes

HMRC has stated that MPs cannot claim a deduction for:

- mortgage interest on an office or part of a residence used as an office;
- newspapers, books and periodicals;
- charitable subscriptions;
- constituency newsletters and other circulars relating to party political activities, canvassing literature, election expenses or Christmas cards;
- entertaining constituents or others;
- extra costs arising out of late night sittings;
- expenses incurred by spouses or civil partners, eg in deputising for or accompanying MPs;
- accountancy fees incurred in the preparation of the SA tax return or related expenses claims.

37.9.2 MPs' pensions

Parliamentary pensions accrue at the rate of 1/50th final remuneration for every year of service. MPs can buy extra years' pension by making regular contributions or by paying a lump sum within 12 months of election to the House of Commons. This is a final salary pension scheme and MPs can choose to set contributions at 5.9% of their salary with a current 'accrual' rate – the proportion of salary received for each year of service – of 1/60th, at 7.9% of salary for a 1/50th accrual rate, or 11.9% of salary for a 1/40th accrual rate.

Ministers are able to pay contributions into a personal pension scheme if their ministerial salary is not pensionable under the Parliamentary Pension Scheme.

37.10 UNIVERSITY LECTURERS

37.10.1 Allowable deductions

A lecturer may claim a deduction for annual subscriptions to a learned society such as the Royal Society of Chemistry. Annual subscriptions to bodies such as the Association of Teachers and Lecturers and the National Association of Teachers in Further and Higher Education are also allowable (for details of the professional subscriptions that are allowable see www.hmrc.gov.uk/list3/index.htm).

The cost of academic dress is also an allowable deduction. Where a lecturer is required to demonstrate in a laboratory or do other laboratory based work, the cost of a lab coat, goggles and other protective clothing can also be claimed. For guidance on these, and other expenses, agreed with the Association of University Teachers, by HMRC, see www.hmrc.gov.uk/manuals/eimanual/EIM70705.htm.

37.10.2 Study allowance

Where a lecturer is required to undertake research work, he or she may be able to secure a study allowance reflecting extra expenditure on light and heat and the cost of office equipment such as a photocopier or fax machine. HMRC accepts that giving a deduction for a study does not result in any restriction of the CGT main residence exemption.

37.10.3 Shares in university spin-outs

Some university lecturers may be offered the opportunity to acquire shares in companies that exploit their research (university spin-outs). The acquisition of such shares could give rise to tax charges on employment income under the FA 2003 legislation (see 6.6). FA 2005 added new

Chapter 4A to Part 7, ITEPA 2003. This legislation ensures that where intellectual property is transferred from a research institution to a company, the relevant transfer will not give rise to an employment-related security tax charge unless employer and employee choose that treatment. The employee is therefore placed in an enviable position. If the venture fails, he or she will be able to exit without facing a tax liability; if it succeeds he or she will pay CGT on the profit, rather than being caught within the employment-related securities net.

The exemption only applies to the value of intellectual property transferred. In situations where the company has other inherent value, for example as a result of funding, a charge to income tax and NIC could still apply to the element that is not related to the intellectual property.

The relieving provisions apply where the individual acquires shares, or the intellectual property is transferred after 1 December 2004 and the individual acquires his or her shares within a period of six months before and after the date of an agreement under which the university or other research institution transfers intellectual property to the company.

37.11 VENTURE CAPITALISTS AND PARTICIPANTS IN MBOs

A concern for managers involved in MBOs (management buy-outs) is whether they may be subject to an income tax charge on their shares. Similarly, individuals who work for venture capital firms are able to participate in investments, either alongside the fund through 'co-investment schemes' or through a shareholding in the venture capital company, or by being a partner in a limited partnership.

HMRC has published a memorandum setting out a 'safe harbour' whereby such investments will be subject only to CGT rather than income tax if certain conditions are satisfied. See *The memorandum of understanding between the Revenue and the BVCA* online at admin.bvca. co.uk/library/documents/PDF_ 2.pdf.

For more information on the taxation of MBOs see www.pkf.co.uk/pkf/ services/corporate_finance/management_buyouts_guide/key_mbo_tax_ questions

37.12 SEAFARERS

(ss 378–385 ITEPA 2003)

A 100% deduction can be claimed by seafarers where they spend a continuous period of 365 days working outside the UK and they are resident and ordinarily resident in the UK during that period. Section 4 FA (No. 3) 2010 extends this treatment to seafarers who are EU or EEA residents. Journeys starting or ending outside the UK are treated as periods working outside the UK. A day of absence is a day when the seafarer is outside the UK at midnight. Shorter periods can be aggregated to make up a 365-day period provided that UK days in between do not make up more than one half of the combined period.

Although the definition of 'seafarer' is somewhat loose, employees who work on jack-up rigs or similar structures in the offshore oil and gas industry are not treated as seafarers and are therefore not entitled to the 100% deduction.

37.13 ENTERTAINERS

Individuals who are employed as entertainers are entitled to claim a deduction for fees paid to agents of up to 17.5% of their earnings (s 722 ITEPA 2003).

The question is 'who is an entertainer?' In June 2006, the Special Commissioners upheld a claim by chat show hosts Richard Madeley and Judy Finnigan that they fell into this category.

37.14 HMRC'S TACTICAL AND INFORMATION PACKAGES

Even if there is no special legislation that governs the way in which your particular occupation is taxed, you may well find it interesting to see the background information HMRC provides to its staff. The old Business Economic Notes (which are now dated) have been replaced by Tactical and Information Packages (TIPs) for many sectors. Although none of these is available via HMRC's website, TIPs for a few sectors have been obtained under the Freedom of Information Act and the following can currently be accessed online at www.accountingweb.co.uk/item/176475:

> TIP 14 – Confectioners, Tobacconists and Newsagents (CTNs)
> TIP 15 – Estate Agents
> TIP 49 – Waste Disposal & Landfill Sites
> TIP 56 – Bookmakers
> TIP 62 – Construction Industry
> TIP 73 – Field Sports
> TIP 114 – Franchises
> TIP 130 – Licensed Trade
> TIP 155 – Mortgage Brokers

SPECIFIC RULES FOR CERTAIN TYPES OF INDIVIDUALS

37.15 CROWN SERVANTS WORKING OVERSEAS

A Crown servant is an individual who is an employee of the Crown whose remuneration is payable out of UK or Northern Ireland public revenue (ie a civil servant or member of HM Forces). The remuneration is treated as arising from work performed in the UK even though all work may actually be carried out overseas.

Crown servants may receive foreign service allowances, which are intended to represent compensation for the extra cost of having to live outside the UK in order to perform the duties of the employment. These foreign service allowances are specifically exempted from UK tax (s 299 ITEPA 2003). In practice, these foreign service allowances may include allowances for boarding school education for the Crown servant's children.

The value of any living accommodation occupied abroad is not subject to income tax as employment income. This is because Crown servants are regarded as representative occupiers required to live in the accommodation to do their job properly.

Most double-taxation agreements provide an exemption from foreign tax for Crown servants living and working in the overseas country concerned.

Crown servants are allowed to take out certain tax-privileged investments such as ISAs and stakeholder pension plans even though they are not resident in the UK. A Crown servant may also be eligible to claim tax credits.

37.16 IRISH NATIONALS LIVING IN THE UK

An Irish national who resides in the UK is normally subject to UK tax on overseas investment income only to the extent that he or she remits such income to the UK (subject to paying the remittance basis charge where appropriate, see 35.12). Moreover, this treatment now applies to investment income received from Irish sources (the position was different for 2007–08 and earlier years).

Similarly, an Irish national who is employed by a non-resident employer, and who carries out all the duties of the employment overseas, will be able to be taxed on the remittance basis. Since 2008–09 this has also applied to employments with Irish resident employers.

CHARITIES AND NOT FOR PROFIT ORGANISATIONS

SARAH CAMPBELL

Most of this book is concerned with paying tax. However, many organisations enjoy exemptions, and their main involvement with HMRC is in reclaiming tax.

This chapter considers the following:

(1) Charities
(2) Community amateur sports clubs
(3) Mutual associations
(4) Holiday clubs and thrift funds
(5) Investment clubs

38.1   CHARITIES

Charities are dealt with by:

HMRC (Charities)
St John's House
Merton Road
Bootle
Merseyside L69 9BB
Tel: 08453 02 02 03

In Scotland, the address is:

HMRC (Charities)
Meldrum House
15 Drumsheugh Gardens
Edinburgh EH3 7UL
Tel: 08453 02 02 03.

38.1.1 A charity must exist exclusively for charitable purposes

To qualify for UK tax exemptions a charity must be charitable for the purposes of English law. Finance Act (No.1) 2010 extended UK charitable tax reliefs to certain organisations in the EU, Norway and Iceland providing the overseas organisations meet the definition of a charity under English and Welsh law as set out in the Charities Act 2006 and are regulated by an equivalent body to the Charity Commission in the UK. The new legislation also requires charities to be managed by 'fit and proper persons'.

Tax notes

Some charities operating in Scotland have recently been told that they must amend their governing document (trust deed or articles of association) to ensure that everything they do conforms with Scottish law on charities as well as English law.

38.1.2 Exemption from income tax and CGT

Charities are exempt from income tax on most income other than trading income (see 38.1.5), provided the income is applied for charitable purposes. Similarly, charities are exempt from CGT.

The exemption can be restricted where a charity has incurred non-charitable expenditure. For chargeable periods commencing on or after 22 March 2006 all charities that incur (or are treated as incurring) non-charitable expenditure will lose tax exemption on an equivalent amount of their income or gains.

The CGT exemption does not cover capital gains realised by personal representatives where the charity is a residuary legatee. In such cases, it may be more tax efficient for the executors to vest the assets in the charity before they are sold to a third party.

38.1.3 Tax credits on dividends

Tax credits on UK dividends are not reclaimable.

38.1.4 Life policies held by charitable trusts

Provisions which took effect from 9 April 2003 ensure that trustees of charitable trusts do not have to pay any tax on most UK policies and no more than basic rate tax on gains from foreign policies.

38.1.5 Trading profits

Trading income is exempt only if the trade is exercised in the course of carrying out a primary purpose of the charity or if the work is carried out mainly by its beneficiaries. The exemption also extends to the sale of donated goods, albeit there can be VAT issues linked with Gift Aid claims on donated goods. A problem area in the past has been the tax treatment of profits from other types of trading.

Small fundraising events

(ESC C4 and HMRC notice CWL4)

HMRC has issued a leaflet (CWL 4), Fundraising events: Exemption for charities and other qualifying bodies, which covers both the direct tax and VAT issues.

ESC C4 has applied for many years. The concession provides exemption for trading profits from fundraising events provided:

- the public are aware that the purpose of the event is to raise funds for charity; and
- the charity holds no more than 15 events of a similar type in the same location each year.

Small events with gross takings of up to £1,000 each do not count towards this total provided they are no more frequent than weekly. Such activities carried out more than once or twice a week are likely to be trading activities and not eligible for exemption.

Exemption for charity's trading profits

There is also a specific tax exemption for the profits of certain small trading activities carried on by a charity that are not otherwise already exempt from tax. This means that, for tax purposes, a charity no longer has to set up a trading company to carry on these activities.

This exemption applies to the profits of all trading activities that are not already exempt from tax, provided:

- the total turnover from all of the activities does not exceed the annual turnover limit, or
- if the total turnover exceeds the annual turnover limit, the charity had a reasonable expectation that it would not do so, and
- the profits are used solely for the purposes of the charity.

The annual turnover limit is:

- £5,000, or
- if the turnover is greater than £5,000, 25% of the charity's 'incoming resources', subject to an overall limit of £50,000.

For this purpose, 'incoming resources' has a very wide meaning. It means the total receipts of the charity for the year from all sources (grants, donations, investment income, etc). The small trading exemption does not apply to VAT.

Example – Turnover limits

A charity sells Christmas cards to raise funds and the sales in the year total £4,000. Assuming this is the only taxable fundraising activity, any profits will be exempt from tax because the turnover does not exceed £5,000.

However, suppose the sales in the year total £40,000 instead of £4,000. Any profits will still be exempt from tax provided the charity's incoming resources are at least £160,000, because the turnover does not exceed either:

- 25% of the incoming resources (£160,000 x 25% = £40,000), or
- the overall limit of £50,000.

Even if, in the example above, the charity's incoming resources are below £160,000, so that the turnover exceeds the annual turnover limit, the profits will still be exempt from tax if it had a reasonable expectation at the start of the year that the turnover would not exceed the limit. Thus, suppose the sales in the year total £60,000. This exceeds the overall annual turnover limit of £50,000. Any profits will still be exempt from tax if there was a reasonable expectation at the start of the year that the turnover would not exceed the limit.

The reasonable expectation test

If the total turnover of the taxable trading activities for any tax year exceeds the annual turnover limit, any profits will still be exempt from tax if it can be shown that, at the start of the tax year, it was reasonable to expect that the turnover would not exceed the limit. This might be because:

- the turnover was expected to be lower, or
- the charity's incoming resources proved to be lower than expected.

HMRC will consider any evidence the charity may have to satisfy this test. For example, if a charity has carried on an activity for a number of years, it may be able to show that the turnover increased unexpectedly compared with earlier years. If it started carrying on the activity in the year, it might be able to show that the turnover was higher than forecast when it was decided to start the activity. Also, it might be able to show that its incoming resources were lower than forecast, perhaps because a grant it was expecting to receive was not paid in the year. Evidence might include minutes of meetings at which these matters were discussed, copies of cash flow forecasts and business plans, and copies of previous years' accounts.

Tax notes

The Charity Commission has confirmed that a charity which is governed by one of the Commission's model governing documents (which contain prohibitions on 'any substantial permanent trading activity') may lawfully carry on the activities falling within the tax exemption without having to set up a trading company. If the charity has some other governing document, it should check that it permits it to carry on a fundraising trade before doing so.

Trading profits not covered by the exemption

If trading profits are not likely to be covered by the above exemption, consideration should be given to the establishment of a company that would carry on the trading activities and then pay away the profits to the charity by a Gift Aid donation. Professional advice should be taken on this.

38.1.6 Gift Aid donations by companies

Companies (including those owned by a charity and unincorporated associations, such as clubs and societies) do not:

- deduct tax from their Gift Aid donations; or
- have to give charities a formal Gift Aid declaration.

38.1.7 Gift Aid donations by individuals

Individuals still have to deduct basic rate tax from their Gift Aid donations and provide a Gift Aid declaration. The charity can reclaim this (and for 2008–09 to 2010–11, could also claim a supplement of 2% of the grossed-up Gift Aid donation).

The guidance below regarding tax reclaims and Gift Aid declarations applies only to donations by individuals.

38.1.8 Gift Aid declarations

Before a charity can reclaim tax on a donation by an individual, it must have received a Gift Aid declaration from the donor containing certain information and confirming that the donation is to be treated as a Gift Aid donation.

Donors can give a declaration:

- in advance of, at the time of or at any time after their donation (subject to the normal time limit within which a charity can reclaim tax – now four years);
- to cover a single donation or any number of donations;
- in writing (eg by post, by fax or through a website) or orally (eg over the telephone).

The amount of information required on a Gift Aid declaration has been kept to the minimum consistent with proper administration of the tax relief and the need for the charity to be able to show an audit trail. A charity can design its own Gift Aid declaration, but must ensure that it satisfies all the requirements set out below and any other legal requirements under the Data Protection Act, the Charities Act, etc. HMRC's approval is not needed for an own-design declaration, but HMRC (Charities) will be happy to approve it if required.

However, from April 2013 charities receiving small donations of £10 or less will no longer need to obtain signed declarations for the first £5,000 of such donations per annum for Gift Aid to apply. To qualify for this new style of repayment, charities will need to have been recognised by HMRC for Gift Aid purposes for at least three years and have been operating Gift Aid during this period with a good compliance history. There will be a consultation with the charity sector during summer 2011 to consider the precise details of the scheme.

Online filing for Gift Aid is to be introduced for charities in 2012–13 to simplify registering for Gift Aid and making Gift Aid claims. As a first step, HMRC will publish four new forms which will contain automatic checks to improve the accuracy of information that charities submit to HMRC.

What a Gift Aid declaration must contain

All Gift Aid declarations must contain:

- the donor's name;
- the donor's address;
- the charity's name;
- a description of the donations to which the declaration relates;
- a declaration that the donations are to be treated as Gift Aid donations; and, except in the case of a declaration given orally:
  - a note explaining the requirement that the donor must pay an amount of income tax or CGT equal to the tax deducted from his or her donations;
  - the date of the declaration.

There is no requirement for a declaration to contain the donor's signature.

In the case of a written declaration, the charity may pre-print the information (eg the charity's name) on the declaration form. In the case of an oral declaration, the information may be recited to the donor for him or her to confirm it, rather than asking the donor to recite the information.

Written records of oral declarations

If a charity receives an oral declaration it must send the donor a written record of the declaration showing:

- all the details provided by the donor in his or her oral declaration;
- a note explaining the requirement that the donor must pay an amount of income tax or CGT equal to the tax deducted from his or her donations;
- a note explaining the donor's entitlement to cancel the declaration retrospectively;
- the date on which the donor gave the declaration; and
- the date on which the written record was sent to the donor.

An oral declaration will not be effective unless and until the donor is sent the written record. This means that a charity cannot reclaim tax in respect of a donation covered by an oral declaration until it has sent the written record. Once it has sent the written record, it can reclaim tax in respect of any donations covered by the declaration, even if it received them before sending the written record.

Tax notes

A charity cannot reclaim tax in respect of a donation covered by an oral declaration until it has sent the written record.

Cancellation of declarations

Donors are entitled to cancel their declaration at any time. They may do so by notifying the charity in any form of communication. The charity should keep a record of the cancellation, including the date of the donor's notification. Cancellation has effect only in relation to donations received by the charity on or after:

- the date on which the donor notifies the cancellation, or
- such later date as the donor may specify.

The charity must not reclaim tax in respect of such donations. Any donations received up to the date of the donor's notification still qualify as Gift Aid donations.

If a donor who has given an oral declaration cancels it within 30 days of being sent the written record, the cancellation will have retrospective effect, so that it will be as if the declaration had never been made. The charity does not have to wait for the 30-day period to expire before reclaiming tax in respect of donations received. But if it reclaims tax and the donor subsequently cancels his or her declaration within the 30-day period, it must pay the tax back to HMRC. It may be possible for the charity to pay the tax back by deducting it from its next tax reclaim and it should contact HMRC Charities regarding this.

38.1.9 Gift Aid donations by partnerships

In England, Wales and Northern Ireland a partnership does not have legal personality, so a donation by a partnership is treated as made by the underlying partners. One partner may make a Gift Aid declaration on behalf of all the partners, provided he or she has the power to do so under the terms of the partnership agreement, in which case it will be sufficient for the declaration to show the name and address of the partnership. Otherwise, it will be necessary for each partner to make his or her own Gift Aid declaration, in which case he or she may do so on the same declaration form, provided it lists all the partners' names and addresses.

In Scotland, a partnership is a legal person, so in all cases one of the partners may make a Gift Aid declaration on behalf of the partnership, showing the name and address of the partnership.

To claim higher rate relief, the partners should each enter their share of the donation on their own SA returns. How the donation is apportioned between the partners is a matter for them, but normally will be in accordance with their share of the partnership profits.

38.1.10 Forms for claiming repayments

Completion of a simple claim form and schedules enable charities to reclaim tax on Gift Aid donations by individuals. HMRC Charities issues them automatically when it receives a tax reclaim. Charities can also obtain them from the Forms Orderline 0151 472 6293.

The charity has to enter the following details on the new schedule for each donor:

- the donor's name;
- the date of the donation or, where the claim covers more than one donation by the donor, the date of the last donation;
- the total amount of donations by the donor on which the charity is claiming in the schedule.

The charity will have to complete a separate schedule for each tax year, or part tax year, included in the claim. It is not necessary to calculate the tax relating to each donation separately. The charity can simply calculate the total tax reclaimed for all the donations shown on each schedule. HMRC intends to implement rules to limit the number of in-year repayment claims a charity can submit, from a date to be appointed, following consultation with the sector.

38.1.11 Keeping records

A charity must keep sufficient records to show that its tax reclaims are accurate. In other words, it must keep records that enable it to show:

- an audit trail linking each donation to an identifiable donor who has given a valid Gift Aid declaration; and
- that all the other conditions for the tax relief are satisfied.

If a charity does not keep adequate records it may be required to pay back to HMRC the tax it has reclaimed, with interest. It may also be liable to a penalty. The one area where some latitude has been introduced is in relation to small charities that reclaim less than £2,500 on Gift Aid donations. From 10 March 2008, HMRC has operated a 4% *de minimis* error level.

The form of records that must be kept is not prescribed in the legislation. In practice, it will depend on the size of the charity, the number of donors and the kind of systems used.

In the event that HMRC audit a tax reclaim, the auditor will usually ask to see in respect of a donation:

- any written Gift Aid declaration;
- in the case of an oral Gift Aid declaration, a copy of the written record sent to the donor;
- any correspondence to or from the donor that relates to the donation, including:
  - any notification of a change of name or change of address;
  - any notification of the cancellation of the Gift Aid declaration;
- the charity's bank statements;
- its paying-in book stubs showing details of cheques and cash banked;
- statements received from credit card companies showing details of credit card donations;
- a cash book recording the receipt of cash donations;
- if the charity uses envelopes to collect cash donations, a sample of the envelopes and a record of the sums enclosed;
- any other records kept relating to the donation.

A charity does not have to keep records on paper. They may be held on the hard drive of a computer, floppy disc or CD-ROM, or stored on microfiche.

Tax notes

If a charity does not keep adequate records it may be required to pay back to HMRC the tax it has reclaimed, with interest. It may also be liable to a penalty.

How long must records be kept?

If the charity is a charitable trust, it must keep records until the later of:

- the 31 January next but one after the end of the tax year to which the tax reclaim relates (eg if it makes a tax reclaim for the tax year 2011–12, until 31 January 2014);

- one year after it makes its tax reclaim, rounded to the end of the next quarter (eg in the case of a tax reclaim on 25 May 2011, until 30 June 2012); or
- when HMRC Charities completes any audit it has commenced.

If the charity is a company, it must keep records until six years after the end of the accounting period to which the tax reclaim relates.

These are the minimum periods for which a charity must keep records. In the event that HMRC Charities audits a tax reclaim and the auditor identifies errors, he or she may reopen tax reclaims for earlier years. Therefore, it may be in the charity's interests to keep records for longer than the minimum period. Since 1 April 2010 the number of years that can be re-opened on an enquiry has been limited to four, unless HMRC alleges careless or deliberate behaviour, in which case, the limits remain six years and 20 years respectively.

Using envelopes to collect cash donations

A charity may choose to collect cash donations in envelopes (eg church stewardship envelopes) so it can show an audit trail linking the donation to the donor. For one-off donations, it may choose to pre-print the Gift Aid declaration on the envelope for completion by the donor. If the donor is a regular supporter, the charity may already hold his or her Gift Aid declaration, in which case the envelope need simply contain either:

- the donor's name, or
- some other unique identifier, such as a number that can be cross-referenced to a donor register.

Where a reference number is used, this should be unique to the donor. In practice, where envelopes containing the same unique identifier are used by the donor and his or her spouse and minor children, a charity can assume that all the donations are from the donor.

When the envelope is opened and the contents are counted, an official of the charity should record the sum that it contained:

- on the envelope, and
- in a donor record.

A charity should retain all envelopes on which a Gift Aid declaration is printed for the periods set out above, together with a sample of other envelopes (normally for one month of the year) and the donor record.

38.1.12 Donations from joint bank accounts, etc

If a charity receives a donation drawn on a joint bank account, and it has not been given a Gift Aid declaration by all of the account holders, it will need to determine whether the donation is from a donor who has given a

Gift Aid declaration. It is normally safe to assume that the donation is from the account holder who signs the cheque, debit card slip or direct debit/ standing order mandate. In the case of a donation received over the phone or online, a charity can normally assume that the donation is from the account holder who authorised the transaction.

Similarly, if a charity receives a credit card donation drawn on an account in respect of which there is more than one authorised signatory, it can normally assume that the donation is from the authorised signatory who signs the credit card slip. In the case of a donation received over the phone or online, it can normally assume that the donation is from the person who authorises the transaction.

If there is any doubt whether the donation is from the person who signs the cheque, etc, or authorises the transaction, the charity should ask the person concerned to confirm whether the donation is from him or her.

38.1.13   Gift Aid donations of tax rebates

Since April 2004, self-assessment taxpayers have been able to donate their tax repayments to charities. If a charity wishes to participate in this scheme it can register with HMRC Charities, SA Donate. However, at the 2011 Budget, it was announced that SA Donate is to be withdrawn for repayments of tax due on tax returns for 2011–12 and all subsequent years as well as for any repayments made in respect of earlier tax years on or after 6 April 2012. Since its introduction in 2005, SA Donate has apparently not been widely used and it is estimated that only £400,000 was donated to charities in most years. HMRC operates a helpline on 0845 302 0203 or you can e-mail your query to charities@hmrc.gov.uk (for all queries other than those concerning VAT reliefs for charities).

38.1.14   Gifts of goods and Gift Aid

HMRC has issued guidance on the Gift Aid position where goods are donated to charity by an individual.

Gift Aid applies only to gifts of money. However, where a charity or its subsidiary company sells goods on behalf of an individual, Gift Aid relief can apply to a subsequent donation of the proceeds. It is recommended that professional advice is taken.

38.1.15   Permissible benefits for Gift Aid donors

A charity may wish to give a token of its appreciation to donors by way of thanks for their donations. Modest benefits received in consequence of making a donation will not stop the donation from qualifying as a Gift Aid donation, provided their value does not exceed certain limits. If a charity wishes to provide benefits to donors (eg as part of a membership scheme) it should consider whether the proposed benefits fall within the limits in the donor benefit rules. If they exceed the limits, the membership subscriptions cannot qualify as Gift Aid donations.

At the 2011 Budget, the Chancellor announced changes to the donor benefit limits for Gift Aid. As part of measures to encourage charitable giving, the benefit limit for donations over £10,000 has been increased. The current rule that any benefits to the donor must not exceed 5% of the donation will remain but the upper limit has been increased from £500 to £2,500. This measure will enable charities to thank their larger donors in a more generous way, without disqualifying the donation from Gift Aid.

The following points need to be considered to decide whether a donation can qualify as a Gift Aid donation:

- whether the donor, or a person connected with him or her, receives any benefits in consequence of making the donation; and
- if so, whether their value exceeds the limits in the donor benefit rules.

Tax notes

Modest gifts given as a token of appreciation to donors will not stop the donation from qualifying for Gift Aid donation, provided their value does not exceed certain limits.

38.1.16 Donor benefit rules

The rules contain two limits for the value of benefits that a donor or a person connected with him or her, may receive in consequence of making a donation. If such value:

- exceeds the limits in 38.1.17 (the relevant value test); or
- including the value of any benefits received in consequence of any Gift Aid donations made by the same donor to the same charity earlier in the same tax year, exceeds £500 (for donations over £10,000, £2,500) – the aggregate value test;

the donation will not qualify as a Gift Aid donation. However, there is a special exemption for heritage and conservation charities (see 38.1.20 below).

38.1.17 The relevant value test

Since 2006–07, the limits for the relevant value test have been:

Amount of donation	Value of benefits
£0–100	25% of the donation
£101–1,000	£25
£1,001–10,000	5% of the donation

38.1.18 The aggregate value test

In addition to satisfying the relevant value test, the value of benefits received in consequence of a donation must also satisfy the aggregate value test if the donation is to qualify as a Gift Aid donation. In other words:

- the value of benefits received in consequence of making the donation;
- plus the value of any benefits received in consequence of any Gift Aid donations by the same donor to the same charity earlier in the same tax year;
- must not exceed £500 or 5% of the gift for donations under £10,000;
- must not exceed £2,500 or 5% of the gift for donations over £10,000.

38.1.19 Application of these rules to corporate donors

These rules also apply for both close and non-close companies that make Gift Aid donations.

38.1.20 Heritage and conservation charities

Some heritage charities allow Gift Aid on donations that attract a right of free admission. Or, to put it another way, they invite the visitor to make a Gift Aid donation and in return they are granted admission to the charitable property. Since 2006–07, Gift Aid relief has been available only for donations amounting to at least 110% of the amount that would be charged for the admission right or where the donation secures free admission for a period of 12 months.

38.1.21 Tainted charity donations rules

The anti-avoidance legislation on substantial donors was introduced in 2006 and was designed to address the perceived abuse of charitable tax reliefs. The charity sector has campaigned for many years for a change in the rules, which were regarded as administratively time-consuming, caught unintended transactions and potentially discouraged donors from making large donations. From 1 April 2011, the substantial donor rules are replaced by the 'tainted charity donation' rules. There is no longer a 'donation threshold' over which the rules will apply and therefore the concept of a substantial donor has been removed.

The tainted charity donations rules will only apply to donors who enter into arrangements to obtain an advantage from a charity and under the new rules it is the donor who will be penalised rather than the charity.

The new legislation removes the entitlement to tax reliefs where a person makes a relievable charity donation (meaning a donation eligible for tax relief) which is a tainted donation.

A tainted donation exists if Conditions A, B *and* C are met:

A. The donor (or persons connected with the donor) enters into arrangements (either before or after the donation is made) and it is reasonable to assume that the donation would not have been made and the arrangements would not have been entered into independently of one another.

B. The main purpose, or one of the main purposes of the person entering into the arrangements, is to obtain an advantage either directly or indirectly from the charity to which the donation is made or a connected charity.

C. The donor is not a company wholly owned by one or more charities, at least one of which is the charity to which the donation is being made.

38.1.22 Payroll giving schemes

(s 713 ITEPA 2003)

Under a payroll giving scheme an employee asks his or her employer to deduct an amount from his or her wage or salary and pay that amount over to a charity (usually a clearing house such as the Charities Aid Foundation). PAYE is then operated by the employer as if the employee's wage or salary had been the amount remaining after the charitable donation, which has the effect of granting tax relief at the highest rate paid.

An employer is not obliged to offer a payroll giving scheme and, if a scheme is offered, employees may decide individually whether they wish to participate. Usually, each employee will specify particular charities to the clearing house, but in some cases the money is paid into a fund administered by a workplace committee. Such funds can cause difficulties, especially where the fund's name suggests that it was established by the generosity of the employer, rather than the employees themselves.

38.1.23 Gifts of shares and land

The reliefs due where an individual gives shares or land to a charity are covered at 11.10–11.11, including the anti-avoidance rules introduced in FA (No.1) 2010.

38.1.24 Useful links

Further information on charities can be found at www.hmrc.gov.uk/charities.

38.2 COMMUNITY AMATEUR SPORTS CLUBS

A package of tax reliefs was introduced for community amateur sports clubs (CASCs) in FA 2002. The relief is designed for those clubs that do not wish to, or cannot, apply for charitable status. See Table 38.1.

Table 38.1 – Comparison of charitable status with community amateur sports clubs

	Charitable status	*Community amateur sports clubs*
Direct taxes	Primary purpose trading income exempt from tax	Gross income from fund raising and trading exempt from tax where turnover is less than £30,000 (all such income is taxable if the threshold is exceeded)
	All rental income exempt	Gross income from property exempt from tax where less than £20,000 (all such income is taxable if the threshold is exceeded)
	80% mandatory relief from uniform business rates	80% mandatory relief from uniform business rates
Incentives to give	Gift Aid on individual and company donations	Gift Aid on individual donations only
	Payroll giving	No payroll giving
	Income tax relief on gift of shares	No income tax relief on gift of shares
	Inheritance tax relief on gifts	Inheritance tax relief on gifts
	Gift of assets on no-gain no-loss basis for capital gains	Gift of assets on no-gain no-loss basis for capital gains
Fundraising	Business: relief on gifts of equipment or trading stock	Business: relief on gifts of equipment or trading stock
	Grants available from other charities, eg community foundations and other bodies supporting charities	Will not attract charitable sources of funding
Regulation	Charity Commission regulation and audit	HMRC regulation and audit
	Public recognition of and trust in 'charity' and 'Gift Aid' concepts	Public awareness of community amateur sports clubs 'brand' to be developed
	Charity Commission definition based on health	HMRC definition based on the value of sport as a factor in community cohesion
	Sports must be capable of improving physical health and fitness	Likely to adopt Sports Council's list of adopted sports
	Significant social activity to be kept separate from charitable activities	Social membership permitted

By kind permission of David Bertram

To qualify for these reliefs, CASCs must be open to the whole community, organised on an amateur basis, and their main purpose must be to provide facilities for, and promote participation in, an eligible sport. An eligible sport is defined as one of those currently recognised by the National Sports Council. The reliefs consist of exemption from:

- tax on interest income;
- tax on rental income up to £20,000;
- tax on trading income up to £30,000;
- CGT.

If the CASC's turnover from trading activities is more than £30,000, or rental income before allowable deductions is over £20,000, it will not get any tax relief for these types of income. In such cases it will have to pay tax on the full amount after any allowable deductions.

In addition, when giving to CASCs, donors are able to take advantage of the following:

- Gift Aid for individual donors;
- relief from IHT;
- business tax relief on gifts of trading stock;
- relief from CGT for gifts of assets from both individuals and businesses.

These measures are designed to provide a boost for community sport activities.

38.3   MUTUAL ASSOCIATIONS

Mutual trading arises where a company or association (eg a club) trades with its members. Profits from such trading are exempt from tax under s 1070 CTA 2010 thus, if a member receives a dividend paid out of profits from mutual trading, he or she is not liable for tax on it.

Problems are apt to arise if there is a mixture of mutual trading (exempt) and trading with non-members (which is taxable), for example, a golf club that also receives green fees from non-members and makes bar profits from them. HMRC's views are set out www.hmrc.gov.uk/manuals/bimmanual/BIM24215.htm. You should consult a professional adviser if you are responsible for running a mutual company or association and the level of turnover is starting to become substantial.

If a company or association receives investment income, it will be subject to corporation tax in the normal way.

> **Tax notes**
>
> Problems are apt to arise if there is a mixture of mutual trading (exempt) and trading with non-members (which is taxable); for example, a golf club that receives green fees from non-members and makes bar profits from them.

38.3.1 CGT roll-over relief

(ss 158(1), (1A), (1B) TCGA 1992)

Roll-over relief may be due to an unincorporated association, the activities of which are not wholly or mainly carried on for profit, if it replaces an asset (eg a hockey club that sells its ground and uses the proceeds to purchase fresh headquarters). Where an asset is owned by a company of which 90% of its shares are held by such an unincorporated association or its members, roll-over relief may be due provided the other conditions are satisfied.

38.4 HOLIDAY CLUBS AND THRIFT FUNDS

In strictness, a holiday club could be regarded as an unincorporated association. For tax purposes it is regarded as a corporate entity and is charged to corporation tax on any profits in the normal manner.

38.5 INVESTMENT CLUBS

Investment clubs are usually formed by a group of friends, neighbours or work colleagues who pool their resources to buy and sell shares on the stock market. Capital gains and allowable losses are apportioned among the members and should be included in their tax returns. Every club member should declare his or her apportioned share of income or gains received from investments made by the club on his or her self-assessment return.

However, a member does not have to declare their share of investment club gains to HMRC provided that those gains, together with any other chargeable gains of the year, are less than the annual exemption (£10,600 for 2011–12) and his or her share of the proceeds from the sale of shares by the club in the tax year, together with any other proceeds from the disposal of other assets, is less than twice the annual exemption.

39

STAMP TAXES

GRAHAM CHASE, OLSWANG LLP

Stamp duty first appeared in England in 1694. It is a charge on documents, with duty stamps physically impressed to show payment. Unlike modern taxes the pressures to stamp are indirect.

The proposed move to paperless share trading was reflected in the introduction of Stamp Duty Reserve Tax (SDRT) in 1986 which tax charges agreements to transfer securities. The importance of stamp duty was further diminished as various categories of asset (eg intellectual property) were excluded from charge. The most significant change occurred in 2003 with the introduction of Stamp Duty Land Tax (SDLT), which applies to land transactions.

In each case legislative changes over the years have resulted in complex rules. Professional advice is recommended before entering into any transaction, particularly in the context of mitigation.

This chapter contains the following sections.

(1) Stamp duty
(2) Stamp Duty Reserve Tax
(3) Stamp Duty Land Tax
(4) Reliefs

39.1   STAMP DUTY

Stamp duty is not a compulsory tax, there are no self-assessment obligations and HMRC cannot issue an assessment. Instead, the pressures to stamp are indirect in that an unstamped document cannot be produced for any purpose. So in the context of an unstamped share transfer the company secretary of the share target should object to any insufficiency of stamp.

39.1.1   Scope of charge

When SDLT was introduced in 2003 the scope of stamp duty was restricted significantly. It is now limited to a transfer on sale of stock or marketable securities at the rate of 0.5% of the amount or value of the consideration, rounded up to the nearest £5. Stamp duty is not chargeable if the amount or value of the consideration for the sale is £1,000 or less and the instrument is certified.

Most forms of loan capital are excluded, but not convertible debt or certain other specified categories.

39.1.2 Transfer on sale

The charge to duty is not limited to stock transfer forms, it can apply to any instrument the effect of which is to transfer stock or marketable securities on sale; for example, a declaration of trust might be so treated, it is a case of considering the legal effect of the instrument. A transfer does not include an issue of securities, whether by way of subscription for new monies or by way of rights or bonus.

To be 'on sale' requires chargeable consideration to be given. This will usually be money but can also include the assumption of debt or the issue of consideration shares. A transfer for no consideration (a gift) is not liable to duty; there is no market value rule. If the consideration comprises an issue of shares then valuation will be relevant.

39.1.3 Territorial scope

Stamp duty applies where the subject matter of the transaction is situated in the UK. A transfer of stock or marketable securities issued by a UK company is therefore within the scope of charge.

Shares issued by a company incorporated and registered outside the UK are situated outside the UK. In practice no stamp duty charge or transfer is expected. However, the territorial scope of stamp duty is wide as the charging provisions refer to any instrument executed in the UK or relating to any property situated or to any matter or thing done or to be done in the UK. In other words, a transfer of shares in a foreign company can be subject to stamp duty if the transfer is executed in the UK or, for example, the purchase price is received in the UK.

39.1.4 Payment and interaction with SDRT

Where stamp duty is paid on a transfer then provision is made for the repayment or cancellation of SDRT paid on any agreement. There is no double charge, provided that the transfer occurs not later than six years after the agreement.

Transfers should be submitted for stamping no later than 30 days after execution, otherwise interest and penalties may be relevant. Taxpayers are normally advised to allow at least three working days in case of postal delays.

39.2 STAMP DUTY RESERVE TAX

Unlike stamp duty, SDRT is a compulsory tax which applies where one person agrees with another to transfer 'chargeable securities' for consideration in money or money's worth.

39.2.1 **Principles**

Usually the charge to SDRT arises when the agreement is made. If the agreement is conditional the charge arises when the condition is satisfied. Tax is charged at 0.5% of the amount or value of the consideration (there is no rounding).

The charge arises irrespective of how it is documented; SDRT is a tax on transactions unlike stamp duty which is a charge on documents. Where shares are traded in de-materialised form (eg CREST on the London Stock Exchange) then SDRT only is relevant as there is no instrument capable of attracting stamp duty.

For chargeable securities of companies not traded on any exchange the due date for SDRT payment is the seventh day of the month following the month in which the charge is incurred.

39.2.2 **Chargeable securities**

SDRT can apply to stocks, shares and loan capital together with certain interests in the same including rights to subscribe and options, as well as units under a unit trust scheme. Most non-UK stocks are excluded but the provisions are complex, so for example shares issued by a non-UK company which are UK registered or paired with shares issued by a UK company fall within the scope of charge.

Loan capital exempted from stamp duty is also exempt from charge to SDRT, as are most units in offshore unit trusts.

39.3 STAMP DUTY LAND TAX

The charging provisions for land transactions were fundamentally recast in 2003 with the introduction of SDLT, a compulsory tax on a self-assessment basis. The tax is wider in scope than stamp duty, with increased financial reporting and record keeping obligations on taxpayers. Subject to transitional provisions it applies to transactions with an effective date on or after 1 December 2003.

39.3.1 **Land transactions**

The charging provisions operate by reference to land transactions, meaning any acquisition of a chargeable interest. The parties to any land transaction are referred to as vendor and purchaser, whether the transaction is a freehold sale, leasehold grant, surrender or assignment. It is the purchaser who is obliged to file a return and pay the tax self-assessed in it.

In most cases the effective date is completion of the transaction. The effective date might occur earlier by reason of a contract being substantially performed; this is a reference to a substantial amount of the consideration being paid or provided, in the context of a lease, any rent being paid, or the purchaser taking possession. So for example, a lessee in respect of a new lease grant might become liable to SDLT at the time of entering premises to effect tenant works in advance of actual completion.

39.3.2 Chargeable interests

SDLT is charged upon the acquisition of any 'chargeable interest', which term relates to UK real property. A chargeable interest is widely defined to include freehold and leasehold interests as well as any interest right or power over land, or the benefit of an obligation, restriction or condition affecting the value of land. The grant of an option or pre-emption right falls within the scope of charge, as would any surrender or release of rights.

The position is more complex in relation to lease variations because only a variation taking effect as, or treated as a new lease grant, or where the rent or term is reduced, is regarded as falling within the scope of charge.

39.3.3 Rates of SDLT

Unlike stamp duty and SDRT, SDLT is charged on the chargeable consideration for a land transaction at different rates. The rates are tiered, so that tax is payable on the entire purchase price at the rate indicated: Rates of charge are as follows for residential property:

Consideration	Rate
Up to £125,000	Nil
More than £125,000 but not more than £250,000 *	1%
More than £250,000 but not more than £500,000	3%
More than £500,000	4%
More than £1m (residential property only)**	5%

* In March 2010 it was announced that first time buyers would enjoy exemption on the acquisition of residential property up to £250,000. The temporary relief is for acquisitions in the two-year period ending before 25 March 2012. This relief is currently subject to a review, the results of which are expected to be announced in autumn 2011.
**The 5% rate applies where the effective date of the transaction is on or after 6 April 2011 unless the transitional provisions are relevant, in which case, the previous 4% rate will apply. Transitional provisions are relevant in relation to contracts entered into before 25 March 2010.

In the case of non-residential property the nil rate is applicable to land transactions for chargeable consideration up to £150,000; thereafter the bands are the same, except that the highest rate is 4%.

Linked transaction rules apply if several properties are bought as part of a single scheme, arrangement or series of transactions between the same vendor and purchaser or persons connected with either. In these circumstances the charge is based on the aggregate consideration rather than the rate otherwise applicable to each individual purchase in isolation.

Finance Act 2011 provides relief for purchasers of residential property who acquire an interest in more than one dwelling. The effect of the relief is that SDLT will be calculated on the mean consideration paid for the properties, subject to a minimum rate of 1% instead of on the aggregate consideration pursuant to the linked transaction rules. This relief will come into effect from the date of Royal Assent to Finance Bill 2011.

39.3.4 Compliance

There are wide-ranging requirements relating to the filing of SDLT land transaction returns, payment, provision of information and record-keeping. The purchaser is responsible for notifying HMRC within 30 days of the effective date of a transaction and for paying the SDLT at that time. HMRC has the power to enquire into returns, to require the production of documents, to issue assessments for a failure to pay all or any SDLT, as well as to charge property in the event of a failure to pay, or underpayment. In addition to various fixed penalties interest is charged on late payment, there are also tax related penalties in certain circumstances.

HMRC may usually enquire within nine months from the last date on which a return could be made, or if later when the return was actually made. Discovery assessments may also be made no later than six years after the effective date (21 years in a case involving fraud or negligence).

39.3.5 Consideration

SDLT is chargeable on the total consideration provided, whether monetary or non-monetary. Detailed provisions provide for chargeable consideration to include any VAT, as well as the value of certain services or works. Deferred consideration is included without discount, although a payment postponement may be available. Land exchanges give rise to SDLT for both sides of the transaction, usually calculated on a market value basis. For land exchanges with an effective date on or after 24 March 2011, the Finance Act 2011 provides for the charge to be due on the greater of market value and the actual consideration paid, to prevent avoidance. As for stamp duty the assumption of indebtedness comprises chargeable consideration.

Where consideration is contingent, SDLT is payable on the basis that the amount will become payable, or that sums will continue to be payable. Where consideration is uncertain or unascertained, it should be valued at the best current estimate. Once the contingency occurs or consideration is otherwise ascertained then the purchaser will normally be obliged to file a further return, with a corresponding adjustment by way of payment or repayment of the SDLT.

There is no consideration for SDLT purposes in a number of circumstances, which include simple gifts (unless the market value rule applies as referred to below) and gifts of land where the donee agrees to pay capital gains tax or inheritance tax.

Exemption from SDLT is available for certain purchases of a property in the context of employment relocation.

39.3.6 Market value imputations

Market value may be imputed in the context of certain partnership transactions as well as transactions involving a connected company. So for example, a gift of land by an individual to a company owned by that person will give rise to SDLT based on the market value of the land so gifted.

39.3.7 Leases

The SDLT provisions in relation to leases tend to be far more onerous than was the case for stamp duty. Tax is charged on the net present value of the lease – calculated by reference to rent reserved over the entire term of the lease, discounted at a statutory rate (3.5%). The formula is available by way of an online calculator on the HMRC Stamp Taxes website.

Tax is charged at the rate of 1% of the net present value. In the case of residential property the first £125,000 of chargeable consideration is exempted (£150,000 for commercial property).

Rents are calculated by reference to the actual rents reserved in the first five years, thereafter by reference to the highest amount of rent payable in any consecutive 12-month period in the first five years. Where rents are contingent, uncertain or unascertained then a reasonable estimate is required, which should then be subject to a subsequent filing and adjustment.

There are detailed rules to cater for tenants holding over, leases for indefinite terms and rent reviews within the first five years of grant amongst others. A targeted anti-avoidance rule applicable to 'abnormal' increases in rent seeks to prevent the manipulation of rental obligations after the first five years.

39.3.8 Partnerships

Partnerships have proved to be a particularly difficult and complex area. When SDLT was first introduced transfers of partnership interests were excluded, but this changed in 2004.

Charges now potentially apply whenever a land interest is brought into or out of a partnership, (meaning any general partnership, limited partnership or limited liability partnership) or where individual partnership income profit sharing ratios change. Charges are based on the market value of the relevant proportion of the underlying land interest.

For example, if a farming partnership was formed by two individuals (who were not connected) on an equal profit share basis, with one of those partners introducing farmland and buildings, half of the value of this property would be subject to a SDLT charge.

In the case of corporate partners, a form of group relief may be applicable for certain partnership transactions where the partners have the necessary degree of connection.

A transfer of an interest in a partnership that includes an interest in land potentially attracts a SDLT charge. This rule has affected many situations where profit-sharing ratios change regularly, for example in the context of professional partnerships it is usual to change profit sharing ratios each year with potential for SDLT charges, valuation and filing obligations.

In this context several changes and simplifications have been introduced. First, a transfer of a partnership interest will now usually only trigger a charge if it comprises an interest in a property investment partnership, meaning a partnership whose sole or main activity is investing or dealing in chargeable interests.

Since 19 July 2007 a transfer of an interest in a property investment partnership it is necessary to consider the type of transfer.

'Type A transfers' continue to attract SDLT by reference to a proportion of the market value of UK land held by the partnership immediately before the transfer, namely the proportion (determined by reference to income profit entitlements) of the interest transferred. The charge arises where consideration for the transfer is given or there is a withdrawal of money or money's worth by the partner who leaves the partnership or who has a reduced interest as a result.

'Type B transfers' are more restrictive as to the scope of charge, with the important result that property acquired by a partnership subject to full SDLT is excluded when calculating relevant partnership property subject to charge on a transfer of a partnership interest.

39.3.9 Anti-avoidance

In addition to targeted rules, a general anti-avoidance rule was introduced with effect from 6 December 2006. For the rule to operate there must be a disposal by one person of a chargeable interest and an acquisition by another of it, or an interest derived from it; a number of transactions involved in connection with the disposal and acquisition; and for less SDLT to be payable than on a direct notional land transaction. There is no motive test.

The rule removes a large number of mitigation opportunities but also impacts on commercial transactions. Where it applies the purchaser is liable to SDLT on a notional transaction the consideration for which is the largest amount given or received for scheme transactions.

The rule reflects the continuing efforts of HMRC to prevent avoidance, with the threat of targeted avoidance to counter specific structures which come to its notice as a result of SDLT disclosure obligations.

39.4 RELIEFS

Each of stamp duty, SDRT and SDLT are subject to various reliefs, the more commonly encountered of which are outlined below.

39.4.1 Group relief

Exemption from stamp duty and SDLT is available for transactions between companies with the requisite degree of connection – so called 'group relief'. The required relationship is that:

- one company is the 75% subsidiary of the other; or
- both are 75% subsidiaries of a third company.

Economic tests relating to dividends and assets on a winding-up must be satisfied in addition to ownership of ordinary share capital. Non-UK companies can satisfy these tests provided they have share capital.

There are complex provisions designed to prevent avoidance in the context of exit and finance arrangements with third parties. In relation to SDLT only, targeted anti-avoidance provisions have been developed so as to deny relief if the transaction is not effected for bona fide commercial reasons, or forms part of arrangements the main or one of the main purposes of which is specified tax avoidance. In addition, withdrawal of relief can occur by reference to subsequent changes in the group relationship within, or pursuant to arrangements within, a three-year period – this rule is designed to prevent the sale of property indirectly following a group transfer.

The precise scope of such provisions can be difficult to determine: Stamp Office practice is therefore extremely relevant.

39.4.2 Reconstructions

Relief from stamp duty and SDLT is available in the context of certain reconstructions, where the whole or part of an undertaking of another company is acquired in qualifying circumstances.

For this exemption to apply, consideration must consist of or include the issue of non-redeemable shares in the acquiring company to the shareholders of the target company. The transaction must be effected for a bona fide commercial purpose not forming part of a scheme or arrangement, the main or one of the main purposes of which is the avoidance of specified taxes.

39.4.3 Acquisition relief

A reduced rate of 0.5% applies in the context of SDLT where the whole or part of the undertaking of another company is acquired in qualifying circumstances. This requires the consideration to include the issue of non-redeemable shares in the acquiring company to the target or the target shareholders.

39.4.4 Charities

No SDLT is payable by a charity on the purchase of a property used for the furtherance of the charity's objects or to hold as an investment the return from which will be used for the furtherance of the charity's objectives. The exemption does not apply if the involvement of the charity is part of an SDLT avoidance scheme.

39.4.5 Registered providers of social housing

A land transaction under which the purchaser is a profit-making registered provider of social housing is exempt from charge to SDLT where the funding of the transaction is assisted by public subsidy. This extension, introduced in 2009, added to an existing exemption for registered social landlords.

39.4.6 Alternative property finance

The Government has stated that it intends to promote the UK as a leading centre for Islamic finance and therefore is working towards a level playing field for conventional and alternative finance structures.

Very broadly the sale of land to a financial institution and its lease back to the vendor (in other words the 'borrower'; the rent reflecting interest that would otherwise be charged on a loan) is exempted from charge to SDLT provided that the vendor is also granted a call option right (once the 'finance' is repaid the land may be reacquired).

40

SOCIAL SECURITY BENEFITS

SUE PARR

In this chapter, we look at the following:

(1) Taxable benefits
(2) Non-taxable benefits
(3) Tax credits

40.1 TAXABLE BENEFITS

The following benefits are taxed as earned income under ITEPA 2003:

● Bereavement allowance ● Certain payments of incapacity benefit ● Certain payments of income support ● Contributions based employment and support allowance ● Industrial death benefit paid as pension ● Carer's allowance ● Jobseeker's allowance ● The state pension ● Statutory maternity pay ● Statutory paternity pay ● Statutory adoption pay ● Statutory sick pay ● Widowed parent's allowance ● Widowed mother's allowance ● Widow's pension

40.2 NON-TAXABLE BENEFITS

The following benefits are not taxable:

● Attendance allowance ● Back to work bonus ● Bereavement payment ● Child benefit ● Child's special allowance ● Christmas bonus for pensioners ● Cold weather payment ● Council tax benefit (administered by local authorities) ● Disability living allowance ● Employment rehabilitation allowance ● Fares to school ● Guardian's allowance ● Industrial injuries benefit ● Invalidity benefit ● Maternity allowance ● Severe disablement allowance ● Employment training allowance ● War orphan's pension ● War widow's pension ● Widow's payment ● Winter fuel payment

Means-tested benefits

● Child tax credit ● Educational maintenance allowance ● Family credit
● Hospital patients' travelling expenses ● Housing benefit ● In work credit
● Income support ● Social fund payments ● State pension credit ● Uniform
and clothing grants ● Working tax credit

Armed Forces compensation scheme/War disablement benefits

● Lump sum in-service compensation payments and other benefits payable
under new Armed Forces Pension, Compensation and Early Departure
Payments Schemes ● War disablement pension, and the following
allowances when paid in addition to a War disablement pension: Age
allowance – Unemployability supplement (including additions for wife and
family) – Invalidity allowance – Constant attendance allowance – Allowance
for lowered standard of occupation – Severe disablement occupational
allowance – Exceptionally severe disablement allowance – Comforts
allowance – Age 80 age addition – War pensioner's mobility supplement

40.3   TAX CREDITS

The role of employers in paying tax credits was removed with effect from
1 April 2006. HMRC now pays tax credits direct to all claimants whether
they are employed or self-employed.

Table 40.1 – Taxable social security benefits

	2009–10	2010–11	2011–12
	£	£	£
Retirement pension			
single category A or B	95.25	97.65	102.15
category B (lower)	57.05	58.50	61.20
Incapacity benefit			
Long-term benefit	89.80	91.40	94.25
increase for age higher	15.65	15.00	13.80
increase for age lower	6.55	5.80	5.60
Short-term benefit – under pension age			
lower rate	67.75	68.95	71.10
higher rate	80.15	81.60	84.15

Table 40.1 – Continued

Incapacity benefit			
Short-term benefit			
over pension age			
lower rate	86.20	87.75	90.45
higher rate	89.80	91.40	94.25
Income support			
Single/lone parent			
single, under 25, or lone parent under 18	50.95	51.85	53.45
single, 25 or over, or lone parent over 18	64.30	65.45	67.50
Couple			
both under 18	50.95	51.85	53.85
both 18 or over	100.95	102.75	105.95
Statutory sick pay			
earnings threshold	95.00	97.00	102.00
standard rate	79.15	79.15	81.60
Statutory maternity, paternity and adoption pay			
earnings threshold	95.00	97.00	102.00
lower rate	123.06	124.88	128.73
Jobseeker's allowance			
single people under 25	50.95	51.85	53.45
single people 25 and over	64.30	65.45	67.50
Widow's payment			
widowed parent's allowance	95.25	97.65	100.70
widow's pension (standard)	95.25	97.65	100.70

Table 40.2 – Non-taxable social security benefits

	2008–09 £	2009–10 £	2010–11 £
Attendance allowance			
higher rate	70.35	71.40	73.60
lower rate	47.10	47.80	49.30
Child benefit			
first or only child	20.00	20.30	20.30
each subsequent child	13.20	13.40	13.40
Severe disablement allowance			
Basic rate	57.45	59.45	62.95
Age-related addition			
higher rate	15.65	15.00	13.80
Middle rate	9.10	8.40	7.10
lower rate	5.35	5.45	5.60
Bereavement payment			
single lump sum	2,000.00	2,000.00	2,000.00
Christmas bonus			
single annual payment	10.00	10.00	10.00

41

TAX TABLES

SUE PARR

Table 41.1 – Rates of income tax

2011–12	Rate	Taxable income £
Starting rate*	10%	0–2,560
Basic rate	20%	0–35,000
Higher rate	40%	35,001–150,000
Additional rate	50%	Over 150,000
2010–11		
Starting rate*	10%	0–2,440
Basic rate	20%	0–37,400
Higher rate	40%	37,401–150,000
Additional rate	50%	Over 150,000
2009–10		
Starting rate*	10%	0–2,440
Basic rate	20%	0–37,400
Higher rate	40%	Over 37,400
2008–09		
Starting rate*	10%	0–2,320
Basic rate	20%	2,321–34,800
Higher rate	40%	Over 34,800
2007–08		
Lower rate	10%	0–2,230
Basic rate	22%	2,231–34,600
Higher rate	40%	Over 34,600

The rates of tax applicable to dividends are 10% for income below the higher rate threshold and 32.5% for income above it for all years in Table 41.1. From 2010–11, there is a new dividend rate of 42.5% for dividend income falling into the additional rate band.

* From 2008–09 there is a new 10% starting rate for savings income only. If an individual's taxable non-savings income is above the starting rate limit then the 10% savings rate will not be applicable.

Table 41.2 – Personal allowances and reliefs (see Chapter 12)

Allowances (£s)	2007–08 £	2008–09 £	2009–10 £	2010–11 £	2011–12 £
– under 65[1,4]	5,225	6,035	6,475	6,475	7,475
– 65–74[1,2]	7,550	9,030	9,490	9,490	9,940
– 75 plus[1,2]	7,690	9,180	9,640	9,640	10,090
– income limit	n/a	n/a	n/a	100,000	100,000
Married couple's allowance[3]					
– either spouse 65 plus	6,285	6,535	n/a	n/a	n/a
– either spouse 75 plus[1,2]	6,365	6,625	6,965	6,965	7,295
– income limit for age-related allowances	20,900	21,800	22,900	22,900	24,000
Blind person's allowance	1,730	1,800	1,890	1,890	1,980

(1) From 2010–11 the personal allowance reduces where the income is above £100,000 – by £1 for every £2 of income above the £100,000 limit. This reduction applies irrespective of age. For 2011–12, once income reaches £114,950, the personal allowance reduces to nil.

(2) These allowances reduce where the income is above the income limit – by £1 for every £2 of income above the limit. For earlier tax years it was never less than the basic personal allowance or minimum amount of married couple's allowance. However, from 2010–11, the personal allowance for people aged 65 and over will be reduced below the basic personal allowance where the income is above £100,000.

(3) Tax relief for the married couple's allowance is given at the rate of 10%.

(4) The personal allowance will increase to £8,105 in 2012–13.

Table 41.3 – 'Official rate' of interest for beneficial loans (see 4.7)

Average rate for year	%
2011–12	4.00*
2010–11	4.00
2009–10	4.75
2008–09	6.10
2007–08	6.25
2006–07	5.00
2005–06	5.00

Actual rate from	%
From 06.04.10	4.00
01.03.09 to 05.04.10	4.75
06.04.07 to 28.02.09	6.25
06.01.02 to 05.04.07	5.00

*The official rate of interest is set in advance by Treasury regulations for the whole of the following tax year, subject to review if necessary.

Table 41.4 – Pension contributions

Maximum contribution	2009–10 £	2010–11 £	2011–12 £
Individual – 100% of relevant earnings up to maximum of	245,000	255,000	50,000
Employer – unlimited but triggers benefit in kind if total pension contributions from both employee and employer are over	245,000	255,000	50,000
Individual's lifetime allowance	1.75m	1.8m	1.8m (£1.5m from April 2012)

A special annual allowance charge applied between 22 April 2009 (for those earning over £150,000 including employer contributions), or 9 December 2009 (for those earning over £130,000 excluding employer contributions), and 5 April 2011.

Table 41.5 – Rates of capital gains tax

	2008–09	2009–10	2010–11[2]	2010–11[1]	2011–12
Annual exemptions					
Individuals	£9,600	£10,100	£10,100	£10,100	£10,600
Trusts divided by the number of trusts settled by the same settlor up to a maximum of 5 (ie minimum exemption 1/10 individual annual exemption)	£4,800	£5,050	£5,050	£5,050	£5,300
Entrepreneurs' relief lifetime limit	£1m	£1m	£2m[2]	£5m[1]	£10m
Rates of tax					
2008–09 onwards flat rate	18%	18%	18%[2]		n/a
2008–09 onwards entrepreneurs' rate (available on certain disposals of business assets)	10%	10%	10%	10%	10%
Individuals					
Gains are effectively taxed as top slice of income					
Gain less than basic rate limit	n/a	n/a	n/a	18%[1]	18%
Gain greater than basic rate limit	n/a	n/a	n/a	28%[1]	28%
Trusts					
Discretionary (including accumulation and maintenance)	18%	18%	18%[2]	28%[1]	28%
Interest in possession	18%	18%	18%[2]	28%[1]	28%

[1] From 23 June 2010. [2] To 22 June 2010.

Table 41.6 – Capital gains tax indexation allowance

	RETAIL PRICE INDEX FIGURES					
	1982	*1983*	*1984*	*1985*	*1986*	*1987*
Jan		325.9	342.6	359.8	379.7	394.5/100.0
Feb		327.3	344.0	362.9	381.1	100.4
Mar	313.4	327.9	345.1	366.1	381.6	100.6
Apr	319.7	332.5	349.7	373.9	385.3	101.8
May	322.0	333.9	351.0	375.6	386.0	101.9
June	322.9	334.7	351.9	376.4	385.8	101.9
July	320.0	336.5	351.5	375.5	384.7	101.8
Aug	323.1	338.0	354.8	376.7	385.9	102.1
Sep	322.9	339.5	355.5	376.5	387.8	102.4
Oct	324.5	340.7	357.7	377.1	388.4	102.9
Nov	326.1	341.9	358.8	378.4	391.7	103.4
Dec	325.5	342.8	358.5	378.9	393.0	103.3
	1988	*1989*	*1990*	*1991*	*1992*	*1993*
Jan	103.3	111.0	119.5	130.2	135.6	137.9
Feb	103.7	111.8	120.2	130.9	136.3	138.8
Mar	104.1	112.3	121.4	131.4	136.7	139.3
Apr	105.8	114.3	125.1	133.1	138.8	140.6
May	106.2	115.0	126.2	133.5	139.3	141.1
June	106.6	115.4	126.7	134.1	139.3	141.0
July	106.7	115.5	126.8	133.8	138.8	140.7
Aug	107.9	115.8	128.1	134.1	138.9	141.3
Sep	108.4	116.6	129.3	134.6	139.4	141.9
Oct	109.5	117.5	130.3	135.1	139.9	141.8
Nov	110.0	118.5	130.0	135.6	139.7	141.6
Dec	110.3	118.8	129.9	135.7	139.2	141.9

			RETAIL PRICE INDEX FIGURES			
	1994	*1995*	*1996*	*1997*	*1998*	*1999*
Jan	141.3	146.0	150.2	154.4	159.5	163.4
Feb	142.1	146.9	150.9	155.0	160.3	163.7
Mar	142.5	147.5	151.5	155.4	160.8	164.1
Apr	144.2	149.0	152.6	156.3	162.6	165.2
May	144.7	149.6	152.9	156.9	163.5	165.6
June	144.7	149.8	153.0	157.5	163.4	165.6
July	144.0	149.1	152.4	157.5	163.0	165.1
Aug	144.7	149.9	153.1	158.5	163.7	165.5
Sep	145.0	150.6	153.8	159.3	164.4	166.2
Oct	145.2	149.8	153.8	159.5	164.5	166.5
Nov	145.3	149.8	153.9	159.6	164.4	166.7
Dec	146.0	150.7	154.4	160.0	164.4	167.3
	2000	*2001*	*2002*	*2003*	*2004*	*2005*
Jan	166.6	171.1	173.3	178.4	183.1	188.9
Feb	167.5	172.0	173.8	179.3	183.8	189.6
Mar	168.4	172.2	174.5	179.9	184.6	190.5
Apr	170.1	173.1	175.7	181.2	185.7	191.6
May	170.7	174.2	176.2	181.5	186.5	192.0
June	171.1	174.4	176.2	181.3	186.8	192.2
July	170.5	173.3	175.9	181.3	186.8	192.2
Aug	170.5	174.0	176.4	181.6	187.4	192.6
Sep	171.7	174.6	177.6	182.5	188.1	193.1
Oct	171.6	174.3	177.9	182.6	188.6	193.3
Nov	172.1	173.6	178.2	182.7	189.0	193.6
Dec	172.2	173.4	178.5	183.5	189.9	194.1

RETAIL PRICE INDEX FIGURES						
	2006	*2007*	*2008*	*2009*	*2010*	2011
Jan	193.4	201.6	209.8	210.1	217.9	229.0
Feb	194.2	203.1	211.4	211.4	219.2	231.3
Mar	195.0	204.4	212.1	211.3	220.7	232.5
Apr	196.5	205.4	214.0	211.5	222.8	
May	197.7	206.2	215.1	212.8	223.6	
June	198.5	207.3	216.8	213.4	224.1	
July	198.5	206.1	216.5	213.4	223.6	
Aug	199.2	207.3	217.2	214.4	224.5	
Sept	200.1	208.0	218.4	215.3	225.3	
Oct	200.4	208.9	217.7	216.0	225.8	
Nov	201.1	209.7	216.0	216.6	226.8	
Dec	202.7	210.9	212.9	218.0	228.4	

Table 41.7 – Rates of interest on overdue tax/repayment supplement

Rates from 6 September 2006:	
For overdue income and capital gains tax	7.5%
For overpaid income and capital gains tax	3.0%
Rates from 6 August 2007:	
For overdue income and capital gains tax	8.5%
For overpaid income and capital gains tax	4.0%
Rates from 6 January 2008:	
For overdue income and capital gains tax	7.5%
For overpaid income and capital gains tax	3.0%
Rates from 6 November 2008:	
For overdue income and capital gains tax	6.5%
For overpaid income and capital gains tax	2.25%
Rates 6 December 2008:	
For overdue income and capital gains tax	5.5%
For overpaid income and capital gains tax	1.5%
Rates from 6 January 2009:	
For overdue income and capital gains tax	4.5%
For overpaid income and capital gains tax	0.75%
Rates from 27 January 2009:	
For overdue income and capital gains tax	3.5%
For overpaid income and capital gains tax	0%
Rates from 24 March 2009:	
For overdue income and capital gains tax	2.5%
For overpaid income and capital gains tax	0%
Rates from 29 September 2009:	
For overdue income, inheritance and capital gains tax	3%
For overpaid income, inheritance and capital gains tax	0.5%

Table 41.8 – Rates of corporation tax

Financial year starting on 1 April	2006	2007	2008–10	2011
Full rate (see 18.4.2)	30%	30%	28%	26%
Small companies rate (see 18.4.3)	19%	20%	21%	20%
Small companies rate – limit	£300,000	£300,000	£300,000	£300,000
Small companies marginal rate limit	£1.5m	£1.5m	£1.5m	£1.5m
Marginal rate	32.75%	32.5%	29.75%	27.5%
Fraction	11/400	1/40	7/400	3/200

The main rate of corporation tax will reduce to 25% in 2012–13, 24% in 2013–14 and 23% in 2014–15.

Table 41.9 – Rates of inheritance tax

	TRANSFERS ON DEATH	LIFETIME TRANSFERS
Cumulative chargeable transfers £	Rate on gross % age	Rate on gross % age
from 6 April 2005		
0–275,000	nil	nil
over 275,000	40	20
from 6 April 2006		
0–285,000	nil	nil
over 285,000	40	20
from 6 April 2007		
0–300,000	nil	nil
over 300,000	40	20
from 6 April 2008		
0–312,000	nil	nil
over 312,000	40	20
from 6 April 2009 – 5 April 2015		
0–325,000	nil	nil
over 325,000	40	20

For married couples and civil partners, it is possible to carry forward the proportion of the nil-rate band unused on the first death to the death of the second spouse or civil partner on or after 9 October 2007. A reduced rate of IHT is to apply for deaths occurring on or after 6 April 2012 where 10% or more of a deceased's net estate (after the deduction of all IHT exemptions, reliefs and the nil rate band) is left to charity. In such cases, the current rate of 40% will be reduced to 36%.

INDEX

VAT 8.11
wear and tear allowance 8.2.11
woodlands 8.9
see also furnished holiday accommodation; investment properties
proportionate charge 31.5.18–20
protective trusts 31.8
provisional figures 2.1.5
provisions against liabilities 16.1.9

qualifying corporate bonds *see* gilts and loan stock
qualifying recognised overseas pension schemes (QROPS) 26.8
quick succession relief 30.11.9
quoted property companies 27.6

rail strike costs 4.4.8
Ramsay principle 33.19
readily convertible assets 21.1.2
Real Estate Investment Trusts (REITs) 9.8.4, 18.15, 27.6.2
    capital gains tax 18.7.4
reasonable care 3.5.5
reasonable expectation test 38.1.5
receipts basis 4.1.2
record keeping 1.5, 3.3.2, 3.6
    charities 38.1.11
    employees 1.3.2
recycling lump sums 26.2.6
redeemable shares 9.9.3
reduced-rate supplies 22.3.2
redundancy payments 4.14
    see also termination payments
registration
    of pension schemes 26.1.1
    for VAT 22.4.1
        group registration 22.5.5
        late registration 22.7.2
reinvestment relief 29.6
relevant value test 38.1.17
relief by aggregation 7.7.4
relocation expenses 4.4.8
remission of tax by HMRC 3.8
remittance basis
    bank account organisation 35.15
    capital gains tax 35.16
    claims 35.1.3
    constructive remittances 35.4.2
    definition of a remittance 35.4
    disguised remuneration 5.8.2
    five-year rule 35.4.5
    foreign dividends and interest 9.10.5
    gifts of unremitted income 35.4.6, 35.4.7
    investment income 35.13
    Irish nationals 37.16
    loss relief (capital gains tax) 35.16.2
    mixed fund remittances 35.4.8
    special charge 35.2, 35.3
    unauthorised remittances 35.4.3
    see also domicile
renewals 8.2.5, 8.2.8
Renovation Allowance 8.2.7
rent-a-room relief 8.4
rent-free periods 8.2.3
rental income 8.2.1
    corporation tax 18.3.2
    overseas property 10.1, 36.4.1
    see also property income
repairs, maintenance and renewals 8.2.5, 8.2.8
replacement assets *see* roll-over relief
replacement expenditure 16.2.9
reporting requirements
    approved share options 6.3.3, 6.3.9, 6.3.12
    benefits-in-kind 4.4.2
    enterprise management incentives 6.3.14
    non-approved share options 6.2.5
representative accommodation 4.4.8
research and development 18.17, 19.6.2
reservation of benefit rules 30.7
residence
    accommodation availability 34.4.2
    allowances and reliefs 34.6.6
    bank and building society interest 34.6.2
    capital gains tax 13.3.1, 13.3.2, 34.6, 34.6.7
    ceasing to be UK resident 34.5
    consequences of UK residency 34.1
    days counted as UK days 34.2.3
    determining residence status 34.2
    disguised remuneration 5.8
    education visits 34.4.4
    employment income 4.1.1, 34.3.1, 34.6.1, 34.6.5
    entertainers 21.6, 34.8.1
    exempt gilts 34.6.3
    income received by non-residents 34.6
    intentions to make a permanent home 34.4.1
    interest income 34.6.6
    investment companies 34.7
    involuntary residence 34.5.2
    living accommodation 34.4.1, 34.4.2
    living overseas 34.5.3
    non-resident landlord scheme 21.5, 34.8.2
    options schemes 6.2.3, 6.2.4
    ordinarily resident rules 5.8.2, 34.3, 34.4
    personal allowances 34.6.6
    planning points 24.4.2
    property income 34.6.4
    regular visitors 34.4.3
    self-employment 7.3.1
    selling a company 29.9.3
    and share incentives 6.5
    six-month rule 33.2.2
    sportsmen 21.6, 34.8.1

INDEX